# Data Analysis in Plain English with Microsoft Excel

# Data Analysis in Plain English with Microsoft Excel

### HARVEY J. BRIGHTMAN
#### GEORGIA STATE UNIVERSITY

Duxbury Press

*An Imprint of Brooks/Cole Publishing Company*

I(T)P® An International Thomson Publishing Company

Pacific Grove • Albany • Belmont • Bonn • Boston • Cincinnati • Detroit • London • Madrid • Melbourne
Mexico City • New York • Paris • San Francisco • Singapore • Tokyo • Toronto • Washington

Sponsoring Editor: *Curt Hinrichs*
Marketing Team: *Laura Hubrich and Jean Thompson*
Project Development Editor: *Cynthia Mazow*
Editorial Assistant: *Rita Jaramillo*

Production Editor: *Tom Novack*
Cover Design: *Kelly Jean Harvey*
Composition: *GEX Publishing Services*
Printing and Binding: *Webcom*

Windows is a registered trademark of Microsoft Corporation.

BROOKS/COLE PUBLISHING COMPANY
511 Forest Lodge Road
Pacific Grove, CA 93950
USA

International Thomson Editores
Seneca 53
Col. Polanco
11560 México, D. F., México

International Thomson Publishing Europe
Berkshire House 168–173
High Holborn
London WCIV 7AA
England

International Thomson Publishing GmbH
Königswinterer Strasse 418
53227 Bonn
Germany

Thomas Nelson Australia
102 Dodds Street
South Melbourne, 3205
Victoria, Australia

International Thomson Publishing Asia
60 Albert Street
#15-01 Albert Complex
Singapore 189969

Nelson Canada
1120 Birchmount Road
Scarborough, Ontario
Canada M1K 5G4

International Thomson Publishing Japan
Hirakawacho Kyowa Building, 3F
2-2-1 Hirakawacho
Chiyoda-ku, Tokyo 102
Japan

Printed in Canada

10   9   8   7   6

**Library of Congress Cataloging-in-Publication Data**

Brightman, Harvey J.
    Data analysis in plain English with Microsoft Excel / Harvey J.
    Brightman
        p.   cm.
    Includes bibliographical references and index.
    ISBN 0-534-52650-0
    1. Social sciences—Statistical methods.   2. Microsoft Excel
(Computer file)   I. Title.
HA29.B8258   1999
519.5'0285'5369—dc21

98-28206

I would like to dedicate this book to my two grandchildren, Stuart and Rachel Ascher.
If I had known how wonderful grandchildren are, we would have had them first.

# Brief Contents

# CONTENTS

# PREFACE

Formulas are not the everyday language of most students and professionals. Yet many statistics books present the subject in a mathematical manner. I believe that statistics should be presented in a way that students or professionals learn best: through the use of words and pictures while leaving the number crunching to Excel and the mindnumbing formulas for the theorists.

Instead of relying heavily on formulas, this text uses the graphical and computational power of Excel to visualize and compute statistics and plain English to explain statistics. My two goals are to help you to (1) identify the proper statistical tools, apply them, and interpret their output and (2) accurately translate statistical ideas into your own words.

## AUDIENCE

You can use this text for a first course in statistics for students of business or public administration. You can use it for a one-quarter, one-semester, or two-quarter course. Given the widespread use of Excel in business, managers will also find the text a valuable resource in helping them to collect and analyze data.

## FEATURES

The most important feature is the text's clarity and writing style. Like its predecessor, *Statistics in Plain English*, I've tried to keep a light, friendly tone. I explain ideas clearly and always present "the why of the subject before the what." Furthermore, the minimal use of formulas aids understanding and subject mastery. Also many chapters have excellent summaries that provide integrating frameworks that help the reader to distinguish the statistical tools.

A second important and innovative feature is the integration of Microsoft Excel into the text. Excel is an excellent tool to visualize, explore, and analyze data. Each chapter includes the dialog boxes for all function wizards and the detailed step-by-step procedures for using the data analysis tools. The text also includes a discussion of the specialized functions, the PivotTable, and Chart Wizards. You will find a complete listing of all function wizards, chart wizards, data analysis tools, and special tools included in each chapter's appendix.

Appendix I of Chapter 1 describes where to find the function wizards and chart wizard on the Excel opening screen and how to activate Excel's data analysis tools. All the step-by-step instructions and screen shots are based on Microsoft Excel 97. The instructions will work equally well for Excel for Windows 95, version 7.0.

A third important feature is the set of management scenarios at the beginning of each chapter. This provides the reader with the typical questions that the chapter will address. Also included are the data sets that are used throughout the chapter. The management scenarios will motivate the reader to learn the statistical tools within the chapter.

A fourth important feature is the end-of-chapter problems. The problems address all the functional fields including Accounting, Finance, Management, Operations Management, Real Estate, Marketing, and Law. Also included are short essay questions because my philosophy is "if you can't say it in plain English, you don't know it." Data sets are available at www.duxbury.com. Click on Data Library and select this text.

A fifth important feature is the inclusion of behavioral objectives at the beginning of most sections. I have found the Bloom et al.[1] taxonomy of cognitive objectives very useful in designing my courses and writing this book. It provides readers with a specific set of observable skills that they should have mastered by the end of each unit.

A sixth important feature is the inclusion of extended examples, or mini-cases, for all the chapters except Chapter 1. These cases will allow your students to explore the data in creative and unstructured ways. It will also provide them an opportunity to write reports on their findings.

Finally, solutions to the exercises are available for adopting professors. Contact your ITP sales representative.

---

[1] Bloom, B. and others, *Taxonomy of Educational Objectives: Handbook I, The Cognitive Domain*, Longmans Green, 1956.

# TEXT'S ORGANIZATION

After an introductory chapter, the text covers three major areas. Part I covers univariate data. Chapter 2 fowcuses on how to visualize the data, compute descriptive statistics, and detect outliers for a specific sample of univariate cross-sectional or time-ordered data. Chapters 3–4 provide a streamlined version of probability and sampling distributions to master both confidence intervals and hypothesis testing. Chapters 5–6 present how to draw conclusions from a specific sample of univariate data and apply it to the population.

Part II covers multivariate data. Chapter 7 presents how to analyze a specific sample of multivariate cross-sectional or time-ordered data. The chapter helps you look for relationships between a quantitative and qualitative variable, two qualitative variables, and two quantitative variables. Chapter 8 presents how to draw conclusions about the differences between two populations. Chapter 9 presents multiple regression analysis and the chi-square test for independence. Both help you draw conclusions about a relationship within the population. Chapter 10 discusses forecasting methods for both meandering and seasonal patterns.

Part III covers the quality area. Chapter 11 presents the "Big 8" quality improvement tools. It also presents mean, standard deviation, proportion, and demerit control charting. Chapter 12 shows how to design and analyze one-factor and two-factor studies.

# ACKNOWLEDGMENTS

I wish to thank the many reviewers who provided insightful comments on the manuscript. The reviewers included

James M. Grayson, Augusta State University

Robert L. Jackson, University of Western Ontario

Ken Lawrence, New Jersey Institute of Technology

Donald Marx, University of Alaska, Anchorage

Herb Moskowitz, Purdue University

J. Wayne Patterson, Clemson University

Donald N. Stengle, CSU @ Fresno

Mike Wegmann, Keller Graduate School of Business

Jeffrey Wilson, Arizona State University @ Tempe

Mustafa Yilmaz, Northeastern University

Christopher Zappe, Bucknell University

*Harvey S. Brightman*

# DATA ANALYSIS FOR IMPROVED DECISION MAKING

## INTRODUCTION

Managers and business professionals are busy people. According to management theorist Henry Mintzberg,[1] approximately every nine minutes a manager's work day is interrupted. A colleague stops by the office, the phone rings, or a subordinate needs direction. There is not much time for reflection. Nor is there much time for managers to sift through the mass (or mess) of data that accumulates on their desks. Computers can generate data at a rate faster than most of us can absorb. Managers must learn to organize, summarize, and interpret data quickly and accurately. In short, they must learn the art and science of data analysis. That is the purpose of this book.

---

[1]Mintzberg, H., *The Nature of Managerial Work*. New York: Harper & Row, 1973.

# TYPES OF PROBLEMS

Solving problems and making decisions quickly are essential to business and personal success. Business professionals face two types of problems. A disturbance, or crisis, problem is a gap between an historic, expected, or budgeted level of performance and the present performance level. For example, a retail department's sales show a sudden and dramatic decline from the previous quarter or from the forecasted value. You must diagnose the problem's causes and take corrective action to solve the problem. A managerial problem, on the other hand, is a gap between the present level and a desired higher level of performance. Internal or external customers define what a "higher performance level" means. For example, bank personnel presently take over 30 minutes to resolve customers' inquiries about their accounts. Customers desire quicker responses. Thus the regional manager identifies an improvement project and sets a new target—15 minutes or less. This is a managerial problem, and you must seek ways to improve performance. In summary, solving a disturbance problem means asking, "How can you restore performance to previous levels?" Solving a managerial problem or opportunity means asking, "How can you improve performance to the desired level?" In short, our mottoes should be:

For Disturbance Problems ⟶ If it's broken, fix it.

For Managerial Problems ⟶ If it's not broken, improve it.

# MENTAL MODELS AND EFFECTIVE PROBLEM SOLVING

How do managers detect emerging disturbance problems or sense managerial opportunities? Managers must learn how to develop **mental models**.

---

**DEFINITION**    A mental model describes how a process, department, or firm is doing, where the opportunities lie, and what the emerging problems are.

---

Mental models need not be complex or mathematical. Rather, they should be simple, verbal, or visual. Data analysis plays an essential role in building these mental models.

Let's illustrate how a manager can use data to build a verbal mental model. Table 1.1 contains the proportion of weekly invoices that have one or more errors—incorrect part numbers, number of items purchased, customer name or address, or the unit cost—for the 13 weeks of the first quarter.

| Week of | Proportion (%) | Week of | Proportion (%) |
|---------|----------------|---------|----------------|
| 1/2 | 1.0 | 2/19 | 1.2 |
| 1/8 | 0.9 | 2/26 | 1.1 |
| 1/15 | 1.2 | 3/4 | 0.9 |
| 1/22 | 0.9 | 3/11 | 1.0 |
| 1/29 | 1.2 | 3/18 | 0.8 |
| 2/5 | 1.0 | 3/25 | 1.2 |
| 2/12 | 0.8 | | |

**Table 1.1**
Quarterly Report on
Proportion of Incorrect
Invoices

How might a manager use Table 1.1 to develop a mental model of the
invoice billing process? Since there are 13 weeks of data, let's first construct
a *line graph*. Assign weekly proportion of errors to the vertical axis and
weeks to the horizontal axis. Examining Figure 1.1, the manager could
develop the following mental model.

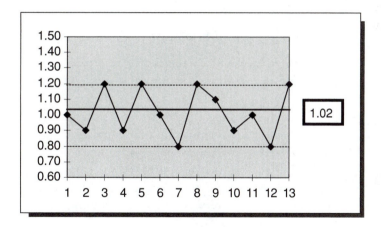

**Figure 1.1**
Line Graph of Weekly
Error Rate Proportions

### How process has operated

In the first quarter the proportion of errors varied between 0.8% and 1.2%.
The mean was about 1%, and there was no upward, downward, or systematic
pattern in the data.

### How process should operate

As management has not planned any intervention for the second quarter, the
weekly proportion of errors should be similar to quarter 1.

### Rules for engaging in disturbance problem solving:

1. If a weekly proportion is above 1.2%, this indicates an unusually high error rate. The manager must determine why the abnormally high error rate happened and take quick and corrective action.[2]

2. If any weekly proportion is below 0.8%, this indicates an unusually low error rate. The manager must determine why it happened to reduce permanently the error rate.

In summary, the mental model consists of Figure 1.1 (visual) and the accompanying text (verbal) and is certainly simple.

Managers can also use the data in Table 1.1 to initiate managerial problem solving. Suppose that a mean error rate of 1% costs the company yearly over $100,000 (and irate customers, too). To recover that cost the firm must generate an additional $1.5 million in sales. The manager might now develop the following mental model.

### How Process Should Operate

Given the high cost of invoice processing errors, the department must initiate an improvement project to minimize the error rate. Our weekly target will be 0.70% or less.

What steps should the department now undertake? First, *flowchart* the invoicing process to determine the sequence of steps to complete an invoice. Then determine what steps in the sequence produce the most errors and redesign the most error-prone steps or institute additional training for supervisors and operating personnel. The manager must then track the impact of the interventions by continuing the line graph shown in Figure 1.1 for periods 14–26.

In summary, mental models are effective for describing the past and present performance of a process, area, or firm. Mental models also articulate a manager's rules for engaging in disturbance problem solving or managerial improvement projects.

## TYPES OF VARIATION

Often in building mental models, managers implicitly define two important concepts in data analysis—**random,** or **common-cause,** variation and **assignable,** or **special-cause**, variation. Random variation is a *minor* departure from the mean historical level of performance. Random variation

---

[2]Using the Kepner and Tregoe method (Kepner, C. and Tregoe, B., *The New Rational Manager,* Princeton, NJ: Princeton Research Press, 1988) or some other problem diagnostic tool greatly increases your chances of determining the root causes for an abnormally high proportion.

results from the thousands of factors that make it impossible to predict exactly the weekly error rate percentage. The manager assumed that error rates between 0.8% and 1.2% were so close to the mean of 1% that they were merely due to random variation.

**D** E F I N I T I O N   Common-cause variation is the result of many small changes that occur in the everyday operation of a process. These small changes create natural variation in a process.

Assignable-cause variation is a *major* departure from the mean historical level of performance. The manager assumed those error rates below 0.8% or above 1.2% for the second quarter would be "so far" from the mean that these would signify a major departure. In short, the manager defined a major departure as any weekly error rate that is greater than ± 0.2% away from the previous quarter's mean level.

**D** E F I N I T I O N   Assignable, or special-cause, variation is due to specific causes, and is *unnatural* variation in a process. Turnover in the workforce and changing vendors are possible causes of assignable-cause variation in a process.

When dealing with data collected over time (see Figure 1.1), assignable-cause variation is also present when the data display any *systematic* pattern. Figures 1.2 and 1.3 display the presence of assignable-cause variation.

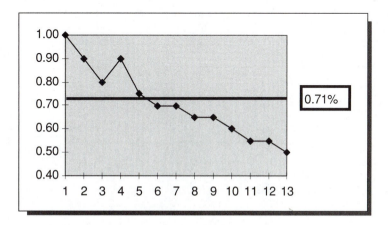

**Figure 1.2**
Data Exhibiting Trend

The data in Figure 1.2 exhibit assignable-cause variation. There is clearly a downward trend over the 13 weeks. Compare this to Figure 1.1 where the *swarm of data points* is reasonably parallel to the horizontal axis over the 13 weeks.

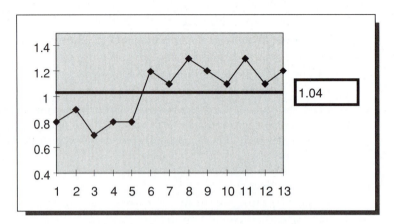

**Figure 1.3**
Data Exhibiting a
Systematic Pattern

The data in Figure 1.3 also exhibit assignable-cause variation. There is clearly a systematic pattern. The first five weekly error rates are all below the mean of 1.04%, and the last eight data points are all above the mean.

There is a simple way to detect assignable-cause variation in data collected over time. First, compute the mean. Second, construct a line graph and count the *string lengths* (the number of sequential data points either above or below the mean). When only random, or common-cause, variation is present, all string lengths should be no larger than three to five and most should be one or two. Assignable-cause variation is probably present when all string lengths are either of length one or when some are of length eight or higher.

The redrawn Figure 1.1 shown below displays the string lengths for the 13 data points. In Table 1.2, the symbol "B" stands for "below the mean" and the symbol "A" stands for "above the mean."

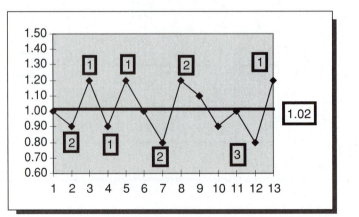

**Figure 1.4**
String Lengths for
Invoicing Error Rate Data

| Figure | String Lengths |
|---|---|
| Figure 1.4 (Figure 1.1) | B2, A1, B1, A1, B2, A2, B3, A1 |
| Figure 1.2 | A5, B8 |
| Figure 1.3 | B5, A8 |

The long string lengths for Figures 1.2 and 1.3 indicate that assignable-cause variation is probably present.

Why do long string lengths indicate the presence of assignable-cause variation? If only common cause variation is present, the likelihood of a data value falling either above or below the mean is 0.5, the same as getting a head (or tail) in a single coin flip. Thus a string length of eight is equivalent to flipping a coin eight times and getting eight heads. Is this likely to happen? No, and if it did, you would suspect the coin's fairness. Likewise string lengths of eight or more should cause you to suspect that assignable-cause variation is present.

Why do *all* string lengths of one indicate the presence of assignable-cause variation? If only common-cause variation is present, it is unlikely that the data will exhibit a "sawtooth" pattern. The "sawtooth" pattern in Figure 1.5 is equivalent to the probability of flipping a fair coin 18 times and getting a succession of heads and tails. Even with a fair coin you would occasionally expect to obtain two or three heads (or tails) in a row. That is, you would expect several string lengths to be greater than one.

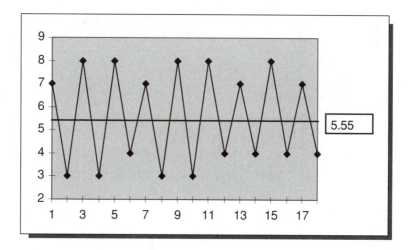

**Figure 1.5**
Sawtooth Data Pattern

Business professionals must determine why assignable-cause variation is present. For example, in Figure 1.2, what factor(s) account for the downward trend in invoice error rates? A correct diagnosis could permanently reduce the error rates. If you don't discover what caused the downward trend, it could reverse itself in the future.

Detecting assignable-cause variation and taking corrective action can (1) fix a process when it temporarily deteriorates or (2) permanently improve a process. In either case, the firm and its customers win.

In summary, for data collected over multiple time periods, only common-cause variation is present when the swarm of data points exhibits (1) no upward or downward pattern over time or (2) no other type of systematic pattern over time. For data collected either over a single period or multiple time periods, only common-cause variation is present when all the data points are "close to" the mean.[3]

# TYPES OF DATA BUSINESS PROFESSIONALS USE

Business professionals use four types of data. Data are (1) cross sectional or time ordered and (2) univariate or multivariate. Distinguishing the four types of data is important because it dictates, in part, the appropriate data-analysis method.

## CROSS-SECTIONAL DATA

Consider the following two tables that contain marketing data for seven sales regions for the first quarter of a year.

| Sales Region | Share of Market |
|---|---|
| Atlanta | 21% |
| Charlotte | 34% |
| New Orleans | 5% |
| Washington | 65% |
| Chicago | 15% |
| Denver | 23% |
| Seattle | 45% |

**Table 1.3**
Cross-Sectional
Univariate Data

---

[3] Yes, the term "close to the mean" is vague. However, until you learn the data-analysis methods in Chapter 2 we cannot be more precise.

| Sales Region | Share of Market | Manager's Performance Rating | Retail Structure in Region |
|---|---|---|---|
| Atlanta | 21% | Average | Franchise |
| Charlotte | 34% | Below average | Chain |
| New Orleans | 5% | Above average | Independent |
| Washington | 65% | Excellent | Franchise |
| Chicago | 15% | Poor | Independent |
| Denver | 23% | Above average | Chain |
| Seattle | 45% | Average | Franchise |

**Table 1.4**
Cross-Sectional
Multivariate Data

**DEFINITION**    Cross-sectional data are measurements taken at *one time period*. The measurements can be on different persons, places, or things, such as 8 sales regions, 50 workers, or several departments.

The cross-sectional data in the two tables are similar. Both tables display measurements on seven sales regions at one point in time (March 31). Compare these two tables to Table 1.1 that illustrates data over 13 time periods.

The cross-sectional data in the two tables differ. Table 1.3 contains only one variable, market share. A variable is a quantity that can take on different values.

**DEFINITION**    When we use one variable to describe a person, place, or thing, the data are **univariate**.

The data in Table 1.4 are *multivariate* because we measure each sales region by three variables. Note that the units of the three variables need not be the same.

**DEFINITION**    When we use two or more variables to measure a person, place, or thing, the data are **multivariate**.

## TIME-ORDERED DATA

Figures 1.1–1.3 contain time-ordered data, weekly error proportions *over 13 time* periods.

**DEFINITION**    Time-ordered, or time-series, data are data collected over time, in chronological sequence.

The time-ordered data in these figures are univariate because for each time period the manager only recorded a single variable—weekly error proportion. The data would be multivariate if the manager had recorded data on several variables such as the proportion of incorrect invoices, the number of overtime hours for invoicing personnel, and hours of computer downtime.

In summary, there are four types of data: (1) univariate cross sectional, (2) multivariate cross sectional, (3) univariate time ordered, and (4) multivariate time ordered.

# DATA MEASUREMENT SCALES

Table 1.4 illustrates three of four *measurement scales* used to describe variables. In increasing order of precision, the scales are nominal, ordinal, interval, or ratio.[4] Distinguishing the four measurement scales is important because it dictates, in part, the appropriate data-analysis method.

## NOMINAL SCALE

When you classify people, products, regions, etc., into categories, you are using a nominal, or naming, scale measurement. In Table 1.4 we measure the retail structure on a nominal scale. The retail structure is (1) independent, (2) chain, or (3) franchise. The classifications or categories must be mutually exclusive and exhaustive.

The nominal scale is the weakest of the four measurement scales. We classify a variable into categories, but one category is not greater than or less than the others, or better or worse than the others. The categories are merely different.

## ORDINAL OR RANKING SCALE

When you *rank* people, products, regions, etc., you are using an ordinal or rank measurement scale. You can arrange the data in some meaningful order that corresponds to their relative value. For example, in Table 1.4 we classified managers' performance ratings along an ascending order of value: Poor, Below Average, Average, Above Average, and Excellent. In sum, an ordinal scale is a nominal scale that you can arrange in some meaningful order.

---

[4] Stevens, S. S., *Handbook of Experimental Psychology*. New York: Wiley, 1951.

Ordinal-scale variables are often represented by rank data. A sales manager ranks the effectiveness of her 30 salespeople. She assigns a rank of 1 to the most productive person and a rank of 30 to her least productive salesperson. Do not treat the ranks as true numbers. That is, the lowest ranked salesperson (rank = 30) is not necessarily 1/30th as effective as the highest ranked person. Indeed, the sales manager could have assigned any 30 ascending numbers to represent her 30 salespeople: −2, 5, 34, 45, 345, 456, . . . , 2343. It is merely common practice to assign successive integers starting with 1. However, you *cannot* meaningfully add, subtract, multiply, or divide such numbers.

## INTERVAL SCALE

An interval scale requires that (1) you can rank the data (ordinal) and that (2) differences between data values are meaningful. Temperature is an example of an interval-scale variable. Consider three temperatures: 30 degrees, 60 degrees, and 90 degrees. Temperature is measured on an interval scale because you can rank the three temperatures from coolest to warmest. Second, the difference in warmth between 30 degrees and 60 degrees is the same as the difference between 60 degrees and 90 degrees. However, 90 degrees is not three times as warm as 30 degrees. That would only be true if temperature were measured on a ratio scale.

## RATIO SCALE

When we measure variables on a ratio scale, the ratio of two numbers is meaningful. Height, weight, share of market, sales, or distance are ratio-scale variables. A 180-pound person weighs twice as much as a 90-pound person. For a given region, a 40% share of market is twice as large as a 20% share of market. What makes height, weight, market share, or distance ratio-scale variables is the possibility of having no (zero) height, weight, market share, or distance. You can add, subtract, multiply, or divide data that represent ratio-scale variables. In summary, you measure variables on either an interval or ratio scale when you can say at least how much larger or better one person, product, or region is over another.

In summary, interval- or ratio-scale variables are called **quantitative** variables. Nominal or ordinal scale variables are called **categorical,** or **qualitative**, variables.

Table 1.5 summarizes the important characteristics of the four measurement scales.

| Scale | What Scale Does | Examples |
|-------|-----------------|----------|
| Nominal | Names results | Gender, state of incorporation |
| Ordinal | Ranks results | Socioeconomic class, ranking of overseas markets |
| Interval | Provides equal intervals between successive values of a variable | Temperature in degrees Fahrenheit, some professionally designed survey instruments |
| Ratio | Provides equal intervals plus a true zero point | Dollar value, weight, length of time to complete a project |

**Table 1.5**
Stevens' Four
Measurement Scales

# DATA SOURCES FOR IMPROVED DECISION MAKING

How do managers obtain data? They have three sources. They already have it within their organization, create it themselves, or buy it from firms that specialize in selling data. A firm's management information system (MIS) provides the first type of data, such as routine reports. Reports such as Table 1.1 contain financial, accounting, marketing, and operations data and describe the state of the firm.

Managers create data by conducting *surveys* and *planned-change studies*. A survey (think of the Gallup Poll) is a representative sampling of facts or opinions that we use to approximate what a complete collection and analysis might reveal. Typical business examples include customer satisfaction surveys and marketing research studies.

For example, the Director of Automotive Safety at Alliance Motors is considering installing a Global Positioning System (GPS) in the firm's top-of-the-line car model, the Alliance Luxor. Presently there are no data on potential buyers' attitudes towards car-installed GPSs. He will conduct a market research survey on a sample of potential buyers.

Managers also seek ways to improve departmental or firm performance by running planned-change studies and analyzing the results. A manager redesigns a process, runs a study, and then compares the study's results to the present performance level. If the redesigned process improves productivity and quality or reduces cost or waste, the manager then permanently implements the process changes.

For example, the Director of Marketing wants to determine which of two advertising strategies—comparative or competitive—would be more effective for a particular market segment. She will conduct a planned-change study. She will select a sample of potential consumers and present them with the two types of advertisements.

Finally, managers can either buy data from outside sources or use data published by public agencies. Often their own management information systems do not contain external data on industry-wide sales or local or national economic data. Thus, firms purchase data from bureaus that sell specialized databases.

For example, Information Resources, Inc., tracks every TV commercial played in the homes of its panelists and every purchase they make at the supermarket. Marketing managers find this information crucial in managing their products.

# DATA COLLECTION THROUGH SURVEYS

Begin by defining the **target population**.

---

**DEFINITION**   A **target population** is the collection of all people or elements about which we wish to draw a conclusion. It is the set of people or elements that **should** be sampled.

---

The target population for the survey for the Luxor car with a global positioning system is all potential purchasers of the firm's Luxor car model.
Next, determine the **sampling frame**.

---

**DEFINITION**   A **sampling frame** is a list of all people or elements that actually can be sampled from the target population.

---

Here the sampling frame is a list of all present Luxor owners as well as owners of competitors' luxury cars. It should also include owners of all near-luxury cars—both American and foreign—who might consider upgrading to a top-of-the-line car model.

## SAMPLING DESIGNS AND SURVEY METHODS

Two critical issues in conducting surveys are selecting (1) a sampling design and (2) a survey method. A sampling design determines how to select respondents from the sampling frame. Its purpose is to ensure that the selected sample is representative of the target population. Sampling designs include simple random sampling, stratified random sampling, cluster sampling, systematic sampling, and rational subgrouping. Simple random sampling is the most basic sampling design.

**DEFINITION**    **Simple random sampling** occurs when every possible sample of size *n* has the same chance of being selected from the sampling frame of *N* people or elements.

To select a simple random sample, begin by assigning each person or element of the sampling frame with sequential numbers starting at 1. Suppose that in the Luxor/GPS marketing research study Alliance Motors had identified $N = 30,000$ people as its sampling frame. The number 1 represents the first person, the number 2 represents the second person, and the number 30,000 represents the 30,000th person. The firm wishes to take a simple random sample, $n = 10$.

Table 1.6 is a **random numbers table** constructed using Excel's Random Number Generation Data Analysis Tool. Figure 1.6 shows the dialog box used to generate 50 uniform random numbers between 1 and 30,000. We used the TRUNC wizard to obtain integer values.

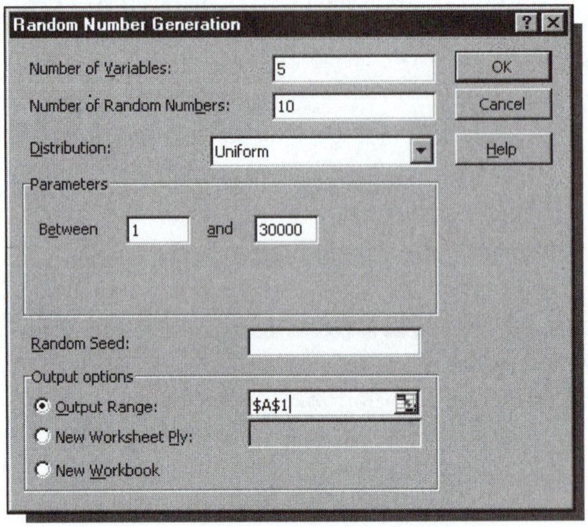

**Figure 1.6**
Random Number
Generation Dialog Box

| | | | | |
|---|---|---|---|---|
| 13606 | 17091 | 5414 | 1436 | 3403 |
| 3306 | 12980 | 9273 | 9050 | 16671 |
| 9213 | 11604 | 671 | 10870 | 14723 |
| 14873 | 9106 | 27936 | 25145 | 12563 |
| 7743 | 1171 | 5147 | 21913 | 16135 |
| 3137 | 18442 | 12640 | 17567 | 1657 |
| 3479 | 28612 | 17795 | 2390 | 9506 |
| 8405 | 17110 | 1373 | 12691 | 25700 |
| 12938 | 25975 | 6993 | 5412 | 15146 |
| 17717 | 29460 | 26550 | 11260 | 15385 |

**Table 1.6**
A Small Random
Numbers Table

Reading across the rows, Alliance Motors selects persons 13606, 17091, 5414, 1436, 3403, 3306, 12980, 9273, 9050, and 16671. These ten people are a simple random sample from the sampling frame.

In summary, a random numbers table ensures that every possible sample of size $n$ has the same chance of being selected from the target population of $N$ people or elements.

The second critical element of a survey is the survey method. A survey method determines how to collect the data from the respondents. Personal interviews, telephone interviews, or mailed questionnaires (or email) are three survey methods.

Table 1.7 displays the strengths and weaknesses of the three methods.

|  | Strengths | Weaknesses |
|---|---|---|
| **Personal Interview** | 1. Permits detailed questions.<br>2. Likely to obtain interview. | 1. Is a slow method.<br>2. Is an expensive method.<br>3. Interviewer can bias respondents' answers. |
| **Telephone Interview** | 1. Is a fast method.<br>2. Useful if respondents are widely dispersed. | 1. Does not permit detailed questions.<br>2. Voice inflection can bias respondents' answers. |
| **Mail Questionnaire (Including email)** | 1. High in obtaining honest opinions.<br>2. Email is a fast method.<br>3. Questionnaire is an inexpensive method. | 1. High nonresponse rate is likely.<br>2. May not reach intended respondents.<br>3. Requires very careful construction. |

**Table 1.7**
Strengths and Weaknesses of Three Survey Methods

Writing survey questions is more an art than a science. Follow these five rules.

1. Write questions that the respondents can understand. Match questions to the respondents' intelligence levels.

2. Avoid vague questions. For example, asking people, "Do you ingurgitate beer regularly?" fails on two accounts. Replace the term "ingurgitate" with "drink." Moreover, what does the term "regularly" mean? It's too vague.

3. Don't ask questions that will cause the respondents to guess rather than admit they do not know the answer. For example, asking people what brand of tires is on their cars often causes guessing. Do you know what brand of tires is on your car?

4.  Avoid questions that invade people's privacy. For example, avoid asking people how often they brush their teeth.

5.  Make sure the questionnaire wording ensures accurate answers. If not, do not trust the data.

Before analyzing the survey data, managers should always question how the data were collected. If the sample isn't representative of the target population, don't trust the data. Make sure that the best survey method for the particular survey was chosen. If not, don't trust the data.

## S U M M A R Y

Data exploration and analysis are powerful concepts. Through data analysis managers can:

1.  separate opinions from facts;

2.  develop mental models of departmental performance and sense emerging problems long before they become crises;

3.  prevent overreaction to common-cause variation;

4.  diagnose problems better by tracing causality, thus countering the tendency to jump from symptoms to false conclusions; and

5.  make better decisions.

In summary, statistics is a way of thinking about and improving business problem solving. It is too useful for only statisticians.

## E X E R C I S E S

1. Managers at Zentron, Inc., maintain a database on the number of personal hours taken in the plant at the end of each month. They want to determine the trend over the past two years. They also want to determine the usual or normal number of hours taken so they can identify a month when the number of hours may have been out of line. If so, they will investigate. The number of workers has remained constant for the past two years and is expected to do so into the future. The data are contained in the 11.xls spreadsheet.

a.  Use Excel's ChartWizard and plot the data in a line graph.

b.  Compute the mean.

c.  Develop a mental model of how the process has operated over the past two years.

**d.** Compute the string lengths for the line graph. Does it appear that only common-cause variation is present? Explain.

**e.** If in the following January, workers took over 100 hours, what might this mean?

**2.** Generate a set of variables to describe the following groups.

| Group | Quantitative | Ordinal Scale |
|---|---|---|
| Hospitals | | |
| Apartment Complexes | | |
| White-Collar Personnel | | |
| Banks | | |

**3.** The American Arbitration Association collects cross-sectional data on the number of grievances filed by plants with between 200 and 300 workers. The data are contained in the 13.xls spreadsheet. The association wants to identify firms with exceptionally low and high numbers of filed grievances. It plans to study these firms.

**a.** Compute the mean.

**b.** Develop a mental model that defines the terms *exceptionally low* and *exceptionally high* numbers of filed grievances. That is, how will you define a *major departure* from the mean? Defend the reasonableness of your mental model.

**c.** Why couldn't you use Excel's ChartWizard to line-graph the data?

**4.** A manufacturer produces a product that is supposed to be 100 cm wide. After hundreds of measurements, she has found that

**1.** 68% of the items measured between 99.9 cm and 100.1 cm (34% between 99.9 and 100 cm and 34% between 100 and 100.1 cm);

**2.** 95% measured between 99.8 cm and 100.2 cm (47.5% between 99.8 and 100 cm and 47.5% between 100 and 100.2 cm); and

**3.** all of the measurements fell within the interval 99.7 cm to 100.3 cm.

Using historical experience, should she conclude there is a disturbance problem if a selected item measures 100.7 cm? 99.5 cm? 99.1 cm? 100.05 cm? Why?

**5.** Data in the 15.xls spreadsheet show the percentage of dollar value of returned items over 12 quarters.

**a.** Use Excel's ChartWizard and plot the data in a line graph.

**b.** Compute the mean.

**c.** Develop a mental model of how the process has operated over the past two years.

**d.** Notice that the data exhibit a pattern. The second and fourth quarters of each year are higher than the first and third quarters respectively. This is called a seasonal pattern. On average, how much greater is the fourth quarter versus the third quarter? On average, how much greater is the second quarter versus the first quarter?

**6.** Spreadsheet 16.xls contains time-ordered market-share data and advertising expenditure data for 16 months.

**a.** Use Excel's ChartWizard and plot two line graphs, market share and advertising expenditures.

**b.** Does it appear that advertising expenditures affect market share? Explain.

7. Spreadsheet 17.xls contains time-ordered data on quarterly profit margin, the net profit after taxes divided by sales for the past 16 quarters.

   **a.** Use Excel's ChartWizard and plot the data in a line graph.

   **b.** Compute the mean.

   **c.** Develop a mental model of how the process has operated over the past four years.

   **d.** Based on the "string length" concept, does it appear that only common-cause variation is present? Explain.

8. Below are a set of variables. Describe the measurement scale for each variable.
   Bond rating
   Number of errors in 100 invoices
   Current assets/Current liabilities
   Net profit
   Type of financial institution
   SAT score
   Gender
   Airlines on-time rankings

9. Financial analysts agree that for an industrial bond to be a safe investment, the firm's total income should be more than three or four times its interest payment. Spreadsheet 19.xls contains the interest-coverage data, total income divided by bond interest, for the past ten years.

   **a.** Use Excel's ChartWizard and plot the interest-coverage data.

   **b.** Develop a mental model of the interest coverage for the past ten years.

   **c.** Suppose in year 11 the interest coverage drops to 5.6. Even though financial analysts would still rate the bonds as a safe investment, what action, if any, should the firm take?

10. Length-of-tenure discounts are the difference between the rents charged longtime tenants and newer tenants. Landlords give discounts because they want to keep good tenants and minimize turnover. The American Housing Group wants to know the size of the discount in Houston. It collects the cross-sectional data in spreadsheet 110.xls, the percentage discounts at selected complexes in Houston.

    **a.** Compute the mean.

    **b.** Develop a mental model that defines the terms *exceptionally low* and *exceptionally high* length-of-tenure discounts. That is, how will you define a *major departure* from the mean? Defend the reasonableness of your mental model.

11. Describe a situation in (1) banking, (2) manufacturing, and (3) the public sector where you would be interested

    **a.** *only* in the specific sample information.

    **b.** in drawing conclusions about the population from which the sample was taken.

12. Suppose the string lengths for a time-ordered data set all equal three. Would this indicate the presence of common-cause or special-cause variation? Explain.

13. One measure of software quality is the error rate per 1000 lines of code (KLOC). Shown below is the number of errors per KLOC from daily test logs in a software company for 30 days (read across the table).

| | | | | | | | | | |
|---|---|---|---|---|---|---|---|---|---|
| 4 | 5 | 4 | 5 | 3 | 5 | 1 | 0 | 6 | 5 |
| 7 | 2 | 4 | 5 | 5 | 7 | 4 | 2 | 3 | 6 |
| 1 | 4 | 5 | 9 | 5 | 7 | 3 | 3 | 4 | 4 |

    **a.** Use Excel's ChartWizard to plot the time-ordered data.

**b.** Compute the mean number of errors per KLOC.

**c.** Based on the "string length" concept, do the error per KLOC data exhibit common-cause variation only? Discuss.

**14.** The quantitative variable, annual income, could be transformed into a categorical variable with six levels as follows:

less than 20,000

20,000 to 39,999.99

40,000 to 59,999.99

60,000 to 79,999.99

80,000 to 99,999.99

100,000 and above

Note all the levels, with the exception of the last level, are of equal width ($20,000). Also note that the six levels capture all the possible annual incomes.

**a.** Transform annual income into a categorical variable with only three levels.

**b.** Is it possible to transform a categorical variable, such as gender or type of financial institution, into a meaningful quantitative variable? Discuss.

**15.** Suggest a disturbance problem and a managerial opportunity in the fields of (1) banking, (2) health care, and (3) the public sector. In terms of the desired goals, what is the major difference between a disturbance problem and a managerial opportunity?

**16.** Use Table 1.6 to select a simple random sample of five from a sampling frame that contains 5000 elements, numbered 0001 to 4999. Read across the rows of the table.

**17.** What, if anything, is wrong with the following questions in a market-research study? Rewrite the question.

**a.** How much income did you make last year?

**b.** This store's merchandise is reasonably priced.
YES                NO

**c.** Has your spouse read the latest issue of *Time*?
YES                NO

**d.** How many cans of beer do you consume each week, on the average?

**e.** Do you attend church regularly?
YES                NO

**18.** The five most common reasons why firms acquire other firms are

| Synergy | to increase the value of the combined enterprises |
| Tax consideration | to shelter the income of the acquiring firm |
| Assets | to obtain assets whose replacement value is higher than their market value |
| Diversification | to stabilize the firm's earnings stream |
| Control | to gain control of the firm |

You wish to conduct a survey to determine why large American and foreign firms in the electronics industry (in excess of sales of $2 billion) have acquired American electronics firms whose sales are between $50 million to $200 million.

**a.** What is the sampling frame?

**b.** Describe how you would take a simple random sample.

**19.** Your target population is all voters in a city. Your sampling frame is the list of telephone numbers in the city directory. Why doesn't your sampling frame properly reflect the target population? How could you correct this?

**20.** When asked what sampling method would be used in an upcoming survey, the marketing manager said, "We will use simple random sampling." Did the manager answer the question? Explain.

**21.** Describe the following data sets along the cross-sectional vs. time-ordered dimension and the univariate vs. multivariate dimension.

**a.** Closing prices of IBM for the past 30 trading days.

**b.** For January, the sales price, the number of square feet, and the number of bathrooms of houses that have sold in the 30350 zip code.

**c.** Closing prices of Dow Jones, S&P 500, and NASDQ stock exchanges.

**d.** For quarter 2, the share of market-sales data for eight regions.

# CHAPTER 1
# APPENDICES

## I. GETTING STARTED IN EXCEL

In this book you will use two types of statistical tools: function wizards and data-analysis tools. Figure 1.7 indicates where to locate the function wizard in a workbook. When the mouse pointer rests on the function wizard tool button (or any toolbar button) for about one second (without clicking), you will see a short description of the tool in a small text box below the button. When you click on the function wizard, you will see many function categories. In this book you will only use the statistical function wizards to analyze your data.

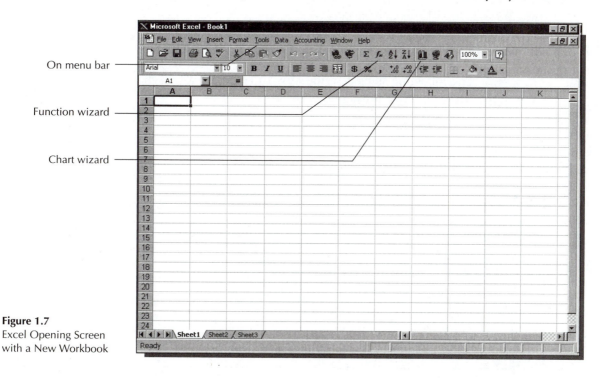

On menu bar

Function wizard

Chart wizard

**Figure 1.7**
Excel Opening Screen with a New Workbook

To activate the data-analysis tools, click on Tools on the menu bar (see Figure 1.7). On the pull-down menu you will see Add-Ins. Click on it. Second, click on the Analysis ToolPak and Analysis ToolPak–VBA boxes. Third, click on OK. You have just activated the data-analysis tool pack.

Click again on Tools on the menu bar. Click on Data Analysis on the pull-down menu and you will see Figure 1.8. You are now ready to use Excel's data-analysis tools.

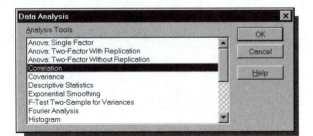

**Figure 1.8**
Data-Analysis Screen

# II. LISTING OF EXCEL TOOLS FOR CHAPTER

1. ChartWizard Line Graph

2. Random Number Generator Data-Analysis Tool

# III. LINE CHARTS FOR TIME-ORDERED DATA

The following steps describe how to construct a line chart for the weekly error proportion data, shown below.

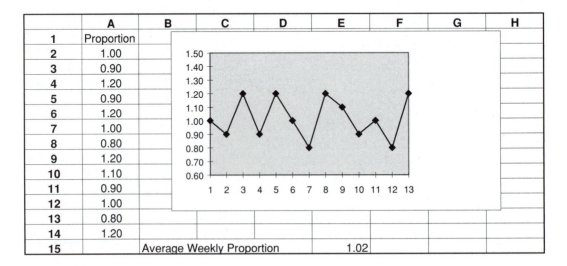

|   | A | B | C | D | E | F | G | H |
|---|---|---|---|---|---|---|---|---|
| 1 | Proportion | | | | | | | |
| 2 | 1.00 | | | | | | | |
| 3 | 0.90 | | | | | | | |
| 4 | 1.20 | | | | | | | |
| 5 | 0.90 | | | | | | | |
| 6 | 1.20 | | | | | | | |
| 7 | 1.00 | | | | | | | |
| 8 | 0.80 | | | | | | | |
| 9 | 1.20 | | | | | | | |
| 10 | 1.10 | | | | | | | |
| 11 | 0.90 | | | | | | | |
| 12 | 1.00 | | | | | | | |
| 13 | 0.80 | | | | | | | |
| 14 | 1.20 | | | | | | | |
| 15 | | Average Weekly Proportion | | | 1.02 | | | |

1. Enter the data in column A of a worksheet as shown. The data are the proportion of invoices with one or more errors. You need not enter time periods 1,2, . . .13.

2. Select the sales data (cells A2:A14); don't include the label in cell A1. Click the *ChartWizard* button. Click on the Line chart type and then click Next.

3. In step 2 click Next. In step 3 you could add a chart title and label the *x* and *y* axes. Click on Legend and click on Show legend box to deactivate the legend. Then click on Next. In step 4 click on Finish. The chart will appear on the worksheet.

4. You can add embellishments such as a chart title, a category (*X*) axis title, a value (*Y*) axis title.

# IV. Computing the Mean

The following steps describe how to compute the mean weekly proportion error rate.

1. Place the cursor in cell E15.

2. Click the Function Wizard tool. Click the statistical function category. Click the Average function name. Click OK.

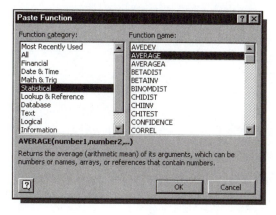

```
┌─AVERAGE──────────────────────────────────────────────────────┐
│    Number1  │A2:A14│                        ▦  = {1;0.9;1.2;0.9;1.2;1 │
│    Number2  │                              │  ▦  = number          │
│                                                                 │
│                                          = 1.015384615          │
│  Returns the average (arithmetic mean) of its arguments, which can be numbers or names, │
│  arrays, or references that contain numbers.                    │
│      Number1: number1,number2,... are 1 to 30 numeric arguments for which you want │
│              the average.                                       │
│  ┌──┐                                        ┌──────┐  ┌──────┐ │
│  │ ? │   Formula result =1.015384615          │  OK   │  │ Cancel │ │
│  └──┘                                        └──────┘  └──────┘ │
└─────────────────────────────────────────────────────────────┘
```

**3.** Select the sales data (cells A2:A14); don't include the label in cell A1.

**4.** Click on OK.

# Chapter 2

# DESCRIBING UNIVARIATE DATA

## INTRODUCTION

Aspiring managers must learn to identify opportunities as well as potential problems. Problem and opportunity sensing are crucial managerial activities because you cannot solve a problem until you know it exists. Effective managers detect emerging problems long before they become crises; they also uncover opportunities before others do.

How can managers more effectively sense problems? As noted in Chapter 1, they must learn to organize, summarize, and interpret large quantities of data. Once managers uncover problems, they must diagnose them quickly and accurately. For disturbance problems, diagnosis is the ability to understand the problem and discover its root causes. Many managers are poor diagnosticians who jump to conclusions about problem causality, blame others, or totally ignore problem diagnosis in their rush to solve a problem. For managerial opportunities, diagnosis is the ability to articulate challenging, but achievable, goals. Simple descriptive statistics that organize and summarize data can help managers sense, diagnose, and solve problems.

In this chapter you will learn how to sense potential problems or opportunities by organizing, summarizing, and interpreting one *specific* sample of univariate data. You will only be interested in drawing conclusions about the specific sample selected.

# MANAGEMENT SCENARIOS AND DATA SETS

Table 2.1 presents the three management situations used in this chapter. These illustrate how managers organize, summarize, and interpret both cross-sectional and time-ordered **univariate** data. Recall from Chapter 1 that univariate data represent observations on one variable that you measure in the same units, such as dollars, units produced, or downtime hours. Also recall from Chapter 1 that cross-sectional data are measurements taken at one time period, and time-ordered, or time-series, data are collected over time. The cases also illustrate three of four measurement scales discussed in Chapter 1.

| Data Type | Data Set | Typical Questions |
|---|---|---|
| Cross Sectional for Quantitative Variables | Productivity and hours downtime for 36 workers in one plant | What is the average and spread in worker productivity or hours of downtime? Are any workers exceptionally low or high performers? Which equipment had very few or very many hours of downtime? |
| Cross Sectional for Qualitative Variables | Firm's quality ranking and type of financial institution | How many firms in the sample were commercial banks? What proportions of firms are in the two highest quality categories? |
| Time Ordered for Quantitative Variables | Personal hours taken (%) in one plant over four years | What has happened to percentage of personal hours taken over the past four years? Were personal hours taken unusually low or high in any months? And if so, why? |

**Table 2.1**
Scenarios and Data Sets for Chapter 2

Scenario I presents cross-sectional data on two quantitative variables. Table 2.2 consists of productivity and downtime hour data for 36 workers and their associated work stations within a single department for one quarter. The firm measures productivity as the total number of *conforming* units produced during the quarter. Worker productivity ranged from 8900 (89) to 12,300 (123) conforming units. Downtime hours for the work stations ranged from 2.34 to 8.12. Both variables are measurable on a ratio scale.

Scenario II presents cross-sectional data on two qualitative variables. The database (see Table 2.3) provides information on the "state of quality" within banks for the past year. A firm's quality rank is an ordinal-scale measure—poor (1), below average (2), average (3), above average (4), excellent (5).[1] The second variable is the type of financial institution—commercial bank versus other types (savings and loans, credit unions, etc.).

---

[1]The improvement in quality between two successive values on the five-point scale is not necessarily equal along the five-point rating scale. If the researchers had designed their instrument with the above property, quality ratings would have been an interval-scale variable.

| Worker | 1 | 2 | 3 | 4 | 5 | 6 | 7 | 8 | 9 | 10 |
|---|---|---|---|---|---|---|---|---|---|---|
| Productivity | 106 | 95 | 103 | 91 | 94 | 92 | 95 | 93 | 102 | 89 |
| Hours of Downtime | 6.41 | 8.12 | 5.36 | 3.51 | 5.05 | 5.15 | 6.77 | 5.45 | 6.14 | 7.02 |
| | | | | | | | | | | |
| Worker | 11 | 12 | 13 | 14 | 15 | 16 | 17 | 18 | 19 | 20 |
| Productivity | 95 | 98 | 107 | 100 | 95 | 101 | 97 | 93 | 92 | 123 |
| Hours of Downtime | 5.84 | 6.42 | 6.50 | 7.86 | 4.56 | 6.10 | 4.40 | 4.42 | 6.47 | 4.42 |
| | | | | | | | | | | |
| Worker | 21 | 22 | 23 | 24 | 25 | 26 | 27 | 28 | 29 | 30 |
| Productivity | 92 | 93 | 94 | 92 | 97 | 94 | 94 | 102 | 106 | 93 |
| Hours of Downtime | 6.10 | 5.81 | 4.71 | 5.03 | 5.35 | 2.34 | 5.05 | 4.21 | 5.00 | 5.46 |
| | | | | | | | | | | |
| Worker | 31 | 32 | 33 | 34 | 35 | 36 | | | | |
| Productivity | 114 | 101 | 95 | 91 | 94 | 95 | | | | |
| Hours of Downtime | 5.28 | 5.71 | 4.22 | 6.07 | 5.34 | 3.74 | | | | |

**Table 2.2**
Productivity and
Downtime Hour Data

Scenario III involves time-ordered data on one quantitative variable. The database (Table 2.4) consists of the percentage of personal hours taken over 48 months. Percentage of personal hours is the number of personal hours taken in the plant divided by the total number of hours worked in the month. Percentage hours taken varied from 0.50% to 4.00%.

# DISPLAYING CROSS-SECTIONAL DATA FOR QUANTITATIVE VARIABLES

After collecting the data, use *graphical methods* to explore it. The appropriate graphical method depends on the type of data.

**Recommendation** Use frequency tables and histograms to display *large* data sets consisting of cross-sectional data for quantitative variables.

Displaying data helps managers see its underlying structure and thereby determine the appropriate statistical measures to summarize the data. By the end of this section you should be able to

1. construct and interpret a frequency table;

2. recognize symmetric, bell-shaped, and skewed histograms; and

3. make a rudimentary assessment if one or more data values are outliers.

| Firm | 1 | 2 | 3 | 4 | 5 | 6 | 7 | 8 | 9 | 10 |
|---|---|---|---|---|---|---|---|---|---|---|
| Type of Institution | Bank | Other | Bank | Bank | Bank | Other | Other | Bank | Bank | Other |
| Quality Rank | 4 | 2 | 5 | 4 | 5 | 1 | 2 | 4 | 5 | 3 |
| | | | | | | | | | | |
| Firm | 11 | 12 | 13 | 14 | 15 | 16 | 17 | 18 | 19 | 20 |
| Type of Institution | Other | Other | Other | Bank | Bank | Bank | Other | Bank | Bank | Bank |
| Quality Rank | 1 | 1 | 3 | 4 | 4 | 5 | 2 | 5 | 4 | 3 |
| | | | | | | | | | | |
| Firm | 21 | 22 | 23 | 24 | 25 | 26 | 27 | 28 | 29 | 30 |
| Type of Institution | Other | Bank | Bank | Bank | Bank | Other | Other | Other | Bank | Bank |
| Quality Rank | 2 | 3 | 4 | 4 | 3 | 1 | 1 | 2 | 5 | 5 |
| | | | | | | | | | | |
| Firm | 31 | 32 | 33 | 34 | 35 | 36 | 37 | 38 | 39 | 40 |
| Type of Institution | Bank | Other | Bank | Other | Bank | Other | Other | Bank | Bank | Bank |
| Quality Rank | 4 | 2 | 3 | 3 | 1 | 2 | 2 | 3 | 4 | 4 |
| | | | | | | | | | | |
| Firm | 41 | 42 | 43 | 44 | 45 | 46 | 47 | 48 | 49 | 50 |
| Type of Institution | Bank | Other | Bank | Other | Other | Other | Other | Bank | Bank | Bank |
| Quality Rank | 5 | 3 | 3 | 2 | 1 | 1 | 2 | 3 | 4 | 5 |

**Table 2.3**
Qualitative Data on Quality Rating and Type of Financial Institution

| Months | 1 | 2 | 3 | 4 | 5 | 6 | 7 | 8 | 9 | 10 | 11 | 12 |
|---|---|---|---|---|---|---|---|---|---|---|---|---|
| % | 0.50 | 1.20 | 0.60 | 1.50 | 0.80 | 1.80 | 0.50 | 1.20 | 2.50 | 1.30 | 1.90 | 3.90 |
| | | | | | | | | | | | | |
| Months | 13 | 14 | 15 | 16 | 17 | 18 | 19 | 20 | 21 | 22 | 23 | 24 |
| % | 1.20 | 2.00 | 2.70 | 1.50 | 2.80 | 2.90 | 2.00 | 3.50 | 3.00 | 3.10 | 4.00 | 3.50 |
| | | | | | | | | | | | | |
| Months | 25 | 26 | 27 | 28 | 29 | 30 | 31 | 32 | 33 | 34 | 35 | 36 |
| % | 3.00 | 3.75 | 2.50 | 3.50 | 2.00 | 1.50 | 2.50 | 1.40 | 1.00 | 1.90 | 1.70 | 1.50 |
| | | | | | | | | | | | | |
| Months | 37 | 38 | 39 | 40 | 41 | 42 | 43 | 44 | 45 | 46 | 47 | 48 |
| % | 2.50 | 2.00 | 1.50 | 1.70 | 2.70 | 1.70 | 2.00 | 3.00 | 1.50 | 2.50 | 2.50 | 2.00 |

**Table 2.4**
Percentage of Personal Hours Taken over 48 Months

## FREQUENCY TABLES

An effective graphing method for large cross-sectional data sets is the *histogram*.[2] A histogram is a graph of a *frequency table* that shows the number of observations that fall into subintervals called classes (or bins in Excel).

---

[2]A large data set contains at least 30 data values. For smaller data sets, use the **dot scale** presented in the next section to display the data.

Begin by constructing a frequency table for the productivity data in Table 2.2. Table 2.5 contains the frequency table developed from Excel's histogram data–analysis tool.

**Table 2.5**
Frequency Table for 36 Productivity Values

| Bin | Frequency | Bin | Frequency |
|-----|-----------|-----|-----------|
| 90  | 1         | 110 | 3         |
| 95  | 21        | 115 | 1         |
| 100 | 4         | 120 | 0         |
| 105 | 5         | 125 | 1         |

The steps in constructing a frequency table are as follows.

1. **Choose the width of each class.**

   The class widths should (1) be equal, (2) be easily interpretable, and (3) allow for between 5 and 15 classes. Table 2.5 has a class width of five because it is easily interpretable. This necessitates eight classes. A class width of 4.56 is definitely not easily interpretable.

2. **Choose an *upper* limit for the first class so that the smallest data value in the data set falls slightly below the upper limit.**

   In Table 2.2, the smallest productivity data value is 89. Thus, the upper limit for the first class is 90. It's a more convenient starting point than 90.5, 91, or 92.

3. **Given the class width, determine the upper limits for all classes needed to include all the data.**

   As the largest data value is 123 you will need the following upper class limits: 90, 95, 100, 105, 110, 115, 120, 125. Generally 5 to 15 classes are appropriate. The number of classes affects our ability to see the data's structure and its detail. For example, a frequency table based on either 2 or 30 classes would not have revealed much information on the data in Table 2.2. Consider 10–15 classes when you have 60 or more data values. Consider 5–10 classes when you have 30 to 60 data values.

Thus, Table 2.5 contains the following eight classes. Except for the first class (called an *open class*), all class widths are five.

| | |
|---|---|
| class 1 | less than or equal to 90 |
| class 2 | greater than  90 and less than or equal to 95 |
| class 3 | greater than  95 and less than or equal to 100 |
| class 4 | greater than 100 and less than or equal to 105 |
| class 5 | greater than 105 and less than or equal to 110 |
| class 6 | greater than 110 and less than or equal to 115 |
| class 7 | greater than 115 and less than or equal to 120 |
| class 8 | greater than 120 and less than or equal to 125 |

## HISTOGRAMS

Figure 2.1 is a histogram of the frequency table in Table 2.5. From it, the manager might formulate the following assessment of worker productivity.

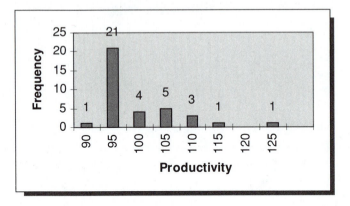

**Figure 2.1**
Histogram of 36
Productivity
Data Values

For the past quarters, 21 of 36 workers produced between 9001 and 9500 conforming units. Only two workers produced more than 11,000 units and only one produced more than 11,500 units.

Figure 2.2 displays a histogram of downtime hours from Table 2.2. Please note that the shape of the productivity and downtime histograms is different. Next, we examine how to characterize the shape of a histogram.

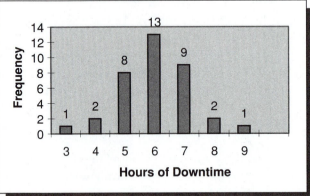

**Figure 2.2**
Histogram of 36
Downtime Hours Values

## DATA SKEWNESS: SHAPE OF HISTOGRAMS

The appropriate data-analysis methods depend on the histogram's shape. Histograms can be symmetric, bell shaped, or skewed.

***Symmetric Histograms.*** How can you determine if Figure 2.2 is a symmetric histogram? Begin by finding the center, or balance point. Think of the number of observations in each class or bin as weights and the horizontal axis of the histogram as a wooden board. Below the wooden board is a steel rod. Move the rod back and forth. The point where the board balances is the center of the frequency histogram and the approximate mean of the data points. The balance point for the histogram in Figure 2.2 is in the class labeled six hours. The classes to the right of the class that contains the center are almost mirror images of the classes to the left. It is the mirror image characteristic of the histogram that makes it symmetric.

***Bell-Shaped Histograms.*** The bell-shaped histogram is one special type of symmetric histogram. In addition to being a symmetric histogram, Figure 2.3 shows Figure 2.2 is also near bell shaped. Notice the following features:

**1.** Many of the data values are at or near the class that contains the center.

**2.** Moving in either direction from the class that contains the center, the numbers of data values first drop off slowly, then more rapidly, and then more slowly again.

The bell-shaped histogram is very important in data analysis because it allows us to make precise statements regarding how far particular data values are from the histogram's center. (More on that later.)

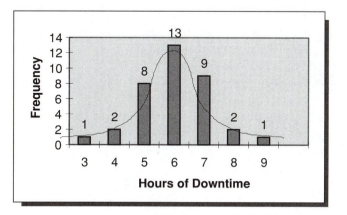

**Figure 2.3**
Bell-Shaped Histogram

**Recommendation** When a histogram is near bell shaped, use the **mean** and **standard deviation** to measure the center and the spread in the data.

***Skewed or Nonsymmetric Histograms.*** Skewed histograms are not symmetric and can be either positively or negatively skewed. To determine the type of skewness, look at the class with the highest frequency (the bin labeled 95) in Figure 2.1. If *more* classes lie to the left of this class than to the right, then the distribution is skewed to the left. That is, the data values fall off more slowly toward the left than toward the right. A skewed-to-the-left distribution is a *negatively skewed* distribution. If a histogram falls off more slowly toward larger values, it is skewed to the right, or positively skewed. The productivity histogram in Figure 2.1 is *positively skewed.*

---

**Recommendation** When a histogram is either positively or negatively skewed[3] or symmetric but not bell shaped, the mean and standard deviation may not be the appropriate measures of the center and spread. (We explain this shortly.) Use the median as the measure of the center and the interquartile range as the measure of the spread.

---

***Outliers.*** A rudimentary definition of an outlier is any data value that is much larger or smaller than most of the other values. Outliers *can* signify major deviations from standard or historical performance, and thus are essential to effective problem sensing. There are three possible explanations for an extreme data value.

**1.** It is due to a coding error.

**2.** It is due to common-cause variation. That is, the data point is really not "so far" from the center that you can rule out chance variation.

**3.** It signifies a problem or an opportunity—assignable-cause variation. The data point is really very far from the center.

How far from the center must data values lie before they are outliers? From Figure 2.1, should the two workers who produced more than 11,000 (110) conforming units be considered outliers? From Figure 2.2, should the equipment with less than 3 hours of downtime or more than 8 hours of downtime be considered outliers?

In Figure 2.1. only 2/36, or 5.5%, of the workers produced more than 11,000 units. Only 2.7% (1/36) of the workers produced more than 11,500 units. While these percentages are small, are they sufficiently small to rule out common-cause, or random, variation above the mean? Some managers use the following rule.

---

[3]Excel provides a measure of the data's skewness in its descriptive-statistics data-analysis tool, presented shortly.

| DEFINITION | If the percentage associated with an event is less than 0.05, consider the event an outlier. |
|---|---|

Using the above definition, only the worker who produced more than 11,500 conforming units is an outlier; he is an extraordinary performer.

Later in this chapter we present two additional rules—the 3-Sigma rule and Tukey's rule—for identifying outliers. These rules help determine data values that are outliers.

In summary, knowing a histogram's shape is informative. It suggests which summarizing statistics to use.

# SUMMARIZING CROSS-SECTIONAL DATA FOR QUANTITATIVE VARIABLES

Summarizing cross-sectional data helps problem solvers answer the following questions:

How are we doing on average?

Is there much variation from one plant to the next, one worker to the next? If so, how much?

The previous section presented how to *organize* cross-sectional data measured on a quantitative scale by developing histograms. Now you will learn how to *summarize* the data to help answer the above questions. By the end of this section, you should be able to

1. compute and interpret two measures of the center of a data set: the sample mean and sample median;

2. explain the need for a measure of spread or variation;

3. compute and interpret three measures of the spread in a data set: the sample range, sample standard deviation, and sample interquartile range; and

4. explain why the mean and standard deviation are appropriate for a bell-shaped data set and why the median and interquartile range are appropriate for a skewed data set or a symmetric but not bell-shaped data set.

# MEAN, RANGE, AND STANDARD DEVIATION

Let's begin by computing the most commonly used measure of the center—the sample mean.

**Sample Mean.** The sample mean is the best measure of the data's center when its histogram is near bell shaped. Since the downtime data are bell shaped, let's use the descriptive-statistics data-analysis tool from Excel to compute the sample mean. Table 2.6 shows a partial output.

|  |  |
|---|---|
| Mean | 5.428 |
| Minimum | 2.340 |
| Maximum | 8.120 |
| Range | 5.780 |
| Standard Deviation | 1.171 |
| Skewness | −0.061 |
| Kurtosis | 0.753 |

**Table 2.6**
Mean, Range, and
Standard Deviation

Use Expression (2.1) to calculate the sample mean.

$$\bar{x} = \frac{\sum_i x_i}{n}$$

(2.1)

The numerator in Expression (2.1) simply says to sum all the data values where $x_{i=1}$ represents the first data value, $x_{i=2}$ represents the second data value, etc.

$$\bar{x} = \frac{6.41 + 8.12 + 5.36 + \ldots + 5.34 + 3.74}{36} = 5.428 \text{ hours}$$

The mean number of downtime hours in the first quarter is 5.428 hours.

Even when you haven't drawn a bell-shaped histogram you can still determine if the data are near bell shaped. Excel's descriptive data-analysis tool provides two important measures—skewness and kurtosis[4] that assess if the data are near bell shaped.

---

[4]Skewness characterizes the degree of asymmetry of a distribution around its mean. Positive skewness indicates a distribution with its long tail extending toward more positive values. Negative skewness indicates a distribution with its long tail extending toward more negative values.

Kurtosis characterizes the relative peakedness or flatness of a distribution compared to the normal distribution. Positive kurtosis indicates a relatively peaked distribution. Negative kurtosis indicates a relatively flat distribution. A kurtosis of zero indicates a bell-shaped peakedness.

**D** E F I N I T I O N          A data set is near bell shaped if:
                                 −1 ≤ skewness ≤ +1 and −1 ≤ kurtosis ≤ +1

For the hours of downtime data in Table 2.2, the skewness and kurtosis are −0.061 and 0.75, respectively. The hours of downtime data are indeed near bell shaped.

You learned previously that the mean is the *balance point* for a histogram. The balance point idea extends to the raw data itself. Consider the following small data set of current ratios—current assets divided by current liabilities—of five firms: 0.8, 2.3, 1.8, 2.6, 1.9. Figure 2.4 is a *dot scale* that illustrates that the mean of 1.88 is the balance point for the data set. So when you hear the term "mean," think balance point.

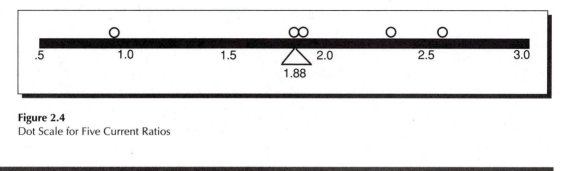

**Figure 2.4**
Dot Scale for Five Current Ratios

**D** E F I N I T I O N          The mean is the **balance point** for a data set.

**Sample Range.** Not all 36 downtime data values are the same as the mean. How different are the data values? The simplest measure of the variation or spread in a data set is the range. It equals the difference between the largest and smallest data values. The range for the downtime data set is 8.12 − 2.34 or 5.78 hours.

The range as a measure of spread has two weaknesses. First, it uses only two data values, ignoring the remaining data. Because of this, the range can provide a misleading assessment of a data set's variation. Figure 2.5 illustrates this. While the range for the three data sets is the same, the variation within the data sets differs. At best, the range is a quick estimate of spread.

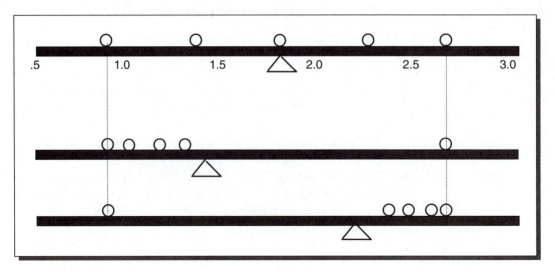

**Figure 2.5**
Three Data Sets with the Same Range

The range also has a second weakness. It ignores the mean in calculating the spread in a data set. A useful measure of spread should tell us how close the data values are to the mean. Why? In Chapter 1 we defined common-cause variation as a minor departure from the mean and assignable-cause variation as a major departure from the mean. Thus to help distinguish common-cause and assignable-cause variation, we should have a measure of spread that reflects how far the data values are from the mean.

***Sample Standard Deviation.*** The sample standard deviation overcomes the two weaknesses of the range and is the best measure of spread when the data's histogram is near bell shaped. The sample standard deviation is the square root of the sum of the squared differences between each observation and the sample mean divided by the sample size minus 1:

$$s = \sqrt{\frac{\sum_i \left[ \left(x_1 - \bar{x}\right)^2 + \ldots + \left(x_n - \bar{x}\right)^2 \right]}{n-1}}$$

(2.2)

The numerator of Expression (2.2) is the *sum of squares*. The sum of squares computations for the downtime-hour data in Table 2.2 are shown below. The denominator of Expression (2.2) is the *degrees of freedom* and is the sample size minus 1.[5]

---

[5]You use the divisor $(n - 1)$ instead of $n$ because you obtain a better estimate of the variance of the population from which the sample was taken. The better estimate is important for constructing confidence intervals (Chapter 5) and performing hypothesis testing (Chapter 6).

| Data Values | Sum of Differences | Sum of Squares |
|:---:|:---:|:---:|
| 6.41 | (6.41 − 5.428) | (6.41 − 5.428)$^2$ |
| 8.12 | (8.12 − 5.428) | (8.12 − 5.428)$^2$ |
| 5.36 | (5.36 − 5.428) | (5.36 − 5.428)$^2$ |
| . | . | |
| . | . | |
| 6.07 | (6.07 − 5.428) | (6.07 − 5.428)$^2$ |
| 5.34 | (5.34 − 5.428) | (5.34 − 5.428)$^2$ |
| 3.74 | (3.74 − 5.428) | (3.74 − 5.428)$^2$ |
| Sum | 0.000 | 48.000 |

$$s = \sqrt{\frac{\left(6.41 - 5.428\right)^2 + \ldots + \left(3.74 - 5.428\right)^2}{36 - 1}}$$

$$s = 1.171 \text{ hours}$$

The sum of the differences will always equal zero (negative sums cancel out positive sums). The sum of squares will always be greater than or equal to zero because we square the differences.

What does the standard deviation tell us? If all the data values are the same, the sum of squares and the standard deviation will equal zero. The larger the standard deviation, the greater is the spread in hours of downtime *around the mean*. Shortly you will learn how to determine outliers for bell-shaped data sets using the sample mean and standard deviation.

**DEFINITION**     The standard deviation measures the squared variation of the data values around the mean. It is expressed in the same units as the original data.

## DATA SKEWNESS

The mean and standard deviation are excellent measures of the center and spread when the data are approximately near bell shaped. However, sometimes the mean (and therefore the standard deviation) can be misleading. Suppose a law firm has eight professionals with the following annual salaries (see Figure 2.6). Can you guess who the partners are? Would the mean salary of almost $74,000 be a meaningful measure of the "average" salary of the eight lawyers? I don't think so!

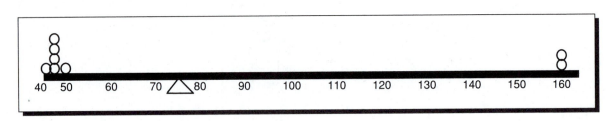

**Figure 2.6**
Dot Scale for Eight Lawyers' Salaries

Why did the mean fail to give an accurate picture of the "average" salary? It's because the salary data are highly skewed! Excel's descriptive-statistics data-analysis tool provides a measure of the data's skewness. For the salary data, the skewness equals +1.43. The following guidelines apply to Excel's measure of skewness.

| **D E F I N I T I O N** | If skewness < −1 | negatively skewed |
| | −1 ≤ skewness ≤ +1 | approximately symmetric |
| | if skewness > +1 | positively skewed |

When data are either negatively or positively skewed, the mean and therefore the standard deviation can be misleading. You must use other measures of the center and variation.

## MEDIAN AND INTERQUARTILE RANGE

An alternative measure to the mean is the median, the middle data value in an *ordered* data set; that is, ordered from the lowest to highest value. If there are no ties, half of the data values will be smaller and half will be larger than the median. Table 2.7 shows a partial output from the descriptive analysis tool for the productivity data.

| | |
|---|---|
| Mean | 97.44 |
| Median | 95 |
| Range | 34 |
| Minimum | 89 |
| Maximum | 123 |
| Skewness | 1.88 |

**Table 2.7**
Mean, Median, Range, and Skewness

*Median.* The productivity data in Figure 2.1 are positively skewed (+1.88). The median productivity is 9500 units.

Table 2.8 shows how the descriptive-statistics tool determines the median. Column 1 contains the raw data for the 36 workers. Column 2 is an **ordered array** of the raw data. The median is the data value that corresponds to the

$\frac{n+1}{2}$ th ordered observation. For a data set of $n = 36$ observations, the median

is the 18.5th ordered, or largest, observation. The median is halfway between the 18th largest data value (95) and the 19th largest data value (95). The median worker productivity for the first quarter is 9500 conforming units.

What is the major difference between how we compute the mean and how we determine the median? In determining the median, we are not concerned with the actual data values that lie above and below the median. We are concerned only that the number of observations that lie at or above the median be the same as the number that lie at or below the median. In computing the mean, we sum the actual data values and divide by the sample size.

The median is not affected by any extreme observation in a data set. For example, if the highest productivity had been 16,300, and not 12,300, the median would still be 9500. Of course, the mean would have changed from its present 9744. That's because the extreme observation would have shifted the balance point to the right (or toward the higher values). In short, the mean is the balance point, and the median is not.

---

**D E F I N I T I O N**   The median is the middle data value in an *ordered* data set, ordered from the lowest to highest value.

---

The mean and median are the two most commonly used measures of the center. Other measures include the trimmed mean or midrange.[6] Neither has been widely adopted in industry.

---

[6]A 10% **trimmed mean** requires eliminating the lowest 10% and the highest 10% of the *ordered* data and then computing the mean for the remaining 80% of the data values. The trimmed mean is used in diving competition to determine a diver's mean score. Perhaps the trimmed mean has not caught on because it requires discarding a portion of the data, data that might have been costly to obtain. However, Excel does provide a function wizard called TRIMMEAN.

The **midrange** is the average of the smallest and largest data values. As with the range, it uses only two values and thus might provide a misleading measure of the center. The descriptive-statistics tool provides the minimum and maximum values from which you can compute the midrange. Weather forecasters use midrange when providing the "average" temperature for a day.

| Raw Data | Ordered Data | Ordered Observation | |
|---|---|---|---|
| 106 | 89 | 1 | |
| 95 | 91 | 2 | |
| 103 | 91 | 3 | |
| 91 | 92 | 4 | |
| 94 | 92 | 5 | |
| 92 | 92 | 6 | |
| 95 | 92 | 7 | |
| 93 | 93 | 8 | |
| 102 | 93 | 9 | $Q_1$ is 9.75th largest data value. |
| 89 | 93 | 10 | |
| 95 | 93 | 11 | |
| 98 | 94 | 12 | |
| 107 | 94 | 13 | |
| 100 | 94 | 14 | |
| 95 | 94 | 15 | |
| 101 | 94 | 16 | |
| 97 | 94 | 17 | |
| 93 | 95 | 18 | Median is 18.5th largest value. |
| 92 | 95 | 19 | |
| 123 | 95 | 20 | IQR = 101 − 93 |
| 92 | 95 | 21 | |
| 93 | 95 | 22 | |
| 94 | 97 | 23 | |
| 92 | 97 | 24 | |
| 97 | 98 | 25 | |
| 94 | 100 | 26 | |
| 94 | 101 | 27 | $Q_3$ is 27.25th largest data value. |
| 102 | 101 | 28 | |
| 106 | 102 | 29 | |
| 93 | 102 | 30 | |
| 114 | 103 | 31 | |
| 101 | 106 | 32 | |
| 95 | 106 | 33 | |
| 91 | 107 | 34 | |
| 94 | 114 | 35 | |
| 95 | 123 | 36 | |

**Table 2.8**
Determining the Median

***Interquartile Range.*** The interquartile range is the measure of spread that accompanies the median. It is easy to interpret and is unaffected by extreme date values. Begin by defining the *quartiles*.

<table>
<tr><td>DEFINITION</td><td>First Quartile</td><td>$Q_1$</td><td>The data value such that about 25% of the ordered data are smaller than it. $Q_1$ is the 25th percentile.</td></tr>
<tr><td></td><td>Second Quartile</td><td>$Q_2$</td><td>The data value such that about 50% of the ordered data are smaller than it. $Q_2$ is the median and the 50th percentile.</td></tr>
<tr><td></td><td>Third Quartile</td><td>$Q_3$</td><td>The data value such that about 75% of the ordered data are smaller than it. $Q_3$ is the 75th percentile.</td></tr>
</table>

Using Excel's QUARTILE function wizard, $Q_1$ equals 93, $Q_2$ (median) equals 95, and $Q_3$ equals 101.

The QUARTILE function wizard uses Expression (2.3) to determine *first* the rank of the first quartile value and then its associated data value.

$$\text{Rank of } Q_1 = \frac{1 + \text{Rank of Median}}{2}$$

(2.3)

For the productivity data, the rank of the median is 18.5; that is, the median was the 18.5th largest value. The rank of the first quartile value is thus $(1 + 18.5)/2$ or 9.75. The first quartile value is the 9.75th ordered, or largest, observation. In other words, $Q_1$ is 3/4th of the way between the 9th and 10th largest data values (see Table 2.8). Since the 9th and 10th data values are the same, $Q_1$ is 9300 units.

The QUARTILE function wizard uses Expression (2.4) to determine first the *rank* of the third quartile value and then its associated data value.

$$\text{Rank of } Q_3 = \frac{\text{Rank of Median} + n}{2}$$

(2.4)

For the productivity data, the sample size, $n$, is 36. The rank of the third quartile is thus $(18.5 + 36)/2$, or 27.25. The third quartile value is the 27.25th ordered observation. In plain English, $Q_3$ is 1/4th of the way between the 27th and 28th largest data values (see Table 2.8). Since the 27th and 28th data values are the same, $Q_3$ is 10,100 units.

The interquartile range (IQR) measures the width of the middle 50% of the *ordered* data values. Approximately 75% of the ordered data values lie below $Q_3$. Approximately 25% of the ordered data values lie below $Q_1$. Thus the middle 50% of the ordered data values lie between $Q_1$ and $Q_3$. Use Expression (2.5) to compute the IQR.

$$\boxed{IQR = Q_3 - Q_1}$$

(2.5)

For the productivity data, the middle 50% of the *ordered* data values lie between 9300 and 10,100 units. The IQR is 800 units.

What does the IQR tell us? As the IQR becomes smaller, the middle 50% of the ordered data values become "bunched up." A frequency histogram would have a peaked distribution. For an IQR of zero, there would be no variation for the middle 50% of the ordered data values. As the IQR becomes larger, the middle 50% of the ordered data values become "spread out." A frequency histogram would have a flat distribution.

What doesn't the IQR tell us? It does not measure the spread around the median. For the productivity data, the IQR is 800 units, and the middle 50% of the ordered data values lie between 9300 and 10,100 units. The IQR does not directly measure the spread around the median of 9500 units. However, a diagram of the interquartile range and median for the productivity data does reveal important information about the spread of the data around the median.

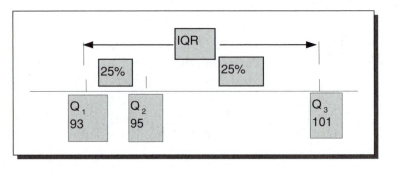

**Figure 2.7**
IQR and the Median for the Productivity Data

About 25% of the data values lie between 9300 and 9500 units (see Figure 2.7). About 25% of the data values lie between 9500 and 10,100 units. Thus the IQR of 800 units consists of two segments: (1) a 200–unit variation "on the downside" below the median plus (2) a 600–unit variation "on the upside" above the median.

To understand how the QUARTILE function wizard works, consider the following data set with $n = 6$ observations.

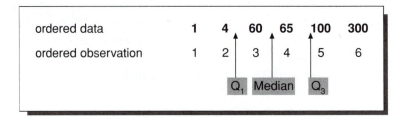

$Q_2$, the median, is the (6+1)/2, or 3.5th ordered observation. The median is halfway between the third largest value (60) and fourth largest value (65). The median is 62.5.

The **rank** of the first quartile is (1 + 3.5)/2 or 2.25. This is 1/4th of the way between the second largest data value (4) and the third largest data value (60). QUARTILE determines this value as

$$4 + \frac{1}{4}\left(60 - 4\right) = 18.$$

The **rank** of the third quartile is (3.5 + 6)/2 or 4.75. This corresponds to 3/4th of the way between the fourth largest data value (65) and the fifth largest data values (100). QUARTILE determines this value as

$$65 + \frac{3}{4}\left(100 - 65\right) = 91.25.$$

QUARTILE

| Array | A1:A6 | = {1;4;60;65;100;300} |
| Quart | 3 | = 3 |

= 91.25

Returns the quartile of a data set.

**Quart** is a number: minimum value = 0; 1st quartile = 1; median value = 2; 3rd quartile = 3; maximum value = 4.

Formula result = 91.25          OK     Cancel

In summary, when the data are near bell shaped, use the mean and standard deviation to measure the central tendency and spread in the data. When the data are either positively or negatively skewed or symmetric but not bell shaped, use the median and interquartile range to summarize the data.

# ASSESSING ASSIGNABLE-CAUSE VARIATION: CROSS-SECTIONAL DATA FOR QUANTITATIVE VARIABLES

An important step in interpreting a data set is the ability to identify outliers, the presence of assignable-cause variation. Assignable-cause variation is a "major" departure from the historical mean performance level. Now that you have learned to compute descriptive statistics, you will learn two additional rules for determining the presence of outliers. The appropriate rule depends on the data's shape.

| | |
|---|---|
| Near bell-shaped data | 3-sigma rule |
| Positively or negatively skewed data or symmetric, but not bell-shaped, data | Tukey's rule |

By the end of this section you should be able to

1. identify outliers using the 3-sigma rule;

2. identify outliers using Tukey's rule; and

3. draw a box-and-whisker plot to visualize the important features of a data set.

## BELL-SHAPED DATA, 3-SIGMA RULE, AND OUTLIERS

When a data set is near bell shaped, use the 3-sigma rule to detect outliers.

**DEFINITION**   An outlier is any data value that is more than three standard deviations either above or below the mean. Such a data value is a "major departure" from the mean.

The 3-sigma rule derives from the properties of the normal distribution presented in Chapter 4. For bell-shaped data, 99.73% (.9973) of the data values will lie between the mean minus three standard deviations and the mean plus three standard deviations (3-sigma). Thus by chance alone, the likelihood of a data value outside of 3-sigma from the mean is only $1 - .9973 = .0027$. That is a very small probability—only 27 in 10,000. Thus, any data value outside of 3-sigma from the mean is an outlier that is due to an assignable cause.

Figure 2.2 suggests that the downtime data are near bell shaped. Thus from Table 2.6, an outlier is any data value that is

1. less than the   mean minus 3-sigma
$5.428 - 3(1.171) = 1.915$ hours.  Lower limit

2. greater than the   mean plus 3-sigma
$5.428 + 3(1.171) = 8.941$ hours.  Upper limit

From Table 2.6, the minimum and maximum values of 2.34 or 8.12 downtime hours should therefore not be considered outliers.

One must apply common sense to the 3-sigma rule. For example, in quarter one, worker #2's work station was down for 8.12 hours. Not an outlier! However, if downtime hours for this worker's station should be close to the upper limit in the second and third quarters, management should probably investigate. Three data values close to either the lower or upper 3-sigma limit should also signal the presence of assignable-cause variation. The 3-sigma rule is not a substitute for common sense.

## SKEWED DATA, TUKEY'S RULE, OUTLIERS, AND BOX PLOTS

John Tukey, the creator of exploratory data analysis, developed an approach to determine outliers for skewed or symmetric, but not bell-shaped, data sets. He used the interquartile range and the first and third quartiles to define outliers.

**DEFINITION**    An outlier is more than one step below the first quartile value, or more than one step above the third quartile value. A step equals $1.5 \cdot$ IQR. These constitute "major" departures from the median.

For the productivity data from Table 2.8, $Q_3 = 10,100$ and $Q_1 = 9300$. The interquartile range is 800 units. A step for the productivity data equals

$$1.5 \cdot \text{IQR}$$
$$1.5 \cdot 800 = 1200$$

Thus outliers are workers whose productivity is

less than
[First quartile value − One step] or $9300 − 1200 = 8100$ units

greater than
[Third quartile value + One step] $10,100 + 1200 = 11,300$ units

According to Tukey's rule, workers #31 and #20 were exceptionally high producers at 11,400 and 12,300 conforming units, respectively. Management should interview the two workers to determine how they achieved their high productivity. Perhaps management can apply the lessons learned to the other 34 workers. In time, the department could increase its productivity.

***Box-and-Whisker Plots.*** Even though Excel does not draw box-and-whisker plots, they are easy to construct.[7] Use Excel's QUARTILE function wizard to develop a five-number summary that consists of

$x_{\text{smallest}}$          $Q_1$          median          $Q_3$          $x_{\text{largest}}$

---

[7]You can draw a box plot using Excel's Drawing toolbar. This is shown in the appendix.

Here is the five-number summary for the productivity data in Table 2.2.

| 8900 | 9300 | 9500 | 10,100 | 12,300 |
|------|------|------|--------|--------|
| $x_{smallest}$ | $Q_1$ | median | $Q_3$ | $x_{largest}$ |

A box plot is a picture of the five-number summary.

Figure 2.8 is a box-and-whisker plot of the productivity data.

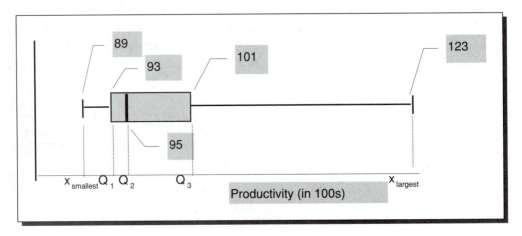

**Figure 2.8**
Box Plot of Productivity Data

Approximately 25% of the 36 productivity data values fall between the following four sets of values: 89 to 93, 93 to 95, 95 to 101, and 101 to 123 (see Figure 2.9).

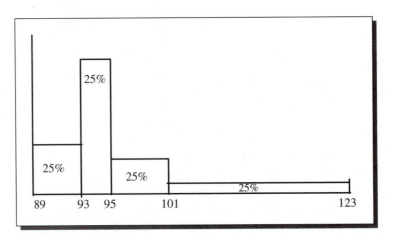

**Figure 2.9**
Block Diagram of the
Box-and-Whisker Plot

I think you will agree that the data's positive, or right, skewness jumps out at you. Pictures are always worth 10,000 words.

You can draw a box-and-whisker plot for any data set. Consider the downtime data that are near bell shaped. While the mean and standard deviation are the most appropriate descriptive statistics, you could construct a box plot to reveal the data's shape.

Figure 2.10 is a box-and-whisker plot of the downtime data. QUARTILE provided the following five-number summary—2.34, 4.67, 5.36, 6.11, 8.12.

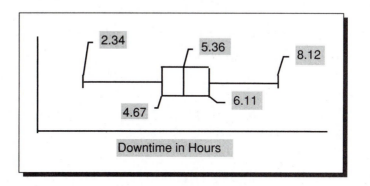

**Figure 2.10**
Box-and-Whisker Plot for
Downtime Hours Data

Approximately 25% of the downtime hours are between the following four sets of values: 2.34 to 4.67, 4.67 to 5.36, 5.36 to 6.11, and 6.11 to 8.12 hours (see Figure 2.11).

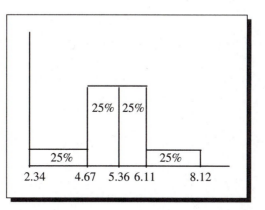

**Figure 2.11**
Block Diagram of the
Box-and-Whisker Plot

Compare and contrast Figures 2.8 and 2.10. Don't the box plots quickly reveal the differences in the shapes of the two distributions?

To this point you have learned how to organize, summarize, and interpret cross-sectional data for quantitative variables. You have also learned how to detect outliers using either the 3-sigma rule or Tukey's rule. Next, you will learn how to display and summarize cross-sectional data for qualitative variables.

# CROSS-SECTIONAL DATA FOR QUALITATIVE VARIABLES

Qualitative, or categorical, variables are only measurable on either a nominal or ordinal scale. You cannot add, subtract, multiply, or divide data measured on a nominal or ordinal scale. This severely limits how to display and summarize the data. By the end of this section you should be able to

1. construct and interpret a single-variable-tally table;

2. construct and interpret a column chart; and

3. compute and interpret a measure of the center for nominal variables and a measure of the center and spread for ordinal variables.

## DISPLAYING DATA THROUGH TALLY TABLES AND COLUMN CHARTS

You cannot use histograms or dot scales to display cross-sectional data for qualitative variables. After all, the numbers assigned to nominal- or ordinal-scale variables are arbitrary. For example, in Table 2.3, type of financial institution is a nominal variable. You can code commercial banks as zero and other institutions as one, but the numbers themselves have no meaning. Rather than histograms, use tally tables and column charts to display data for qualitative variables.

***Tally Tables.*** Tally tables show the number (or percentage) of occurrences of each category in a data set. The tally table answers the following types of questions:

1. How many (or what percentage) of the firms in Table 2.3 were commercial banks?

2. How many financial institutions received an excellent quality rating?

3. How many financial institutions received a poor quality rating?

For large databases, developing tally tables can be time consuming. Fortunately, Excel provides a single-variable-tally tool called PivotTable.[8]

Tables 2.9 and 2.10 are tally tables for the type of institution and quality ratings of the 50 firms in Table 2.3. Type of institution has two categories and quality rating has five categories.

---

[8] See instructions for developing a PivotTable in the Appendix.

**Table 2.9**
Tally Table (Count) for Quality Rating of 50 Financial Institutions (banks and other institutions)

| Count of Quality Rating | | |
|---|---|---|
| Quality Rating | | Total |
| Poor | 1 | 8 |
| | 2 | 10 |
| | 3 | 11 |
| | 4 | 12 |
| Excellent | 5 | 9 |
| Grand Total | | 50 |

**Table 2.10**
Tally Table (Percentage) for Type of Financial Institution

| Count of Type of Institution | |
|---|---|
| Type of Institution | Total |
| Bank | 58.00% |
| Other | 42.00% |
| Grand Total | 100.00% |
| | |

Would the mean quality rating for the 50 financial institutions in Table 2.9 be a meaningful number? Given the 1 through 5 rating scores, you may be tempted to compute a mean. Do not succumb to temptation! You could have used any five ascending numbers to represent the five quality ratings. Unless you measure a variable on an interval or ratio scale, do not compute means (or standard deviations). Shortly, we present the most effective measures.

***Column Charts.*** Column charts are pictures of tally tables. As with histograms, dot scales, and box-and-whisker plots for quantitative variables, column charts help show the data's underlying structure.

Figures 2.12 and 2.13 are column charts for the type of institution (percentage) and quality rating (count) tally table created by Excel's ChartWizard. Alternatively, we could have used pie charts or bar charts to graphically display the data.

Column charts and frequency histograms are similar, yet different. Both display the number of observations for each class or bin. However, the data in a single class of a histogram are not the same value. For example, in Figure 2.2, there are eight observations in the class labeled "5." This class contains the downtime data values that are greater than 4.0 hours but less than 5.0 hours. The data in a single class of a column chart will all be the same value. For example, in Figure 2.12, there are eight observations in the class labeled "1." All eight data values that equaled 1 represented eight banks that had a poor level of service quality.

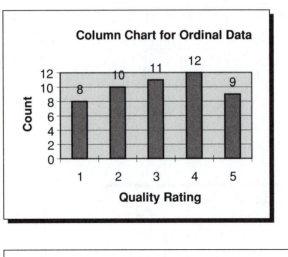

**Figure 2.12**
Column Chart for
Quality Rating Data

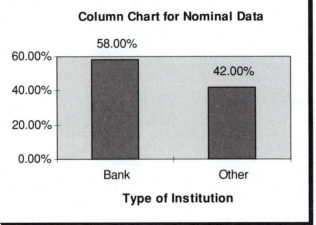

**Figure 2.13**
Column Chart for Type
of Institution Data

## SUMMARIZING THE CENTER AND SPREAD FOR QUALITATIVE VARIABLES

The appropriate measures of the center and the spread differ for nominal and ordinal variables. But keep in mind that given the scales' limitations, you cannot compute means or standard deviations.

***Mode.*** The best measure of the center for nominal variables is the *mode*. The mode is the outcome that occurs most frequently in a data set. For the type of institution data, commercial banks were the modal outcome. 58% of the banks (or 29 banks) were commercial banks versus only 42% (or 21 banks) that were other types of financial institutions. Although the binomial standard deviation is the measure of the variability of nominal variables, managers do not often use it because it is difficult to interpret and thus will not be presented here.

***Median and IQR for Ordinal Variables.*** For ordinal variables, order or ranking is meaningful. The most appropriate measure of the center is the median. The median quality rating, $Q_2$, of the 50 firms in Table 2.3 is the 25.5th largest value in the ranked data and equals 3. That indicates average quality.

$$\text{Median} = \frac{1 + 50}{2} = 25.5 \text{th \textbf{largest value}}$$

The interquartile range is an appropriate measure of the spread. From QUARTILE, the first quartile ($Q_1$) equals 2 (a below-average quality rating). The third quartile ($Q_3$) equals 4 (an above-average quality rating). Thus the middle 50% of the **ordered** quality ratings are between a below-average and above-average quality rating.[9]

In summary, commercial banks were the most common, or modal, type of financial institution in the survey. The median quality level for the 50 institutions was average and 50% of the financial institutions had between a below-average to an above-average quality rating.

***Stretching Assumptions.*** Can we treat ordinal variables as we do quantitative variables? It depends on the specific situation. For a given survey or rating instrument, we must ask how far off is the survey scale from an interval scale. For the quality rating data, ask the following question.

Is the increase in quality between a firm with a rating of 1 versus 2 the same as between any two successive rating scores on the five-point scale?

If the answer is "almost" then we can probably treat the ordinal variable as if it were quantitative. Thus if the data set was near bell shaped, you could meaningfully compute the mean and standard deviation in the quality ranking scores. Although sometimes we treat ordinal variables as if they were quantitative, do not do this "stretching" for nominal variables. This is because the numbers attached to categories of nominal variables have no meaning.

Table 2.11 shows the appropriate measures of the center and spread for each type of variable. You can use the descriptive measures listed to the right (and below) of the corresponding measurement scale.

---

[9]Others prefer to use the difference in the 95th and 5th percentiles. This measures the spread in the middle 90% of the **ordered** data values. Excel provides a PERCENTILE function wizard.

| Measurement Scale | Measures of Center | Measures of Spread |
|---|---|---|
| Quantitative | Mean or Median | Standard Deviation or Interquartile Range |
| Ordinal | Median | Interquartile Range |
| Nominal | Mode | --------------- |

**Table 2.11**
Descriptive Measures
for Measurement Scales

# DISPLAYING TIME-ORDERED DATA

For cross-sectional data you develop histograms, dot scales, or box-and-whisker plots. For time-ordered data, you draw line graphs. By the end of this section you should be able to

**1.** draw and interpet a line graph; and

**2.** explain the difference between stationary and nonstationary time-ordered data.

Figure 2.14 is a line graph of the percentage of personal hours taken data from Table 2.4. The horizontal axis measures time in months, and the vertical axis is the percentage of personal hours taken.

What does the line graph reveal? The data are **nonstationary** because there is a trend over time. Personal hours increased up to the 23rd month, then dropped over the next 10 months, and then began to rise slowly again.

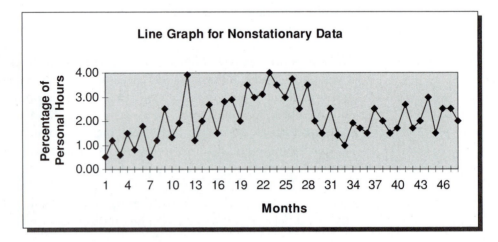

**Figure 2.14**
Line Graph of Percentage of Personal Hours Taken

**DEFINITION**     Data are nonstationary when the data exhibit an upward or downward trend or a systematic pattern. Nonstationary data contain assignable-cause variation. Assignable causes produce the trend or pattern.

By contrast, the number of coding errors per 1000 lines of code (KLOC) data in Figure 2.15 are **stationary** because the general level of the data remains constant over the entire time period. The values of the stationary data fluctuate around a constant mean value of 2.24 errors per thousand lines of code.

**DEFINITION**     Data are stationary when the swarm of data points is horizontal and exhibits no systematic pattern. Stationary data contain only common-cause variation.

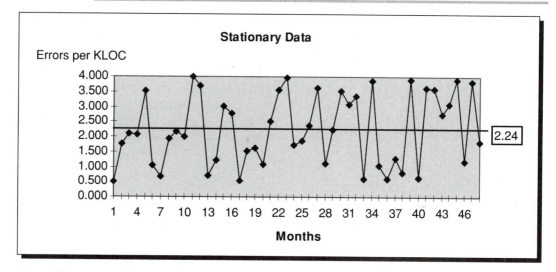

**Figure 2.15**
Stationary Time-Ordered Data

In summary, managers describe cross-sectional data as symmetric, bell shaped, or skewed. Managers describe time-ordered data as stationary or nonstationary.

# SUMMARIZING TIME-ORDERED DATA

After drawing a line graph you should summarize the time-ordered data. Summarizing time-ordered data enables business professionals to answer the following questions:

How are we doing, on average, *over time*?

Is our department's performance declining, staying the same, or improving *over time*?

Is there any pattern to our department's performance *over time*? When do we do well? When do we do poorly?

By the end of this section you should be able to

1. explain why the mean and standard deviation, or the median and interquartile range, should *not* be used to summarize nonstationary time-ordered data; and

2. compute and interpret a single moving average, MA($n$).

## ARE THE MEAN OR MEDIAN INFORMATIVE FOR NONSTATIONARY DATA?

Figure 2.14 (also Table 2.4) contains four years of nonstationary data. We have computed the mean and median for each year and for the overall four-year period, as shown in Table 2.12. Use the appropriate function wizards and verify the calculations.

**Table 2.12**

Comparison of Means and Medians for Percentage Hours Data over Four Years

|  | Mean | Median |
|---|---|---|
| **Year 1** | 1.48% | 1.25% |
| **Year 2** | 2.68% | 2.85% |
| **Year 3** | 2.19% | 1.95% |
| **Year 4** | 2.13% | 2.00% |
| **Over Four Years** | 2.12% | 2.00% |

The overall four-year mean and median are not informative or useful for summarizing the percentage personal hours data. Why? Think about it before continuing.

An "average" should accurately summarize the data. It should provide a typical value that summarizes the 48 months of data. The overall four-year mean or median values are too high for the first year and too low for the second year. In short, do not use the mean or median to summarize time-ordered data that are nonstationary. Nonstationary data do not have a constant mean or median over time. Nor do they have a constant variance or IQR over time.

If the data are stationary, the overall mean or median will accurately reflect the average performance each and every year. Thus, you can use the mean and standard deviation or the median and interquartile range for stationary time-ordered data. In conclusion:

> Summarize stationary time-ordered data by computing either the mean and standard deviation or the median and interquartile range. Use the latter pair of statistics when the data are skewed or symmetric, but not bell shaped. Use the mean and standard deviation when the data are near bell shaped. Treat stationary time-ordered data the same as cross-sectional data.

> Do not compute the mean and standard deviation or median and interquartile range for nonstationary time-ordered data.

How then can we describe nonstationary time-ordered data? A solution is to use a moving average series.

## MOVING AVERAGES

A moving average replaces each data value with a mean of what is happening around it. Use a moving average of three, five, or seven time periods (days, weeks, months, years, or the like) to **smooth** time-ordered data.[10]

Table 2.13, which contains only one of the four years of personal hours data, illustrates how to construct a single moving average of three months, MA(3). We used the moving average data-analysis tool from EXCEL to generate the moving average values.[11]

For an MA(3), a period's moving average value is the mean of the values for that period, the period before, and the period after. Thus, February's moving average value is the mean of the January, February, and March data values. March's moving average value is the mean of March and its neighbors, February and April.

You cannot compute a moving average for January of the first year (see Table 2.13, #NA entry) and for December of the last year (not shown), since there are no values before the first data point or after the last data point. Two data values are "lost" when computing a single moving average of length three.

---

[10]Here the sole purpose is to *smooth* the data, not to *forecast* future values. See Chapter 10 for information on using moving averages to prepare forecasts.

[11]See instructions for constructing a MA(3) in the appendix.

| Months | Personal Hours Taken (%) | Moving Average |
|--------|--------------------------|----------------|
| Jan.   | 0.50                     | #N/A           |
| Feb.   | 1.20                     | 0.77           |
| March  | 0.60                     | 1.10           |
| April  | 1.50                     | 0.97           |
| May    | 0.80                     | 1.37           |
| June   | 1.80                     | 1.03           |
| July   | 0.50                     | 1.17           |
| August | 1.20                     | 1.40           |
| Sept.  | 2.50                     | 1.67           |
| Oct.   | 1.30                     | 1.90           |
| Nov.   | 1.90                     | 2.37           |
| Dec.   | 3.90                     | 2.33           |

(.50+1.20+.60)/3=.77

**Table 2.13**
MA(3) for Year One of Percentage Personal Hours Data[12]

***Smoothing by Moving Averages.*** Moving averages expose underlying trends that tell whether the time-ordered data are increasing or decreasing over the long term. Sometimes the raw data contain many peaks and valleys, and it may be difficult to see the long-term upward or downward changes over time. Figure 2.16 displays the actual percentage personal hours taken and its MA(3).

What does the MA(3) in Figure 2.16 reveal? It shows that the percentage of personal hours increased from under 1% in February of the first year to about 3.50% in November of the second year, when it peaked. The percentage then dropped quickly and reached a low of about 1.50% in September of the third year. Then the percentage of personal hours increased to about 2.40%.

It's not that you couldn't see the pattern from the rough, or original, data, but it was somewhat hidden and more difficult to detect. The underlying data pattern is more obvious in the moving average "smoothed" line graph.

---

[12]The moving average data-analysis tool incorrectly places the first moving average value for a MA($n$). The first value for a MA(3) should be placed in February as shown in Table 2.13, but the tool places the first value in March. The first value of MA(5) should be placed in March, but the tool places the first value in May. The first value for an MA(7) should be placed in April, but the tool places the first value in July. Watch out for these misplacements and correct them in your spreadsheets.

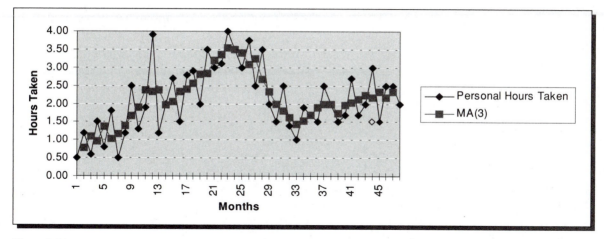

**Figure 2.16**
Original Data and Moving Average[13]

Moving averages of lengths greater than three are common in business. Consider an MA(7). A period's moving average value is the mean of the value for that period, the three periods before, and the three periods after. Thus, Table 2.14 shows that April's moving average value is the mean of January through July's data values, and May's moving average value is the mean of February through August's data values.

| Months | Personal Hours Taken (%) | MA(7) |
|---|---|---|
| Jan. | 0.50 | #N/A |
| Feb. | 1.20 | #N/A |
| March | 0.60 | #N/A |
| April | 1.50 | 0.99 |
| May | 0.80 | 1.09 |
| June | 1.80 | 1.27 |
| July | 0.50 | 1.37 |
| August | 1.20 | 1.43 |
| Sept. | 2.50 | 1.87 |
| Oct. | 1.30 | 1.79 |
| Nov. | 1.90 | 2.00 |
| Dec. | 3.90 | 2.21 |

**Table 2.14**
Constructing an MA(7)

For an MA(7), you cannot compute a moving average for January through March for the first year or October through December of the fourth year.

---

[13]The graph was not done by the charting option for the moving average data-analysis tool. It places the first value of the moving average in the third period (March, see above) rather than in the second period, February. Instead, we used the ChartWizard line-graph option.

Six data values are "lost" when computing a single moving average of length seven.

Figure 2.17 shows that constructing a moving average of length seven will smooth the data even more than an MA(3). In general, the greater the length of the moving average, the greater is the smoothing of the original data set.

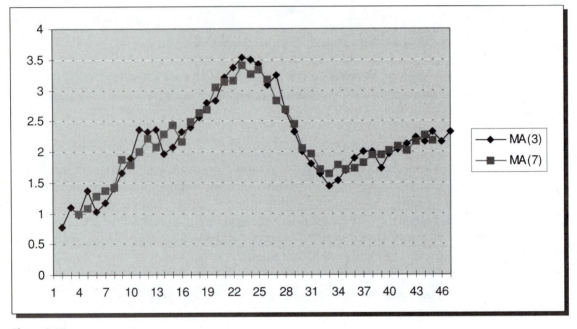

**Figure 2.17**
MA(3) versus MA(7)

In summary, what should the moving average length be? For data *smoothing*, lengths of three, five, or seven are common. For an MA(3), you obtain some smoothing and only "lose" two data points. For an MA(5), you obtain more smoothing, but "lose" four data points. For an MA(7), you obtain even more smoothing, but "lose" six data points. It's a trade-off between the amount of smoothing and the amount of "lost data" you can tolerate. Consider the following rule of thumb: The rougher—more peaks and valleys—the original data, the larger the order, or length (*n*), the moving average must be to see the data's pattern.

# ASSESSING ASSIGNABLE-CAUSE VARIATION FOR TIME-ORDERED DATA

The smoothed line graph is a crucial step in seeing the data's underlying structure, but it is not the last step. You must also analyze the **residuals**—the differences between the original data (rough data) and the moving average (smooth data). Residuals help detect outliers. By the end of this section you should be able to

1. compute and interpret a residual graph;

2. explain how outliers can distort the residuals; and

3. compute and interpret a moving median.

## RESIDUAL GRAPH

Table 2.15 shows the calculated residuals, the original rough-data value minus its corresponding smoothed value, for the 48 months of the percentage of personal hours data.

| Period | 1 | 2 | 3 | 4 | 5 | 6 | 7 | 8 | 9 | 10 | 11 | 12 |
|---|---|---|---|---|---|---|---|---|---|---|---|---|
| Rough | 0.50 | 1.20 | 0.60 | 1.50 | 0.80 | 1.80 | 0.50 | 1.20 | 2.50 | 1.30 | 1.90 | 3.90 |
| Smooth | | 0.77 | 1.10 | 0.97 | 1.37 | 1.03 | 1.17 | 1.40 | 1.67 | 1.90 | 2.37 | 2.33 |
| Residual | | 0.43 | −0.50 | 0.53 | −0.57 | 0.77 | −0.67 | −0.20 | 0.83 | −0.60 | −0.47 | **1.57** |

| Period | 13 | 14 | 15 | 16 | 17 | 18 | 19 | 20 | 21 | 22 | 23 | 24 |
|---|---|---|---|---|---|---|---|---|---|---|---|---|
| Rough | 1.20 | 2.00 | 2.70 | 1.50 | 2.80 | 2.90 | 2.00 | 3.50 | 3.00 | 3.10 | 4.00 | 3.50 |
| Smooth | 2.37 | 1.97 | 2.07 | 2.33 | 2.40 | 2.57 | 2.80 | 2.83 | 3.20 | 3.37 | 3.53 | 3.50 |
| Residual | **−1.17** | 0.03 | 0.63 | −0.83 | 0.40 | 0.33 | −0.80 | 0.67 | −0.20 | −0.27 | 0.47 | 0.00 |

| Period | 25 | 26 | 27 | 28 | 29 | 30 | 31 | 32 | 33 | 34 | 35 | 36 |
|---|---|---|---|---|---|---|---|---|---|---|---|---|
| Rough | 3.00 | 3.75 | 2.50 | 3.50 | 2.00 | 1.50 | 2.50 | 1.40 | 1.00 | 1.90 | 1.70 | 1.70 |
| Smooth | 3.42 | 3.08 | 3.25 | 2.67 | 2.33 | 2.00 | 1.80 | 1.63 | 1.43 | 1.53 | 1.70 | 1.70 |
| Residual | −0.42 | 0.67 | −0.75 | 0.83 | −0.33 | −0.50 | 0.70 | −0.23 | −0.43 | 0.37 | 0.00 | 0.00 |

| Period | 37 | 38 | 39 | 40 | 41 | 42 | 43 | 44 | 45 | 46 | 47 | 48 |
|---|---|---|---|---|---|---|---|---|---|---|---|---|
| Rough | 2.50 | 2.00 | 1.50 | 1.70 | 2.70 | 1.70 | 2.00 | 3.00 | 1.50 | 2.50 | 2.50 | 2.00 |
| Smooth | 2.00 | 2.00 | 1.73 | 1.97 | 2.03 | 2.13 | 2.23 | 2.17 | 2.33 | 2.17 | 2.50 | |
| Residual | 0.50 | 0.00 | −0.23 | −0.27 | 0.67 | −0.43 | −0.23 | 0.83 | −0.83 | 0.33 | 0.00 | |

**Table 2.15**
Residuals for Percentage of Personal Hours Data

Figure 2.18 is a graph for the 46 residual data values. Time is on the horizontal axis, and the residuals are on the vertical axis.

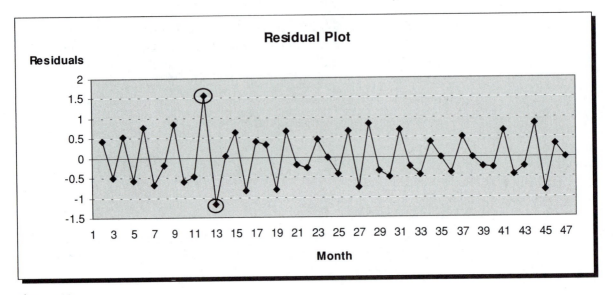

**Figure 2.18**
Residual Graph for the Percentage of Personal Hours Data

Look for large positive or negative residuals. They suggest that something out of the ordinary could have happened. In Figure 2.18, two large residuals stand out from the rest. In December of the first year, the actual percentage of personal hours taken was much higher than the moving average. In the following month, the actual percentage of personal hours taken was much lower than the moving average. Do these large residuals indicate outliers?

Given that the residual plot is stationary (a horizontal swarm of data points), you can treat the data as cross sectional. Excel's data-analysis tool indicated that the 46 residual values are near bell shaped distributed— skewness = 0.29 and kurtosis = −0.48. Given that the residual data are near bell shaped, we use the 3-sigma rule, not Tukey's rule, to detect outliers. An outlier is any data value that is more than three standard deviations below or above the mean. The mean of the 46 residuals is zero and the standard deviation is 0.593. As none of the residuals are less than −1.78 or greater than +1.78, there are no outliers. So management should not label December's residual and January's residual as outliers. The variation from the mean of zero is simply due to common-cause variation.

Had these two residuals been outliers, what should have been done next? Effective business professionals ask what could account for the large positive or negative residuals. Did this occur during the time when the firm considered and then rejected a wage cut? Did the accounting department mistakenly credit some of January's hours to December? Was there a flu epidemic? Effective managers should investigate any residuals that are outliers, determine their causes, and correct them.

## MOVING MEDIAN

Sometimes large residuals from a moving average are merely due to "averaging." The new time-ordered data set in Table 2.16 illustrates this. The original data contain one extreme value (period 5). What impact does it have on an MA(3) and its residuals?

The residual column indicates large negative and positive residuals for periods 4–6. But there was only one extreme value, namely, in period 5. Due to the smoothing by averages of three, the extreme value's impact was spread over three periods. Remember that one data value affects three moving average calculations.

So what is the point? Residuals that are outliers may not be due to assignable causes. They may simply be due to smoothing by averages of three; that is, they may be due to the way you construct a moving average.

| Period | Data | MA(3) | Residual |
|--------|------|-------|----------|
| 1 | 10 | | |
| 2 | 12 | 11.67 | 0.33 |
| 3 | 13 | 12.33 | 0.67 |
| 4 | 12 | 25.00 | **−13.00** |
| 5 | **50** | 25.67 | **24.33** |
| 6 | 15 | 27.00 | **−12.00** |
| 7 | 16 | 15.00 | 1.00 |
| 8 | 14 | 15.67 | −1.67 |
| 9 | 17 | 16.33 | 0.67 |
| 10 | 18 | 18.00 | 0.00 |
| 11 | 19 | 19.00 | 0.00 |
| 12 | 20 | | |

**Table 2.16**
Impact of Extreme
Value on Residuals

Constructing a moving median (MM) series can minimize spurious extreme residuals. Table 2.17 illustrates a moving median of length three.

| Period | Data | Moving Median | Residual |
|--------|------|---------------|----------|
| 1 | 10 | | |
| 2 | 12 | 12 | 0 ——— Median of 10, 12, 13 is 12 |
| 3 | 13 | 12 | 1 ——— Median of 12, 13, 12 is 12 |
| 4 | 12 | 13 | −1 |
| 5 | 50 | 15 | 35 |
| 6 | 15 | 16 | −1 |
| 7 | 16 | 15 | 1 |
| 8 | 14 | 16 | −2 |
| 9 | 17 | 17 | 0 |
| 10 | 18 | 18 | 0 |
| 11 | 19 | 19 | 0 ——— Median of 18, 19, 20 is 19 |
| 12 | 20 | | |

**Table 2.17**
Moving Median of
Length Three

Construct a moving median of length three [MM(3)] as follows:[14]

1. Determine the median of the first three values. Place the median opposite the middle of the three numbers. This is centering and we did this when constructing an MA($n$).

2. Delete the first value and add the fourth data value. Determine the median of these three numbers. Place the median opposite the middle of these three numbers.

3. Continue to do this until you have determined all the medians.

Now only one residual (period 5) indicates the possible presence of an outlier. That's because a median ignores the magnitude of the data values. The median for period 5 was the median for the three values—12, 15, and 50—or 15. It would still have been 15 if the data value for period 5 was 5000. While the median does not change, three moving average values would have been affected very much. So when you obtain a large residual from a moving median, you can eliminate the possibility that it is a spurious large residual. It cannot be due to "averaging."

In summary, moving averages and moving medians help smooth rough time-ordered data. This permits us to see the data's underlying structure.

---

[14]You can use Excel's median function wizard to construct a moving median series. Use it to determine the median for the first three values and then copy and paste the cell expression for the remaining periods.

Residual graphs help detect possible outliers that are due to assignable causes. Both tools are essential for analyzing time-ordered data for quantitative variables.

# GUIDE TO DATA-ANALYSIS METHODS

Figure 2.19 presents an overview of the graphical and analytical methods presented in this chapter. It should help integrate and link the material within Chapter 2. You learned how to organize and summarize the three types of univariate data used in business and to determine outliers.

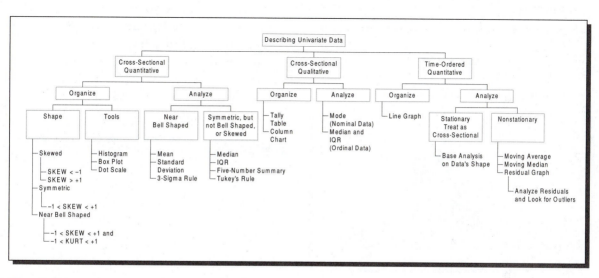

**Figure 2.19**
Integrating Framework for Chapter 2

# EXERCISES

**1.** Explain the logic of the 3-sigma rule that defines an outlier as an observation that is more than three standard deviations away from the mean.

**2.** Is it possible for the first quartile, median, and third quartile to be the same value? If so, what does that indicate about the data?

**3.** Without resorting to math, how could you quickly approximate the mean of a histogram?

**4.** Why is it not possible to add, subtract, multiply, or divide data measured on a nominal scale?

**5.** What problems will you have if you use the mean and standard deviation or the median and interquartile range to summarize nonstationary time-ordered data?

**6.** How does a residual plot aid in detecting problems or opportunities?

**7.** Which box plot suggests that the data are symmetrically distributed and which box plot suggests that the data are skewed?

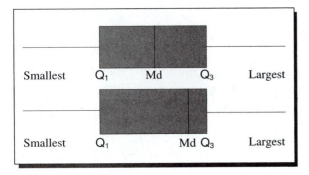

**8.** Below is a frequency histogram of 30 data values. Estimate the data's mean. Are the data symmetric or skewed? Discuss.

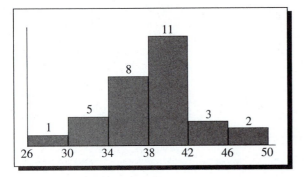

**9.** Given the box plot shown here, determine, if possible, the following values.

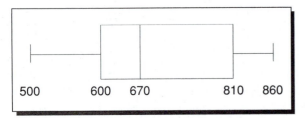

  **a.** the 75th percentile

  **b.** the range that contains the middle 50% of the data values

  **c.** the range that contains the upper 75% of the data values

  **d.** the range that contains the data from the 50th to the 75th percentiles

  **e.** the mean

*Use Excel's Function Wizards, Data-Analysis Tools, and ChartWizard for the following exercises.*

**10.** Best Dairy, Inc., has segmented its market into eight groups. Among these separate markets are the Machos and the Status Seekers. Machos are young, male, blue-collar workers with high school degrees who live in the city. Status Seekers are young, male, white-collar workers with college degrees who live in the suburbs. Best Dairy, Inc., takes a sample of ten from both market segments and asks each person his annual income. The data follow. Are there any differences in incomes between the Machos and Status Seekers?

| Machos | Status Seekers |
|--------|----------------|
| $22,500 | $29,000 |
| 22,000 | 28,500 |
| 21,000 | 28,000 |
| 22,000 | 27,500 |
| 23,000 | 28,500 |
| 23,750 | 29,000 |
| 20,000 | 27,500 |
| 22,500 | 28,000 |
| 23,500 | 28,000 |
| 21,500 | 28,000 |

  **a.** Develop two histograms and two dot scales.

  **b.** Compute the skewness and kurtosis for both data sets.

  **c.** Compute the appropriate measures of the center and spread.

  **d.** What are the differences between the two segments?

**11.** The administrator of the emergency room in Safehaven Hospital in Chicago has recorded the amount of time a patient waits before receiving treatment. The length of time that a patient must wait for treatment is important in determining the size of the emergency room staff. He records the wait times for 200 patients in a typical week. The data follow.

| Class | Frequency |
|-------|-----------|
| Less than 10 minutes | 5 |
| 10 up to 15 minutes | 25 |
| 15 up to 20 minutes | 70 |
| 20 up to 25 minutes | 70 |
| 25 up to 30 minutes | 25 |
| 30 or more minutes | 5 |

**a.** What percentage of patients receives treatment in less than 10 minutes?

**b.** What percentage of patients receives treatment after 30 or more minutes?

**c.** Experience indicates that if 30% of wait times are less than 10 minutes, the emergency room is overstaffed. If 20% of the wait times are 30 or more minutes, the emergency room is understaffed. What can you conclude about Safehaven's emergency staffing?

**d.** Construct a frequency table that would suggest that the emergency room is at times both understaffed and overstaffed.

**12.** The Gallup Poll conducts a survey to determine attitudes toward a balanced budget amendment to the U.S. Constitution. We interview a random sample of 1500 voters and obtain the following results.

Yes     950
No      550

**a.** Draw a column chart for the responses.

**b.** Determine the mode.

**c.** Would it be meaningful to compute the standard deviation?

**13.** The financial manager at a firm wants to know how profit margins—net profit after taxes divided by sales—have done for the past 16 quarters. The data follow.

| Quarter | Profit Margin |
|---------|---------------|
| 1 | 5.05 |
| 2 | 4.10 |
| 3 | 5.15 |
| 4 | 5.20 |
| 5 | 6.75 |
| 6 | 5.30 |
| 7 | 5.35 |
| 8 | 5.40 |
| 9 | 5.95 |
| 10 | 5.50 |
| 11 | 5.15 |
| 12 | 5.60 |
| 13 | 5.65 |
| 14 | 6.70 |
| 15 | 5.75 |
| 16 | 5.80 |

**a.** Develop a line graph.

**b.** Smooth the data using an MA(3).

**c.** Describe the MA(3) in terms a manager could understand.

**d.** Develop a residual plot.

**e.** Based on your answer to part c, what do you expect should happen to profit margin for the next four quarters? If your expectations are not met, what might that mean?

**14.** Minnesota Video wants to compare the sales-to-salary ratio for salespeople in two of its southern sales regions—Charlotte and New Orleans. Sales-to-salary ratio is an employee's sales divided by his or her base salary. Historically, New Orleans has had the highest sales-to-salary ratios. Recently, the Charlotte region has taken measures to increase the ratio. Five-number summaries for all employees in both regions are presented.

| | New Orleans | Charlotte | Charlotte (one year ago) |
|---|---|---|---|
| Minimum | 9 | 9 | 3 |
| Maximum | 25 | 24 | 15 |
| First quartile | 10 | 10 | 7 |
| Median | 12 | 11 | 7 |
| Third quartile | 15 | 15 | 11 |

**a.** Has Charlotte been successful in improving its sales-to-salary ratio? Defend your position.

**b.** How would you attempt to further improve both Charlotte's and New Orleans' sales-to-salary ratio?

**15.** Consider the following time-ordered data of quarterly sales (in thousands) for three years.

| Q1 | Q2 | Q3 | Q4 | Q5 | Q6 |
|---|---|---|---|---|---|
| 25 | 35 | 30 | 120 | 40 | 45 |

| Q7 | Q8 | Q9 | Q10 | Q11 | Q12 |
|---|---|---|---|---|---|
| 40 | 50 | 55 | 60 | 65 | 70 |

**a.** Plot the quarterly data.

**b.** Construct a three-quarter moving average and a residual graph.

**c.** What impact did quarter four's extreme value have on the residuals? Discuss.

**d.** What type of smoothed series should you construct and why?

**e.** Construct the appropriate smoothed series and residual plot you recommended in part d.

**e.** Explain the difference in the two sets of residuals. Which residual graph is more informative and why?

**16.** Historically, over 40% of the accounts receivable at Apex, Inc., have been in excess of 35 days. Apex recently started a program of inducements to reduce the age of the accounts receivable. Two months later a sample of 15 accounts receivable is taken. Given the following data, has the age of the accounts receivable been reduced?

| Number of Days | | | | |
|---|---|---|---|---|
| 20 | 15 | 20 | 16 | 19 |
| 15 | 22 | 21 | 20 | 17 |
| 21 | 30 | 20 | 18 | 15 |

**a.** Develop a histogram for the data and a dot scale.

**b.** Compute the skewness and kurtosis.

**c.** Compute the appropriate measures of the center and spread.

**d.** Has the inducements program been successful? Explain.

**17.** In a survey, 100 Gatemax Computer customers are asked to describe their level of satisfaction with their recently purchased multimedia computer system.

| Very Dissatisfied | 1 |
|---|---|
| Somewhat Dissatisfied | 5 |
| Somewhat Satisfied | 40 |
| Very Satisfied | 54 |

**a.** Determine the median and interquartile range for the 100 responses.

**b.** Suppose we assign scores of 1–4 to the four response categories. Do you see any problems with calculating the mean and standard deviation for the 100 responses?

**18.** The Arbitration Association collects data on the number of grievances filed by plants with between 200 and 300 workers. Shown are the data for the January survey. They want to identify firms with exceptionally low and high numbers of filed grievances. They plan to study these firms.

| Firms | Grievances |
|-------|------------|
| 1 | 70 |
| 2 | 74 |
| 3 | 65 |
| 4 | 45 |
| 5 | 78 |
| 6 | 69 |
| 7 | 99 |
| 8 | 76 |
| 9 | 72 |
| 10 | 62 |

**a.** Compute the median and interquartile range.

**b.** Draw a box-and-whisker plot.

**c.** Identify outliers and label the box plot.

**d.** Having identified two plants that are outliers, what would you do next?

**19.** The given data set is the number of children per household in a survey of ten families.

0  1  1  1  9  2  2  2  3  3

**a.** Compute the mean and the median.

**b.** Given the two values, what does that imply about the data set?

**c.** Compute the most appropriate measure of the variation.

**20.** Managers at Zentron, Inc., maintain a database on the number of personal hours taken in the plant at the end of each month. They want to determine the trend over the past two years. They also want to determine a normal number of hours taken so they can identify a month when the number of hours is out of line. If so, they will investigate.

| Month | Number of Hours Taken | Month | Number of Hours Taken |
|-------|------------------------|-------|------------------------|
| January | 74 | January | 49 |
| February | 51 | February | 63 |
| March | 64 | March | 74 |
| April | 66 | April | 53 |
| May | 50 | May | 69 |
| June | 55 | June | 63 |
| July | 60 | July | 60 |
| August | 72 | August | 63 |
| September | 63 | September | 50 |
| October | 64 | October | 74 |
| November | 60 | November | 51 |
| December | 60 | December | 64 |

**a.** Plot a line graph.

**b.** Are the time-ordered data stationary? Why?

**c.** Compute the mean and standard deviation.

**d.** Assume that no changes occur within the plant. Use the 3-sigma rule to determine how many personal hours taken you should expect in 99.73% of the months.

**e.** If, in the following January, workers took over 90 hours, what might that mean? Why?

**21.** A large health maintenance organization maintains data on men and women who have died in the past ten years. The data include (1) age at death, (2) smoking status, (3) height, (4) weight, (5) amount of exercise per week, (6) blood pressure at last annual physical, and (7) type of diet (fat free, salt free, meat-and-potatoes, etc.). For each of the six risk factors, indicate the scale used to measure each variable.

**22.** Each day the process-control group takes ten cans of the company's best-selling beverage and checks to see if the cans contain 300 mL. The mean results for a ten-day period on the filling volume are listed. This procedure is to ensure that proper filling volume is maintained.

| Day | Filling Volume | Day | Filling Volume |
|-----|-----|-----|-----|
| 1 | 301 | 6 | 295 |
| 2 | 300 | 7 | 290 |
| 3 | 297 | 8 | 291 |
| 4 | 299 | 9 | 287 |
| 5 | 295 | 10 | 285 |

   **a.** Plot the daily means of the filling volumes in a line graph.

   **b.** Compute an MA(3) and plot it.

   **c.** Does it appear that the firm is having trouble with its filling operation? What action should the firm take? Explain your position.

**23.** Spreadsheet 223.xls contains the results of a survey of customer satisfaction with new-car purchases. The database contains the type of car purchased, the level of satisfaction with the car, and the level of satisfaction with the maintenance staff and facilities. Use Excel's PivotTable to complete the exercise.

   **a.** Determine a count and percentage for the three qualitative variables.

   **b.** Describe the general level of satisfaction with the car and with the service facilities and staff.

   **c.** From the tally table, which car was purchased most in the sample of 100 customers?

   **d.** Determine the median level of car satisfaction and median level of customer service satisfaction.

   **e.** Determine the interquartile range for both satisfaction variables.

   **f.** Describe, in plain English, what you learned from parts d and e.

**24.** Financial analysts agree that for an industrial bond to be a safe investment, the firm's total income should be more than three or four times its interest payment. Shown are the interest coverage data, total income divided by bond interest, for the past ten years. Are the firm's bonds a safe investment?

| Year | Interest Coverage* |
|-----|-----|
| 1 | 8.5 |
| 2 | 7.9 |
| 3 | 8.2 |
| 4 | 6.5 |
| 5 | 6.6 |
| 6 | 5.7 |
| 7 | 5.8 |
| 8 | 6.9 |
| 9 | 7.5 |
| 10 | 8.5 |

   **a.** Plot the interest coverage data for the past ten years.

   **b.** Compute an MA(3) and plot it.

   **c.** Describe the overall pattern of the interest coverage ratio for the past ten years. Using only the above time-ordered data, have the firm's industrial bonds been a safe investment for the past ten years?

**25.** The sales of motor homes for Mobile Homes, Inc., for a 20-month period are shown. The sales manager wants to develop a model of sales for the past 20 months. The

---

* In 1982 the firm's total income was 8.5 times as large as its interest on bonds.

manager may use the model to make predictions for the next several months.

| Month | Sales in Units | Month | Sales in Units |
|---|---|---|---|
| 1 | 628 | 11 | 1117 |
| 2 | 652 | 12 | 1214 |
| 3 | 495 | 13 | 762 |
| 4 | 344 | 14 | 846 |
| 5 | 405 | 15 | 1228 |
| 6 | 586 | 16 | 937 |
| 7 | 403 | 17 | 1396 |
| 8 | 700 | 18 | 1174 |
| 9 | 837 | 19 | 628 |
| 10 | 1224 | 20 | 1753 |

**a.** Plot the raw data.

**b.** Compute the mean, standard deviation, median, and interquartile range.

**c.** Do any of the measures summarize the data accurately? Why?

**d.** Compute an MA(3) series and plot it. Are the time-ordered data stationary? Describe the overall pattern of the moving average series.

**26.** Length-of-tenure discounts are the difference between the rents charged longtime tenants and newer tenants. Landlords give discounts because they want to keep good tenants and minimize turnover. The American Housing Group wants to know if the size of the discount is the same in Atlanta and Houston. It collects the following data, which are the percentage discounts at selected apartment complexes in the two cities. Do the discounts differ in the two cities?

| Atlanta | | Houston | |
|---|---|---|---|
| 3.4 | 1.5 | 6.2 | 3.5 |
| 6.5 | 2.0 | 7.2 | 4.6 |
| 11.5 | 3.4 | 5.4 | 5.3 |
| 2.7 | 2.5 | 6.8 | 4.2 |
| 2.3 | 3.9 | 7.1 | 6.9 |
| 2.9 | 1.1 | 10.9 | 7.4 |
| 3.9 | 2.2 | 23.0 | 5.6 |
| 3.2 | | 5.8 | |

**a.** Construct box-and-whisker plots for the two cities.

**b.** Compute the appropriate measures of the center and spread.

**c.** Do the discounts differ between Atlanta and Houston? How?

**d.** What economic and demographic variables might account for the difference between Atlanta and Houston length-of-tenure discounts?

**27.** The product life cycle tells us that the sales for a product are slow right after introduction, increase at an increasing rate, increase at a constant rate, begin to level off, and may even decline. Do the following sales data behave as the life cycle predicts?

| Year | Sales (in thousands) | Year | Sales (in thousands) |
|---|---|---|---|
| 1 | 5 | 10 | 54 |
| 2 | 7 | 11 | 57 |
| 3 | 10 | 12 | 61 |
| 4 | 19 | 13 | 60 |
| 5 | 31 | 14 | 59 |
| 6 | 47 | 15 | 57 |
| 7 | 49 | 16 | 55 |
| 8 | 52 | 17 | 56 |
| 9 | 50 | 18 | 54 |

**a.** Compute an MA(3) for the yearly sales and plot it.

**b.** Use the moving average series to describe the growth of your product. Do sales follow the product life-cycle model?

**c.** Given the product's stage in year 18, what actions should the firm consider?

**28.** Spreadsheet 228.xls contains two financial ratios—current ratio and net sales to net worth—of 50 firms within an industry.

**a.** Develop a histogram for both variables.

**b.** Based on the skewness and kurtosis of each variable, compute the appropriate measure of the center and the spread.

**c.** Are any of the current ratio data values or net sales-to-net worth data values outliers? Discuss.

**29.** Spreadsheet 229.xls contains 60 months of time-ordered data on the sales in thousands of units.

**a.** Compute and interpret an MA(3) and an MA(5).

**b.** Develop residual graphs for both moving averages.

**c.** What do the residual plots indicate? Discuss.

**30.** Spreadsheet 230.xls contains qualitative data from a survey of 30 hospitals. The data are hospital type and patients' ratings of the quality of hospital services along a seven-point scale (1 = poor to 7 = outstanding).

**a.** Determine the modal hospital type.

**b.** Determine the median and interquartile range for the quality of hospital services.

**31.** Below are time-ordered data on the number of customer complaints per month before and after the implementation of a total quality management program (TQM). The goal of TQM is to reduce complaints, improve service, and ultimately increase net profits.

| Before | | | | | | | | | | | |
|---|---|---|---|---|---|---|---|---|---|---|---|
| J | F | M | A | MY | J | JL | AU | SE | O | N | D |
| 46 | 46 | 45 | 45 | 43 | 46 | 47 | 42 | 45 | 43 | 48 | 43 |

| After | | | | | | | | | | | |
|---|---|---|---|---|---|---|---|---|---|---|---|
| J | F | M | A | MY | J | JL | AU | SE | O | N | D |
| 41 | 39 | 40 | 37 | 36 | 35 | 35 | 36 | 31 | 31 | 28 | 29 |

**a.** Develop a line graph for the two years of data.

**b.** Has TQM been successful? Why?

**32.** Consider the following time-ordered data set consisting of quarterly sales data (in thousands) for three years.

| Q1 | Q2 | Q3 | Q4 | Q5 | Q6 |
|---|---|---|---|---|---|
| 25 | 35 | 30 | 120 | 40 | 45 |
| Q7 | Q8 | Q9 | Q10 | Q11 | Q12 |
| 40 | 50 | 55 | 60 | 65 | 70 |

**a.** Plot the data and compute an MA(3).

**b.** Determine the residuals.

**c.** Is it necessary to construct an MM(3)? Why not?

**33.** American Breakfast sells 10-ounce boxes of its cereals. Each hour the Statistical Process Control Department takes a sample of four boxes from the production line and weighs the contents. This is to ensure that it does have 10 ounces in its boxes.

| Hour | Weight of Four Boxes off the Line | | | |
|------|------|------|------|------|
| 0800–0900 | 9.8 | 10.0 | 10.1 | 9.9 |
| 0900–1000 | 9.9 | 10.0 | 10.2 | 10.0 |
| 1000–1100 | 9.8 | 10.0 | 9.7 | 10.2 |
| 1100–1200 | 10.1 | 10.0 | 9.9 | 9.8 |
| 1200–1300 | 9.7 | 10.0 | 9.9 | 10.0 |
| 1300–1400 | 10.4 | 10.0 | 9.8 | 9.8 |
| 1400–1500 | 9.9 | 10.2 | 9.7 | 10.3 |
| 1500–1600 | 9.8 | 10.0 | 10.0 | 10.0 |
| 1600–1700 | 10.0 | 9.9 | 9.8 | 10.2 |
| 1700–1800 | 9.9 | 10.0 | 10.1 | 10.0 |

a. Compute the ten hourly means and ranges. Plot the ten hourly means and ranges in two separate line graphs.

b. Compute the mean and standard deviation of the ten hourly sample means and ranges.

Assuming that the means and ranges are bell shaped, 99.73% of the hourly means (and hourly ranges) should lie within a distance of three standard deviations from their respective means.

c. Suppose that the hourly mean weight of the four boxes for hour 1900–2000 is 9.5 ounces. What might that signify? Why?

d. Suppose that the hourly range is 1.8 ounces for hour 2100–2200. What might that signify? Why?

e. Given your answers to parts c and d, what action would you take if you were the plant manager?

34. Below is a data set of incomes of a "sociables" market segment for an upscale bottled water firm.

| | | | | | |
|--------|--------|--------|--------|--------|--------|
| 45,500 | 47,000 | 50,000 | 45,500 | 52,500 | 40,000 |
| 51,000 | 43,000 | 94,500 | 82,500 | 55,000 | 47,000 |
| 46,000 | 54,500 | 57,500 | 42,000 | 51,000 | 45,000 |

a. Construct a histogram and a dot scale.

b. Based on the histogram and data's skewness and kurtosis, compute the appropriate measures of the center and the spread.

c. Construct and interpret a box-and-whisker plot.

d. Based on the box plot, do any of the incomes qualify as outliers? Discuss.

35. A measure of a stock's volatility relative to an average stock is the beta coefficient. A beta of one means that the stock tends to move up and down in step with a market index such as the S&P 500. Below are 25 beta coefficients for firms in one industry.

| | | | | |
|------|------|------|------|------|
| 1.74 | 1.14 | 1.57 | 0.88 | 1.09 |
| 1.19 | 0.98 | 0.96 | 1.36 | 1.28 |
| 0.63 | 1.09 | 0.63 | 0.77 | 0.75 |
| 1.27 | 1.46 | 0.70 | 0.71 | 1.37 |
| 0.90 | 1.18 | 0.72 | 0.98 | 0.97 |

a. Construct a histogram and a dot scale.

b. Based on the histogram and data's skewness and kurtosis, compute the appropriate measures of the center and the spread.

c. Based on the appropriate rule for detecting outliers, do any of the beta coefficients qualify as outliers? Discuss.

36. Firms buy or sell foreign currencies as a means of **hedging exchange rate exposure**. For example, a U.S. firm purchases 5000 watches for 1 million Swiss francs to be paid in 180 days. The firm would like to take advantage of the trade credit for 180 days. However, if the firm thought that the franc would appreciate against the dollar, it might purchase 1 million francs for delivery in 180 days for a known amount of U.S. dollars. The firm has protected itself against the possibility of the Swiss franc appreciating against the U.S. dollar. This device passes the exchange-rate risk for a price on to a

professional risk taker. Below are data on 15 firms that use or don't use hedging.

| Firm | Use Hedging | Sales in Millions |
|------|-------------|-------------------|
| 1 | yes | 2100 |
| 2 | yes | 4500 |
| 3 | no | 450 |
| 4 | no | 750 |
| 5 | yes | 5450 |
| 6 | yes | 5155 |
| 7 | no | 3020 |
| 8 | no | 350 |
| 9 | yes | 7500 |
| 10 | no | 245 |
| 11 | yes | 4500 |
| 12 | yes | 4000 |
| 13 | no | 550 |
| 14 | no | 600 |
| 15 | yes | 3500 |

**a.** Determine a count and percentage for those firms that use hedging.

**b.** Compute the mean and standard deviation for those firms that do and do not hedge. Describe the differences. What conclusions can you draw about the specific 15 firms in the study?

**37.** Shown here are the daily closing prices of the Kaufman Fund, a highly successful aggressive-growth mutual fund, over a 30-day period—mid-July to mid-August 1997. Read across.

| | | | | | | | |
|---|---|---|---|---|---|---|---|
| $6.16 | 6.15 | 6.15 | 6.20 | 6.20 | 6.22 | 6.23 | 6.25 |
| 6.30 | 6.33 | 6.35 | 6.40 | 6.37 | 6.35 | 6.34 | 6.33 |
| 6.37 | 6.39 | 6.40 | 6.40 | 6.39 | 6.41 | 6.43 | 6.45 |
| 6.49 | 6.50 | 6.78 | 6.49 | 6.50 | 6.53 | | |

**a.** Plot the time series.

**b.** Develop an MA(3). Describe the behavior of the Kaufman Fund during the 30-day period.

**c.** Develop a residual graph. Compute the skewness and kurtosis of the residuals. Were any closing prices outliers?

## CASE STUDY

Rachel Stuart, HR director at Computer Technics, is conducting a wage and salary review of the AS/400 programmer/analyst position. She wants to ensure that the firm remains competitive in hiring and retaining AS/400 analysts. Table 2.18 contains a breakdown of salaries by number of years of experience.

| Salary + Bonus × $1000 | Mean |
|------------------------|------|
| Less than 1 Year | 35 |
| 1–2 Years | 38 |
| 3–4 Years | 41 |
| 5–6 Years | 43 |
| 7–8 Years | 52 |
| 9+ Years | 58 |

**Table 2.18**   Salary Structure for AS/400 Analysts

She compares the firm's salary structure with a recent Nate Vialli Associates' survey conducted for *Midrange Computing Magazine*.

See http://www.midrangecomputing.com/salary/prg97/fall.htm for entire data set.

| Salary + Bonus × $1000 | Mean | Mean of Top 20% | Median | 80th Percentile |
|---|---|---|---|---|
| Less than 1 Year | 36.6 | 50.4 | 35.0 | 45.0 |
| 1–2 Years | 35.8 | 49.1 | 34.8 | 42.3 |
| 3–4 Years | 39.8 | 55.0 | 38.5 | 47.9 |
| 5–6 Years | 43.2 | 58.1 | 42.4 | 50.0 |
| 7–8 Years | 46.6 | 61.2 | 44.8 | 54.5 |
| 9+ Years | 50.0 | 68.1 | 48.0 | 58.2 |

**Table 2.19**  Vialli Survey Findings

What action, if any, should Ms. Stuart recommend to the firm's CFO? Prepare a one-page report. Use the data to support your position.

# CHAPTER 2
# APPENDICES

## I. LISTING OF EXCEL TOOLS USED IN CHAPTER

1. Histogram data-analysis tool
2. Descriptive Statistics data-analysis tool
3. QUARTILE function wizard
4. SKEW function wizard
5. KURT function wizard
6. ChartWizard: Column Chart
7. ChartWizard: Line Graph
8. PivotTable
9. Moving Average data-analysis tool

## II. FREQUENCY TABLE AND HISTOGRAM

1. Enter bins as a label in cell D1, enter 90 in cell D2, and enter 95 in cell D3. Select D2:D3. Drag the Autofill square in the lower right of the selected range down to cell D8.

Bins and Data for Histogram Tool Analysis

|    | A | B | C | D | E | F | G |
|----|---|---|---|---|---|---|---|
| 1  | Productivity | Hours of Downtime |  | Bins |  |  |  |
| 2  | 106 | 6.41 |  | 90 |  |  |  |
| 3  | 95  | 8.12 |  | 95 |  |  |  |
| 4  | 103 | 5.36 |  | 100 |  |  |  |
| 5  | 91  | 3.51 |  | 105 |  |  |  |
| 6  | 94  | 5.05 |  | 110 |  |  |  |
| 7  | 92  | 5.15 |  | 115 |  |  |  |
| 8  | 95  | 6.77 |  | 120 |  |  |  |
| 9  | 93  | 5.45 |  |  |  |  |  |
| 10 | 102 | 6.14 |  |  |  |  |  |
| 11 | 89  | 7.02 |  |  |  |  |  |
| 12 | 95  | 5.84 |  |  |  |  |  |
| 13 | 98  | 6.42 |  |  |  |  |  |

**2.** From the Tools menu, choose the Data Analysis command and choose the Histogram from the Analysis Tools list box.

**3. Input Range** Enter the range of cells containing the productivity data (A1:A37) including the label.

**4. Bin Range** Enter the range of cells containing the values that indicate the upper limits of each class (D1:D8) including the label. The bins must be in ascending order.

**5. Labels** Check this box to indicate that labels have been included in the Input Range and Bin Range.

**6. Output Range** Enter the upper left-cell of the range where you want the output table to appear (E1).

**7. Chart Output** Check this box to obtain a histogram. If left unchecked, you obtain a frequency table only.

Frequency Table for Productivity Data

| | A | B | C | D | E | F | G |
|---|---|---|---|---|---|---|---|
| 1 | Productivity | Hours of Downtime | | Bins | Bin | Frequency | |
| 2 | 106 | 6.41 | | 90 | 90 | 1 | |
| 3 | 95 | 8.12 | | 95 | 95 | 21 | |
| 4 | 103 | 5.36 | | 100 | 100 | 4 | |
| 5 | 91 | 3.51 | | 105 | 105 | 5 | |
| 6 | 94 | 5.05 | | 110 | 110 | 3 | |
| 7 | 92 | 5.15 | | 115 | 115 | 1 | |
| 8 | 95 | 6.77 | | 120 | 120 | 0 | |
| 9 | 93 | 5.45 | | | More | 1 | |
| 10 | 102 | 6.14 | | | | | |
| 11 | 89 | 7.02 | | | | | |
| 12 | 95 | 5.84 | | | | | |
| 13 | 98 | 6.42 | | | | | |
| 14 | 107 | 6.50 | | | | | |

You also obtain a histogram (not shown here).

# III. DESCRIPTIVE DATA-ANALYSIS TOOL

1. From the Tools menu, choose the Data Analysis command and choose Descriptive Statistics from the Analysis Tools list box.

2. **Input Range** Enter the range of cells containing the hours of downtime data (B1:B37) including the label.

3. **Labels** Check this box to indicate that the label has been included in the Input Range.

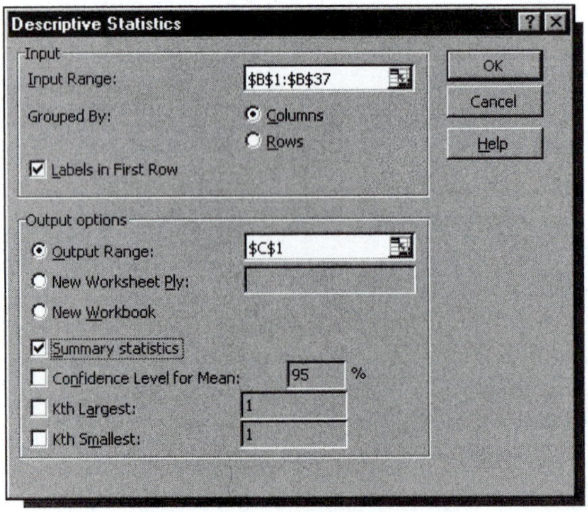

4. **Output Range** Enter the upper left-cell of the range where you want the output table to appear (C1).

5. **Summary Statistics** Check this box for descriptive statistics.

Descriptive Statistics Output for Downtime Hours

| | A | B | C | D | E | F | G |
|---|---|---|---|---|---|---|---|
| 1 | Productivity | Hours of Downtime | *Hours of Downtime* | | | | |
| 2 | 106 | 6.41 | | | | | |
| 3 | 95 | 8.12 | Mean | 5.428175 | | | |
| 4 | 103 | 5.36 | Standard Error | 0.195197 | | | |
| 5 | 91 | 3.51 | Median | 5.353945 | | | |
| 6 | 94 | 5.05 | Mode | 5.05 | | | |
| 7 | 92 | 5.15 | Standard Deviation | 1.171184 | | | |
| 8 | 95 | 6.77 | Sample Variance | 1.371672 | | | |
| 9 | 93 | 5.45 | Kurtosis | 0.753006 | | | |
| 10 | 102 | 6.14 | Skewness | −0.0616 | | | |
| 11 | 89 | 7.02 | Range | 5.78 | | | |
| 12 | 95 | 5.84 | Minimum | 2.34 | | | |
| 13 | 98 | 6.42 | Maximum | 8.12 | | | |
| 14 | 107 | 6.50 | Sum | 195.4143 | | | |
| 15 | 100 | 7.86 | Count | 36 | | | |
| 16 | 95 | 4.56 | Confidence Level (95.000%) | 0.382579 | | | |

# IV. PIVOTTABLE WIZARD

1. Select a cell anywhere in the database so that Excel will automatically determine the range of data you want to use. From the Data menu, choose the PivotTable Report command.

Data for Two Qualitative Variables

| | A | B | C |
|---|---|---|---|
| 1 | Type of Institution | Quality Rating | |
| 2 | Bank | 4 | |
| 3 | Other | 2 | |
| 4 | Bank | 5 | |
| 5 | Bank | 4 | |
| 6 | Bank | 5 | |
| 7 | Other | 1 | |
| 8 | Other | 2 | |
| 9 | Bank | 4 | |
| 10 | Bank | 5 | |
| 11 | Other | 3 | |
| 12 | Other | 1 | |
| 13 | Other | 1 | |

**2.** In step 1 of 4, select the radio button (if not already selected) for Microsoft Excel List or Database, and click Next.

**3.** In step 2 verify that Excel has selected the appropriate range (A1:B51), and click Next.

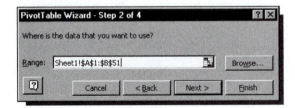

**4.** In step 3, click the Type of Institution field button on the right and drag it to the ROW area on the left and release it. Click the Type of Institution field button again and drag it to the DATA area. When you release the mouse button, the Type of Institution becomes "Count of Type of Institution" as shown below. If the button in the DATA area isn't labeled "Count of" double click it. In the "Summarize by" list box that next appears, select Count and click OK.

**5.** In step 4, click the existing worksheet and then type in C1 to place the pivot table. Click Finish.

**6.** Shown below is the finished product. The tally table shown is a count table for the Type of Institution data.

Output from PivotTable

|    | A | B | C | D | E |
|----|---|---|---|---|---|
| 1  | Type of Institution | Quality Rating | Count of Type of Institution | | |
| 2  | Bank | 4 | Type of Ins | Total | |
| 3  | Other | 2 | Bank | 29 | |
| 4  | Bank | 5 | Other | 21 | |
| 5  | Bank | 4 | Grand Total | 50 | |
| 6  | Bank | 5 | | | |
| 7  | Other | 1 | | | |
| 8  | Other | 2 | | | |
| 9  | Bank | 4 | | | |
| 10 | Bank | 5 | | | |

**7.** To obtain a percentage table, select a cell in the pivot table containing a count (in column D). Click the right mouse button, and choose PivotTable Field. To display additional options, click the Options button. In the Show Data as: drop-down list box, select % of total. Click OK.

# V. MOVING AVERAGE

**1.** From the Tools menu, choose Data Analysis. Click on the Moving Average in the Analysis Tools list box, and click OK. The Moving Average dialog box shown below appears.

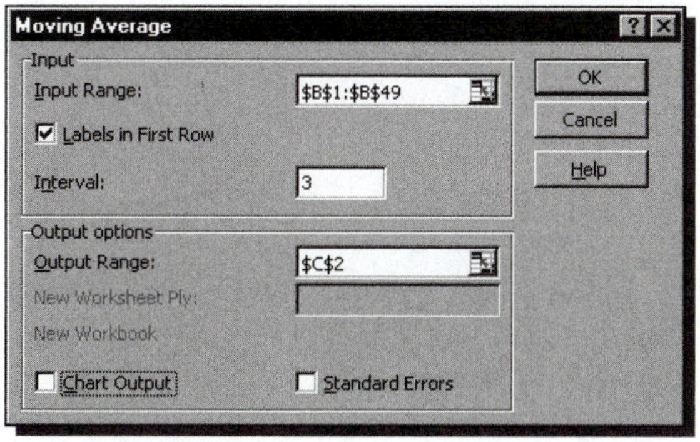

**2.** Complete the dialog box as shown. For smoothing data, do not click the Chart Output or Standard Errors boxes. Click OK.

**3.** Shown is the completed and uncorrected moving average series.

|  | A | B | C |
|---|---|---|---|
| 1 |  | Personal Hours Taken (%) |  |
| 2 | Jan | 0.50 | #N/A |
| 3 | Feb | 1.20 | #N/A |
| 4 | Mar | 0.60 | 0.77 |
| 5 | Apr | 1.50 | 1.10 |
| 6 | May | 0.80 | 0.97 |
| 7 | Jun | 1.80 | 1.37 |
| 8 | Jul | 0.50 | 1.03 |
| 9 | Aug | 1.20 | 1.17 |
| 10 | Sep | 2.50 | 1.40 |
| 11 | Oct | 1.30 | 1.67 |

Misplaced. It should line up with February.

Notice how the tool misplaced 0.77. It should be the moving average for February, but it placed it in March.

Cut the moving average series, starting in cell C4, and paste it into cell C3.

Moving Average Series (Corrected)

|  | A | B | C |
|---|---|---|---|
| 1 |  | Personal Hours Taken (%) |  |
| 2 | Jan | 0.50 | #N/A |
| 3 | Feb | 1.20 | 0.77 |
| 4 | Mar | 0.60 | 1.10 |
| 5 | Apr | 1.50 | 0.97 |
| 6 | May | 0.80 | 1.37 |
| 7 | Jun | 1.80 | 1.03 |
| 8 | Jul | 0.50 | 1.17 |
| 9 | Aug | 1.20 | 1.40 |
| 10 | Sep | 2.50 | 1.67 |
| 11 | Oct | 1.30 | 1.90 |

Now it does line up with February.

# VI. FIVE-NUMBER SUMMARY AND BOX PLOT

1. Use Excel's QUARTILE function wizard to determine the five-number summary for the downtime data shown in B2:B37. Place the five-number summary in cells C1 through G1, one at a time. Insert 0 for the desired quart to obtain the minimum value, insert 1 for the desired quart to obtain the first quartile value, and so forth. Insert 4 to obtain the maximum value.

**2.** In cell C4 type 85 and in cell D4 type 90. Select cells C4 and D4 and then point to the fill handle in cell D4. The pointer changes to a cross. Drag the fill handle to cell K4 (not shown).

|     | A          | B            | C  | D  | E  | F   | G   | H   |
|-----|------------|--------------|----|----|----|-----|-----|-----|
| 1   | Worker     | Productivity | 89 | 93 | 95 | 101 | 123 |     |
| 2   | 1          | 106          |    |    |    |     |     |     |
| 3   | 2          | 95           |    |    |    |     |     |     |
| 4   | 3          | 103          | 85 | 90 | 95 | 100 | 105 | 110 |
| 5   | 4          | 91           |    |    |    |     |     |     |
| 6   | 5          | 94           |    |    |    |     |     |     |
| 7   | 6          | 92           |    |    |    |     |     |     |
| 8   | 7          | 95           |    |    |    |     |     |     |
| 9   | 8          | 93           |    |    |    |     |     |     |
| 10  | 9          | 102          |    |    |    |     |     |     |
| 11  | 10         | 89           |    |    |    |     |     |     |
| 12  | 11         | 95           |    |    |    |     |     |     |
| 13  | 12         | 98           |    |    |    |     |     |     |

**3.** Click on the line button and while holding down the shift key draw a vertical line at the minimum value of 89. Also draw a vertical line at the median value and maximum value.

**4.** Click on rectangle button and click at first quartile value of 93 and drag rectangle to the third quartile value of 101.

**5.** Click on line button and while holding down the shift key draw a horizontal line from minimum value to the first quartile value (left side of rectangle). Draw line from the third quartile value (right side of rectangle) to the maximum value of 123.

# Chapter 3

# BASIC PROBABILITY
# CONCEPTS AND PROBLEMS
# IN ASSESSING PROBABILITIES

## INTRODUCTION

Chapter 3 provides tools to accomplish three goals. First, you will learn how to compute probabilities to make estimates or judgments under uncertain conditions. Second, you will learn how to determine if two factors such as gender (male or female) and promotion status (promoted or not promoted) are related *for a specific sample*. Finally, you will learn how to reduce the chances of making a common managerial error of judgment, the noncoherency error.

Consider the following situation. Five years ago a firm hired 200 entry-level programmers for a new department. There were 120 males and 80 females. Five years later, the firm promoted 70 people—60 males and 10 females. *For the specific sample of 200 employees*, does one's gender affect one's chance of being promoted? That is, does it appear that the firm is guilty of violating the 1964 Civil Rights Act that extended to women the legal rights enjoyed by men? You will be able to answer this question by the chapter's end.

Figure 3.1 is a *frequency tree* that displays the gender and promotion data presented above. Note that the top branch displays the total sample size of 200 employees. Of these, 120 are males and 80 are females. These are at the tree's second level—the "children" of the top branch. Of the 120 males, 60 were promoted (and 60 were not). These are at the tree's third level—the "children" of the 120 males' branch. Of the 80 females, 10 were promoted (and 70 were not). These are at the third level—the "children" of the 80 females' branch.

The four bottom boxes provide two important pieces of information. First, they tell us how many promoted males (60), not promoted males (60), promoted females (10), and not promoted females (70) there were in the study. Second, adding the two boxes partially labeled *Promoted* tell us that 70 people were promoted and 130 were not. You will use Figure 3.1 later in the chapter to compute probabilities.

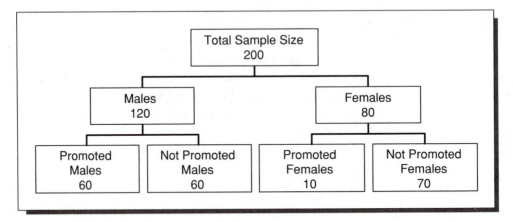

**Figure 3.1**
Frequency Tree for Gender and Promotion Study Data

---

**D E F I N I T I O N**    A frequency tree portrays the number, or frequency, of people or elements classified by two or more attributes.

---

We can redraw Figure 3.1 and place the promoted versus not promoted attribute as the second level of the tree. Figure 3.2 is the redrawn frequency tree.

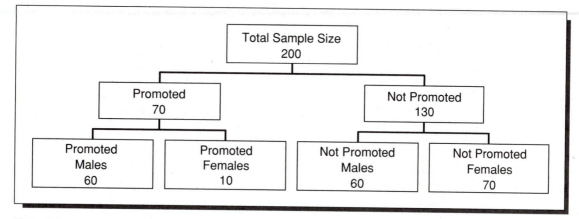

**Figure 3.2**
Redrawn Frequency Tree for Gender and Promotion Study Data

Consider a second situation. The director of planning for a utility company must determine if additional power plants are needed in the next ten years. She believes that it depends on whether (1) consumers will increase conservation efforts beyond present levels and (2) the federal government will permit taxpayers to deduct conservation costs from their tax bills.

The director estimates that there is a 0.50 chance of increased conservation efforts and a 0.60 chance that the taxpayers will be able to deduct conservation costs. Further, if the tax policy does permit deductions for conservation costs, the chance of increased conservation efforts will be higher than her 0.50 estimate—say, 0.85.

The three chance estimates—0.50, 0.60, 0.85—cannot all be correct. You will know why by the chapter's end.

## TYPES OF PROBABILITY

Probabilities are numbers between 0 and 1. Rare events, those that are not likely to occur, will have probabilities close to 0. Common events, those that are likely to occur, will have probabilities close to 1. By the end of this section you should be able to

1. distinguish between personal and relative-frequency probabilities and

2. compute unconditional, joint, and union probabilities using a frequency tree.

Managers use two methods to estimate probabilities. First, they can **assess** or "guestimate" personal probabilities. Or they can **compute** relative-frequency probabilities.

## ASSESSING PERSONAL PROBABILITIES

Managers use personal probabilities when assessing the chances of either never-before-happened events or events about which they have little or no information. What is the probability that the federal government will permit taxpayers to deduct conservation costs on their tax bills within the next ten years? What is the probability that an alien spacecraft landed in Roswell, New Mexico, in 1947?

Personal probabilities reflect one's personal beliefs and biases about the chance of an event happening. You would assign a probability of 0 if you were absolutely certain that the event would not occur; you would assign a probability of 1 if you were absolutely certain that the event would occur. The more certain you are that an event will occur, the greater is your personal probability of the event.

There is good news and bad news regarding personal probabilities. The good news is that they are very easy to assign. The bad news is that they are easy to assign. Irrelevant factors often influence a manager's personal probability estimates.

Let's illustrate how irrelevant factors can affect personal probability estimates. For example, is a person more likely to die from an accidental fall or from the accidental discharge of a firearm? What are your personal probability estimates for both events?

Many people assign a higher probability to death by the accidental discharge of a firearm. That is because such deaths make the evening news! According to the U.S. Public Health Service, the probability of death from an accidental fall is many times greater than from the accidental discharge of a firearm. People's probability estimates can be biased by the amount of media exposure—surely an irrelevant factor.

Managers often develop erroneous personal probability estimates. This was true of the three estimates the director of planning developed in the second case presented earlier. While her three estimates—0.50, 0.60, and 0.85—reflect her thinking about the future, they are not valid. Later you will know why they violate the most fundamental rule of probability.

## COMPUTING RELATIVE-FREQUENCY PROBABILITIES

Often managers use data to estimate probabilities based on computing relative frequencies.[1] In the gender and promotion study, the manager had data on 200 employees over a five-year period (see Figure 3.1). When valid data

---

[1]Technically, relative frequencies only estimate probabilities. A probability is a fixed and unchanging number between zero and one. It represents the relative frequency of an event based on an infinite sample size.

are available, managers use Expression (3.1) to estimate probabilities based on relative frequencies.

$$P\left(A\right) \approx \text{Relative frequency}\left(A\right) = \frac{\text{Frequency}\left(A\right)}{\text{Total Sample Size}}$$

(3.1)

Let's use Figure 3.1 and Expression (3.1) to compute three different types of probabilities.

**D E F I N I T I O N**      An **unconditional** probability is the probability of one event A, P(A).

The four unconditional probabilities in the gender and promotion study are

P(Male)              P(Promoted)

P(Female)            P(Not Promoted)

The denominator for Expression (3.1) is 200 employees for the four above probabilities. Figure 3.1 reproduced here provides the numerators (shown in a larger font in bold italic) for the two calculations shown here.

P(Male) = 120/200 = 0.60   P(Promoted) = (60 + 10)/200 = 0.35

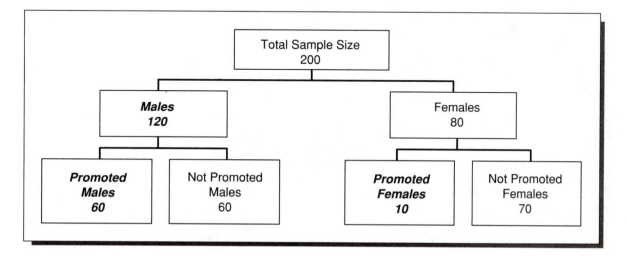

In summary, unconditional probabilities focus on a *single* event—male, promoted, etc. These will be critical in later determining if gender and promotion are related in the specific sample of 200 employees.

---

**DEFINITION**    A **joint** probability is the probability of two (or more) events, P(A **AND** B).

---

The four joint probabilities in the gender and promotion study are

P(Male AND Promoted)

P(Male AND Not Promoted)

P(Female AND Promoted)

P(Female AND Not Promoted)

You can rewrite the four joint probabilities into a more managerially friendly form as follows:

| Traditional Format | Managerially Friendly Format |
|---|---|
| P(Male AND Promoted) | P(Promoted Male) |
| P(Male AND Not Promoted) | P(Not Promoted Male) |
| P(Female AND Promoted) | P(Promoted Female) |
| P(Female AND Not Promoted) | P(Not Promoted Female) |

Note that in the managerially friendly format, each probability represents two events or employee descriptors. For example, a Promoted Male is both a *male and promoted* employee.

Use Expression (3.1) to compute joint probabilities. The denominator for Expression (3.1) is still 200 employees for the four joint–probability calculations in the gender and promotion study. Figure 3.1 reproduced here provides the numerators (shown in a larger font in bold italic) for the two calculations shown here.

$$P\left(\text{Promoted Male}\right) = 60/200 = 0.30 \quad P\left(\text{Not Promoted Female}\right) = 70/200 = 0.35$$

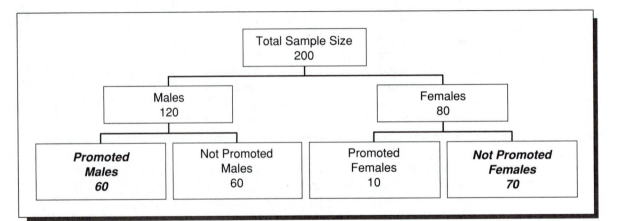

In summary, you can always find the numerators for computing joint probabilities at the bottom level of a frequency tree. Joint probabilities are not critical in determining if gender and promotion are related in the sample of 200 employees.

---

**D E F I N I T I O N**          A **union** probability is the probability of two (or more) events, P(A **OR** B).

The four union probabilities in the gender and promotion study are

P(Male OR Promoted)

P(Male OR Not Promoted)

P(Female OR Promoted)

P(Female OR Not Promoted)

Again, use Expression (3.1) to compute union probabilities. The denominator for Expression (3.1) is still 200 employees for the four union-probability calculations in the gender and promotion study. Figure 3.1 reproduced here provides the numerators (shown in a larger font in bold italic) for the calculation shown here.

$$P\left(\textbf{Male OR Promoted}\right) = \frac{60 + 60 + 10}{200} = 0.65$$

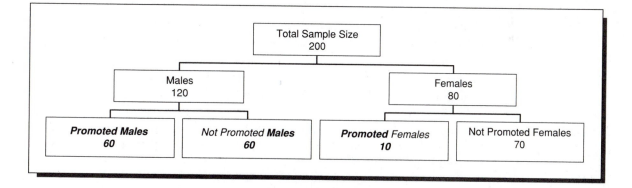

The frequency of Males OR Promoted Employees includes the 120 males and 10 promoted females for a total of 130 employees. We only excluded the Not Promoted Female group from the numerator.

In summary, use the bottom level of a frequency tree to compute the numerators for union probabilities. These, too, are not critical in determining if gender and promotion are related in the sample of 200 employees.

# COMPUTING CONDITIONAL PROBABILITIES AND STATISTICAL INDEPENDENCE

Is promotion status related to gender? Does one's gender affect the likelihood of being promoted? Or in general, are two attributes or descriptors related? This section introduces **conditional probability**. The combination of computed unconditional and conditional probabilities will help determine if two attributes are related. By the end of this section you should be able to

1. distinguish between unconditional and conditional probability;

2. explain, in your own words, what statistical independence is;

3. compute conditional probabilities using a frequency tree; and

4. determine if, for a specific sample, two attributes are related to one another.

## CONDITIONAL PROBABILITY

Here are three probabilities regarding the gender and promotion data:

1. Select one person from the 200 employees. Given no other information, what is the probability that the person has been promoted?

2. Select one person from the 200 employees. Suppose that employee is a male. Now what is the probability that the person has been promoted?

3. Select one person from the 200 employees. Suppose that employee has a size 7C shoe. Now what is the probability that the person has been promoted?

What is different about these three probabilities? The first probability provides no information about the employee beyond promotion status. The first probability describes an unconditional probability. The last two probabilities provide information about the employee's gender and shoe size, respectively. The last two probabilities are **conditional probabilities**.

---

**DEFINITION**    A **conditional** probability is the probability of event A, **given** that event B is known, P(A | B).

---

Event B in the second probability is that the employee is a male. Event B in the third probability is that the employee has a size 7C shoe. Following are the three statements translated into probability notation.

1. P(Promoted)                    Unconditional Probability

2. P(Promoted | Male)             Conditional Probability

3. P(Promoted | Shoe Size is 7C)  Conditional Probability

Read the probability notation as follows. P(Promoted) is simply the probability of being promoted. P(Promoted | Male) is the probability of being promoted *given* or *if* you are male. That is, read the symbol, | , as "given" or "if."

From Figures 3.1 or 3.2 you already know that the P(Promoted) is 70/200 = 0.35. The third probability tells us that the employee has a shoe size of 7C. What would you logically say is the conditional probability of being promoted knowing this fact? Please think about it before reading on.

Presumably you would not change the probability figure of 0.35 upon knowing the employee's shoe size. After all, an employee's shoe size does not affect the likelihood of being promoted. Thus you would probably conclude that

$$P(\text{Promoted} \mid \text{Shoe Size is 7C}) = 0.35$$

So what have you learned? You have *logically* concluded that one's chance of being promoted and one's shoe size are *statistically independent* events. Knowing that event B happened did not cause you to revise the original unconditional probability of being promoted from 0.35.

## STATISTICAL INDEPENDENCE AND DEPENDENCE

Two events can be statistically independent or dependent. The following table distinguishes independent and dependent events.

| Independent Events | Dependent Events |
| --- | --- |
| P(A \| B) = P(A) | P(A \| B) ≠ P(A) |
| The probability of the occurrence of A does not change if event B is known. | The probability of the occurrence of A does change if event B is known. |
| P(B \| A) = P(B) | P(B \| A) ≠ P(B) |
| The probability of the occurrence of B does not change if event A is known. | The probability of the occurrence of B does change if event A is known. |

In plain English, when the conditional probability, P(A|B), and the unconditional probability, P(A), are equal, event B is independent of event A. Knowing event B does not affect the probability that event A occurs. In business and the courts, if the conditional probability, P(A|B), and the unconditional probability, P(A), are *nearly* equal, event B is independent of event A.

On the other hand, when the conditional probability, P(A), and the unconditional probability, P(A|B), are *not* the same, knowing event B has caused us to revise the probability that event A will occur. In business and the courts, if the P(A|B) and the P(A) differ greatly (not just differ), the two events are related.

Probability revision means that we believe that the two events, A and B, are statistically dependent. When event B is pertinent information, we should increase or decrease the probability of event A from its unconditional probability value. However, when the event B information is irrelevant, we should not revise the unconditional probability. The two events are statistically independent.

In summary, one's shoe size is irrelevant information with respect to one's chances of being promoted. So if based on the data, the P(Promoted) is 0.35, the P(Promoted | Shoe Size is 7C) should remain 0.35. Logically, shoe size and promotion are statistically independent events.

## COMPUTING CONDITIONAL PROBABILITIES

In the business world we do not use logic or intuition to determine statistical dependence; we compute conditional probabilities.

We will continue to use the gender and promotion data. We already know the unconditional probability of being promoted, 0.35. To determine if promotion and gender are related, we must compute the following two conditional probabilities.

1. P(**Promoted**)           =0.35

2. P(**Promoted** | Male)   = ?

3. P(**Promoted** | Female) = ?

Why compute the above two conditional probabilities? Because if the two conditional probabilities do not equal 0.35, it means that gender impacts one's chances of being promoted.

The frequency tree, Figure 3.1, which is reproduced here, provides the necessary data for computing the two conditional probabilities. We must adjust Expression (3.1) to compute conditional probabilities.

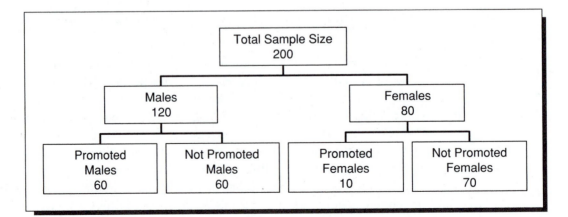

In Expression (3.1) the denominator was the total sample size in the study. When computing a conditional probability we are not interested in the total sample size; we are only interested in the number of event-B people. Thus from Figure 3.1

$$P\left(\textbf{Promoted} \mid \text{Male}\right) \qquad = \frac{}{120}$$

$$P\left(\textbf{Promoted} \mid \text{Female}\right) \qquad = \frac{}{80}$$

For the first conditional probability, we are not interested in all 200 employees; only those that are *males*—120. In the second conditional probability, we are also not interested in all 200 employees; only those that are *females*—80.

Let's now determine the two numerators for the above probabilities. Of the 120 males, how many were promoted? Sixty. So 60 is the numerator.

$$P\left(\textbf{Promoted} \mid \text{Male}\right) \qquad = \frac{60}{120} = 0.50$$

Of the 80 females, how many were promoted? Ten. So 10 is the numerator.

$$P\left(\textbf{Promoted} \mid \text{Female}\right) \qquad = \frac{10}{80} = 0.125$$

1. P(**Promoted**) = 0.350
2. P(**Promoted** | Male) = 0.500
3. P(**Promoted** | Female) = 0.125

For those who desire a formula, use Expression (3.2) to compute conditional probabilities.

$$P\left(A \mid B\right) = \frac{\text{Frequency}\left(A \textbf{ AND } B\right)}{\text{Frequency}\left(B\right)}$$

**(3.2)**

The three probabilities of being promoted differ. First, note that neither conditional probability equals the unconditional probability of being promoted, 0.35. From the earlier discussion of statistical independence, this means that gender and promotion are statistically related for the *specific sample of 200*.

Now let's focus on the two conditional probabilities. These will reveal the nature of the statistical dependence. If ("|") you are male, the probability of being promoted is 0.500. If ("|") you are a female, the probability of being promoted is 0.125. Men are four times more likely to be promoted than females.

The firm does appear to be in violation of the 1964 Civil Rights Act. Or is it? The next section presents an argument the firm could make that it is not in violation of the 1964 Civil Rights Act. However, before presenting it, let's compute several more conditional probabilities from the gender and promotion study and analyze one more case. Please compute the following probability.

$$P(\text{Not Promoted} \mid \text{Female}) = ?$$

From Figure 3.1, there are 80 females. So the denominator is 80. Of these 80 females, 70 were not promoted. So the numerator is 70. Thus

$$P(\text{Not Promoted} \mid \text{Female}) = \frac{70}{80} = 0.875$$

$$P(\text{Male} \mid \text{Promoted}) = ?$$

How many people did the firm promote? From Figure 3.1, there are 60 promoted males and 10 promoted females. So there are 70 promoted people. The denominator is 70. Of the 70 promoted people, 60 are males. So the numerator is 60.

$$P(\text{Male} \mid \text{Promoted}) = \frac{60}{70} = 0.857$$

## CASE STUDY

**Impact of Market Segment on Milk Preferences.** Best Dairy, Inc., has segmented its market into eight groups. Among these separate markets are the Machos and Status Seekers. Machos are young males, blue-collar workers, with high school degrees. Status Seekers are young males, white-collar workers with college degrees. Best Dairy, Inc., interviews all members of both segments in a small town and asks each to state their preference for whole milk, 2%, or skim milk. Figure 3.3 contains a frequency tree for the study.

Are market segment and milk preference statistically dependent? We can use the following three probabilities to answer that question: (1) P(**Whole Milk**), (2) P(**Whole Milk** | Macho), and (3) P(**Whole Milk** | Status Seeker). Compute these before reading on.

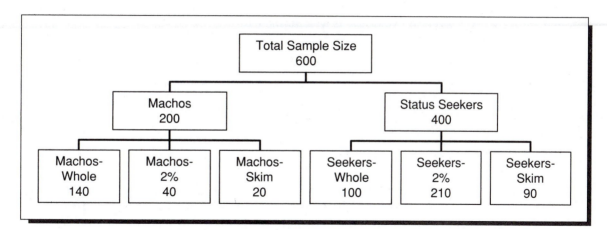

**Figure 3.3**    Frequency Tree of Market Segment and Milk Preference Study

Using Expressions (3.1) and (3.2):

$$P\left(\textbf{Prefer Whole Milk}\right) = \frac{140+100}{600} = 0.40$$

$$P\left(\textbf{Prefer Whole Milk} \mid \textbf{Macho}\right) = \frac{140}{200} = 0.70$$

$$P\left(\textbf{Prefer Whole Milk} \mid \textbf{ Status Seeker}\right) = \frac{100}{400} = 0.25$$

The three probabilities differ. Market segment and milk preference are statistically dependent for the specific sample of 600 consumers. One's preference for whole milk depends upon one's market segment.

Alternatively, we could have used the following four probabilities to assess statistical dependence.

P(**Macho**)
P(**Macho** | Prefer Whole Milk)
P(**Macho** | Prefer 2% Milk)
P(**Macho** | Prefer Skim Milk)

To determine statistical independence compute the following probabilities.

P(**A**)

P(**A** | B₁)

$\cdot$
$\cdot$
$\cdot$

P(**A** | Bₖ)

Where if event "A" is Macho or Status Seeker, event $B_1$ = Prefer Whole Milk, $B_2$ = Prefer 2%, or $B_3$ = Prefer Skim Milk. Or if event "A" is Prefer Whole Milk, Prefer 2%, or Prefer Skim Milk, events $B_1$ = Macho, and $B_2$ = Status Seeker.

If the several probabilities greatly differ (a judgment call), events A and B are statistically dependent for the specific sample.

## INTERVENING VARIABLES

Let's return to the gender and promotion study. The firm could argue that it is true that males are four times more likely to be promoted than females—P(Promoted | Male) = 0.50 and P(Promoted | Female) = 0.125—but the difference in probabilities is not due to gender. Suppose that most promotions went to programmers who were certified in the C++ language because the firm had developed many new applications in that language over the past five years. Furthermore, suppose that a higher percentage of males had completed C++ certification than females. The firm might argue, therefore, that the men were better qualified and thus more deserving of promotion. The firm has argued that promotion is related to C++ certification, not gender. The firm is suggesting that C++ certification is an **intervening variable**.

To prove its point, the firm provides the court with the following frequency tree in which it has included the intervening variable, C++ certification (see Figure 3.4).

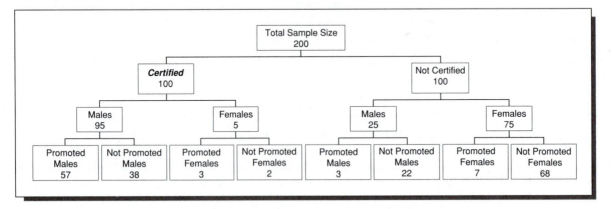

**Figure 3.4**
Frequency Tree for Gender and Promotion Study Data with Intervening Variable, C++ Certification

Let's recompute P(**Promoted** | Male) and P(**Promoted** | Female) for those employees that have been C++ certified. Let's focus on the 100 employees who were certified in the C++ language (left side of tree). Of these 100 employees, 95 were males and 5 were females. Thus,

$$P\left(\textbf{Promoted} \mid \text{Male}\right) \qquad = \frac{57}{95} = 0.60$$

$$P\left(\textbf{Promoted} \mid \text{Female}\right) \qquad = \frac{3}{5} = 0.60$$

Let's also recompute P(**Promoted** | Male) and P(**Promoted** | Female) for those employees that have not been C++ certified. Of these 100 noncertified employees (right side of tree), 25 were males and 75 were females. Thus,

$$P\left(\textbf{Promoted} \mid \text{Male}\right) \qquad = \frac{3}{25} = 0.12$$

$$P\left(\textbf{Promoted} \mid \text{Female}\right) \qquad = \frac{7}{75} = 0.093$$

With the inclusion of the intervening variable, the conditional probabilities of being promoted for those employees who were certified are the same, 0.60. Also, the conditional probabilities of being promoted for those employees who were not certified are about the same. Gender and promotion are statistically independent with the inclusion of the intervening variable.

**D E F I N I T I O N**    An **intervening** variable accounts for the impact of one attribute upon another. Including the intervening variable in the analysis eliminates the apparent relationship between the two attributes.

How would a judge rule in the discrimination case? The judge must evaluate the reasonableness of the intervening variable. A variable such as C++ certification could be reasonably related to promotion because many of the firm's new products were written in that language. The judge would probably also look for evidence of past discrimination in the firm. Given that the intervening variable is reasonable and assuming that the company has no history of discrimination, the judge might rule in favor of the firm.

One final point remains. How do we determine potential intervening variables? They do not just appear out of thin air. Rather we must consider possible *logical variables* that might account for the differences in promotion probabilities of males and females. Bear in mind that intervening variables must pass the reasonableness test.

# USING PROBABILITY TREES TO REDUCE MANAGERIAL JUDGMENT ERRORS

Managers have difficulties making assessments involving personal probability data. Inconsistency and systematic error often plague their judgments. One common error is noncoherency. Managers can construct **probability trees** to minimize this error. A probability tree is similar to a frequency tree except that it contains probabilities, not frequencies. By the end of this unit you should be able to

1. construct a probability tree to test for the noncoherency error and

2. explain, in your own words, the noncoherency error.

## NONCOHERENCY ERROR

At the beginning of the chapter a director of planning had assessed three personal probabilities. Her three personal probability estimates are restated here:

P(Increased Conservation)                                    = 0.50  Unconditional Probability

P(Deduct Expenses)                                           = 0.60  Unconditional Probability

P(Increased Conservation | Deduct Expenses) = 0.85  Conditional Probability

The three probabilities seem to make sense. All her estimates fell between 0 and 1. Furthermore, the director increased the probability of increased conservation efforts from 0.50 to 0.85 if the federal government permits taxpayers to deduct conservation expenses. That, too, seems reasonable. And yet the three probabilities are not valid. These probabilities will subsequently generate a negative probability—clearly an impossible condition.

Begin by constructing a *probability tree*. Whereas the total sample size is at the top level of a frequency tree, place the probability of 1.0 at the top of the probability tree. There are two choices as to what to place at the second level of the tree—the increased conservation versus the not increased conservation boxes or the deduct expenses versus the not deduct expenses boxes.

For reasons that we present later, place the deduct expenses and not deduct expenses boxes as the tree's second level. Insert the unconditional probability of 0.60 in the deduct expenses box and $1.00 - 0.60 = 0.40$ in the not deduct box.

Figure 3.5 is a partially completed probability tree for the conservation problem. The probabilities in the lowest level of this tree are the following four joint probabilities.

P(Deduct Expenses AND Increased Conservation)

P(Deduct Expenses AND Not Increased Conservation)

P(Not Deduct Expenses AND Increased Conservation)

P(Not Deduct Expensed AND Not Increased Conservation)

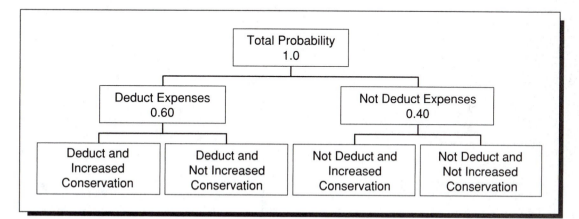

**Figure 3.5**
Partially Completed Probability Tree for the Conservation Problem

How can we compute the four joint probabilities? For the previous frequency trees we provided the reader with the joint frequencies for the four boxes. But now all you have is one conditional probability:

P(Increased Conservation | Deduct Expenses) = 0.85

Determine the joint probabilities using a variation of Expression (3.2) shown as Expression (3.3) here. Whereas Expression (3.2) uses frequencies, Expression (3.3) uses probabilities to calculate a conditional probability:

$$P\!\left(A \mid B\right) = \frac{P\!\left(A \text{ AND } B\right)}{P\!\left(B\right)}$$

**(3.3)**

Letting A = Increased Conservation and B = Deduct Expenses, we have

$$P\!\left(\text{Increased Conservation} \mid \text{Deduct Expenses}\right) = \frac{P\!\left(\text{Increased Conservation AND Deduct Expenses}\right)}{P\!\left(\text{Deduct Expenses}\right)}$$

You already know two of the three probabilities in Expression (3.3). Simply solve for the unknown joint probability.

$$.85 = \frac{P\left(\text{Increased Conservation } \textbf{AND } \text{Deduct Expenses}\right)}{.60}$$

P(Increased Conservation and Deduct Expenses) = 0.51

Let's insert the joint probability of 0.51 into Figure 3.6. Subtract .60 − .51 = .09. This is the joint probability of deducting expenses and no increased conservation.

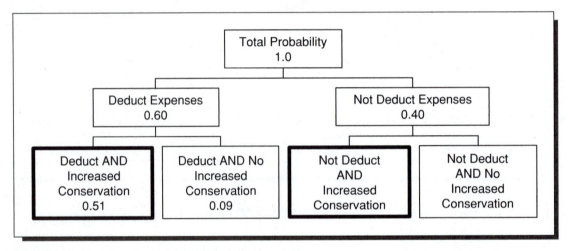

**Figure 3.6**
Completed Probability Tree for the Conservation Problem

The sum of the two joint probabilities in the two boxes with the thick borders represents the unconditional probability of increased conservation efforts.[2]

**P(Increased Conservation) = P(Deduct Expenses AND *Increased Conservation*) + P(Not Deduct Expenses AND *Increased Conservation*)**

Recall that the director of planning estimated that the unconditional probability of increased conservation efforts was 0.50. Thus,

$$\mathbf{0.50 = 0.51 + \left[-0.01\right]}$$

---

[2]In general, we can say that P(A) = P(A AND B) + P(A AND Not B) or
P(B) = P(B AND A) + P(B AND Not A)

Thus, the joint probability of Not Deduct Expenses AND Increased Conservation must equal −0.01. But a negative probability is impossible! Therefore, the three personal probabilities are not valid or coherent. The director must change one or more of the personal probabilities and reexamine them using the probability tree.

It's time to explain why the second level of the tree in Figure 3.6 contained the deduct expenses versus not deduct expenses rather than the increased conservation versus not increased conservation boxes. The director assessed the conditional probability shown below as 0.85. To solve for the joint probability (the numerator), it was necessary to have already placed in the tree the probability of deducting expenses (the denominator of the calculation)

$$P\left(\text{Increased Conservation} \mid \text{Deduct Expenses}\right) = \frac{P\left(\text{Increased Conservation } \textbf{AND} \text{ Deduct Expenses}\right)}{P\left(\text{Deduct Expenses}\right)}$$

When testing for noncoherent probabilities, select event B from the assessed conditional probability as the second level of the tree. Otherwise you will not be able to use Expression (3.3) to compute any joint probability.

The director reassesses her probability estimates and generates the following three revised personal probabilities.

P(Increased Conservation) = 0.50 Unconditional Probability

P(Deducting Expenses) = 0.60 Unconditional Probability

P(Increased Conservation | Deducting Expenses) = 0.65 Conditional Probability

Complete the partially completed probability tree shown below using the above probabilities. You will see that none of the four joint probabilities will be negative. Thus the three assessed personal probabilities are valid or coherent.

One final note: Valid probabilities are not necessarily accurate probabilities. Valid means that the three assessed probabilities do not force one or more joint probabilities to be negative. The accuracy of the probabilities is a different matter. Because the director is assessing probabilities of future events, she will not know their accuracy for some time into the future. Let's consider a second case that examines for the noncoherency error.

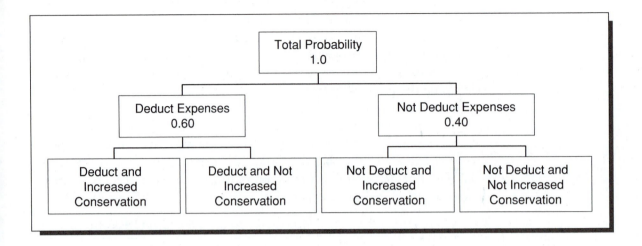

## CASE STUDY

**The Impact of Technology on Market Entrance.** A firm's senior management is discussing the possibility of entering a new market. It believes that its chances of successfully entering the market depend on whether it can develop a new technology (breakthrough) that will significantly reduce its cost. The group has made the following personal probability assessments:

P(successful entry)                                    = .70 Unconditional probability

P(breakthrough)                                         = .20 Unconditional probability

P(successful entry | breakthrough) = .95 Conditional probability

Be sure that your tree has the breakthrough and no breakthrough boxes as its second level. Try constructing the probability tree before reading on. Then compare your tree to that in Figure 3.7.

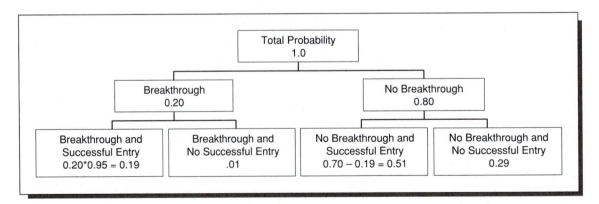

**Figure 3.7**    Completed Probability Tree for Market Entry Study

The team assessed the P(Successful Entry) as 0.70. Thus,

P(Successful Entry) = P(Successful Entry AND Breakthrough)
                    + P(Successful Entry AND No Breakthrough)

0.70 = .19 + P(Successful Entry AND No Breakthrough)

P(Successful Entry AND No Breakthrough) = 0.51

When the table is completed, all four joint probabilities are positive. The team has not committed the noncoherency error.

The probability tree is effective in assessing noncoherency. Business professionals can overcome other errors by simply knowing that they exist. Here we present three common judgment errors.

Please answer the following question:

According to the Georgia Bureau of Investigation, for the years 1993–1996, in what year, if any, did the most bombings occur in Georgia?

Most people respond 1996. According to the GBI, the number of bombings was constant over that four-year period. When asked why they chose 1996, most people usually say that they can recall the Olympic Park bombing and that influenced their judgment. These people have committed the **availability error**.

<table>
<tr><td>**D E F I N I T I O N**</td><td>The availability error occurs when our ability to recall specific instances affects our assessment of events.</td></tr>
</table>

Before assessing the likelihood of events, seek out information to make your judgment. Do not rely solely on recall.

When U.S. Surgical stock entered the market, many people passed up the opportunity to buy it at $50 per share. They thought it was overpriced and too expensive. Over the next year the stock went to $130 and then plummeted back to about $50. At that point many buyers thought that it was a "steal" and purchased it. After climbing to about $70, it again dropped to less than $30. Most buyers at $50 then bailed out. These stock pundits had committed the **anchoring error**.

<table>
<tr><td>**D E F I N I T I O N**</td><td>Anchoring occurs when we evaluate an event based on an arbitrary base or anchor.</td></tr>
</table>

The stock pundits anchored U.S. Surgical as a $130 stock that was now underpriced, even though they did not consider purchasing it when it was $50 on the way up. Given the anchor of $130, the stock seemed underpriced to them. And so they purchased it, only to see the stock drop to about $30 in less than a year. The moral of the story is, choose your anchor wisely. Better yet, realize that you are basing your assessment on an anchor and seek better data before making a judgment or investment. Remember that the stock market can be an expensive place to learn about anchoring.

Joe is about to purchase an older model of a particular car. He reads in *Consumer Reports* that the model he is interested in is a Best Buy. However, his friend, who had that model, tells Joe that it had been the worst car he had ever owned. Joe decides not to purchase the model. Joe has just committed the **concreteness error**.

---

**D E F I N I T I O N**     The concreteness error occurs when a person values a sample of one, based on vivid or personal experiences, over a large impersonal database.

---

What causes us to succumb to the concreteness bias? Joe did not know the tens of thousands of people surveyed for *Consumer Reports*, but he did know his friend. That latter datum was thus more meaningful and important in his final assessment.

Do not value personal data more than impersonal survey data. Rather, what is important is the validity of each and the amount of evidence that supports each position. One of the enduring lessons of statistics you will learn is that large-size samples are more informative than small-size samples.

# KEY IDEAS

Except in statistics books, managers are not given probabilities. So where do they come from? There are two methods for either computing or assigning probabilities:

**1.** computing relative-frequency probabilities and

**2.** assigning personal probabilities.

Experience is the basis for the relative-frequency approach. We use data from studies to estimate probabilities. We can use this frequency data to assess statistical independence for a specific sample.

Statistical independence is a critical idea. A successful manager is one who detects relationships between events before others. Use frequency trees to compute an unconditional probability, P(A), and the appropriate conditional probabilities, $P(A \mid B_1)$ and $P(A \mid B_2)$, to assess the statistical independence of two events for a specific sample.

Intuition is the basis for personal probabilities. A business professional estimates a probability based on knowledge and insight about an event. Be forewarned that it is relatively easy to make errors in assessing personal probabilities. Probability trees are helpful in assessing noncoherency, but many other judgment errors are not detectable by trees.

# EXERCISES

**1.** Do relative frequencies of events exactly equal their probabilities? Explain.

**2.** Under what conditions, if any, can a joint probability be less than 0?

**3.** If P(Promotion | Male) equals P(Promotion), what can you conclude about the impact of gender on promotion?

**4.** If P(Promotion | Male) equals P(Male), what can you conclude about the impact of gender on promotion?

**5.** In your own words, what is the noncoherency error?

**6.** Develop a rule that explains which of the unconditional probabilities should be placed in the second level of a probability tree when assessing noncoherency.

**7.** Identify the type of probability—unconditional, conditional, joint, or union—in the following statements. An employee who is

   **a.** promoted

   **b.** promoted or male

   **c.** a promoted female

   **d.** promoted if a male

   **e.** a not promoted female

   **f.** female given the employee has been promoted

**8.** Best Dairy, Inc., has collected the following frequency data on market segment and milk preference. For the specific sample of 200 customers, do different segments have different milk preferences?

| | |
|---|---|
| Machos and Skim | 30 |
| Machos and Whole | 70 |
| Status Seekers and Skim | 80 |
| Status Seekers and Whole | 20 |

   **a.** Develop a frequency tree from the data.

   **b.** What is P(preferring skim milk OR being a Status Seeker)?

   **c.** What is P(preferring whole milk AND being a Macho)?

   **d.** What is the following unconditional probability: P(being a Macho)?

   **e.** What is the following conditional probability: P(being a Macho | preferring whole milk)?

   **f.** Based on your answers to parts d–e, does milk preference appear to be independent of market segment for the specific sample of 200? Explain.

9. An organizational-behavior consulting firm has collected the following data on leadership style for 200 firms in the United States and Canada. For the specific sample of 200 firms, do American and Canadian firms prefer the same leadership styles?

| | |
|---|---|
| U.S. firm and participative leadership | 30 |
| U.S. firm and autocratic leadership | 70 |
| Canadian firm and participative leadership | 50 |
| Canadian firm and autocratic leadership | 50 |

a. What is P(having participative leadership)?

b. What is P(having participative leadership | firm in United States)?

c. Based on your answers to parts a and b, is leadership style independent of the country where the firm is located? Explain in terms that a manager could understand.

d. Determine P(U.S. firm AND an autocratic leadership style).

e. Determine P(Canadian firm OR participative leadership style).

10. Cablebest is preparing to apply to the Federal Communications Commission (FCC) for a license. The FCC has three options: (1) grant a restricted license, (2) grant an unrestricted license, (3) do not grant a license. Cablebest believes that the FCC ruling will depend on its ability to recruit a knowledgeable general manager. Cablebest is presently seeking such a person. The firm is not sure whether it will have such a person when it submits the application. Following are the firm's personal probability estimates.

| | |
|---|---|
| P(will recruit) | 0.70 |
| P(won't recruit) | 0.30 |
| P(unrestricted license) | 0.50 |
| P(restricted license) | 0.40 |
| P(no license) | 0.10 |

The firm also estimates that P(unrestricted license | will recruit) = 0.90. Are all the probability estimates valid or coherent? Develop a probability tree.

11. The Sagman Test is a newly discovered method for early detection of a disease. Which of the following probabilities is most appropriate to determine the test's effectiveness? Explain.

P(have disease X | test says you have the disease)

P(test says you have the disease | have the disease)

P(test says you have the disease)

12. A civil rights group has collected the following hypothetical probability data on hiring practices in an industry:

| | |
|---|---|
| P(hiring an applicant) | = 0.10 |
| P(hiring an applicant \| applicant is white male) | = 0.10 |
| P(hiring an applicant \| applicant is an African American male) | = 0.10 |

The Civil Rights Act says that a person cannot be discriminated against in hiring based on sex, race, creed, or place of national origin. For the specific data, are hiring and the applicant's race statistically independent in the industry? Explain.

**13.** You are told that men and women have the same chances of being promoted in a firm.

  **a.** What must be true about the following three probabilities? Explain in simple terms.

  P(promoted)

  P(promoted | male)

  P(promoted | female)

  **b.** Must the following two probabilities equal one another for gender and promotion to be statistically independent? Explain.

  P(promoted | female)

  P(female | promoted)

**14.** Do company-run stress management programs minimize absenteeism? ABC Research collects the following data on firms that (1) have a program or (2) don't have a program versus level of absenteeism. Low absenteeism is defined as less than 1% of total personnel-hours lost.

  Have program and low absenteeism    40

  Have program and high absenteeism    60

  Don't have program and
    low absenteeism    10

  Don't have program and
    high absenteeism    90

  **a.** Develop a frequency tree from the data.

  **b.** Does having a stress reduction program impact the level of absenteeism for the specific sample of 200? Explain.

**15.** A firm uses two different strategies to sell its product—comparative versus competitive advertising. Three hundred white Americans, 200 African Americans, and 100 Asian Americans are shown the same ad using the two marketing strategies presented above. Here are the study's data.

  White Americans who prefer the
    comparative ad    180

  White Americans who prefer the
    competitive ad    120

  African Americans who prefer the
    comparative ad    118

  African Americans who prefer the
    competitive ad    82

  Asian Americans who prefer the
    comparative ad    61

  Asian Americans who prefer the
    competitive ad    39

  **a.** Develop a frequency tree from the data.

  **b.** What is P(selecting a white American OR having the person prefer the comparative ad)?

  **c.** What is P(selecting an Asian American AND having the person prefer the competitive ad)?

  **d.** What is P(preferring the comparative ad)?

  **e.** What is P(preferring the comparative ad | white American)?

  **f.** What is P(preferring the comparative ad | African American)?

  **g.** What is P(preferring the comparative ad | Asian American)?

  **h.** Based on your answers to parts d–g, is race related to advertisement preference for the specific sample of 600? Explain.

**16.** An economist estimates that the probability that American exports will exceed imports next year is 0.10. She also estimates that the probability that Japan will have a major recession is 0.20. However, if Japan does have a major recession, she estimates that the probability that American exports will exceed imports will increase to 0.50. Draw a probability tree and determine if the three probabilities are coherent.

**17.** Does having internships during college help obtain desired jobs upon graduation from college? A university tracks 500 students over a four-year period. It obtains the following data:

Had no internship and obtained
    desired job within six months    160

Had no internship and didn't obtain
    desired job within six months    190

Had internship and obtained
    desired job within six months    140

Had internship and didn't obtain
    desired job within six months    10

**a.** Develop a frequency tree from the data.

**b.** What is P(having an internship OR obtaining desired job)?

**c.** What is P(having an internship AND not obtaining desired job)?

**d.** What is P(obtaining desired job)?

**e.** What is P(obtaining desired job | no internship)?

**f.** What is P(obtaining desired job | internship)?

**g.** Based on your answers to parts d–f, is having an internship statistically independent of obtaining desired jobs within six months of graduation for the specific sample of 500? Explain.

**18.** A major bank wishes to determine if years with present firm affects one's credit rating. They collect the following data:

Good credit rating and less than
    five years at present firm    250

Good credit rating and five years
    or more at present firm    600

Bad credit rating and less than five
    years at present firm    100

Bad credit rating and five years
    or more at present firm    50

**a.** Develop a frequency tree from the data.

**b.** Is having a good credit rating statistically independent of years at present firm for the specific sample of 1000? Explain.

**19.** An economist makes the following personal probability estimates. (High inflation is an inflation rate over 5%.)

P(high inflation next year)    0.20

P(no slack in productive plant
    capacity next year)    0.40

P(high inflation next year | no slack in
    productive plant capacity next year) 0.30

**a.** Are the three probabilities coherent? Use a probability tree to support your position.

**b.** Given the above data, what is P(high inflation next year | slack in productive plant capacity next year)?

**20.** A college determines that of its 2000 business majors, 1400 are extroverted and 600 are introverted based on the Myers-Briggs Type Indicator. Of the college's 3000 Arts and Science majors, 1800 are introverted and 1200 are extroverted.

**a.** Develop a frequency tree from the data.

**b.** For the specific sample of 5000, is one's choice of a business or A&S major statistically independent of one's preference for extroversion versus introversion? Explain.

**21.** Because of the high risk and high cost of introducing new products, many firms seek to extend the life of their established products. Firms use several brand-extension strategies to either increase share of market or delay the decline stage of the product life cycle. Below are a product manager's personal probabilities.

P(Delaying declining market share for product)    = 0.15

P(Developing creative varied usage brand-extension campaign)    = 0.60

P(Delaying | developing creative campaign)    = 0.45

Are the three probabilities coherent? Use a probability tree to support your position.

**22.** Does magnitude of profit margin on sales ratios affect stock analysts' opinions of firms in the retail industry? One hundred stock analysts are provided data on firms with varying profit margins and asked to make either a positive or negative *stock buy* recommendation.

Positive recommendation and firm at or above industry average    45

Positive recommendation and firm below industry average    25

Negative recommendation and firm at or above industry average    5

Negative recommendation and firm below industry average    25

**23.** One questionable tactic that firms undertake to make themselves unattractive to potential buyers is a **poison pill** strategy. For example, a firm threatens to give huge retirement bonuses (which represents a large part of the firm's wealth) to its senior management if it is taken over. A stock analyst provides the following personal probability estimates that Carltex, Inc., will use the poison pill strategy in the next year.

P(use poison pill)    0.20

P(Carltex stock drops by more than 25%)    0.25

P(use poison pill | Carltex stock drops by more than 25%)    0.50

Are the three probabilities coherent? Use a probability tree to support your position.

**24.** Consider the following occupancy data at 100 urban and rural hospitals.

Urban hospital and at least 60% of beds occupied    25

Urban hospital and less than 60% occupied    20

Rural hospital and at least 60% of beds occupied    15

Rural hospital and less than 60% occupied    40

**a.** Calculate P(at least 60% occupied | urban hospital).

**b.** Calculate P(at least 60% occupied | rural hospital).

**c.** Are the events—at least 60% occupied and location of hospital—statistically independent?

**25.** Do frozen pizza marketers in the Midwest use different marketing channels than their counterparts on the West Coast? An industry association collects the following data. For the specific sample of 130, are the marketer location and marketing channels used statistically related?

Midwest marketer and food broker    20

Midwest marketer and truck-driver salesperson    50

West Coast marketer and food broker    50

West Coast marketer and truck-driver salesperson    10

## CASE STUDY

Recently MidAmerica Bank has been concerned that many of its services can be obtained through mutual fund companies or discount brokerage firms. Discount brokerage asset-management accounts offer unlimited check writing, automatic teller machine cards, and credit cards. They take direct deposit of customers' paychecks and can automatically pay a number of bills. Moreover, customers have access to a wide array of no-load mutual funds and money market funds that often pay higher interest than many banks. Plus, their customers get a consolidated statement that lists all deposits, withdrawals, and investment activities. Recently, Citibank had introduced a $125-a-year account for major depositors that has many of the same features.

MidAmerica is considering introducing its own asset-management account. It must decide if it wants to offer it to all its customers or first do a six-month market research study to determine its likely effectiveness. A survey will require an expenditure of $150K for the marketing and systems-development effort. Depending on the success of the market research study, MidAmerica would then decide whether to offer the program to all its customers. If it markets the program, it will spend an additional $750K. If demand for the product is high, MidAmerica's inflow should be $2000K. If demand is low, MidAmerica's inflow should be only $500K.

The project manager has prepared a diagram of the decisions facing MidAmerica, as shown on the page 111.

The program manager argues that the optimal decisions are obvious. First, do no market survey and then launch the project. He argues that there is no advantage to doing the survey because all the outcomes that follow the "do survey" branch are lower than the corresponding outcomes for the "don't do survey" branch. He also argues that if the firm does nothing it has a zero gain. If it launches the product, it could gain $1,350,000 or lose $250,000. The upside potential is much greater than the downside potential.

**a.** Comment on the manager's reasoning.

The CEO then asks the project manager to estimate several probabilities. He provides the following personal estimates.

**1.** The probability of high demand is 0.60

**2.** The probability of a favorable outcome from the market survey is 0.70

**3.** The probability of high demand if the market survey is favorable is 0.80

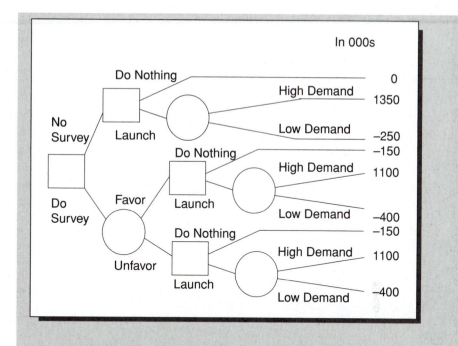

**b.** Comment on the manager's probabilities.

Given the above probabilities and the decision diagram, what actions would you recommend that MidAmerica take? Should it do a market survey? Should it launch the product?

# SAMPLING AND SAMPLING DISTRIBUTIONS

## THE NEED FOR STATISTICAL INFERENCE METHODS

Managers use descriptive statistics to build mental models, sense and understand problems and opportunities, seek root causes, and make decisions. They do this by asking the right questions. For example,

What is our customers' mean income level?

What proportion of the firm's employees favor a flex-time system?

What is the consistency in delivery times from a vendor?

Managers realize it would be too costly to survey all customers, interview all employees, or review all shipping records to answer their questions. They can, however, take a *representative* sample from each target population and compute descriptive statistics, the sample mean, proportion, or variance.

Chapter 5 will use descriptive statistics and the method of *confidence intervals* to *estimate* a population's mean, proportion, or variance. If you follow politics, you are already familiar with confidence intervals. For example, a polling firm interviews a representative sample of 1500 voters across the nation and concludes it is 95% confident that a candidate will receive 57% ± 3% of the vote. The population percentage of voters supporting the candidate could vary by ± 3% from the sample result of 57%—from 54% to 60% of the votes. It's amazing that polling organizations can be so accurate and confident when they interview only 1500 voters out of a population of over 90 million voters. And yet polling organizations rarely make incorrect predictions!

By the end of this section you should be able to

**1.** distinguish between a population parameter and a sample statistic; and

**2.** explain what margin of error is and why it should be as small as possible.

## IMPORTANT DEFINITIONS

To understand confidence intervals and statistical inference, let's begin with some very important definitions.

**DEFINITION**    A **target population** is the entire group of elements about which you want information. An **element** is an object or subject on which you take a measurement. It is the set of people or elements that **should** be sampled.

For example, all the employees in a firm, all the firm's customers, and all the shipping records from a vendor are target populations. An element would be a particular employee or customer (subject) or shipping record (object). The measurement could be a customer's income level, an employee's attitude towards flex-time, or the delivery time of parts from a vendor in hours.[1]

Do not confuse the sampling frame and target population. Recall the following from Chapter 1:

**DEFINITION**    A **sampling frame** is a list of all people or elements that you can actually sample from the target population.

**DEFINITION**    A **population parameter** is a number that describes a target population. It could be the mean ($\mu$), median, proportion ($p$), or variance ($\sigma^2$).

---

[1]The term *population* also refers to the set of measurements themselves. Thus, you can refer to a population distribution of ages or a population distribution of salaries for a target population of customers (elements).

Population parameters are constant values and are generally unknown and unknowable. For example, population parameters are the mean income of *all* customers in the target population, the variance in *all* the delivery times, or the proportion of *all* employees within the firm that favor flex–time.

**D E F I N I T I O N**    A **sample** is a part of a target population.

You gain knowledge about a target population from the sample. For example, 100 randomly selected customers or 200 randomly selected employees are samples.

**D E F I N I T I O N**    A **sampling design** describes how to select the sample from a sampling frame.

In Chapter 1 we presented simple random sampling. Recall that simple random sampling occurs when every possible sample of size $n$ has the same chance of being selected from the sampling frame of $N$ people or elements. Use an Excel-generated random numbers table (see Table 1.6) to select a simple random sample.

**D E F I N I T I O N**    **Sample statistics** describe samples and estimate unknown population parameters. Important sample statistics are the sample mean ($\bar{x}$), sample proportion ($\hat{p}$), or sample variance ($s^2$).

While the population parameter is a constant value, a sample statistic will vary from sample to sample. For example, the sample mean income of 100 customers will vary from one sample to the next.

**D E F I N I T I O N**    A **statistical inference method** is a process of using sample statistics based on one representative sample from a target population to make an assertion, or *inference,* about an entire target population.

Chapters 5–6 will present two common statistical inference methods—confidence intervals and hypothesis testing.

**Margin of error** is the possible difference between the sample result and the result that you would obtain if you surveyed the target population.

For example, the margin of error in the polling illustration above was $\pm$ 3%.

## MARGIN OF ERROR AND CONFIDENCE LEVEL

Meaningful inferences about population parameters should have small margins of error. What would be the value of knowing that a candidate will receive 57% $\pm$ 30% of the votes? The margin of error would be too wide to draw useful conclusions.

The confidence level for an inference is also very important. Higher levels of confidence are more meaningful. For example, it is not very informative to be 20% confident that a candidate will receive 57% $\pm$ 3% of the votes. No one will listen to (or pay) an organization that is not very confident of its inferences. Many organizations construct 95% confidence intervals. They can accept a 5% chance that their inferences about the population parameter can be wrong. However, there is nothing sacred about a 95% level of confidence.

In summary, sample statistics describe samples and parameters describe populations. You estimate population parameters from sample statistics using statistical inference methods such as the method of confidence intervals. Constructing confidence intervals requires that you first understand sampling distributions.

## INTRODUCTION TO SAMPLING DISTRIBUTIONS

Just what is a sampling distribution? Suppose you take one random sample of $n$ customers from a sampling frame and determine the sample mean family income. Because this is one of many possible samples, the sample mean, $\bar{x}$, will probably not equal the population mean, $\mu$. The two means will differ because of the variation within the population. Likewise, if you took many other samples, all the sample means would probably differ from the first sample mean and each other. In short, if you took repeated samples of size $n$ you would obtain a sampling distribution of the mean.

In the business world, firms do not take repeated samples; they take a single sample of size $n$. Yet knowing the properties of a sampling distribution—its shape, mean, and standard deviation—the firm can construct confidence intervals to draw conclusions about a target population from a single sample. Figure 4.1 illustrates the statistical inference process.

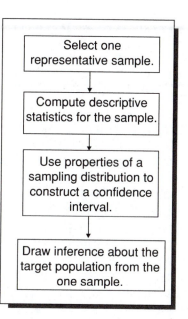

**Figure 4.1**
Statistical Inference
Process

This chapter discusses the shape, mean, and standard deviation of three important sampling distributions. These are the distribution of the (1) sample mean, (2) sample proportion, and (3) sample variance.

# EXPLORING THE DISTRIBUTION OF THE SAMPLE MEAN

The most commonly used sampling distribution is the distribution of the sample mean. By the end of this section you should be able to

1. distinguish between the population distribution and a distribution of the sample mean;

2. distinguish between the mean and standard deviation of (1) a population, (2) a sample, and (3) the distribution of the sample mean;

3. explain why the standard deviation of the distribution of the sample mean, or standard error of the mean, must be smaller than the standard deviation of the population or of a single sample;

4. explain how the shape, mean, and standard error of the mean are useful in estimating an unknown population mean; and

5. explain why the distribution of the sample mean will be near normally distributed, provided the sample size is sufficiently large.

# THE DISTRIBUTION OF A POPULATION

Suppose a firm has only 300 customers. Table 4.1 represents the population of customers' incomes generated by using Excel's Random Number Generation data-analysis tool (see Appendix for dialog box).

| | | | | | | | | | |
|---|---|---|---|---|---|---|---|---|---|
| $46,254 | $54,485 | $56,131 | $53,916 | $56,948 | $51,778 | $56,004 | $55,444 | $52,219 | $56,507 |
| $45,851 | $52,308 | $51,369 | $44,922 | $55,214 | $47,259 | $48,791 | $46,165 | $47,460 | $45,069 |
| $55,271 | $53,806 | $51,857 | $56,272 | $47,976 | $49,308 | $54,349 | $55,244 | $57,369 | $46,731 |
| $54,168 | $48,334 | $45,536 | $47,689 | $52,117 | $49,933 | $47,146 | $45,390 | $53,655 | $54,670 |
| $52,055 | $47,790 | $55,122 | $46,660 | $46,754 | $56,152 | $55,736 | $52,961 | $44,684 | $50,077 |
| $50,206 | $52,675 | $50,109 | $50,283 | $44,567 | $45,865 | $55,578 | $53,691 | $50,120 | $53,193 |
| $44,667 | $47,114 | $44,052 | $53,477 | $46,020 | $56,085 | $54,130 | $48,569 | $48,395 | $57,138 |
| $45,548 | $46,727 | $52,227 | $47,581 | $50,812 | $45,919 | $53,919 | $47,047 | $45,251 | $51,211 |
| $49,355 | $54,890 | $49,533 | $45,671 | $55,373 | $48,206 | $56,274 | $56,964 | $46,677 | $44,541 |
| $46,122 | $50,051 | $49,923 | $44,066 | $54,909 | $44,669 | $49,463 | $50,776 | $44,230 | $53,017 |
| $54,487 | $55,015 | $50,079 | $47,305 | $49,536 | $55,357 | $51,369 | $52,118 | $56,637 | $56,161 |
| $46,478 | $44,727 | $44,522 | $51,326 | $49,651 | $55,304 | $48,191 | $52,061 | $49,895 | $55,691 |
| $45,283 | $47,701 | $49,202 | $55,658 | $46,996 | $51,882 | $47,228 | $49,311 | $44,545 | $55,604 |
| $48,774 | $55,080 | $52,888 | $52,997 | $55,688 | $53,957 | $54,704 | $55,827 | $52,038 | $55,901 |
| $45,854 | $46,529 | $52,181 | $45,089 | $52,824 | $55,843 | $45,066 | $47,432 | $53,366 | $44,818 |
| $52,895 | $44,026 | $48,829 | $47,248 | $56,502 | $54,960 | $57,418 | $49,839 | $46,050 | $49,658 |
| $47,365 | $52,640 | $57,417 | $48,671 | $51,737 | $57,049 | $47,862 | $46,092 | $51,872 | $45,935 |
| $51,859 | $50,018 | $46,688 | $54,173 | $52,175 | $45,733 | $56,824 | $56,632 | $47,580 | $44,022 |
| $48,871 | $55,432 | $49,285 | $46,309 | $55,168 | $52,995 | $55,460 | $48,515 | $55,894 | $49,702 |
| $46,460 | $50,330 | $47,446 | $49,693 | $50,109 | $56,812 | $52,841 | $51,615 | $49,639 | $52,480 |
| $52,608 | $48,362 | $53,670 | $56,333 | $50,930 | $53,098 | $46,816 | $48,958 | $53,004 | $54,117 |
| $45,793 | $55,653 | $46,851 | $50,841 | $47,124 | $55,241 | $49,077 | $46,487 | $50,813 | $52,489 |
| $51,299 | $55,218 | $54,092 | $51,303 | $48,232 | $53,305 | $51,099 | $50,634 | $51,683 | $53,629 |
| $54,099 | $56,751 | $55,397 | $44,021 | $50,605 | $44,816 | $44,041 | $49,793 | $47,013 | $52,419 |
| $51,769 | $47,458 | $45,602 | $54,508 | $53,125 | $57,468 | $51,518 | $45,380 | $56,255 | $48,505 |
| $51,095 | $44,658 | $46,180 | $48,617 | $44,623 | $47,913 | $53,590 | $55,254 | $47,931 | $57,377 |
| $50,916 | $45,003 | $51,371 | $51,394 | $45,649 | $53,059 | $53,097 | $55,049 | $45,655 | $56,232 |
| $47,218 | $49,133 | $50,447 | $48,048 | $56,699 | $55,383 | $53,680 | $53,222 | $51,118 | $54,145 |
| $48,822 | $51,565 | $55,135 | $45,407 | $50,259 | $44,617 | $44,782 | $44,356 | $54,307 | $46,050 |
| $45,447 | $52,392 | $46,864 | $53,640 | $55,630 | $51,256 | $49,696 | $53,859 | $48,373 | $47,719 |

**Table 4.1**
Population of 300 Customers' Incomes

***Shape.*** Figure 4.2 displays the population histogram for the 300 customers' incomes from Table 4.1. One thing is clear—the population's distribution is not normal shaped. The data values shown above the bars are the number of customers with incomes in each class or bin. For example, 56 customers have incomes that are less than or equal to $45,000. Thirty-nine customers have incomes that are greater than $45,000 but less than or equal to $47,500.

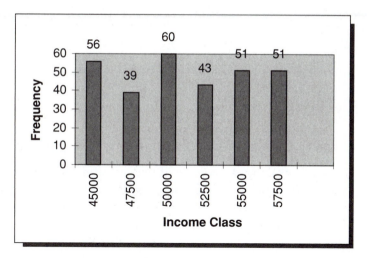

**Figure 4.2**
Histogram for a
Population of 300
Customers' Incomes

***Population Parameters.*** Using the descriptive-statistics data-analysis tool on Table 4.1, the population shown in Figure 4.2 has a mean income, $\mu$, of $50,667 and standard deviation, $\sigma$, of $3,885.

Please understand that in the "real world" you would never know these two population parameters. To know them with certainty would require collecting data on the entire target population. However, to understand the properties of sampling distributions, let's assume that we know the population parameters, $\mu$ and $\sigma$.

## DATA FROM ONE SAMPLE

Now let's select one simple random sample of size $n = 5$ from the population of $N = 300$ family incomes—from Table 4.1. Using Excel's Sampling data-analysis tool, we obtained the five family incomes in Table 4.2 (see Appendix III for dialog box).

**Table 4.2**
Data from One Sample
of Size Five

| $55,135 | $53,680 | $49,533 | $52,608 | $45,655 |

***Sample Statistics.*** Using Excel's function wizards, the sample mean income (AVERAGE), $\bar{x}$, is $51,322 and the sample standard deviation (STDEV), $s$, is $3,777.

So what have you learned to this point? If you take one representative sample of size $n$ from a target population:

**1.** the sample mean, $\bar{x}$, and population mean, $\mu$, will differ, but $\bar{x}$ is reasonably close to $\mu$; and

**2.** the sample standard deviation, $s$, and population standard deviation, $\sigma$, will differ, but $s$ is reasonably close to $\sigma$.

Any sample mean will be close to the population mean, $\mu$, of $50,667. But how close is close? You cannot answer that question until we present the properties of the distribution of the sample mean.

## THE DISTRIBUTION OF THE SAMPLE MEAN

Instead of taking one sample of size five from the 300 family income data values, *imagine* you took *all possible samples of size five with replacement from the population* and computed the sample means.[2] This would generate a **distribution of the sample mean** for samples of size five. We use the word "imagine" because managers never construct a distribution of the sample mean. It would be too costly and time consuming. Yet knowing the properties of the "imaginary" distribution will help you understand confidence intervals and hypothesis testing in the next two chapters.

Let's construct an **approximate** distribution of the sample mean. Table 4.3 shows the five observations taken from the population for samples 1–10 and sample 100.

| Sample | Obs. 1 | Obs. 2 | Obs. 3 | Obs. 4 | Obs.5 | | **Mean** |
|---|---|---|---|---|---|---|---|
| 1 | $55,135 | $53,680 | $49,533 | $52,608 | $45,655 | | $51,322 |
| 2 | $55,135 | $44,658 | $46,816 | $44,818 | $53,691 | | $49,024 |
| 3 | $49,651 | $52,995 | $45,447 | $46,688 | $46,122 | | $48,181 |
| 4 | $55,630 | $50,930 | $50,018 | $51,769 | $48,206 | | $51,311 |
| 5 | $57,418 | $56,948 | $50,259 | $51,299 | $45,069 | | $52,198 |
| 6 | $52,055 | $47,305 | $53,098 | $55,218 | $45,733 | | $50,682 |
| 7 | $56,004 | $43,567 | $51,394 | $56,948 | $56,004 | | $52,783 |
| 8 | $50,109 | $50,120 | $50,813 | $47,446 | $46,180 | | $48,934 |
| 9 | $51,095 | $46,529 | $44,658 | $56,502 | $51,099 | | $49,976 |
| 10 | $57,418 | $53,629 | $45,456 | $54,487 | $53,919 | | $52,982 |
| . | | | | | | | . |
| . | | | | | | | . |
| 100 | $44,667 | $52,419 | $50,018 | $46,460 | $50,605 | | $48,834 |

**Table 4.3**
100 Random Samples of Size Five Taken from a Population of 300 Customers

---

[2] The actual number of possible samples of size five with replacement from a population of only 300 customers is a number far greater than $10^{12}$.

***The Central Limit Theorem.*** How does the shape of the distribution of 100 sample means of size five compare to the histogram of the population of 300 customers' incomes that was not bell shaped? Figure 4.3 is a histogram of the 100 **sample means** from Table 4.3 (the right-most column of data).

Notice how the shape of the approximate sampling distribution for samples of size five is somewhat bell shaped or **normal**. That probably is surprising! We selected 100 samples of size five from a population that is not bell shaped (Figure 4.2). Yet the histogram of the 100 sample means looks somewhat normal. Why is this happening?

Figure 4.3 illustrates a very important idea in statistics, the **Central Limit Theorem**.

**Theorem**    *The Central Limit Theorem states:*

Regardless of the shape of the population's distribution, the distribution of the sample mean based on samples of size *n* approaches a bell-shaped, or normal, curve as the sample size *n* increases.

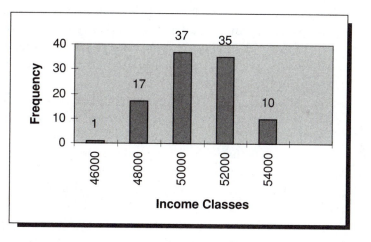

**Figure 4.3**
Histogram of the Distribution of 100 Sample Means for *n* = 5 Shown in Table 4.3

What must the sample size, *n*, be to ensure that the distribution of the sample mean is near normal? That depends on the shape of the population distribution. For population distributions that are symmetric, even a sample size as small as four or five will ensure that the distribution of the sample mean is almost normal. As the population histogram becomes more skewed, you will need a sample size of 30 or more.

Figure 4.4 is a histogram of 100 sample means based on samples of size 20 taken from the population in Figure 4.2, the population of 300 incomes. Given the Central Limit Theorem, we should expect that this distribution would closely resemble a normal curve. And it does!

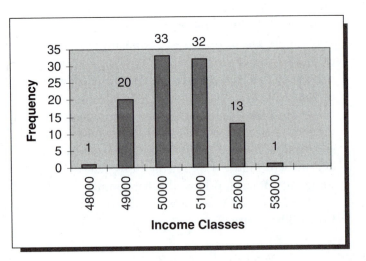

**Figure 4.4**
Histogram of the
Distribution of 100
Sample Means for *n* = 20
Taken from Table 4.1

But why does the Central Limit Theorem work? From Table 4.3 note that most sample means are near the population mean of $50,667. This occurs because of the "averaging effect." For example, in sample #2, one customer had an income of over $55,000. Another customer in the same sample had a relatively low income of $44,658. The mean of the five data values tended toward the middle between the two extremes. This happened in most samples of size five. Thus, many sample means, $\bar{x}$, were very close to the population mean, $\mu$, of $50,667.

The number of sample means fell off rapidly in either direction from the population mean of $50,667. Here's why. To obtain a sample mean, $\bar{x}$, of less than $46,000, all five randomly selected customers must have relatively low incomes. While this was possible, it wasn't very likely given the histogram of the population (see Figure 4.2) and it didn't occur. To obtain a sample mean, $\bar{x}$, of more than $54,000, all five randomly selected families must have relatively high incomes. While it was possible, it never did occur.

In other words, most sample means fell near the population mean. The number of sample means fell off rapidly both above and below the population mean of $50,667. Isn't that a description of a bell-shaped curve?

So the distribution of the sample mean is near bell shaped provided you take a large enough sample of size *n*. So what? Well, you can use the 3-Sigma rule from Chapter 2 to make some statements about how close any sample mean, $\bar{x}$, is likely to be to the population mean, $\mu$. Before doing that let's investigate the other two properties of the distribution of the sample mean, its mean and standard deviation.

**Mean of the Sampling Distribution.** The mean of the approximate distribution of the 100 sample means in Table 4.3 equals $50,650. It is very close to the population mean of $50,667. The mean of the true distribution of the sample mean, $\mu_{\bar{x}}$, would have equaled the population mean, $\mu$.[3] In summary,

**the mean of the distribution of the sample mean is the same as the mean of the population.**

$$\mu = \mu_{\bar{x}}$$

**Standard Deviation of the Sampling Distribution.** Table 4.4 (Table 4.3 redrawn) illustrates what the standard deviation of the sampling distribution, $\sigma_{\bar{x}}$, measures versus what the sample standard deviation, $s$, measures.

| Sample | Obs. 1 | Obs. 2 | Obs. 3 | Obs. 4 | Obs.5 | | Mean | s |
|---|---|---|---|---|---|---|---|---|
| 1 | $55,135 | $53,680 | $49,533 | $52,608 | $45,655 | | $51,322 | $3777 |
| 2 | | | | | | | $49,024 | |
| 3 | The sample standard deviation (s) for sample | | | | | | $48,181 | |
| 4 | one measures the variation of the five | | | | | | $51,311 | |
| 5 | incomes around $51,322. It equals $3,777. | | | | | | $52,198 | |
| 6 | | | | | | | $50,682 | |
| 7 | | | | | | | $52,783 | |
| 8 | | | | | | | $48,934 | |
| 9 | | | | | | | $49,976 | |
| 10 | | | | | | | $52,982 | |
| . | | | | | | | . | |
| . | | | | | | | . | |
| 100 | $44,667 | $52,419 | $50,018 | $46,460 | $50,605 | | $48,834 | |

**Table 4.4**
Distinguishing the Sample Standard Deviation and the Standard Error

From Table 4.4 note that the sample standard deviation (STDEV) measures the variation in the five incomes around the mean of the one sample of size five; for example, $\bar{x}$ = $51,322. It measures the variation in the five observations shown within the nondotted line. The sample standard deviation for sample one is $3,777. The sample standard deviation varies from one sample to the next.

The standard error of the mean, $\sigma_{\bar{x}}$, measures the spread of all possible sample means around the population mean, $50,667. Note that Table 4.4

---

[3] Again that would have required generating over $10^{12}$ different samples of size five.

displays only 100 sample means, not all possible sample means. Do not confuse the standard error of the mean, $\sigma_{\bar{x}}$, with the sample standard deviation, $s$.

If we actually took 100 samples of size five (see Table 4.4) you could *estimate* the standard error of the mean as follows:

$$\sigma_{\bar{x}} \approx \sqrt{\frac{\left(51,322 - 50,667\right)^2 + \dots + \left(48,834 - 50,667\right)^2}{100 - 1}}$$

But in practice you actually take only one sample of size five. How then can you determine the standard error of the mean, $\sigma_{\bar{x}}$?

Expression (4.1) represents the relationship between the population standard deviation, $\sigma$, and the standard error of the mean $\sigma_{\bar{x}}$. Recall from our discussion of Figure 4.2, the population standard deviation equals $3,885.

$$\sigma_{\bar{x}} = \frac{\sigma}{\sqrt{n}}$$

**(4.1)**

From Expression (4.1), the standard error of the mean for a sample of size five is

$$\sigma_{\bar{x}} = \frac{3,885}{\sqrt{5}} = \$1,737.43$$

By increasing the sample size to $n = 20$, the standard error of the mean shrinks to $\dfrac{3,885}{\sqrt{20}}$, or \$868.71. In short:

**the standard error of the mean decreases as the sample size, *n*, increases.**

Expression (4.1) is amazing. To compute the standard error of the mean you do *not* have to take billions of samples of size $n$ from the population, compute their sample means, and then compute the standard deviation of all the sample means. Rather, all you need is Expression (4.1).

What happens if you do not know the population standard deviation, $\sigma$? You still don't have to take billions of samples of size $n$. Since you already know that the sample standard deviation, $s$, will be reasonably close to the population standard deviation, $\sigma$, you can compute the *estimated* standard error of the mean,$\hat{\sigma}_{\bar{x}}$.[4] You will use Expression (4.2) in Chapters 5 and 6 when constructing confidence intervals and doing hypothesis testing.

$$\hat{\sigma}_{\bar{x}} = \frac{s}{\sqrt{n}}$$

(4.2)

## LESSONS LEARNED FROM THE EXPLORATION

How close is any sample mean likely to be to the population mean? You can apply the 3-Sigma rule to the distribution of the sample mean. From Chapter 2, for bell-shaped data, 99.73% of the data values will lie between the mean minus three standard errors and the mean plus three standard errors (3-sigma).

**Table 4.5**
Applying the 3-Sigma Rule to the Distribution of the Sample Mean

| | |
|---|---|
| 99.73% of the sample means will lie within a distance of three standard errors on either side of the population mean ($\mu$). | For a sample of size $n = 5$, 99.73% of all sample means will lie between $$\$50,667 \pm 3 \cdot \frac{3885}{\sqrt{5}}$$ For $n = 20$, 99.73% of all sample means will lie between $$\$50,667 \pm 3 \cdot \frac{3885}{\sqrt{20}}$$ |

Figure 4.5 displays the information contained in Table 4.5. 99.73% of the sample means will lie between $45,455 and $55,879. Or 49.865% (99.73/2) of the sample means will fall between $45,455 and $50,667, and 49.865% of the sample means will fall between $50,667 and $55,879.

Figure 4.5 also includes the sample incomes—$48,930 and $52,404—that are one standard error away from the mean. The **1-Sigma** rule tells us that 68.26% of the sample means will fall between $48,930 and $52,404. Or 34.13% of the sample means will fall between $48,930 and $50,667 and 34.13% of the sample means will fall between $50,667 and $52,404. Finally, the **2-Sigma** rule tells us that 95.44% of the sample means will fall between $50,667 $\pm$ 2 standard errors.

Because of the Central Limit Theorem, the distribution of the sample mean is normal, provided your one sample of size $n$ is sufficiently large. In the next section, let's explore the normal curve more fully.

---

[4] The symbol $^\wedge$ indicates that you are estimating the standard error of the mean. That is, $\hat{\sigma}_{\bar{x}}$ is an estimate of $\sigma_{\bar{x}}$.

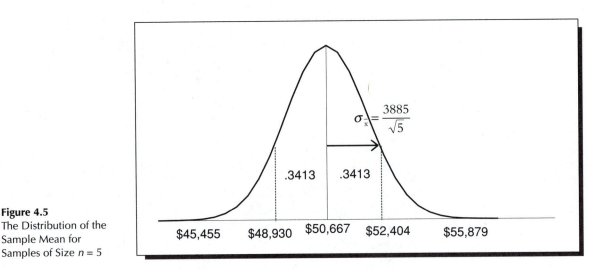

**Figure 4.5**
The Distribution of the
Sample Mean for
Samples of Size $n = 5$

# THE NORMAL DISTRIBUTION

Suppose you wanted to know the probability that the sample mean income based on one sample of size five is

1. less than $52,000

2. between $47,000 and $52,500

3. more than $51,000

4. equal to $51,745

Because of the importance of the Central Limit Theorem, we must more fully explore the normal distribution.[5] By the end of this section, you should be able to

1. draw a sketch to estimate the desired probability; and

2. use Excel's NORMDIST function wizard to compute and interpret normal probabilities.

The normal distribution is a family of bell-shaped curves. All have the same basic bell shape and differ only in their population mean, $\mu$, and standard error of the mean, $\sigma_{\bar{x}}$. The population mean determines the location of the center of the bell, and the standard error of the mean determines the spread of the bell. Figure 4.6 presents three characteristic shapes. As the population mean increases, the distribution shifts to the right. See curves A and B for

---

[5] The normal distribution is also an approximation for the distributions of many variables such as IQ, height, grade-point average, blood pressure, and the diameter of machined parts.

comparison. As the standard error increases, the distribution spreads out or flattens about the population mean; see curves A and C.

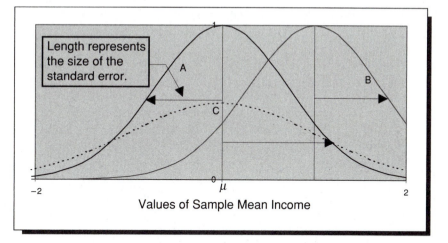

**Figure 4.6**
Three Normal Curves

The standard error of the mean is the distance from the centerline to the *point of inflection* on the normal curve. That is where the curve changes from "convex from below" to "concave from below." Thus, the greater the standard error of the mean, the flatter is the normal curve.

All normal curves have the following characteristics:

**1.** They are symmetric.

**2.** *Probabilities are areas under the normal curve.* The total area under the curve is 1.00.

**3.** The normal curve is asymptotic to the horizontal axis. The curve gets closer to this axis as the values of a sample mean (for example, mean income) get very large or small, but only touches the horizontal axis at plus and minus infinity.

**4.** The probability that the values of a sample mean will fall below (above) the population mean, $\mu$, is 0.5.

So how can we compute the three probabilities at the beginning of this section? Probabilities are areas under a normal curve. Because computing these areas requires calculus, Excel provides an important function wizard, NORMDIST, to determine areas underneath the normal curve. Let's explore how it works by determining the three probabilities.

**EXAMPLE**  **1**  Based on one simple random sample of size $n = 5$, what is the probability that the sample mean income will be less than \$52,000? Assume the population is normal. Mathematically, we can represent this area underneath the normal curve as

$$P\left(\bar{x}_5 < \$52,000\right)$$

Before using Excel's NORMDIST function wizard it is good practice to draw a picture of the normal curve. This will help visualize the probability. Furthermore, you can use your picture to estimate the desired probability. Figure 4.5 is redrawn below.

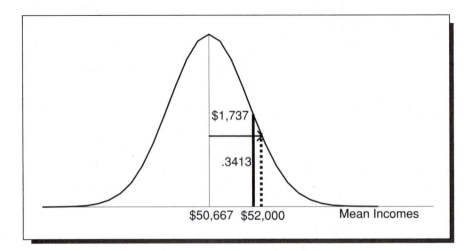

Place \$52,000 on the horizontal axis and draw a vertical line (heavy line) from the horizontal axis to the normal curve. The desired probability equals the area under the curve to the left (less than) of \$52,000. The desired area or probability consists of two parts.

**1.** The area below the mean of \$50,667 is 0.50 because half of the area under the normal curve is below the mean.

**2.** The distance between \$50,667 and \$52,000 is slightly less than one standard error. One standard error above the mean is at \$52,404. From the redrawn Figure 4.5 the area between \$50,667 and \$52,000 is slightly less than 0.3413; say, 0.30.

Thus the desired probability is approximately $0.50 + 0.30 = 0.80$.

Now use the NORMDIST function wizard to determine the desired probability.

NORMDIST requires four inputs. Type in

1. *x*, the value for which you want the **cumulative** probability—52,000,

2. mean, the known population mean—50,667;

3. standard_dev, the known standard error—1737.43;[6] and

4. TRUE, as the fourth entry.

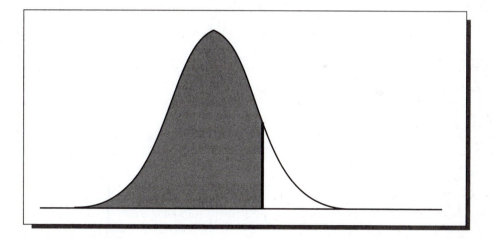

The NORMDIST function wizard provides the *cumulative* area under the curve shown in Figure 4.7.

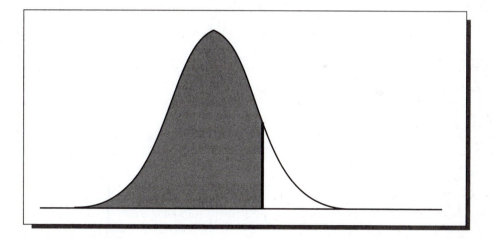

**Figure 4.7**
Area Represented by
$P\left(\overline{x}_5 < \$52,000\right)$
Calculation

---

[6] NORMDIST converts the value, 52,000, into a **z-score** to determine the cumulative probability. A z-score for a value is simply *the number of standard errors that the value is from the mean.* z-score = (value − mean)/standard error. Thus 52,000 converts to (52,000 − 50,667)/ 1737.43 = +0.77. $52,000 is 0.77 standard errors above (+) the mean of $50,667.

---

**DEFINITION**    Cumulative probability is the area under the curve from minus infinity to any value of the sample mean.

---

That is, Excel's NORMDIST function wizard provides the area under the curve from where the normal curve touches the horizontal axis at minus infinity to $52,000. As this was the requested probability for Example 1, the probability is 0.7785. In plain English, if we take one sample of size five, the probability that the sample mean income is less than $52,000 is 0.7785.

The NORMDIST function wizard provides *cumulative* probabilities. But you can use NORMDIST even if you do not desire to compute a cumulative probability. The next example demonstrates this.

**EXAMPLE**    2    Based on one simple random sample of size $n = 5$, what is the probability that the sample mean income will be between $47,000 and $52,500? Assume the population is normal. Mathematically, we can represent the area underneath the normal curve as

$$P\left(\$47,000 < \bar{x}_5 < \$52,500\right)$$

Again we can use a redrawn Figure 4.5 to estimate the desired probability.

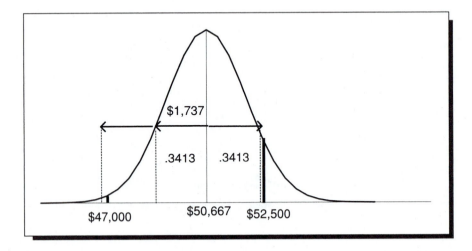

The desired area consists of two parts. Place $47,000 on the horizontal axis and draw a vertical line (heavy line) from the horizontal axis to the normal curve. The area between $47,000 and the mean of $50,667 is much greater than 0.3413, but less than 0.50. Let's say 0.45. Now place $52,500 on the horizontal axis and draw a vertical line (heavy line) from the horizontal axis to the normal curve. The distance between $50,667 and $52,500 is just over one standard error. From the above figure that area is about 0.35. Thus the desired probability is about 0.45 + 0.35, or 0.80.

How can we use the cumulative probability distribution of the NORMDIST function wizard to determine the desired probability? Look at the above figure and think about it before reading on.

Compute the desired probability in three steps.

**1.** Determine the cumulative probability associated with $52,500. That is the area shown below in Figure 4.8A. That is the area underneath the normal curve to the left of $52,500.

**2.** Then determine the area underneath the normal curve to the left of $47,000 (Figure 4.8B).

**3.** The difference in the two areas equals the desired probability—the area between $47,000 and $52,500.

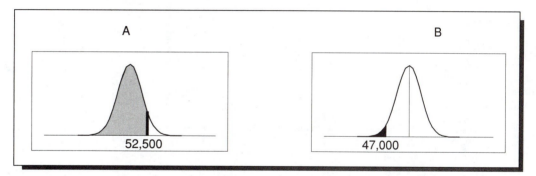

**Figure 4.8**
Areas Represented by $P\left(\$47,000 < \bar{x}_5 < \$52,500\right)$ Calculation

Please use NORMDIST and verify that the desired probability is

$$0.8543 - 0.0174 = 0.8369$$

---

**EXAMPLE**    **3**   Based on one simple random sample of size $n = 5$, what is the probability that the sample mean income is more than $51,000? Assume the population is normal. Mathematically, we can represent the area underneath the normal curve as

$$P\left(\bar{x}_5 > \$51,000\right)$$

Again we can use Figure 4.5 to estimate the desired probability. The desired area underneath the curve is to the *right* of $51,000. Place $51,000 on the horizontal axis and draw a vertical line from the horizontal axis to the normal curve. Figure 4.5 suggests that the area between the mean and $51,000 is small; say 0.05. Thus the area underneath the curve above $51,000 should be about 0.50 − 0.05 = 0.45. Remember that half the area under the normal curve lies above its mean.

How can we use the cumulative probability distribution of NORMDIST to determine the desired probability? Look at Figure 4.5 and think about it before reading on.

We compute the desired probability in two steps.

**1.** First, determine the cumulative probability associated with $51,000. That is the area underneath the normal curve from minus infinity to $51,000 shown in Figure 4.9. We want the remaining area underneath the curve.

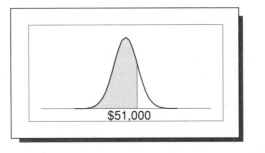

**Figure 4.9**
Area Represented by
$P\left(\overline{x}_5 > \$51,000\right)$
Calculation

**2.** Since the total area under the normal curve is 1.0, the desired probability is 1.0 − cumulative probability that the sample mean income is less than $51,000.

Use NORMDIST and verify that the desired probability is

$$1.000 - 0.5760 = 0.4240$$

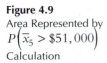

**EXAMPLE**     4     Based on one simple random sample of size $n = 5$, what is the probability that the sample mean income equals $51,745? Assume the population is normal. Mathematically, we can represent the desired probability as

$$P\left(\overline{x}_5 = \$51,745\right)$$

You should not use the NORMDIST function wizard to determine the answer. Why not? Think about it before continuing.

▶ **WARNING** Probability is the area *under* the normal curve. How much area lies underneath the curve at $51,745? There is no area under a single point! So the probability is zero. You can only compute probabilities for ranges of values—as in Examples 1–3.

You could use the NORMDIST function wizard in Examples 1–3 because the population was normal. For sample sizes under 30 you cannot use the NORMDIST wizard unless the population distribution is normally distributed. For sample sizes greater than 30, the distribution of the sample mean will be normally distributed because of the Central Limit Theorem, and you could use NORMDIST even if the population distribution was not normal.

In summary, the implications of Central Limit Theorem are astounding. In the real world, the distribution of incomes (and other business variables) is highly skewed (think of the high incomes of athletes or rock stars). Yet we take one sample of size $n$ from this skewed population and provided the sample size is sufficiently large, the Central Limit Theorem tells us that the *distribution of the sample mean* will be normal. This allows us to use the NORMDIST function wizard to compute probabilities. If the Central Limit Theorem were not true, then the distribution of the sample mean would only be normal if the distribution of the target population from which we took the sample was itself normal.

In this section we have used the Central Limit Theorem and the normal distribution to compute probabilities that a sample mean will take on certain values. In Chapter 5 we will use these two concepts to estimate an unknown population mean, $\mu$, based on one sample mean for a sample of size $n$ taken from a target population.

# EXPLORING THE DISTRIBUTION OF THE SAMPLE PROPORTION

The distribution of the sample mean is not the only sampling distribution that managers must know. Suppose you take a random sample of CEOs and determine that 0.62 of them use company profitability to determine their employees' yearly bonuses. Because this is one of many possible samples, the sample proportion, $\hat{p}$ (a sample statistic), will probably not equal the population proportion, $p$ (a population parameter). The two proportions will differ because of the variation within the population and because the composition of samples varies. However, most sample proportions will be close to the population proportion because of the properties of the distribution of the sample proportion. By the end of this section you should be able to

1. explain why the distribution of the sample proportion will be near normally distributed, provided the sample size is sufficiently large;

2. use the NORMDIST function wizard to compute the probabilities regarding the sample proportion; and

3. compare and contrast the distributions of the sample mean and the sample proportion.

## THE DISTRIBUTION OF A POPULATION

Suppose that a firm that provides electronic information services wants to know the proportion of present and future customers who would favor a new charge plan for connecting to the Internet. While the firm does not know the proportion of customers in the target population of $N = 5000$ that favor the new charge plan, let's assume that we do—0.30. Based on a single sample of size 125, how close can the firm estimate the population proportion in favor of the new plan?

*Shape.* The column chart using Excel's chart wizard for the proportion of customers who favor the plan in the target population appears in Figure 4.10. One thing is clear—the distribution of the population is not normal shaped. The population proportion, $p$, who favor the plan is 0.30.

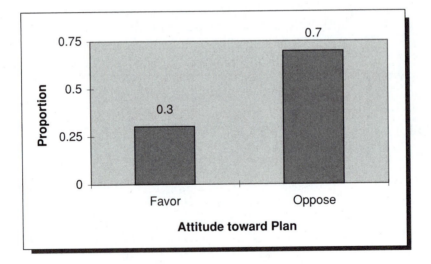

**Figure 4.10**
Column Chart on
Attitude toward Plan
within the Population

## DATA FROM ONE SAMPLE

Now select one simple random sample of size $n = 125$ from the population of $N = 5000$ customers and then determine the sample proportion, $\hat{p}$, who favor the plan. It will not equal the population proportion, $p = 0.30$, but it should be relatively close. We selected the 125 observations from a spreadsheet containing 5000 attitudes towards the plan (favor or oppose) in which

30% favored the plan. For obvious reasons, the 5000 values aren't shown here. However, Table 4.6 displays the survey results. Of the 125 interviewed, 39 favored the plan.

| Favor | Oppose | Oppose | Favor | Oppose | Oppose | Oppose | Oppose | Oppose | Favor | Favor | Oppose | Oppose |
|---|---|---|---|---|---|---|---|---|---|---|---|---|
| Oppose | Favor | Oppose | Oppose | Oppose | Oppose | Oppose | Oppose | Oppose | Oppose | Oppose | Favor | Oppose |
| Favor | Oppose | Oppose | Oppose | Oppose | Favor | Oppose | Oppose | Favor | Oppose | Oppose | Oppose | Oppose |
| Oppose | Favor | Favor | Oppose | Favor | Oppose | Favor | Favor | Oppose | Oppose | Favor | Oppose | Oppose |
| Favor | Oppose | Oppose | Oppose | Oppose | Favor | Oppose | Oppose | Favor | Oppose | Favor | Oppose | Oppose |
| Favor | Oppose | Oppose | Favor | Favor | Favor | Oppose | Favor | Favor | Favor | Oppose | Favor | |
| Oppose | Favor | Oppose | Favor | Favor | Oppose | Oppose | Oppose | Oppose | Oppose | Oppose | Oppose | |
| Favor | Oppose | Oppose | Oppose | Oppose | Oppose | Favor | Oppose | Oppose | Oppose | Oppose | Favor | |
| Oppose | Oppose | Oppose | Oppose | Favor | Oppose | Oppose | Oppose | Oppose | Favor | Oppose | Oppose | |
| Oppose | Oppose | Oppose | Oppose | Favor | Oppose | Favor | Oppose | Favor | Oppose | Favor | Oppose | |

**Table 4.6**
Results of Survey of 125 Customers

Use Expression (4.3) to compute a sample proportion.

$$\hat{p} = \frac{n_{YES}}{n}$$

(4.3)

where $n$ is the total sample size and $n_{YES}$ is the number who said YES to the survey question.

For the Internet charge study, the sample proportion who favors the plan is

$$\hat{p} = \frac{39}{125} = 0.312$$

Note that the sample proportion, $\hat{p}$, of 0.312 is relatively close to the unknown, and generally unknowable, population proportion, $p = 0.30$.

## THE DISTRIBUTION OF THE SAMPLE PROPORTION

Instead of taking one sample of size 125, *imagine* taking *all possible samples of size 125* with replacement from the population of $N = 5000$ customers and computing the sample proportions. This would generate a distribution of the sample proportion for samples of size 125. We use the word "imagine" because managers never construct such a distribution. It would be too costly and time consuming.

Table 4.7 displays the 100 sample proportions based on 125 observations each taken from the population of $N = 5000$ where 30% of the customers favor the new plan.

The shape of the distribution of the sample proportion will be normal, provided the sample size is sufficiently large, because of the Central Limit Theorem.

| | | | | | | | | | |
|----|-------|----|-------|----|-------|----|-------|-----|-------|
| 1  | 0.312 | 21 | 0.264 | 41 | 0.288 | 61 | 0.256 | 81  | 0.256 |
| 2  | 0.248 | 22 | 0.344 | 42 | 0.256 | 62 | 0.280 | 82  | 0.320 |
| 3  | 0.272 | 23 | 0.304 | 43 | 0.256 | 63 | 0.272 | 83  | 0.288 |
| 4  | 0.328 | 24 | 0.232 | 44 | 0.208 | 64 | 0.344 | 84  | 0.216 |
| 5  | 0.312 | 25 | 0.328 | 45 | 0.264 | 65 | 0.376 | 85  | 0.280 |
| 6  | 0.328 | 26 | 0.304 | 46 | 0.280 | 66 | 0.312 | 86  | 0.272 |
| 7  | 0.360 | 27 | 0.304 | 47 | 0.296 | 67 | 0.304 | 87  | 0.248 |
| 8  | 0.304 | 28 | 0.328 | 48 | 0.272 | 68 | 0.264 | 88  | 0.368 |
| 9  | 0.216 | 29 | 0.328 | 49 | 0.352 | 69 | 0.384 | 89  | 0.256 |
| 10 | 0.328 | 30 | 0.304 | 50 | 0.264 | 70 | 0.288 | 90  | 0.344 |
| 11 | 0.272 | 31 | 0.296 | 51 | 0.272 | 71 | 0.320 | 91  | 0.384 |
| 12 | 0.280 | 32 | 0.312 | 52 | 0.304 | 72 | 0.304 | 92  | 0.328 |
| 13 | 0.248 | 33 | 0.232 | 53 | 0.368 | 73 | 0.296 | 93  | 0.296 |
| 14 | 0.272 | 34 | 0.280 | 54 | 0.280 | 74 | 0.312 | 94  | 0.368 |
| 15 | 0.328 | 35 | 0.280 | 55 | 0.360 | 75 | 0.304 | 95  | 0.320 |
| 16 | 0.304 | 36 | 0.304 | 56 | 0.328 | 76 | 0.304 | 96  | 0.280 |
| 17 | 0.272 | 37 | 0.296 | 57 | 0.304 | 77 | 0.408 | 97  | 0.280 |
| 18 | 0.336 | 38 | 0.328 | 58 | 0.344 | 78 | 0.296 | 98  | 0.352 |
| 19 | 0.336 | 39 | 0.376 | 59 | 0.392 | 79 | 0.280 | 99  | 0.336 |
| 20 | 0.296 | 40 | 0.304 | 60 | 0.224 | 80 | 0.328 | 100 | 0.352 |

**Table 4.7**
Table of 100 Sample Proportions Each Based on $n = 125$

Figure 4.11 displays the distribution of the 100 sample proportions based on samples of $n = 125$. Note that the shape is near normal.

How large must the sample size be such that the distribution of the sample proportion is near normal? Table 4.8 presents Cochran's Rules on the normality of the distribution of the sample proportion.

**Table 4.8**
Cochran's Rules for Normality of the Distribution of the Sample Proportion

| If Population Proportion Is | Sample Size Needed to Ensure Normality |
|------------------------------|----------------------------------------|
| .5          | 30   |
| .40 or .60  | 50   |
| .30 or .70  | 80   |
| .20 or .80  | 200  |
| .10 or .90  | 600  |
| .05 or .95  | 1400 |

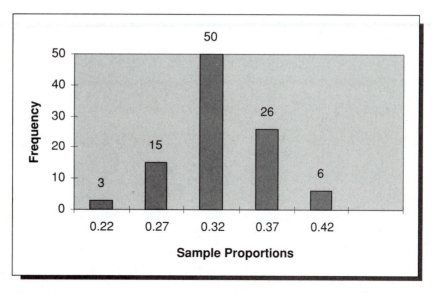

**Figure 4.11**
Distribution of the Sample Proportion for $n = 125$

Given a population proportion of 0.30, the distribution of the sample proportion based on $n = 125$ should have been normal by Cochran's Rule. And Figure 4.11 indicates that it was!

The standard error of the proportion measures the variation in all (or from Table 4.7, the 100) sample proportions around the population proportion of 0.30. If all the sample proportions had equaled 0.30, the standard error of the proportion would be zero. You could use Table 4.7 to estimate the standard error of the proportion as follows:

$$\sigma_{\hat{p}} \approx \sqrt{\frac{\left(.312 - .30\right)^2 + \left(.248 - .30\right)^2 + \left(.272 - .30\right)^2 + \ldots + \left(.352 - .30\right)^2}{100 - 1}}$$

But in practice you only take one sample of size 125. How, then, can you determine the standard error of the proportion? You can use Expression (4.4) to determine it.

$$\sigma_{\hat{p}} = \sqrt{\frac{p \cdot q}{n}}$$

**(4.4)**

From Expression (4.4), the standard error of the proportion for a sample of size 125 is

$$\sigma_{\hat{p}} = \sqrt{\frac{(0.30) \cdot (0.70)}{125}} = .0410$$

Expression (4.4) is quite amazing. To compute the standard error of the proportion you do *not* have to take millions of samples of size $n$ from the population, compute the sample proportions, and then compute the standard deviation of all the sample proportions. Rather, all you need to know is the population proportion in favor of the plan ($p$) and population proportion opposed to the plan ($q = 1 - p$) and the size of the one sample you plan to take from the population. Expression (4.4) then generates the standard error of the proportion.

What happens if you do not know the population proportion, $p$? You still don't have to take repeated samples of size $n$. You can compute the *estimated* standard error of the proportion. You substitute the sample proportion $\hat{p}$ for $p$ and $\hat{q}$ for $q$. In Chapters 5 and 6, you will use Expression (4.5) to construct confidence intervals on the population proportion, $p$, and do hypothesis testing on a population proportion.

$$\hat{\sigma}_{\hat{p}} = \sqrt{\frac{\hat{p} \cdot \hat{q}}{n}}$$

(4.5)

## LESSONS LEARNED FROM THE EXPLORATION

You now know how close any sample proportion is likely to be to the population proportion because:

1. The Central Limit Theorem states that the distribution of the sample proportion is normal even if the population from which you took the sample was not, provided the sample size is sufficiently large. Use Cochran's Rule (Table 4.8) to determine the minimum sample size.

2. You can apply the NORMDIST function wizard to compute the desired probability.

Before computing normal probabilities, Figure 4.12 should help you estimate normal probabilities before using the NORMDIST function wizard. The figure is based upon the 3–Sigma rule.

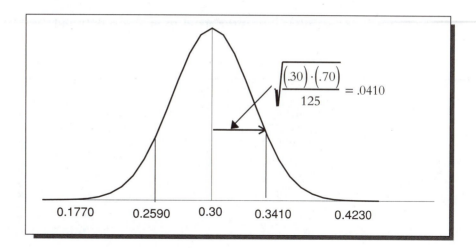

**Figure 4.12**
The Distribution of the Sample Proportion for $n = 125$

Figure 4.12 shows that 68.26% of the sample proportions will lie between 0.2590 and 0.3410. The figure also shows 99.73% of the sample proportions will lie between 0.1770 and 0.4230. And 50% of the sample proportions will be below 0.30.

## COMPUTING PROBABILITIES USING THE NORMAL DISTRIBUTION

Given that the distribution of the sample proportion is normal, you can use Excel's NORMDIST function wizard to compute normal probabilities.

**EXAMPLE**

**5**  Based on one simple random sample of size $n = 125$, what is the probability that the sample proportion who favors the charge plan will be less than .285 (say, the financial break-even point)? Mathematically you can represent this area underneath the normal curve as

$$P\left(\hat{p}_{125} < 0.285\right)$$

Place 0.285 on the horizontal axis and draw a vertical line from the horizontal axis to the normal curve. From Figure 4.12, the desired probability equals the area under the curve to the left (less than) of the sample proportion, 0.285. The area between 0.285 and 0.30 is about 0.15. So the area below the sample proportion of 0.285 is about $0.50 - 0.15$ or 0.35.

Below is the NORMDIST function wizard used to determine the desired probability. Type in

**1.** $x$ is the value for which you want the cumulative probability—0.285,

**2.** mean is the population proportion—0.30;

3. standard_dev is the standard error—.0410; and

4. TRUE is always the fourth entry.

NORMDIST

| | | |
|---|---|---|
| **X** | .285 | = 0.285 |
| **Mean** | .300 | = 0.3 |
| **Standard_dev** | .0410 | = 0.0410 |
| **Cumulative** | TRUE | = TRUE |

= 0.356903494

Returns the normal cumulative distribution for the specified mean and standard deviation.

**Cumulative** is a logical value: for the cumulative distribution function, use TRUE; for the probability mass function, use FALSE.

Formula result =0.356903494          OK          Cancel

$$P\left(\hat{p}_{125} < 0.285\right) = 0.3569$$

---

**EXAMPLE**

6  Based on one simple random sample of size $n = 125$, what is the probability that the sample proportion who favors the charge plan will be between 0.2590 and 0.3410? Mathematically, you can represent this area underneath the normal curve as:

$$P\left(0.2590 < \hat{p}_{125} < 0.3410\right)$$

Compute the desired probability in three steps.

1. First, determine the cumulative probability associated with 0.3410. That is the area underneath the normal curve to the left of 0.3410.

2. Then determine the area underneath the normal curve to the left of 0.2590.

3. The difference in the two areas equals the desired probability—the area between 0.2590 and 0.3410.

Use NORMDIST and verify that the desired probability is

$$0.8413 - 0.1586 = 0.6827$$

This section concludes with a comparison of the two sampling distributions presented so far (see Table 4.9).

| Bases for Comparison | Distribution of the Sample Mean | Distribution of the Sample Proportion |
|---|---|---|
| Shape | Will be normal if the sample size is greater than 30. Can be normal for a sample size of four or five. | Will be normal if the sample size exceeds Cochran's Rules. The minimum sample size depends on value of $p$ (or $\hat{p}$ as the population proportion is unknown and unknowable). |
| Standard Error | As the sample size increases, the standard error of the mean decreases. | As the sample size increases, the standard error of the proportion decreases. |
| Formula for Standard Error | $\sigma_{\bar{x}} = \dfrac{\sigma}{\sqrt{n}}$ | $\sigma_{\hat{p}} = \sqrt{\dfrac{p \cdot q}{n}}$ |

**Table 4.9**
Comparing Two
Sampling Distributions

# EXPLORING THE DISTRIBUTION OF THE SAMPLE VARIANCE

This section introduces the distribution of the sample variance. Suppose you take a random sample of blue-collar workers and compute the sample variance in the number of hours of training in the past quarter. Because this is one of many possible samples, the sample variance in training hours, $s^2$, will probably not equal the population variance, $\sigma^2$. The two variances will differ because of the variation within the population and because the composition of samples varies. However, most sample variances will be close to the population variance because of the properties of the distribution of the sample variance. By the end of this section you should be able to

**1.** explain why the distribution of the sample variance will *not* be normally distributed, irrespective of the sample size;

**2.** explain why the standard error of the variance becomes smaller as the sample size increases; and

**3.** compute and interpret chi-square probabilities.

## THE DISTRIBUTION OF A POPULATION

Suppose a firm wants to know the variance in number of training hours among all blue-collar workers in a plant with $N = 4000$ workers. While the firm does not know the variance, let's assume that we do. Assume that the population mean number of training hours ($\mu$) is 10 and the population variance ($\sigma^2$) is 1.[7] Furthermore, assume the number of training hours is normally distributed in the target population. Let's see how close the firm, based on a single random sample of size five, can estimate the population variance.

## DATA FROM ONE SAMPLE

Select one simple random sample of size $n = 5$ from the population of $N = 4000$ workers and compute the sample mean, $\bar{x}$, and sample variance, $s^2$. The sample variance is unlikely to equal the population variance, $\sigma^2 = 1.00$, but it should be relatively close. Below are the number of training hours of five randomly selected blue-collar workers. These five observations are from a spreadsheet containing 4000 workers' number of training hours. For obvious reasons, we have chosen not to show the spreadsheet. The sample mean number of training hours is 10.46 hours.

| 10.16 | 10.66 | 9.56 | 11.32 | 10.60 | 10.46 |
|-------|-------|------|-------|-------|-------|

Using the variance function wizard (VAR) or Expression (4.6), the sample variance, $s^2$, equals 0.4248. As expected, it is reasonably close to the population variance, $\sigma^2$, of 1.00, but the two variances do differ.

$$s^2 = \frac{\sum_i \left(x_i - \bar{x}\right)^2}{n - 1}$$

**(4.6)**

$$s^2 = \frac{\left(10.16 - 10.46\right)^2 + \ldots + \left(10.60 - 10.46\right)^2}{5 - 1} = 0.4248$$

## THE DISTRIBUTION OF THE SAMPLE VARIANCE

Instead of taking one sample of size five, imagine taking all possible samples of size five with replacement from the population in the spreadsheet of 4000 workers and computing the sample variances. This would generate a distribution of the sample variance for samples of size five. We use the word "imagine" because managers never construct a sampling distribution. It would be too costly and time consuming.

Using Excel we generated 100 random samples of size five from a spreadsheet that contains a population of $N = 4000$ workers with a mean,

---

[7] The units for variance is hour$^2$. The units for standard deviation would thus be in hours, a more understandable quantity.

$\mu$, of 10 training hours and a variance, $\sigma^2$, of 1.00. Table 4.10 only displays 22 (of the 100) sample variances based on five observations each. Note that many of the sample variances are relatively close to 1.00. For the 22 sample variances shown, the smallest sample variance was 0.0373 and the largest was 4.1144. Remember that the variance of the target population, $\sigma^2$, is 1.00.

What will the shape of the distribution of the sample variances (shown within the heavy lines) be? Will it be normal? Figure 4.13 that displays the distribution of 100 sample variances for samples of size five may surprise you.

| Sample | Obs. 1 | Obs. 2 | Obs. 3 | Obs. 4 | Obs. 5 | Sample Variance for $n = 5$ |
|---|---|---|---|---|---|---|
| 1 | 10.16 | 10.66 | 9.56 | 11.32 | 10.60 | 0.4248 |
| 2 | 11.58 | 11.79 | 10.47 | 9.50 | 10.33 | 0.8966 |
| 3 | 9.46 | 9.98 | 9.77 | 9.64 | 9.63 | 0.0373 |
| 4 | 9.19 | 9.63 | 9.72 | 12.00 | 9.71 | 1.2358 |
| 5 | 9.42 | 9.85 | 10.13 | 11.34 | 10.03 | 0.5134 |
| 6 | 8.91 | 8.77 | 9.30 | 9.10 | 10.47 | 0.4519 |
| 7 | 8.67 | 9.07 | 10.76 | 9.44 | 11.38 | 1.3342 |
| 8 | 10.29 | 11.22 | 9.68 | 9.72 | 10.49 | 0.4004 |
| 9 | 8.85 | 10.38 | 10.72 | 8.49 | 8.21 | 1.3063 |
| 10 | 10.45 | 11.04 | 9.80 | 8.90 | 11.55 | 1.0828 |
| 11 | 10.74 | 10.11 | 10.98 | 10.95 | 12.02 | 0.4737 |
| 12 | 9.84 | 9.75 | 10.07 | 8.89 | 9.38 | 0.2131 |
| 13 | 10.81 | 10.50 | 9.98 | 10.29 | 9.36 | 0.3059 |
| 14 | 10.43 | 7.76 | 11.69 | 9.45 | 10.07 | 2.0735 |
| 15 | 8.81 | 11.05 | 8.63 | 10.80 | 10.48 | 1.3138 |
| 16 | 10.05 | 10.50 | 10.24 | 10.08 | 9.62 | 0.1032 |
| 17 | 11.11 | 10.52 | 9.82 | 10.14 | 11.03 | 0.3106 |
| 18 | 7.48 | 10.75 | 12.46 | 10.03 | 8.20 | 3.9930 |
| 19 | 9.38 | 10.62 | 13.95 | 10.96 | 8.68 | 4.1144 |
| 20 | 12.09 | 10.01 | 11.28 | 9.49 | 11.63 | 1.2184 |
| 21 | 9.5 | 10.74 | 10.75 | 10.80 | 9.79 | 0.3862 |
| 22 | 11.13 | 8.37 | 9.46 | 8.81 | 8.64 | 1.2284 |

standard error measures the standard deviation of all the sample variances around a population variance of 1.00.

**Table 4.10**
Table of 22 Sample Variances Based on $n = 5$

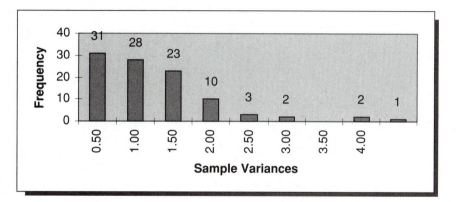

**Figure 4.13**
Histogram of the Distribution of the 100 Sample Variances for Samples of Size Five

The distribution of the sample variance is not normal. You may be thinking that if you had increased the sample size, the distribution would become normal. Figure 4.14 indicates that the distribution of the sample variance is still not normal for samples of size 20.

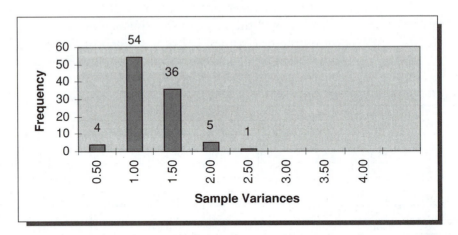

**Figure 4.14**
Histogram of the Distribution of the 100 Sample Variances for Samples of Size 20

Irrespective of the sample size, the distribution of the sample variance will *never* be normal. In short, the Central Limit Theorem does not apply to the distribution of the sample variance.

Here's why the distribution of the sample variance cannot be normally distributed. Under no circumstances can a sample variance be less than zero [see Expression (4.6)]. However, there is no *theoretical* upper limit to the maximum size of a sample variance. Doesn't that suggest that the distribution of the sample variance must be *positively skewed* toward the right or larger values?

The distribution of the sample variance, $s^2$, is positively skewed. If you multiply the sample variance by $(n-1)$ and then divide by the population variance, $\sigma^2$, the resulting statistic is **chi-square** distributed.

$$\frac{(n-1) \cdot s^2}{\sigma^2} \text{ is } X^2_{n-1} \text{ distributed,}$$

(4.7)

where $n$ is the size of the one sample taken from the population.

The chi-square distribution is an important family of skewed distributions. Its degree of skewness decreases as $(n-1)$ increases.[8] Shortly you will use the chi-square distribution to determine how close a sample variance is to the population variance based on one sample of size $n$. Before doing this, you must understand the standard error of the variance.

---

[8] The sample size minus one is called the degrees of freedom and is discussed in Chapter 5.

What does the standard error of the variance, $\sigma_{s^2}$, measure? Does it decrease as the sample size, $n$, increases as do the standard errors of the mean and the proportion?

Table 4.10 displays what the standard error of the variance measures. It measures the standard deviation in the sample variances (22 of which are shown) around the population variance of 1.00. If all the sample variances equaled 1.00, the standard error of the variance would be zero. Because the sample variances in Table 4.10 differ from the population variance of 1.00, the standard error of the variance cannot be zero for that distribution.

From Figures 4.13 and 4.14, increasing the sample size from five to 20 reduced the standard error of the variance. Note the *tighter* spread around the distribution's center in Figure 4.14 versus Figure 4.13. Although we have not provided an expression for calculating the standard error of the variance, it does get smaller as the sample size increases. In short, it behaves like the standard error of the mean and the standard error of the proportion.

## LESSONS LEARNED FROM THE EXPLORATION

The distribution of the sample variance is positively skewed. The statistic, $\dfrac{(n-1) \cdot s^2}{\sigma^2}$, is chi-square distributed. In the next chapter you will use the chi-square statistic to construct confidence intervals on an unknown, and generally unknowable, population variance.

Your estimate of the population variance will improve as the sample size increases. This happens because the standard error of the variance becomes smaller as you increase the sample size. In plain English, this means that as $n$ increases, any sample variance is likely to be close to the unknown population variance.

## COMPUTING PROBABILITIES USING THE CHI-SQUARE DISTRIBUTION

Given that the statistic $\dfrac{(n-1) \cdot s^2}{\sigma^2}$ is chi-squared distributed, you can use Excel's CHIDIST function wizard to compute chi-square probabilities.

**EXAMPLE**

**7**  Based on one simple random sample of size $n = 11$, what is the probability that the sample variance in training hours will be greater than 2?

Recall that the population variance, $\sigma^2$ is 1.00. Mathematically, you can represent this area underneath the chi-square curve as

$$P\left[s_{11}^2 > 2\right]$$

$$P\left[\frac{(n-1)\cdot s_{11}^2}{\sigma^2 = 1} > \frac{(n-1)\cdot 2}{1}\right]$$

$$P\left[10\cdot s_{11}^2 > 20\right]$$

Remember that $s^2$ is *not* chi-square distributed. Only $\dfrac{(n-1)\cdot s^2}{\sigma^2}$ is chi-square distributed. Thus, the second and third equations convert $s^2$ into a statistic that is chi-square distributed.

Figure 4.15 is a chi-square distribution for $11 - 1$ degrees of freedom. The total area underneath the curve equals 1.00. The desired probability equals the area under the curve to the *right* (greater than) of 20.00. The area is about .05.

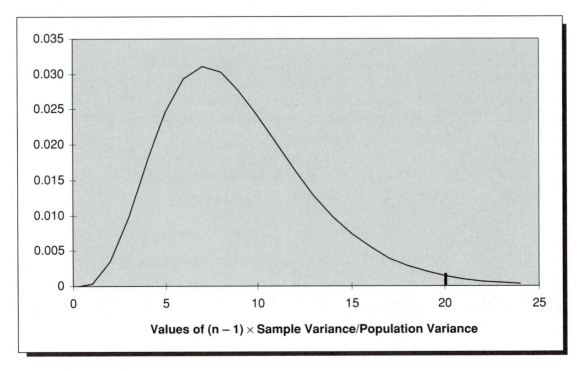

**Figure 4.15**
Chi-Square Curve for $n - 1$, or 10, Degrees of Freedom

Below is the CHIDIST function wizard to determine the desired probability. You must type in two inputs:

1. $x$ is the value for which you want the area underneath the curve *that lies to the right* of a value—in this example, 20. Unlike NORMDIST, the CHIDIST wizard provides the area in the *upper tail* of the chi-square curve. That is, CHIDIST provides the area under the curve from some value, $k$ (here 20), to infinity.

2. degrees of freedom is sample size minus one—10;

```
┌─CHIDIST────────────────────────────────────────────────┐
│           X  20                              ▦ = 20      │
│   Deg_freedom 10                             ▦ = 10      │
│                                    = 0.029252688         │
│   Returns the one-tailed probability of the chi-squared distribution. │
│                                                          │
│     Deg_freedom is the number of degrees of freedom, a number between 1 and 10^10, │
│                excluding 10^10.                          │
│   ┌─┐                                                    │
│   │?│   Formula result =0.029252688      [  OK  ] [ Cancel ] │
│   └─┘                                                    │
└────────────────────────────────────────────────────────┘
```

The desired probability is 0.029. Thus, if the population variance equals 1.00, the probability of obtaining a sample variance greater than 2.00 is only 0.029. That is, only 2.9% of the sample variances will be greater than 2.00 when the population variance is 1.00.

---

**EXAMPLE**    **8**    Based on one simple random sample of size $n = 11$, what is the probability that the sample variance in training hours *will be less than* 1.5? Mathematically, you can represent this area underneath the chi-square curve as

$$P\left[s_{11}^2 < 1.5\right]$$

$$P\left[\frac{(n-1)\cdot s_{11}^2}{\sigma^2 = 1} < \frac{(n-1)\cdot 1.5}{1}\right]$$

$$P\left[10\cdot s_{11}^2 < 15\right]$$

From Figure 4.15, the desired probability equals the area *to the left* of 15. It's about 0.85.

Here is how to determine the actual probability. The CHIDIST function wizard provides the area in the upper tail of the chi-square curve (above 15). Use CHIDIST to find the area to the right of 15.00 and then subtract that area from 1.00. From the CHIDIST function wizard, the area in the upper tail above 15.00 for 10 degrees of freedom is 0.132062. Thus the desired probability is

$$1 - 0.132062 = 0.867938$$

Given that the population variance equals 1.00, the probability that a sample variance will be less than 1.50 is about 0.87. In other words, 87% of all sample variances will be between zero and 1.5. In short, 87% of all sample variances will be very close to the population variance of 1.00.

---

**EXAMPLE**    **9**    Based on one simple random sample of size $n = 11$, what is the probability that the sample variance in training hours *will be between* 0.8 and 1.2? Mathematically, you can represent this area underneath the chi-square curve as

$$P\left[.80 < s_{11}^2 < 1.2\right]$$

$$P\left[\frac{(n-1)\cdot 0.8}{1} < \frac{(n-1)\cdot s_{11}^2}{\sigma^2 = 1} < \frac{(n-1)\cdot 1.2}{1}\right]$$

$$P\left(8 < 10s_{11}^2 < 12\right)$$

Since the CHIDIST function wizard provides the area in the upper tail of the chi-square curve, you will need three steps to determine the desired probability.

1.  First, use CHIDIST to find the area to the right of 8.00. From the CHIDIST function wizard, the area in the upper tail above 8.00 for 10 degrees of freedom is 0.628837.

2.  Next use CHIDIST to find the area to the right of 12.00. The area in the upper tail above 12.00 for 10 degrees of freedom is 0.285057.

3.  Then subtract the two areas. Thus the desired probability is

$$0.628837 - 0.285057 = 0.34378$$

In this section you have used the statistic $\dfrac{(n-1)s^2}{\sigma^2}$ to compute chi-square probabilities. In Chapter 5 you will use the statistic to construct confidence intervals on an unknown population variance.

# KEY IDEAS AND OVERVIEW

This chapter concludes with Figure 4.16, a redrawn Figure 4.1 that illustrates the statistical inference process. The redrawn figure includes the key ideas presented in the chapter.

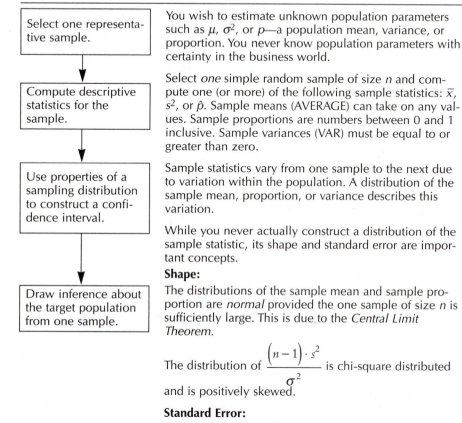

You wish to estimate unknown population parameters such as $\mu$, $\sigma^2$, or $p$—a population mean, variance, or proportion. You never know population parameters with certainty in the business world.

Select *one* simple random sample of size $n$ and compute one (or more) of the following sample statistics: $\bar{x}$, $s^2$, or $\hat{p}$. Sample means (AVERAGE) can take on any values. Sample proportions are numbers between 0 and 1 inclusive. Sample variances (VAR) must be equal to or greater than zero.

Sample statistics vary from one sample to the next due to variation within the population. A distribution of the sample mean, proportion, or variance describes this variation.

While you never actually construct a distribution of the sample statistic, its shape and standard error are important concepts.

**Shape:**

The distributions of the sample mean and sample proportion are *normal* provided the one sample of size $n$ is sufficiently large. This is due to the *Central Limit Theorem.*

The distribution of $\dfrac{(n-1) \cdot s^2}{\sigma^2}$ is chi-square distributed and is positively skewed.

**Standard Error:**

The standard error of the mean, proportion, or variance becomes smaller as you increase the sample size. Thus, the value of any sample statistic is likely to be close to its corresponding population parameter.

**Figure 4.16**
The Statistical Inference
Process Revisited

# EXERCISES

1. How do a sample statistic and population parameter differ?

2. Correct, if necessary, the following statement: We use known population parameters to estimate unknown sample statistics.

3. Correct, if necessary, the following statement: We use known population statistics to estimate unknown sample parameters.

4. Correct, if necessary, the following statement: We use known sample statistics to estimate unknown sample parameters.

5. Explain why the standard error of the mean will be less than the standard deviation of the population? Do *not* use Expression (4.1) to support your argument.

6. Is it necessary to construct a distribution of the sample mean to determine the standard error of the mean? If not, how can you do so without constructing a distribution of the sample mean?

7. Critique and correct if necessary: The Central Limit Theorem tells us that the distribution of the population will be normal provided the sample size is sufficiently large.

8. Is it likely that a sample variance based on $n = 30$ will equal the population variance? If you increase the sample size from 30 to 300, which sample variance is likely to be closer to the population variance? Why?

9. A population consists of 100,000 consumers whose incomes you wish to estimate. Explain to a marketing manager how to

   a. Compute the mean and standard deviation of the population. How costly and time consuming would it be to determine the population mean and standard deviation? What are the symbols for the population parameters?

   b. Compute a sample mean and a sample standard deviation. What are the sample statistics' symbols?

   c. Construct a distribution of the sample mean for samples of size 30. How costly and time consuming would it be to construct a sampling distribution? What are the symbols that represent the mean and standard error of the mean?

10. Time to complete a project is normally distributed with a mean time of 40 hours and a standard deviation of 16 hours.

   a. What is the mean of the distribution of the sample mean for samples of size 30?

   b. Determine the standard error.

   c. Would the standard error be smaller if a sample of 100 were taken? Why?

   d. Is the distribution of the sample mean normal shaped? Why?

11. Time to complete a project is not normally distributed with a mean time of 100 hours and a standard deviation of 10 hours.

   a. What is the mean of the distribution of the sample mean for samples of size 40?

   b. Determine the standard error.

   c. Would the standard error be smaller if a sample of 400 were taken? Why?

   d. Is the distribution of the sample mean normal shaped? Why?

12. Family incomes in Akron, Ohio, are not normally distributed. The population mean income is $35,500 and the standard deviation is $5,000. Select one sample of 100 families and determine the sample mean. Use the NORMDIST function wizard to compute the desired probabilities.

**a.** Determine the standard error of the mean.

**b.** $P(\bar{x}_{100} > \$36,500)$

**c.** $P(\bar{x}_{100} < \$34,000)$

**d.** $P(\$35,000 < \bar{x}_{100} < \$35,750)$

**e.** $P(\bar{x}_{100} > \$35,100)$

**f.** $P(\$35,600 < \bar{x}_{100} < \$35,900)$

**g.** $P(\bar{x}_{100} < \$38,125)$

Also draw a picture of the distribution of the sample mean and use it to estimate the six desired probabilities.

**13.** The population of mileages for a radial tire is normally distributed with a mean of 52,000 miles and a standard deviation of 3000 miles. Take one sample of size 900.

**a.** Determine the standard error.

**b.** $P(\bar{x}_{900} > 52,100 \text{ miles})$

**c.** $P(\bar{x}_{900} < 50,850 \text{ miles})$

**d.** $P(51,900 < \bar{x}_{900} < 52,100)$

**e.** $P(51,950 < \bar{x}_{900} < 52,050)$

**f.** $P(\bar{x}_{900} < 52,150 \text{ miles})$

**g.** $P(\bar{x}_{900} > 51,700 \text{ miles})$

Also draw a picture of the distribution of the sample mean and use it to estimate the six desired probabilities.

**14.** Using standard methods, a trained worker can complete a task in 12.0 minutes with a standard deviation of 2.1 minutes. An industrial engineer specializing in time and method studies suggests a new way of completing the task. A sample of 49 trained workers complete the task using the new system in a mean time of 11.4 minutes.

**a.** If the new method is no better than the standard method, what is the probability of obtaining a sample mean of 11.4 minutes or less?

**b.** Based on your answer to part (a), is the new method faster than the existing method? Explain.

**15.** Use Excel's data–analysis random number generator tool to demonstrate how the Central Limit Theorem affects the distribution of the sample mean.

**a.** Use a uniform distribution to generate a population of data values with the following properties.

| | |
|---|---|
| number of variables | 10 |
| number of random numbers | 100 |
| uniform distribution between 40,000 and 50,000 |

**b.** Use the descriptive-statistics tool to determine the minimum and maximum data values in the population. This will help establish your bins or classes for your histogram.

**c.** Using the data-analysis histogram tool, develop a histogram of the population of 1000 data values. What is its shape?

**d.** Compute the 100 sample means, each based on $n = 10$ observations. The 100 sample means are an approximate distribution of the sample mean.

**e.** Use the descriptive-statistics tool to determine the minimum and maximum data values for the distribution of the sample mean. This will help establish your bins or classes for your histogram.

**f.** Using the data-analysis histogram tool, develop a histogram of the 100 sample means. What is its shape?

**g.** Examine the variation in the 100 sample means. If you increased the sample size from 10 to 25, would the variation in the sample means decrease, stay the same, or increase? Use the standard error of the mean to defend your argument.

**h.** Now verify your answer in part (g) by generating a second approximate distribution of the sample mean based on the following properties.

| number of variables | 25 |
|---|---|
| number of random numbers | 100 |
| uniform distribution between 40,000 and 50,000 | |

Compare the two distributions of the sample mean. Which distribution exhibits less variation in the sample mean?

**16.** Refer to Exercises 12 and 13. If the Central Limit Theorem did not exist, could you have solved these two exercises using the NORMDIST function wizard? Discuss.

**17.** Refer to Exercise 12. According to the 3–Sigma rule, 99.73% of all sample means should fall between what two specific numbers?

**18.** The population proportion of CEOs that use the firm's profitability to determine employees' bonuses is 0.65.

**a.** Compute the standard error of the proportion.

You take one simple random sample of 500 CEOs. Use the NORMDIST wizard to compute the following probabilities. Determine the probability that the sample proportion will be

**b.** greater than .63.

**c.** less than .68.

**d.** between .62 and .70.

**e.** greater than .695.

**f.** less than .64.

**g.** between .61 and .63.

Also draw a picture of the distribution of the sample proportion and use it to estimate the six desired probabilities.

**h.** Given the population proportion and the sample size, are you justified in using the NORMDIST function wizard to compute the desired probabilities?

**19.** An attempted hostile takeover occurs when a target firm's management resists acquisition. Maximizing share price is an effective way to resist. Then the acquiring firm may have to pay too steep a price for the acquisition.

An investment banking house knows that the proportion of firms in the industry that use the maximize share price strategy is .80.

**a.** Compute the standard error of the proportion.

Based on one sample of size of 1000 firms, determine the probability that the sample proportion who use a maximizing share price strategy will be

**b.** greater than .83.

**c.** less than .785.

**d.** between .80 and .82.

**e.** greater than .785.

**f.** less than .825.

**g.** between .788 and .812.

Also draw a picture of the distribution of the sample proportion and use it to estimate the six desired probabilities.

**h.** Given the population proportion and the sample size, are you justified in using the NORMDIST function wizard to compute the desired probabilities?

**20.** Refer to Exercise 18. Between what two specific numbers will 99.73% of all the sample proportions fall?

**21.** Refer to Exercise 18. Suppose you increase the sample size from 500 CEOs to 2000 CEOs. Now determine between what two specific numbers will 99.73% of all the sample proportions fall. Use the standard error of the proportion to explain why this happened.

**22.** Use Excel's data-analysis random number generator tool to demonstrate how the Central Limit Theorem affects the distribution of the sample proportion.

    **a.** Use a Bernoulli distribution to generate a population of data values with the following properties.

| | |
|---|---|
| number of variables | 50 |
| number of random numbers | 100 |
| Bernoulli $p = .40$ | |

    **b.** Use a column chart to display the population of 5000 data values. What is its shape?

    **c.** Compute the 100 sample proportion, each based on $n = 50$. The 100 samples are an approximate distribution of the sample proportion.

    **d.** Use the descriptive-statistics tool to determine the minimum and maximum data values for the distribution of the sample proportion. This will help establish your bins or classes for your histogram.

    **e.** Using the data-analysis histogram tool, develop a histogram of the 100 sample proportions. What is its shape?

    **f.** Examine the variation in the 100 sample proportions. If you increased the sample size from 50 to 150, would the variation in the sample proportions decrease, stay the same, or increase? Use the standard error of the proportion to defend your argument.

    **g.** Now verify your answer in part (f) by generating a second approximate distribution of the sample proportion based on the following properties.

| | |
|---|---|
| number of variables | 150 |
| number of random numbers | 100 |
| Bernoulli $p = .40$ | |

Compare the two distributions of the sample proportion. Which distribution exhibits less variation in the sample proportion?

**23.** The population variance, $\sigma^2$ equals 9. Based on one sample of size 11 (ten degrees of freedom), use the CHIDIST function wizard to determine the following probabilities.

    **a.** $P(s^2 > 10.5)$

    **b.** $P(s^2 > 4.0)$

    **c.** $P(s^2 < 8.1)$

    **d.** $P(8 < s^2 < 10)$

    **e.** $P(3 < s^2 < 14)$

**24.** Excessive variation is a major battle manufacturing industries have today in achieving high product quality. At American Eyeglass the process variance in the tensile strength of its eyeglass frames has been 22,500 squared ppsi (pounds per square inch). An hourly worker recently made a suggestion that could reduce the variance in tensile strength. After implementing the change, the firm runs a pilot study (sample size is 121) and determines that the process variance is now 15,129 squared ppsi.

    **a.** Compute the following probability. $P(s^2 < 15,129)$.

    **b.** Given your answer in part (a), does it appear that the worker's suggestion reduced the process variance? Discuss.

**25.** For a sample size of 11 and $\sigma^2 = 1$, determine the following probabilities.

**a.** $P(s^2 < 0.934)$

**b.** $P(s^2 < 1.250)$

**c.** $P(s^2 < 1.599)$

**d.** $P(s^2 < 1.830)$

**e.** $P(s^2 < 2.048)$

**f.** $P(s^2 < 2.321)$

**g.** $P(s^2 < 2.519)$

**26.** Refer to Exercise 23. Suppose you increase the sample size from 11 to 121. Compute the $P(8 < s^2 < 10)$. Compare this answer to your answer in Exercise 23. Why must the probability in Exercise 26 be larger than in Exercise 23?

**27.** Use Excel's data-analysis random number generator tool to demonstrate how the Central Limit Theorem does *not* apply to the distribution of the sample variance.

**a.** Use a normal distribution to generate a population of data values with the following properties.

| | |
|---|---|
| number of variables | 10 |
| number of random numbers | 100 |
| normal distribution, mean of 40,000 and standard deviation of 1000 | |

**b.** Compute the 100 sample variances, each based on $n = 10$. The 100 sample variances are an approximate distribution of the sample variance.

**c.** Use the descriptive-statistics tool to determine the minimum and maximum data values for the distribution of the sample variance. This will help establish your bins or classes for your histogram.

**d.** Using the data-analysis histogram tool, develop a histogram of the approximate distribution of the sample variance. What is its shape? In plain English, why is the distribution not normally distributed?

**e.** Examine the variation in the 100 sample variances. If you increased the sample size from 10 to 25, would the variation in the sample variances decrease, stay the same, or increase? Use the standard error of the variance to defend your argument.

**f.** Now verify your answer in part (e) by generating a second approximate distribution of the sample variance based on the following properties.

| | |
|---|---|
| number of variables | 25 |
| number of random numbers | 100 |
| normal distribution, mean of 40,000 and standard deviation of 1000 | |

Compare the two distributions of the sample variance. Which distribution is "tighter"; that is, exhibits less variation or has the smaller standard error of the sample variance?

**28.** A firm has recently installed a just–in–time (JIT) inventory system. The firm does not stockpile the materials needed to produce its product. Instead it relies on vendors to deliver materials needed for daily production at 6:00 AM. The firm's vendors have agreed to a delivery schedule with a standard deviation of 30 minutes or a variance of 900 squared minutes. Assume that the firm's vendors can actually meet their agreed–upon variation in delivery times. If you select one sample of $n = 10$ deliveries, compute the following probabilities.

**a.** $P(625 < s^2 < 1225)$

**b.** $P(s^2 > 900)$

**c.** $P(s^2 < 1600)$

**d.** $P(841 < s^2 < 906.01)$

**e.** $P(s^2 < 400)$

**29.** A wave soldering machine can solder the 800 connections of a printed circuit board in 140 milliseconds with a standard deviation of 4 milliseconds.

**a.** If you take one sample of 10 boards, compute the $P(15 < s^2 < 16)$.

**b.** If you take one sample of 50 boards, compute the $P(15 < s^2 < 16)$.

**c.** If you take one sample of 100 boards, compute the $P(15 < s^2 < 16)$.

**d.** Why does the probability that the variance will be between 15 and 16 squared milliseconds increase as we increase the sample size?

**30.** The weight of parcels delivered by an overnight carrier is not normally distributed. Its population mean is 4.50 pounds and the standard deviation is 2.50 pounds.

**a.** Select one parcel at random from the population. You cannot use the NORMDIST function wizard to compute the following probability, $P(x > 4.85$ pounds). Why?

**b.** Select a random sample of 50 parcels. You can use the NORMDIST function wizard to compute the following probability, $P(\bar{x}_{50} > 4.85$ pounds). Why?

**c.** Compute the probability in part (b).

**31.** Under what conditions, if any, can the standard error of the mean be less than zero? Can the standard error of the mean equal zero? If this happened, describe the variation in the distribution of the sample means.

**32.** According to industry-wide data, 45% (0.45) of all industries do "benchmarking" in which they compare their business practices to the best in the world. Select one random sample of 700 firms. Compute the following probabilities.

**a.** $P(\hat{p} > .465)$

**b.** $P(\hat{p} < .445)$

**c.** $P(.445 < \hat{p} < .453)$

**d.** $P(\hat{p} < .461)$

**e.** $P(\hat{p} > .438)$

**33.** The soldering time for a printed circuit board is not normally distributed. Its mean is 140 milliseconds and its standard deviation is 3.5 milliseconds.

**a.** Select one circuit board at random from the population. It is not possible to compute the following probability, $P(x > 145$ milliseconds). Why?

**b.** Select a random sample of 30 boards. It is possible to compute the following probability, $P(\bar{x}_{30} > 145$ milliseconds). Why?

**c.** Compute the probability in part (b).

**34.** According to census data, the population proportion of homeless people in metropolitan areas is about 0.049. A social welfare agency interviews a random sample of 3000 people in the downtown area. Compute the following probabilities.

**a.** $P(\hat{p} > .05)$

**b.** $P(\hat{p} < .01)$

**c.** $P(.025 < \hat{p} < .031)$

**d.** $P(\hat{p} < .032)$

**e.** $P(\hat{p} > .024)$

**f.** Why is the distribution of the sample proportion normally distributed? Discuss.

**35.** Under what conditions will the sample variance equal the population variance? Discuss.

**36.** The population standard deviation for soldering time for the 800 connections of a printed circuit board is 4.0 milliseconds. After making potential process improvements, the quality team conducts a study to determine if it has reduced the standard deviation in soldering times, a major goal in its process improvement program. The team selects a sample of 50 boards and determines the sample mean and standard deviation soldering time—140 milliseconds and 2.75 milliseconds. If the population standard deviation were still 4.0 milliseconds, what is the probability of obtaining a standard deviation of 2.75 milliseconds or less? Given your answer, has the quality team reduced the population standard deviation? Discuss.

**37.** Industry-wide statistics state that for a particular industry the mean average collection period (value of accounts receivable divided by average sales per day) is 35.5 days and the standard deviation is 1.5 days. If this is true, then what is the probability of randomly selecting 50 firms and finding that the mean average collection period for the 50 firms is

**a.** greater than 35.8 days?

**b.** less than 34.9 days?

**c.** between 35.4 and 35.6 days?

**d.** Why is the distribution of the sample mean normally distributed? Discuss.

**e.** Under what condition could you compute the probability that the average collection period for *one* firm will be less than 36.2 days?

**38.** According to the Strategic Resources Institute, firms that do formal strategic planning obtain higher returns on total assets (net income after taxes divided by total assets) than firms that do not do formal strategic planning. Firms that do planning have a population mean return of 11.4% and a standard deviation of 3.5%. Thirty firms are selected that either all do planning or don't do planning. Based on the sample mean return on total assets, you believe you can correctly classify them as planners or nonplanners. The sample mean is 9.55%.

**a.** What is the probability of obtaining a sample mean of 9.55% or less if the 30 firms all do planning?

**b.** Based on your answer in part (a), does it appear that the 30 firms all do strategic planning? Discuss.

**c.** What permitted you to use the NORMDIST function wizard in part (a)? Explain.

**39.** The population proportion of "travelers" (paperwork that tracks the progress of "built to order" systems) that have one or more errors in a firm is 0.055. Each day the firm selects a random sample of 500 travelers and checks them for accuracy.

**a.** Use the 3-Sigma rule to determine the range within which 99.73% of the daily sample proportions of travelers with one or more errors will fall.

**b.** Suppose the daily proportion for March 13 falls below the lower limit of the range computed in part (a)—0.055 minus 3-sigma. Should such a value be considered an outlier? That is, is assignable cause present?

c. Assuming a data value below the lower limit of the range is an outlier, is the occurrence a problem or an opportunity? Discuss.

d. Suppose the daily proportion for March 13 falls above the upper limit of the range computed in part (a)—0.055 plus 3-sigma. Should such a value be considered an outlier? That is, is assignable cause present?

e. Assuming a data value above the upper limit of the range is an outlier, is the occurrence a problem or an opportunity? Discuss.

**40.** Market segmentation is a process of identifying smaller markets that exist within a larger market. These groups are called market segments. Best Dairy, Inc., knows that the population mean income of its Status Seeker market segment is $77,000 and the population standard deviation in incomes is $5000. Best Dairy selects one random sample of 100 customers. Given the above information, compute the following probabilities.

a. $P(\bar{x}_{100} > \$77,500)$

b. $P(\bar{x}_{100} < \$78,100)$

c. $P(\$77,000 < \bar{x}_{100} < \$78,000)$

d. $P(\bar{x}_{100} < \$76,250)$

e. $P(\bar{x}_{100} > \$75,800)$

f. What permitted you to legitimately use the NORMDIST function wizard to solve the exercises?

g. Suppose Best Dairy wished to determine if one customer would have an income in excess of $78,500. Under what condition could that probability be computed using the NORMDIST function wizard?

## CASE STUDY

Allison Zhang is owner of ZRS, a relay switch company. Just yesterday she learned that the Boeing Company is seeking to purchase about 645 switches a day from a U.S. manufacturer for its new generation of commercial aircraft. The contract calls for a 100-day supply. The due date for submission is in two months. The contract states that the vendor will pay a penalty of $10,000 if the daily production is less than 645 switches. However, Zhang's anticipated net margin per switch is $10.20. Thus, she would like to submit a proposal.

For several years, ZRS has been developing a new generation of relay switches that would be superior to any product currently on the market. However, Zhang is unsure if her production team can produce the 645 switches per day needed by Boeing. Recently the firm has made some manufacturing runs and has only produced about 630 per day. Of course, ZRS could add a third shift a day to increase capacity. However, the two-month time horizon is not sufficient to hire and train additional personnel.

Recently a worker suggested a manufacturing change that should increase daily production to over 655 units per day, well above the minimum of 645 needed for the Boeing contract. Preliminary analysis revealed that the change might work and would add no extra cost to the process. However, the vice president of engineering is not sure if the suggested process will be under statistical control. That is, the process output may not be stationary over time. Nor is he convinced that the output data will be normally distributed.

Zhang suggests implementing the worker's suggestion for 30 shifts, or 15 days. If the process changes really do achieve at least 645 switches per day, ZRS can then submit a bid. If not, it still could develop alternative approaches.

Here are the data for the 15 days (two shifts per day).

| Shift | Switches | Shift | Switches | Shift | Switches |
|-------|----------|-------|----------|-------|----------|
| 1 | 660 | 11 | 657 | 21 | 659 |
| 2 | 657 | 12 | 665 | 22 | 656 |
| 3 | 657 | 13 | 658 | 23 | 656 |
| 4 | 660 | 14 | 654 | 24 | 660 |
| 5 | 658 | 15 | 664 | 25 | 657 |
| 6 | 655 | 16 | 656 | 26 | 658 |
| 7 | 663 | 17 | 657 | 27 | 656 |
| 8 | 654 | 18 | 663 | 28 | 660 |
| 9 | 656 | 19 | 654 | 29 | 660 |
| 10 | 653 | 20 | 654 | 30 | 653 |

Prepare a one-page report that addresses the following issues.

1. Were the vice president's concerns over the process stability and normality justified?

2. Should ZRS submit a proposal?

3. If it obtains the contract what is its anticipated total profit?

4. How likely is it that ZRS will have to pay the $10,000 daily penalty?

Use the data to support your position.

# CHAPTER 4
# APPENDICES

## I. LISTING OF EXCEL TOOLS FOR CHAPTER

**1.** Random Number Generator Data–Analysis Tool

**2.** Sampling Data-Analysis Tool

**3.** NORMDIST function wizard

**4.** CHIDIST function wizard

## II. DIALOG BOX FOR GENERATING TARGET POPULATION OF 300 CUSTOMERS' INCOMES

This dialog box generates 30 rows of 10 observations each. See Table 4.1. The smallest possible value is $44,000, and the highest possible value is $57,500. The distribution requested is a uniform distribution. After obtaining the 300 values, we used the TRUNC wizard to obtain integer values.

# III. DIALOG BOX FOR GENERATING REPEATED SAMPLES OF SIZE FIVE FROM A TARGET POPULATION: DEVELOPING AN APPROXIMATE DISTRIBUTION OF THE SAMPLE MEANS

The population database is in cells A1 to J30. The above dialog box is used to select a simple random sample of size five from the database. The five random observations are placed in cells A50 to A54.

To obtain a second sample of size five, change the output range to B50 and execute. The second five observations are placed in cells B50 to B54.

Continue the sampling, each time changing the output range.

# STATISTICAL INFERENCE I: CONFIDENCE INTERVALS

## THE STATISTICAL INFERENCE PROCESS

In Chapter 2, you learned how to organize, summarize, and interpret one specific sample of univariate data. For example,

**1.** What was the mean (and standard deviation) downtime hours for the 36 machines in quarter 1?

**2.** What proportion of the 50 financial institutions had an excellent quality rating?

The managers were only interested in the specific sample (the 36 machines or the 50 financial institutions) selected. They computed the sample mean, proportion, or standard deviation that are descriptive statistics. They were *not* interested in using the descriptive statistics from the specific sample to draw conclusions about a target population's parameters.

By contrast, in Chapter 5 we are not interested in the specific sample. Rather, we select a *representative* sample, compute the descriptive statistics, and then use them to estimate a target population's parameters: its mean ($\mu$), variance ($\sigma^2$), or proportion ($p$).

**DEFINITION**    Statistical inference is a process of drawing valid conclusions about a population's parameter based on one representative sample from the target population.

An effective estimate of a population parameter should include(1) an interval and (2) a measure of assurance that the parameter value lies within the interval. For example, based on one relatively small sample, the Bureau of Labor Statistics estimates the number of unemployed to be $5.2 \pm .3$ million, feeling rather sure that the actual number is between 4.9 and 5.5 million. Table 5.1 contrasts Chapters 2 and 5.

| Bases for Comparison | Chapter 2 | Chapter 5 |
|---|---|---|
| Number of Samples | One sample from a population. | One sample from a population. |
| How Sample Selected | Select a *specific* sample. | Select a *random*, or representative, sample. |
| First Step in Analysis | Compute *descriptive statistics* for the sample. | Compute *descriptive statistics* for the sample. |
| Second Step in Analysis | There is no second step. We are only interested in the one sample. | Draw conclusions about a population's parameters from the one sample. |
| Degree of Assurance about Conclusions | 100% regarding the specific sample's descriptive statistics. | Less than 100% confident about the population's parameters. |

**Table 5.1**
Compare and Contrast
of Chapters 2 and 5

In Chapter 5 the statistical inference method you will learn is called **confidence intervals.** In Chapter 6 the statistical inference method you will learn is called **hypothesis testing**.

**DEFINITION**    A confidence interval provides a range estimate and an associated level of confidence that a population parameter lies within that range.

# MANAGEMENT SCENARIOS AND DATA SETS

The four scenarios in Table 5.2 illustrate how managers use **univariate** (one column of data) cross-sectional data to draw conclusions about unknown population parameters—$\mu$, $\sigma^2$, and $p$.

Table 5.3 displays the length-of-tenure discount data for 20 randomly selected renters in Dallas. Length-of-tenure discount is the percent reduction in rent for those renters who have lived at an apartment complex for five or more years. A Dallas-based apartment rental firm wants to know if its discounts are in line with published data on other apartment rental firms within the city.

| Data Type | Database (Random Sample) | Typical Questions |
|---|---|---|
| Cross-Sectional for a Ratio-Scale Variable | 50 family incomes from a census tract. | At most, what is the population *mean* family income in the census tract? We desire a 95% confidence level. |
| Cross-Sectional for a Ratio-Scale Variable | Length-of-tenure discounts for 20 renters in Dallas. | At the 99% assurance, or confidence, level, what is the population *mean* length-of-tenure discount for an apartment rental firm in Dallas? |
| Cross-Sectional for a Qualitative (Yes/No) Variable | 900 potential customers from a target population. | At a minimum, what is the population *proportion* of potential customers that would purchase our dental plaque-removal system for $89? We desire a 99.5% confidence level. |
| Cross-Sectional for a Ratio-Scale Variable | Weight of the galvanized coatings of 20 pipes from a production line. | At the 95% confidence level, what is the population *standard deviation* in weight of the galvanized coatings of all pipes manufactured in that shift? |

**Table 5.2**
Scenarios and Databases for Chapter 5

Using the AVERAGE and STDEV function wizards, the sample mean discount and sample standard deviation were 8.85% and 1.30%, respectively.

**Table 5.3**
Length-of-Tenure Discount Survey Data

| | | | | |
|---|---|---|---|---|
| 5.96 | 8.03 | 11.48 | 9.49 | 9.58 |
| 8.84 | 7.29 | 10.68 | 8.51 | 8.15 |
| 8.84 | 9.47 | 7.75 | 7.68 | 9.11 |
| 10.95 | 8.37 | 8.38 | 9.91 | 8.60 |

Table 5.4 displays the incomes of 50 randomly selected families within a census tract. Based upon the sample, the federal government will determine if the *entire* census tract is eligible for aid. Eligibility requires that the mean family income for the entire tract must not exceed $12,000.

Using the AVERAGE and STDEV function wizards, the sample mean income and sample standard deviation were $11,480.10 and $571.76, respectively.

In the third case study, a firm wants to estimate the proportion of potential customers who would purchase its plaque-removal system for $89. It conducts a market research study and interviews 900 randomly selected potential customers.

The data are qualitative, Yes/No, data. The data are coded 1 if customers say YES they would purchase the system and 0 if customers say NO they would not purchase the system. Of the 900 potential customers interviewed, 212 indicate they would purchase the system. The sample proportion, $\hat{p}$, is 212/900, or 0.2356.

| | | | | |
|---|---|---|---|---|
| $10,744 | $11,680 | $12,368 | $11,105 | $10,927 |
| $11,204 | $11,609 | $11,678 | $10,137 | $12,066 |
| $11,848 | $11,710 | $11,594 | $11,685 | $10,980 |
| $11,293 | $11,060 | $10,827 | $12,008 | $11,937 |
| $11,294 | $10,942 | $11,211 | $11,514 | $11,475 |
| $10,793 | $11,471 | $12,252 | $11,502 | $12,396 |
| $11,274 | $11,995 | $12,111 | $12,043 | $11,324 |
| $11,773 | $9,862 | $12,683 | $12,226 | $11,692 |
| $11,968 | $11,333 | $10,922 | $12,145 | $11,416 |
| $11,611 | $11,185 | $11,621 | $10,818 | $10,693 |

**Table 5.4**
Family Income
Survey Data

Table 5.5 displays the weights of galvanized coatings of 20 randomly selected pipes produced in one shift. The specification requires that each pipe have 200 pounds of coating. The firm wants to estimate the consistency of the coating weights.

Using the AVERAGE and STDEV function wizards, the sample mean coating weight and sample standard deviation were 200.76 and 4.59 pounds per pipe, respectively.

**Table 5.5**
Weight of Galvanized
Coatings of 20
Randomly Selected
Pipes

| | | | | |
|---|---|---|---|---|
| 202.25 | 193.87 | 199.66 | 199.82 | 197.01 |
| 195.52 | 200.59 | 203.58 | 201.77 | 208.80 |
| 199.27 | 197.97 | 210.59 | 204.55 | 204.23 |
| 192.77 | 201.75 | 201.26 | 204.05 | 195.82 |

The four scenarios illustrate the statistical inference process. Since the firms cannot obtain all the data from their respective target populations, they must use descriptive statistics and the method of confidence intervals to estimate the unknown population parameters.

# GENERAL PRINCIPLES OF CONFIDENCE INTERVALS

Glance at Figure 5.3 on page 190 that contains the expressions for constructing confidence intervals. You might conclude that the expressions for generating the confidence intervals on $\mu$, $\sigma^2$, and $p$ are totally different. This section demonstrates that these expressions reflect five general principles. Although we use a confidence interval on an unknown population mean to introduce these principles, they apply to all three population parameters. By the end of this section you should be able to

1. explain what a confidence interval is and how it is derived from a distribution of a sample statistic;

2. interpret a confidence interval and especially the meaning of the confidence level;

3. explain the relationship between confidence level and the width of the confidence interval;

4. explain the impact of increasing the sample size on the width of the confidence interval;

5. explain why you cannot construct confidence intervals on non stationary time-ordered data; and

6. explain when to construct *one-sided* versus *two-sided* intervals.

## CONFIDENCE INTERVALS AND THE PROPERTIES OF THE SAMPLING DISTRIBUTION

Consider the following situation. A tire manufacturer will shortly announce a new tire. The company must know the mean tire life so that it can set the limits for its tread wear warranty. If the company sets the warranty too low, it may lose its competitive advantage. If it is too high, the company will have to replace too many tires.

The only way you could know the mean tire life, $\mu$, with absolute certainty is to test each and every tire. Clearly this is not a practical approach. It takes too long, is too costly, and there would be no tires left to sell.

A practical alternative is to estimate the population parameter, $\mu_{\text{tire life}}$. The boss asks how we will arrive at an estimate, and we respond that we will take one simple random sample of size 900 from the population of tires in the warehouse. In a simple random sample, each possible collection of 900 tires has an equal chance of being selected. The boss nods in agreement.

We test the sample of 900 tires in a laboratory until the tread thickness is below federal standards. Here are the sample statistics:

$$\bar{x} = 47,500 \text{ miles}$$
$$s = 3000 \text{ miles}$$

The unknown population mean, $\mu_{\text{tire life}}$, is not 47,500 miles. Nor is the unknown population standard deviation, $\sigma$, 3000 miles. That is, if we took another simple random sample of 900 tires, we would not get a sample mean of 47,500 miles or a sample standard deviation of 3000 miles again.

We tell the boss to imagine that instead of taking one sample of 900, we took all possible samples of 900 from the population and tested the tires. When the boss complains that this is impractical, we respond that we aren't really going to do this; just imagine it.

We then explain that from the Central Limit Theorem, the distribution of the sample mean based on 900 observations will be normally distributed and its mean is the same as the unknown population mean. The boss is not impressed. She says that if she does not know the population mean, then she does not know the mean of the sampling distribution either. We tell her that the important point is that in estimating the mean of the distribution of the sample mean, we are also estimating the unknown population parameter, $\mu_{\text{tire life}}$. She nods her head in agreement.

Next we tell the boss that the standard error of the mean is much smaller than the population standard deviation. But since we do not know $\sigma$, we do not know the standard error of the mean either. However, we can estimate it by using the *estimated* standard error, $\hat{\sigma}_{\bar{x}} = \dfrac{s}{\sqrt{n}}$. The estimated standard error is

$$\frac{s}{\sqrt{n}} = \frac{3000}{\sqrt{900}} = 100 \text{ miles}$$

Figure 5.1 shows a distribution for the sample mean based on a sample of 900 *if we had taken repeated samples*. From the 2-Sigma rule, 95.44% of the sample means will lie within two estimated standard errors, or 200 miles, of the unknown population mean.

The boss says that is a lovely picture, but she still does not know the population mean, so what good is it? We present the following facts:

1. 95.44% of all sample means will be within two estimated standard errors [2(100) = 200 miles] of the unknown population mean, $\mu_{\text{tire life}}$ .

2. The probability is 0.9544 that *any* sample mean will be within 200 miles of the unknown population mean.

3. We are 95.44% confident that *our* sample mean of 47,500 miles will be within 200 miles of the unknown population mean.

4. We are 95.44% confident that the interval 47,500 ± 200 miles contains the unknown population mean.

The interval 47,500 ± 200, or 47,300 to 47,700 miles, is a 95.44% confidence interval. We are 95.44% certain that the unknown population mean lies somewhere within this interval. There is only a 4.56% chance that we are wrong. The interval's width is 400 miles.

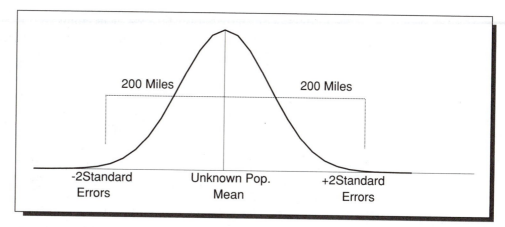

**Figure 5.1**
Distribution of the Sample Mean for $n = 900$

Another way to interpret confidence level is through odds. The confidence level tells us the odds that the unknown and unknowable population parameter lies somewhere within the confidence interval. Use Expression (5.1) to compute the odds.

$$\text{Odds} = \frac{\text{Confidence Level}}{1 - \text{Confidence Level}}$$

**(5.1)**

So a 95.44% confidence level translates into .9544/.0456 or 21 to 1 odds that the unknown population mean tire life, $\mu_{\text{tire life}}$, lies somewhere within the confidence interval—47,300 to 47,700 miles.

In summary, we constructed our confidence interval using two important principles first learned in Chapter 4. First, we do not have to take repeated samples of size $n$ to compute the estimated standard error. All we need to know is the sample standard deviation and the sample size, $\frac{s}{\sqrt{n}}$.

Second, because the distribution of the sample mean is normal for samples greater than 30 (Central Limit Theorem), we can construct confidence intervals using probabilities from the normal distribution.

## CONFIDENCE LEVEL AND THE WIDTH OF THE CONFIDENCE INTERVAL

What happens to the interval's width as we increase the confidence level? For the tire life study, a 95.44% confidence level generated an interval width of ± 200 or 400 miles. What would the interval's width be for a 99.73% confidence level? Please think about it before reading on.

From the normal distribution, 99.73% of all sample means will be within three estimated standard errors of the unknown population mean. Thus a 99.73% confidence interval would be

$$47,500 \pm 3 \cdot \frac{3000}{\sqrt{900}}$$

$$47,500 \pm 300 \text{ miles}$$

Notice that the confidence interval's width increased from 400 to 600 miles as the confidence level increased from 95.44% to 99.73%. This leads to our first general principle:

**Lesson 1:**    *Increasing the confidence level increases the width of the confidence interval.*

Is it better to be 99.73% confident than 95.44% confident? Is it better to be 95.44% confident than 80% confident that an interval will contain the unknown population mean?

Lesson 1 tells us that increasing the confidence level increases the interval's width. Wider confidence intervals provide less meaningful information. For example, how meaningful is it to be 99.99% confident that a population mean tire life is 47,500 ± 15,000 miles? The good news is that we are highly confident. The bad news is that the interval's width of 30,000 miles is so wide that it is practically useless.

We have two choices in constructing a confidence interval. *Keeping the sample size constant*, we can construct either a narrow interval with a relatively low level of confidence or a wide interval with a relatively high level of confidence. Many firms use 90% or 95% confidence levels. However, there is no magic number to use. Each manager must decide upon the trade-off between confidence level and interval width.

## IMPACT OF SAMPLE SIZE ON WIDTH OF CONFIDENCE INTERVAL

Can we have narrow confidence intervals with high levels of confidence? Yes, by increasing the study's sample size. For the tire study, let's determine the impact of increasing the sample size from 900 to 3600 tires. Assume that the sample standard deviation for the one sample of 3600 tires is still 3000 miles and the sample mean is still 47,500 miles. Increasing the sample size to 3600 tires reduces the estimated standard error of the mean to $\frac{3,000}{\sqrt{3600}} = 50 \text{ miles}$ .

That is, quadrupling the sample size reduced the estimated standard error by one-half. A 95.44% confidence interval would now be

$$47,500 \pm 2 \cdot 50$$

$$47,400 \text{ to } 47,600 \text{ miles}$$

This leads to our second lesson:

**Lesson 2:**    *Increasing the sample size reduces the width of the confidence interval.*

Lesson 2, in turn, suggests another important principle:

**Lesson 3:**    *As you consider increasing the desired confidence level, consider increasing the sample size to maintain a meaningful (and relatively narrow) interval width.*

Increasing the sample size does have its downside. First, it increases the cost of the study. Second, the impact of increasing the sample size is painfully slow. To reduce the interval's width by one-half, you have to increase the sample size fourfold. This is due to the square root term in the denominator of the estimated standard error of the mean. Nevertheless, avoid wide confidence intervals, as they do not provide meaningful information.

Table 5.6 displays the relationship between sample size, confidence level, and interval width. The sample mean is 47,500 miles and a sample standard deviation is 3000 miles for all table entries.

**Table 5.6**
The Impact of Sample Size and Confidence Level on Interval Width

|          | $n = 900$          | $n = 3600$        |
|----------|--------------------|-------------------|
| 68.26%   | $47,500 \pm 1 \cdot 100$ | $47,500 \pm 1 \cdot 50$ |
| 95.44%   | $47,500 \pm 2 \cdot 100$ | $47,500 \pm 2 \cdot 50$ |
| 99.73%   | $47,500 \pm 3 \cdot 100$ | $47,500 \pm 3 \cdot 50$ |

## CONFIDENCE INTERVALS AND NONSTATIONARY DATA

In Chapter 2 you learned that the sample mean and sample standard deviation summarize cross-sectional and stationary time-ordered data. A line graph for stationary time-ordered data will show no upward or downward pattern over time. It will show no exploding or dampening pattern. It will show no pattern at all! Sample values fluctuate around a *constant mean with a constant variance*. Because the population mean and variance are constant, you can construct confidence intervals to estimate both parameters. Nonstationary data do not have a constant mean or constant variance. There is no constant population mean or variance to estimate. This leads to Lesson 4.

**Lesson 4:**     *Construct confidence intervals only for cross-sectional data or stationary time-ordered data.*

## ONE-SIDED VERSUS TWO-SIDED CONFIDENCE INTERVALS

Up to now, all confidence intervals have been two sided; they extended an equal amount on each side of the sample mean (i.e., 47,500 ± 200 miles). Two-sided intervals have a lower and an upper limit. Sometimes you want to make statements such as: "I am 95% confident that the mean amount of personal time taken per week is *at most* 1.5 hours" or "I am 90% confident that the mean work group productivity is *at least* 30 units per hour." These are examples of one-sided confidence intervals; they do not extend an equal amount on each side of the sample mean. They do not have a lower and upper limit.

There are two types of one-sided intervals. *At most* intervals only have an upper limit. *At least* intervals only have a lower limit.

When should you use one-sided versus two-sided intervals? When the situation dictates the need to estimate *between* what two values a population parameter is likely to lie, use a two-sided interval. When the situation dictates the need to estimate either the highest or lowest possible value for a population parameter, use a one-sided interval. If the situation doesn't clearly dictate, construct a two-sided interval.

These ideas lead to the fifth and final lesson of this section:

**Lesson 5:**     *Construct one-sided intervals when you want to make either* at least *or* at most *statements about population parameters. Construct two-sided intervals when you want to determine* between *which two values a population parameter will lie.*

The five lessons apply to confidence intervals on a population mean, proportion, or variance. Perhaps the most important practical lesson is to construct relatively narrow confidence intervals with relatively high levels of confidence. Otherwise your confidence intervals will not be meaningful or useful.

# CONFIDENCE INTERVALS ON AN UNKNOWN POPULATION MEAN

In this section you will learn how to construct confidence intervals on an unknown population mean, $\mu$, based on a relatively large sample ($n \geq 30$) or on a relatively small sample ($n < 30$). You will use the normal distribution first learned in Chapter 4 for constructing confidence intervals for a sample size of 30 or greater. You will learn a new distribution—the $t$ distribution, or TINV function wizard—for constructing confidence intervals for a sample size less than 30. By the end of this section you should be able to

1. construct and interpret *large-sample* confidence intervals using the NORMSINV function wizard;

2. construct and interpret *small-sample* confidence intervals using the TINV function wizard; and

3. explain when you should transform the data using a logarithmic or square root transformation.

## LARGE-SAMPLE INTERVAL ON THE POPULATION MEAN $\mu$

For sample sizes greater than 30, the distribution of the sample mean is approximately normal from the Central Limit Theorem. That allows us to use the normal curve for constructing confidence intervals as we did in the previous section.

Use Expression (5.2) for constructing two-sided intervals on an unknown population mean, $\mu$, when the sample size is 30 or greater.

$$
\begin{array}{l}
\bar{x} \pm \text{ Margin of Error} \\[4pt]
\bar{x} \pm \text{ Reliability factor} \cdot \text{ Estimated standard error} \\[4pt]
\bar{x} \pm \text{NORMSINV}_{\,CL + \frac{1 - CL}{2}} \cdot \frac{s}{\sqrt{n}}
\end{array}
$$

(5.2)

where CL is the desired confidence level expressed as a number between 0 and 1, "$n$" is the sample size, and "$s$" is the standard deviation of the one sample of size $n$.

Use Expression (5.3) for constructing one-sided intervals on the unknown population mean, $\mu$, when the sample size is 30 or greater.

| | |
|---|---|
| At Most Intervals | $\bar{x} + \text{NORMSINV}_{CL} \cdot \dfrac{s}{\sqrt{n}}$ |
| At Least Intervals | $\bar{x} - \text{NORMSINV}_{CL} \cdot \dfrac{s}{\sqrt{n}}$ |

(5.3)

## CASE STUDY

**Census Tract Study.** Is a census tract containing 20,000 families eligible for aid under a specific federal program? Program eligibility requires that the population mean income be *at most* $12,000. Only during a census year would the population mean income be known with certainty. In other years, the program administrator must determine eligibility by estimating the unknown population mean using confidence intervals.

The administrator will select a simple random sample of 50 families, a relatively large sample. He desires a 98% confidence level. From Table 5.4, the sample mean income for the 50 families is $11,480.10 and the sample standard deviation is $571.76. Note: The program's eligibility requirement dictates a one-sided "at most" confidence interval.

Substituting into Expression (5.3),

$$\bar{x} + \text{NORMSINV}_{CL} \cdot \frac{s}{\sqrt{n}}$$

$$11480.10 + \text{NORMSINV}_{.98} \cdot \frac{571.76}{\sqrt{50}}$$

You must now use the NORMSINV wizard to compute the confidence interval. There is only one input necessary: probability = CL = .98. The NORMSINV wizard generates a value of 2.05.

$$11480.10 + 2.05 \cdot \frac{571.76}{\sqrt{50}}$$

Upper Limit: $11,645.86

NORMSINV
Probability  .98                            = 0.98
= 2.053748176
Returns the inverse of the standard normal cumulative distribution (has a mean of zero and a standard deviation of one).
**Probability** is a probability corresponding to the normal distribution, a number between 0 and 1 inclusive.
Formula result = 2.053748176        OK      Cancel

*Interpretation:* The program administrator is 98% confident that the unknown population mean income in the census tract is *at most* $11,645.86. Since the maximum population mean family income for eligibility is $12,000, the census tract is eligible for federal aid under the program.

Suppose the computed at most upper limit had been $12,100. Would the census tract be eligible under this program? No, because the population mean could be over $12,000. In order to be eligible, the upper limit of the confidence interval must be less than $12,000.

---

**EXAMPLE**

**1**   A tire firm wishes to construct a two-sided 90% confidence interval on the population mean tire life on its new Milemaster tire. The firm takes a simple random sample of 900 tires and tests them until tread thickness is below federal standards. Here are the descriptive statistics for the sample of 900:

$$\bar{x} = 47,500 \text{ miles}$$
$$s = 3000 \text{ miles}$$

Substitute the data into Expression (5.2).

$$47,500 \pm \text{NORMSINV}_{.90 + \frac{1 - .90}{2}} \cdot \frac{3000}{\sqrt{900}}$$

$$47,500 \pm 1.645 \cdot 100$$

$$47,500 \pm 164.50 \text{ miles}$$

*Interpretation:* The firm is 90% confident (9:1 odds) that the *population* mean tire life of all Milemaster tires will be somewhere between $47,500 - 164.50$ miles and $47,500 + 164.50$ miles. There is a 0.10 probability that the population mean does not lie within the above interval.

Before leaving large sample intervals, Table 5.7 provides the reliability factors for the most-common one-sided and two-sided intervals.

**Table 5.7**
Table of NORMSINV
Reliability Factors

|                     | 90%   | 95%   | 99%   |
|---------------------|-------|-------|-------|
| One-Sided Intervals | 1.282 | 1.645 | 2.326 |
| Two-Sided Intervals | 1.645 | 1.960 | 2.576 |

When the sample size is less than 30, we have two problems in constructing confidence intervals.

**Problem 1**     The distribution of the sample mean may not be normal, because the Central Limit Theorem may not apply to sample sizes smaller than 30.

**Problem 2**     We cannot assume that the sample standard deviation, $s$, is a good approximation of the population standard deviation, $\sigma$. Thus, we cannot use the normal curve, or NORMSINV, to determine the reliability factor in computing confidence intervals.

**Solution to Problem 1**     We mentioned in Chapter 4 that the distribution of the sample mean will be approximately normal for samples as small as four or five if the target population itself is near normal. To determine this, compute the skewness and kurtosis of the sample data. If the sample data are near normal, the population from which you selected the sample will also be normal. And the distribution of the sample mean will be approximately normal even for sample sizes as small as four or five.

**Solution to Problem 2**     You must use a new distribution for the reliability factor in Expressions (5.2) or (5.3). It is the $t$-distribution—the TINV function wizard in Excel.

## SMALL-SAMPLE INTERVAL ON THE POPULATION MEAN, $\mu$

When your sample size is less than 30, first apply the SKEW and KURT function wizards presented in Chapter 2 to determine if the sample data are reasonably bell shaped. If so, then the population from which you took the sample is also reasonably bell shaped. Under this condition you can construct a confidence interval using the two expressions below. If the sample data are not reasonably bell shaped, you ought not to construct confidence intervals immediately; you should first consider transforming the data. More on that later.

Use Expression (5.4) to construct a two-sided confidence interval on an unknown population mean when the sample size is less than 30.

$$
\begin{array}{l}
\bar{x} \pm \text{Margin of Error} \\[4pt]
\bar{x} \pm \text{Reliability factor} \cdot \text{ Estimated standard error} \\[4pt]
\bar{x} \pm \text{TINV}_{1\,-\,\text{CL},\,n\,-\,1} \cdot \dfrac{s}{\sqrt{n}}
\end{array}
$$

**(5.4)**

where CL is the desired confidence level expressed as a number between 0 and 1, $n - 1$ is the degrees of freedom, and $s$ is the standard deviation of the one sample.

Note that the TINV wizard has two required inputs: (1) probability which equals $1 - CL$ and (2) degrees of freedom which is $n - 1$.

Use Expression (5.5) for constructing one-sided intervals on the unknown population mean, $\mu$, when the sample size is less than 30.

$$
\begin{array}{ll}
\text{At Most Intervals} & \bar{x} + \text{TINV}_{2(1-CL),\,n-1} \cdot \dfrac{s}{\sqrt{n}} \\[2em]
\text{At Least Intervals} & \bar{x} - \text{TINV}_{2(1-CL),\,n-1} \cdot \dfrac{s}{\sqrt{n}}
\end{array}
$$

$$(5.5)$$

## CASE STUDY

**Length-of-Tenure Discount Study.** In the length-of-tenure study, the Daltex apartment rental firm wanted to know if its discounts are in line with other apartment rental firms within the city, about 7.7%. The rental firm desires a two-sided 95% confidence interval on the population mean discount. It selects a simple random sample of $n = 20$ of its apartment dwellers. See Table 5.3 for the data. The sample mean and sample standard deviation are 8.85% and 1.30%, respectively.

Since the sample size is less than 30, let's determine the shape of the population of tenure discounts. Apply the SKEW and KURT function wizards to the 20 data values.

| | |
|---|---|
| Skewness: | 0.087 |
| Kurtosis: | 0.452 |

From Chapter 2 the sample data are reasonably bell shaped. Thus, we will construct a confidence interval.

▶ **WARNING** If

$$\text{SKEW} < -1 \text{ or SKEW} > 1 \textbf{ AND}$$
$$\text{KURT} < -1 \text{ or KURT} > 1,$$

do not construct a confidence interval as the population distribution is so "unbell shaped" that the Central Limit Theorem cannot guarantee the normality of the distribution of the sample mean. Shortly we present how to transform the data to normalize it.

Substituting into Expression (5.4) and using the TINV function wizard:

$$\bar{x} \pm \text{TINV}_{1-.95, 19} \cdot \frac{s}{\sqrt{n}}$$

$$8.85 \pm 2.093 \cdot \frac{1.30}{\sqrt{20}}$$

Lower limit: 8.24%

Upper limit: 9.46%

*Interpretation*: Daltex is 95% confident that its unknown population mean tenure discount is between 8.24% and 9.46%. This interval does not include the 7.7% mean discount of the other apartment rental firms in Dallas. Daltex's tenure discount is *not* in line with its competitors. It will now have to decide if it wishes to maintain a discount rate higher than its competitors.

Daltex's confidence interval is rather wide, $8.85 \pm 0.61$. How might it have narrowed the 0.61? Think about it before reading on.

From Lesson 2, Daltex could have selected a larger sample. Increasing the sample size from 20 to 80 renters (fourfold) would have reduced the width of the confidence interval by one-half. Also, had the sample size been 80, Daltex would have used Expression (5.2) to construct the interval, not Expression (5.4).

Before leaving small-sample intervals, Table 5.8 provides the reliability factors for several one-sided and two-sided intervals.

**Table 5.8**
Table of TINV
Reliability Factors

| one-Sided | 95.00% | 97.50% | 99.50% |
|---|---|---|---|
| two-Sided | 90.00% | 95.00% | 99.00% |
| **n − 1** | | | |
| 5 | 2.015049 | 2.570578 | 4.032117 |
| 10 | 1.812462 | 2.228139 | 3.169262 |
| 15 | 1.753051 | 2.131451 | 2.946726 |
| 20 | 1.724718 | 2.085962 | 2.845336 |
| 25 | 1.708140 | 2.059537 | 2.787438 |

## COMPARISON OF **NORMSINV** AND **TINV** WIZARDS

Examine the NORMSINV and TINV values in Tables 5.7 and 5.8. For example, compare the magnitudes of the two reliability factors for a two-sided 95% confidence level. How do they compare?

You will notice that the corresponding TINV wizard values are always greater than the NORMSINV wizard value of 1.960. Why is this important? Expression (5.2) shows that as the reliability factor increases, the width of the confidence interval also increases. And wide confidence intervals are less meaningful.

Why are the TINV wizard values greater than their corresponding NORMSINV wizard value? The answer is simple. There is more uncertainty when using samples of size less than 30. The price you pay is a wider, and thus less meaningful, confidence interval. Let me demonstrate the increased uncertainty.

Large Samples    You don't know the population mean, uncertainty #1. But because the sample size is large, the standard deviation of the sample, $s$, is likely to be close to the population standard deviation, $\sigma$. Think of this situation as having only one uncertainty.

Small Samples    You don't know the population mean, uncertainty #1. But because the sample size is small, the standard deviation of the sample, $s$, is *not* likely to be close to the population standard deviation, $\sigma$. That's uncertainty #2.

The greater the uncertainty, the wider is your confidence interval.

In summary, you now have two reasons for selecting large sample sizes. First, as the sample size increases, the estimated standard error of the mean, $\frac{s}{\sqrt{n}}$ decreases. From Expression (5.2) that reduces the confidence interval's width. Second, large sample sizes permit you to use the NORMSINV wizard to determine the reliability factor, which also reduces the confidence interval's width.

## DATA TRANSFORMATIONS

What can you do when the sample data are not reasonably bell shaped and the sample is under 30? One obvious choice is to increase the sample size. If that is not economically possible, consider *transforming* the sample data. Transforming the data simply means changing the measurement scale. To make the sample data more bell shaped, use either the square root or logarithmic transformations. Both transformations work provided the data consists of only positive numbers.[1] We illustrate the transformation approach below.

Transforming the data simply means changing the measurement scale. The square root and logarithmic transformations tend to make the data more bell shaped. Table 5.9 displays the square root and log transformations to rescale the nonnormal data in column 1.

| Original | Square Root | Log$_{10}$ |
|---|---|---|
| 12 | 3.464102 | 1.079181 |
| 14 | 3.741657 | 1.146128 |
| 17 | 4.123106 | 1.230449 |
| 19 | 4.358899 | 1.278754 |
| 19 | 4.358899 | 1.278754 |
| 23 | 4.795832 | 1.361728 |
| 26 | 5.099020 | 1.414973 |
| 32 | 5.656854 | 1.505150 |
| 41 | 6.403124 | 1.612784 |
| 75 | 8.660254 | 1.875061 |
| 2.075777 | 1.56054646 | 0.974110 |
| 4.736621 | 2.69337129 | 0.922938 |

**Table 5.9**
Transformation by Square Root and Logarithm

The original data were not bell shaped (SKEW = 2.08, KURT = 4.74). The log data are near bell shaped, and the distribution of their sample mean will be reasonably normal. Consult a professional statistician to help you develop a confidence interval for the transformed data.

# CONFIDENCE INTERVALS ON AN UNKNOWN POPULATION PROPORTION

We have been dealing with quantitative (ratio-scale) data up to this point. This section focuses on yes or no qualitative data—data often (but not solely) used to code responses to survey questionnaires. Typical yes or no questions include

1. Would you purchase this dental plaque-removal system for $89?

2. Did a surgical patient have postoperative complications?

3. Did a "traveler" (paperwork that tracks the progress of built to order systems) have one or more errors?

---

[1] Positive data values are necessary because the log or square root of a negative number is undefined.

In Chapter 2, you learned to organize and summarize yes or no data. In Chapter 4 you learned the distribution of the sample proportion. Now let's use its properties to construct one- or two-sided confidence intervals on an unknown population proportion, a number between 0 and 1. By the end of this section you should be able to

1. distinguish between a sample mean and a sample proportion; and

2. construct and interpret confidence intervals on an unknown population proportion.

## DISTRIBUTION OF THE SAMPLE PROPORTION

Recall from Chapter 4 the sample proportion, $\hat{p}$, is the number of *yes* responses divided by the sample size. Use Expression (5.6) to compute the sample proportion.

$$\hat{p} = \frac{n_{Yes}}{n}$$

(5.6)

where $n_{yes}$ is the number of yes responses and $n$ is the total sample size.

From Chapter 4, use Expression (5.7) to compute the estimated standard error of the sample proportion. Recall that $\hat{q}$ is the sample proportion of the *no* responses.

$$\hat{\sigma}_{\hat{p}} = \sqrt{\frac{\hat{p} \cdot \hat{q}}{n}}$$

(5.7)

The distribution of the sample proportion will be normal provided the sample size is sufficiently large. Table 4.8 provided Cochran's sample size guidelines to ensure the normality of the distribution of the sample proportion.

With this brief review, let's construct confidence intervals on an unknown population proportion.

## EXPRESSIONS FOR CONSTRUCTING CONFIDENCE INTERVALS

Use the following expressions to construct confidence intervals on an unknown population proportion, $p$.

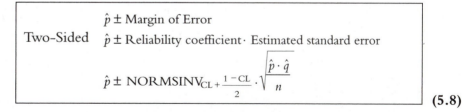

Two-Sided

$\hat{p} \pm$ Margin of Error

$\hat{p} \pm$ Reliability coefficient $\cdot$ Estimated standard error

$\hat{p} \pm \text{NORMSINV}_{CL + \frac{1 - CL}{2}} \cdot \sqrt{\frac{\hat{p} \cdot \hat{q}}{n}}$

(5.8)

| | |
|---|---|
| One-Sided: At least | $\hat{p}$ − Reliability coefficient · Estimated standard error <br><br> $\hat{p} - \text{NORMSINV}_{CL} \sqrt{\dfrac{\hat{p} \cdot \hat{q}}{n}}$ |
| One-Sided: At most | $\hat{p}$ + Reliability coefficient · Estimated standard error <br><br> $\hat{p} + \text{NORMSINV}_{CL} \sqrt{\dfrac{\hat{p} \cdot \hat{q}}{n}}$ |

**(5.9)**

## CASE STUDY

**Dental Plaque System Survey.** A firm wants to estimate the proportion of potential customers who will purchase its plaque-removal system for $89. The firm will only market the product if *at least* 20% (.20) of the potential customers indicate that they will purchase the product. The firm desires a 95% confidence interval.

The data are yes or no data. The data are coded 1 if the customer would purchase the system and 0 if the customer would not purchase the system. Of the 900 potential customers interviewed, 212 indicate they would purchase the system. The *sample* proportion is 212/900, or .2356.

$$\hat{p} = \frac{212}{900} = 0.2356$$

$$\hat{\sigma}_{\hat{p}} = \sqrt{\frac{.2356 \cdot \left(1 - .2356\right)}{900}} = .0141$$

Given a sample proportion of .2356, a sample of 900 is more than four times the minimum sample size necessary to ensure normality of the distribution of the sample proportion (see Table 4.8).

The *sample* proportion, $\hat{p}$, is above 0.200. However, the firm wants to know if the *population* proportion, $p$, is above 0.200. From Expression (5.9), the one-sided "at least" 95% confidence interval on the unknown population proportion is

$$.2356 - \text{NORMSINV}_{.95} \cdot \sqrt{\frac{.2356 \cdot .7644}{900}}$$

$$.2356 - 1.6449 \cdot .0141$$

Lower Limit: .2123

*Interpretation*: The firm is 95% confident that at least 21.23% (0.2123) of potential customers will purchase the plaque-removal system. As this is above its break-even point of 0.200, the firm will market the product.

In summary, just as you use the sample mean to estimate a population mean, you use the sample proportion to estimate the population proportion.

▶ **WARNING** You should not construct confidence intervals on the population proportion for sample sizes that are less than Cochran's minimum recommendations. If your present sample size is insufficient to ensure normality of the distribution of the sample proportion, increase it.

# DETERMINING THE SAMPLE SIZE

Early in a study, a project manager must determine the sample size. This section discusses how to determine the sample size so that you can be confident that the sample statistic, $\bar{x}$ or $\hat{p}$, will differ from the population parameter, $\mu$ or $p$, by no more than an amount that you specify. By the end of this section you should be able to

1. determine the sample size to limit the margin of error to some maximum value in estimating an unknown population mean;

2. determine the sample size to limit the margin of error to some maximum value in estimating an unknown population proportion; and

3. Determine the sample size needed for one-sided or two-sided confidence intervals.

## SAMPLE SIZE FOR AN UNKNOWN POPULATION MEAN

To set up a two-sided confidence interval on an unknown population mean, you have used the following expression.

$$\bar{x} \pm \text{NORMSINV}_{CL + \frac{1-CL}{2}} \cdot \frac{s}{\sqrt{n}}$$

The expression $\text{NORMSINV} \cdot \dfrac{s}{\sqrt{n}}$ is simply the margin of error. To determine the necessary sample size, set $\text{NORMSINV} \cdot \dfrac{s}{\sqrt{n}}$ equal to the desired margin of error and solve for $n$. This leads to Expression (5.10).

$$\text{Desired Margin of Error (DME)} = \text{NORMSINV}_{\text{CL}+\frac{1-\text{CL}}{2}} \cdot \frac{s}{\sqrt{n}}$$

**(5.10)**

The term $s$ is the sample standard deviation. You will not know what it is until you have taken the sample. But at this point you do not even know the sample size! So you must estimate the sample standard deviation. Three common approaches are to

**1.** use the sample standard deviation from a small *pilot study*;

**2.** use the sample standard deviation from similar studies; or

**3.** estimate the range of the data. Then divide the range by 6 to estimate the sample standard deviation.

Approach #1 is probably the best method.

**EXAMPLE**    **2**    Let's revisit the Milemaster tire study first presented on page 173. Milemaster, Inc., must estimate the population mean tire life. Milemaster estimates the sample standard deviation is 850 miles from a pilot study of 10 tires. At the 98% confidence level, what must the sample size be such that the sample mean, $\bar{x}$, will be within 100 miles of the unknown population mean, $\mu$? That is, the firm wants the desired margin of error to be 100 miles.

Substituting into Expression (5.10),

$$\text{DME} = \text{NORMSINV}_{.98+\frac{1-.98}{2}} \cdot \frac{850}{\sqrt{n}}$$

$$\text{DME} = \text{NORMSINV}_{.99} \cdot \frac{850}{\sqrt{n}}$$

$$100 = 2.326 \cdot \frac{850}{\sqrt{n}}$$

$$\sqrt{n} = \frac{1977.1}{100} = 19.771$$

$$n = 390.89$$

A simple random sample of 391 tires (always round up) will allow Milemaster, Inc., to be 98% confident that the sample mean will be within 100 miles of the unknown population mean. The 10 tires in the pilot study count toward the 391 tires. Thus Milemaster, Inc., will need only an additional 381 tires to complete the study.

We can extend sample size determination to one-sided confidence intervals. The only change is that in using the NORMSINV wizard the probability input is CL rather than $CL + \frac{1-CL}{2}$. This leads to Expression (5.11).

$$DME = NORMSINV_{CL} \cdot \frac{s}{\sqrt{n}}$$

**(5.11)**

## SAMPLE SIZE FOR AN UNKNOWN POPULATION PROPORTION

To determine the sample size necessary, use one of the following two expressions.

$$\text{Two-sided interval} \quad DME = NORMSINV_{CL + \frac{1-CL}{2}} \cdot \sqrt{\frac{\hat{p} \cdot \hat{q}}{n}}$$

**(5.12)**

$$\text{One-sided interval} \quad DME = NORMSINV_{CL} \cdot \sqrt{\frac{\hat{p} \cdot \hat{q}}{n}}$$

**(5.13)**

To determine the sample size, set the left-hand side of the equation to the desired margin of error—a manager's prerogative—and solve for $n$.

Do you see a problem with using Expressions (5.12) or (5.13)? The problem is that you do not know what $\hat{p}$ is and you will not know it until you have selected the sample. So you must estimate $\hat{p}$. Three common approaches are to

**1.** use the sample proportion from a small-scale pilot study;

**2.** use the sample proportion from similar studies;

**3.** estimate the minimum and maximum possible values of $\hat{p}$ using managerial intuition. Use both estimates and determine the respective sample sizes. Select the larger sample size.

<table>
<tr><td>**EXAMPLE**</td><td>**3**</td><td>Let's revisit the marketing decision for the dental plaque-removal system. The firm must estimate the population proportion of customers who are likely to purchase the unit. At the 95% confidence level, what must the sample size be such that the sample proportion *will be no further away than .02 below* the unknown population proportion? The italicized phrasing indicates that a one-sided interval is appropriate.</td></tr>
</table>

The firm estimates that the minimum and maximum possible values of $\hat{p}$ are 0.15 to 0.25. Insert both estimates into Expression (5.13).

$$.02 = \text{NORMSINV}_{.95} \cdot \sqrt{\frac{(.15) \cdot (.85)}{n}}$$

For $\hat{p} = .15$ 

$$.02 = 1.645 \cdot \sqrt{\frac{.1275}{n}}$$

$$n = \frac{0.345018187}{0.0004} = 862.55$$

$$.02 = \text{NORMSINV}_{.95} \cdot \sqrt{\frac{(.25) \cdot (.75)}{n}}$$

For $\hat{p} = .25$ 

$$.02 = 1.645 \cdot \sqrt{\frac{.1875}{n}}$$

$$n = \frac{0.507379687}{0.0004} = 1268.45$$

Select the larger of the two sample sizes, namely 1,269 potential customers.

In summary, first set a maximum distance that the sample statistic can be from the population parameter and the desired confidence level. Then determine the sample size to estimate the population mean or proportion.

# CONFIDENCE INTERVALS ON AN UNKNOWN POPULATION VARIANCE

Up to this point, you have drawn inferences about a population's center. For qualitative *yes* or *no* data you constructed confidence intervals on the population proportion. For quantitative data you constructed confidence intervals on the population mean. Sometimes you are interested in making inferences about the population's variability rather than its mean value. By the end of this section you should be able to construct and interpret confidence intervals on the population variance or standard deviation.

## THE CHI-SQUARE DISTRIBUTION REVISITED

In Chapter 4 you learned that the statistic, $(n-1) \cdot s^2 / \sigma^2$, is $X^2$ distributed.

The chi-square distribution is actually a family of skewed distributions. The degree of skewness depends on $n - 1$, the degrees of freedom. Here you will use the chi-square distribution to construct confidence intervals on an unknown, and generally unknowable, population variance, $\sigma^2$—the term in the denominator of the statistic shown above.

Figure 5.2 displays a chi-square distribution for 19 degrees of freedom. The total area underneath the curve is 1.00. To construct a two-sided 95% confidence interval you must determine the values $a$ and $b$ such that 95% of the $(n-1) \cdot s^2 / \sigma^2$ values, or area, lie between the two values.

Begin by subdividing the area $1 - 95/100 = .05$ into .025 of the area below the value of $a$ and .025 of the area above the value of $b$. The probability that the confidence interval will not contain the unknown population variance is .05.

Determine $a$ and $b$ using the CHIINV function wizard (see below). The Excel developers designed the CHIINV wizard to provide the area under the chi-square curve *above* any value. That is, CHIINV provides the area in the upper tail of the chi-square distribution.

Determination of value of $a$    The area below $a$ is .025. Thus the area above $a$ is .95 + .025 = .975. Set the probability value for the CHIINV wizard to .975. Degrees of freedom are 19.

Determination of value of $b$    The area above $b$ is .025. Set the probability value for the CHIINV wizard to .025. Degrees of freedom are 19.

The CHIINV wizard indicates that 97.5% of the area under the chi-square curve in Figure 5.2 lies above $a$ = 8.91 and 2.5% of the area lies above $b$ = 32.85. Thus 95% of the area under the chi-square distribution for 19 degrees of freedom lies between the two values, $a$ = 8.91 and $b$ = 32.85.

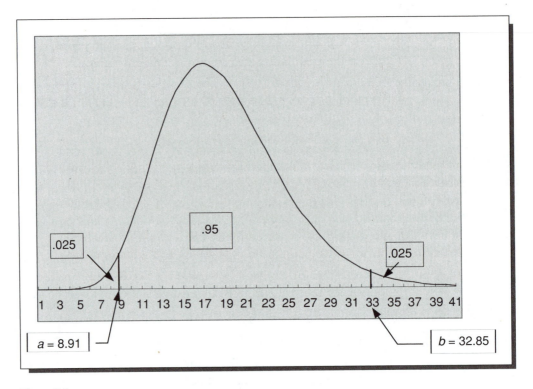

**Figure 5.2**
Chi-Square Distribution for 19 Degrees of Freedom

From Figure 5.2

$$P\left[8.91 < \frac{(n-1) \cdot s}{\sigma^2} < 32.85\right] = .95$$

We want to estimate the $\sigma^2$ term in the denominator. So we "flip" the expression, and in doing so we obtain the following:

$$P\left[\frac{1}{32.85} < \frac{\sigma^2}{(n-1) \cdot s^2} < \frac{1}{8.91}\right] = .95$$

Cross-multiplication leads to our final expression:

$$P\left[\frac{(n-1) \cdot s^2}{32.85} < \sigma^2 < \frac{(n-1) \cdot s^2}{8.91}\right] = .95$$

The lower limit of the confidence interval for the population variance, $\sigma^2$, is $\frac{(n-1) \cdot s^2}{32.85}$. The upper limit of the confidence interval for the population variance, $\sigma^2$, is $\frac{(n-1) \cdot s^2}{8.91}$.

## CASE STUDY

**Galvanized Coatings Weight.**  Let's use the above expression to construct a two-sided 95% confidence interval on the unknown population variance, $\sigma^2$, for the galvanized coating study. Table 5.5 displays the weights of galvanized coatings of $n = 20$ randomly selected pipes produced in one shift. From the AVERAGE and STDEV wizards, the sample mean and sample standard deviation are 200.76 and 4.59 pounds per pipe, respectively. The variance for galvanized coating is $s^2 = 4.59^2$.

Management desires a two-sided 95% confidence interval on the standard deviation. The specification calls for a population standard deviation of 4.50 pounds per pipe. Does the shift's production meet the standard deviation specification?

A two-sided 95% interval on the population variance for the coating weights is

$$P\left[\frac{(n-1)\cdot s^2}{32.85} < \sigma^2 < \frac{(n-1)\cdot s^2}{8.91}\right] = .95$$

$$P\left[\frac{19\cdot 4.59^2}{32.85} < \sigma^2 < \frac{19\cdot 4.59^2}{8.91}\right] = .95$$

$$P\left[12.186 < \sigma^2 < 44.926\right] = .95$$

The operations manager is 95% confident that the population variance in coating weights is between 12.186 and 44.926. Since the firm set the variability specification using the standard deviation, the manager then constructed a confidence interval on the standard deviation. To do this he simply took the square root of the lower and upper limits:

$$P\left(\sqrt{12.186} < \sigma < \sqrt{44.926}\right) = .95$$
$$P\left(3.49 < \sigma < 6.70\right) = .95$$

*Interpretation:* The manager is 95% confident that the population standard deviation in coating weights is between 3.49 pounds per pipe and 6.70 pounds per pipe. Since the interval includes the target value of 4.50 pounds, the engineering specification on variability has been met.

## EXPRESSIONS FOR CONSTRUCTING CONFIDENCE INTERVALS

As with all other confidence intervals you can construct either one-sided or two-sided intervals. Below are the necessary expressions.

$$\text{Two-sided:} \quad \frac{(n-1)\cdot s^2}{CHIINV(\frac{\alpha}{2},n-1)} \text{ to } \frac{(n-1)\cdot s^2}{CHIINV(1-\frac{\alpha}{2},n-1)}$$

**(5.14)**

$$\text{One-Sided At Least} \quad \frac{(n-1)\cdot s^2}{CHIINV(\alpha,n-1)}$$

**(5.15)**

$$\text{One-Sided At Most} \quad \frac{(n-1)\cdot s^2}{CHIINV(1-\alpha,n-1)}$$

**(5.16)**

where $\alpha = 1 - \left(\text{CL}/100\right)$ is the probability that the confidence interval will *not* contain the unknown population variance or standard deviation.

In summary, it's not enough to construct confidence intervals on a population's mean. Sometimes drawing conclusions about a population's variation is also important. Think confidence intervals for a population variance or standard deviation.

# KEY IDEAS AND OVERVIEW

Why must you construct confidence intervals on population parameters? You need to know these parameters to make decisions or gain insight into a problem or opportunity. But unless you sample the entire population,

$\bar{x}$ *will not equal* $\mu$,

$s^2$ *will not equal* $\sigma^2$,

$\hat{p}$ *will not equal p.*

Confidence interval methods *estimate* unknown population parameters with a high degree of confidence. These are essential techniques for a manager's analytical tool kit.

Figure 5.3 is an overview of the chapter's confidence interval procedures. It should help you determine the appropriate procedure to use. Included are the expressions for two-sided confidence intervals on the population mean, proportion, and variance.

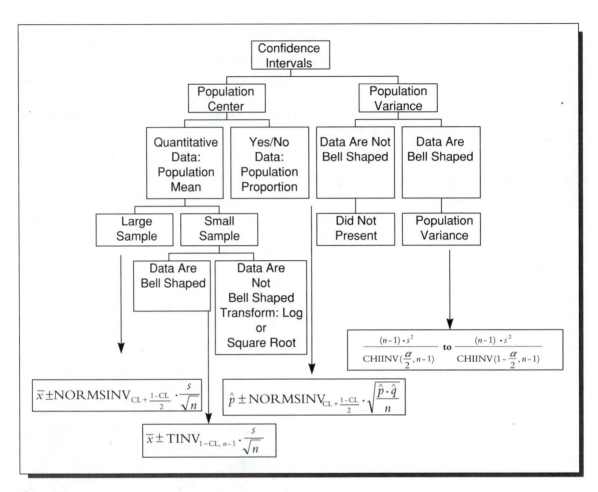

**Figure 5.3**
Overview of Chapter 5

# EXERCISES

1. Suppose the Central Limit Theorem was not true. What impact, if any, would this have on constructing confidence intervals on $\mu$?

2. The margin of error for estimating a population mean for large samples is

    $$\text{NORMSINV} \cdot \frac{s}{\sqrt{n}}.$$ Without changing the

    level of confidence, what is a practical way to reduce the margin of error?

3. Why would you want to reduce the margin of error?

4. What would the limits be for a 100% confidence interval on the population mean?

5. What is a one-sided confidence interval? When is it necessary?

6. Why does increasing the confidence level increase the margin of error?

7. Under what two conditions is it necessary to transform the data before constructing confidence intervals on the population mean?

8. Provide an example different from those in the book where it would be important to estimate an unknown population standard deviation.

9. Correct, if necessary, the following statements: As the sample size increases from $n = 10$ to $n = 1000$,

    a. the estimated standard error decreases.

    b. the sample standard deviation decreases.

    c. the reliability factor decreases.

    d. the sample mean decreases.

    e. the margin of error increases.

10. An attempted hostile takeover occurs when the target firm's management resists acquisition. Maximizing share price is the most effective way to resist. Then the acquiring firm may have to pay too steep a price for the acquisition. Other less effective approaches are taking a poison pill or using greenmail.

    An investment banking house wants to estimate the proportion of firms that use the first strategy to maximize share price. It takes a simple random sample of 1000 firms. Eight hundred indicate that they use the strategy to maximize share price. Set up and interpret a 90% confidence interval on the population proportion that uses this strategy.

11. A firm is presently using family branding on a consumer product and selling about 1750 cartons per store per week in the southeast United States. The marketing group has developed a new media campaign that it believes will increase sales substantially. It convinces management to try individual branding for six months. After the test period the firm selects a simple random sample of 400 stores and finds that these stores have sold a mean of 1760 cartons per store per week; the sample standard deviation is 2000 cartons per week.

    a. Set up and interpret a 95% confidence interval.

    b. Based on the confidence interval, can you conclude that the individual branding has increased the mean level of sales?

12. A vice president of a large manufacturing firm wants to estimate the mean productivity rate of his 2000 work teams. He selects a simple random sample of nine teams and obtains the following productivity data as a percentage of standard:

    92% 95% 89% 96% 94% 97% 99% 92% 101%

Are the population data likely to be near bell shaped? If so, set up and interpret a 95% confidence interval. Why is it important to assess the shape of the population distribution?

13. The second stage in the marketing adoption decision is product interest. The consumer searches for information about the new product. Kinsu Knives wants to know if an innovative ad has helped potential consumers obtain correct information on the product's (deluxe steak knife) attributes. Kinsu Knives interviews 225 people who have seen the ad at least four times in the past month and records the number of product attributes correctly identified.

$$\bar{x} = 2.15 \text{ attributes}$$
$$s^2 = .75$$
$$n = 225$$

Kinsu Knives will consider the ad successful if consumers, on average, can recall at least 2.20 attributes. Using a 95% confidence level, has the ad been successful?

14. A human resources manager wants to know the proportion of firms in the United States that have day-care facilities on their premises. His pilot study of 30 plants indicates that 0.20 have day-care facilities. What is the sample size needed to be 95% confident that the sample proportion will be within 0.05 of the unknown population proportion?

15. A manager wants to estimate how much variability there is in job climate among all blue-collar workers. She selects a simple random sample of 12 workers and obtains the following data on a 10-point job climate scale (higher numbers mean a more positive attitude toward the firm).

5 6 6 7 6 5 7 6 6 5 7 6

a. Set up and interpret a 90% confidence interval on the standard deviation in job climate among all blue-collar workers.

b. Why must she set up a confidence interval? After all, she knows the sample standard deviation of the 12 blue-collar workers. Explain.

16. Koca Kola wants to estimate the mean income of its blue-collar market segment. It selects ten families from the segment and obtains the following income data.

| | |
|---|---|
| $24,500 | $30,500 |
| 26,700 | 32,100 |
| 31,000 | 30,675 |
| 26,000 | 27,750 |
| 28,500 | 25,500 |

a. Use Excel's function wizards to compute the family income sample mean and standard deviation.

b. Compute the estimated standard error.

c. Is the population from which the sample was taken reasonably bell shaped? Why is this important?

d. The marketing manager believes that the population mean income for the bluecollar segment is at least $21,500. Should the manager construct a one- or two-sided interval? Explain.

e. Construct a 99% confidence interval on the population mean income.

f. Based on your answer in part (e), was the manager's belief justified? Explain.

17. Just-in-Time, Inc., is a stock-market timing service. It is interested in knowing the percentage of business economists who believe there will be a recession next year. Using the membership list of 4500 members in the American Association of Business

Economists as a sampling frame, the service calls 150 randomly selected members. Forty-three believe the country will experience a recession next year.

Construct and interpret a 95% confidence interval to estimate the proportion of business economists who believe there will be a recession next year.

18. AirComm inspects a sample of 1500 cellular handsets per day. If a handset has a surface blemish, it is defective and the blemishes must be corrected before shipment. Consider the following data over the past ten shifts.

| Shift | Proportion Defective |
|-------|---------------------|
| 1 | .08 |
| 2 | .06 |
| 3 | .09 |
| 4 | .08 |
| 5 | .08 |
| 6 | .09 |
| 7 | .08 |
| 8 | .06 |
| 9 | .08 |
| 10 | .09 |

a. Are the daily proportion defective time-ordered data stationary? Use Excel's line-graph chart wizard to graph the data.

b. If the data are stationary, determine the average proportion defective by summing the ten proportion defectives and dividing by 10.

c. Use the average proportion in place of $\hat{p}$. Construct and interpret a two-sided 99.73% confidence interval. In control charting the lower and upper limits are called the lower and upper *control* limits. When the daily proportion defective is above the upper control limit or below the lower control limit, the operator investigates the causes. Data values outside the control limits are considered outliers,

and the operator must seek assignable causes. Are any of the $\hat{p}$ values outliers?

19. Excessive variation is the major battle manufacturing industries have today in achieving high product quality. At the B&L Optical Company, the process standard deviation in the tensile strength of its eyeglass frames has been 150 pounds per square inch (ppsi). Based on suggestions from its hourly production workers, B&L has made what it thinks are major process improvements. First B&L ensures that the new process has been stabilized—the standard deviation over 15 successive shifts is neither increasing or decreasing over time. Then it takes a random sample of 121 eyeglass frames from a production shift and determines that the sample standard deviation is now 123 ppsi.

a. Construct and interpret a 95% confidence interval on the population standard deviation.

b. Have these improvements reduced the process standard deviation from the previous 150-ppsi level?

20. A goal of the Division of Tuberculosis Elimination (DTBE) in Atlanta is to reduce patient waiting time in TB clinics to at most an average of 75 minutes. It collects data on a simple random sample of clinics in ten cities and obtains the following data.

| City | Minutes |
|------|---------|
| Hartford | 53 |
| Birmingham | 65 |
| Denver | 57 |
| Seattle | 65 |
| San Antonio | 57 |
| Columbia | 58 |
| Madison | 51 |
| Columbus | 72 |
| San Francisco | 68 |
| New York City | 77 |

Is the population from which the sample was taken reasonably bell shaped? If so, construct a 95% confidence interval. Has DTBE been successful? Discuss.

**21.** Below are profit margins on sales—net income after taxes divided by sales—for ten firms. Can you construct a 95% confidence interval on the population mean? If not, why not?

5.0% 5.1% 5.5% 5.9% 6% 6.3% 6.6% 6.8% 7.7% 11.4%

**22.** Fine Foods, Inc., wishes to estimate the mean income of its most affluent consumer market segment. It suspects that income within this segment is not normally distributed. Below is a random sample of 20 families taken from the affluent market segment.

| | | | | |
|---|---|---|---|---|
| $ 75,750 | $ 77,050 | $ 80,750 | $ | 82,450 |
| 85,675 | 91,000 | 96,000 | | 97,750 |
| 150,000 | 155,750 | 157,250 | | 160,500 |
| 165,500 | 175,000 | 190,500 | | 495,500 |
| 510,000 | 650,000 | 750,500 | | 1,250,500 |

**a.** Use the SKEW and KURT function wizards. Do the income data appear to be reasonably bell shaped?

**b.** Apply a log transformation to the data. Are the transformed sample data now reasonably bell shaped? Discuss.

**23.** The manager of a repair center must estimate the population mean travel time between customers for an 800-person repair force. From other repair firms' data, he estimates the standard deviation in travel times will be about 20 minutes. What size sample must he take so that he can be 90% confident that the sample mean will not vary from the population mean by more than 6 minutes?

**24.** Refer to Exercise 22. Construct a two-sided 95% confidence interval on the log of the population mean income.

**25.** A product may advertise that it has no fat if it contains at most 0.1 grams per serving. Can Know-Fat cheese advertise that it contains no fat? Use a 90% level of confidence. Here are sample data from an FDA study.

$$\bar{x} = 0.06 \text{ grams}$$

$$s^2 = 0.16$$

$$n = 400 \text{ cheese square servings}$$

**26.** AirComm's quality control department has set the mean impact resistance standard for plastic headphones at 4660 pounds per square inch (ppsi). It has set the standard deviation in impact resistance at 22 pounds per square inch. During each shift the quality control department takes a sample of ten phones (about one every 45 minutes) and tests their impact resistance. Shown below are the data for one shift:

| Impact Resistance (ppsi) | |
|---|---|
| 1 | 4650 |
| 2 | 4650 |
| 3 | 4600 |
| 4 | 4700 |
| 5 | 4650 |
| 6 | 4650 |
| 7 | 4700 |
| 8 | 4650 |
| 9 | 4600 |
| 10 | 4650 |

**a.** Draw a line graph. Do the time-ordered data appear to be stationary?

**b.** Determine if the population from which the sample was taken was reasonably bell shaped. If so, set up and interpret a 95% confidence interval on the population mean.

**c.** Set up and interpret a 95% confidence interval on the standard deviation.

**d.** Are both manufacturing standards being met on this shift? Explain.

**e.** As a manager, what problem-solving action should you take?

**27.** In an antitrust case, *U.S. v. United Shoe Machinery Corp.*, the government estimated the market share United Shoe held on a variety of machines for the shoe industry. Using a simple random sample of 55 firms, United Shoe's sample proportion of fitting room machines was 0.41. Set up and interpret a 95% two-sided confidence interval on the population proportion (market dominance) of United Shoe's fitting room machines.

**28.** The Securities and Exchange Commission (SEC) requires companies to file annual reports concerning their financial status. Firms cannot audit every account receivable, so the SEC permits firms to estimate the true, or population, mean. Suppose the SEC requires that a reported sample mean be within $5 of the population mean with 95% confidence. Given a small sample of 20, a firm estimates the standard deviation to be $50. What must the total sample size be so that the firm can be 95% confident that the sample mean will be within $5 of the population mean?

**29.** In *Swain v. Alabama*, the U.S. Supreme Court compared the fraction of grand jurors who are African American (about 12%) with their fraction in the community (about 26%). The Court decided that the difference in percentages was insufficient to create a prima facie case of racial discrimination. Prima facie means that the evidence appears to indicate that discrimination is occurring. If the plaintiffs demonstrate a prima facie case, then the burden of proof shifts to the defendant to explain or justify the apparent discrimination.

Assume that African Americans formed 12% of the 2000 jurors over the past ten years.

**a.** Assume for the moment that the population proportion of African Americans in the community is unknown. Set up an "at most" 95% confidence interval on the unknown population proportion of African Americans in the community based on the 12% figure.

**b.** Relying on census data, the court knew that the population proportion of African Americans in the community was 26%. Given your answer in part (a), what could the court have concluded about the potential for racial discrimination in selecting juries?

**30.** A manufacturer makes a machine that injects a specified amount of heart stimulant into a patient's bloodstream. The manufacturer claims that the standard deviation of the amount injected is at most .05 milliliter. If the standard deviation is greater than .05, the patient may not get enough stimulant or get too much stimulant and die. The variance in a sample of ten injections was .00587.

**a.** Construct a 99% confidence interval to estimate the standard deviation of the amount injected.

**b.** Keeping in mind that people's lives depend on your decision, would you conclude that the machine is safe to use? Defend your position.

**31.** What proportion of industrial distributors or jobbers are merchant wholesalers? The American Marketing Association commissions a study to determine the proportion. Here are the sample data.

$$\hat{p} = .80$$
$$n = 1000$$

Set up and interpret a 99% confidence interval on the unknown population proportion of merchant wholesalers.

**32.** The times interest earned (TIE) is determined by dividing a firm's earnings before interest and taxes by its interest charge. A financial association wishes to construct a 90% confidence interval on the population mean TIE in an industry. It selects 50 firms at random and obtains their times interest earned data. Here are the sample data.

$$\bar{x} = 5.7 \text{ times}$$
$$s = 2.5$$

Construct a two-sided 95% confidence interval. Why isn't it necessary to determine if the population distribution from which the sample was taken is reasonably bell shaped?

**33.** One hundred economic forecasters are interviewed and asked to make predictions as to whether the budget deficit will be reduced next year. The 95% confidence interval on the population proportion of forecasters who predict that the budget deficit will be reduced is 0.49 to 0.53.

   **a.** Can we say at a 95% level of confidence that a majority of the economic forecasters in the United States believe that the deficit will be reduced next year? Explain.

   **b.** Suppose the answer in part (a) does not allow you to say that a majority of forecasters believe that the deficit will be reduced next year. Would reducing the margin of error help, and, if so, how can it be reduced without changing the confidence level? Explain.

**34.** Industrial psychologists believe that stress is curvilinearly related to performance. That is, too little stress produces no drive to excel. Too much stress causes anxiety that reduces performance. For the past two years a firm worked to optimize the level of stress within a plant. The firm's psychologist selects a sim-

ple random sample of 50 workers from the 20,000 employees and administers a stress test. The mean level of stress is 5.35 with a sample variance of 0.36.

   **a.** Construct a 99% confidence interval for the mean stress level for the plant.

   **b.** Does it appear that the mean stress level is at the optimum level of 5.0?

   **c.** Is it necessary to determine if the population distribution is near bell shaped? Discuss.

**35.** Spreadsheet 535.xls contains the amount of time to complete a task for 50 randomly selected customer service representatives. The firm has implemented a quality improvement program to reduce the amount of time to complete the task. The program's goal was to reduce the mean time to at most 7.5 minutes.

   **a.** Use Excel's function wizards or descriptive-statistics data-analysis tool to determine the sample mean and sample standard deviation number of minutes to complete the task.

   **b.** Construct a 95% confidence interval, and determine if the quality improvement program has been successful.

**36.** In *Sears, Roebuck and Co. v. City of Inglewood*, Sears claimed that it had overpaid its sales tax because of an erroneous definition of what constituted an out-of-city sale. The law read that sales made to persons in the city limits were not subject to the tax. To support its claim, Sears selected a simple random sample of 900 sales slips and found that 330 of them were for sales to persons within the city and thus not subject to the sales tax. Set up and interpret a two-sided 95% confidence interval on the population proportion of sales to persons within the city.

**37.** The First National Bank of Minneapolis wishes to estimate the mean inquiry resolution time to obtain mortgage information. It desires a margin of error of $\pm 5$ minutes and a two-sided 90% confidence interval. Based on industry-wide data, the estimated sample standard deviation is 24.5 minutes. Determine the necessary sample size.

**38.** Spreadsheet 538.xls contains data on the profit margins, net profit after taxes divided by sales, for 60 randomly selected firms in an industry. Construct and interpret a two-sided 99% confidence interval on the appropriate measure of the population's center.

**39.** In the process of chrome plating, parts immersed in a chemical bath containing nickel receive a thin plating when small electric currents are running through the bath. Metals used in plating solutions are called "electroless nickel" and its concentration is measured in oz/gallon.

Spreadsheet 539.xls contains data on the concentration of electroless nickel at the beginning of a shift over a 30-day period. Since there are three shifts per day, there are 90 measurements.

  **a.** Use Excel's line-graph chart wizard and determine if the concentration data are stationary over the 30-day period.

  **b.** If the data are stationary, construct a 99.73% confidence interval on the population mean concentration and the population variance in concentration.

**40.** One measure of software quality is the error rate per 1000 lines of code (KLOC). The data in spreadsheet 540.xls show the errors per KLOC from daily test logs over a 30-day period.

  **a.** Use Excel's line-graph chart wizard and determine if the time-ordered errors per KLOC are stationary over the 30-day period.

  **b.** If the data are stationary, construct a 99.73% confidence interval on the population mean number of errors per KLOC and the population variance in errors per KLOC.

**41.** The American Society for Quality wishes to estimate the population proportion of American firms that have been ISO certified. Unless companies are certified they cannot conduct business in the European Common Market. ASQ selects a simple random sample of 800 firms and finds that 217 have been certified. Construct and interpret a two-sided 99% confidence interval.

**42.** Spreadsheet 542.xls contains data on the weight loss for a one-month period experienced by 100 randomly selected customers of Jenny Krug. The firm claims that customers will lose, on average, at least 10 pounds in the first month. Is the firm's claim justified? Construct a 95% interval to evaluate the claim.

**43.** Spreadsheet 543.xls contains data on 50 randomly selected used-car loans from the bank's loan portfolio. The bank wishes to construct a confidence interval on the population mean size loan. Construct and interpret a two-sided 95% confidence interval.

**44.** A firm wants to reduce the amount of time to test a product. It believes that if it provides ergonomic work stations for its workers, it can reduce testing time by at least 5 minutes. After installing the work stations, the firm records the reduction in testing time of 75 randomly selected workers. Spreadsheet 544.xls contains the data.

**a.** Construct and interpret a 95% confidence interval on the population reduction in testing time.

**b.** You actually didn't need to compute the lower limit of the interval to realize that the ergonomic work stations had not reduced testing time by at least 5 minutes. How could you tell after only computing the sample mean reduction in time?

**45.** According to published data, 19.1 million Americans belonged to a health club this past year. A national health club wants to estimate the percentage of its clientele that has never shown up once during the past year. The firm selects a simple random sample of 1000 paid-up members. The records indicate that 22 never showed up once during the year. Construct and interpret a two-sided 95% confidence interval on the population proportion.

**46.** Dunky Donut wants to estimate the population mean number of doughnuts sold every minute at its 1000 stores across the nation. It selects ten stores and records the number of doughnuts sold during a 30-minute randomly selected time of day. During the test period, the ten stores sold the following number of doughnuts per minute.

0 2 2 1 1 2 2 1 1 3

**a.** Is it necessary to determine if the population from which the sample was taken is near bell shaped? Why? Can you construct a confidence interval on the population mean?

**b.** Construct a 99% confidence interval on the population mean number of doughnuts sold per 30 minutes.

**47.** Five years ago a study revealed that 45% of Americans exercise less than twice a week.

An insurance company wants to know if the percentage has dropped since the study. It interviews a simple random sample of 1500 adult Americans, and finds that 635 exercise less than twice a week. Construct and interpret a two-sided 95% confidence interval on the population proportion. Has the percentage dropped from the 45% figure of five years ago? Discuss.

**48.** If the lower limit of a confidence interval on the population variance were less than zero, what should you conclude? Discuss.

**49.** The United Way wishes to estimate the mean percentage of an American's salary that goes to charity. It interviews a simple random sample of 100 adult Americans and determines that the sample mean and standard deviation are 1.95% and 1.45%. Construct and interpret a 90% confidence interval on the population mean percentage of an American's salary that goes to charity.

**50.** Best Dairy, Inc., has segmented its market into eight groups. One such market segment is the Status Seekers. They are young, male, white-collar workers with college degrees who live in the suburbs. Shown below are ten incomes of Status Seekers.

| | | | | |
|---|---|---|---|---|
| $45,665 | $43,553 | $46,104 | $43,516 | $46,175 |
| $44,824 | $44,858 | $44,563 | $46,376 | $45,154 |

**a.** Are the population data from which the sample was taken reasonably normally distributed? Show all work.

**b.** If so, construct and interpret a two-sided 95% confidence interval on the population mean income and the population standard deviation in incomes of the Status Seeker market segment.

## CASE STUDY

The vice president of DairyBest Products received an urgent call from the plant manager of its major customer in the Midwest. The manager of Reliable Foods complained that the butterfat he had recently received from DairyBest's Midwest plant had such high levels of *salmonella* that it had ruined the company's food products. In the last two days, merchants had been complaining and health officers had impounded Reliable Food's products made with DairyBest butterfat. The plant manager at Reliable then checked every bag of butterfat from DairyBest and found that many bags had *salmonella* bacteria counts above acceptable limits, 2–3 cells. While some of the bags were okay, many bags were putrid and had apparently been running bad for the past week. See data in columns 6 and 7 in the database on page 201.

Reliable Foods was DairyBest's major customer in the Midwest. DairyBest sold four truckloads of butterfat per day. DairyBest operators skimmed the butterfat, put it into sterilized 38-pound bags, heat-sealed the bags, placed them on wooden pallets, froze the bags to −20 degrees, and then shipped the pallets in prechilled trucks. There were 45 bags to a pallet, nine per level and five deep. The distance between the two plants was about 100 miles. During the trip the temperature of the butterfat rose to about −15 degrees. This was still far below the temperature necessary for the *salmonella* bacteria to multiply and the butterfat to become putrid. DairyBest's quality control department checked several samples from each wooden pallet for high bacteria count before shipping. Reliable Foods also checked several samples per pallet for high bacteria count before accepting each pallet.

DairyBest also shipped butterfat to many other customers throughout the United States. Because the sales volume was low, DairyBest did not palletize the bags. Rather, it heat-sealed the bags and then froze them to −20 degrees. The vice president of DairyBest planned to check a random sample of the butterfat received by these companies later in the day. Finally, Reliable Foods also purchased butterfat from other suppliers. The Reliable Foods (RL) plant manager promised to check a random sample of bags for *salmonella* from other suppliers and report back to the vice president of DairyBest (DB).

| DairyBest—Reliable Process | DairyBest—Other Customers |
|---|---|
| Skim butterfat | Skim butterfat |
| Fill 38-pound bags and heat-seal | Fill 38-pound bags and heat-seal |
| Place on pallet and then freeze pallet | Freeze bag |
| DB outgoing inspection | DB outgoing inspection |
| Ship in precooled vans | Ship in precooled vans |
| RL incoming inspection | Customer incoming inspection |
| RL uses butterfat in variety of its products | Customer uses butterfat |
| Ship in vans to supermarkets | No *salmonella* present |
| Complaint in stores—RL products putrid and due to DB's butterfat (high *salmonella* counts) | |

Based on a preliminary evaluation the DairyBest vice president concluded that the *salmonella* outbreak was probably due to recent process changes at Reliable Foods.

Write a one-page report that addresses the following issues.

1. Evaluate the claim made by DairyBest's vice president.

2. Discuss and evaluate other possible root causes of the *salmonella* outbreak.

Use the data to support your position.

## Database for Salmonella Outbreak

| Other DB Customers | | Other Butterfat Suppliers | | | Bags at RF | |
| --- | --- | --- | --- | --- | --- | --- |
| Sample | Cell Count | Sample | Cell Count | | Sample | Cell Count |
| 1 | 1.19 | 1 | 1.02 | | 1 | 28.61 |
| 2 | 1.23 | 2 | 1.06 | | 2 | 28.04 |
| 3 | 1.21 | 3 | 1.13 | | 3 | 29.80 |
| 4 | 1.26 | 4 | 1.18 | | 4 | 13.48 |
| 5 | 1.34 | 5 | 1.23 | | 5 | 29.52 |
| 6 | 1.10 | 6 | 1.01 | | 6 | 7.10 |
| 7 | 1.19 | 7 | 1.06 | | 7 | 14.93 |
| 8 | 1.19 | 8 | 1.08 | | 8 | 16.72 |
| 9 | 1.40 | 9 | 1.27 | | 9 | 24.09 |
| 10 | 1.15 | 10 | 1.15 | | 10 | 17.78 |
| 11 | 1.30 | 11 | 1.08 | | 11 | 15.81 |
| 12 | 1.30 | 12 | 1.09 | | 12 | 26.04 |
| 13 | 1.40 | 13 | 1.14 | | 13 | 16.02 |
| 14 | 1.24 | 14 | 1.18 | | 14 | 16.93 |
| 15 | 1.38 | 15 | 1.18 | | 15 | 32.06 |
| 16 | 1.16 | 16 | 1.09 | | 16 | 10.35 |
| 17 | 1.45 | 17 | 1.17 | | 17 | 18.04 |
| 18 | 1.07 | 18 | 1.08 | | 18 | 17.43 |
| 19 | 1.27 | 19 | 1.23 | | 19 | 23.93 |
| 20 | 1.30 | 20 | 1.16 | | 20 | 29.91 |
| 21 | 1.23 | 21 | 0.97 | | 21 | 8.56 |
| 22 | 1.37 | 22 | 1.10 | | 22 | 12.20 |
| 23 | 1.35 | 23 | 1.16 | | 23 | 13.41 |
| 24 | 1.20 | 24 | 1.09 | | 24 | 11.53 |
| 25 | 1.17 | 25 | 1.14 | | 25 | 23.94 |
| 26 | 1.03 | 26 | 1.10 | | 26 | 19.74 |
| 27 | 1.37 | 27 | 1.17 | | 27 | 24.05 |
| 28 | 1.18 | 28 | 1.21 | | 28 | 17.23 |
| 29 | 1.17 | 29 | 1.16 | | 29 | 28.84 |
| 30 | 1.24 | 30 | 1.16 | | 30 | 23.14 |
| 31 | 1.21 | 31 | 1.10 | | 31 | 10.84 |
| 32 | 1.14 | 32 | 1.18 | | 32 | 26.32 |
| 33 | 1.22 | 33 | 1.01 | | 33 | 30.44 |
| 34 | 1.22 | 34 | 1.04 | | 34 | 18.58 |
| 35 | 1.14 | 35 | 1.16 | | 35 | 7.82 |

# CHAPTER 5
# APPENDICES

## I. LISTING OF EXCEL TOOLS FOR CHAPTER

1. AVERAGE function wizard
2. STDEV function wizard
3. NORMSINV function wizard
4. TINV function wizard
5. CHIINV function wizard

## II. DESCRIPTIVE-STATISTICS DATA-ANALYSIS TOOL

Instead of using several separate function wizards you may use the descriptive-statistics data-analysis tool to help construct confidence intervals on an unknown population mean (see Figure 5.4).

|  | A | B | C | D |
|---|---|---|---|---|
| 1 | $45,665 |  | **Column1** |  |
| 2 | $44,824 |  |  |  |
| 3 | $43,553 |  | **Mean** | 45,078.8 |
| 4 | $44,858 |  | **Standard Error** | 323.777 |
| 5 | $46,104 |  | Median | 45006 |
| 6 | $44,563 |  | Mode | N/A |
| 7 | $43,516 |  | StandardDeviation | 1023.873 |
| 8 | $46,376 |  | SampleVariance | 1048315 |
| 9 | $46,175 |  | **Kurtosis** | −0.97091 |
| 10 | $45,154 |  | **Skewness** | −0.35638 |
| 11 |  |  | Range | 2860 |
| 12 |  |  | Minimum | 43516 |
| 13 |  |  | Maximum | 46376 |
| 14 |  |  | Sum | 450788 |
| 15 |  |  | Count | 10 |
| 16 |  |  |  |  |

**Figure 5.4**
Using the Descriptive-Statistics Data-Analysis Tool

1. Enter the data in column A, rows 1–10, of a worksheet as shown in Figure 5.4. The data are family incomes in a census tract.

2. Place the cursor in cell C1.

3. Click on Tools and then on Data Analysis. Then click on Descriptive Statistics and click on OK.

4. Type in the following entries for the descriptive-statistics tool.

Click on Summary statistics box and then click OK.

5. The critical outputs from the descriptive-statistics tool are bold-faced in Figure 5.4. Note the skewness and kurtosis indicate that the data are reasonably normal. All you now need is the value of the TINV function wizard (because the sample size is under 30). Multiply the value of the TINV function wizard by the standard error to obtain the margin of error.

You probably noticed that the descriptive-statistics data-analysis tool allows you to obtain the margin of error directly by checking the confidence level for mean box on the descriptive-statistics input screen. The tool provides the correct width of the confidence interval for two-sided intervals on the mean for *sample sizes less than 30* where you should use the TINV function wizard to compute the margin of error. However, the tool always uses the TINV wizard for computing the margin of error even when you should use the NORMSINV function for computing the margin of error.

▶ **WARNING** Do not use the margin of error from the descriptive-statistics data-analysis tool when computing two-sided confidence intervals on the population mean for sample sizes of 30 or greater. Your margin of error will be incorrect.

# Chapter

# STATISTICAL INFERENCE II: HYPOTHESIS TESTING ON ONE POPULATION PARAMETER

## INTRODUCTION

To this point two chapters have focused on univariate data—data on one variable. Chapter 2 described how to organize, visualize, and analyze one *specific* sample of data. Chapter 5 presented how to estimate an unknown and unknowable population parameter based upon constructing confidence intervals on one *random,* or *representative*, sample from the population. This chapter presents a second method for estimating an unknown and unknowable population parameter—hypothesis testing.

Hypothesis testing evaluates claims made by others—internal or external customers, vendors, superiors, and so forth who are trying to influence you—the decision maker. To verify his or her claim, the decision maker takes a representative sample from the population and based on the sample evidence evaluates the claim's truth.

Table 6.1 displays how Chapters 2, 5, and 6 are similar and different.

| Basis | Chapter 2 Descriptive Statistics | Chapter 5 Confidence Intervals | Chapter 6 Hypothesis Testing |
|---|---|---|---|
| How Sample Is Selected | Select one *specific* sample from the population. | Select one *random*, or representative, sample from the population. | Select one *random*, or representative, sample from the population. |
| First Step in Analysis | Compute descriptive statistics for the sample. | Compute descriptive statistics for the sample. | Compute descriptive statistics for the sample. |
| Second Step in Analysis | There is no second step. We are only interested in the specific sample. | Draw conclusions about a population parameter from the one sample. | Draw conclusions about a population parameter from the one sample. |
| Method of Drawing Conclusions about Population | None, because we are only interested in the specific sample. | Construct a *confidence interval*. | Conduct *hypothesis testing*. |
| Degree of Assurance of Conclusion about Population Parameter | Not applicable or relevant. | Analyst selects a *confidence level*. Cannot be 100% confident about the value of the population parameter. | Analyst selects a *significance level*. Cannot be 100% confident about the truth of the hypothesis, or claim. |

**Table 6.1**
Compare and Contrast of Chapters 2, 5, and 6

# MANAGEMENT SCENARIOS AND DATA SETS

In Scenario I, a project manager must decide whether or not to market a new tire that the engineering group *claims* will have a population mean tire life greater than 47,000 miles. If that claim is true, the new tire would have a major competitive advantage over other brands. What makes the decision—to market or not to market the tire—difficult is the project manager's uncertainty of how long the tires will really last on average.

The manager selects a random sample of 1000 tires and determines the tread life on a test track. Here are the statistics from the study.

| | |
|---|---|
| Sample mean | $\bar{x}_{1000} = 47,300$ miles |
| Sample standard deviation | $s_{1000} = 3162$ miles |
| Sample size | $n = 1000$ tires |

In Scenario II, a marketing manager seeks to reduce consumers' levels of postpurchase doubt for his product, a high-end sports car. This arises when the buyer chooses one purchase alternate and rejects others although each has some desirable unique features. The consumer, in effect, asks, "Did I make the right decision?" Unless the doubt is dissipated, future purchases from that firm are doubtful. Marketers can reduce postpurchase doubt by developing an effective advertising campaign. .

Historically the mean level of postpurchase doubt for the QW4 sports car has been 20 on a 1 (no doubt) to 100 (absolute doubt) scale. The advertising design team claims that a new ad will reduce the mean level of postpurchase doubt below the present level of 20. It runs the ad in one test market. Then the marketing manager selects a random sample of 25 consumers from the test market who recently purchased the QW4 sports car and who say that they have seen the new ad more than three times. Through a customer feedback questionnaire he obtains postpurchase doubt data on the 25 customers. Here are the statistics:

| | |
|---|---|
| Sample mean | $\bar{x}_{25} = 19.6$ |
| Sample standard deviation | $s_{25} = 2.50$ |
| Sample size | $n = 25$ customers |

Scenario III examines whether a critical financial ratio has changed that could impact an industry's bond ratings. Historically, the *times interest earned* (TIE) ratio for the metal fabrication industry has been 5.7 times. The ratio is earnings before interest and taxes divided by the interest charges. A ratio of 5.7 means that earnings before interest and taxes are 5.7 times larger than annual interest charges. The TIE ratio measures the extent to which earnings can decline before a firm is unable to meet its annual interest costs.

A research group claims that the ratio has changed in the industry from the historical level of 5.7 times. If so, this change could cause either Moody's Investors Services or Standard and Poor's Corporation to change bond ratings of firms within the industry.

The controller for a firm within the industry wishes to assess the claim of the research group. She selects a random sample of 40 publicly traded firms within the industry and computes their TIE ratio data.

| Sample mean | $\bar{x}_{40} = 5.99$ times |
| Sample standard deviation | $s_{40} = 0.75$ times |
| Sample size | $n = 40$ firms |

In Scenario IV, a product manager at RBC seeks to increase the proportion of customers in a small, but potentially explosive, market segment. RBC sells a line of nonalcoholic beverages. Currently about 8% (.08) of its customers are in the "fitness-conscious" market segment. This segment includes young males and females with college degrees who live in the suburbs and make over $45,000 per year. They avoid overindulgence, jog, play tennis, and are "me" oriented. They are light to moderate product users who almost never drink the brand with meals. They exhibit some brand loyalty.

A marketing team at RBC has finalized a specific marketing mix that it claims is tailored to the fitness-conscious market segment. The mix includes minor product changes, distribution channel modifications, a new promotion campaign, and a 3% price increase. As director of marketing at RBC, you must make the final decision on the marketing mix. You plan to test the marketing team's mix in one city before implementing it nationwide.

After implementing the marketing mix in Denver, the director conducts a survey to determine if the proportion of RBC customers who are in the fitness-conscious market segment is now greater than 0.08. The team interviews 500 RBC customers in Denver and obtains the following results. From Expression (5.6),

$$n = 500 \text{ RBC customers}$$
$$n_{yes} = 55 \text{ fitness-conscious customers}$$
$$\text{Sample proportion} \quad \hat{p} = \frac{55}{500} = .11$$

# HYPOTHESIS TESTING ON ONE POPULATION MEAN

This section introduces hypothesis testing on an unknown and unknowable population mean. By the end of this section you should be able to

1. State hypotheses and associated managerial actions;

2. Determine the Type I and Type II error and explain why two errors are possible before collecting the data;

3. Set a significance level and explain it in nontechnical language;

4. Explain in plain English what the test statistic means;

5. Use the NORMSDIST wizard to choose between the null and alternative hypotheses for large-size samples of 30 or more;

6. Use the TDIST function wizard to choose between the null and alternative hypotheses for small-size samples of less than 30; and

7. Explain a study's computed *p*-value in nontechnical language.

# LARGE SAMPLE HYPOTHESIS TESTING

**EXAMPLE**

**1　Milemaster Product Introduction Decision.** Based on a competitive analysis, Milemaster will market a new tire recently developed by the engineering group only if the *population* mean tread life exceeds 47,000 miles. The engineering group believes that the population mean tread life exceeds 47,000 miles. However, the project manager is still unsure if the population mean is less than, equal to, or greater than 47,000 miles. The uncertainty is making her decision difficult.

Let's apply the five-step hypothesis testing approach to evaluate the engineering group's claim and decide whether or not to market the tire.

**STEP 1:** **State Hypotheses and Managerial Actions**

The first step is to develop two hypotheses about the unknown population mean tread life, $\mu_{\text{tread life}}$. These are the **null** and **alternative** hypotheses. A hypothesis is simply a testable claim or statement.

The null hypothesis is almost always the opposite of the claim made by others who wish to influence the decision maker. A vendor claims its product is better than what your firm is currently using; the decision maker's null hypothesis is that the product is not better. A prosecuting attorney claims a defendant is guilty; the jury's null hypothesis is that the defendant is not guilty. In short, the decision maker's null hypothesis is the "I-don't-believe-your-claim" hypothesis.

Here is the logic behind the "I-don't-believe-your-claim" null hypothesis. Decision makers often hear claims by others inside and outside the firm who want to influence a decision. The decision maker must be skeptical of these claims. After all, have you ever heard anyone claim that his or her product or service is worse than what is currently being used? The null hypothesis reflects the decision maker's skepticism about claims made by others.

**DEFINITION**

The null hypothesis is the claim initially favored by the *decision maker*. It generally is the opposite of the claim made by others who are trying to influence the decision maker.

For the Milemaster project, the engineering group claims that the population mean tread life, $\mu_{\text{tread life}}$, will exceed 47,000 miles. Thus, in words, the decision maker's null hypothesis is the opposite of that claim; namely,

$H_0$: The population mean tread life will not exceed 47,000 miles.

Using symbols we can write the null hypothesis as

$$H_0: \mu_{\text{tread life}} \leq 47,000 \text{ miles}$$

The decision maker assumes that the null hypothesis is true until proven otherwise. This idea is already familiar to you. In a jury trial, the judge tells the jury that it must assume the defendant is not guilty. The jury may only reject this hypothesis when the evidence proves beyond a reasonable doubt that the defendant is guilty.

The alternative hypothesis is almost always the claim made by others. In the Milemaster study, the alternative hypothesis is the engineering group's claim. That is, the population mean tread life will exceed 47,000 miles.

$$H_1: \mu_{\text{tread life}} > 47,000 \text{ miles}$$

In summary, here are the null and alternative hypotheses and their associated managerial actions for the Milemaster study.

| Hypotheses | Managerial Actions |
|---|---|
| $H_0: \mu_{\text{tread life}} \leq 47,000$ miles | Failure to reject the null hypothesis means the firm *will not* market the Milemaster tire. |
| $H_1: \mu_{\text{tread life}} > 47,000$ miles | Rejecting the null hypothesis means the firm *will* market the Milemaster tire. |

Note several important features of the two hypotheses. First, the project manager has stated what action to take if she fails to reject or if she rejects the null hypothesis. Clearly, hypothesis testing is action oriented. Second, the two hypotheses are mutually exclusive and exhaustive. Either the unknown population mean tread life is less than, equal to, or greater than 47,000 miles. Both the null and alternative hypotheses cannot be true, but one must be true. Third, both hypotheses make claims about an unknown (and unknowable) population mean. Unless the firm tested all its tires, it must rely on sample data to test hypotheses.

There is one remaining, but very important, point. Managers always hope that based on the study's data they can reject the null hypothesis. The null hypothesis is generally the "do nothing" hypothesis. In the Milemaster study, failure to reject the null hypothesis means *not* marketing the tire. The alternative hypothesis generally reflects the "take action" hypothesis. So managers would like to reject the null hypothesis in favor of the alternative hypothesis.

In conclusion, upon completing the first step in hypothesis testing, you will develop one of the following three sets of hypotheses.

Set I:        $H_0$: $\mu \geq k$

$H_1$: $\mu < k$

This is a **one-sided, lower-tail** (or **one-tail**) test. Use it to test someone else's claim that a population mean is *less than* the value of $k$. This is similar to a one-sided confidence interval.

Set II:        $H_0$: $\mu \leq k$

$H_1$: $\mu > k$

This is a **one-sided, upper-tail** (or **one-tail) test**. Use it to test someone else's claim that the population mean is *greater than* the value of $k$. This set reflects the Milemaster tire example with $k = 47,000$ miles. This too is similar to a one-sided confidence interval.

Set III:        $H_0$: $\mu = k$

$H_1$: $\mu \neq k$

This is a **two-sided,** or **two-tail**, test. Use it to test someone else's claim that the population mean *differs* or *has changed* from the value of $k$. This is similar to a two-sided confidence interval.

---

| STEP 2: | **Determine the Consequences of the Decision-Making Errors** |

We can be either right or wrong when we make statistical inferences about an unknown population mean. Table 6.2 shows that there are *two* ways to be right and *two* ways to be wrong in hypothesis testing.

**Table 6.2**
Types of Errors in
Milemaster Study

| After Running the Study the Manager | But Null Hypothesis Is True | But Null Hypothesis Is False |
|---|---|---|
| Does not reject the null | Correct decision | **Type II Error** |
| Rejects the null | **Type I Error** | Correct decision |

After running the study the manager will either reject the null hypothesis or not reject it. Then only one error is possible. If she does not reject the null hypothesis, she will have either (1) made a correct decision or (2) made a Type II error. If she rejects the null hypothesis, she will have either (1) made a correct decision or (2) made a Type I error. Before running the study, the manager must be concerned about the possibility of both errors and their associated costs because they affect the next step of hypothesis testing.

Here we determine the two types of possible errors and their associated costs for the Milemaster study.

| | |
|---|---|
| Type I Error: | **Reject the null hypothesis when the null hypothesis is true.** |
| Translation of Type I Error | "Reject the null" means that the firm believes the alternative is true. It will market the Milemaster tire because it thinks that the population mean tread life exceeds 47,000 miles. |
| | "Null is true" means the population mean tread life is truly less than or equal to 47,000 miles. The firm should not have marketed the tire. |
| Description of Type I Error | **The firm markets the tire, but it should not have.** |
| Type II Error: | **Do not reject the null hypothesis when the null is false.** |
| Translation of Type II Error | "Do not reject the null" means that the firm does not market the tire because it thinks the population mean is less than or equal to 47,000 miles. |
| | "Null is false" means the population mean tread life truly exceeds 47,000 miles. It should have marketed the tire. |
| Description of Type II Error | **The firm does not market the tire when it should have. This is a lost marketing opportunity.** |

Business errors are generally costly. What costs are associated with the Type I and Type II errors in the Milemaster project study?

***Costs of a Type I Error.***    The firm markets the tire and after the tires have been in the marketplace several years the firm realizes that the population mean tread life is less than or equal to 47,000 miles. Then problems will begin. Possible costs include reduced consumer confidence in the company, expensive tire replacements under the tread warranty, and possible class-action suits filed by irate customers. A Type I error could be very costly.

***Costs of a Type II Error.***   In failing to market the Milemaster tire, the firm would have lost a major marketing opportunity. The potential loss would depend on how good the new tire truly is. If the population mean tread life, $\mu_{\text{tread life}}$, were only 48,000 miles, the firm's losses might be small. However, if $\mu_{\text{tread life}}$ were 75,000 miles, then failure to market this tire would be very costly in terms of lost profit.

While there is a single Type I error cost, the cost of a Type II error depends on the magnitude of the lost opportunity. Since the engineering team believed that the mean tread life could be as high as 55,000 miles, the *most likely* Type II error cost would be high. In summary, for this example the potential costs of the Type I error and the *most likely* Type II error are both very high.

## STEP 3:   Set a Significance Level and Determine the Sample Size

The third step requires setting a **significance level**, $\alpha$. Base it on the relative costs of making the Type I error and most likely Type II error from the previous step.

No one likes making errors. However, when testing hypotheses, there is always the chance of making either a Type I or Type II error. The significance level, $\alpha$, addresses the probability of making a Type I error.

**DEFINITION**    The significance level, $\alpha$, is the *maximum* probability of making a Type I error that the decision maker can accept or "live with." Base it on the relative costs of making the Type I error and the most likely Type II error.

Decision makers rely on judgment to set the $\alpha$ level. How should they do it?

As shown in this chapter's appendix, the probabilities of making the Type I error and Type II error are inversely related. For a given sample size, reducing the probability of making a Type I error, $\alpha$, increases the probability of making the most likely Type II error. This inverse relationship leads to the following three guidelines:

PRINCIPLE 1          If the Type I error is costly (or serious) and the most likely Type II error is not costly, set a low significance level—an $\alpha$ of .01 or less. A low $\alpha$ level protects the decision maker from making a costly Type I error. Do not worry about making the most likely Type II error if it is not costly or serious.

PRINCIPLE 2          If the most likely Type II error is costly and the Type I error is not as serious or costly, set $\alpha$ higher —at .15 or above. This reduces the probability of making a costly Type II error.

PRINCIPLE 3    When both errors are costly, set the significance level, $\alpha$, at .05 or .01. Reduce the probability of making the most likely Type II error by increasing the sample size of the study.

Given the relative costs, the project manager applied Principle 3 and set the significance level low, an $\alpha$ of .01. If she rejects the null hypothesis, the probability of making the costly Type I error is *at most* 1 in 100. Thus she can be *at least* $100(1 - \alpha)\%$, or 99%, confident of having made a correct decision. The project manager will use the significance level, $\alpha = .01$, in step #5 of hypothesis testing.

To minimize the possibility of making a costly Type II error, the project manager should select the largest possible sample size that the initial project budget and time will allow. If this does not reduce sufficiently the probability of making the most likely Type II error (see this chapter's appendix), the manager should increase the sample size. In the tire study, the project manager chose a sample size of 1000 tires.

## STEP 4:    Conduct Study or Survey

The project manager ran the study. She randomly selected 1000 tires and mounted them on 250 randomly selected cars. She controlled the cars by radio frequency. All cars were run continually at 60 miles per hour, and every hour the test group checked the tires for tread wear and air pressure. The test group maintained an air pressure of 32 ppsi in all tires. All tires were tested on the same test track and under the same conditions (a predefined combination of wet and dry track) over a six-week period. The test group recorded the mileage at which each tire failed to meet federal standards for tread wear. Here are the study's sample statistics:

Sample mean    $\bar{x}_{1000} = 47,300$ miles

Sample standard deviation    $s_{1000} = 3162$ miles

Sample size    $n = 1000$ tires

Estimated standard error    $\dfrac{s}{\sqrt{n}} = \dfrac{3162}{\sqrt{1000}} = 100$ miles

## STEP 5:    Compute Test Statistic and Choose between the Null and Alternative Hypotheses

For the specific sample, the sample mean tire life ($\bar{x}_{1000}$) was 47,300 miles. Thus, you may be thinking that the project manager should *automatically* reject the null hypothesis. It is true that $\bar{x}_{1000}$ is greater than 47,000 miles.

However, she cannot even consider saying that the mean tread life for *all* Milemaster tires will be greater than 47,000 miles ($\mu_{\text{tread life}} > 47,000$) until completing this step. And even if she does conclude that the population mean is greater than 47,000 miles, she will not be able to say this with 100% certainty!

The sample results are based on only 1000 tires. So she must ask: "Does a *sample* mean of 47,300 miles favor the alternative hypothesis that $\mu_{\text{tread life}} > 47,000$ miles or the null hypothesis, $\mu_{\text{tread life}} \leq 47,000$ miles?"

To *possibly* reject the null hypothesis, the sample mean must be greater than 47,000 miles.[1] To reject the null hypothesis, the sample mean mileage must be *significantly greater than* 47,000 miles. The sample mean is 300 miles greater than the population mean of 47,000 miles based on the null hypothesis.

$$\text{difference} = 47,300 - 47,000 = 300 \text{ miles}$$

To determine if a 300-mile difference is *significant*, we compare it to the study's estimated standard error of 100 miles, $3162 / \sqrt{1000}$ .

What accounts for the size of the estimated standard error? It is due to **extraneous factors** present in the study that affect tire mileage. These include car-to-car differences, day-to-day differences, unintended variations in the car track surface throughout the study, variation in tire air pressure, and so forth. All these extraneous factors (above and beyond the tire itself) affect tire mileage.

**DEFINITION**     **Extraneous factors** are factors that the project manager does not (or cannot) control in a study. These factors can, however, impact the variable of interest.

Since it is impossible to hold all extraneous factors constant within a study, the 1000 tread mileage data values varied. Their net impact results in the estimated standard error of 100 miles, $3162 / \sqrt{1000}$ .

To test the null hypothesis, compute the following **test statistic**.

$$\frac{\text{Sample mean} - \text{Population mean (H}_0)}{\text{Estimated standard error}}$$

**(6.1)**

---

[1] If the *sample* mean were less than 47,000 miles, the project manager need not complete step #5. She cannot reject the null hypothesis.

The test statistic measures the impact of the engineering group's claim (the numerator) versus the impact of all extraneous factors (the denominator) on tread mileage. The test statistic for the Milemaster study is +3.00.

$$\textbf{Test Statistic} = \frac{47,300 - 47,000}{100} = +3.00$$

From Figure 6.1, the "weight" of the engineering group's claim is 300 miles. The "weight" of the impact of extraneous factors on tread mileage is only 100 miles. All the extraneous factors account only for a variation in tread life of 100 miles, so the impact of the new tire was three times larger. Thus, the scale seems to favor the engineering group's claim that the population mean tread life is greater than 47,000 miles—the alternative hypothesis.

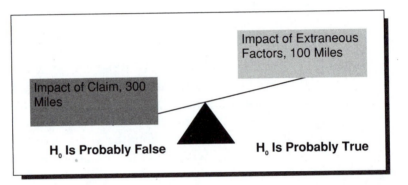

**Figure 6.1**
The Impact of the Claim versus Variation due to Extraneous Factors

Is a test statistic of +3.00 sufficient evidence to reject the null hypothesis *at an α level of .01?* That means that if the project manager rejects the null hypothesis, there is *at most* a .01, or 1%, probability of making a Type I error. In summary, she must compute the probability of obtaining a test statistic of +3.00 *or greater.*

Because the sample size in the study is 30 or greater, use Excel's NORMSDIST function wizard to determine the probability of obtaining a test statistic of +3.00 or greater.[2] The NORMSDIST function wizard requires one input, the value of the test statistic.

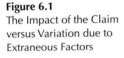

Probability that test statistic is **less than** +3.00.

---

[2]If the sample size is less than 30 as in the third case presented shortly, use the TDIST function wizard to evaluate the null hypothesis.

The value from NORMSDIST tells us that if the null hypothesis were true, the probability of obtaining a test statistic *of less than* +3.00 is 0.99865. So the probability of getting a test statistic of *+3.00 or greater* is $1 - 0.99865 = 0.00135$.

The *computed p-value* for the study is 0.00135. The computed $p$-value is the probability that the null hypothesis is true given the study's data. Given a sample mean of 47,300 miles and an estimated standard error of 100 miles, the probability that the null hypothesis is true is only .00135 or 135 in 100,000—a very low probability.

Is the computed $p$-value sufficiently small to reject the null hypothesis? You evaluate the null hypothesis using one of the following three decision rules.

**Rule I for an Upper Tail Test,**          $H_0: \mu \leq k$
                                             $H_1: \mu > k$

Reject the null hypothesis and accept the alternative hypothesis if the
        $p$-value $= 1 -$ NORMSDIST(test statistic)
is less than or equal to the significance level, $\alpha$, set in Step 3. Otherwise do not reject the null hypothesis.

**Rule II for a Lower Tail Test,**          $H_0: \mu \geq k$
                                            $H_1: \mu < k$

Reject the null hypothesis and accept the alternative hypothesis if the
        $p$-value $=$ NORMSDIST(test statistic)
is less than or equal to the significance level, $\alpha$, set in Step 3. Otherwise do not reject the null hypothesis.

**Rule III for a Two-Tail Test,**          $H_0: \mu = k$
                                           $H_1: \mu \neq k$

Reject the null hypothesis and accept the alternative hypothesis
a. For a test statistic less than zero if
        $p$-value $= 2 \cdot$ NORMSDIST(test statistic)
is less than or equal to the significance level, $\alpha$, set in Step 3. Otherwise do not reject the null hypothesis.

b. For a test statistic greater than zero if
        $p$-value $= 2 \cdot [1 -$ NORMSDIST(test statistic)]
is less than or equal to the significance level, $\alpha$, set in Step 3. Otherwise do not reject the null hypothesis.

From Rule 1, because the computed $p$-value of .00135 is less than $\alpha = .0100$, the project manager should reject the null hypothesis and accept the alternative hypothesis—the engineering group's claim. She should market the Milemaster tire.

## Decision-Making Consequences

See Table 6.2. Having rejected the null hypothesis, the project manager has either made a Type I error (probability = .00135) or a correct decision (probability = 1 − .00135 = .99865). The project manager can be 99.865% confident she has made a correct decision. Alternatively, the odds of having made a correct decision are .99865 / .00135 ≈ 740:1 . Not bad odds!

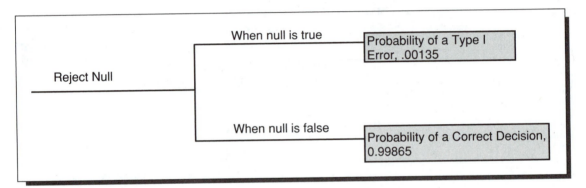

**Figure 6.2**
Consequences of Rejecting a Null Hypothesis

The $p$-value and $\alpha$ significance level are different. The decision maker *sets* the $\alpha$ level using the three principles from Step #3 *before* collecting the data. The decision maker *computes* the $p$-value (from the NORMSDIST function wizard) based on the sample data *after* completing the study. The $\alpha$ level is the *maximum* probability of making a Type I error that a decision maker can accept. The $p$-value is the *actual* probability of making a Type I error.

**D E F I N I T I O N**    The $p$-value is the probability that the null hypothesis is true based on the sample data. You can only determine it after computing the sample mean, estimated standard error, and test statistic.

Figure 6.3 displays the $p$-value graphically for the Milemaster study.

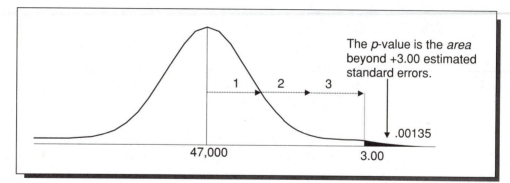

**Figure 6.3**
The *p*-Value as Area under the Distribution of the Sample Mean Assuming the Null Hypothesis Is True—$\mu$ is at most 47,000 miles

In summary, reject the null hypothesis if the *p*-value is less than or equal to $\alpha$, the significance level. Do not reject the null hypothesis if the *p*-value is greater than the significance level.

If the study's computed *p*-value had been 0.22, the project manager would not have rejected the null hypothesis. Why? Because there would have been a 22% chance that the null hypothesis is true. If she rejected the null hypothesis there would have been a 22% chance that she had just committed a Type I error, rejecting the null when the null is true. But in Step 3 the project manager set the maximum chance of making a Type I error at only 1%—the significance level. So she could not reject the null hypothesis.

One final note: Given that the project manager has rejected the null hypothesis and will market the tire, what is the probability of having made a Type II error? Think about it before reading on.

The probability of making a Type II error is now zero because the project manager rejected the null hypothesis. To *possibly* make a Type II error, the decision maker must fail to reject the null hypothesis.

**EXAMPLE**

**2   Times Interest Earned Ratio Claim.** Over the past several years, the TIE ratio for the metal fabrication industry has been 5.7 times. A research group claims that the ratio is no longer 5.7 times. The controller for Metalfabx, Inc., wishes to assess the research group's claim. She selects a random sample of 40 publicly traded firms within the industry and computes their TIE ratio data.

For the TIE study, the research group claims that the population mean TIE ratio, $\mu_{TIE}$, has *changed* from 5.7 times. Thus, in words, the decision maker's null hypothesis is the opposite of that claim. Here are the null and alternative hypotheses for the times interest earned ratio study.

| STEP 1: | State Hypotheses |

$H_0$: The population mean TIE ratio has *not changed* from 5.7 times.
$H_0: \mu_{TIE} = 5.7$ times

$H_1$: The population mean TIE ratio has *changed* from 5.7 times.
$H_1: \mu_{TIE} = 5.7$ times

This is a **two-sided** (or **two-tail**) test. Use it to test someone else's claim that a population mean is not equal to some value of $k$, say $k = 5.7$.

| STEP 2: | Determine the Consequences of the Decision-Making Errors |

Next we determine the Type I and Type II errors.

Type I Error:    **Reject the null hypothesis when the null hypothesis is true.**

Conclude that the population mean TIE ratio has changed from 5.7 times when it has not.

Type II Error:    **Do not reject the null hypothesis when the null is false.**

Conclude that the mean population TIE ratio is still 5.7 times when it is not.

| STEP 3: | Set a Significance Level and Determine the Sample Size |

In this example, no decision needs to be made. The controller simply wants to evaluate the claim made by the research group. It will provide insight whether major rating agencies in the future might change bond ratings within the industry. Hence, it is difficult to assess costs associated with the Type I error and the most likely Type II error. When assessing costs is difficult, consider setting the significance level at 0.05, a standard for many business and governmental applications. Consequently, the controller set the significance level, $\alpha$, at 0.05.

| STEP 4: | Conduct Study or Survey |

Here are the study's data:

| | |
|---|---|
| Sample mean | $\bar{x}_{40} = 5.99$ times |
| Sample standard deviation | $s_{40} = 0.75$ times |
| Sample size | $n = 40$ firms |
| Estimated standard error | $\dfrac{0.75}{\sqrt{40}} = 0.1186$ times |

### STEP 5: Compute Test Statistic and Choose between the Null and Alternative Hypotheses

To *possibly* reject the null hypothesis, the sample mean must be different from 5.70. To reject the null hypothesis, the sample mean must be *significantly different from* 5.70. The sample mean is 0.29 more than the population mean of 5.70 based on the null hypothesis.

$$\text{difference} = 5.99 - 5.70 = 0.29$$

To determine if a 0.29 difference is *significant,* we compare it to the study's estimated standard error of 0.1186.

From Expression (6.1), the test statistic for the TIE study is +2.44.

$$\text{Test Statistic} = \frac{5.99 - 5.70}{0.1186} = +2.44$$

Figure 6.4 displays the impact of the research group's claim versus the impact of extraneous factors on the TIE data. Figure 6.4 suggests that the controller should reject the null hypothesis.

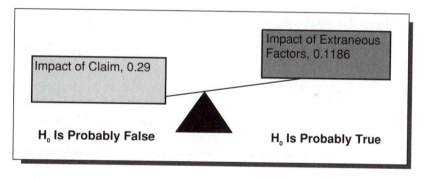

**Figure 6.4**
The Impact of the Claim versus Variation due to Extraneous Factors

Is a test statistic of +2.44 sufficient evidence to reject the null hypothesis *at an α level of .05?* That means if the controller rejects the null hypothesis, there is *at most* a .05, or 5%, probability of being wrong.

Use Rule IIIb from page 217 reproduced below to test the null hypothesis. As the test statistic is positive (+2.44), the decision rule is:

Reject the null hypothesis if
 *p*-value = 2·[1 − NORMSDIST(test statistic)]
is less than or equal to the significance level, α, set in Step 3. Otherwise do not reject the null hypothesis.

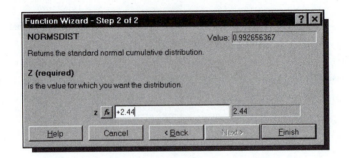

The *p*-value equals $2 \cdot (1 - 0.99266) = 2 \cdot (.00734) = .01468$. The *p*-value is the probability that the null hypothesis is true given the sample data. Given a sample mean of 5.99 times and an estimated standard error of 0.1186 times, the probability that the null hypothesis is true is only 0.01468.

Since the computed *p*-value of 0.01468 is less than $\alpha = .05$, the controller should reject the null hypothesis. The mean TIE ratio for the industry has *changed* from the historical level of 5.70 times.

Figure 6.5 displays the *p*-value graphically for the TIE ratio study.

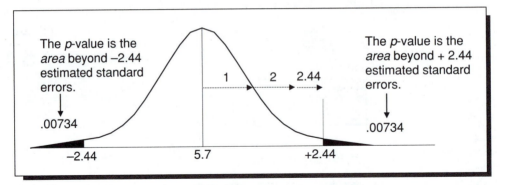

**Figure 6.5**
The *p*-Value as Area under the Distribution of the Sample Mean Assuming the Null Hypothesis Is True—$\mu$ equals 5.7 times

Note one difference in the *p*-value for a two-tailed test. The *p*-value is the sum of *two* areas under the curve. The *p*-value equals the area below −2.44 estimated standard errors (probability = 0.00734) and the area above +2.44 estimated standard errors (probability = 0.00734). The total area is thus 0.01468.

Having rejected the null hypothesis, the project manager has either made a Type I error (probability = .01468) or a correct decision (probability = $1 - .01468 = .98532$). The odds of having made a correct decision are $\left(.98532 / .01468\right) \approx 67:1$.

You can conduct hypothesis testing under the following two conditions:

**1.** You select a random sample from the population.

**2.** You must select a sample (1) from a population that is normally distributed or (2) that is sufficiently large to invoke the Central Limit Theorem.

To this point, the sample sizes have been greater than 30. Thus, by the Central Limit Theorem, the distribution of the sample mean was near normal and you could use the NORMSDIST wizard to compute *p*-values.

## SMALL SAMPLE HYPOTHESIS TESTING

When the sample size is less than 30, the distribution of the sample mean may not be normal. Then we must determine if the population is normal. As in Chapter 5, apply Excel's KURT and SKEW function wizards to the data set. The population is reasonably normal if the following conditions are both met. If so, do hypothesis testing.

**1.** $-1 < \text{KURT} < +1$

**2.** $-1 < \text{SKEW} < +1$

If the SKEW and KURT values are not both between $-1$ and $+1$, you have two choices. You can increase the sample size beyond 30 or you can transform the data by using either a square root or logarithmic base 10 transformation. Please review Confidence Intervals on an Unknown Population Mean in Chapter 5, pages 177–178, for a discussion of transformations. You can then perform hypothesis testing on the normalized data.

▶ **WARNING** For sample sizes less than 30, you cannot use the NORMSDIST wizard to compute the *p*-value. As in Chapter 5, you must use the *t*-distribution. However, you still apply the five-step hypothesis testing method. We illustrate small sample hypothesis testing next.

---

**EXAMPLE**     **3   Reducing Postpurchase Doubt.** A marketing manager wishes to reduce the consumers' levels of postpurchase doubt for his product. Marketers can reduce postpurchase doubt through advertising. An advertising team claims its new ad will reduce the population mean level of consumer postpurchase doubt for the QW4 sports car below its present level of 20 on a 1 to 100 scale. The director of marketing is not convinced. He conducts a market research study to evaluate the advertising team's claim.

Let's apply the five-step hypothesis testing approach to evaluate the advertising team's claim and to decide whether or not to implement the new ad *nationwide*.

### STEP 1:    State Hypotheses and Managerial Actions

The advertising team claims that the population mean doubt level, $\mu_{\text{doubt}}$, will be less than 20 on a 1 to 100 scale. Thus, the decision maker's null hypothesis is the opposite of that claim; namely,

$$H_0: \mu_{\text{doubt}} \geq 20$$

Because the null and alternative hypotheses must be mutually exclusive and exhaustive, we can write the alternative hypothesis as

$$H_1: \mu_{\text{doubt}} < 20$$

| Hypotheses | Managerial Actions |
|---|---|
| $H_0: \mu_{\text{doubt}} \geq 20$ | Failure to reject the null hypothesis means the firm *will not* implement the new ad nationwide. |
| $H_1: \mu_{\text{doubt}} < 20$ | Rejecting the null hypothesis means the firm *will* implement the new ad nationwide. |

This is a **one-sided, lower-tail** (or **one-tail**) test. Use it to test someone else's claim that a population mean is less than the value of $k$; say, $k = 20$ on the 1 to 100 doubt measurement scale.

### STEP 2:    Determine the Consequences of the Decision–Making Errors

Below are the formal definitions of the two errors and their translations into the study.

| | |
|---|---|
| Type I Error: | **Reject the null hypothesis when the null hypothesis is true.** |
| Translation of Type I Error | "Reject the null" means that the manager believes the alternative is true. He will implement the new ad nationwide because he thinks that the population mean doubt level is less than 20—an improvement over previous ads. |

"Null is true" means the population mean doubt level is truly greater than or equal to 20. The manager should not implement the ad nationwide.

| | |
|---|---|
| Description of Type I Error | **The firm implements the ad nationwide when it should not have.** |
| Type II Error: | **Do not reject the null hypothesis when the null is false.** |
| Translation of Type II Error | "Do not reject the null" means that the manager does not implement the ad nationwide because he thinks the population mean doubt level is 20 or higher. |
| | "Null is false" means the population mean doubt level really is less than 20. He should have implemented the ad nationwide. |
| Description of Type II Error | **The manager does not implement the ad nationwide when he should have. This is a lost marketing opportunity.** |

**STEP 3:**  **Set a Significance Level and Determine the Sample Size**

Using the three principles presented earlier, the manager sets the significance level, $\alpha$, at 0.10. This is the maximum probability of making a Type I error that the manager can accept. He sets the sample size at 25 customers.

**STEP 4:**  **Conduct Study or Survey**

Here are the study's sample statistics:

| | |
|---|---|
| Sample mean | $\bar{x}_{25} = 19.6$ |
| Sample standard deviation | $s_{25} = 2.50$ |
| Sample size | $n = 25$ customers |
| Estimated standard error | $\dfrac{s}{\sqrt{n}} = \dfrac{2.50}{\sqrt{25}} = 0.50$ |

Because the sample size was under 30, the manager also computed the data's skewness and kurtosis. Both descriptive measures were between −1 and +1. Thus, the population is reasonably bell shaped, and the manager can proceed with hypothesis testing.

> **STEP 5:** **Compute Test Statistic and Choose between the Null and Alternative Hypotheses**

The sample results are based on only 25 customers. So the director of marketing must ask: "Does a *sample* mean of 19.6 favor the alternative hypothesis that $\mu_{doubt} < 20$ or the null hypothesis, $\mu_{doubt} \geq 20$?"

To *possibly* reject the null hypothesis, the sample mean must be less than 20.[3] To reject the null hypothesis, the sample mean must be *significantly less than* 20. The sample mean is 0.40 less than the population mean of 20 based on the null hypothesis.

$$\text{difference} = 19.6 - 20 = -0.40$$

To determine if a 0.40 difference is *significant*, we compare it to the study's estimated standard error of 0.50.

From Expression (6.1), the test statistic for the study is −0.80.

$$\text{Test Statistic} = \frac{19.6 - 20}{0.50} = -0.80$$

Figure 6.6 displays the impact of the advertising team's claim versus the impact of extraneous factors on doubt level. Figure 6.6 suggests that the director of marketing should not reject the null hypothesis.

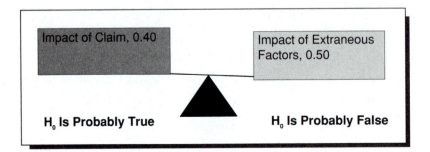

**Figure 6.6**
The Impact of the Claim versus Variation due to Extraneous Factors

Is a test statistic of −0.80 sufficient evidence to reject the null hypothesis *at an* $\alpha$ *level of .10?* That means if the manager rejects the null hypothesis, there is *at most* a .10, or 10%, probability of being wrong.

---

[3]If the sample mean were greater than 20 the project manager need not complete step #5. He cannot reject the null hypothesis.

Because the sample size is less than 30, use Excel's TDIST function wizard to determine if the test statistic of –0.80 is sufficient evidence to reject the null hypothesis. The function wizard requires three inputs:

1. value of the test statistic $0.80$[4] labeled $x$

2. degrees of freedom which is $25 - 1 = 24$

3. number of tails. Since this is a one-sided lower-tail alternative hypothesis, the number of tails equals 1.

```
┌─ TDIST ──────────────────────────────────────────────────┐
│              X │.8                            │ = 0.8     │
│   Deg_freedom │24                            │ = 24      │
│         Tails │1                             │ = 1       │
│                                                           │
│                                         = 0.215779273     │
│  Returns the Student's t-distribution.                    │
│                                                           │
│        Tails specifies the number of distribution tails to return: one-tailed distribution │
│               = 1; two-tailed distribution = 2.           │
│                                                           │
│   ?   Formula result =0.215779273        [ OK ]  [ Cancel ]│
└──────────────────────────────────────────────────────────┘
```

The TDIST wizard returns the **p-value**. The p-value is the probability that the null hypothesis is true given the study's data. Given a sample mean of 19.6 and an estimated standard error of 0.50, the probability that the null hypothesis is true is 0.2158, or approximately 22%.

Is the computed p-value sufficiently small to reject the null hypothesis? You evaluate the null hypothesis using one of the following three decision rules.

**Rule I for an Upper–Tail Test,**          $H_0: \mu \le k$

$H_1: \mu > k$

Reject the null hypothesis and accept the
alternative hypothesis if the
    p-value = TDIST(test statistic, df, 1)
is less than or equal to the significance level, $\alpha$,
set in Step 3. Otherwise do not reject the null
hypothesis.

---

[4] You must take the absolute value, ABS, of the test statistic. The TDIST wizard will not accept a negative test statistic value.

**Rule II for a Lower-Tail Test,**     $H_0$: $\mu \geq k$

$H_1$: $\mu < k$

Reject the null hypothesis and accept the alternative hypothesis if the

$p$-value = TDIST(ABS[test statistic], df, 1)

is less than or equal to the significance level, $\alpha$, set in Step 3. Otherwise do not reject the null hypothesis.

**Rule III for a Two-Tail Test,**     $H_0$: $\mu = k$

$H_1$: $\mu \neq k$

Reject the null hypothesis and accept the alternative hypothesis if

$p$-value = 2· TDIST(test statistic, df, 2)

is less than or equal to the significance level, $\alpha$, set in Step 3. Otherwise do not reject the null hypothesis.

From Rule 2, since the computed $p$-value of 0.2158 is greater than $\alpha$ = .10, the manager should not reject the null hypothesis. He should *not* implement the ad nationwide.

Although the sample mean was less than 20, it was *not* significantly less than 20 (for $\alpha$ = 0.10). If the marketing manager had rejected the null, there would have been a 22% chance of making a Type I error, (see Figure 6.7). But from Step 3, he said he could only accept a 10% maximum probability of making a Type I error. That is why he failed to reject the null hypothesis! Having failed to reject the null hypothesis, the manager has either made a Type II error or a correct decision.

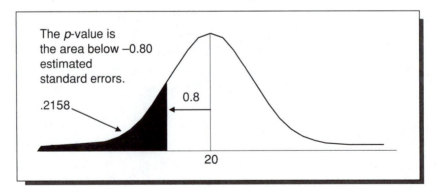

**Figure 6.7**
The *p*-Value as Area under the Distribution of the Sample Mean Assuming the Null Hypothesis Is True—
$\mu \geq 20$

# HYPOTHESIS TESTING ON ONE POPULATION PROPORTION

We have been dealing with *quantitative* (ratio–scale) data up to this point. This section focuses on *yes or no qualitative* (or *proportion*) data. Typical yes or no questions include

1. Is this customer a member of a particular market segment?

2. Did a printed circuit board have one or more failed soldered connections?

3. Does your firm offer a flexible medical spending account?

In Chapter 2, you learned to organize and summarize proportion data, a number between 0 and 1. In Chapter 4 you learned the distribution of the sample proportion. In Chapter 5 you constructed one- or two-sided confidence intervals on an unknown population proportion. By the end of this section you should be able to use the five-step hypothesis-testing framework to test a claim about an unknown and unknowable population proportion.

There is only one difference between this section and the previous one. Earlier, you tested claims about an unknown population mean, $\mu$. In this section, you will test claims about an unknown population proportion, $p$.

---

**EXAMPLE**

4  **RBC Marketing Mix Decision.** A product manager at RBC seeks to increase the proportion of customers in its "fitness-conscious" market segment. The segment presently contains 8% (.08) of the market. A marketing team claims that its new marketing mix will increase the proportion of RBC customers in this segment.

After implementing the mix in Denver, the Director conducts a survey to determine the proportion of RBC customers who are in the fitness-conscious market segment.

**STEP 1:**  **State Hypotheses and Managerial Actions**

For the RBC marketing mix study, the marketing team claims that the population **proportion**, $p_{\text{fitness}}$, will be greater than 0.08. Thus, the decision maker's null hypothesis is the opposite of that claim, namely

$$H_0: p_{\text{fitness}} \leq .08$$

| Hypotheses | Managerial Actions |
|---|---|
| $H_0: p_{fitness} \leq .08$ | Failure to reject the null hypothesis means the firm *will not* implement the new marketing mix nationwide. |
| $H_1: p_{fitness} > .08$ | Rejecting the null hypothesis means the firm *will* implement the new marketing mix nationwide. |

This is a **one-sided, upper-tail** (or **one-tail**) test. Use it to test someone else's claim that a population proportion is greater than the value of $k$, say $k = 0.08$.

---

**STEP 2:**    **Determine the Consequences of the Decision-Making Errors**

Below are the formal definitions of the two errors and their translations into the RBC marketing mix study setting.

| | |
|---|---|
| Type I Error: | **Reject the null hypothesis when the null hypothesis is true.** |
| Translation of Type I Error | "Reject the null" means that the manager believes the alternative is true. He will implement the new marketing mix nationwide because he thinks that the *population proportion* of fitness-conscious consumers is greater than 0.08.

"Null is true" means the *population proportion* of fitness-conscious consumers is really less than or equal to 0.08. The manager should not implement the mix nationwide. |
| Description of Type I Error | **The firm implements the mix nationwide when it should not have.** |
| Type II Error: | **Do not reject the null hypothesis when the null is false.** |
| Translation of Type II Error | "Do not reject the null" means that the manager does not implement the marketing mix nationwide because he thinks the *population proportion* of fitness-conscious customers is less than or equal to 0.08.

"Null is false" means the *population proportion* really is greater than 0.08. He should have implemented the marketing mix nationwide. |
| Description of Type II Error | **The manager does not implement the mix nationwide when he should have. This is a lost marketing opportunity.** |

**STEP 3:**  **Set a Significance Level and Determine the Sample Size**

Using the three principles presented earlier, the manager sets the significance level, $\alpha$, at 0.025. This is the maximum probability of making a Type I error that the manager can accept. He selects a sample size of 500.

**STEP 4:**  **Conduct Study or Survey**

Here are the study's sample statistics:

$$n = 500 \text{ RBC customers}$$

$$n_{yes} = 55 \text{ fitness-conscious customers}$$

$$\text{Sample proportion} \quad \hat{p} = \frac{55}{500} = .11$$

**STEP 5:**  **Compute Test Statistic and Choose between the Null and Alternative Hypotheses**

The sample results are based on only 500 customers. So the marketing manager must ask: "Does a *sample* proportion of 0.11 favor the alternative hypothesis that $p_{fitness} > 0.08$ or the null hypothesis, $p_{fitness} \leq 0.08$?"

To *possibly* reject the null hypothesis, the sample proportion must be greater than 0.08. To reject the null hypothesis, the sample proportion of fitness-conscious customers must be *significantly greater* than 0.08. The sample proportion is 0.03 greater than the population proportion of 0.08 based on the null hypothesis.

$$\text{difference} = 0.11 - 0.08 = 0.03$$

To determine if a 0.03 difference is *significant,* we compare it to the study's standard error.

We use Expression (6.2) shown below to compute the standard error. Expression (6.2) uses the hypothesized value of the population proportion. We label it $p_0$. For this study $p_0 = 0.08$. Remember, we assume that the null hypothesis is true until proven otherwise. In short, the hypothesized standard error is

$$\boxed{\sqrt{\frac{p_0 q_0}{n}}}$$

$$\text{(6.2)}$$

The hypothesized standard error for the study is

$$\sqrt{\frac{0.08 \cdot 0.92}{500}} = 0.01213$$

$$\text{Test Statistic} = \frac{0.11 - 0.08}{0.01213} = +2.473$$

Figure 6.8 displays the impact of the advertising team's claim versus the impact of extraneous factors. Figure 6.8 suggests that you should reject the null hypothesis.

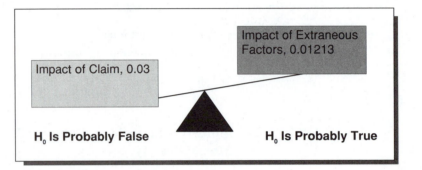

**Figure 6.8**
The Impact of the Claim versus Variation due to Extraneous Factors

Is a test statistic of +2.473 sufficient evidence to reject the null hypothesis *at an α level of .025*? That means if the manager rejects the null hypothesis, there is *at most* a .025, or 2.5%, probability of being wrong.

Use Excel's NORMSDIST function wizard to determine if a test statistic of +2.473 is sufficient evidence to reject the null hypothesis. The function wizard requires one input, the test statistic value.

Use Rule I reproduced below to test the null hypothesis:

> Reject the null hypothesis and accept the alternative hypothesis if the
>     $p$-value = 1 − NORMSDIST(test statistic)
> is less than or equal to the significance level, $\alpha$, set in Step 3. Otherwise do not reject the null hypothesis.

```
NORMSDIST
        z  +2.473                            = 2.473

                                     = 0.993300784
Returns the standard normal cumulative distribution (has a mean of zero and a standard
deviation of one).
        Z is the value for which you want the distribution.

   ?     Formula result = 0.993300784        OK        Cancel
```

Since the computed $p$-value = 1 − 0.9933 = .0067 is less than $\alpha$ = .0250, the director of marketing should reject the null hypothesis and accept the alternative hypothesis—the marketing group's claim. He should implement the marketing mix to increase the fitness-conscious market segment nationwide.

Having rejected the null hypothesis, the director of marketing has either made a Type I error (probability $= .0067$) or a correct decision (probability $= 1 - .0067 = .9933$). The odds of having made a correct decision are $\frac{.9933}{.0067} \approx 148{:}1$. Having rejected the null hypothesis, the probability of a Type II error is zero.

# KEY IDEAS AND SUMMARY

This chapter has presented the five-step hypothesis-testing framework for assessing claims about an unknown and unknowable *population mean* or *population proportion*.

Hypothesis testing and confidence intervals are two different methods that accomplish similar purposes. Both are important methods in your statistical arsenal of tools. Table 6.3 compares and contrasts these two statistical inference methods used to draw conclusions about an unknown and unknowable population parameter from sample data.

**Table 6.3**

Compare and Contrast Table for Confidence Intervals and Hypothesis Testing

| Bases for Comparison | Confidence Intervals | Hypothesis Testing |
|---|---|---|
| Draw Conclusions about Population Parameter from Sample Data? | Yes | Yes |
| Tests Claims? | Can Be Used | Should Be Used |
| Can Population Parameter Be Known with Certainty? | No | No |
| Two Errors Considered? | No | Yes |
| Level of Confidence/ Significance Level Connection? | 95% | $100(1 - \alpha = .05)\%$ $\alpha$ is the significance level |

# EXERCISES

1. What are the advantages of hypothesis testing over the confidence interval method?

2. What, if anything, is wrong with the following hypotheses?

$$H_0{:}\ \bar{x} > 4.5$$
$$H_1{:}\ \bar{x} < 4.5$$

3. Why is it possible to make either a Type I or Type II error before a study, but only one type of error after the study?

4. In nontechnical language, describe what the numerator and denominator of the test statistic measure.

5. What information does the *p*-value provide?

**6.** Suppose $H_1 : \mu > 30$ minutes and the computed sample mean is 35 minutes. Why is it necessary to do hypothesis testing before rejecting the null in favor of the alternative hypothesis? After all, a sample mean of 35 minutes is greater than 30 minutes.

**7.** Given the following hypotheses, describe your subordinate's claim about the proportion defective in a process.

$$H_0: p \ge .01$$
$$H_1: p < .01$$

**8.** How do the *p*-value and significance level differ?

**9.** Historically, the population mean age of accounts payable has been 22 days. For the past six months the firm has tried several ways to reduce the age of accounts payable. The accounting team now believes that it has been successful.

   **a.** Set up the appropriate null and alternative hypotheses.

   **b.** In the problem context, what are the Type I and Type II errors?

   The accounting supervisor selects a simple random sample of 225 accounts payable. The sample mean age is 20.5 days and the sample standard deviation is 7.5 days.

   **c.** Given an $\alpha$ of .05, evaluate the accounting team's claim.

**10.** A firm is presently using *family branding* on a consumer product and selling about 1750 cartons per week in the southeast United States. The marketing group believes that using *individual branding* will increase sales substantially. It convinces management to try individual branding in one test market for six months. Assume you must make the final decision as to whether to use individual branding nationwide.

   **a.** Set up the appropriate null and alternative hypotheses.

   **b.** In the problem context, what are the Type I and Type II errors?

   After the test period the firm selects a random sample of 400 and finds that these stores have sold a mean of 1760 cartons per week; the sample standard deviation is 200 cartons per week.

   **c.** Given an $\alpha$ level of 0.10, evaluate the marketing team's claim.

   **d.** Is it now possible to make a Type II error? Explain.

**11.** Industrial psychologists believe that stress is curvilinearly related to performance; that is, too little stress produces no drive to excel. Too much stress causes anxiety that reduces performance. Over the past several years, a firm worked to optimize the level of stress within a plant. At the beginning of the period, the level of stress was at 5 (on a scale of 1 to 10)—the optimal level. However, in the past nine months several things have happened that may have caused a change in the stress level.

   **a.** Set up the appropriate null and alternative hypotheses.

   **b.** In the problem context, what are the Type I and Type II errors?

   The firm's psychologist selects a simple random sample of 50 workers from the 1000 employees and administers a stress test. The mean level of stress is 5.35 with a sample variance of 0.79.

   **c.** Given an $\alpha$ of .01, what can the psychologist conclude? Should the null hypothesis be rejected?

12. Just-in-time (JIT) inventory means that subassemblies arrive at the plant as they are needed in the production process. JIT almost eliminates the need for inventorying subassemblies. In the past, parts have been delivered late only 2% of the time at Metfabx. Due to personnel changes at the vendor, the operations manager believes that the percentage of late deliveries has recently increased. He does not want to talk to the vendor until he has more evidence.

   a. Set up the null and alternative hypotheses and the associated managerial actions.

   b. Describe the Type I and Type II errors and their associated costs.

   c. Of the next 100 deliveries five are late. At the .05 significance level, evaluate the manager's claim. What action should he take now?

13. The comptroller wants to know how his firm compares with the industry mean on the fixed-asset utilization ratio. This ratio is sales divided by net fixed assets and indicates how effective a firm is in using its fixed assets. If his firm's ratio is low compared to the industry's, he will probably be denied funds for new capital investment in the next planning cycle. The comptroller believes that the industry mean exceeds 3.0. The claim must be evaluated.

   a. Set up the null and alternative hypotheses and managerial actions.

   b. Describe the Type I and Type II errors and their associated costs.

   The comptroller selects 30 publicly traded firms at random and obtains the following data.

$$\bar{x}_{30} = 3.12 \text{ times}$$
$$s_{30} = 1.56 \text{ times}$$
$$n = 30$$

   c. At $\alpha = .01$, evaluate the comptroller's claim. What can you conclude?

14. An economist claims that the proportion of consumers with a favorable attitude toward the economy's growth is at least 0.65. She selects a random sample of 1500 consumers and finds that 1020 have a favorable attitude. At a significance level of .05, evaluate the economist's claim.

15. Over the past year, 95% of the guests at the Hilmark Hotel have indicated they are satisfied with their stay and service. The executive director wants to increase the percentage of satisfied customers. Based upon guest feedback surveys, he has increased the number of nonsmoking rooms, reduced delays at check-in, and offered low-fat entree alternatives in the restaurant. He believes these extra services have increased the percentage of satisfied customers. Based on a random sample of 2000 recent guests, 1960 indicated they are satisfied with their stay. Let $\alpha = .05$. Evaluate the director's claim.

16. The engineering manager in the St. Louis division believes that recent improvements in the department's procedures have reduced the mean time to make engineering blueprint changes from its historical level of 6.40 hours. Let $\alpha = .05$.

   a. Set up the appropriate null and alternative hypotheses and associated managerial actions.

   b. In the problem context, what are the Type I and Type II errors?

After implementing the changes, he records the amount of time to make changes in 50 randomly selected blueprints. The following sample data are collected.

$$\bar{x}_{50} = 6.70 \text{ hours}$$
$$s_{50} = 2.56 \text{ hours}$$
$$n = 50$$

Even without doing Step #5 of hypothesis testing, the supervisor already knows the improvements have not reduced the population mean time to make blueprint changes. Why?

17. The engineering manager in the St. Louis division believes that recent improvements in the department's procedures have reduced the mean time to make engineering blueprints changes from its historical level of 6.40 hours. Let $\alpha = .05$.

    a. Set up the appropriate null and alternative hypotheses and associated managerial actions.

    b. In the problem context, what are the Type I and Type II errors?

    After implementing the changes, she records the amount of time to make changes in 50 randomly selected blueprints. The following sample data are collected:

    $$\bar{x}_{50} = 6.30 \text{ hours}$$
    $$s_{50} = 2.56 \text{ hours}$$
    $$n = 50$$

    Evaluate the engineering manager's claim.

18. According to Philip Crosby, an expert in the quality field, an essential ingredient in a total quality management program is internal communications. The director of

quality in a firm believes he has taken action to improve internal communications. Historically, the average communication score was 70 on a 0 to 100 point-scale instrument. The director randomly selects 16 workers and asks them to rate the internal communication within the firm. Here are the sample data (assume the sample data are normally distributed):

$$\bar{x}_{16} = 74.5$$
$$s_{16} = 5.25$$
$$n = 16$$

Let $\alpha = .10$.

a. Set up the appropriate null and alternative hypotheses and the associated managerial actions.

b. In the problem context, what are the Type I and Type II errors?

c. Evaluate the director's claim. After rejecting the null hypothesis, what are the odds that the director has drawn a correct conclusion?

d. Why did you have to assume the population from which the sample was taken was near normally distributed?

19. A soft drink dispenser dispenses, on average, exactly 12.0 oz into a container. Recently customers have been complaining that either the drink overflows the container or does not fill the container. Is the soft drink dispenser no longer dispensing, on average, 12.0 oz? Let $\alpha = .01$.

a. Set up the appropriate null and alternative hypotheses.

b. In the problem context, what are the Type I and Type II errors?

The firm runs a test on the dispenser. Here are the sample data:

$$\bar{x}_{20} = 12.1 \text{ oz}$$
$$s_{20} = 4.2 \text{ oz}$$
$$n = 20 \text{ word disj}$$

**c.** Suppose the sample data were not normal; could you have used hypothesis testing on the above data? Explain.

**d.** Evaluate the customers' claim that the drink overflows the container or does not fill the container.

**e.** Is it possible to now make a Type II error?

**20.** Little Rock's division manager claims that a greater proportion of her employees (versus the firm as a whole) believe the policies are clear and unambiguous. According to a recent internal survey, the population proportion of all the firm's employees who believe the policies are clear and unambiguous is 0.82.

**a.** Set up the appropriate null and alternative hypotheses.

**b.** In the problem context, what are the Type I and Type II errors?

**c.** She selects a random sample of 100 people, and 91 respond the policies are clear and unambiguous. Let $\alpha = .01$. Evaluate the manager's claim.

**21.** A credit manager claims that the proportion of people filing for personal bankruptcy in the state has changed from the last published data available, namely, 0.08. He selects a random sample of 500 people and finds that 50 have filed for personal bankruptcy.

**a.** Set up the appropriate null and alternative hypotheses.

**b.** Evaluate the claim at a 5% significance level.

**22.** The tensile strength of an eyeglass temple (the part that fits around your ear) should be 4750 pounds per square inch (ppsi). The operations manager believes that the population mean tensile strength has changed over the past several hours. If true, he must make process adjustments.

**a.** Set up the appropriate null and alternative hypotheses.

**b.** In the problem context, what are the Type I and Type II errors?

He selects 20 random temples and determines the tensile strength. Here are the data:

$$\bar{x}_{20} = 4775 \text{ ppsi}$$
$$s_{20} = 100 \text{ ppsi}$$
$$n = 20$$
$$\text{Let } \alpha = .05$$

**c.** Evaluate the operations manager's claim. What action should the operations manager take?

**d.** Based upon part (c), is it possible to make a Type II error? Discuss.

**e.** What should the manager have done to ensure that he could properly apply hypothesis testing? Discuss.

**23.** First Bancorp has been attempting to reduce the amount of time needed to provide mortgage information to its customers. First Bancorp has implemented several programs to reduce the time to under ten minutes. Has it been successful? Here are the time-ordered data over a random sample of 21 recent customers. Let $\alpha = .025$.

| Customer | Time | Customer | Time |
|----------|------|----------|------|
| 1 | 8.50 | 12 | 8.70 |
| 2 | 8.70 | 13 | 8.10 |
| 3 | 9.40 | 14 | 9.30 |
| 4 | 9.35 | 15 | 8.20 |
| 5 | 8.50 | 16 | 8.80 |
| 6 | 8.75 | 17 | 7.95 |
| 7 | 8.20 | 18 | 8.90 |
| 8 | 8.60 | 19 | 9.15 |
| 9 | 7.90 | 20 | 8.30 |
| 10 | 9.30 | 21 | 8.75 |
| 11 | 8.55 | | |

**a.** Set up the appropriate null and alternative hypotheses.

**b.** In the problem context, what are the Type I and Type II errors?

**c.** Evaluate First Bancorp's claim that the mean processing time is now under 10 minutes. Is it necessary to assess if the data are near normally distributed? If so, do it.

**24.** Firms such as NameLab, Inc., develop and test brand names. For example, NameLab invented the COMPAQ personal computer brand name. Suppose NameLab has suggested CLIMTEC for a new day-hiking boot. It claims that over 65% of potential customers will like the new name. The boot manufacturer evaluates the new name. It asks 100 potential customers to react to the CLIMTEC brand name. Seventy-five customers report that they like the new name. Let $\alpha = .10$.

**a.** Set up the appropriate null and alternative hypotheses.

**b.** In the problem context, what are the Type I and Type II errors?

**c.** Evaluate NameLab's claim that over 65% of potential customers will like the new name.

**25.** An educational researcher claims a teacher's lecture and organization clarity is the most important factor in influencing how students do on a common final. Dr. X, the most organized teacher in the department, teaches a class of 30. Over the past several semesters, the average grade on the final exam for similar size classes taught at the same time of day has been 77. Here are Dr. X's results for the most recent 30 sections:

| | | |
|----|----|----|
| 83 | 86 | 83 |
| 80 | 81 | 85 |
| 79 | 86 | 77 |
| 80 | 82 | 80 |
| 88 | 87 | 76 |
| 84 | 91 | 85 |
| 84 | 79 | 77 |
| 80 | 81 | 81 |
| 86 | 79 | 81 |
| 81 | 86 | 83 |

Evaluate the educational researcher's claim at the .05 significance level.

**26.** Benchmarking is the continuous process of measuring products, processes, and services against companies recognized as industry leaders. Through benchmarking, firms learn from the best, copy or modify their practices, and implement these practices. The American Society for Quality Control (ASQC) believes that over 42% of the firms within the electronics industry are doing benchmarking. To test its claim, ASQC conducts a study and obtains the following data:

| | |
|----------------------------------|-----|
| Number of firms doing benchmarking | 113 |
| Sample size | 250 |

Let $\alpha = .05$. Evaluate the ASQC's claim.

**27.** The mean income for master plumbers in a city has been $850 per week. Recently several changes have occurred that cause the local union leader to believe that the mean income has changed (adjusted for inflation). She conducts a study to evaluate her claim.

**a.** Set up the appropriate null and alternative hypotheses.

**b.** In the problem context, what are the Type I and Type II errors?

Here are the sample data:

$$\bar{x}_{25} = \$845$$
$$s_{25} = \$25$$
$$n = 25$$

**c.** Evaluate the union leader's claim at a 15% significance level.

**d.** Under what conditions would a 15% significance level make sense?

**e.** Suppose the SKEW and KURT were both greater than one. What impact, if any, would this have on your analysis?

**28.** A marketing manager believes that magazine and newspaper coupons are effective in stimulating spending on a product. Without any coupons the mean weekly dollar amount of purchase of a product is $9.50.

**a.** Set up the appropriate null and alternative hypotheses.

**b.** In the problem context, what are the Type I and Type II errors?

Based on a sample of 30 customers who use coupons, the manager obtains the following data:

| | | |
|---|---|---|
| $10.49 | $10.43 | $ 9.50 |
| $ 9.66 | $ 9.39 | $10.04 |
| $ 9.51 | $10.63 | $11.01 |
| $ 9.20 | $ 9.53 | $ 9.78 |
| $10.10 | $ 9.66 | $ 9.77 |
| $ 9.87 | $ 9.62 | $ 9.83 |
| $10.03 | $10.52 | $10.87 |
| $10.38 | $ 9.92 | $ 9.78 |
| $10.50 | $10.29 | $10.39 |
| $10.63 | $10.04 | $ 9.41 |

**c.** Evaluate the marketing manager's claim at a .005 significance level.

**29.** Personnel in the operations department and research/development department have always had difficulty talking to one another. A senior manager believes that one reason is that operating group personnel are detail and fact oriented whereas research personnel are big-picture oriented. When the two groups get together, it sounds like the day workers at the Tower of Babel. The senior manager knows that 65% of the operating personnel are detail oriented. She claims that less than 65% of the research personnel are detail oriented. She gives the Myers-Briggs Type Indicator (MBTI) to a sample of 100 researchers. Fifty-five researchers are detail oriented as measured by the MBTI. Let $\alpha = .05$. Evaluate the senior manager's claim.

**30.** Most businesses experience seasonal and/or cyclical fluctuations. This requires temporary current assets. The manner in which permanent and temporary current assets are financed constitutes the firm's working capital financing policy. There are three financial policies: maturity matching, the aggressive approach, and the conservative approach. In the conservative approach permanent capital is used to finance all permanent asset requirements and some of the temporary current assets. A financial analyst claims that recent economic developments have caused the proportion of firms that use the conservative approach to change from 0.22. He selects a random sample of 250 firms, and determines that 63 are presently using the conservative approach. At a significance level of 1%, evaluate the analyst's claim.

**31.** In the electronics industry, the common practice is that sales terms call for payment within 30 days. Recently a financial analysis at Painn–Weaver claims that the average collection period for the industry is over 30 days. The average collection period (ACP) ratio is computed by dividing average sales per day into accounts receivable. It indicates the average amount of time (in days) the firm must wait after making a sale before receiving payment. He selects a random sample of 16 firms from the industry and obtains the following data. Are the data normally distributed, and why is it important?

**a.** Set up the appropriate null and alternative hypotheses.

**b.** In the problem context, what are the Type I and Type II errors?

**c.** Evaluate the financial analyst's claim at the 5% significance level.

| ACP Data (in days) | |
|---|---|
| 32.67 | 36.18 |
| 35.26 | 34.68 |
| 34.67 | 36.45 |
| 34.72 | 36.60 |
| 35.85 | 34.21 |
| 36.38 | 35.25 |
| 34.57 | 33.61 |
| 34.87 | 33.09 |

**32.** Suppose that in the previous exercise your alternative hypothesis is

$$\mu > 30 \text{ days.}$$

If the sample mean is 28.5 days you don't have to compute a test statistic to know that you will fail to reject the null hypothesis. Explain.

**33.** Corporations purchase foreign currencies as a means of hedging exchange rate exposure. For example, a jewelry chain buys 5000 watches from a Swiss manufacturer for 1 million Swiss francs. Payment is to be made in Swiss francs in 180 days. The chain is apprehensive that the dollar will weaken over the next 180 days, and that it will have to pay more in U.S. dollars because each dollar will purchase fewer Swiss francs. On the other hand, the firm doesn't want to pay cash today and forgo the 180 days of free trade credit. It can take the trade credit and protect itself by purchasing 1 million Swiss francs from a bank for delivery in 180 days at a fixed price. The chain has covered its trade payable by a *forward market hedge.*

Historically 90% of the firms purchasing products in Switzerland have used the forward market hedge. Recently the American dollar has been strong against the Swiss franc. An analyst claims that this has reduced the need for the forward market hedge, and that less than 90% of firms are now using it. To evaluate the claim, he randomly selects 100 firms doing business in Switzerland, and determines that 82 are now using the forward market hedge. Evaluate his claim at the 1% significance level.

**34.** The chamber of commerce knows that over the past two years, conference attendees spend, on average, about $150 per day (excluding hotel room charges). Recently the city and local businesses attempted to make downtown more attractive to out-of-town visitors by creating pedestrian walkways, outdoor cafes, and "green" areas. Have these additions led to increased spending by conference attendees? The chamber of commerce thinks so.

**a.** Set up the appropriate null and alternative hypotheses.

**b.** In the problem context, what are the Type I and Type II errors?

After implementing the changes, the chamber randomly selected 50 conference attendees and asks them to record their daily expenditures. Here are the data:

| | | | | |
|---|---|---|---|---|
| $166 | $164 | $161 | $165 | $161 |
| $167 | $171 | $167 | $163 | $159 |
| $168 | $161 | $160 | $162 | $162 |
| $166 | $172 | $165 | $165 | $155 |
| $160 | $153 | $167 | $166 | $157 |
| $166 | $163 | $166 | $160 | $174 |
| $167 | $170 | $169 | $164 | $159 |
| $156 | $168 | $159 | $165 | $175 |
| $170 | $165 | $165 | $162 | $158 |
| $165 | $164 | $171 | $162 | $164 |

**c.** At a 10% significance level, have the city's efforts to increase daily spending above $150 been successful? Explain.

**35.** A manager sets the significance level for a study at 0.05. The computed $p$-value is 0.11. Why can't she reject the null hypothesis? Discuss.

**36.** Construct business scenarios for the following sets of hypotheses:

$H_0: \mu \leq 4.2$ recalled product attributes

$H_1: \mu > 4.2$ recalled product attributes

$H_0: \mu \geq 4.5$ errors per 1000 lines of code

$H_1: \mu < 4.5$ errors per 1000 lines of code

$H_0: p \geq .05$ circuit boards with one or more failed solder connections

$H_1: p < .05$ circuit boards with one or more failed solder connections

**37.** A city manager claims that the population mean income within a particular zip code is over $50,000. Given the following data, what can she conclude at a .01 significance level? If a census has just been taken, would it have been necessary to perform hypothesis testing? Discuss.

| | | | | |
|---|---|---|---|---|
| $52,432 | $53,912 | $51,555 | $53,768 | $53,136 |
| $51,706 | $51,111 | $51,371 | $52,732 | $52,486 |
| $50,163 | $53,064 | $50,688 | $53,745 | $52,166 |
| $54,953 | $52,667 | $52,039 | $52,963 | $53,335 |
| $50,308 | $52,829 | $53,884 | $53,507 | $52,395 |
| $51,409 | $52,843 | $52,160 | $52,531 | $53,421 |
| $53,877 | $52,266 | $52,112 | $52,275 | $51,726 |
| $53,100 | $51,552 | $52,472 | $52,759 | $52,750 |
| $52,058 | $52,305 | $53,337 | $52,594 | $53,524 |
| $50,585 | $52,314 | $54,003 | $52,141 | $52,366 |

**38.** A financial analyst claims that the population mean acid ratio within an industry is no longer 1.80. Given the following data and an $\alpha$ level of 0.05, what can he conclude?

| | | | | |
|---|---|---|---|---|
| 1.67 | 1.60 | 2.02 | 1.81 | 1.90 |
| 4.05 | 1.84 | 1.67 | 2.09 | 1.60 |
| 1.52 | 1.66 | 1.97 | 1.88 | 1.73 |
| 2.14 | 1.87 | 0.90 | 2.56 | 1.83 |
| 1.76 | 2.11 | 1.94 | 1.75 | 0.85 |

**39.** A manager claims that by using computer automated drawing software the firm can reduce architectural drawing time from its present 32 hours. Given the following data and an $\alpha$ level of 0.01, what can she conclude?

| | | | | |
|---|---|---|---|---|
| 30.53 | 31.45 | 29.45 | 30.23 | 30.27 |
| 29.64 | 29.25 | 30.21 | 30.06 | 30.94 |
| 30.02 | 29.29 | 30.09 | 30.40 | 30.70 |
| 30.37 | 30.33 | 30.89 | 29.36 | 29.81 |
| 28.99 | 29.54 | 29.69 | 29.67 | 29.31 |

## CASE STUDY

The headquarters for MidAmerica Bank Corporation is in Columbus, Ohio. The corporation has 230 branches in six Midwestern states. The Executive Committee reviews representative samples of the daily operating results of all branches monthly. At the September review, it appeared that the Middletown branch had a volume of transactions slightly below target. All other branches of similar size in Indiana were either at or above target. The Committee agreed to monitor carefully the suburban Middletown branch's performance over the next several months. In October through December it appeared that the branch continued to slip behind target, although all other Indiana branches were still at or above target.

| Transaction Volume: Percent of Target | Middletown Branch | | | |
|---|---|---|---|---|
| | September | October | November | December |
| Sample 1 | 98.93 | 99.11 | 99.11 | 96.77 |
| Sample 2 | 100.45 | 97.67 | 97.67 | 95.30 |
| Sample 3 | 99.59 | 99.05 | 99.05 | 95.36 |
| Sample 4 | 100.41 | 97.86 | 97.86 | 95.49 |
| Sample 5 | 99.46 | 97.47 | 97.47 | 95.69 |
| Sample 6 | 99.85 | 97.41 | 97.41 | 96.28 |
| Sample 7 | 99.00 | 97.77 | 97.77 | 96.11 |
| Sample 8 | 100.22 | 98.01 | 98.01 | 95.97 |
| Sample 9 | 99.35 | 98.92 | 98.92 | 96.43 |
| Sample 10 | 100.05 | 98.45 | 98.45 | 95.91 |

At the January 7 meeting an Executive Committee member suggested that a new manager had started in August and that subsequently the branch's level of transactions had begun to decline. He said: "Look, Jones represents a change at that branch. Before he arrived, the branch was meeting its target. Within six weeks of his arrival, the branch dropped below target. I thought we had made a mistake when we promoted him." Another member noted that Jones had been promoted to the Middletown "Class A" bank even though he did not have the prerequisite number of years of banking experience. The group then began to discuss possible replacements for Jones. At this point the chair of the Executive Committee asked for a short recess to reconsider the Jones decision.

Prepare a one-page paper that addresses the following issues.

1. Has the mean transaction volume for the Middletown branch dropped over the past four months?

2. Characterize the Executive Committee's problem diagnostic skills.

3. What would you recommend to improve the Executive Committee's effectiveness?

4. Should Jones be fired?

Use the data to support your position.

# CHAPTER 6
# APPENDICES

## I. LISTING OF EXCEL TOOLS

1. NORMSDIST function wizard
2. TDIST function wizard
3. KURT function wizard
4. SKEW function wizard

## II. RELATIONSHIP BETWEEN TYPE I AND TYPE II ERRORS

### IMPACT OF INCREASING THE PROBABILITY OF MAKING A TYPE I ERROR ON THE PROBABILITY OF MAKING A TYPE II ERROR

Figure 6.9A (upper panel) shows the distribution of the sample mean for the Milemaster study when the null hypothesis is true—that is, when the population mean is at most 47,000 miles. Figure 6.9B shows one of many possible distributions of the sample mean where the alternative hypothesis is true, and the population mean is greater than 47,000 miles. We have assumed that the population mean for the lower panel is 48,000 miles.

Suppose the computed $p$-value was just larger than 0.01—just to the left of the significance level = .01 line in the upper panel. Then we would *not* reject the null hypothesis. Is it possible that the null hypothesis is false, and the population mean is truly greater than 47,000 miles—say 48,000 miles? According to the lower panel, the answer is yes, and the shaded area represents that probability. In summary, the shaded area is the probability of failing to reject the null hypothesis when the null hypothesis is false (population mean equals 48,000 miles).

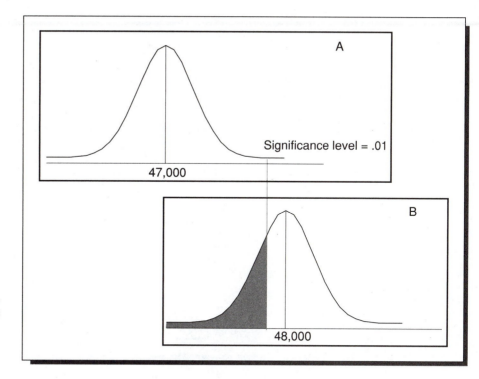

**Figure 6.9**
Probability of Type II Error for Significance Level of 0.01, Sample Size of 1000, and Population Mean of 48,000 Miles

Now suppose we increase the probability of making a Type I error, the significance level. This will shift the significance level to the left in the upper panel (more area equals a greater probability of making a Type I error). See the upper panel in Figure 6.10.

Suppose the computed *p*-value was just larger than 0.15—just to the left of the significance level = 0.15 line in the upper panel of Figure 6.10. Then we would *not* reject the null hypothesis. Now the probability of making a Type II error is smaller—the shaded area represents that probability. In summary, as you increase the significance level, the probability of making a Type I error, you reduce the probability of making a Type II error.

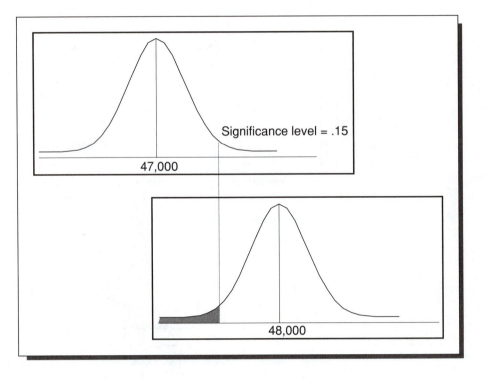

**Figure 6.10**
Probability of Type II Error for Significance Level of 0.15, Sample Size of 1000, and Population Mean of 48,000 Miles

## IMPACT OF SAMPLE SIZE ON THE PROBABILITY OF MAKING A TYPE II ERROR

We can also reduce the probability of making a Type II error for a given significance level by increasing the sample size. Look at Figure 6.10. Suppose you increase the sample size in the study from 1000 tires to 4000 tires. What will happen to the shapes of the distributions in the two panels?

As you increase the sample size four fold, the estimated standard error shrinks by one-half. This causes the two distributions in Figure 6.10 to become "tighter" around their respective means. As the distributions become tighter, the probability of making a Type II error decreases for a given probability of making a Type I error. See Figure 6.11.

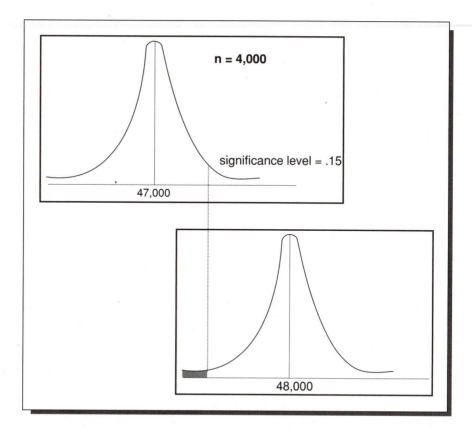

**Figure 6.11**
Probability of Making
a Type II Error for a
Significance Level of
0.15, Sample Size of
4000, and a Population
Mean of 48,000 Miles

In summary:

1. Increasing the probability of making a Type I error (the significance level, $\alpha$) reduces the probability of making a Type II error.

2. For a constant $\alpha$ level, increasing the sample size reduces the probability of making a Type II error.

# Chapter 7

# DESCRIBING
# MULTIVARIATE DATA

## INTRODUCTION

This chapter presents how to analyze two or more columns of data. For example, suppose you have monthly data on market share and advertising expenditures and want to determine if advertising expenditures affect market share in the current or the following months. Alternatively, say you have data on 100 workers—such as their job satisfaction level, number of training hours, and productivity for the past quarter. You want to know if level of job satisfaction and number of training hours influence productivity. You will learn how to determine which variables, if any, **affect** or are **related to** an important business variable you wish to predict, control, or improve. Think of Chapter 7 as "looking for relationships or differences" within a specific sample.

Chapter 7 and Chapter 2 are similar. Both chapters focus on analyzing **specific** samples. We are *not* interested in drawing conclusions about the population from which the sample was taken.[1] Both chapters present how to organize, summarize, and interpret both quantitative and categorical cross-sectional and time-ordered data.

---

[1] In Chapters 5 and 6 we were interested in drawing conclusions about the population from which we selected a sample.

The major difference in the two chapters is one of focus. The techniques of Chapter 2 described one sample or variable—its shape, center, and variation. The techniques of Chapter 7 determine if one or more variables affect or are related to an important business variable we wish to predict, control, or improve.

There are several other differences. Chapter 2 focused on *univariate* data; Chapter 7 focuses on *multivariate* data. Recall that we can either describe a person, place, or thing by a single variable (univariate data) or by two or more variables (multivariate data).[2] Also, Chapter 7 presents new methods for organizing data—the **contingency table** and the **scatter plot**. It includes new methods for analyzing data including **joint** or **row percentages**, the **correlation coefficient** and **correlation matrix,** and **least squares trendlines**.

In assessing relationships you must distinguish between an explanatory (also known as a predictor or independent) variable and a dependent variable. A dependent variable is the variable you wish to predict, control, or improve. It is the effect. An explanatory variable is the variable you believe affects or influences the dependent variable. It is the cause. Unlike dependent variables, explanatory variables do not depend on any other variables.

In summary, consider this chapter when you are only interested in a *specific* sample and you wish to determine if one or more variables affect an important business variable you wish to predict, control, or improve.

# MANAGEMENT SCENARIOS AND DATA SETS

Table 7.1 presents the five scenarios used in this chapter. These illustrate how managers use both cross-sectional (from one time period) and time-ordered (from multiple time periods) multivariate data to determine what explanatory variables affect an important dependent variable. Again, note that we are only interested in the specific sample we select. The cases also illustrate three of the four measurement scales discussed in Chapter 1.

Scenario I presents cross-sectional data for a **mixed data set.** Management wants to determine which of three types of creativity training is most effective. The explanatory variable is **qualitative**, type of creativity training, and the dependent variable is **quantitative**, the number of solutions generated during problem solving.

**DEFINITION**    A **mixed data set** consists of qualitative and quantitative variables.

---

[2] For example, we can describe a sales region using either univariate data (25% market share) or multivariate data (25% market share, 105 employees, regional headquarters).

The data set (see Table 7.2) is the number of solutions produced with three different types of training. Workers trained in traditional brainstorming averaged 38.45 solutions, and the number of solutions ranged from 10 to 55. Workers trained in computerized brainstorming averaged 65.55 solutions and the number of solutions ranged from 51 to 99. Workers who received no training averaged only 6.09 solutions and the number of solutions ranged from 3 to 14. The dependent variable, number of solutions, is measurable on a ratio scale.

| Data Type | Explanatory | Dependent | Database | Typical Questions |
|---|---|---|---|---|
| Cross-Sectional | Qualitative | Quantitative | Results from three types of creativity training for 33 workers. | Does type of training affect the number of solutions generated? |
| Cross-Sectional | Qualitative | Qualitative | HR database that includes gender and whether worker has been promoted. | For a specific sample of 200 workers, does gender affect the likelihood of promotion? |
| Cross-Sectional | Quantitative | Quantitative | Marketing database on five economic variables for 12 sales regions for one quarter. | Which explanatory variables affect market share? Can the relationship between each explanatory variable and dependent variable be described by a straight line? |
| Time-Ordered | Quantitative | Quantitative | Sales database over 16 quarters that includes three economic variables. | What explanatory variables affect market share over time? Does advertising in one quarter affect market share in the next quarter? Two quarters later? |
| Time-Ordered | Quantitative | Quantitative | Sales database over 16 quarters. Only contains a single variable, sales. | Do sales in one quarter affect sales in the next quarter? Two quarters later? |

**Table 7.1**
Management Scenarios and Data Sets

| Brainstorm | Brainstorm Computerized | No Creative Method |
|---|---|---|
| 45 | 65 | 8 |
| 38 | 68 | 7 |
| 36 | 70 | 6 |
| 10 | 68 | 5 |
| 55 | 58 | 4 |
| 43 | 56 | 5 |
| 41 | 51 | 3 |
| 37 | 99 | 14 |
| 34 | 53 | 6 |
| 35 | 56 | 5 |
| 49 | 77 | 4 |

**Table 7.2**
Database for Study on Total Number of Solutions versus Three Types of Creativity Training

Scenario II presents cross-sectional data where both variables are qualitative. Five years ago a firm hired 200 entry-level white-collar employees; Table 7.3 contains data on 20 of the employees. Recently the firm has received complaints from female employees of the original group that it has discriminated against them in awarding promotions.

The organization records each employee's gender and whether he or she has been promoted. Although the organization assigns numbers to gender (Female = 0, Male = 1 or vice versa) and promoted status (Not = 0, Yes = 1 or vice versa), the numbers are not meaningful. We cannot add, subtract, multiply, or divide them. The numbers simply make it easier to *code* the data into the database (see Table 7.3).

Next, the organization designates the explanatory and dependent variables for the HR study. The question that generated the study was, "Does gender affect one's chances of promotion?" Therefore, "gender" is the explanatory variable and "promoted status" is the dependent variable. From the database of 200 workers, the firm will determine if the women's complaints are justified.

Scenario III presents cross-sectional data from a marketing database on five variables for 12 sales regions for the first quarter of a year; see Table 7.4. The dependent variable is quantitative, as are three of the four explanatory variables. Each sales region is represented by five variables. For example, the Atlanta region spent $130,000 on advertising; its level of closeness of supervision was 3 on the following scale (1 = very lax to 25 = very close); its region was highly competitive; its price list was, on average, 1.50 times higher than the mean of its competitors; and its market share was 20%.

What might have prompted the vice president to assemble Table 7.4? She receives a quarterly report on market share for the 12 sales regions (column #6 of Table 7.4). While the mean market share for the 12 regions was 29.42%, market share varied widely. It varied from a low of 5% in Washington to a high of 55% in Dallas. She might have asked herself: "What variables could account for the wide dispersion in market share?" She and her staff brainstormed and generated the four potential explanatory variables in Table 7.4.

| Employee | Gender | Promoted | |
|----------|--------|----------|---|
| 1 | 0 | 1 | →Promoted Female |
| 2 | 0 | 1 | |
| 3 | 1 | 0 | |
| 4 | 0 | 1 | |
| 5 | 0 | 1 | |
| 6 | 1 | 0 | →Not Promoted Male |
| 7 | 0 | 1 | |
| 8 | 1 | 1 | |
| 9 | 0 | 0 | |
| 10 | 0 | 0 | |
| 11 | 1 | 0 | |
| 12 | 0 | 1 | |
| 13 | 1 | 0 | |
| 14 | 0 | 1 | |
| 15 | 1 | 1 | →Promoted Male |
| 16 | 0 | 1 | |
| 17 | 1 | 0 | |
| 18 | 0 | 1 | |
| 19 | 0 | 0 | →Not Promoted Female |
| 20 | 1 | 0 | |

**Table 7.3**
Portion of Database on Gender and Promoted Status

| Region | Adv-Last Qtr ($0000) | Closeness | Competitive? | Rel. Price | Market Share |
|--------|----------------------|-----------|--------------|------------|--------------|
| ATLANTA | 13 | 3 | 1 | 1.50 | 20 |
| BRMHM | 28 | 15 | 0 | 0.60 | 50 |
| CHAR | 17 | 20 | 1 | 1.00 | 30 |
| JACK | 8 | 1 | 1 | 1.75 | 10 |
| NO | 16 | 23 | 1 | 1.30 | 25 |
| ORLANDO | 18 | 4 | 0 | 0.90 | 30 |
| MIAMI | 21 | 19 | 0 | 2.00 | 35 |
| WASH | 6 | 25 | 1 | 2.90 | 5 |
| BALT | 25 | 7 | 0 | 1.50 | 45 |
| DALLAS | 32 | 11 | 0 | 1.10 | 55 |
| HOUSTON | 11 | 2 | 1 | 2.50 | 20 |
| AUSTIN | 16 | 20 | 1 | 2.25 | 28 |

**Table 7.4**
Marketing Database on Share of Market and Four Possible Explanatory Variables

Competitiveness level is a qualitative variable and measures the degree of competition in the region. The vice president coded the variable as follows: $0$ = not highly competitive and $1$ = highly competitive region.

Scenario IV presents **time-ordered** data where all the variables are quantitative. Table 7.5 contains advertising expenditure data, relative price data, and market-share data for one sales region *over 16 quarters*. While the mean market share was 20.56%, it varied from a low of 15% to a high of 25% (see column 4).

The curious and effective manager asked what variables might affect the variation in market share. The sales manager suggested relative price and advertising. The former is the ratio of the firm's product price to the mean of its competitors' prices.

The manager can use the data set to determine if either explanatory variable affects market share in the same time period or in later time periods. An explanatory variable that affects a dependent variable in the same time period is a **coincident indicator**. An explanatory variable that affects a dependent variable in one or more later time periods is a **leading indicator**.

We denote time-ordered variables using the symbol ($t$). For example, the notation Adv (1) represents the level of advertising in quarter 1. Likewise, market share (2) represents market share in quarter 2. The notation becomes crucial when determining if an explanatory variable in one period affects the dependent variable in subsequent time periods. The ($t$) notation clarifies whether the explanatory variable is a coincident or leading indicator. Lastly, all three variables are measured on a ratio scale.

| Quarter | Adv($t$) in (0000) | Rel. Price ($t$) | Market Share ($t$) |
|---|---|---|---|
| 1 | 13 | 1.15 | 24 |
| 2 | 11 | 1.65 | 18 |
| 3 | 17 | 1.80 | 16 |
| 4 | 20 | 1.45 | 22 |
| 5 | 20 | 1.20 | 24 |
| 6 | 16 | 1.25 | 24 |
| 7 | 15 | 1.40 | 20 |
| 8 | 13 | 1.45 | 21 |
| 9 | 17 | 1.65 | 18 |
| 10 | 11 | 1.35 | 22 |
| 11 | 19 | 1.70 | 16 |
| 12 | 15 | 1.18 | 24 |
| 13 | 21 | 1.54 | 20 |
| 14 | 10 | 1.20 | 25 |
| 15 | 15 | 1.90 | 15 |
| 16 | 13 | 1.47 | 20 |

**Table 7.5**
Marketing Database for Time-Ordered Quantitative Variables

Scenario V presents time-ordered data on a single variable. Here we ask the question: "Does the value of a variable in one time period affect the value of the same variable in subsequent time periods?" For example, can we use sales in period 1, sales (1), to predict sales in period 2, sales (2)? Can we use sales (1) to predict sales two periods later? To answer these questions, we will use the data from scenario V to build an **autoregressive equation,** or **model** (See Table 7.6).

| Period | Sales (t) | Period | Sales (t) |
|--------|-----------|--------|-----------|
| 1 | 3.40 | 9 | 5.61 |
| 2 | 2.00 | 10 | 4.05 |
| 3 | 1.90 | 11 | 4.63 |
| 4 | 3.20 | 12 | 5.01 |
| 5 | 4.80 | 13 | 6.03 |
| 6 | 3.75 | 14 | 4.61 |
| 7 | 4.13 | 15 | 5.08 |
| 8 | 4.51 | 16 | 5.29 |

**Table 7.6**
Database to Develop an
Autoregressive Model

# ANALYZING MIXED CROSS-SECTIONAL DATA

This section presents how to determine if a qualitative explanatory variable affects a quantitative dependent variable. The pairing of different types of variables creates a *mixed data set*. By the end of this section you should be able to

**1.** explain what a mixed data set is; and

**2.** construct a one-way table or multiple box plot to analyze a mixed data set.

## ONE-WAY TABLE DISPLAY

You have run a study to determine if computerized creativity software program using brainstorming helps generate more solutions than the traditional brainstorming method or no creativity method at all. Table 7.7 is a one-way table that describes the study's results. You can obtain the data in Table 7.7 by applying Excel's descriptive-statistics data-analysis tool and the QUARTILE function wizard to the data in Table 7.2.

For the *specific* sample of 33 employees, the computerized brainstorming system clearly outperformed both the traditional brainstorming and the no creativity groups. The computerized system outproduced the typical brainstorming by almost a 2 to 1 margin. The computerized system outperformed the no creativity group by over 10 to 1.

If the 33 employees were merely a representative sample from the population of the firm's employees, our analysis would not yet be complete. We must then draw conclusions about which creativity training is best for *all* employees. You will learn how to do so in Chapter 12.

| | Traditional Brainstorming | Computerized Brainstorming | No Creative Method |
|---|---|---|---|
| Sample Size | 11 | 11 | 11 |
| Sample Mean | 38.45 | 65.55 | 6.09 |
| Sample Std. Deviation | 11.42 | 13.75 | 2.98 |
| Sample Median | 38 | 65 | 5 |
| Sample IQR | 8.50 | 13 | 2 |

**Table 7.7**
One-Way Table for Type of Creativity versus Number of Solutions Generated

## MULTIPLE BOX PLOT

In Chapter 2 you first learned to construct a box plot. It displays the five-number summary of the data. It indicates the minimum, first quartile, median, third quartile, and the maximum data values. We can also include the Tukey-based fences that help determine the presence of outliers.

This chapter presents the **multiple** box plot. Figure 7.1 is a multiple box plot for the creativity study. Although Excel does not provide a traditional box plot, you can use Excel's XY scatter chart wizard to develop the reasonable facsimile shown in Figure 7.1 (see Appendix Chapter 2).

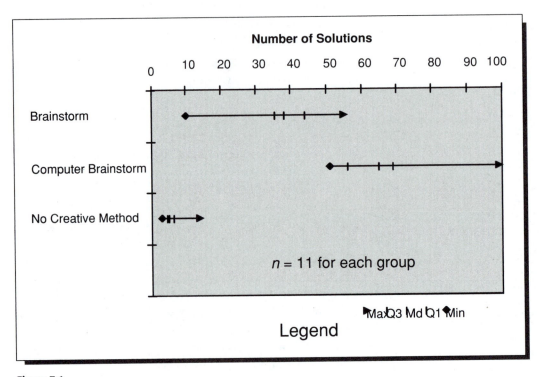

**Figure 7.1**
An Excel-Developed "Multiple Box Plot" without Fences

As with the one-way table, Figure 7.1 indicates that computerized brainstorming is superior to the other two treatments, or conditions.

In summary, when you want to determine if a qualitative explanatory variable affects a quantitative dependent variable, construct either a one-way table or multiple box plot, or both.

# ANALYZING QUALITATIVE CROSS-SECTIONAL DATA

When the explanatory and dependent variables are both categorical, or qualitative, managers use two-way contingency tables to determine whether the two variables are related. By the end of this section you should be able to

1. construct a two-way contingency table;

2. explain row and column percentages in a table;

3. determine if a specific sample of two categorical variables are related to one another by using the row or column percentages;

4. explain why you might need to qualify your conclusion about the relationship between two variables;

5. explain what intervening variables are and how you generate them;

6. control for the impact of an intervening variable; and

7. assess the potential relationship between two variables after accounting for an intervening variable.

## TWO-WAY CONTINGENCY TABLES

A HR manager wants to determine whether an employee's gender affects his/her chances of promotion within the firm. The two categorical variables are gender and promoted status. The subcategories for both categorical variables must be *mutually exclusive and exhaustive*. Classify gender as male or female. Classify promoted status as not promoted or promoted. These two subcategories for each variable generate a 2 × 2 contingency table. Note that the manager could have defined promoted status along three levels: not promoted, promoted one level, or promoted two or more levels. This would have generated a 2 × 3 contingency table.

---

**DEFINITION**     A two-way contingency table displays the number of people or elements cross-classified according to two criteria.

We constructed Table 7.8 from the data shown in Table 7.3. Note that Table 7.3 contained gender and promotion data on only 20, not 200, employees.

**Table 7.8**

Contingency Table for 200 Employees Cross-Classified by Gender and Promoted Status

|  | Promoted | Not Promoted | Total |
|---|---|---|---|
| **Male** | 80 | 30 | 110 |
| **Female** | 25 | 65 | 90 |
| Total | 105 | 95 | 200 |

What do the entries in the body of Table 7.8 represent? The entries represent the number of employees with two attributes—a particular gender *and* a particular promoted status. Thus, of the original group of 200, five years later there were 80 promoted males, 25 promoted females, 30 not promoted males, and 65 not promoted females.

What do the entries in the table's right-most column and bottom row (the margins) represent? They are row and column totals found by summing across rows and down columns. Thus, there were (and still are) 110 males and 90 females in the original group, while there are 105 promoted employees and 95 not promoted employees. Margin entries represent the number of employees with one attribute—a particular gender *or* a particular promoted status.

Having developed the 2 × 2 contingency table, we can now determine whether for the *specific sample of 200 employees,* the two categorical variables are related. Does gender affect one's chance for promotion?

To answer this question, compute the following two important percentage tables:

**1.** Column percentage table

**2.** Row percentage table

Each table highlights a different aspect of the data.

## Column Percentage Tables

Table 7.9 displays the column percentages for the contingency data. To obtain column percentages, divide each entry in Table 7.8 by its *column* total. For example, the top left entry in Table 7.9 is 80/105 = 76.2%. *Note:* The marginal percentages on the right total column are *not* obtained by summing across the rows.

**Table 7.9**
Column Percentage
Table for Gender-
Promotion Study

|  | Promoted | Not Promoted | Total |
|---|---|---|---|
| **Male** | 76.2% | 31.6% | 55% |
| **Female** | 23.8% | 68.4% | 45% |
| Total | 100% | 100% | 100% |

We can analyze either row of the table. Focusing on the male employees in the upper row, we learn the following:

**1.** Overall, 55% of the original group hired five years ago was male.

**2.** Of the promoted employees, 76.2% were males.

**3.** Of the not promoted employees, only 31.6% were males.

If gender were not related to promoted status, all three of the above column percentages would be about 55%.

Likewise, focusing on the female employees in the lower row, we learn the following:

**1.** Overall, 45% of the original group hired five years ago was female.

**2.** Of the promoted employees, only 23.8% were females.

**3.** Of the not promoted employees, 68.4% were females.

If gender were not related to promoted status, all three column percentages would be about 45%.

## Row Percentage Tables

Table 7.10 shows the row percentages. To obtain row percentages, divide each entry in Table 7.8 by its row total. For example, the top left entry in Table 7.10 is $80/110 = 72.7\%$. Again, note that the marginal percentages at the bottom are *not* obtained by summing down the columns.

**Table 7.10**
Row Percentage Table
for Gender-Promotion
Study

|  | Promoted | Not Promoted | Total |
|---|---|---|---|
| **Male** | 72.7% | 27.3% | 100% |
| **Female** | 27.8% | 72.2% | 100% |
| Total | 52.5% | 47.5% | 100% |

We can analyze either *column* of the table. Focusing on the promoted employees in the left column, we learn the following:

**1.** Overall, 52.5% of the employees in the original group were promoted.

**2.** Of the male employees, 72.7% were promoted.

**3.** Of the female employees, only 27.8% were promoted.

If gender were not related to promoted status, all three row percentages would be about 52.5%.

Likewise, focusing on the not promoted employees in the right column, we learn the following:

**1.** Overall, 47.5% of the employees in the original group were not promoted.

**2.** Of the male employees, only 27.3% were not promoted.

**3.** Of the female employees, 72.2% were not promoted.

If gender were not related to promoted status, all three row percentages would be about 47.5%.

Both the row and column percentage tables suggest that gender and promoted status may be related for the specific sample of 200 employees.

You need only compute either a row or column percentage table for both provide the same information on the relationship between the attributes—gender and promotion status. Which you compute is a matter of personal choice.

If gender did not affect one's chances of promotion, what should the cell entries in the body of the contingency table, Table 7.8, be? From the row percentage table, Table 7.10, we note that 52.5% of the original group was promoted during the five-year period, (105/200). Thus 52.5% of the males and the females should have been promoted. Of the 110 males, we should have expected $110(.525) = 57.75$ promotions. There should have been 57.75 promoted males. Of the 90 females, we should have expected $90(.525) = 47.25$ promotions. There should have been 47.25 promoted females. Given the row and the column totals, we can determine the two remaining cell entries in the $2 \times 2$ table in Table 7.11.

**Table 7.11**
Expected Cell Entries if Gender and Promoted Status Were Not Related

| | Promoted | Not Promoted | Total |
|---|---|---|---|
| **Male** | 57.75 | 52.25 | 110 |
| **Female** | 47.25 | 42.75 | 90 |
| Total | 105 | 95 | 200 |

In summary, we can use two approaches to assess whether gender and promoted status are related.

**1.** From Table 7.10, 72.7% of the males in the cohort group were promoted, while only 27.8% of the females were promoted. (Or we could use any other row or column percentage.)

**2.** The actual frequencies (Table 7.8) differ dramatically from the frequencies we would expect (Table 7.11) if gender and promoted status were not related.

It *appears* that gender and promoted status are related for the specific sample of 200 employees. Why should we qualify our conclusion? While there is no question that the promotion rates are very different, the apparent relationship may be due to variables other than gender. We call these **intervening variables**.

### Intervening Variables

Table 7.10 indicates that a higher percentage of men have been promoted than women, but the difference in promotion percentages (72.7% versus 27.8%) may not be based on gender. Suppose that the promotions occurred in the overseas divisions. Furthermore, suppose the men had taken more course work in International Business (IB). Perhaps the men were better qualified and thus more deserving of promotion. The HR manager is suggesting a variable other than gender that could account for the differences in the promotion percentages of each gender.

The HR manager is suggesting that completing International Business course work is an intervening variable. That is, IB course work, not gender, explains the difference in the row percentages of men and women promoted.

---

**DEFINITION**     An intervening variable is an explanatory variable that affects a dependent variable. Including an intervening variable eliminates the apparent relationship between the original explanatory variable and the dependent variable.

---

Can IB course work explain the differential promotion rates of men and women? To answer that question, let's construct a *tree diagram*. Figure 7.2 displays a tree diagram, which is a breakdown of the total sample of 200 according to the categorical variables of interest—IB course work, gender, and promotion status.

To construct a tree diagram, first divide the entire sample of 200 into two groups by the intervening variable, IB course work. That is, determine of the 200 employees how many did and did not take IB course work. Then divide each of these two groups into either male or female and then into promoted or not promoted (or vice versa). Figure 7.2 is the tree diagram for the gender-promotion study in which we examine the impact of the IB course work intervening variable.

Let's explore the tree diagram. One hundred employees had taken IB course work and 100 had not. Of those that did take IB course work, 80%, or 80, were males. Of those who did not take IB course work, 70%, or 70, were females.

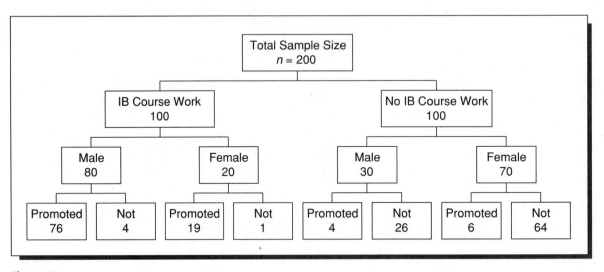

**Figure 7.2**
Tree Diagram for One Intervening Variable: IB Course Work

Let's continue our exploration. Of the 80 males who took IB course work, 76 were promoted. Of the 20 females that took IB course work, 19 were promoted. Of the 30 males who did not take IB course work, 26 were not promoted. Of the 70 females who did not take IB course work, 64 were not promoted.

Table 7.12 displays two contingency (with row percentages) tables, one for each subcategory of the IB course work intervening variable. We constructed these two tables from the lowest level of the tree diagram. Of the 100 employees who had taken IB course work, there were:

**1.** 76 promoted males

**2.** 4 not promoted males

**3.** 19 promoted females, and

**4.** 1 not promoted female.

Of the 100 employees who had not taken IB course work, there were:

**1.** 4 promoted males

**2.** 26 not promoted males

**3.** 6 promoted females, and

**4.** 64 not promoted females.

### IB Course Work Taken

|        | Promoted |       | Not Promoted |       | Total |
|--------|----------|-------|--------------|-------|-------|
| Male   | 76       | (95%) | 4            | (5%)  | 80    |
| Female | 19       | (95%) | 1            | (5%)  | 20    |
| Total  | 95       | (95%) | 5            | (5%)  | 100   |

### No IB Course Work Taken

|        | Promoted |         | Not Promoted |          | Total |
|--------|----------|---------|--------------|----------|-------|
| Male   | 4        | (13.3%) | 26           | (86.7%)  | 30    |
| Female | 6        | (8.57%) | 64           | (91.43%) | 70    |
| Total  | 10       | (10%)   | 90           | (90%)    | 100   |

**Table 7.12**
Two Contingency Tables Using an IB Intervening Variable

What can we conclude from the two tables? Of the males and females that took IB course work, 95% were promoted. Only about 10% of the males and females that did not take IB course work were promoted. When we take into account IB course work, the percentage of males and females who were promoted (or not promoted) is the same or nearly the same. When we take into account IB course work, gender and promoted status do not appear to be related. Rather, promoted status depended on whether or not an employee took IB course work.

How do we evaluate the reasonableness of an intervening variable? The HR manager could make a compelling argument that IB course work should be related to overseas promotions. However, there are many demographic or socioeconomic variables that would not be reasonable intervening variables. For example, an employee's undergraduate major and GPA might not be reasonable intervening variables for the gender-promotion study. An intervening variable must pass the reasonableness test.

There can be more than one intervening variable. For example, the HR manager could classify people by IB course work and overseas experience. Here the manager is using two intervening variables. As you include more intervening variables, the number of contingency tables increases while the sample size for each table decreases. The sample size for *each cell entry* of a table may become so small that the manager cannot reach valid conclusions about potential gender discrimination.

# ANALYZING QUANTITATIVE CROSS-SECTIONAL DATA

One-way tables, multiple box plots, and contingency tables are effective in assessing relationships between two variables when one or more variables are qualitative. However, for quantitative variables, we need an additional tool—the scatter diagram. This tool and its accompanying analyses allows us to determine the type of relationship:

**1.** linear relationship ($y = a + bx$) between two variables,

**2.** nonlinear relationship between two variables ($y = a + bx + cx^2$), and

**3.** clusters or groups of observations that are distinct from one another.

By the end of this section you should be able to

**1.** construct a scatter diagram;

**2.** interpret a scatter diagram;

**3.** apply the "ellipse test" to determine whether two quantitative variables appear to be linearly related;

**4.** explain what a least squares trend line is;

**5.** use Excel's function wizards and trendline option to determine the least squares linear or nonlinear trend line;

**6.** explain what a nonlinear relationship means;

**7.** identify clusters in a scatter diagram; and

**8.** interpret clusters accurately.

From Table 7.4, the vice president desired to explain the variation in the 12 market shares. That is, why does market share vary from a low of 5% in Washington to a high of 55% in Dallas? In short,

Question: Are advertising expenditures, closeness of management supervision, level of competition and relative price **related to** market share?[3]

Answer: Plot scatter diagrams.

---

[3] Establishing a relationship does not establish **cause and effect.** For example, the number of theaters in a city is related to the total amount of alcohol consumed. Cities with greater numbers of theaters also have more alcohol consumption. But we would not say that the presence of theaters causes alcohol consumption.

# LINEAR RELATIONSHIPS

From Table 7.4, is level of advertising expenditures linearly related to market share in the 12 regions? We have three "tools" to answer this question.[4]

**DEFINITION**    A relationship between two variables is linear if as the value of the explanatory variable, $x$, increases, $y$ changes by a constant amount. Describe a linear relationship as $y = a + bx$.

## The Scatter Diagram

Figure 7.3 is a scatter diagram of market share and advertising expenditures for the 12 sales regions in Table 7.4. We used Excel's chart wizard using the XY graph option. Advertising expenditures is the explanatory variable, and market share is the dependent variable.

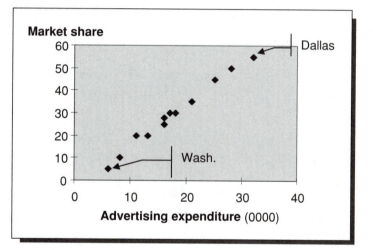

**Figure 7.3**
XY Scatter Plot of
Advertising Expenditures
versus Market Share

The scatter diagram suggests that the two variables are linearly related to one another. As advertising expenditures increase, does market share generally increase by a *constant amount?* Yes. Moreover, there is a *positive* linear relationship; as advertising expenditures increase, so does market share.

## The Circle versus the Ellipse Test

To understand the logic of the ellipse test, look at Figure 7.3. In order to enclose the 12 data points, we need a tight ellipse that is upward sloping

---

[4] When the data are a sample from a population and we wish to determine if there is a relationship *in the population*, we use a fourth tool, the ANalysis Of VAriance (ANOVA). See Chapter 9.

to the right. Figure 7.4 reproduces Figure 7.3, but with an ellipse drawn around the data. The data points lie along a straight line and are tightly clustered. An unbroken straight line running through the data would be upward sloping to the right. This indicates that for the specific data set, the two variables are positively related; that is, as advertising increases, market share increases.

When two variables are linearly related, we can enclose their data points in a *tight* ellipse. The stronger the linear association between the two variables, the tighter the ellipse will be. An upward sloping to-the-right ellipse indicates a positive relationship between two variables. A downward sloping to-the-right ellipse indicates a negative relationship between two variables. When two variables are not linearly related, it will take either a circle or an ellipse parallel to the horizontal axis to enclose the data points.

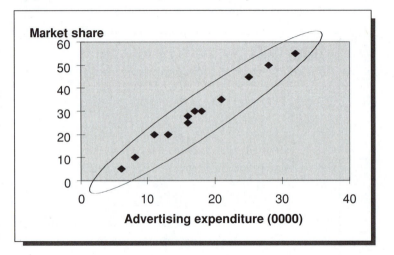

**Figure 7.4**
XY Scatter Plot of
Advertising versus Market
Share with Ellipse Drawn

## Least Squares Equations

We can compute the *best-fitting linear line* for the 12 data points using the least squares equations. Before doing this, let's review some basics about graphing using Figure 7.5.

Start at Point A and move up the line to Point B. The distance along the *x*-axis, four units, is the **run.** The distance along the *y*-axis, three units, is the **rise.** The **sample slope** is the ratio of the rise to the run, better known as "rise over run."

$$\text{sample slope} = \frac{\textbf{rise}}{\textbf{run}} = \frac{3}{4} = +0.75$$

As *x* increases by one unit, *y* will increase by +0.75 units.

The **sample intercept** is the value of $y$ where $x$ equals zero. It is $-2$ in Figure 7.5. The sample intercept and sample slope define a linear relationship. The equation for the line in Figure 7.5 is

$$\hat{y} = a + bx$$
$$\hat{y} = -2 + 0.75 \cdot x$$

where $\hat{y}$ represents the values of $y$ from the equation, $a$ is the sample intercept, and $b$ is the sample slope.

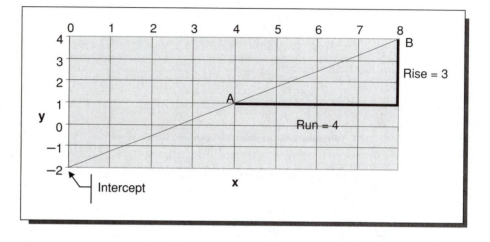

**Figure 7.5**
Defining the Sample Intercept and Sample Slope for a Linear Line

Before illustrating the least squares equations for a simple two-variable case, Figure 7.6 illustrates the goal of the least squares equations.

Figure 7.6 contains five data points (pairs of $x,y$ data values). The best-fitting linear line is the one that minimizes the sum of the squared vertical distances, or deviations, between the line and the data points. The vertical distance equals

$$d_i = y_i - \hat{y}_i$$

**(7.1)**

where for a value of $x$, $y_i$ is the actual value of $y$ and $\hat{y}_i$ is the value of $y$ from the equation, $a + bx$.

Compute the five vertical deviations between the line and the five data points. Label these as $d_1$, $d_2$, $d_3$, $d_4$, and $d_5$. Note that $d_5$ equals $16 - 18$, or $-2$. Now square each of the five values and then sum the squares. This is the sum of the squared vertical deviations for the line. Picture all the linear lines that could represent the data in Figure 7.6. The best-fitting linear line is the one that has the smallest sum of the squared deviations.

Suppose we suggest that the best-fitting line is the line that minimizes the sum of the vertical distances (without squaring them). Do you know why this would not work?

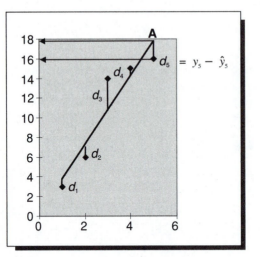

**Figure 7.6**
Illustration of the Goal of the Least Squares Equations

Here's a hint. Vertical deviations can be positive or negative. It will also help if you draw a scatter diagram with only two points and two linear lines. One line should connect the two data points, and the second line should be horizontal, halfway between the two points. Compute the sum of the deviations for each line. Do not look at Figure 7.7.

The sum of the deviations for both lines in Figure 7.7 is zero. However, line B is an awful fit. The reason for the bad fit is that the positive deviation cancels out the negative deviation and their sum is zero. That is why we use the sum of the *squared* deviations criterion.

How do we determine the best-fitting linear line? You could use trial and error to guess at the values of the sample intercept and sample slope, then compute the sum of the squared deviations. You would continue this strategy until you could not further reduce the sum of the squared deviations. As you might suspect, trial and error is mostly trial and aggravation. There has to be a more efficient method.

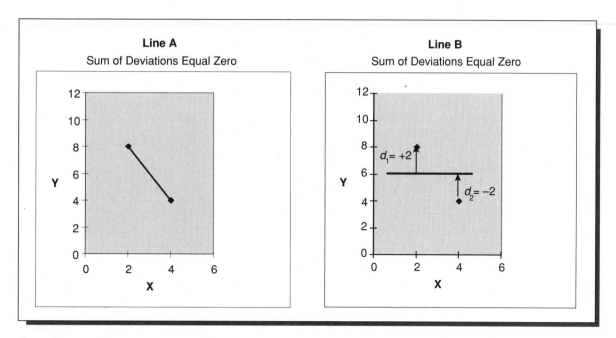

**Figure 7.7**
The Problem with Minimizing the Sum of the Deviations Criterion

Calculus provides a set of equations for the sample intercept and sample slope that guarantee to minimize the sum of the squared deviations. Not surprisingly, these are the **least squares equations.** Here are the equations for the two-variable case for a linear relationship, $\hat{y} = a + b \cdot x$.

| | |
|---|---|
| sample intercept | $a = \bar{y} - (b \cdot \bar{x})$ |
| sample slope | $b = \dfrac{\sum\limits_{i} x_i y_i - n \cdot \bar{x} \cdot \bar{y}}{\sum\limits_{i} x_i^2 - n \cdot \bar{x}^2}$ |

$$(7.2)$$

where $n$ is the sample size, the number of pairs of $x,y$ data values and $\bar{x}$ and $\bar{y}$ are the average of the $x$ and $y$ values.

Let's compute the best-fitting linear line for the data shown below. First, solve for the sample slope ($b$), and use your answer to compute the sample intercept ($a$) (see Table 7.13).

| x | y | xy | x² |
|---|---|---|---|
| 1 | 5 | 5 | 1 |
| 2 | 7 | 14 | 4 |
| 3 | 6 | 18 | 9 |
| 4 | 8 | 32 | 16 |
| 5 | 10 | 50 | 25 |
| Sum   15 | Sum   36 | Sum   119 | Sum   55 |

**Table 7.13**
Computing the Least
Squares Equations

$$b = \frac{119 - \left(5 \cdot \frac{15}{5} \cdot \frac{36}{5}\right)}{55 - \left[5 \cdot \left(\frac{15}{5}\right)^2\right]} = \frac{11}{10} = 1.1 \qquad a = \frac{36}{5} - 1.1 \cdot \frac{15}{5} = 3.9$$

$$\hat{y} = 3.9 + 1.1 \cdot x$$

This is the best-fitting linear line for the five data values in Table 7.13. We can show this by computing the sum of the squared deviations (see Table 7.14).

| x | y | ŷ = 3.9 + 1.1x | Deviation | Deviation² |
|---|---|---|---|---|
| 1 | 5 | 3.9+1.1(1) = 5.0 | .0 | .00 |
| 2 | 7 | 3.9+1.1(2) = 6.1 | .9 | .81 |
| 3 | 6 | 3.9+1.1(3) = 7.2 | −1.2 | 1.44 |
| 4 | 8 | 3.9+1.1(4) = 8.3 | −.3 | .09 |
| 5 | 10 | 3.9+1.1(5) = 9.4 | .6 | .36 |
| | | | | **2.70** |

**Table 7.14**
Computing the Sum of
the Squared Deviations

The sum of the squared deviations is 2.70. No other linear line will produce a smaller sum of the squared deviations than 2.70; the least squares equations guarantee this.

Fortunately, using Excel's function wizards, **INTERCEPT** and **SLOPE,** you will never have to solve the least squares equations manually.

Returning to the market share study, do advertising expenditures affect market share? The scatter plot (see Figure 7.3) and the ellipse versus circle test (see Figure 7.4) certainly suggest that advertising is positively related to market share. That is, increasing advertising is associated with increasing market share.

Let's compute the best-fitting linear line for the advertising and market share data in Table 7.4. Note, advertising expenditures is the explanatory, or x, variable. Market share is the dependent, or y, variable. The sample slope and intercept obtained by the INTERCEPT and SLOPE wizards are show below.

The best–fitting linear line or model is

$$\hat{y} = -4.2802 + 1.9164 \cdot \text{ADV}$$

(7.3)

where $\hat{y}$ represents the market share from the best-fitting linear line and ADV, not the generic term $x$, represents the amount of advertising in tens of thousands of dollars.

What might the vice president conclude from the model? Since the sample intercept is not informative, let us focus on the sample slope. The sample slope is $+1.9164$. This means that as we increase the level of advertising expenditure by \$10,000, on average, the market share increases by 1.92% .[5] Because of the linear relationship, as we increase advertising by \$20,000, market share increases by 3.84%—2(1.92). Of course, at some level of advertising, increased advertising will *not* result in increased market share. But for advertising expenditures in the \$60,000 to \$320,000 range (see Table 7.4, the range of the study), the linear relationship should hold.

In the first quarter the Washington, D.C. region spent \$60,000 on advertising. Expression (7.3) predicts that if the Washington region had expended \$100,000, its predicted market share would have been

$$\hat{y} = -4.2802 + 1.9164 \cdot \text{ADV} = -4.2802 + 1.9164(10) = 14.88\%.$$

---

[5] The units for the $x$ variable are advertising expenditures in *tens of thousands of dollars*.

One note of caution: You can use Expression (7.3) to make predictions on market share for levels of advertising between $60,000 and $320,000. That is the range of advertising dollars from the data set. However, extrapolation is risky. Extrapolation occurs when one uses Expression (7.3) for advertising levels below $60,000 or above $320,000. There is no assurance that the linear model, or equation, will remain valid. You can use Expression (7.3) to make extrapolating predictions only if you can defend why the linear model remains valid in the extrapolation region.

From Table 7.4, the level of the region's competitiveness is a qualitative explanatory variable. The vice president coded the variable as follows: 0 = not highly competitive and 1 = highly competitive region. The dependent variable is market share, which is a quantitative variable. You learned in the section, Analyzing Mixed Cross-Sectional Data, that for mixed data sets use either one-way tables or multiple box plots to analyze the data. We can use the scatter diagram as well when the explanatory variable is qualitative.

### Graphing Indicator Variables

When explanatory variables are qualitative, we call them indicator variables. By assigning the numbers 0 and 1 to the indicator variable, we can then draw a scatter diagram and compute a best-fitting line using the least squares equations.

Figure 7.8 is a scatter diagram of the region's level of competitiveness versus market share. We used Excel's ADD TRENDLINE,[6] rather than the SLOPE and INTERCEPT function wizards, to obtain the best-fitting linear line.

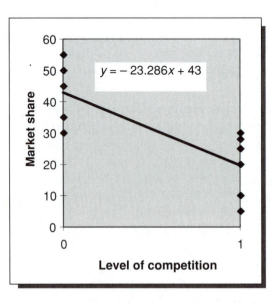

**Figure 7.8**
Scatter Diagram for
Indicator Variable

---

[6] The ADD TRENDLINE option is shown in the chapter's appendix.

The equation for the best-fitting linear line or model is

$$\hat{y} = 43 - 23.286 \cdot \text{COMP}$$

**(7.4)**

For regions that are not highly competitive (COMP = 0), the predicted market share from Expression (7.4) is

$$\hat{y} = 43 - 23.286 \cdot \text{COMP} = 43 - 23.286 \cdot 0 = 43\%$$

For regions that are highly competitive (COMP = 1), the predicted market share from Expression (7.4) is

$$\hat{y} = 43 - 23.286 \cdot \text{COMP} = 43 - 23.286 \cdot 1 = 19.71\%$$

In summary, when you have two (or more) quantitative variables, first determine if the two variables are linearly related.[7] Do this because a linear relationship is the simplest type of relationship and is easy to explain to others. First, plot the two variables in a scatter diagram and use the ellipse versus the circle test to determine if the variables are related or not. Then use Excel's SLOPE and INTERCEPT function wizards or the ADD TRENDLINE option to determine the equation for the best-fitting linear line or model. This equation indicates by the sign of the sample slope whether there is a positive or negative relationship between the two variables. Moreover, the magnitude of the sample slope indicates what change will occur in the dependent variable for a one-unit change in the explanatory variable. Finally, you can use the best-fitting linear line to make predictions about $y$ (for example, market share) for various values of $x$ (for example, level of advertising or level of competitiveness).

Relationships between variables are not always linear. Next, we turn to graphing and analyzing nonlinear relationships.

## NONLINEAR RELATIONSHIPS

Figure 7.9 is a scatter diagram of two quantitative variables, closeness of supervision on a 1 to 25 scale versus market share (see Table 7.4). Closeness of supervision is the explanatory variable and market share is the dependent variable. Are the two variables related?

Clearly there is no linear relationship between closeness of supervision and market share. But there is a **nonlinear** relationship that can be represented by

---

[7] Expression (7.3) indicates how advertising affects market share. Expression (7.4) indicates how level of competition affects market share. We could use Excel's Regression Analysis Data-Analysis Tool to develop one equation that indicates how advertising *and* level of competition affect market share. However, we will postpone this until Chapter 9.

an inverted U. As the closeness of supervision scores increase (supervision becomes more close or vigilant), market share initially increases. Market share, however, peaks for closeness scores of 11 to 13 and then drops.

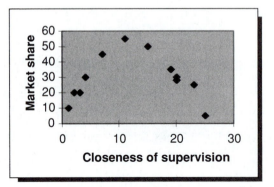

**Figure 7.9**
Scatter Diagram of
Closeness of Supervision
versus Market Share

How can we make sense of the nonlinear relationship? Managers with a lax management style may be too distant from their subordinates to provide effective leadership and mentoring. Managers who are neither too lax nor too close (scores of 11 to 13) may allow their subordinates to work freely and creatively. Managers with a too-tight style may suffocate their subordinates, and in turn, market share decreases. The nonlinear relationship may make sense.

We can use Excel's ADD TRENDLINE option to determine the best-fitting nonlinear line of order 2 (see Figure 7.10).[8]

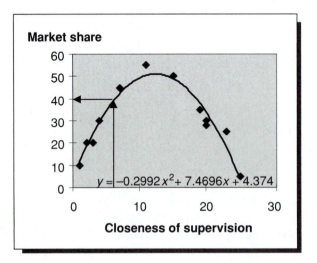

**Figure 7.10**
Best-Fitting Nonlinear
Line of Order 2
(Quadratic Curve) for
Closeness of Supervision
versus Market Share

---

[8] Excel solves three least squares equations with three unknowns ($a$ = intercept, $b$ = slope for linear term, and $c$ = slope for nonlinear term) to determine the best-fitting nonlinear line of order 2. This curve minimizes the sum of the squared deviations, or vertical distances, between it and the 12 data points. A polynomial of order $k$ has the form, $y = a + bx + cx^2 + \ldots + gx^k$.

Substituting the variable CLOSE for $x$ and rearranging terms, the best-fitting nonlinear line of order 2 is

$$\hat{y} = 4.374 + 7.4696 \cdot \text{CLOSE} - 0.2992 \cdot \text{CLOSE}^2$$

**(7.5)**

The vice president could use Expression (7.5) to make predictions on market share for differing closeness of supervision scores. For example, Baltimore's closeness of supervision score was 7. Expression (7.5) predicts that market share will be

$$\hat{y} = 4.374 + [7.4696 \cdot (7.0)] - [0.2992 \cdot (7.0)^2]$$
$$\hat{y} = 4.374 + 52.2872 - 14.6608 = 42.00\%$$

How are Expression (7.5) and its accompanying scatter diagram useful? What managerial action should the vice president take? Think about the possibilities before continuing.

Given the inverted U-shape, the vice president might ask the managers with a too-close management style to give their subordinates additional freedom and those with a too-loose style to provide more proactive leadership. Management should implement training for all but the Dallas regional manager. This is an example of *internal benchmarking* where the firm can improve its overall performance by seeking to emulate best practices within the firm.

Excel can determine the best-fitting nonlinear line for polynomials of order $k$ and logarithmic, power, and exponential curves. Use each type of curve when the scatter diagram indicates that as the explanatory variable increases, the dependent variable either increases or decreases by a *nonconstant* amount (see Table 7.15).

---

**D E F I N I T I O N**    A relationship between two variables is **nonlinear** if as the value of the explanatory variable, $x$, increases, $y$ does not change by a constant amount.

---

Here we illustrate how to select the *best* nonlinear line for a data set. A market research firm wants to know how many times a television viewer would have to see an advertisement before that viewer could recall it. The firm selects ten groups of 100 TV viewers. The firm assigns each group of 100 to one of the following ten conditions—view ad once during test week, view ad twice, ... view ad ten times. One month later, the firm asks all 1000 people to recall the ad. The market research firm records the percentages of each group who could correctly recall the ad.

| Dependent Variable | Type of Curve | General Expression |
|---|---|---|
| first increases (or decreases) and then increases (or decreases) **U-shaped curve** | polynomial of order 2 quadratic curve | $y = a + bx + cx^2$ |
| first increases (decreases) then decreases (increases), and then increases (decreases) **Sine curve** | polynomial of order 3 | $y = a + bx + cx^2 + dx^3$ |
| either increases or decreases by a nonconstant amount | exponential logarithmic power | $y = ae^{bx}$ $y = a + \ln x$ $y = ax^b$ |

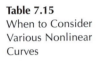

**Table 7.15**
When to Consider Various Nonlinear Curves

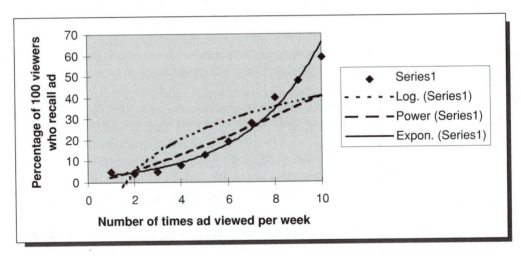

**Figure 7.11**
Number of Times Ad Viewed versus Percentage Recall

Figure 7.11 shows that only about 5% could remember an ad if it was viewed from one to three times a week. But above that level, the percentage increased nonlinearly as the firm aired the commercial more frequently. Thus, the firm considered representing the data by either a logarithmic, power, or exponential curve.

Excel's ADD TRENDLINE option developed the three best-fitting nonlinear lines; each curve is "best of its class." Figure 7.11 shows that the exponential curve is clearly the "best of show." Expression (7.6) is the least squares equation for the exponential curve obtained by the ADD TRENDLINE option.

$$\hat{y} = 2.3587e^{0.3264 \cdot NUMBER}$$

**(7.6)**

Expression (7.6) predicts the percentage of viewers who can recall the ad correctly based on the *NUMBER* of times they viewed the ad. For example, for viewers who saw the ad seven times, Equation (7.6) predicts that 23.17% will recall the ad correctly.

$$\hat{y} = 2.3587e^{0.3264 \cdot 7}$$
$$\hat{y} = 23.17\%$$

The actual percentage of viewers who saw the ad seven times a week was very close to this percentage (see Figure 7.11).

## CLUSTERS

Figure 7.12 is a scatter diagram of market share versus relative price for the 12 sales regions from Table 7.4. At first glance there appears to be no relationship between relative price and market share. We would need a circle or an ellipse parallel to the horizontal axis to enclose all the data points. Moreover, there is no nonlinear relationship. Can we conclude that the two variables are not related? Think about it before continuing.

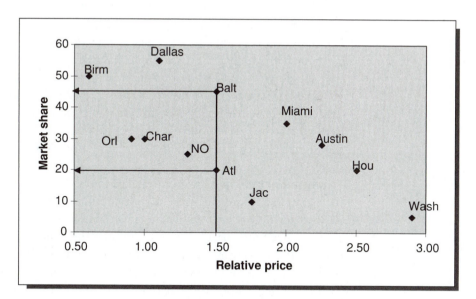

**Figure 7.12**
Relative Price versus
Market Share

Look again carefully at Figure 7.12. There are two distinct clusters, or groups, of data points, each consisting of six cities. The lower cluster includes the Atlanta, Birmingham, Charlotte, Jacksonville, New Orleans, and Orlando sales regions. The upper cluster includes the other six cities. How should we interpret the clusters?

Both clusters slope downward from left to right. Within each cluster, the higher the firm's price versus the mean of its competitors' prices the lower its market share. That makes economic sense. Now compare two cities—one in each cluster that have the same relative price. In the lower cluster, Atlanta has a 1.50 relative price, as does Baltimore in the upper cluster. In both regions, the firm's price is 1.50 times higher than the mean of its competitors. Then why does Baltimore have a 45% market share and Atlanta only a 20% share? There must be other variables that explain the different market shares for the same relative price.

**D E F I N I T I O N**    A **cluster** in a scatter diagram is a swarm of points that form a distinct grouping. If there are two or more clusters, determine what factors could account for the groupings.

Begin the diagnosis. First, what is *similar* about the six cities within each cluster? Second, what is *different* between the two clusters? For example, perhaps sales offices in the upper cluster cities provide better after-sales service, have more effective reward structures, have more efficient sales organizations, or sell to different clientele. Third, have there been any recent *changes* in the six cities in the upper cluster that might account for their superior performance? For example, have they recently run sales promotion campaigns? Have they recently restructured their sales forces?

Sales managers in the lower cluster cities should evaluate these *potential* differences and changes. If they find that the clustering is caused by factors over which they have control, they could raise market share to the level of the higher cluster. They would have found a pathway to higher market share.

In summary, when an important quantitative dependent variable varies, such as market share, begin by identifying potential explanatory variables. Then determine if each explanatory variable is linearly or nonlinearly related to the dependent variable. Finally, examine the scatter diagrams and seek clusters. If they occur, find reasons for the clustering. These graphical and mathematical methods help explain why an important dependent variable varies, and help improve the firm's productivity, profitability, or quality.

# ANALYZING TIME-ORDERED QUANTITATIVE DATA

In this section we continue to examine the relationship between two quantitative variables. We can, of course, use the methods of the previous section. But, because the data are *time ordered,* draw **leading period** scatter diagrams. By the end of this section you should be able to

**1.** construct and interpret leading period scatter diagrams; and

**2.** explain a leading relationship between two variables.

Table 7.5, shown again below, provides marketing data over 16 quarters. Market share varied from 15% to 25%. The sales manager has brainstormed two potential explanatory variables that could explain the variation—advertising expenditures and relative price.

| Quarter | Adv in (0000) | Rel. Price | Market Share |
|---|---|---|---|
| 1 | 13 | 1.15 | 24 |
| 2 | 11 | 1.65 | 18 |
| 3 | 17 | 1.80 | 16 |
| 4 | 20 | 1.45 | 22 |
| 5 | 20 | 1.20 | 24 |
| 6 | 16 | 1.25 | 24 |
| 7 | 15 | 1.40 | 20 |
| 8 | 13 | 1.45 | 21 |
| 9 | 17 | 1.65 | 18 |
| 10 | 11 | 1.35 | 22 |
| 11 | 19 | 1.70 | 16 |
| 12 | 15 | 1.18 | 24 |
| 13 | 21 | 1.54 | 20 |
| 14 | 10 | 1.20 | 25 |
| 15 | 15 | 1.90 | 15 |
| 16 | 13 | 1.47 | 20 |

**Table 7.5**
Marketing Database
for Time-Ordered
Quantitative Variables

Initially treat the data as cross sectional. Begin by plotting a scatter diagram of each explanatory variable and market share. A scatter diagram of relative price versus market share (not shown) indicates that the two variables are linearly and positively related. However, it is clear from Figure 7.13 that there is no linear or nonlinear relationship between advertising expenditures and market share. Nor are there any clusters. In short, the data are totally scattered.

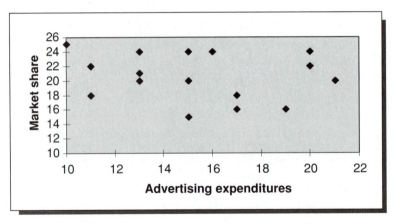

**Figure 7.13**
Advertising versus
Market Share

## DEVELOPING A SCATTER DIAGRAM WITH A LEADING PERIOD OF ONE

Since the data are time ordered, examine if the explanatory variable, advertising expenditures, **leads** market share. That is, does advertising expenditures in one quarter affect (or lead) market share in the next quarter? Or market share two or more quarters later? Marketing practitioners know that advertising's effects often take time to impact market share. Thus, examining for a leading relationship of one or two (or more) quarters makes sense.

| Quarter | Adv in (0000) | Rel. Price | Market Share |
|---------|---------------|------------|--------------|
| 1 | 13 | 1.15 | 24 |
| 2 | 11 | 1.65 | 18 |
| 3 | 17 | 1.80 | 16 |
| 4 | 20 | 1.45 | 22 |
| 5 | 20 | 1.20 | 24 |
| 6 | 16 | 1.25 | 24 |
| 7 | 15 | 1.40 | 20 |
| 8 | 13 | 1.45 | 21 |
| 9 | 17 | 1.65 | 18 |
| 10 | 11 | 1.35 | 22 |
| 11 | 19 | 1.70 | 16 |
| 12 | 15 | 1.18 | 24 |
| 13 | 21 | 1.54 | 20 |
| 14 | 10 | 1.20 | 25 |
| 15 | 15 | 1.90 | 15 |
| 16 | 13 | 1.47 | 20 |

**Table 7.5a**
Marketing Data Set
for Time-Ordered
Quantitative Variables

First, let's determine if advertising expenditures lead market share by one quarter. To draw a scatter diagram with a leading period of one, we must transform Table 7.5a and develop a new data set, Table 7.16. In the row labeled "quarter two" place market share for quarter two and the advertising expenditure for quarter one. Each row represents the market share for the quarter ($t$) and the advertising expenditure from the previous quarter ($t - 1$).

**Table 7.16**
Market Share for Quarter versus Advertising from Previous Quarter

| Quarter ($t$) | Adv($t-1$) | MShare ($t$) | Quarter ($t$) | Adv($t-1$) | MShare ($t$) |
|---|---|---|---|---|---|
| 2 | 13 | 18 | 10 | 17 | 22 |
| 3 | 11 | 16 | 11 | 11 | 16 |
| 4 | 17 | 22 | 12 | 19 | 24 |
| 5 | 20 | 24 | 13 | 15 | 20 |
| 6 | 20 | 24 | 14 | 21 | 25 |
| 7 | 16 | 20 | 15 | 10 | 15 |
| 8 | 15 | 21 | 16 | 15 | 20 |
| 9 | 13 | 18 | | | |

Figure 7.14 shows that market share in one period ($t$) is linearly and positively related to advertising expenditures in the previous quarter ($t - 1$). Using Excel's ADD TRENDLINE option, the equation for the best-fitting linear line is

$$\hat{y}(t) = 6.1929 + 0.9103 \cdot ADV(t - 1)$$

(7.7)

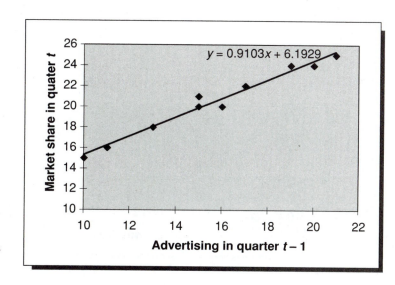

**Figure 7.14**
Market Share ($t$) versus Advertising Expenditures ($t - 1$)

From Expression (7.7), if the firm spends 175,000 (17.5) in a quarter, its market share next quarter should be about:

$$\hat{y}(t) = 6.1929 + [0.9103 \cdot 17.5] = 22.12\%$$

## DEVELOPING A SCATTER DIAGRAM WITH A LEADING PERIOD OF TWO

Next consider where advertising expenditure leads market share by two quarters. Table 7.17 contains the data. For the quarter three row, place market share for quarter three and advertising expenditures for quarter one. Each row represents the market share for the quarter ($t$) and the advertising expenditures from two quarters earlier ($t - 2$).

Figure 7.15 indicates that there is no linear or nonlinear relationship between market share in one quarter and advertising expenditures from two quarters earlier. Nor are there any clusters. In short, the data are totally scattered.

**Table 7.17**
Market Share for Quarter and Advertising from Two Quarters Earlier

| Quarter ($t$) | Adv($t-2$) | MShare ($t$) | Quarter ($t$) | Adv($t-2$) | MShare ($t$) |
|---|---|---|---|---|---|
| 3 | 13 | 16 | 10 | 13 | 22 |
| 4 | 11 | 22 | 11 | 17 | 16 |
| 5 | 17 | 24 | 12 | 11 | 24 |
| 6 | 20 | 24 | 13 | 19 | 20 |
| 7 | 20 | 20 | 14 | 15 | 25 |
| 8 | 16 | 21 | 15 | 21 | 15 |
| 9 | 15 | 18 | 16 | 10 | 20 |

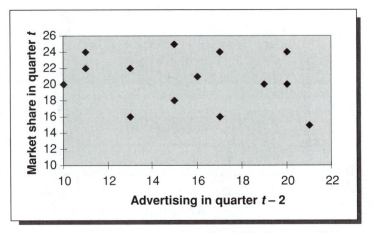

**Figure 7.15**
Market Share ($t$) versus Advertising Expenditures ($t-2$)

We could determine if advertising expenditures lead market share by three, four, or more quarters. For the sake of brevity, we will not present these analyses here.

In summary, with time-ordered data, begin by plotting each explanatory variable and the dependent variable. If you find no relationship, generate scatter diagrams with one or more leading periods. Once you have detected a linear or nonlinear relationship use the ADD TRENDLINE option to determine the best-fitting line or curve. Use the best-fitting line or curve to make predictions on the dependent variable.

# ANALYZING TIME-ORDERED QUANTITATIVE DATA: AUTOREGRESSIVE EQUATIONS

In the previous section we developed leading-period scatter diagrams. These indicated whether the value of a *dependent variable* in one period was affected by the values of an *explanatory variable* from one or more previous periods. Similarly, we could ask if the value of a *dependent variable* in one period is affected by the values of the *dependent variable* from one or more previous periods. We answer the latter question by developing an **autoregressive** equation using Excel's ADD TRENDLINE option. By the end of this section you should be able to develop and interpret an autoregressive equation or model.

**Table 7.6**
Database to Develop an
Autoregressive Equation

| Month | Sales ($t$) (tens of thousands) | Month | Sales ($t$) (tens of thousands) |
|-------|-------------------------------|-------|-------------------------------|
| 1 | 3.40 | 9 | 5.61 |
| 2 | 2.00 | 10 | 4.05 |
| 3 | 1.90 | 11 | 4.63 |
| 4 | 3.20 | 12 | 5.01 |
| 5 | 4.80 | 13 | 6.03 |
| 6 | 3.75 | 14 | 4.61 |
| 7 | 4.13 | 15 | 5.08 |
| 8 | 4.51 | 16 | 5.29 |

Table 7.6, shown again above, contains sales data (in tens of thousands of units) over 16 months. Can we use sales in one month to estimate sales in future months? Before answering that question, let's draw a *line graph* of the data in Table 7.6. Recall from Chapter 2 that the line graph is an essential tool for displaying univariate time-ordered data.

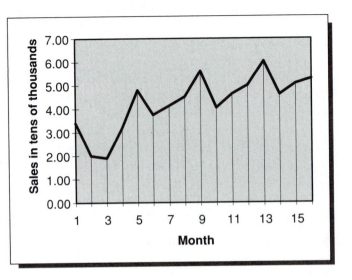

**Figure 7.16**
Line Graph of Sales over
16 Months

Figure 7.16 exhibits a distinct and systematic pattern. Over the 16 months sales have generally increased. More important, sales peaked in months 1, 5, 9, and 13. Sales bottomed out in months 2–3, 6–7, 10–11, and 14–15. Whenever you see any systematic pattern, consider developing an autoregressive model or equation.

**DEFINITION**     An autoregressive model uses data values from one or more previous periods of the dependent variable for its explanatory variables.

## DEVELOPING A ONE-PERIOD LEADING AUTOREGRESSIVE EQUATION

Construct Table 7.18 from Table 7.6a. Starting in month 2, each row in Table 7.18 represents the sales for the previous month $(t-1)$ and the sales for the month $(t)$.

Figure 7.17 is a scatter diagram of sales $(t)$ versus sales $(t-1)$. The explanatory variable is sales $(t-1)$ and the dependent variable is sales $(t)$. The scatter diagram indicates that sales in one month is positively related to sales from the previous month, as the swarm of data points is upward sloping to the right. The ADD TRENDLINE option generated the following best-fitting linear autoregression equation.

$$\hat{y}(t) = 1.6679 + 0.6312 \cdot SALES(t-1)$$

(7.8)

| Month | Sales ($t$) |
|-------|-------------|
| 1 | 3.40 |
| 2 | 2.00 |
| 3 | 1.90 |
| 4 | 3.20 |
| 5 | 4.80 |
| 6 | 3.75 |
| 7 | 4.13 |
| 8 | 4.51 |
| 9 | 5.61 |
| 10 | 4.05 |
| 11 | 4.63 |
| 12 | 5.01 |
| 13 | 6.03 |
| 14 | 4.61 |
| 15 | 5.08 |
| 16 | 5.29 |

**Table 7.6a**
Original Database

| Month ($t$) | Sales ($t-1$) | Sales ($t$) |
|-------------|---------------|-------------|
| 2 | 3.40 | 2.00 |
| 3 | 2.00 | 1.90 |
| 4 | 1.90 | 3.20 |
| 5 | 3.20 | 4.80 |
| 6 | 4.80 | 3.75 |
| 7 | 3.75 | 4.13 |
| 8 | 4.13 | 4.51 |
| 9 | 4.51 | 5.61 |
| 10 | 5.61 | 4.05 |
| 11 | 4.05 | 4.63 |
| 12 | 4.63 | 5.01 |
| 13 | 5.01 | 6.03 |
| 14 | 6.03 | 4.61 |
| 15 | 4.61 | 5.08 |
| 16 | 5.08 | 5.29 |

**Table 7.18**
Sales ($t$) versus Sales ($t-1$)

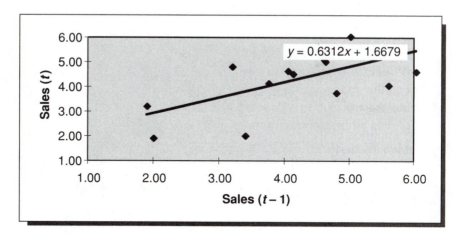

**Figure 7.17**
Scatter Diagram of
Sales ($t$) versus Sales
($t-1$)

Interpret the sample intercept and slope as you would for any other best-fitting linear line. Sales (in tens of thousands of units) in any month are equal to a constant amount (1.6679) plus 63.12% of the sales for the previous month.

Business professionals use autoregressive models or equations for forecasting. If the dependent variable exhibits a systematic pattern (from a line graph), then develop scatter diagrams and their accompanying best-fitting lines to determine if

**1.** sales $(t - 1)$ is related to sales $(t)$,

**2.** sales $(t - 2)$ is related to sales $(t)$,

**3.** .

**4.** .

**k.** sales $(t - k)$ is related to sales $(t)$.

# CORRELATION AND CROSS-CORRELATION

Scatter diagrams are useful in identifying leading or coincident relationships. However, scatter diagrams and their accompanying best-fitting lines do not indicate the strength of the linear relationship between two variables. Correlation and cross-correlation coefficients provide a convenient and simple-to-understand numerical index that measures the degree of the linear association between two variables. By the end of this section you should be able to

**1.** explain what a correlation coefficient measures and why it is useful for cross-sectional data;

**2.** explain how to use the "ellipse versus circle test" to estimate a correlation coefficient;

**3.** define covariance and explain how it relates to the correlation coefficient;

**4.** use Excel's CORREL and COVAR function wizards and interpret their output;

**5.** use Excel's correlation data-analysis tool to compute a correlation matrix; and

**6.** explain when the cross-correlation coefficient should be used and how to interpret it.

## THE CORRELATION COEFFICIENT

The correlation coefficient, $r$, is a numerical measure of the strength of a linear relationship between two variables. Correlation coefficients can vary from $-1$ to $+1$. The graphs in Figure 7.18 show different degrees of linear associations and their correlation values.

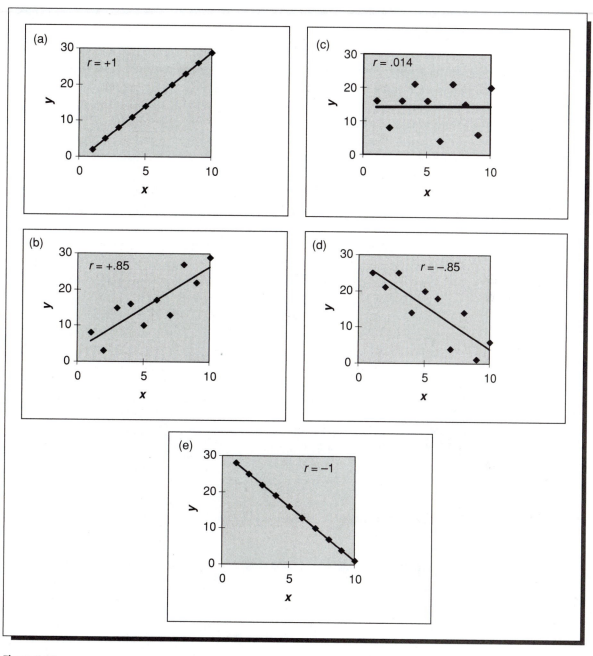

**Figure 7.18**
Scatter Diagrams and Associated Correlation Coefficient Values

In scatter diagram (a), $r = +1$. There is a *perfect positive* linear relationship between the two variables. It is perfect because $r$ equals 1 and positive because of the plus sign. The relationship is perfect in the sense that all the data points fall on an unbroken straight line. If we determine the best-fitting linear line we can predict $y$ values with perfect certainty. The relationship is positive because as variable $x$ increases, variable $y$ also increases. Graph (e) shows a *perfect inverse* linear relationship, and $r$ has a value of $-1$. In both graphs (a) and (e), only variable $x$ affects variable $y$.

Scatter diagrams (b) and (d) show lines that fit the pattern of data points quite well, but not perfectly. A tight ellipse can enclose the data points. Correlation coefficients are close to $+1$ and $-1$. In graphs (b) and (d), variables other than $x$ affect variable y. That is why all ten data values do not lie on the linear line.

Scatter diagram (c) shows a pattern of points that you can enclose by a circle or an ellipse parallel to the $x$-axis. The correlation coefficient is close to 0, indicating no linear relationship. That is, as variable $x$ increases, variable $y$ neither increases nor decreases. The horizontal line indicates the lack of a linear relationship between the two variables.

Let's use Excel's CORREL function wizard to compute the four correlation coefficients between each explanatory variable and the market share dependent variable in Table 7.4. Shown below is the function wizard screen for computing the correlation coefficient between advertising expenditures and market share. Note that $r = +0.99374$, indicating an almost perfect positive linear relationship. Table 7.19 presents the remaining correlation coefficients.

```
CORREL
    Array1  B2:B13                          = {13;28;17;8;16;18;2
    Array2  F2:F13                          = {20;50;30;10;25;30

                                            = 0.993741333
Returns the correlation coefficient between two data sets.

    Array2 is a second cell range of values. The values should be numbers, names,
           arrays, or references that contain numbers.

    ?       Formula result =0.993741333          OK         Cancel
```

| Correlation between | Coefficient | Interpretation |
|---|---|---|
| Adv and Market Share (MS) | $r_{adv,\ mshare} = 0.99374$ | Variables are almost perfectly positively related. |
| Closeness and MS | $r_{close,\ mshare} = 0.00846$ | Variables are not linearly related. |
| Level of Competition and MS | $r_{comp,\ mshare} = -0.79142$ | Variables are strongly negatively related. |
| Relative Price and MS | $r_{price,\ mshare} = -0.64956$ | Variables are strongly negatively related. |

**Table 7.19**
Correlation Coefficients between Explanatory and Dependent Variables in Table 7.4

As informative as the correlation coefficient is, the scatter diagram is also a valuable aid. Two examples demonstrate this. First, the correlation between closeness of supervision and market share is only 0.00846. There is no linear relationship between the two variables. However, Figure 7.10 shows that closeness of supervision is *nonlinearly* related to market share. That is, the overall best-fitting curve is a polynomial of order 2. Second, while the correlation coefficient between relative price and market share indicates a strong negative relationship, it does not tell us of the two distinct clusters in the data (see Figure 7.12).

## VISUALIZING COVARIANCE: A FOUR-QUADRANT ANALYSIS

We will use the advertising expenditure and market-share data from Table 7.4 to explore the connection between correlation, covariance, and the "ellipse versus circle test."

Understanding the equation for calculating the correlation coefficient, Expression (7.9), is helpful.

$$r = \frac{\text{Covariance}(x, y)}{s_x \cdot s_y}$$

(7.9)

The terms, $s_x$ and $s_y$, are the sample standard deviations for the two variables. From Excel's STDEV function wizard, these are 7.85619 (or \$78,561.90) and 15.15 (or 15.15%), respectively.

The numerator, the *covariance*, is an extension of the variance concept. Covariance measures the extent to which the data values of the two variables move together, or covary.

$$\text{Covariance} = \frac{\sum_i \left(x_i - \bar{x}\right) \cdot \left(y_i - \bar{y}\right)}{n - 1}$$

(7.10)

Visualizing the *covariance* is important. Figure 7.19 reproduces Figure 7.3 with two important additions. We have drawn a horizontal line at the mean for market share, 29.42%, and a vertical line at the mean for advertising expenditures, 17.58. Excel's AVERAGE function wizard provided these two means. These two lines divide the scatter diagram into four quadrants labeled A, B, C, and D.

From Expression (7.9), the sign of the covariance determines the sign of the correlation coefficient because the standard deviations in the denominator are always positive. In turn, the sign of the covariance depends on the cross-product term in the numerator of Expression (7.10). To determine the signs of the cross-product terms, use the quadrants in Figure 7.19 to obtain the results shown in Table 7.20.

**Table 7.20**
The Quadrants and Associated Cross-Products Terms

| Quadrant | $x_i - \bar{x}$ | $y_i - \bar{y}$ | Cross-Product Terms $(x_i - \bar{x}) \cdot (y_i - \bar{y})$ |
|---|---|---|---|
| A | Negative | Positive | Negative |
| B | Positive | Positive | Positive |
| C | Negative | Negative | Positive |
| D | Positive | Negative | Negative |

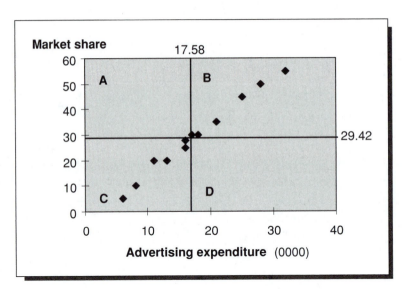

**Figure 7.19**
Advertising Expenditures versus Market Share with Quadrants Drawn

Let's analyze the data in Figure 7.19. In quadrant B, there are six data values where both the advertising expenditures and market-share data values are both larger than their respective means. From Expression (7.10), the cross-product terms for these data points will be positive. In quadrant C, there are also six data points where both the advertising expenditures and market-share data values are less than their respective means. The cross-product terms will also be positive. Given no data values in quadrants A and D, the covariance should be a large positive value and the correlation should be positive.

When there is a positive linear relationship, most data points will lie in quadrants B and C. The covariance terms and thus the correlation coefficient will be positive. When there is a negative linear relationship, most data points will lie in quadrants A and D. The covariance terms and thus the correlation coefficient will be negative. When there is no linear relationship, there are roughly equal numbers of data points in the four quadrants. The positive cross-product terms for data points in quadrants B and C will cancel out the negative cross-product terms from quadrants A and D. The covariance and thus the correlation coefficient will be approximately 0.

## THE CORRELATION MATRIX

Excel's CORREL function wizard has one limitation. It only computes one correlation coefficient at a time. Suppose you wanted to compute the correlation coefficients for *all* pairs of the five variables in Table 7.4. There are ten such pairs of variables, and you would have to use the CORREL function wizard ten times. This is time consuming.

Excel provides a correlation data-analysis tool for this purpose. It produces a **correlation matrix** for all pairs of variables from a database. Below is the dialog box.

| | Adv | Closeness | Competitive? | Rel.Price | MShare |
|---|---|---|---|---|---|
| Adv | 1 | | | | |
| Closeness | 0.035885285 | 1 | | | |
| Competitive? | −0.810877063 | 0.129408232 | 1 | | |
| Rel. Price | −0.656920654 | 0.156343643 | 0.493189351 | 1 | |
| Market Share | **0.993741333** | **0.008458209** | **−0.79142441** | **−0.649557** | 1 |

**Table 7.21**
Correlation Matrix for Table 7.4 Data

Consider Table 7.21. What does the correlation matrix reveal? The intersection of a row and column is the correlation coefficient for the two corresponding variables. Earlier, Excel's CORREL function wizard provided the four bold-faced values in the bottom row of the correlation matrix. These are the correlation coefficients for market share versus the four explanatory variables. The 1s along the matrix's diagonal are the correlation coefficients of a variable versus itself. These are not too informative, and nothing would be lost if they were omitted. The six values within the triangular-shaped area are the correlation coefficients for all pairs of **explanatory** variables. For example, the correlation coefficient between competitiveness level and closeness of supervision is 0.1294.

We have not discussed these six correlation coefficients in this section. However, these will be very important for assessing multicollinearity, a topic that we postpone until regression analysis in Chapter 9.

## THE CROSS-CORRELATION COEFFICIENT

Correlation coefficients measure the linear relationship between two variables. When we ask if an explanatory variable is linearly related to a dependent variable in one or more subsequent time periods, we are interested in computing **cross**-correlations. Of course, you must have time-ordered data to compute cross-correlation coefficients.

The cross-correlation concept is an extension of correlation. We can compute cross-correlations where one variable leads another by one, two, or more time periods. The symbols are $r(1)$, $r(2)$, etc. We interpret a cross-correlation the same as a correlation coefficient. In short, the cross-correlation measures the strength of the linear association between a *leading* explanatory variable and a dependent variable. You can use Excel's CORREL function wizard to compute cross-correlations.

**DEFINITION**    A **cross-correlation coefficient** is a numerical measure of the linear relationship between a dependent variable for time $t$ and an explanatory variable from one or more earlier time periods. Similar to a correlation coefficient, it varies from –1 to +1.

We have reproduced Table 7.16 and 7.17 here. We used these tables to develop scatter diagrams with a leading period of one and a leading period of two earlier in the chapter.

By applying the CORREL wizard to the data in Table 7.16 and 7.17 we obtained the cross-correlation coefficients for market share and advertising expenditures for one or two quarters earlier. The magnitudes of the cross-correlation coefficients are in agreement with Figures 7.14 and 7.15.

| Quarter ($t$) | Adv($t$) | MShare ($t$) |
|:---:|:---:|:---:|
| 2 | 13 | 18 |
| 3 | 11 | 16 |
| 4 | 17 | 22 |
| 5 | 20 | 24 |
| 6 | 20 | 24 |
| 7 | 16 | 20 |
| 8 | 15 | 21 |
| 9 | 13 | 18 |
| 10 | 17 | 22 |
| 11 | 11 | 16 |
| 12 | 19 | 24 |
| 13 | 15 | 20 |
| 14 | 21 | 25 |
| 15 | 10 | 15 |
| 16 | 15 | 20 |

$$r(1) = +.98956$$

**Table 7.16a**
Market Share for Quarter and Advertising
from One Quarter Earlier

| Quarter ($t$) | Adv($t - 2$) | MShare ($t$) |
|:---:|:---:|:---:|
| 3 | 13 | 16 |
| 4 | 11 | 22 |
| 5 | 17 | 24 |
| 6 | 20 | 24 |
| 7 | 20 | 20 |
| 8 | 16 | 21 |
| 9 | 15 | 18 |
| 10 | 13 | 22 |
| 11 | 17 | 16 |
| 12 | 11 | 24 |
| 13 | 19 | 20 |
| 14 | 15 | 25 |
| 15 | 21 | 15 |
| 16 | 10 | 20 |

$$r(2) = -.21340$$

**Table 7.17a**
Market Share for Quarter and Advertising from
Two Quarters Earlier

In summary, when looking for relationships between two variables for which we have time-ordered data, compute cross-correlation coefficients for one, two, or more periods. Try to make sense of the cross-correlations. That is, why should variable $x$ affect variable $y$ in $k$ or more periods later?

# GUIDELINES FOR USING CHAPTER'S DESCRIPTIVE METHODS

In this chapter you have learned many methods for assessing and quantifying relationships between two (or more) variables. Table 7.22 summarizes the descriptive methods presented in this chapter.

| Dependent Variable | Explanatory Variable | Analytical Tools |
|---|---|---|
| Quantitative | Qualitative | Develop one-way tables. Draw multiple box plots. Draw a scatter diagram; code the qualitative explanatory variable as 0 or 1. |
| Qualitative | Qualitative | Develop contingency tables. Compute row or column percentage tables. Examine for impact of intervening variables. |
| Quantitative | Quantitative | **For Cross-Sectional Data** Draw scatter diagrams. Determine best-fitting linear line or nonlinear curve. For linear lines, compute the correlation coefficient. |
| Quantitative | Quantitative | **For Time-Ordered Data** Treat as cross-sectional data. Draw leading-period scatter diagrams. Compute best-fitting linear line or nonlinear curve. For linear lines, compute the cross-correlation coefficients for one, two, or more time periods. Consider an autoregressive equation. |

**Table 7.22**
Guidelines for Using the Statistical and Graphical Methods in Chapter 7

# EXERCISES

**1.** What is the difference between univariate and multivariate data?

**2.** What role do intervening variables play in a contingency-table analysis?

**3.** Does a finding of no linear or nonlinear relationship between two variables mean that the two variables are not related?

**4.** What is the difference between a correlation coefficient and a cross-correlation coefficient?

**5.** The chapter can be subtitled "looking for relationships." Explain why.

**6.** What is meant by the term "best fitting linear line"?

**7.** From the field of finance, suggest two variables where the impact of one variable affects the second variable one or more periods later.

**8.** Does a high correlation mean that one variable causes another variable to vary?

**9.** Distinguish between quantitative and categorical data.

**10.** If the correlation coefficient is 0, does that mean that two variables are not related? Discuss.

**11.** Length-of-tenure discounts are the differences between the rents charged longtime tenants and newer tenants. Landlords give discounts because they want to keep good tenants and minimize turnover. The length-of-tenure discounts in Chicago vary from 1.5% to 11.5%. Why is there so much variability? The American Housing Association believes that it is due to the size of the apartment complex. Larger complexes (more than ten units) are owned by corporations and can afford to have vacant apartments. Thus they give smaller discounts. Small complexes owned by families cannot afford to have unrented apartments and so give higher discounts for tenants to stay.

| Discount | Size of Complex | Discount | Size of Complex |
|----------|-----------------|----------|-----------------|
| 1.5 | Large | 6.5 | Small |
| 2.0 | Large | 11.5 | Small |
| 5.4 | Small | 2.7 | Large |
| 2.5 | Large | 10.7 | Small |
| 3.9 | Large | 2.9 | Large |
| 1.7 | Large | 6.7 | Small |
| 5.5 | Small | 5.2 | Small |
| 3.4 | Large | 8.7 | Small |

**a.** Develop a one-way table and multiple box plot using size of complex as the explanatory variable. For the one-way table, compute only the mean and standard deviation.

**b.** From part (a), does complex size seem to explain why discounts vary widely for the 16 apartment complexes in Chicago?

**c.** Why couldn't you use a scatter diagram to organize and summarize the data?

**12.** An advertising manager wants to determine whether level of advertising is positively related to sales. If so, she may increase advertising. If the two variables are not related, she may reduce advertising. Shown are the most recent 20 months of sales and level of advertising data. Are the two variables related?

**a.** Use Excel's chart wizard to draw a scatter diagram for sales and level of advertising. Use Excel's ADD TRENDLINE option to determine the best-fitting line and the CORREL function wizard to compute the correlation coefficient.

**b.** Draw a scatter diagram for sales and the previous month's advertising. Use Excel's ADD TRENDLINE option to determine the best-fitting line and the CORREL function wizard to compute the correlation coefficient.

**c.** Which scatter diagram is more suggestive of a relationship between sales and level of advertising? Explain the relationship in terms that a marketing manager could understand.

| Month | Sales (000 of units) | Advertising (000 of dollars) |
|-------|----------------------|------------------------------|
| 1 | 210 | 23.0 |
| 2 | 210 | 25.5 |
| 3 | 235 | 26.5 |
| 4 | 220 | 27.0 |
| 5 | 250 | 27.0 |
| 6 | 250 | 32.5 |
| 7 | 270 | 28.0 |
| 8 | 260 | 29.5 |
| 9 | 290 | 34.0 |
| 10 | 320 | 29.0 |
| 11 | 270 | 36.0 |
| 12 | 320 | 33.0 |
| 13 | 310 | 34.0 |
| 14 | 340 | 32.0 |
| 15 | 300 | 38.0 |
| 16 | 360 | 30.0 |
| 17 | 330 | 40.0 |
| 18 | 380 | 43.0 |
| 19 | 410 | 42.0 |
| 20 | 400 | 30.0 |

13. A stock analyst specializing in the retail industry wants to know if chain stores, such as Sears, stress the same focus—service or price—as do independents. He surveys 30 independents and 20 chains and determines if they are price or service oriented. Here are the data.

|  | Service | Price | Total |
|---|---|---|---|
| Independents | 25 | 5 | 30 |
| Chains | 4 | 16 | 20 |

Do independents and chains have the same focus for the 50 stores samples? Defend your position.

14. Shown below are sales in thousands of units over 16 quarters. Each column represents one year of data.

| Year 1 | Year 2 | Year 3 | Year 4 | Year 5 |
|---|---|---|---|---|
| 85 | 136 | 104 | 166 | 112 |
| 133 | 94 | 154 | 115 | 184 |
| 175 | 136 | 210 | 148 | 237 |
| 140 | 205 | 144 | 229 | 170 |

Use Excel's chart wizard to draw a line graph of the data. Do the data appear to have a systematic pattern? If so, explain the pattern in terms a marketing manager could understand.

15. Shown is a specific sample of ten surgeons. We have recorded their annual incomes as the dependent variable. Number of years in practice, and whether they are board certified (passed a certification test similar to the CPA in accounting) are the two explanatory variables.

| Surgeon | Annual Income | Years of Experience | Board-Certified |
|---|---|---|---|
| 1 | $170,000 | 4 | no |
| 2 | 190,000 | 6 | no |
| 3 | 180,000 | 8 | no |
| 4 | 195,000 | 5 | no |
| 5 | 210,000 | 8 | no |
| 6 | 240,000 | 10 | yes |
| 7 | 300,000 | 10 | yes |
| 8 | 370,000 | 12 | yes |
| 9 | 430,000 | 13 | yes |
| 10 | 510,000 | 15 | yes |

Do the appropriate analyses and explain your findings in terms a manager could understand.

16. The Myers–Briggs Type Indicator (MBTI) measures four dimensions of human behavior. One dimension is how people make judgments. They are either thinkers (T) or feelers (F). Thinkers use logic and analysis; feelers stress feelings and impacts on people. Do thinkers and feelers choose different careers? One hundred preschool teachers and 86 computer systems analysts are interviewed. Each completes the MBTI. The contingency table data are shown here. [Source: *Manual: A Guide to the Development of the Myers-Briggs Type Indicator*, I. Myers and M. McCaulley, Palo Alto, CA,1985, pp. 248–250.]

|  | Thinker | Feeler | Total |
|---|---|---|---|
| Preschool Teacher | 21 | 79 | 100 |
| Computer Analyst | 66 | 20 | 86 |

a. Use either row or column percentage tables to determine if the thinker/feeler dimension is related to career preference.

b. Why couldn't you use a one-way table to determine if the two variables are related?

**17.** A financial analyst believes that firms that produce high-quality products have higher returns on investment than those firms that produce low-quality products. Product quality is rated from 50 for low quality to 100 for high quality. Shown are data collected on ten firms.

**a.** Develop a scatter diagram that relates product quality and return on investment.

**b.** Determine the best-fitting line and the correlation coefficient.

**c.** Use the equation for the best-fitting line to predict return on investment for firm 7 that has a product quality score of 100.

**d.** Would you expect the actual and predicted returns on investment to be the same? Discuss.

| Firm | Average Product Quality | Return on Investment (%) |
|------|------|------|
| 1 | 90 | 14.5 |
| 2 | 50 | 8.7 |
| 3 | 50 | 8.8 |
| 4 | 70 | 9.0 |
| 5 | 90 | 13.5 |
| 6 | 70 | 11.4 |
| 7 | 100 | 22.5 |
| 8 | 100 | 17.8 |
| 9 | 60 | 8.5 |
| 10 | 60 | 8.2 |

**18.** Market–research personnel believe that in selling VCRs informative advertising is more effective (higher monthly sales) than persuasive advertising. Below are VCR sales data for 16 stores of a national chain. Informative advertising was used in eight stores in Atlanta, and persuasive advertising was used in eight stores (of similar size and sales history) in Houston.

| Informative | 630 | 644 | 640 | 652 | 632 | 645 | 651 | 638 |
|------|------|------|------|------|------|------|------|------|
| Persuasive | 533 | 546 | 549 | 534 | 527 | 534 | 548 | 529 |

Do the appropriate analyses and explain your findings in terms a manager could understand.

**19.** Below are time-ordered data on the number of quality circle ideas on reducing scrap that were accepted by top management and the percentage of scrap in a production process.

**a.** Develop a scatter diagram of number of ideas ($t$) versus percentage scrap ($t$). Perform an ellipse test. Also compute the correlation coefficient.

**b.** Develop a scatter diagram of number of ideas ($t-1$) versus percentage scrap ($t$). Perform an ellipse test. Also compute the cross-correlation coefficient, $r(1)$.

**c.** Develop a scatter diagram of number of ideas ($t-2$) versus percentage scrap ($t$). Perform an ellipse test. Also compute the cross-correlation coefficient, $r(2)$.

**d.** From the above three analyses what can you conclude about the impact of number of ideas accepted by top management and percentage scrap? Discuss.

| Month | Percentage of Scrap | Number of Ideas |
|------|------|------|
| 1 | 4.5% | 10 |
| 2 | 2.8% | 6 |
| 3 | 3.4% | 2 |
| 4 | 3.9% | 15 |
| 5 | 2.6% | 12 |
| 6 | 2.7% | 3 |
| 7 | 3.7% | 15 |

**20.** Some experts believe that asset size and type of organizational structure affect the number of product innovations. Shown are the data for a study of product innovation in the insurance industry.

| Firm | Number of Innovations over a 3-Year Period | Asset Size (millions) | Decentralized |
|------|------|------|------|
| 1 | 10 | 200 | no |
| 2 | 14 | 300 | no |
| 3 | 12 | 400 | no |
| 4 | 13 | 500 | no |
| 5 | 12 | 600 | no |
| 6 | 10 | 215 | yes |
| 7 | 13 | 290 | yes |
| 8 | 16 | 405 | yes |
| 9 | 19 | 510 | yes |
| 10 | 23 | 580 | yes |

**a.** Develop a scatter diagram between the number of innovations and asset size. Does there appear to be a linear relationship between the two variables?

**b.** Label each point in the scatter diagram as (C)entralized or (D)ecentralized. Are there distinct clusters? What can you conclude about the impact of decentralization on the asset size versus number of product innovations relationship of the ten insurance firms?

**21.** Three years ago 50 new people were hired at plant A and at plant B. A recent review showed that 15 of 50 are still working at plant A and 25 of 50 are still working at plant B.

**Table 1**

|  | Plant A | Plant B | Total |
|------|------|------|------|
| Still Employed | 15 | 25 | 40 |
| Left Employment | 35 | 25 | 60 |
|  | 50 | 50 | 100 |

**Table 2**

| Nonmanagers | Plant A | Plant B | Total |
|------|------|------|------|
| Still Employed | 7 | 9 | 16 |
| Left Employment | 33 | 21 | 54 |
|  | 40 | 30 | 70 |

| Managers | Plant A | Plant B | Total |
|------|------|------|------|
| Still Employed | 8 | 16 | 24 |
| Left Employment | 2 | 4 | 6 |
|  | 10 | 20 | 30 |

**a.** Based on the information in Table 1, does it appear that labor retention is related to place of employment? Explain using either row or column percentages.

**b.** Table 2 shows the same data broken down by whether the new employees were in managerial or nonmanagerial positions. Does it appear that employee retention is related to place of employment after controlling for type of position? Explain.

**c.** Develop two other plausible intervening variables that could explain differential retention rates of the two plants.

**22.** Generate hypothetical data and develop a multiple box plot that shows that performance level—top quartile of performers versus bottom quartile of performers—is related to average annual raise. Your multiple box plot should show that the top-quartile performers had higher median annual raises and lower variability than the bottom-quartile performers.

**23.** Does mean daily patient load determine the number of x-rays at ten nonteaching hospitals in the New York City area?

| Hospital | Number of X-rays | Mean Patient Load |
|----------|------------------|-------------------|
| 1        | 2100             | 65                |
| 2        | 9100             | 90                |
| 3        | 11,400           | 105               |
| 4        | 12,500           | 125               |
| 5        | 15,000           | 160               |
| 6        | 24,500           | 200               |
| 7        | 30,500           | 250               |
| 8        | 35,500           | 240               |
| 9        | 45,000           | 300               |
| 10       | 47,500           | 310               |

**a.** Determine the best-fitting linear line for the above data and the correlation coefficient.

**b.** Determine the sum of the squared deviations.

**c.** Explain what is meant by the term "best-fitting line."

**d.** Use the expression for the best-fitting line to predict hospital 6's number of x-rays.

**e.** Why aren't the actual and predicted number of x-rays the same?

**24.** Spreadsheet 724.xls contains data on sales (000s of units) versus research and development expenditures (0000s of dollars) for the past 28 quarters.

**a.** Draw a scatter diagram of sales ($t$) versus R&D ($t$). Compute the correlation coefficient.

**b.** Draw a scatter diagram of sales ($t$) versus R&D ($t - 1$). Compute the cross-correlation coefficient, $r(1)$.

**c.** Draw a scatter diagram of sales ($t$) versus R&D ($t - 2$). Compute the cross-correlation coefficient, $r(2)$.

**d.** Draw a scatter diagram of sales ($t$) versus R&D ($t - 3$). Compute the cross-correlation coefficient, $r(3)$.

**e.** Based on parts (a)–(d), is R&D related to sales? Discuss.

**25.** Best Dairy, Inc., sells to two market segments. Machos are blue-collar men in their twenties with below-median incomes. Status seekers are families in their thirties who have above-median incomes. Best Dairy wonders if Machos and Status Seekers have different preferences for skim and whole milk. Best Dairy, Inc., interviews 200 customers and cross-classifies them along the following two dimensions:

|       | Machos | Status Seekers | Total |
|-------|--------|----------------|-------|
| Skim  | 30     | 80             | 110   |
| Whole | 70     | 20             | 90    |
|       | 100    | 100            | 200   |

**a.** Compute the row and the column percentages. For the specific sample of 200 customers, do Machos and Status Seekers prefer skim and whole milk equally?

**b.** Suppose we use the weight of the customer as an intervening variable. There are 80 underweight customers and 120 overweight customers in the sample of 200. Develop two type-of-milk versus market-segment contingency tables (one for underweight and one for overweight customers) that would indicate that after controlling for the intervening variable, there is no relationship between type of milk and market segment. The sum of the column totals for both tables must sum to 100 Machos and 100 Status Seekers.

**26.** Spreadsheet 726.xls contains 28 months of data. The dependent variable is sales and the predictor variable is housing starts. An analyst has three beliefs. First, she believes that housing starts is a coincident indicator of sales. Second, she believes that housing starts $(t - 2)$ are related to sales $(t)$. Third, she also believes that sales $(t - 1)$ affects sales $(t)$. Develop the necessary scatter diagrams and compute the correlation and cross-correlation coefficients to verify the analyst's three claims.

27. The Arbitration Association collects data on the number of grievances filed by plants with between 200 and 300 workers. It wonders why the number of grievances varies from 45 to 99 among the ten firms. Could the large variability be related to a firm's use of participative management? It determines whether each firm uses participative management. Shown are the data.

   **a.** Using the absence or presence of participative management as an explanatory variable, construct a one-way table for the mean and standard deviation.

   **b.** Develop a scatter diagram of the type of management (0 = participative and 1 = not participative) versus number of grievances. Determine the best-fitting line and the correlation coefficient.

   **c.** From parts (a)–(b), does it appear that for the ten firms, participative management has an impact on the number of grievances?

| Firms | Grievances | Participative Management |
|-------|-----------|--------------------------|
| 1 | 70 | No |
| 2 | 74 | No |
| 3 | 65 | Yes |
| 4 | 45 | Yes |
| 5 | 78 | No |
| 6 | 69 | Yes |
| 7 | 99 | No |
| 8 | 76 | No |
| 9 | 56 | Yes |
| 10 | 62 | Yes |

28. An HR manager wonders if years of schooling is related to job satisfaction measured on a scale from 1 (very unsatisfied) to 15 (very satisfied) for ten systems analysts in his firm. He obtains the following data.

| Years | Satisfaction |
|-------|--------------|
| 16 | 14 |
| 16 | 14.5 |
| 14 | 15 |
| 15 | 15 |
| 18 | 12 |
| 12 | 11 |
| 19 | 10 |
| 18 | 11 |
| 13 | 13 |
| 15 | 15 |
| 11 | 9 |

Do the appropriate analyses and explain your findings in terms a manager could understand.

29. A sales manager wishes to predict sales based on the dollar value of quotes made by the sales staff. She collects data on the total dollar value of quotes given to prospective clients and also records the dollar volume of sales in that month over the past year. The data are shown.

| Month | Quotes (0000s of dollars) | Sales (0000s of dollars) |
|-------|---------------------------|--------------------------|
| 1 | 20 | 13 |
| 2 | 15 | 12 |
| 3 | 10 | 9 |
| 4 | 17 | 7 |
| 5 | 25 | 11 |
| 6 | 15 | 15 |
| 7 | 18 | 10 |
| 8 | 20 | 12 |
| 9 | 20 | 12 |
| 10 | 14 | 11 |
| 11 | 18 | 9 |
| 12 | 12 | 11 |

**a.** Plot a scatter diagram for Sales volume vs. Quotes volume. Is quotes a coincident indicator of sales? Explain.

**b.** Is quotes volume a leading indicator of sales volume? Calculate the cross-correlation coefficient between sales volume $(t)$ and quotes volume $(t-1)$ and between sales volume $(t)$ and quotes volume $(t-2)$. Plot the two scatter diagrams.

**30.** Which diagnostic method is best in diagnosing a difficult operational problem? A researcher tests three approaches: (1) Kepner-Tregoe method, (2) fishbone diagram method, and (3) a control group. Below are the results of 30 managers from a large firm working on the same problem. A panel of experts determined diagnostic scores that ranged from zero (very poor diagnosis) to 100 (very accurate diagnosis).

Do the appropriate analyses and explain your findings in terms a manager could understand. Could you extend your findings to the several thousand managers within the firm that were not included in the study? Discuss.

| Kepner-Tregoe | Fishbone | Control Group |
|---|---|---|
| 80 | 50 | 35 |
| 85 | 45 | 35 |
| 80 | 60 | 46 |
| 75 | 45 | 5 |
| 90 | 50 | 50 |
| 90 | 40 | 45 |
| 75 | 60 | 35 |
| 85 | 65 | 45 |
| 85 | 60 | 50 |
| 80 | 60 | 40 |

**31.** Shown are the quarterly data on the discount rate charged by the Federal Reserve Bank of New York in the early 1980s. The discount rate is the interest rate that the Fed charges its commercial bank customers to borrow money. It is one of several tools that the Fed uses in managing the overall economy.

| | | | |
|---|---|---|---|
| March 1980 | 13.00% | September | 8.75% |
| June | 11.00 | December | 8.75 |
| September | 11.00 | March 1984 | 9.00 |
| December | 13.00 | June | 9.00 |
| March 1981 | 13.75 | September | 8.50 |
| June | 14.00 | December | 8.00 |
| September | 13.00 | March 1985 | 7.75 |
| December | 12.00 | June | 7.50 |
| March 1982 | 12.00 | September | 7.50 |
| June | 11.50 | December | 7.00 |
| September | 10.00 | March 1986 | 7.00 |
| December | 9.00 | June | 6.00 |
| March 1983 | 8.50 | September | 5.50 |
| June | 8.50 | December | 5.50 |

**a.** Plot a line graph of the discount rate data. Interpret it.

**b.** Given your line graph, develop a prediction model and use it to predict the discount rate for March 1987. Compare it to the actual rate for March 1987.

**c.** Would you expect the two values to be close to one another? Why? Would you expect the two values to be identical? Why?

**32.** Shown below are unit sales over the past 20 quarters.

**a.** Draw a line graph of the data.

**b.** Determine the best-fitting linear line or model and its equation.

**c.** Determine the best-fitting polynomial of order 2 curve and its equation.

**d.** Determine the best-fitting exponential curve and its equation.

**e.** Determine the best-fitting power curve and its equation.

**f.** Use all four models to predict sales (21).

**g.** Which of the four models should you use to make a sales prediction for quarter 21? Defend.

| Quarter | Unit Sales | Quarter | Unit Sales |
|---------|-----------|---------|-----------|
| 1 | 10,581 | 11 | 14,626 |
| 2 | 11,192 | 12 | 17,247 |
| 3 | 11,367 | 13 | 16,930 |
| 4 | 11,580 | 14 | 17,249 |
| 5 | 12,946 | 15 | 17,551 |
| 6 | 12,948 | 16 | 17,741 |
| 7 | 13,874 | 17 | 18,424 |
| 8 | 14,167 | 18 | 19,268 |
| 9 | 13,942 | 19 | 19,808 |
| 10 | 15,482 | 20 | 20,944 |

**33.** Management theory suggests that participative leadership is more effective (higher productivity) than autocratic leadership. Below are 16 workers' production rates for one shift for two supervisors with the same years of experience and similar backgrounds.

| Autocratic | 93 | 94 | 94 | 95 | 95 | 96 | 96 | 98 |
|------------|----|----|----|----|----|----|----|----|
| Participative | 103 | 104 | 104 | 103 | 102 | 103 | 104 | 102 |

Do the appropriate analyses and explain your findings in terms a manager could understand.

**34.** A management consultant wishes to determine if participative decision making leads to a more positive job climate. He obtains the following data on 400 firms.

| Description of Firms | Number |
|---------------------|--------|
| Autocratic and poor job climate | 150 |
| Participative and poor job climate | 50 |
| Autocratic and good job climate | 10 |
| Participative and good job climate | 190 |

**a.** Construct a 2 × 2 contingency table.

**b.** Does it appear that decision-making style and job climate are related for the 400 firms in the study?

**35.** Interpret the following autoregressive model on forecasted earnings per share for a firm for the upcoming quarter.

EPS $(t)$ = 1.75 + 0.5 EPS $(t-1)$ − 0.4 EPS $(t-2)$ + 0.1 EPS $(t-3)$

**36.** Below is a correlation matrix for three variables. The dependent variable is time to complete a house in days. The first explanatory variable is the seniority of the work group measured in total years of experience. The second explanatory variable is the number of days the temperature exceeds 95°.

| | Completion Time | Seniority | Days above 95° |
|---|---|---|---|
| Completion Time | 1 | +0.90 | −0.95 |
| Seniority | | 1 | −0.90 |
| Days above 95° | | | 1 |

**a.** Describe the relationship between the three pairs of variables.

**b.** Develop a data set with ten observations of the three variables (30 numbers in total) that would approximately generate the above correlation matrix.

**c.** Use Excel's correlation data-analysis tool to verify that your data set does approximately generate the above correlation matrix.

**37.** Consider the following two qualitative variables:

| Race | | Promoted Status | |
|------|---|-----------------|---|
| White | = 250 | Not Promoted = 300 | |
| African American | = 150 | Promoted | = 100 |

Construct a 2 × 2 contingency table based on the 400 people above that would indicate that the two variables—race and promoted status—are not related in the sample of 400. Explain how your cell entries indicate that the two variables are not related.

**38.** A survey was done to compare the base salaries (in hundreds of thousands of dollars) of chief executives in two industries. The results are shown.

**a.** Plot salary against company sales for all the data. Does it appear that chief executive officers are paid according to the level of company sales? If so, is the relationship linear or nonlinear? Determine the best-fitting line.

**b.** Is years with the company related to the salary of the chief executive? If so, is the relationship linear or nonlinear? Determine the best-fitting line.

**c.** Does the type of industry (1 versus 2) affect the relationship between sales and salary? Plot two scatter diagrams, one for each type of industry. Determine the best-fitting line for each industry.

| Salary | Company Sales (millions of dollars) | Industry Type | Years with Company |
|--------|--------------------|---------------|--------------------|
| 4.6 | 60 | 1 | 8 |
| 14.3 | 400 | 2 | 3 |
| 5.4 | 90 | 1 | 12 |
| 5.6 | 150 | 1 | 12 |
| 4.1 | 180 | 2 | 18 |
| 4.8 | 75 | 1 | 6 |
| 5.6 | 130 | 1 | 10 |
| 21.5 | 500 | 2 | 9 |
| 3.3 | 130 | 2 | 12 |
| 8.1 | 300 | 2 | 15 |
| 5.7 | 105 | 1 | 16 |
| 5.6 | 100 | 1 | 14 |
| 5.6 | 230 | 2 | 8 |
| 5.7 | 115 | 1 | 15 |
| 9.7 | 330 | 2 | 20 |

## CASE STUDY

Rachel Stuart, HR director at Computer Technics, wishes to determine if the firm's salary structure for AS/400 programmer/analysts with 9+ years of experience reflects different living costs across the nation. She selects economic indicator data on 25 cities. The dependent variable is the median salary of the firms' AS 400 programmers with 9+ years of experience in 25 cities.

City data are from Rhoda Garoogan's *America's Top-Rated Cities: A Statistics Handbook,* 5th ed. 1997, Reference Publications Universal, Boca Raton, FL.

Prepare a one-page report on the firm's salary structure. Does the firm's structure reflect different living costs across the nation? Use the data to support your position.

| City | Salary & Bonus × 1000 | Median Household Income | Tax Burden | Cost of Living Index | Median Price of Home × 1000 |
|---|---|---|---|---|---|
| Baltimore | $61,000 | $36,550 | $10,658 | 100.4 | 131 |
| Boston | $61,500 | $40,491 | $12,628 | 142.5 | 148 |
| San Francisco | $63,650 | $40,494 | $12,451 | 164.3 | 289 |
| New York | $68,210 | $31,659 | $17,144 | 234.5 | 155 |
| Minneapolis | $60,600 | $36,565 | $12,197 | 101.4 | 112 |
| Pittsburgh | $63,210 | $26,700 | $13,926 | 109.5 | 92 |
| Lexington | $56,569 | $36,767 | $9475 | 97.4 | 100 |
| Albuquerque | $53,250 | $35,945 | $6964 | 101.7 | 131 |
| Salt Lake City | $56,785 | $30,882 | $8590 | 96.5 | 146 |
| Chicago | $60,100 | $35,265 | $10,937 | 118 | 144 |
| Indianapolis | $55,250 | $31,655 | $7782 | 95.8 | 121 |
| St. Louis | $56,890 | $41,943 | $8446 | 98.7 | 100 |
| Detroit | $57,383 | $34,612 | $9421 | 113.4 | 112 |
| Washington | $61,995 | $54,939 | $13,235 | 125.4 | 174 |
| Honolulu | $60,100 | $52,041 | $9761 | 174.2 | 238 |
| Las Vegas | $51,005 | $36,301 | $5246 | 104.7 | 123 |
| Nashville | $52,118 | $30,223 | $5187 | 94.2 | 110 |
| Richmond | $55,023 | $40,209 | $7510 | 103 | 111 |
| Atlanta | $57,986 | $36,051 | $9794 | 99.5 | 119 |
| Dallas | $55,229 | $33,277 | $7740 | 98.9 | 116 |
| Orlando | $53,400 | $31,230 | $6363 | 99.4 | 95 |
| Jacksonville | $52,504 | $26,514 | $6363 | 96 | 91 |
| Knoxville | $51,236 | $25,134 | $4877 | 97.5 | 87 |
| Houston | $53,146 | $31,473 | $6435 | 93.9 | 100 |
| LA | $58,995 | $34,965 | $10,497 | 119.7 | 160 |

**Table 7.23**
Salary and Economic Indicator Data for 25 Cities

The tax burden assumes a family with two wage earners and two children.

# CHAPTER 7
# APPENDICES

## I. LISTING OF EXCEL TOOLS FOR CHAPTER

1. INTERCEPT function wizard
2. SLOPE function wizard
3. ADD TRENDLINE (when chart is activated)
4. CORREL function wizard
5. COVAR function wizard
6. STDEV function wizard
7. AVERAGE function wizard
8. Correlation data-analysis tool

# II. DRAWING A MULTIPLE BOX PLOT

The following steps describe how to create a multiple box plot using Excel's ChartWizard.

|    | A | B | C | D | E | F | G | H | I |
|----|---|---|---|---|---|---|---|---|---|
| 1 | Brainstorm | Brainstorm | No Brainstorm | | | | | | |
| 2 | Paper/Pencil | Computer | | | | | | | |
| 3 | 45 | 65 | 8 | | Min | Q1 | Md | Q3 | Max |
| 4 | 38 | 68 | 7 | Brainstorm | 10 | 35.5 | 38 | 44 | 55 |
| 5 | 36 | 70 | 6 | Computer Brainstorm | 51 | 56 | 65 | 69 | 99 |
| 6 | 10 | 68 | 5 | No Brainstorm | 3 | 4.5 | 5 | 6.5 | 14 |
| 7 | 55 | 58 | 4 | | | | | | |
| 8 | 43 | 56 | 5 | | | | | | |
| 9 | 41 | 51 | 3 | | | | | | |
| 10 | 37 | 99 | 14 | | | | | | |
| 11 | 34 | 53 | 6 | | | | | | |
| 12 | 35 | 56 | 5 | | | | | | |
| 13 | 49 | 77 | 4 | | | | | | |

1. Use Excel's QUARTILE function wizard to determine the five-number summaries shown E4 through I6.

2. Select all the values and column labels (D3:I6) and then click on the ChartWizard tool.

3. Select XY (Scatter) as the chart type and click on Next.

4. Click on Series in columns and click on Next.

5. Add a title to Value (x) axis, *Type of Creativity*. Add a title to Value (y) axis, *Number of Solutions*.

6. Click on Gridlines tab and click on Value (x) axis Major gridline. Then click on Finish.

7. Click on Legend and click on None. Then click on Finish.

8. Click on Data Labels and then on Show Value. Then click on Finish.

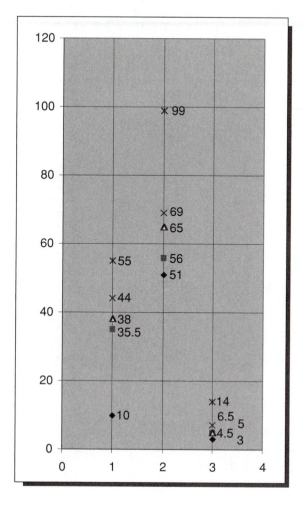

# III. DRAWING AN XY SCATTER DIAGRAM

The following steps describe how to create and embellish a scatter plot using Excel's ChartWizard.

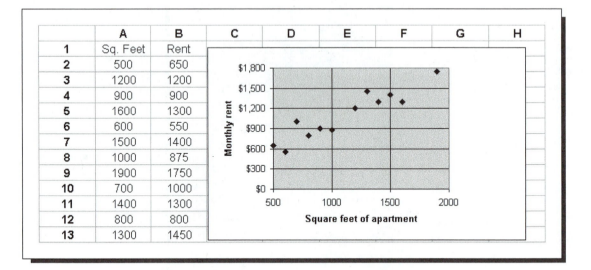

1. Arrange the data in columns on a worksheet with the *x* variable (square feet) on the left and the *y* variable (monthly rental) on the right as shown above.

2. Select all the *x* and *y* variable values (A2:B13). Do not include the labels above the data.

3. Click on the ChartWizard tool.

4. Select XY (Scatter) as the chart type and click on Next.

5. Click on series in columns if not already checked. Click on Next.

6. Add a title to the Value (x) axis, *Square feet of apartment*. Add a title to the Value (y) axis, *Monthly rent*.

7. Click on Legend tab. Click on Show Legend (check disappears). Click Finish.

8. Click the chart to activate it for editing.

9. Change the x-axis to display 500 to 2,000 square feet. Double click the values of the horizontal axis and click on the Scale tab. Clear the Auto check boxes for Minimum and Maximum and type 500 and 2000 in their edit boxes. Then click OK.

10. Change the y-axis to display $0 to $1,800. Double click the values of the vertical axis and click on the Scale tab. Clear the Auto check boxes for Minimum and Maximum and type 000 and 1800 with a major unit of $300 in their edit boxes. Then click OK. Click on the Number tab. Click on Currency with zero decimal places, then click on OK.

# IV. CORRELATION DATA-ANALYSIS TOOL

The following steps describe how to obtain a correlation matrix using the correlation data-analysis tool.

| | A | B | C | D | E | F | G | H |
|---|---|---|---|---|---|---|---|---|
| 1 | Sq. Feet | Bath Rooms | Rent | | | Sq. Feet | Bath Rooms | Rent |
| 2 | 500 | 1 | 650 | | Sq. Feet | 1 | | |
| 3 | 1200 | 1 | 1200 | | Bath Rooms | C.873401 | 1 | |
| 4 | 900 | 1 | 900 | | Rent | C.951016 | 0.82173774 | 1 |
| 5 | 1600 | 2 | 1300 | | | | | |
| 6 | 600 | 1 | 550 | | | | | |
| 7 | 1500 | 2 | 1400 | | | | | |
| 8 | 1000 | 1 | 875 | | | | | |
| 9 | 1900 | 2 | 1750 | | | | | |
| 10 | 700 | 1 | 1000 | | | | | |
| 11 | 1400 | 2 | 1300 | | | | | |
| 12 | 800 | 1 | 800 | | | | | |
| 13 | 1300 | 2 | 1450 | | | | | |

1. Enter the data for two or more variables in a worksheet as shown in columns A through C of the above figure. The upper left-hand corner of the correlation matrix will be in cell E1.

2. From the Tools menu, choose Data Analysis. From the Data-Analysis dialog box, select Correlation in the Analysis Tools list box and press OK.

3. In the Input range section of the Correlation dialog box, specify the location of the data in the input Range edit box, including the labels (A1:C13). Verify that the data is grouped in Columns and be sure the Labels box is checked.

4. In the Output section, click the Output Range button, and specify the upper left cell where the Correlation output will be located (E1).

5. Click OK. The output appears in cells E1:H4 as shown above.

# V. THE ADD TRENDLINE FUNCTION

Let's use the scatter diagram from Appendix III to illustrate the ADD
TRENDLINE function. If you are using Excel 95 version 7.0, you must
use the INSERT TRENDLINE function.

1. Click on the XY chart to activate it.

2. Click on Chart on the menu bar and then click on Add Trendline.

3. Click on Options and then click on Display Equation on Chart.
   Click OK.

4. The best-fitting linear line, or model, and its equation are graphed and
   computed.

5. If you desire a best-fitting nonlinear line, click on the desired graph in
   the Type box.

# Chapter 8

# HYPOTHESIS TESTING ON TWO POPULATION PARAMETERS

## STATISTICAL INFERENCE PROCESS

In the last chapter, we looked for relationships or differences among two or more *specific samples*. We computed the sample mean and standard deviation, contingency tables, the sample intercept and slope of the best-fitting line, or the correlation coefficient. These are descriptive statistics and were appropriate because we were only interested in drawing conclusions about the specific samples that we selected.

By contrast, in this chapter we are not interested in the specific samples. Rather we select *representative* samples, compute the descriptive statistics, and then use them to draw conclusions about the target populations from which we selected the samples. This chapter reacquaints us with the hypothesis–testing framework first learned in Chapter 6.

# MANAGEMENT SCENARIOS AND DATA SETS

Table 8.1 presents the five scenarios used in this chapter. These illustrate how managers use cross-sectional multivariate data to determine if two population means, proportions, or variances differ.[1]

In Scenario I, management seeks to reduce the mean soldering time for the 800 connections of a printed circuit board. Presently the soldering time averages about 135 milliseconds. Engineering claims that it can reduce soldering time by raising the preheat temperature from the present 140° to 160°. Management conducts a **one-factor, two-treatment-level completely random** study to test the claim.

| Explanatory Variable | Dependent Variable | Data Set | Question That Motivates Study |
|---|---|---|---|
| Preheat Temperature | Soldering Time | Soldering times of 50 randomly selected printed circuit boards; 25 boards each at two temperatures. | Can we reduce the mean soldering time for *all* boards by increasing temperature? |
| Presence or Absence of Computerized Planning | Return on Total Assets | Return on total assets for 80 randomly selected firms within an industry; 40 firms do no computerized planning. | For the *entire* industry, does computerized planning, on average, increase a firm's return on total assets? |
| Type of Creativity Training | Number of Alternatives Generated | The number of solutions generated by 20 matched pairs of managers. | Based on one study, which creativity method, on average, generates more solutions for *all* managers within the firm? |
| Employee Classification | Systematic Savings for Retirement—Yes or No | Presence or absence of systematic savings for retirement for 200 randomly selected employees. | Based on one sample of 200, is the percentage of *all* white-collar and blue-collar workers within the firm who save for retirement the same? |
| Experimental versus Present Process | Inside Diameter of Piston Rings | The inside diameter of 30 randomly selected piston rings; 15 each produced by the two processes. | Does the experimental process reduce the variance of the inside diameters of *all* piston rings? |

**Table 8.1**
Scenarios and Data Sets

---

[1] The same methods should be used for **stationary time-ordered data**.

| DEFINITION | A one-factor two-treatment level completely random study examines two variations of one experimental factor to determine their impact on a dependent variable. Use randomization to select experimental units or subjects, to assign them to treatment levels, and to run the study. |

The study team selects a random sample of 50 boards and randomly subdivides them into two groups of 25 each. They select two soldering machines at random and ensure that both have the same settings, except for the preheat temperature. They randomly determine which machines to set to the 140° and 160° temperatures—the two treatment levels of the experimental factor, temperature. One operator will run both groups of 25 boards simultaneously. The use of randomization and holding other factors constant (such as time of day or operators) increases the study's validity.

**Experimental Factor:**   **Treatment Levels:**
**Preheat Temperature**   **140° and 160°**

Table 8.2 displays the 50 soldering times from the study.

**Table 8.2**
Soldering Times in
Milliseconds

| | | | | | | | | | | | | | |
|---|---|---|---|---|---|---|---|---|---|---|---|---|---|
| 140° F | 135 | 136 | 155 | 140 | 135 | 128 | 135 | 147 | 146 | 124 | 127 | 135 | 144 |
| | 127 | 135 | 125 | 144 | 127 | 136 | 148 | 145 | 133 | 134 | 112 | 135 | |
| 160° F | 138 | 121 | 130 | 130 | 120 | 131 | 141 | 113 | 109 | 128 | 140 | 120 | 128 |
| | 119 | 128 | 138 | 144 | 127 | 127 | 128 | 126 | 127 | 140 | 120 | 113 | |

| treatment | sample mean | sample standard deviation |
|---|---|---|
| 140° | 135.52 milliseconds | 9.381 milliseconds |
| 160° | 127.44 milliseconds | 9.269 milliseconds |

For the specific samples, the *sample* mean soldering time was faster at 160°. However, until the firm does **hypothesis testing** it cannot say that the *population* mean soldering time for *all* boards will be faster at 160°. After all, 50 printed circuit boards do not constitute a population!

In Scenario II, 3Com's management must decide whether or not to purchase an expensive computerized planning package from SCM. It claims the firms that use its computerized package have higher returns on total assets (ROA) than firms that do manual planning. 3Com conducts a survey to determine the impact of computerized strategic planning on return on total assets.

**Experimental Factor:**   **Treatment Levels:**
**Planning Package**   **Computerized and Manual Planning**

Table 8.3 contains the survey data.

| SCM Computerized | | | | | | | |
|---|---|---|---|---|---|---|---|
| 10.80 | 11.10 | 11.40 | 11.50 | 11.55 | 11.30 | 10.40 | 11.75 |
| 12.10 | 11.50 | 11.65 | 11.60 | 11.40 | 11.45 | 10.90 | 11.90 |
| 11.20 | 11.30 | 11.00 | 11.80 | 11.30 | 12.10 | 10.90 | 11.10 |
| 10.90 | 10.73 | 11.68 | 11.09 | 11.55 | 11.70 | 11.62 | 11.11 |
| 11.35 | 10.75 | 11.08 | 11.96 | 10.62 | 11.89 | 10.87 | 11.36 |

| Manual | | | | | | | |
|---|---|---|---|---|---|---|---|
| 10.50 | 12.60 | 7.60 | 9.90 | 12.90 | 12.50 | 10.70 | 9.10 |
| 11.10 | 11.50 | 10.70 | 13.00 | 10.30 | 11.60 | 10.10 | 9.50 |
| 10.90 | 10.10 | 13.80 | 9.00 | 10.60 | 11.00 | 10.50 | 12.50 |
| 11.40 | 11.38 | 11.88 | 10.20 | 9.21 | 11.11 | 10.26 | 12.73 |
| 11.40 | 8.50 | 12.67 | 11.45 | 12.65 | 10.79 | 10.38 | 13.50 |

**Table 8.3**
Data from Study of Impact of Computerized Planning on ROA

| treatment | sample mean | sample standard deviation |
|---|---|---|
| Manual Planning | 11.038% | 1.395% |
| Computerized Planning | 11.332% | 0.419% |

For the specific samples, the mean ROA was larger for those firms that use SCM's computerized strategic planning package. However, until 3Com's management does hypothesis testing, it cannot say that, on average, *all* firms that use the vendor's strategic planning package will outperform those that do not.

In Scenario III, the human resource manager evaluates two creativity methods—analogy versus brainstorming—to determine which generates more alternative solutions. Based on one study, the manager will incorporate the more productive method in all subsequent training programs.

Brainstorming and analogy are similar. In brainstorming you quickly generate solutions to a management problem using the principle of deferred judgment. In the analogy method you brainstorm solutions to an action-based concrete story, an analogy, such as "getting a cat off a roof" or "getting into a sold-out sporting event." Then you creatively use the brainstormed solutions from the analogy problem to solve the management problem.

The HR manager could have run a one-factor two-level study. He would have selected a random sample of employees, randomly divided them into two subgroups, and then randomly assigned each subgroup to either the analogy or brainstorming treatment. He would then have provided the appropriate training for each group and counted the number of alternatives generated on the test problem.

**Experimental Factor:**        **Treatment Levels:**
**Creativity Training**          **Brainstorm and Analogy**

He chose not to do so. Here's why. There are many individual differences among employees that could account for differences in the number of solutions generated beyond the experimental factor. The most important **extraneous** factor is "natural" creativity level as measured by a commercially available test.[2] Each employee had already taken the test as part of the firm's career development program. Even using randomization it is possible that the HR manager could have assigned all of the more highly creative people to one of the creativity methods. This would jeopardize the study's validity. When you suspect that one or two extraneous factors have a major impact on the dependent variable, use the matched-pair design rather than the two-level completely random design.

**D**EFINITION    A **matched-pair design** requires selecting pairs of subjects matched on an important extraneous factor that is known to affect the dependent variable. Randomly assign one member of each pair to each treatment level.

The study team conducted a matched-pair design. They selected 20 matched pairs of employees; each matched pair of employees had similar "natural" creativity levels. They then randomly assigned each member of a pair to one of the two creativity methods.

For a given pair of employees, if there are differences in the number of alternatives generated, it cannot be due to their "natural" creativity—an extraneous factor. It must be due to the impact of the different types of creativity training.

Table 8.4 displays the study's data. Pair 19 produced many alternatives, whereas pair 16 produced few alternatives. The study team anticipated there would be large differences in the number of alternatives generated among pairs. That is why they chose the matched-pair design.

The analysis for the matched-pair design begins by computing the difference in the number of solutions for each pair (see Table 8.4, column 4). Then use Excel's AVERAGE function wizard to compute the mean difference. On average, participants generated 2.6 more solutions using analogy than those using brainstorming. Finally, use Excel's STDEV function wizard to compute the standard deviation for the difference data values.

---

[2] You first encountered the idea of extraneous factors in Chapter 6 on hypothesis testing on one population mean.

| Pair | Analogy | Brainstorm | Difference = Analogy – Brainstorm | |
|------|---------|------------|------------------|---|
| 1 | 43 | 40 | 3 | |
| 2 | 32 | 30 | 2 | |
| 3 | 28 | 27 | 1 | |
| 4 | 43 | 40 | 3 | |
| 5 | 32 | 29 | 3 | |
| 6 | 7 | 4 | 3 | |
| 7 | 30 | 29 | 1 | |
| 8 | 25 | 23 | 2 | |
| 9 | 35 | 32 | 3 | |
| 10 | 49 | 46 | 3 | |
| 11 | 25 | 23 | 2 | |
| 12 | 51 | 50 | 1 | |
| 13 | 33 | 29 | 4 | |
| 14 | 18 | 15 | 3 | |
| 15 | 25 | 21 | 4 | |
| 16 | 8 | 4 | 4 | Not Creative Pair |
| 17 | 20 | 17 | 3 | |
| 18 | 36 | 33 | 3 | |
| 19 | 66 | 64 | 2 | Highly Creative Pair |
| 20 | 26 | 24 | 2 | |

**Table 8.4**
Number of
Alternatives Generated
by Analogy and
Brainstorming

| sample mean | sample standard deviation | sample size |
|-------------|---------------------------|-------------|
| 2.6 solutions | 0.9403 solutions | 20 (not 40) |

In Scenario IV, a HR specialist believes that a larger proportion of the firm's white-collar workers is financially planning for retirement than are its blue-collar workers. If so, she will offer additional retirement planning sessions for the blue-collar workers. She conducts a survey on a random sample of blue-collar and white-collar employees within the firm. Each randomly selected employee answers the following question: "Beyond Social Security and the firm's pension plan, are you systematically saving for your retirement?"

**Experimental Factor:**          **Treatment Levels:**
**Worker**                        **White Collar and Blue Collar**

Table 8.5 displays the results. The sample proportion of white-collar workers is $70/100 = 0.70$. The sample proportion of blue-collar workers is only $45/100 = 0.45$.

| 100 White-Collar Workers | | | | | 0 = no systematic saving for retirement, 1 = systematic saving | | | | | | | | | | | | | | |
|---|---|---|---|---|---|---|---|---|---|---|---|---|---|---|---|---|---|---|---|
| 1 | 1 | 0 | 1 | 1 | 0 | 1 | 0 | 0 | 1 | 1 | 0 | 0 | 1 | 1 | 1 | 0 | 1 | 0 | 0 |
| 1 | 1 | 1 | 1 | 1 | 1 | 1 | 1 | 1 | 1 | 1 | 1 | 1 | 0 | 1 | 1 | 1 | 0 | 1 | 1 |
| 1 | 0 | 1 | 1 | 1 | 1 | 1 | 0 | 1 | 1 | 1 | 1 | 1 | 1 | 1 | 0 | 0 | 1 | 1 | 1 |
| 0 | 1 | 0 | 1 | 1 | 0 | 0 | 1 | 1 | 0 | 0 | 1 | 1 | 1 | 1 | 1 | 0 | 1 | 1 | 0 |
| 0 | 0 | 1 | 1 | 1 | 1 | 0 | 1 | 1 | 0 | 1 | 1 | 0 | 1 | 0 | 1 | 1 | 1 | 1 | 0 |

| 100 Blue-Collar Workers | | | | | 0 = no systematic saving for retirement, 1 = systematic saving | | | | | | | | | | | | | | |
|---|---|---|---|---|---|---|---|---|---|---|---|---|---|---|---|---|---|---|---|
| 1 | 1 | 1 | 1 | 0 | 0 | 1 | 0 | 1 | 0 | 0 | 1 | 1 | 1 | 1 | 0 | 1 | 1 | 0 | 1 |
| 1 | 0 | 0 | 1 | 1 | 1 | 0 | 1 | 1 | 0 | 1 | 0 | 0 | 0 | 0 | 1 | 0 | 0 | 1 | 1 |
| 0 | 0 | 1 | 0 | 0 | 0 | 0 | 1 | 0 | 0 | 0 | 1 | 1 | 0 | 0 | 1 | 0 | 0 | 0 | 1 |
| 1 | 1 | 0 | 1 | 0 | 0 | 0 | 1 | 0 | 0 | 0 | 0 | 0 | 0 | 0 | 0 | 0 | 0 | 0 | 0 |
| 0 | 0 | 1 | 0 | 1 | 1 | 0 | 1 | 0 | 1 | 1 | 1 | 0 | 0 | 1 | 0 | 1 | 1 | 1 | 1 |

**Table 8.5**
Survey Results of 200 Randomly Selected Employees

However, the firm cannot say that the proportion of *all* white-collar workers within the firm who systematically save is greater than for *all* blue-collar workers until they have completed hypothesis testing.

In Scenario V, management wants to reduce the variance of the inside diameter measurements for automobile piston rings. This will reduce future engine problems. The target value for the inside diameter is 74.00 millimeters (mm). A quality improvement team has developed a set of process changes that it believes will reduce the variance.

The team conducts a one factor two-treatment-level completely random study. They randomly select 30 piston rings and subdivide the 30 rings into two random subgroups. They randomly assign each subgroup of 15 rings to one of the two processes—present or experimental process. They select two operators with the same years of experience in the department. The operators manufacture the piston rings and measure the inside diameters. The results are given in Table 8.6.

**Experimental Factor:        Treatment Levels:**
**Manufacturing Process        Present and Experimental Process**

For the specific samples, the experimental process has the smaller variance. However, the firm cannot say that the experimental process will produce more consistent inside diameter measurements for *all* piston rings until they have completed hypothesis testing.

| Experimental | Present |
|---|---|
| 73.996 | 73.987 |
| 74.012 | 74.004 |
| 73.997 | 73.975 |
| 74.008 | 73.999 |
| 74.005 | 74.000 |
| 73.989 | 73.986 |
| 74.011 | 73.986 |
| 73.996 | 73.984 |
| 74.007 | 74.003 |
| 74.004 | 73.996 |
| 74.018 | 74.014 |
| 73.994 | 74.007 |
| 74.004 | 73.994 |
| 73.984 | 74.013 |
| 74.000 | 74.000 |

**Table 8.6**
Inside Diameters of
Automobile Piston
Rings

| treatment | sample mean | sample standard deviation | sample variance |
|---|---|---|---|
| Present Process | 73.9965 mm | .0112 mm | .000125 |
| Exp. Process | 74.0017 mm | .0091 mm | .000084 |

# HYPOTHESIS TESTING ON THE DIFFERENCE IN THE MEANS OF TWO INDEPENDENT POPULATIONS HAVING EQUAL VARIANCES

An operations manager wants to reduce soldering time for printed circuit boards. An engineering team believes that raising the preheat temperature from 140° to 160° will reduce soldering time. It persuades management to run a study. By the end of this unit you should be able to conduct the five steps of hypothesis testing first learned in Chapter 6.

### STEP 1: State Hypotheses and Managerial Actions

An engineering team claims that the population mean soldering time at 160°, $\mu_{160}$, will be less than the population mean soldering time at 140°, $\mu_{140}$. The decision maker's null hypothesis is the opposite of that claim; namely,

| Hypothesis | Managerial Actions |
|---|---|
| $H_0: \mu_{160} \geq \mu_{140}$ <br> $\mu_{160} - \mu_{140} \geq 0$ | When applied to *all* boards (in the population), the mean soldering time at 160° is either the same as or greater than the soldering time at 140°. |

The alternative hypothesis is always the claim made by others—in this instance, the engineering team.

$$H_1: \mu_{160} < \mu_{140}$$
$$\mu_{160} - \mu_{140} < 0$$

In summary, here are the null and alternative hypotheses for the soldering time study.

| Hypotheses | Managerial Actions |
| --- | --- |
| $H_0: \mu_{160} - \mu_{140} \geq 0$ | Failure to reject the null hypothesis means the firm will continue to use the 140° preheat temperature. |
| $H_1: \mu_{160} - \mu_{140} < 0$ | Rejecting the null hypothesis means the firm will implement the 160° preheat temperature. |

In conclusion, upon completing the first step in hypothesis testing, you will develop one of the following three sets of hypotheses.

$$\text{Set I:} \quad H_0: \mu_A - \mu_B \geq 0$$
$$H_1: \mu_A - \mu_B < 0$$

This is a **one-sided, lower tail** (or **one-tail**) test. Use it to test someone else's claim that the mean of population "A" is less than the mean of population "B." The soldering time study is a one-sided, lower tail test. Engineering claimed that the population mean soldering time at 160° (A) is less than the population mean soldering time at 140° (B).

$$\text{Set II:} \quad H_0: \mu_A - \mu_B \leq 0$$
$$H_1: \mu_A - \mu_B > 0$$

This is a **one-sided, upper tail** (or **one-tail**) test. Use it to test someone else's claim that the mean of population "A" is greater than the mean of population "B."

$$\text{Set III:} \quad H_0: \mu_A - \mu_B = 0$$
$$H_1: \mu_A - \mu_B \neq 0$$

This is a **two-sided,** or **two-tail**, test. Use it to test someone else's claim that the means of two populations differ.

## STEP 2: Determine the Consequences of the Decision–Making Errors

Recall from Chapter 6 you learned that two errors are possible in hypothesis testing. Below are the formal definitions of the two errors and their translations into the soldering time study setting.

| | |
|---|---|
| Type I Error: | **Reject the null hypothesis when the null hypothesis is true.** |
| Translation of Type I Error | "Reject the null" means that the firm believes the alternative is true. It will increase the temperature to 160° because it thinks that the population mean soldering time will decrease. |
| | "Null is true" means the population mean soldering time at 160° is either the same as or greater than the mean soldering time at 140°. |
| Description of Type I Error | The firm increases the temperature to 160°, but the population mean soldering time does not decrease. |
| Type II Error: | **Do not reject the null hypothesis when the null is false.** |
| Translation of Type II Error | "Do not reject the null" means that the firm believes the null hypothesis is true. Thus, it will maintain the 140° temperature. |
| | "Null is false" means the population mean soldering time at 160° is lower than at 140°. The preheat temperature should be increased to 160°. |
| Description of Type II Error | The firm does not increase the temperature when it should have. It could have reduced mean soldering time. This is a lost opportunity. |

Business errors are always costly. What costs are associated with the Type I and Type II errors in the soldering time study?

***Costs of a Type I Error.*** The firm increases its temperature, and the anticipated reduction in mean soldering time fails to materialize. Costs include installing expensive heating equipment and perhaps a slower (or at best, the same speed) process. The Type I error would be very costly.

***Costs of a Type II Error.*** In failing to increase the preheat temperature, the firm would have lost a major opportunity to reduce soldering time and cost and increase production capacity. The cost of a Type II error depends on the magnitude of the lost opportunity. Since the engineering team believed that soldering times in the 130-millisecond range (only a 5-millisecond reduction from the present time) were possible at the 160° temperature, the *most likely* Type II error cost would not be too high. In summary, the potential cost of the Type I error was very high and that of the most likely Type II error was much lower.

STEP 3:   Set a Significance Level and Determine the Sample Sizes

The third step requires setting a **significance level**, $\alpha$. Base it on the relative costs of making the Type I error and the most likely Type II error.

Using the three principles presented in Chapter 6 on hypothesis testing on one population mean, the manager sets the significance level, $\alpha$, at 0.05. If he rejects the null hypothesis, the probability of making the Type I error is at most 5 in 100. Thus, he can be at least $100(1 - \alpha = .05)\%$, or 95%, confident of having made a correct decision. We will use the significance level, $\alpha = .05$, in Step 5 of hypothesis testing. Since the Type II error was not too costly, the operations manager selected a rather small sample size per treatment level, 25 boards each.

STEP 4:   Conduct Study or Market Survey

The operations manager conducts a one-factor two-treatment-level completely random study discussed earlier. Table 8.7 presents the sample statistics for the raw data in Table 8.2.

**Table 8.7**
Data from the One-Factor Two-Treatment-Level Study on Soldering Time

| Preheat Temperature | Treatment One 140° | Treatment Two 160° |
|---|---|---|
| Sample mean | 135.52 milliseconds | 127.44 milliseconds |
| Sample variance | 88.01 | 85.92 |
| Sample size | 25 | 25 |

***Small- versus Large-Size Sample.***  In Chapters 4–6 you learned that if the sample size is 30 or greater the distribution of sample mean will be near normal because of the Central Limit Theorem. When the sample size is less than 30, you must determine if the population from which you selected the sample is near normal. You do this by computing the sample data's skewness and kurtosis. If both statistics are between −1 and +1, the data are near normal and you can perform hypothesis testing.

Since the **sample size per treatment level** was less than 30 in this study, the operations manager computed the skewness and kurtosis for the data at each treatment level.

|  | 140° Treatment | 160° Treatment |
|---|---|---|
| Skewness | −0.211 | −0.055 |
| Kurtosis | 0.534 | −0.497 |

If the data had not been normal, you could apply a log or square root transformation (see Chapter 5). If that does not normalize the data, do not perform hypothesis testing.

Of course, when the sample size per treatment level is 30 or greater, you need not compute the skewness and kurtosis because of the Central Limit Theorem.

### STEP 5:    Compute the Test Statistic and Choose between the Null and Alternative Hypotheses

For the specific samples, the sample mean soldering time at $160°$ ($\overline{x}_{160}$) was 8.08 milliseconds faster than at $140°$. Compute:

$$\text{Diff} = \overline{x}_{160} - \overline{x}_{140}$$
$$\text{Diff} = 127.44 - 135.52 = -8.08 \text{ milliseconds.}$$

It is true that $\overline{x}_{160} < \overline{x}_{140}$. However, the manager cannot even consider saying that the mean soldering time for *all* boards at $160°$ will be less than at $140°$ ($\mu_{160} < \mu_{140}$) until completing this step. And even then, he will not able to say this with 100% certainty.

To *possibly* reject the null hypothesis, the sample difference must be less than 0. To reject the null hypothesis, the sample difference must be *significantly less than* 0.

As in Chapter 6, we compute a test statistic that measures the impact on soldering time due to the two temperatures (the experimental factor) versus the impact due to all extraneous factors. The numerator of the test statistic measures the impact due to the two temperatures; namely, 8.08 milliseconds. The denominator of the test statistic is the estimated standard error. It measures the impact on soldering time due to all extraneous factors such as differences in soldering flux, operators, ambient conditions in the plant, time of day, circuit board cleanliness, machines, etc. We use the two sample variances from Table 8.7 to estimate the impact on soldering time attributed to extraneous factors.

Assuming that the population variances in soldering times are equal at the $140°$ and $160°$ temperatures, we can use Expression (8.1) to compute a **pooled variance**,

$$s_p^2 = \frac{n_1 \cdot s_1^2 + n_2 \cdot s_2^2}{n_1 + n_2}$$

**(8.1)**

Even without a formal statistical test, it appears from Table 8.7 that the two population variances are the same because the two sample variances are almost equal.[3]

---

[3] You will learn how to test for the equality of two *population* variances on page 340.

For equal sample sizes, the pooled variance is simply the average of the two sample variances. The pooled variance for the soldering time study is

$$\frac{25 \cdot 88.01 + 25 \cdot 85.92}{25 + 25} = 86.97$$

Then use Expression (8.2) to compute the estimated standard error.

$$\sqrt{\frac{s_p^2}{n_1} + \frac{s_p^2}{n_2}}$$

(8.2)

The estimated standard error is:

$$\sqrt{\frac{86.97}{25} + \frac{86.97}{25}} = 2.638 \text{ milliseconds}$$

Now compare the 8.08 millisecond impact on soldering time due to the two preheat temperatures to the 2.638 millisecond variation due to all extraneous factors. As in Chapter 6, compute the following test statistic.

$$\frac{\text{Impact of Experimental Factor}}{\text{Impact of Extraneous Factors}} = \frac{\bar{x}_{160} - \bar{x}_{140}}{\text{Estimated Standard Error}} = \frac{-8.08}{2.638} = -3.06$$

Ignoring the minus sign, the impact of the experimental factor (preheat temperature) on soldering time is 3.06 times larger than the combined impact of all extraneous factors on soldering time.

First presented in Chapter 6, Figure 8.1 is a graphical representation of the impact of the experimental factor versus the extraneous factors on soldering time. Figure 8.1 suggests that the firm should reject the null hypothesis.

**Figure 8.1**
The Impact of the Experimental Factor versus the Impact due to Extraneous Factors on Soldering Time

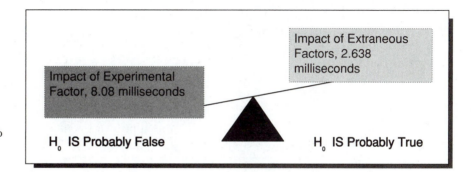

From Chapter 6, you could now use the TDIST function wizard to determine the $p$-value for the study. But it's very time consuming. First, you must use Excel's AVERAGE wizard to obtain the two sample means for the numerator of the test statistic. The denominator requires several steps. Second, you must use Excel's VAR wizard to obtain the two sample variances. Then you must manually calculate the pooled variance from Expression (8.1) and the estimated standard error from Expression (8.2). You must then calculate the test statistic and insert it as the first data entry in the TDIST wizard and then determine the degrees of freedom for this study, $(n_1 - 1) + (n_2 - 1)$, or $(25 - 1) + (25 - 1) = 48$. Fortunately, there is a faster method.

Table 8.8 is the output from Excel's **data–analysis tool, the t-test: two-sample assuming equal variances**. Shown here is the dialog box for the tool.[4]

The data–analysis tool provides all the information to evaluate the null hypothesis. Note the sample mean soldering times in row 1, the pooled variance as computed from Expression (8.2) in row 4, and the test statistic (t Stat) in row 7. Most importantly, it provides the $p$-value statistic, row 8, that determines if we can reject the null hypothesis at a 0.05 significance level.

Use the following decision rule to choose between the null and alternative hypotheses.

---

**Decision Rule:** Reject the null hypothesis and accept the alternative hypothesis if the computed $p$-value is less than or equal to the significance level, $\alpha$, set in Step 3 for the appropriate-tailed test—one or two tailed. Otherwise, do not reject the null hypothesis.

---

[4] See Appendix II for this chapter.

|                             | 160 F    | 140 F        |
|-----------------------------|----------|--------------|
| Mean                        | 127.44   | 135.52       |
| Variance                    | 85.92333 | 88.01        |
| Observations                | 25       | 25           |
| Pooled Variance             | 86.96667 | $s_p^2$      |
| Hypothesized Mean Difference| 0        |              |
| Df                          | 48       | $n_1 + n_2 - 2$ |
| t Stat                      | −3.0633  |              |
| P(T<=t) one-tail            | 0.001792 | **p-value for one-tail test** |
| t Critical one-tail         | 1.677224 |              |
| P(T<=t) two-tail            | 0.003584 | **p-value for two-tail test** |
| t Critical two-tail         | 2.010634 |              |

**Table 8.8**
t-Test: Two-Sample Assuming Equal Variances

Since a p-value of 0.001792 for a one-tailed test ($H_1: \mu_{160} - \mu_{140} < 0$) is less than 0.05, reject the null hypothesis and conclude that increasing preheat temperature does reduce the population mean soldering time.

## DECISION-MAKING CONSEQUENCES

Having rejected the null hypothesis, the operations manager has made a correct decision or has rejected the null hypothesis when the null was true—a Type I error (see Figure 8.2).

Having rejected the null hypothesis, the manager is 99.82% confident that he has made a correct decision. Or the odds of having made a correct decision are .998208/.001792, or 557:1. The chance of making a Type II error is zero because the operations manager rejected the null!

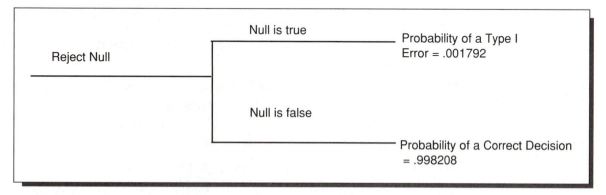

**Figure 8.2**
Consequences of Rejecting a Null Hypothesis

## ASSUMPTIONS UNDERLYING t-TEST: TWO-SAMPLE ASSUMING EQUAL VARIANCES

1. The manager must select random samples from the two populations.

2. Both samples either must be (1) from populations that are normally distributed or (2) sufficiently large to invoke the Central Limit Theorem (30 or greater per treatment level).

3. The variances of the two populations from which the samples were taken must be equal. You will test this assumption formally beginning on page 340.

# HYPOTHESIS TESTING ON THE DIFFERENCE IN THE MEANS OF TWO INDEPENDENT POPULATIONS HAVING UNEQUAL VARIANCES

This section is similar to the previous one in that we test for the differences in the means of two populations. However, here we assume that the populations have unequal variances. The only change is how we compute the estimated standard error.

Strateg–Com (SCM) wants to sell 3Com, Inc., its strategic planning software package and training program that costs about $85,000. SCM claims that firms that use its planning software have higher returns on total assets (ROA) than firms that do manual planning. Since the software package is expensive, 3Com's management conducts a survey. It selects 80 public firms and obtains the ROA data. Forty firms use SCM's planning software and 40 firms do manual planning. Based upon the study's results, 3Com, Inc., will decide whether to purchase the planning software. By the end of this unit you should be able to conduct the five steps of hypothesis testing.

### STEP 1: State Hypotheses and Managerial Actions

SCM claims that firms that use its planning software have higher returns on total assets (ROA) than firms that do manual planning. Thus, 3Com's null hypothesis is the opposite of that claim; namely,

| Hypothesis | Managerial Actions |
|---|---|
| $H_0: \mu_{SCM} - \mu_{NoSCM} \leq 0$ | In the population, firms that use SCM's planning software have ROAs that are equal to or less than firms that do not use the software. |
| | Failure to reject the null hypothesis means that 3Com will not purchase the planning software. |

The alternative hypothesis is always the claim made by others. Thus:

| Hypothesis | Managerial Actions |
|---|---|
| $H_1: \mu_{SCM} - \mu_{NoSCM} > 0$ | In the population, firms that use SCM's planning software have higher ROAs than firms that do not use the software. |
| | Rejecting the null means that 3Com will purchase the planning software. |

This is a one-sided, upper tail (or one-tail) test.

### STEP 2: Determine the Consequences of the Decision-Making Errors

Below are the formal definitions of the two errors and their translations into the return on total assets study setting.

| Type I Error: | **Reject the null hypothesis when the null hypothesis is true.** |
|---|---|
| Translation of Type I Error | "Reject the null" means that 3Com believes the alternative is true. It will purchase the planning software because it thinks it will help increase its ROA. |
| | "Null is true" means the population mean ROA for those firms that use SCM's planning software is no higher than for those who do not use the software (manual planning). |
| Description of Type I Error | 3Com purchases the software but it does not help increase its ROA. |
| Type II Error: | **Do not reject the null hypothesis when the null is false.** |
| Translation of Type II Error | "Do not reject the null" means that 3Com believes the null hypothesis is true. Thus, it will not purchase the planning software. |
| | "Null is false" means the population mean ROA for firms that use SCM's planning software is higher than for firms that do not. 3Com should have purchased the planning software. |
| Description of Type II Error | 3Com does not purchase the planning software when it should have. It could have increased ROA. This is a lost financial opportunity. |

### STEP 3: Set a Significance Level and Determine the Sample Sizes

In this study, both errors are costly. 3Com set the significance level, $\alpha$, at 0.01. If it rejects the null hypothesis, the probability of making a Type I error is at most 1 in 100. Thus, the firm can be at least $100(1 - \alpha = 0.01)\%$, or 99%, confident of having made a correct decision. We will make use of the significance level, $\alpha = 0.01$, in Step 5.

To reduce the chance of a costly Type II error, the firm chose a large sample size of 40 firms per treatment level.

### STEP 4: Conduct Study or Market Survey

3Com conducts the survey study discussed earlier. Table 8.9 presents the sample statistics for the study (see Table 8.3 for raw data).

**Table 8.9**

Data from Study on Impact of SCM's Planning Software on ROA

| Planning Done Using | SCM Software | No SCM Software |
|---|---|---|
| Sample mean | 11.332% | 11.038% |
| Sample variance | 0.175198 | 1.94720 |
| Sample size | 40 | 40 |

Given the large sample sizes per treatment level, there is no need to compute the skewness and kurtosis descriptive statistics.

### STEP 5: Compute Test Statistic and Choose between the Null and Alternative Hypotheses

The sample mean ROA for firms that use SCM's planning software ($\bar{x}_{SCM}$) was 0.294 higher than firms that did not use SCM's software.

$$\text{Diff} = \bar{x}_{SCM} - \bar{x}_{NoSCM}$$
$$\text{Diff} = 11.332 - 11.038 = 0.294$$

To *possibly* reject the null hypothesis, the sample difference must be greater than 0. To reject the null hypothesis, the sample difference must be *significantly greater than* 0.

Compute the test statistic that measures the impact on ROA due to the planning software versus the impact due to all extraneous factors. The numerator of the test statistic measures the impact of the planning software; namely, 0.294%. The denominator is the estimated standard error. It measures the impact on ROA due to all extraneous factors such as varying profit margins on products, the introduction of new products, the ability to control expenses, alternative financing strategies to hold down interest expenses, and so forth. We use the two sample variances from Table 8.9 to estimate the impact on ROA attributed to extraneous factors.

Assuming that the population variances are *not* equal, we can use Expression (8.3) to compute the estimated standard error.

$$\sqrt{\frac{s_1^2}{n_1} + \frac{s_2^2}{n_2}}$$

**(8.3)**

Even without a formal statistical test, it appears from Table 8.9 that the two population variances are not the same because one sample variance is over 11 times larger than the other sample variance.

The estimated standard error is:

$$\sqrt{\frac{0.17520}{40} + \frac{1.9472}{40}} = 0.230\%$$

The test statistic is

$$\frac{\text{Impact of Experimental Factor (Software)}}{\text{Impact of Extraneous Factors}} = \frac{\bar{x}_{\text{SCM}} - \bar{x}_{\text{NoSCM}}}{\text{Est.Std.Error}} = \frac{0.294}{0.230} = 1.28$$

Is a test statistic of 1.28 sufficient evidence to reject the null hypothesis at a $\alpha$ level of 0.01?

Table 8.10 is the output from Excel's data-analysis tool, the **t-test: two-sample assuming unequal variances**. Shown here is the dialog box for the tool.

|  | Computer | Manual |
|---|---|---|
| Mean | 11.3315 | 11.03775 |
| Variance | 0.175198 | 1.947203 |
| Observations | 40 | 40 |
| Hypothesized Mean Difference | 0 | |
| df | 46 | |
| t Stat | 1.275247 | |
| P(T<=t) one-tail | 0.104313 | **p-value for one-tail test** |
| t Critical one-tail | 1.678659 | |
| P(T<=t) two-tail | 0.208625 | |
| t Critical two-tail | 2.012894 | |

**Table 8.10**
t-Test: Two-Sample
Assuming Unequal
Variances

Use the following decision rule to choose between the null and alternative hypotheses.

**Decision Rule:** Reject the null hypothesis and accept the alternative hypothesis if the computed $p$-value is less than or equal to the significance level, $\alpha$, set in Step 3 for the appropriate-tailed test—one or two tailed. Otherwise, do not reject the null hypothesis.

From Table 8.10, the $p$-value equals 0.104313. Since it is larger than the significance level of 0.01, 3Com cannot reject the null hypothesis. It should not purchase the planning software.

Having failed to reject the null hypothesis, 3Com has either made a correct decision or a Type II error. It could not have made a Type I error.

Again, to do hypothesis testing the following assumptions must be true:

1. The manager must select random samples from the two populations.

2. Both samples either must be (1) from populations that are normally distributed or (2) larger than 30 to use the Central Limit Theorem.

3. The variances of the two populations from which the samples were taken must *not* be equal. You will test this assumption formally beginning on page 340.

# TESTING FOR THE DIFFERENCE BETWEEN THE MEANS OF TWO RELATED POPULATIONS: THE PAIRED SAMPLE $t$-TEST FOR THE MATCHED-PAIR DESIGN

A firm is presently teaching brainstorming in its creativity training sessions and it is effective. Several trainers believe that analogy may be a superior creative method. The human resource manager approves a study to compare analogy versus brainstorming to determine which method generates more solutions.

A study team conducts a matched-pair design. They identify pairs of employees who have similar levels of "natural" creativity. They then randomly assign one member of each pair to one of the two treatments (creativity methods) and record the number of solutions.

By the end of this section you should be able to

1. complete the five steps in hypothesis testing; and

2. explain how to use the Pearson correlation coefficient after completing a study to determine if a matched-pair design was the appropriate design for the study.

| STEP 1: | State Hypotheses and Managerial Actions |

The trainers claim that analogy will generate more solutions than brainstorming. The HR manager's null hypothesis is the opposite of that claim. The alternative hypothesis is always the claim made by others. This leads to the following hypotheses.

| Hypotheses | Managerial Actions |
|---|---|
| $H_0: \mu_{AN} - \mu_{BS} \leq 0$ | In the population, the number of solutions generated by analogy is less than or equal to brainstorming. |
| | Failure to reject the null hypothesis means that the firm will continue to teach brainstorming. |
| $H_1: \mu_{AN} - \mu_{BS} > 0$ | In the population, the number of solutions generated by analogy is greater than for brainstorming. |
| | Rejecting the null means that the firm will teach the analogy method. |

This is a **one-tail (upper tail)** test.

| STEPS 2 & 3: | Determine the Consequences of Errors, Set a Significance Level, and Determine the Sample Sizes |
|---|---|

There are costs associated with both errors.

Type I Error    The firm begins teaching the analogy method when, in fact, it is no better than (and perhaps worse than) brainstorming. It was already satisfied with the brainstorming method.

Type II Error   The firm concludes that the analogy method is not superior when, in fact, it is. However, since the firm is very satisfied with brainstorming, the error would not be serious.

Because the Type I error was more costly than the Type II error, the HR manager set the significance level, $\alpha$, at 0.01. If the firm rejects the null hypothesis, the probability of making a Type I error is at most 1 in 100. Thus, the firm can be at least $100(1 - \alpha = 0.01)\%$, or 99%, confident of having made a correct decision. We will make use of the significance level, $\alpha = 0.01$, in Step 5.

Since the Type II error was not too costly the HR manager selected a small sample size. The sample size is 20 pairs of employees *matched* on their "natural" creativity levels.

| STEP 4: | Conduct Study or Market Survey |
|---|---|

The study team conducts the matched-pair study. Table 8.11 presents the sample statistics for the study (see Table 8.4 for the raw data).

**Table 8.11**
Difference Data (Column 4 in Table 8.4) from the Matched-Pair Design

| Number of Solutions | Difference = Analogy – Brainstorm |
|---|---|
| Sample mean | 2.6 Solutions |
| Sample standard deviation | 0.940325 Solutions |
| Number of Pairs | 20 |

On average, the pair member who used analogy generated 2.6 more solutions than his/her matched partner who used brainstorming.

| STEP 5: | Compute the Test Statistic and Choose between the Null and Alternative Hypotheses |
|---|---|

To *possibly* reject the null hypothesis, the sample mean difference must be greater than 0. To reject the null hypothesis, the sample mean difference must be *significantly greater than* 0.

The test statistic measures the impact on the number of solutions due to the two creativity methods (the experimental factor) versus all extraneous factors. The numerator of the test statistic measures the impact due to the two creativity methods; namely, +2.6 solutions. The denominator is the estimated standard error. It measures the impact on the number of solutions due to all extraneous factors such as demographic, personality, and motivational differences among the study's participants. We use Expression (8.4) to compute the estimated standard error.

$$\frac{\text{sample standard deviation of difference data}}{\sqrt{n}}$$

(8.4)

where $n$ is the number of matched pairs in the study

The estimated standard error is:

$$\frac{0.9403}{\sqrt{20}} = 0.210 \text{ solutions}$$

The test statistic is

$$\frac{\text{Impact of Experimental Factor (Method)}}{\text{Impact of Extraneous Factors}} = \frac{2.6}{.210} = 12.4$$

Is a test statistic value of 12.4 sufficient evidence to reject the null hypothesis at an $\alpha$ level of 0.01?

Table 8.12 is the output from Excel's data-analysis tool, the **t-test: paired two samples for mean**. Shown here is the dialog box for the tool.

Use the following decision rule to choose between the null and alternative hypotheses.

**Decision Rule:** Reject the null hypothesis and accept the alternative hypothesis if the computed $p$-value is less than or equal to the significance level, $\alpha$, set in Step 3 for the appropriate-tailed test—one or two tailed. Otherwise, do not reject the null hypothesis.

| | Analogy | Brainstorm |
|---|---|---|
| Mean | 31.6 | 29 |
| Variance | 200.7789 | 209.36842 |
| Observations | 20 | 20 |
| Pearson Correlation | 0.998063 | |
| Hypothesized Mean Difference | 0 | |
| df | 19 | **pairs − 1** |
| t Stat | 12.36547 | |
| P(T<=t) one-tail | 7.79E-11 | **p-value for one-tail test** |
| t Critical one-tail | 1.729131 | |
| P(T<=t) two-tail | 1.56E-10 | |
| t Critical two-tail | 2.093025 | |

**Table 8.12**
t-Test: Paired Two
Sample for Means

From Table 8.12 the p-value of 0.00000000078 is less than the significance level of 0.01. The firm should reject the null hypothesis. In the population, analogy generates more solutions than brainstorming. The HR manager should implement the analogy method in the training programs.

## DECISION-MAKING CONSEQUENCES

The HR manager has made a correct decision or has rejected the null hypothesis when the null was true, a Type I error. The actual probability of having made a Type I error is almost zero. Having rejected the null hypothesis, it is not possible to have now made a Type II error.

## CORRELATION AND THE MATCHED-PAIR DESIGN

Note the Pearson correlation coefficient in Table 8.12. We did not provide this statistic in either of the previous two analyses. From Chapter 7, the correlation coefficient, $r$, is a numerical measure of the strength of a linear relationship between two variables. Correlation coefficients can vary from $-1$ to $+1$.

A correlation of $+0.9981$ indicates a very strong positive relationship among the 20 pairs of data values in Table 8.4. Why should we have expected such a large positive correlation coefficient? Think about it before continuing.

The study team *correctly* determined the appropriate extraneous factor—creativity level—to match participants. So if one member of a pair generated a large number of solutions using one creative method you would expect the other member also to generate many solutions using the other method. And if one member of a pair generated only a few solutions using one creative method you would expect the other member also to generate few solutions. From Table 8.4, that is exactly what happened (for example, see pairs 19 and 16).

In the planning software study discussed in the previous section, the manager selected two totally random samples of firms. What might you expect the correlation coefficient to be between the 40 SCM data values and the 40 No SCM data values from Table 8.3? Think about before continuing.

Since the two groups of firms are not related to one another (have not been matched), we should expect the correlation coefficient to be close to zero. For the return on total asset data, the correlation coefficient (CORREL) is $-0.1278$.

In summary, if you run a matched-pair design and the correlation coefficient is not close to $+1.0$ (zero or *highly* negative) you may have matched pairs on *irrelevant extraneous factors*. At that point, you should either (1) select a truly important extraneous factor(s) to match on and rerun the study or (2) rerun the study as a one-factor two-level completely random design.

Consider also using Excel's data-analysis tool, the t-test: paired two samples for means, when conducting a **repeated-measures** design in which you take multiple measurements on the same individual.

---

**D E F I N I T I O N**      In a **repeated-measures** design you observe each subject under each of the treatment levels.

Below is an example of a repeated-measures design from the advertising area (see Table 8.13). The research team will show each subject the two different ads and obtain his or her preference scores. The firm will use randomization to determine which ad each subject sees first.

| Study Participant | Advertisement A | Advertisement B |
|---|---|---|
| 1 | $score_{1A}$ | $score_{1B}$ |
| 2 | $score_{2A}$ | $score_{2B}$ |
| 3 | $score_{3A}$ | $score_{3B}$ |
| 4 | $score_{4A}$ | $score_{4B}$ |
| . | . | . |
| . | . | . |
| . | . | . |

**Table 8.13**
Layout for a One-Factor Repeated Measures Design

The repeated-measures design is related to the matched-pair design. In the latter we randomly selected two people who are similar on important extraneous factors. But who is most similar to a person? The same person, of course! So in the repeated-measures design we match on the "same person." For both the matched pair or repeated-measures designs, the correlation between the two columns of data should be close to +1.0.

## ASSUMPTIONS UNDERLYING EXCEL'S PAIRED SAMPLE t-TEST FOR THE MATCHED-PAIR DESIGN

1. Assignment of a treatment to each subject within a pair is random for the matched-pair design. The sequencing of presenting the treatments to each subject is random for the repeated-measures design.

2. Both samples must be from populations that are normally distributed.

The skewness and kurtosis for the 20 analogy values and 20 brainstorming values (not shown here) indicated that the two populations are near normally distributed. If the sample data had not been normally distributed, you could transform the data by using either a square root or logarithmic base 10 transformation. You can then do hypothesis testing if the transformed data are near normal.

# TESTING FOR THE DIFFERENCE BETWEEN THE PROPORTIONS OF TWO INDEPENDENT POPULATIONS

An HR specialist believes that a larger proportion of the firm's white-collar workers is financially planning for retirement than are its blue-collar workers.

To evaluate the claim, the HR manager conducts a survey on a random sample of blue-collar and white-collar employees within the firm. Each randomly selected employee answers the following question: "Beyond Social Security and the firm's pension plan, are you systematically saving for your retirement?" Based on study's findings, the HR manager will then decide whether to offer additional retirement planning sessions for all blue-collar workers.

All the ideas in the section beginning on page 318 apply to hypothesis testing on the difference in the proportions of two independent populations. The only distinction is how we compute the estimated standard error for the study. By the end of this unit you should be able to complete the five steps in hypothesis testing.

### STEP 1:   State Hypotheses and Managerial Actions

An HR *specialist* claims that a larger proportion of the firm's white-collar workers is financially planning for retirement than are its blue-collar workers. Thus, the HR *manager's* null hypothesis is

| Hypothesis | Managerial Actions |
|---|---|
| $H_0: P_{WCW} - P_{BCW} \leq 0$ | In the population, the proportion of the firm's white-collar workers that are financially planning for retirement is not greater than for its blue-collar workers. |
| | Failure to reject the null hypothesis means that the firm will not conduct additional retirement planning sessions for all blue-collar workers. |

The alternative hypothesis is always the claim made by others. Thus,

| Hypothesis | Managerial Actions |
|---|---|
| $H_1: P_{WCW} - P_{BCW} > 0$ | In the population, the proportion of the firm's white-collar workers that are financially planning for retirement is greater than for its blue-collar workers. |
| | Rejecting the null means that the firm will conduct additional retirement planning sessions for all blue-collar workers. |

This is a one-sided, upper tail (or one-tail) test.

| STEPS 2 & 3: | Determine the Costs of Errors, Set a Significance Level, and Determine the Sample Sizes |

There are costs associated with both errors.

Type I Error    Conduct additional retirement planning sessions when, in fact, none are needed. Costs include the development of new training materials and the lost productivity of workers attending the sessions.

Type II Error    Do not conduct additional retirement planning sessions when, in fact, sessions are needed. Costs include the long-term consequences to workers who do not have sufficient income for retirement.

Both errors are costly, although the firm "pays" the Type I error cost, while the workers "pay" the costs of a Type II error. The HR manager set the $\alpha$ level at 0.025 and selected two random samples of 100 workers each. If she rejects the null hypothesis, the probability of making the Type I error is at most 2.5 in 100. Thus, she can be at least $100(1 - \alpha = 0.025)\%$, or 97.5%, confident of having made a correct decision. We will use the significance level, $\alpha = 0.025$, in Step 5.

| STEP 4: | Conduct Study or Market Survey |

Table 8.14 presents the sample statistics for the study (see Table 8.5 for the raw data).

**Table 8.14**
Sample Statistics for Retirement Survey

|  | White-Collar Workers | Blue-Collar Workers |
|---|---|---|
| Sample Proportion, $\hat{p}$ | 70/100 = 0.70 | 45/100 = 0.45 |
| Sample Size | 100 | 100 |

| STEP 5: | Compute Test Statistic and Choose between the Null and Alternative Hypotheses |

To *possibly* reject the null hypothesis, the sample difference must be greater than 0. To reject the null hypothesis, the sample difference must be *significantly greater than* 0.

$$\text{Diff} = \hat{p}_{\text{WCW}} - \hat{p}_{\text{BCW}}$$
$$\text{Diff} = 0.70 - 0.45 = 0.25$$

The numerator of the test statistic is 0.25. The denominator is the estimated standard error, the impact on the proportion of workers who have systematic savings for retirement due to all extraneous factors such as demographic, personality, and motivational differences.

To compute the estimated standard error, first compute the pooled estimate of the population proportion. Use Expression (8.5).

$$\bar{p} = \frac{n_1 \cdot \hat{p}_1 + n_2 \cdot \hat{p}_2}{n_1 + n_2}$$

(8.5)

Given that each sample size was 100, the pooled estimate is simply the average of the two sample proportions and equals 0.575.

$$\bar{p} = \frac{(100 \cdot 0.70) + (100 \cdot 0.45)}{200} = 0.575$$

Use Expression (8.6) to compute the estimated standard error.

$$\sqrt{\left[\frac{\bar{p} \cdot (1 - \bar{p})}{n_1}\right] + \left[\frac{\bar{p} \cdot (1 - \bar{p})}{n_2}\right]}$$

(8.6)

The estimated standard error is

$$\sqrt{\left[\frac{0.575 \cdot (0.425)}{100}\right] + \left[\frac{0.575 \cdot (0.425)}{100}\right]} = 0.06991$$

The test statistic is

$$\frac{0.70 - 0.45}{\text{estimated standard error}} = \frac{0.250}{0.06991} = 3.5760$$

Is a test statistic of 3.576 sufficient evidence to reject the null hypothesis at the $\alpha = .025$ level? Use the NORMSDIST function wizard to test the null hypothesis as we did in Chapter 6.

For $z > 0$, the p-value for a one-tail test is 1 − NORMSDIST value.
For $z < 0$, the p-value for a one-tail test is the NORMSDIST value.
For a two-tail test, the p-value is two times the one-tail value.

The *p*-value for the study is $1 - 0.999825515 = 0.00017448$.

Since the *p*-value of 0.00017448 is less than the significance level of 0.025, the HR manager should reject the null hypothesis and accept the alternative hypothesis. She should have her staff develop and implement retirement planning sessions for all blue-collar workers.

## DECISION-MAKING CONSEQUENCES

The HR manager has rejected the null hypothesis. She has either made a correct decision or has made a Type I error. She can be $100(1 - 0.00017) = 99.983\%$ confident that she has made a correct decision. Alternatively, the odds are $0.99983/0.00017 = 5881:1$. The HR manager could not have made a Type II error because she rejected the null hypothesis.

# TESTING FOR THE EQUALITY OF VARIANCES FROM TWO INDEPENDENT POPULATIONS: THE F-TEST

In this section we test for the equality of two population variances. This is important for two reasons. First, in hypothesis testing on the difference in the means of two independent populations, the proper Excel data-analysis tool depends on whether the population variances are equal or differ. We can use the F-test to determine which analysis is appropriate. Second, we use the F-test as an end in itself. Often we are interested in knowing if process or product changes have reduced the variance. In today's competitive marketplace, *variance is the enemy*.

Consider the following situation. The target value for the inside diameter of automotive piston rings is 74.000 millimeters. A quality improvement team has developed a set of process changes that it believes will reduce the variance of the inside diameters of the rings. The operations manager authorizes the team to conduct a one factor two-treatment-level completely random study to evaluate the changes. The two levels are the present process (PP) versus the experimental process (EP). The sample size is 15 observations, or piston rings, per level. By the end of this section you should be able to complete the five steps in hypothesis testing.

| STEP 1: | State Hypotheses and Managerial Actions |

The quality improvement team claims that the experimental process will reduce the process variance. The null hypothesis is always the opposite of the claim made by others who wish to influence the decision maker. The decision maker's hypotheses are:

| Hypothesis | Managerial Actions |
|---|---|
| $H_0: \sigma^2_{EP} > \sigma^2_{PP}$ | In the population, the variance for the experimental process is equal to or greater than for the present process. |
| | Failure to reject the null hypothesis means that the operations manager will not implement the experimental process. |

The alternative hypothesis is always the claim made by others. Thus,

| Hypothesis | Managerial Actions |
|---|---|
| $H_1: \sigma^2_{EP} < \sigma^2_{PP}$ | In the population, the variance for the experimental process is less than for the present process. |
| | Rejecting the null means that the operations manager will implement the experimental process. |

### STEPS 2 & 3:    Determine the Costs of Errors, Set a Significance Level, and Determine the Sample Sizes

There are costs associated with both errors.

| Type I Error | The firm implements the experimental process. It expects the process variance to drop when, in fact, it will not drop. Costs include the actual process changes and their associated downtime costs. |
|---|---|
| Type II Error | The firm does not install the experimental process when, in fact, it would have reduced process variance. This is a lost opportunity. |

Because the Type I error was costly, the operations manager set the significance level, $\alpha$, at 0.03. If the manager rejects the null hypothesis, the probability of making a Type I error is at most 3 in 100. Thus, the firm can be at least $100(1 - \alpha = 0.03)\%$, or 97%, confident of having made a correct decision. We will make use of the significance level, $\alpha = 0.03$, in Step 5.

### STEP 4:    Conduct Study or Market Survey

The quality improvement team conducts the one factor two–treatment–level study discussed earlier. Table 8.15 presents the sample statistics for the study (see Table 8.6 for raw data).

**Table 8.15**
Statistics from One-Factor Two-Level Study on Reducing Variance of Inside Diameters of Automotive Piston Rings

|  | Experimental | Present |
|---|---|---|
| Sample mean | 74.0017 | 73.9965 |
| Sample variance | .0000837 | .000125 |
| Sample size | 15 | 15 |

### STEP 5:    Compute the F Statistic and Choose between the Null and Alternative Hypotheses

For the specific samples, the sample variance for the experimental process

$\left(s_{EP}^2 = 0.0000837\right)$ was less than the sample variance for the present process

$\left(s_{PP}^2 = 0.000125\right)$. However, the manager cannot even considering saying that

$\sigma_{EP}^2 < \sigma_{PP}^2$ until completing Step 5.

In this section we compute the F(isher) statistic. It measures how different the two sample variances are. *Always place the larger variance in the numerator of Expression (8.7).*

$$F = \frac{s_{larger}^2}{s_{smaller}^2}$$

(8.7)

For the piston-ring study, the F ratio is:

$$F = \frac{0.000125}{0.0000837} = 1.49$$

In plain English, the variance for the present process is 1.49 times *larger* than the variance for the experimental process. Is a ratio of 1.49 sufficiently large to reject the null hypothesis at a significance level of 0.03?

Table 8.16 is the output from Excel's **data-analysis tool, F-Test: Two-Sample for Variances.** Shown here is the dialog box for the tool.

* Due to an idiosyncrasy of the tool, the variance of Variable 1 must be greater than the variance of Variable 2. If your output shows the variance of the first variable is less than the second, swap the variable range references in the dialog box and run the tool again.

|  | **Present** | **Experimental** |
|---|---|---|
| Mean | 73.99653 | 74.00167 |
| Variance | 0.000125 | 8.37E-05 |
| Observations | 15 | 15 |
| Df | 14 | 14 |
| F | 1.497211 | |
| P(F<=f) one-tail[5] | 0.229871 | **p-value for one-tail test** |
| F Critical one-tail | 2.483723 | |

**Table 8.16**
F-Test: Two-Sample for Variances

Use the following decision rule to choose between the null and alternative hypotheses.

**Decision Rule:** Reject the null hypothesis and accept the alternative hypothesis if the computed $p$-value is less than or equal to the significance level, $\alpha$, set in Step 3. Otherwise, do not reject the null hypothesis.

Since the $p$-value of 0.2299 is greater than the significance level of 0.03, the operations manager should not reject the null hypothesis. There is insufficient evidence to reject the null hypothesis. He should not implement the experimental process.

The operations manager has failed to reject the null hypothesis. Having failed to reject the null hypothesis, the operations manager has made either a correct decision or a Type II error. He could not have made a Type I error.

---

[5] The correct label for this output row is actually $P(F \geq f)$. This is a technicality but if you plan to show the output to others, correct it.

# USING THE F-TEST PRIOR TO HYPOTHESIS TESTING ON THE DIFFERENCE IN TWO POPULATION MEANS

Also use the F-test as a preliminary test for hypothesis testing on the difference in the means of two independent populations. If the two population variances are equal, then use Excel's t–Test: Two-Sample Assuming Equal Variances data-analysis tool. If the two population variances differ, then use Excel's t–Test: Two-Sample Assuming Unequal Variances data-analysis tool.

In the section beginning on page 318 we assumed that the variances of the two populations were the same. Let's use the F-test to determine if that assumption was justified. Begin by stating the null and alternative hypotheses. When testing for the equality of two population variances (in preparation for hypothesis testing on two population means), the *null is always that the two population variances are the same.*

$$\mathbf{H_0}: \sigma^2_{140} = \sigma^2_{160}$$
$$\mathbf{H_1}: \sigma^2_{140} \neq \sigma^2_{160}$$
$$\alpha = \mathbf{0.05}$$

This is a two-tail test. For a two–tail test, type in $\alpha/2$, not $\alpha$ in the Excel dialog box (see below).[6] This will ensure that the correct *p*-value is determined. *Do this only for two-tail tests.*

The *p*-value for a one-tail test is 0.476808. Because this is a two-tail test, you multiply the *p*-value from the Excel-generated table by 2.

---

[6] This is a second idiosyncrasy of the analytical tool.

Table 8.17 is the output for the F-test.

| F-Test Two-Sample for Variances | | |
|---|---|---|
| | **140 F** | **160 F** |
| Mean | 135.52 | 127.44 |
| Variance | 88.01 | 85.92333 |
| Observations | 25 | 25 |
| Df | 24 | 24 |
| F | 1.024285 | |
| P(F<=f) one-tail | 0.476808 | **p-value for *two-tail* test is 2(.476808) = 0.953616** |
| F Critical one-tail | 2.269275 | |

**Table 8.17**
F-Test for Wave
Soldering Time Data

Since the $p$-value of 0.953616 is greater than the significance level of $\alpha = 0.05$, we cannot reject the null hypothesis. We conclude that the variances of the two populations are the same. Therefore, the operations manager was justified in using Excel's t-Test: Two-Sample Assuming Equal Variances data-analysis tool. Had the null hypothesis been rejected, the manager would have used Excel's t-Test: Two-Sample Assuming Unequal Variances tool.

## ASSUMPTIONS UNDERLYING THE F-TEST TWO-SAMPLE FOR VARIANCES

**1.** The manager must select random samples from the two populations.

**2.** The populations must be normally distributed.

The skewness and kurtosis (not shown) for the data in the variance reduction study and the reduction in wave soldering time study suggested that the populations were all normally distributed. If the populations had not been normally distributed, you should not use the F-test unless the transformed data were near normally distributed.

# ROAD MAP FOR THE CHAPTER

Perhaps the most difficult task for managers is knowing when to use the five different hypothesis-testing Excel tools in this chapter. The chapter concludes with a road map, given in Figure 8.3, that provides useful guidelines.

Regardless of which hypothesis-testing tool you use, for a sample size of less than 30 per treatment level always verify that the populations are near normally distributed. If not, transform the data and determine if the data are now near normally distributed. If not, do not conduct hypothesis testing.

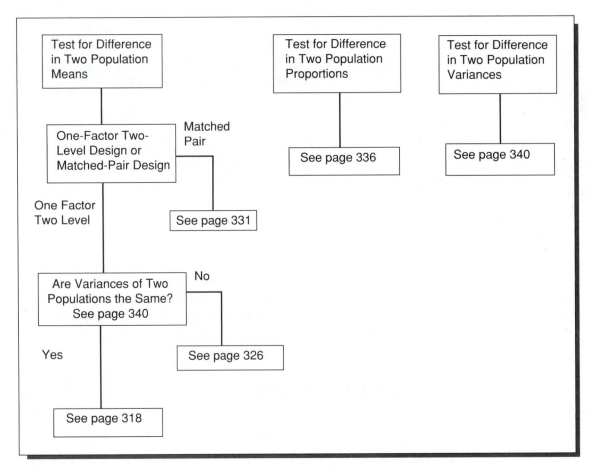

**Figure 8.3**
Road Map for Chapter's Statistical Methods

# EXERCISES

**1.** Correct, if necessary, the following sets of hypotheses.

**a.** $H_0: \bar{x}_1 \le \bar{x}_2$
$H_1: \bar{x}_1 > \bar{x}_2$

**b.** $H_0: \mu_1 < \mu_2$
$H_1: \mu_1 > \mu_2$

**c.** $H_0: \mu_1 \ge \sigma_2^2$
$H_1: \mu_1 < \sigma_2^2$

**2.** Why is it possible to make either a Type I or Type II error before a study, but only one of these errors after the study?

**3.** If the most likely Type II error is costly but the Type I error is not, why might you set the significance level, $\alpha$, at 0.15 or higher?

**4.** What does the $p$-value tell you?

**5.** Suppose you set the $\alpha$ level at 0.05 for a one-tail test. You obtain the following Excel output: P(T <= t) one tail = 0.0786956. Should you reject the null hypothesis? Why?

**6.** Under what conditions should you use a matched-pair or repeated-measures design?

**7.** Suppose $H_1: p_1 > p_2$. Suppose that $\hat{p}_1 = .67 > \hat{p}_2 = .60$. Why can't we immediately reject the null hypothesis and accept the alternative hypothesis? Why is it necessary to do hypothesis testing?

**8.** Develop a hypothetical problem that is consistent with each of the following alternative hypotheses.

   **a.** $H_1: \sigma^2_{\text{portfolio A}} < \sigma^2_{\text{portfolio B}}$

   **b.** $H_1: \mu_{\text{cost per day in Alabama}} < \mu_{\text{cost per day in Florida}}$

   **c.** $H_1: p_{\text{business travelers after promotion}} > p_{\text{business travelers before promotion}}$

**9.** A Koger senior manager claims that Koger has lower prices than Cab Foods. He selects $n = 10$ pairs of products and then determines the prices of these products at both food chains. Let $\alpha = 0.05$. Assume the data are normally distributed.

| Product | Koger | Cab Foods |
|---|---|---|
| Jam | $1.31 | $1.34 |
| Milk | 1.74 | 1.89 |
| Juice | 1.47 | 1.50 |
| Ice Cream | 4.23 | 4.50 |
| Oranges | 0.97 | 1.00 |
| Lettuce | 0.99 | 0.99 |
| Battery | 3.45 | 3.60 |
| Health Bars | 2.65 | 2.60 |
| Popcorn 6-Pak | 1.89 | 2.00 |
| Total Cereal | 3.45 | 3.69 |

   **a.** Set up the null and alternative hypotheses and the associated managerial actions.

   **b.** Describe the Type I and Type II errors.

   **c.** Use the study's $p$-value to evaluate the senior manager's claim.

**10.** A medical consumer watchdog agency claims that the mean hospitalization cost per day in Alabama is greater than in the neighboring state of Mississippi. It randomly selects hospitals (the same mix of not-for-profit and profit hospitals) in both states and obtains the daily cost data found in spreadsheet 810.xls.

   **a.** Before doing hypothesis testing on the difference on the means of two independent populations, conduct an F-test on the equality of the variances of the two populations. Let $\alpha = 0.05$.

   **b.** Set up the null and alternative hypotheses and the associated managerial actions for testing the agency's claim.

   **c.** Describe the Type I and Type II errors.

   **d.** Based on your answer from part (a), use the appropriate hypothesis-testing tool to evaluate the agency's claim at the $\alpha = 0.05$ level.

**11.** A quality engineer for a cellular phone manufacturer claims that she has reduced process variance by switching to a new material vendor. Has she reduced the process variance in tensile strength of phone handsets? She collects production data before and after the process change. Assume the data are normally distributed.

| Old Vendor | New Vendor |
|---|---|
| 4975 | 4770 |
| 4625 | 4800 |
| 4750 | 4675 |
| 4900 | 4800 |
| 4700 | 4775 |
| 4550 | 4700 |
| 4800 | 4780 |
| 4775 | 4650 |
| 4500 | 4750 |
| 4975 | 4800 |

**a.** Compute descriptive statistics for the two processes.

**b.** Conduct an F-test to evaluate the engineer's claim. Let $\alpha = 0.10$.

**c.** Given the study's findings, is it possible to have made a Type II error?

**d.** Are the two populations from which the data were taken truly normally distributed? Discuss.

**12.** An educational researcher believes that average student performance on a common final examination will improve if an instructor uses in-class, small-group exercises. To test his claim, he teaches two sections of statistics. In one section, he uses a straight lecture method. In the other section, he uses small groups. Both classes follow the same course syllabus and take the same common final. Assume that the students in the two classes are random samples. Spreadsheet 812.xls contains the study data.

**a.** Before doing hypothesis testing on the difference in the means of two independent populations, conduct an F-test on the equality of the variances of the two populations. Let $\alpha = 0.05$.

**b.** Set up the null and alternative hypotheses and the associated managerial actions for testing the researcher's claim.

**c.** Describe the Type I and II errors.

**d.** Let $\alpha = 0.05$. Based on your findings from part (a), evaluate the researcher's claim.

**13.** An economist believes that a greater proportion of married couples between 25–34 years of age systematically purchase mutual funds than their single counterparts. The economist randomly selects two samples of 500 each in the 25–34 age bracket and asks them, "Have you systematically purchased mutual funds over the past three years?" Here are the data.

| Couples | Singles |
|---|---|
| $\hat{p}_c = 0.17$ | $\hat{p}_s = 0.09$ |

**a.** Set up the null and alternative hypotheses and the associated managerial actions.

**b.** Let $\alpha = 0.05$. Evaluate the economist's claim.

**14.** In a just-in-time delivery system, vendors' parts arrive at a plant just before they are needed in production. This reduces a firm's inventory storage costs. But vendors' parts must arrive at or very near the scheduled time; otherwise, production is stopped. Consistent (low-variance) delivery times are preferred to inconsistent (high-variance) delivery times. Zander Manufacturing has arranged with Hiteck, Inc., that electronic parts should arrive daily at noon for a particular production line. For over six months, Hiteck had trouble meeting the schedule. A joint problem-solving team made several recommendations it claimed would reduce on-time variance. Below are the arrival data for two random ten-day periods before and after the joint problem-solving effort. Zander records the number of hours off the noon target (*Note: a + 2 means that a shipment arrived at 2:00 pm.*). Assume the data are normally distributed.

| Before | +3 | +2 | −3 | 0 | 0 | −4 | 0 | 0 | −2 | +4 |
|---|---|---|---|---|---|---|---|---|---|---|
| After | −1 | 0 | +1 | −1 | +1 | 0 | +1 | −1 | 0 | 0 |

**a.** Set up the null and alternative hypotheses and the associated managerial actions.

**b.** Describe the Type I and Type II errors.

**c.** Evaluate the problem-solving team's claim that the variance has been reduced. Let $\alpha = 0.01$.

**15.** An accounting firm wants to compare two CPA training methods. It believes that a "live classroom" is superior to a videotape course. It selects ten pairs of accountants matched in terms of years of experience and grade-point average in upper division accounting courses. Each member of each pair is randomly assigned to one of the two training methods—videotape or live classroom lecture. After completing the training, all 20 accountants take a common exam. Assume the data are normally distributed. Here are their scores.

| Pair | 1 | 2 | 3 | 4 | 5 | 6 | 7 | 8 | 9 | 10 |
|---|---|---|---|---|---|---|---|---|---|---|
| Videotape | 75 | 90 | 40 | 80 | 70 | 90 | 87 | 45 | 78 | 94 |
| Live Classroom | 84 | 95 | 50 | 85 | 76 | 92 | 92 | 52 | 81 | 100 |

**a.** Look at the ten pairs of scores. Does it appear that matching on experience and grade-point average was successful? Use the Pearson correlation coefficient to defend your answer.

**b.** Use the appropriate Excel data-analysis tool to evaluate the firm's claim. Let $\alpha = 0.05$.

**c.** Are the two populations normally distributed? Discuss.

**16.** A financial analyst claims that the mean average collections period (value of accounts receivable divided by average sales per day) is different for two industries. He randomly selects two samples of firms, one from each industry, and obtains the data shown in spreadsheet 816.xls. Show all work. Let $\alpha = 0.05$.

**17.** The manager of Quik Speed bicycle messenger service claims that her service can, on average, deliver a letter faster than her major competitor, Velocity, Inc. As a customer, you must now evaluate that claim. You give both services 60 letters to deliver that require a similar mix of distances, times of day, and street conditions. The data are in spreadsheet 817.xls. Show all work. Let $\alpha = 0.025$.

**18.** A manager uses a matched-pair design to test two different advertising approaches. He selects ten pairs of consumers between the ages of 25 and 34 matched in terms of gender and socioeconomic class. One member of each pair sees a MTV–style advertising presentation and the other member sees a traditional advertising presentation for the same product. He records the number of product features that each can correctly recall one week later. The manager believes that consumers who view the MTV–style ad will, on average, recall more product features. Assume the data are normally distributed.

| Pair | 1 | 2 | 3 | 4 | 5 | 6 | 7 | 8 | 9 | 10 |
|---|---|---|---|---|---|---|---|---|---|---|
| MTV | 4 | 3 | 4 | 5 | 4 | 2 | 4 | 4 | 5 | 4 |
| Trad | 1 | 0 | 2 | 1 | 0 | 2 | 1 | 0 | 2 | 0 |

Evaluate the marketing manager's claim at the $\alpha = 0.025$ level.

**19.** A marketing manager believes that magazine and newspaper coupons are more effective, on average, than proof-of-purchase refund offers in stimulating product sales. Based on two samples of 45 randomly selected customers, the manager obtains the data shown in spreadsheet 819.xls. The data are the weekly amount of purchases of a product using the two sales promotion methods.

**a.** Conduct a preliminary F-test to determine if the variances of the two populations are the same or differ. Let $\alpha = 0.075$.

**b.** Evaluate the marketing manager's claim at the $\alpha = 0.075$ level.

**20.** The St. Louis engineering division manager claims that his staff, on average, takes longer to document engineering changes in a product than the Dayton division personnel. If correct, he will determine why the Dayton personnel are faster, and then implement their practices in St. Louis. He randomly selects 50 similar engineering changes in the two divisions and records the time in hours to document them. Spreadsheet 820.xls contains the data from the study.

**a.** Conduct a preliminary F-test to determine if the variances of the two populations are the same or differ. Let $\alpha = 0.01$.

**b.** Set up the null and alternative hypotheses and the associated managerial actions to test the division manager's claim.

**c.** Describe the Type I and Type II errors.

**d.** Evaluate the engineering manager's claim at the $\alpha = 0.01$ level.

**21.** To attract older people to her community, the city manager of St. Petersburg claims that her city has a higher proportion of retirees than Boca Raton.

|  | St. Petersburg | Boca Raton |
|---|---|---|
| Number of Retirees | 714 | 689 |
| Sample Size | 1,000 | 1,000 |

**a.** Set up the null and alternative hypotheses and the associated managerial actions.

**b.** Describe the Type I and Type II errors.

**c.** Let $\alpha = 0.05$. Evaluate the city manager's claim.

**22.** Little Rock's division manager claims that a greater proportion of her employees believe the policies on quality are clear than do Salt Lake City employees. To assess her claim, she randomly selects 100 employees in both divisions and asks them: "Are the policies on quality clear?"

|  | Little Rock | Salt Lake City |
|---|---|---|
| Number of Yes Responses | 91 | 82 |
| Sample Size | 100 | 100 |

Evaluate the division manager's claim.

**23.** A firm that conducts SAT and GMAT review courses claims that student will improve their SAT scores by taking its half-day course. To prove this, it takes $n = 10$ students and records their SAT scores before and after taking the SAT review course. Each student is paired with himself or herself. Assume that SAT scores are normally distributed in the population. Let $\alpha = 0.05$.

| Student | 1 | 2 | 3 | 4 | 5 |
|---|---|---|---|---|---|
| Before | 700 | 1140 | 900 | 940 | 1000 |
| After | 740 | 1130 | 970 | 1000 | 1010 |

| Student | 6 | 7 | 8 | 9 | 10 |
|---|---|---|---|---|---|
| Before | 890 | 1100 | 790 | 1050 | 1100 |
| After | 890 | 1120 | 820 | 1040 | 1150 |

**a.** Set up the null and alternative hypotheses and the associated managerial actions.

**b.** Describe the Type I and Type II errors.

**c.** Let $\alpha = 0.05$. Evaluate the firm's claim.

**d.** Using the Pearson correlation coefficient, was the repeated-measures design a good design choice? Discuss.

**e.** Now determine if the two populations are normally distributed. Discuss.

**24.** An electronics firm wishes to reduce the wave soldering time for its printed circuit boards. Presently the mean soldering time is about 124 milliseconds. The engineering team runs a one-factor two-level study in which it varies the conveyor belt speed that carries the boards to the soldering station.

The two treatment levels are five feet per minute (present conditions) and seven feet per minute (experimental conditions). The team claims that by increasing the conveyor speed it can reduce the average soldering time. See spreadsheet 824.xls for the study's data.

**a.** Conduct a preliminary F-test to determine if the variances of the two populations are the same or differ. Let $\alpha = 0.10$.

**b.** Set up the null and alternative hypotheses and the associated managerial actions for testing the team's claim.

**c.** Describe the Type I and Type II errors.

**d.** Let $\alpha = 0.10$. Based on part (a), use the appropriate hypothesis-testing procedure to evaluate the team's claim.

**25.** The marketing manager claims that the population mean income of two of his company's marketing segments, Machos and Dinks, differs. To prove this, he selects two random samples from each market segment and determines their incomes. See spreadsheet 825.xls for the survey's data.

**a.** Before doing hypothesis testing on the difference in the means of two independent populations, conduct an F-test on the equality of the variances of the two populations. Let $\alpha = 0.05$.

**b.** Set up the null and alternative hypotheses and the associated managerial actions for testing the marketing manager's claim.

**c.** Describe the Type I and Type II errors.

**d.** Let $\alpha = 0.05$. Evaluate the marketing manager's claim using the appropriate hypothesis-testing method from (a).

**e.** Given the analysis, is it possible to have made a Type I error? Discuss.

**f.** Given the analysis, is it possible to have made a Type II error? Discuss.

**26.** A pharmaceutical firm purchases the same raw material from two suppliers. The company is concerned that the mean level of impurities from Vendor A is considerably greater than from Vendor B. This could affect the quality of its end product. To compare the mean level of impurities between the two suppliers, the company selects 20 shipments from each supplier and measures the percentage of impurities on each shipment. Spreadsheet 826.xls contains the data for the study.

**a.** Before doing hypothesis testing on the difference in the means of two independent populations, conduct an F-test on the equality of the variances of the two populations. Let $\alpha = 0.02$.

**b.** Set up the null and alternative hypotheses and the associated managerial actions for testing the firm's claim.

**c.** Describe the Type I and Type II errors.

**d.** Let $\alpha = 0.02$. Evaluate the firm's claim using the appropriate hypothesis-testing method from (a).

**e.** Given the analysis, is it possible to have made a Type I error? Discuss.

**f.** Given the analysis, is it possible to have made a Type II error? Discuss.

**27.** The American Housing Group claims that smaller complexes offer larger length-of-tenure discounts than do larger complexes. That is the discount on rent (in percent) given to long-term renters. AHG selects a simple random sample of 50 small and 50 large complexes and computes the length-of-tenure discounts for tenants who have lived at each complex for more than five years. Spreadsheet 827.xls contains the survey data.

**a.** Before doing hypothesis testing on the difference in the means of two independent populations, conduct an F-test on the equality of the variances of the two populations. Let $\alpha = 0.075$.

**b.** Set up the null and alternative hypotheses and the associated managerial actions for testing the group's claim.

**c.** Describe the Type I and Type II errors.

**d.** Let $\alpha = 0.075$. Evaluate the AHG claim using the appropriate hypothesis-testing method from (a).

**e.** Given the analysis, is it possible to have made a Type I error? Discuss.

**f.** Given the analysis, is it possible to have made a Type II error? Discuss.

**28.** A human resource manager claims that the proportion of extroverted managers in the United States is greater than in the European division. She selects two random samples of 100 managers and has them take the Myers–Briggs Type Indicator. Do the following data support her claim?

|  | U.S. Division | European Division |
|---|---|---|
| Number of Extroverts | 65 | 45 |
| Sample Size | 100 | 100 |

**a.** Set up the null and alternative hypotheses and the associated managerial actions.

**b.** Describe the Type I and Type II errors.

**c.** Let $\alpha = 0.05$. Evaluate the human resource manager's claim.

**d.** Given the analysis, is it possible to have made a Type I error? Discuss.

**e.** Given the analysis, is it possible to have made a Type II error? Discuss.

**29.** Degree of financial leverage (DFL) is the percentage change in earnings per share (EPS) that is associated with a given change in earnings before interest and taxes (EBIT). A DFL of 1.43 means that a 100% increase in EBIT would result in a 143% increase in EPS. A financial analyst claims that similar firms in the United States and the European Community have different mean DFLs. The data from the survey are in spreadsheet 829.xls.

**a.** Before doing hypothesis testing on the difference in the means of two independent populations, conduct an F-test on the equality of the variances of the two populations. Let $\alpha = 0.15$.

**b.** Set up the null and alternative hypotheses and the associated managerial actions for testing the analyst's claim.

**c.** Describe the Type I and Type II errors.

**d.** Let $\alpha = 0.15$. Evaluate the analyst's claim using the appropriate hypothesis-testing method based on (a).

**e.** Given the analysis, is it possible to have made a Type I error? Discuss.

**f.** Given the analysis, is it possible to have made a Type II error? Discuss.

**30.** American firms that sell their products to European firms have to conform to a quality standard called ISO-9000. An international consultant claims that there is a difference in the proportion of firms in the hardware and software industries that have already implemented the ISO-9000 quality standard. The consultant obtains the following survey data.

|  | Hardware Firms | Software Firms |
|---|---|---|
| Sample Size | 200 | 200 |
| $\hat{p}$ | 0.75 | 0.61 |

Evaluate the consultant's claim using the appropriate hypothesis-testing method. Given the analysis, is it possible to have made a Type I error? Discuss. Given the analysis, is it possible to have made a Type II error? Discuss.

**31.** A pharmaceutical firm purchases the same raw material from two suppliers. The company believes that the variance in the level of impurities from Vendor A is considerably greater than from Vendor B. This could affect the quality of its end product. To compare the variances in the levels of impurities between the two suppliers, the company selects 16 shipments from each supplier and measures the percentage of impurities in each shipment. Spreadsheet 831.xls contains the data for the study.

   **a.** Set up the null and alternative hypotheses and the associated managerial actions.

   **b.** Describe the Type I and Type II errors.

   **c.** Let $\alpha = 0.01$. Evaluate the firm's claim.

   **d.** Given the analysis, is it possible to have made a Type I error? Discuss.

   **e.** Given the analysis, is it possible to have made a Type II error? Discuss.

**32.** The Environmental Protection Agency (EPA) routinely checks to ensure that Anderson Metals is treating its toxic waste before discharging it into the Ohio River. Anderson Metals claims the mean bacteria count downstream from its plant is actually lower than the count upstream from its plant. That is, the water after the Anderson Metals plant is actually purer than before the plant. The EPA investigates Anderson's claim. The EPA selects 40 samples; 20 are upstream from the plant and 20 are downstream from the plant. Spreadsheet 832.xls contains the data.

   **a.** Before doing hypothesis testing on the difference in the means of two independent populations, conduct an F-test on the equality of the variances of the two populations. Let $\alpha = 0.015$.

   **b.** Set up the null and alternative hypotheses and the associated managerial actions for testing Anderson Metal's claim.

   **c.** Describe the Type I and Type II errors.

   **d.** Let $\alpha = 0.015$. Evaluate Anderson Metal's claim using the appropriate hypothesis-testing method based on (a).

   **e.** Given the analysis, is it possible to have made a Type I error? Discuss.

   **f.** Given the analysis, is it possible to have made a Type II error? Discuss.

**33.** An engineering team claims that a new gas additive will improve mileage. The team selects $n = 15$ pairs of cars matched on horsepower, weight, and type of transmission. For each pair, the team randomly assigns one car to the gasoline with the additive and one car to the gasoline without the additive. The team runs each car using ten gallons of gas under the same track conditions and determines the miles per gallon. Assume the data are normally distributed. Spreadsheet 833.xls contains the data.

   **a.** Set up the null and alternative hypotheses and the associated managerial actions.

   **b.** Describe the Type I and Type II errors.

   **c.** Let $\alpha = 0.05$. Evaluate the team's claim.

   **d.** Using the Pearson correlation coefficient, was the matched-pair design a good design choice? Discuss.

   **e.** Are the data from the two populations normally distributed? Discuss.

**34.** A financial analyst claims that the population proportion of firms that *forward market hedge* foreign currencies has dropped over the past several years as the dollar has rebounded in strength against European currencies. To evaluate that claim, his superior selects 200 firms and asks 100 of them the following question: "Five years ago did you generally use the forward market hedge when purchasing products in Europe?"

The other 100 firms are asked the following question: "Today are you generally using the forward market hedge when purchasing products in Europe?"

Here are the sample percentage data of firms that use the forward market hedge:

| Five Years Ago | Today |
|---|---|
| $\hat{p}_{FIVE} = 0.44$ | $\hat{p}_{TODAY} = 0.41$ |

**a.** Set up the null and alternative hypotheses and the associated managerial actions.

**b.** Describe the Type I and Type II errors.

**c.** Let $\alpha = 0.05$. Evaluate the claim using the appropriate hypothesis-testing method.

**d.** Given the analysis, is it possible to have made a Type I error? Discuss.

**e.** Given the analysis, is it possible to have made a Type II error? Discuss.

**35.** Sears was the first firm to open a retail dentistry practice in 1977. Other major firms such as DentalHealth and United Dental Network, among others, have joined this trend. Analysts claim that the proportion of franchised dentistry practices has increased in the past five years. To evaluate this claim, the American Dental Association selects a sample of 250 dental practices across the United States today and another sample of 250 from five years ago. Shown here are the proportion data for those practices that are franchised.

| Today | Five Years Ago |
|---|---|
| $\hat{p}_{TODAY} = 0.26$ | $\hat{p}_{FIVE} = 0.14$ |

**a.** Set up the null and alternative hypotheses and the associated managerial actions.

**b.** Describe the Type I and Type II errors.

**c.** Let $\alpha = 0.05$. Evaluate the claim using the appropriate hypothesis-testing method.

**d.** Given the analysis, is it possible to have made a Type I error? Discuss.

**e.** Given the analysis, is it possible to have made a Type II error? Discuss.

## CASE STUDY

Apex produces three sizes of drawers or compartments for computer tables sold by Contemporary Office Furniture. Model A has a four-inch-deep drawer, model B has a seven-inch-deep drawer, and model C has a ten-inch-deep drawer.

There are three steps in manufacturing drawers. At blanking, workers cut the raw material to the approximate drawer size. Next, workers use stamping presses that bend the blanked metal to form the drawer. Stamping press 3 makes the four-inch drawer, presses 1 and 4 make the seven-inch drawer, and press 2 makes the ten-inch drawer. Finally, workers inspect for cracks and other damage. Apex then ships defect-free drawers to Contemporary Office Furniture.

Cracking sometimes happens during stamping. It occurs at the lower corners of the drawer where the metal undergoes the maximum deformation and therefore stress. Over the past several months, 1% of the drawers had cracks.

On Tuesday, the plant manager, David Ascher, calls in his staff at 10:45 am to discuss a crisis in his plant.

Ascher    I've called you in here because we're in real trouble if we can't solve this reject problem fast. The company needs all the drawers we can ship, and more, if it's going to catch up with this new-model market. So let's get all the facts out on the table and run this thing down before lunch. Jones here tells me Line #1 started putting out excessive rejects about three minutes after the end of the 10 o'clock relief break and line #4 went wild about 10:30. Line 2 also went crazy about the same time.

Jones    Yeah, it's really weird. But Line 3 is holding steady. Its reject rate is still running around 1%.

Salvina    Tyson, the supervisor on Line #2, says he's checked several times to see if these cracks in the drawers are being caused by something in the sheets, but he hasn't found anything suspicious. The sheets all look nice and clean going into the press, but many come out with cracks. He says the inspectors discovered that rejects rose from the normal 1% to 8%. On Line #1, Rachel Stuart says her reject rate is about 4%, and she can't figure it out—it just started up suddenly after the relief break. The same is true for Line #4.

Ascher    Could the increases be due to sabotage? You know we had that problem with sabotage a few years back. How are our relations with the operating personnel?

Jones    Relations are strained but nothing out of the ordinary. I really don't think that is the problem. But you never know!

Salvina    Has anyone checked the presses?

Jones    Engineering did check the presses right after the problem started. They found no problems. They made some minor adjustments but it hasn't affected the reject rates.

Ascher    Well, something is causing it! We are not leaving this room until we have a game plan.

Jones    Do you think it could be the new material we started using today?

Ascher    It could, but why didn't the problem start at the beginning of the shift? And why aren't we having the problem on Line #3? It's turning out the usual 1% cracking.

Salvina    I think we may have had some stacks of old material at the presses at the beginning of the shift. Maybe as they were depleted and we started using the new material the reject rate climbed.

Ascher    That is a possibility. Do we have any material from our previous vendor in stock?

Jones    I bet we can find some in the plant.

Ascher    That still doesn't explain why Line #3 is still only turning out 1% rejects. It's got to be more than the new material. But let's check the new versus old material on Line #2— our worst production line. Let's meet in two hours after running the study.

| Line 2 | New Material | Old Material |
|---|---|---|
| 1100–1110 | 8.00 | 0.96 |
| 1110–1120 | 8.00 | 1.37 |
| 1120–1130 | 8.40 | 0.68 |
| 1130–1140 | 7.23 | 0.69 |
| 1140–1150 | 7.92 | 1.40 |
| 1150–1200 | 8.14 | 0.78 |
| 1200–1210 | 8.27 | 1.08 |
| 1210–1220 | 9.27 | 0.91 |
| 1220–1230 | 7.84 | 0.99 |
| 1230–1240 | 7.87 | 1.27 |
| 1240–1250 | 7.11 | 0.56 |
| 1250–100 | 8.95 | 0.91 |

Prepare a one-page report for Ascher. Your memo should answer the following questions.

**1.** Is the new material a cause of the problem?

**2.** Is the new material the only cause of the problem?

**3.** Can you rule out sabotage as a possible cause?

**4.** What additional information do you need to determine all the root causes?

**5.** What short-term and long-term actions should Ascher take?

# CHAPTER 8
# APPENDICES

## I. LISTING OF EXCEL TOOLS USED IN THIS CHAPTER

1. AVERAGE function wizard
2. Descriptive Statistics data-analysis tool
3. STDEV function wizard
4. t-Test: Two-Sample Equal Variance data-analysis tool
5. t-Test Two-Sample with Unequal Variance data-analysis tool
6. F-test Two-Sample for Variances data-analysis tool
7. t-Test Paired Two-Sample for Mean data-analysis tool
8. NORMSDIST function wizard

## II. HYPOTHESIS TESTING ON THE DIFFERENCE IN THE MEANS OF TWO INDEPENDENT POPULATIONS t-TEST: TWO-SAMPLE EQUAL VARIANCES

1. From the tools menu choose Data Analysis. In the Data-Analysis dialog box, scroll the tools list box and select t-Test: Two-Sample Assuming Equal Variances. Click OK. The dialog box shown below will appear.

2. For the Variable 1 Range, point to the cells on the worksheet (click and drag) containing the 160° data, or type **A1:A26**. For the Variable 2 Range, select the 140° data, or type **B1:B26**.

3. Type 0 (zero) in the Hypothesized Mean Difference text box, check the box for Labels, and type 0.05 in the Alpha (level of significance) text box.

**t-Test: Two-Sample Assuming Equal Variances**

Input
Variable 1 Range:     $A$1:$A$26
Variable 2 Range:     $B$1:$B$26

Hypothesized Mean Difference:    0

☑ Labels
Alpha:  0.05

Output options
◉ Output Range:    $D$1
○ New Worksheet Ply:
○ New Workbook

OK
Cancel
Help

**4.** Click the radio button for Output Range, select its text box, and point to cell D1 (or type in **D1**) on the worksheet. Click OK.

| | A | B | C | D | E | F |
|---|---|---|---|---|---|---|
| 1 | 160 F | 140 F | | t-Test: Two-Sample Assuming Equal Variances | | |
| 2 | 138 | 135 | | | | |
| 3 | 121 | 136 | | | 160 F | 140 F |
| 4 | 130 | 155 | | Mean | 127.44 | 135.52 |
| 5 | 130 | 140 | | Variance | 85.92333 | 88.01 |
| 6 | 120 | 135 | | Observations | 25 | 25 |
| 7 | 131 | 128 | | Pooled Variance | 86.96667 | |
| 8 | 141 | 135 | | Hypothesized Mean Difference | 0 | |
| 9 | 113 | 147 | | df | 48 | |
| 10 | 109 | 146 | | t Stat | −3.0633 | |
| 11 | 128 | 124 | | P(T<=t) one-tail | 0.001792 | |
| 12 | 140 | 127 | | t Critical one-tail | 1.677224 | |
| 13 | 120 | 135 | | P(T<=t) two-tail | 0.003584 | |
| 14 | 128 | 144 | | t Critical two-tail | 2.010634 | |
| 15 | 119 | 127 | | | | |
| 16 | 128 | 135 | | | | |
| 17 | 138 | 125 | | | | |
| 18 | 144 | 144 | | | | |
| 19 | 127 | 127 | | | | |
| 20 | 127 | 136 | | | | |
| 21 | 128 | 148 | | | | |
| 22 | 126 | 145 | | | | |
| 23 | 127 | 133 | | | | |
| 24 | 140 | 134 | | | | |
| 25 | 120 | 112 | | | | |
| 26 | 113 | 135 | | | | |

# REGRESSION ANALYSIS AND CHI-SQUARE TEST OF INDEPENDENCE

## INTRODUCTION

This chapter is about "looking for relationships." Effective managers determine which factors affect, or are related to, important business variables that they wish to understand, predict, or control. These important business variables are called dependent variables. Managers then identify predictor variables that they believe affect a dependent variable. Perhaps a worker's quarterly review, gender, or years of schooling affect his or her percentage increase in salary. Perhaps annual income or marital status affects the amount of life insurance owned. Perhaps race or gender affects whether a brand is recognized or not. By determining which predictor variables affect important dependent variables, managers can improve their departments' performance. In short, this chapter answers the question, "What affects what?"

The appropriate "relationship-detection" tool depends, in part, on the measurement scales used for the dependent and predictor variables. From Chapter 1, a categorical variable is measurable on either a nominal or ordinal scale. Race (White or Not White) and gender (Male or Female) are nominal variables. Ordinal-scale variables are measured on a nominal scale that we can arrange in some meaningful order. For example, tire performance is rated as good, superior, or outstanding. Quantitative variables are measured on a numerical scale. Annual income, months on the job, market share, and years of schooling are quantitative variables. Let's begin this chapter by comparing two relationship-detection tools.

# MANAGEMENT SCENARIOS AND DATA SETS

In Case I, a product manager wants to know if a customer's race affects brand recognition for her product. Brand recognition is the dependent variable and race is the predictor variable. Both variables are categorical. She interviews 500 potential customers, asks them if they recognize the brand name, and displays the results in a *contingency* table (see Table 9.1). For example, 100 potential customers were White and recognized the brand name. For the specific sample, it appears that race is related to brand recognition. Of the 200 White customers, 100, or 50%, recognized the product. Of the 200 African American customers only 50, or 25%, recognized the product. And only 5, or 5%, of the 100 Other customers recognized the product.

**Table 9.1**
3 × 2 Contingency Table on Race versus Brand Recognition

|  | White | African American | Other | Total |
|---|---|---|---|---|
| Recognized | 100 | 50 | 5 | 155 |
| Not Recognized | 100 | 150 | 95 | 345 |
| Total | 200 | 200 | 100 | 500 |

To draw conclusions about the race–brand recognition relationship for *all* potential customers, the product manager uses the **chi-square test of independence**, a statistical inference method presented in the section, "Chi-Square Test of Independence" beginning on page 405.[1]

**DEFINITION**    Use the **chi-square test** to determine if two categorical variables are related in the population.

---

[1]Review the section, "Analyzing Qualitative Cross-Sectional Data" in Chapter 7 before reading this section.

In Case II a consultant wants to know which variables affect the speed at which firms adopt a particular type of Internet software. Adoption time, the dependent variable, is the number of months from the product's inception to its permanent installation within a firm. She believes that firm size (measured by sales in millions of dollars) and type of industry—health care versus electronics—impact adoption time. Furthermore, she believes that for firms in the health care (HC) industry, adoption time drops with increasing size. However, for firms in the electronics (E) industry adoption time actually increases with increasing size. She randomly selects 16 firms, eight from each industry, records their sales, and determines the time in months to install new software. See Table 9.2.

| Firm | Sales | Industry | Adoption Time |
|------|-------|----------|---------------|
| 1 | 200 | E | 8.16 |
| 2 | 150 | E | 5.44 |
| 3 | 250 | E | 10.62 |
| 4 | 300 | E | 13.43 |
| 5 | 340 | E | 14.65 |
| 6 | 250 | E | 12.07 |
| 7 | 175 | E | 5.89 |
| 8 | 405 | E | 11.10 |
| 9 | 235 | HC | 9.75 |
| 10 | 325 | HC | 6.50 |
| 11 | 205 | HC | 10.05 |
| 12 | 395 | HC | 4.55 |
| 13 | 155 | HC | 12.35 |
| 14 | 175 | HC | 14.55 |
| 15 | 305 | HC | 7.00 |
| 16 | 400 | HC | 2.50 |

**Table 9.2**
Software Adoption-
Time Study

In Case III, an HR manager wants to know which variables affect the percent increase in auditors' salaries, the dependent variable. Ultimately he wants to predict percentage increase in salaries. He randomly selects 30 auditors and records their percent increase in salary for the past year. He then identifies and collects data on five predictor variables. See Table 9.3.

| | | Predictor Variables | | | | |
|---|---|---|---|---|---|---|
| Employee | Gender | Education | Avg. Quarterly Rating | Stress Level | Goal-Set Level | Percent Increase |
| 1 | F | 17.7 | 55 | 10 | 1.5 | 4.40000 |
| 2 | F | 16.5 | 60 | 80 | 1.5 | 4.40000 |
| 3 | F | 15.3 | 75 | 15 | 2.5 | 5.36667 |
| 4 | F | 15.7 | 85 | 20 | 3.2 | 5.91667 |
| 5 | F | 17.6 | 80 | 27 | 6.5 | 6.20000 |
| 6 | F | 15.6 | 60 | 14 | 3.5 | 4.88333 |
| 7 | F | 17.2 | 75 | 28 | 2.9 | 5.71667 |
| 8 | F | 15.7 | 73 | 85 | 4.6 | 4.63333 |
| 9 | F | 17.7 | 67 | 81 | 2.1 | 5.00000 |
| 10 | F | 15.5 | 90 | 76 | 3.5 | 6.25000 |
| 11 | F | 15.2 | 60 | 80 | 4.5 | 5.00000 |
| 12 | F | 16.5 | 50 | 82 | 1.4 | 4.36667 |
| 13 | F | 16.0 | 58 | 82 | 1.9 | 4.81667 |
| 14 | F | 17.3 | 95 | 28 | 4.0 | 6.66667 |
| 15 | F | 17.8 | 95 | 78 | 7.5 | 6.91667 |
| 16 | M | 16.4 | 60 | 30 | 5.3 | 7.83000 |
| 17 | M | 17.0 | 75 | 36 | 6.2 | 8.63000 |
| 18 | M | 15.6 | 67 | 78 | 5.4 | 7.95000 |
| 19 | M | 16.5 | 76 | 75 | 6.3 | 8.70000 |
| 20 | M | 17.7 | 65 | 77 | 4.9 | 7.45000 |
| 21 | M | 16.1 | 72 | 75 | 6.5 | 8.17000 |
| 22 | M | 16.9 | 70 | 35 | 5.9 | 8.33000 |
| 23 | M | 17.4 | 65 | 30 | 5.5 | 8.00000 |
| 24 | M | 15.8 | 85 | 56 | 9.7 | 11.77000 |
| 25 | M | 17.8 | 95 | 55 | 9.5 | 11.50000 |
| 26 | M | 16.6 | 78 | 70 | 7.4 | 9.73000 |
| 27 | M | 16.1 | 80 | 39 | 7.5 | 9.75000 |
| 28 | M | 15.4 | 82 | 38 | 5.5 | 9.35000 |
| 29 | M | 15.8 | 90 | 30 | 5.5 | 8.00000 |
| 30 | M | 16.1 | 85 | 71 | 7.8 | 10.05000 |

**Table 9.3**
Salary Increase
Study Data

Four of the five predictor variables are quantitative.

**Gender**     There may be gender discrimination if gender is related to percentage increase in salary.

**Education**     Education is the number of years of schooling completed. Most auditors are completing undergraduate and graduate accounting programs in the evening.

**Rating**     Rating is the average of an auditor's past four quarterly reviews. Scores for a single review can range from 40 to 100.

| Stress | Stress is measured on a commercially available instrument. The scale ranges from zero (no stress) to 100 (dangerously high stress levels). |
|---|---|
| **Goal-Set Level** | Goal set measures the level of each auditor's yearly goal set. Each auditor's goal set is compared to the "norm" developed by the firm for an entry-level auditor. Ambitious goal sets receive scores between 6.4 and 9.9. Unambitious goal sets receive scores between 1.0 and 4.5. Goal sets that meet the norm receive scores between 4.6 and 6.3. |

For the moment, let's focus on one of the four predictor variables, average quarterly rating. For the specific sample, it appears that average quarterly rating is related to percent increase. The higher the rating, the greater was an auditor's percent salary increase. The HR manager could use Excel's function wizards, INTERCEPT and SLOPE, and the data in columns 4 and 7 of Table 9.3 to obtain the estimated regression equation, or model.[2]

$$\hat{y} = 0.3548 + 0.0923 \cdot \text{RAT}$$

**(9.1)**

where $\hat{y}$ represents the predicted percent increase in salary and RAT is the average of an auditor's last four quarterly performance ratings

The HR manager could use Model (9.1) to predict percent increase in salary *for these 30 auditors* in the study.

If the HR manager is interested in determining if *all* five predictor variables are related to the percent increase for *all the firm's auditors* (population), he must use **regression analysis**.

---

**D E F I N I T I O N**     **Regression analysis** determines the estimated equation, or model, for one or more predictor variables *and* provides inference methods to draw conclusions about a population based on one sample of size *n*.

---

In summary, to determine if two or more variables are related in the population, consider two "relationship-detection" tools. When both the predictor and dependent variables are categorical, use the chi-square test of independence. When the dependent variable is quantitative, and the predictor variables are either categorical or quantitative, use regression analysis.

---

[2]Review the section, "Analyzing Qualitative Cross-Sectional Data" in Chapter 7 before reading the next section in this chapter, "Introduction to Regression Analysis."

# INTRODUCTION TO REGRESSION ANALYSIS

Suppose you believe that firm size is linearly related to adoption time for new software. You want to develop a model, or equation, that helps you predict, for a given size firm, the expected adoption time. You select one sample of size $n$. For each firm you record the firm's size (sales in millions of dollars) and the actual adoption time. To test your belief, you need regression analysis. By the end of this section you should be able to

1. interpret a first-order multiple regression model;

2. interpret the population parameters for both quantitative and categorical variables;

3. explain the terms *simple and multiple regression*, *linear in the parameters*, and *linear in the predictor variables*;

4. distinguish population parameters from sample regression coefficients based on the least squares equations;

5. distinguish a regression model from an *estimated* regression model;

6. code categorical variables with two or more classes; and

7. interpret the interaction terms and quadratic terms of a multiple regression model.

## First-Order Models

Consider a **simple** linear regression model where $y$ = adoption time, there is only one predictor variable ($x_1$ = firm size), and the regression function is linear. Suppose you selected every firm of size 250 million dollars sales and determined adoption times for a particular software. Would all the times be the same? No! Suppose you then selected every firm of size 300 million dollars and every firm of size 340 million dollars and determined their adoption times. Would all the times at each firm size be the same? Again no! Thus, for any value of $x_1$, there will be a probability distribution of adoption times. With this in mind, let's discuss Figure 9.1, a pictorial representation of a simple linear regression model.

1. There is a linear statistical relationship between $y$ = adoption time and $x_1$ = firm size. Note that the relationship is not perfect because for any value of $x_1$, there is a distribution of $y$ values. Thus, factors other than firm size such as type of industry, firm profitability, level of competition, etc., also affect adoption time. If the relationship were perfect, then for any value of $x_1$ there would only be one value for $y$.

2. Each distribution of $y$ values is normally distributed and of constant variance.

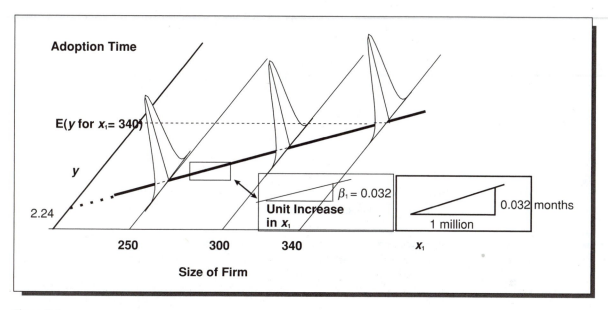

**Figure 9.1**
Simple Linear Regression Model

**3.** The means of the distributions, $E(y)$, lie on a linear population regression line. The equation is

$$E(y) = \beta_0 + \beta_1 \cdot x_1$$

**(9.2)**

**4.** Model (9.2) is *simple, linear in the parameters,* and *linear in the predictor variable.* It is simple because it contains a single predictor variable. It is linear in the parameters because $\beta_0$ or $\beta_1$ does not appear as an exponent. It is linear in the predictor variable, or first order, because the predictor variable is only raised to the first power.

**5.** Interpret $\beta_1$ as follows: As $x_1$ increases by one million dollars, mean adoption time increases by 0.032 months. If $x_1$ increases by 100 million dollars, mean adoption time increases by $100(0.032) = 3.2$ months.

**6.** $\beta_0$ and $\beta_1$ are *population parameters,* the population intercept and population slope respectively. Although shown in Figure 9.1 as 2.24 and 0.032, respectively, they can never be known for sure unless the study included all firms. That is clearly not practical. Thus $\beta_0$ and $\beta_1$ are unknown and unknowable.

While you can never know $\beta_0$ and $\beta_1$ with certainty, you can estimate these parameters from the least squares equations first presented in Chapter 7.

A statistical relationship can contain more than one predictor variable. Model (9.3) is a *multiple* linear, or first-order, regression model with $k$ predictor variables. It is both linear in the parameters and linear in the predictor variables.

$$E(y) = \beta_0 + \beta_1 \cdot x_1 + \beta_2 \cdot x_2 + \ldots + \beta_k \cdot x_k$$

**(9.3)**

$\beta_i$ measures the mean change in $y$ for a one-unit increase in $x_i$ *holding all other predictor variables in the model constant.*

**DEFINITION**    In a first-order model the parameters $(\beta_i)$ do not appear as exponents and the predictor variables appear only in the first power.

## Coding and Interpreting Categorical Variables

Suppose an analyst believes that, in addition to firm size $(x_1)$, adoption times differ for the firms in the electronics versus the health care industry $(x_2)$. The first predictor variable is quantitative and has already been discussed. How do we code the categorical variable, Type of Industry? It is a categorical variable with two classes or categories. We can represent it as follows:

$$x_2 = 1 \quad \text{if health care industry}$$
$$0 \quad \text{if electronics industry}[3]$$

Model (9.4) is a first-order multiple regression model that includes two predictor variables, Size $(x_1)$ and Type of Industry $(x_2)$.

$$E(y) = \beta_0 + \beta_1 \cdot x_1 + \beta_2 \cdot x_2$$

**(9.4)**

How do we interpret $\beta_2$? First consider firms in the electronics industry. For such firms, $x_2 = 0$ and Model (9.4) becomes

$$E(y) = \beta_0 + \beta_1 \cdot x_1 + \beta_2 \cdot 0 = \beta_0 + \beta_1 \cdot x_1 \qquad \text{Firms in Electronics Industry}$$

---

[3]Or we code 1 = if electronics industry and 0 = if health care industry.

Thus the equation for a firm in the electronics industry is a linear line, with an $y$ intercept of $\beta_0$ and slope of $\beta_1$. See Figure 9.2.

Now consider a firm in the health care industry. For such firms, $x_2 = 1$, and model (9.4) becomes

$$E(y) = \beta_0 + \beta_1 \cdot x_1 + \beta_2 \cdot 1 = \left(\beta_0 + \beta_2\right) + \beta_1 \cdot x_1 \qquad \text{Firms in Health Care Industry}$$

This is also a linear line, with the same slope $\beta_1$, but with a $y$ intercept of $\beta_0 + \beta_2$ (see Figure 9.2).

The interpretation of the $\beta_2$ parameter is straightforward. If $\beta_2$ is positive, firms in the health care industry take more time to adopt software than do firms in the electronics industry. If $\beta_2$ is negative, firms in the health care industry take less time. And because the two lines are parallel, the difference in adoption time does *not* depend on the firm's size. There is a constant time differential in months, $\beta_2$, between firms in the two industries. In short, $\beta_2$ shows how much higher (lower) the mean adoption time is for firms coded 1 than for firms coded 0.

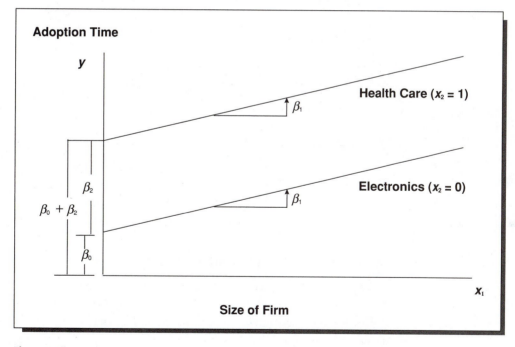

**Figure 9.2**
Multiple Regression Model with a Categorical Variable

Suppose that in the adoption study we include three industries: electronics, health care, and retail. The categorical variable contains three classes. Since type of industry has three classes, we must create two indicator variables, $x_2$ and $x_3$. One way to represent the type of industry categorical variable is as follows:

$$x_2 = 1 \quad \text{if health care industry}$$
$$0 \quad \text{if not health care industry}$$

$$x_3 = 1 \quad \text{if retail industry}$$
$$0 \quad \text{if not retail industry}$$

Firms in the health care industry are coded as $x_2 = 1$ and $x_3 = 0$. Firms in the retail industry are coded as $x_2 = 0$ and $x_3 = 1$. Firms in the electronics industry are coded as $x_2 = 0$ and $x_3 = 0$, as they are neither in the health care or retail industries.

We could have coded the Type of Industry categorical variable using other schemes. For example,

| | | | |
|---|---|---|---|
| $x_2 = 1$  if retail | $x_2 = 1$  if electronics | $x_2 = 1$  if health care | |
| $\quad 0$  if not retail | $\quad 0$  if not electronics | $\quad 0$  not health care | |
| $x_3 = 1$  if electronics | $x_3 = 1$  if health care | $x_3 = 1$  if retail | |
| $\quad 0$  if not electronics | $\quad 0$  if not health care | $\quad 0$  if not retail | |

In general:

We represent a categorical variable with $C$ classes by $C - 1$ indicator variables, each taking on a value of 0 or 1.

Model (9.5) is a first-order multiple regression model that includes three predictor variables, Sales ($x_1$) and Type of Industry ($x_2$, $x_3$).

$$E(y) = \beta_0 + \beta_1 \cdot x_1 + \beta_2 \cdot x_2 + \beta_3 \cdot x_3$$

(9.5)

### First-Order Models with Interaction Terms

In Figure 9.2 the impact of type of industry on adoption time did not depend on the firm size. Health care firms took $\beta_2$ more months to adopt the software than electronics firms *irrespective of firm size*. There was *no interaction* between type of industry and firm size. The two lines were parallel.

Suppose that small health care firms had longer adoption times than small electronics firms, but large health care firms had shorter adoption times than large electronics firms. This suggests an *interaction between type of industry and firm size* (see Figure 9.3).

Note several important features of Figure 9.3.

1. As firm size increases, firms in the health care industry take less adoption time.

2. As firm size increases, firms in the electronics industry take more adoption time.

3. Thus, the impact of firm size on adoption time *depends* upon the type of industry.

4. The two lines are clearly *not* parallel. There is an interaction effect between firm size and type of industry. For an interaction to be present it is not necessary that the two regression lines cross; they simply cannot be parallel, as in Figure 9.2.

We can develop a model that reflects Figure 9.3 by adding an **interaction term** to the model represented by Figure 9.2, which is reproduced here for comparison.

$$E(y) = \beta_0 + \beta_1 \cdot x_1 + \beta_2 \cdot x_2 \qquad\qquad \text{No Interaction Term}$$

$$E(y) = \beta_0 + \beta_1 \cdot x_1 + \beta_2 \cdot x_2 + \beta_{12} \cdot x_1 x_2 \qquad \text{Interaction Term}$$

**(9.6)**

How do we interpret $\beta_{12}$? First consider firms in the electronics industry where the following coding scheme has been used.

$$x_2 = 1 \quad \text{if health care industry}$$
$$0 \quad \text{if electronics industry}$$

For firms in the electronics industry, $x_2 = 0$ and thus $x_1 x_2 = 0$, and Model (9.6) becomes

$$E(y) = \beta_0 + \beta_1 \cdot x_1 + \beta_2 \cdot 0 + \beta_{12} \cdot 0 = \beta_0 + \beta_1 \cdot x_1$$

Thus the equation for a firm in the electronics industry is a linear line, with a $y$-intercept of $\beta_0$ and slope of $\beta_1$ (see Figure 9.3).

Now consider a firm in the health care industry. For such firms, $x_2 = 1$ and $x_1 x_2 = x_1$, and Model (9.6) becomes

$$E(y) = \beta_0 + \beta_1 \cdot x_1 + \beta_2 \cdot 1 + \beta_{12} \cdot x_1 = \left(\beta_0 + \beta_2\right) + \left(\beta_1 + \beta_{12}\right) \cdot x_1$$

Thus the equation for a firm in the health care industry is a linear line with a $y$-intercept of $\beta_0 + \beta_2$ and slope of $\beta_1 + \beta_{12}$. See Figure 9.3 where $\beta_2$ is a positive value and $\beta_{12}$ is a negative value and is larger than $\beta_1$.

So how do we interpret $\beta_{12}$ in Figure 9.3? Since it is *negative*, and larger than the value of $\beta_1$,

As the size of firms in the health care industry increases their adoption time decreases.

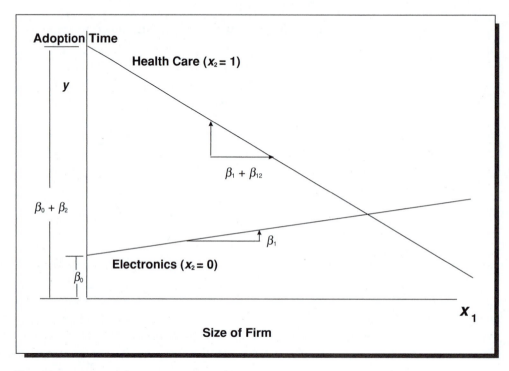

**Figure 9.3**
First-Order Model with an Interaction Term

In summary, when should you include interaction terms in a model? Do so when logic, theory, or the actual data suggest that the impact of one predictor variable on the dependent variable *depends upon* another predictor variable.

### Second-Order Models

A statistical relationship need not be linear. Figure 9.4 illustrates a curvilinear relationship, a polynomial of order 2. The means of the distributions of $y$ values lie on a curvilinear regression line. The equation for that model is

$$E(y) = \beta_0 + \beta_1 \cdot x_1 + \beta_{11} \cdot x_1^2$$

(9.7)

Model (9.7) is linear in the parameters but nonlinear in the predictor variable because of the squared term.[4] Model (9.7) is a second-order model. The linear effect regression coefficient is $\beta_1$ and $\beta_{11}$ is the curvature effect regression coefficient.

<hr>

**D E F I N I T I O N**    In a **second-order model** a **predictor**, or **explanatory**, **variable** appears in the second degree. A second-order model is called quadratic and has the familiar U-shape of a parabola.

<hr>

Consider a second-order (or higher) model when logic, theory, or the actual data suggest that the impact of a predictor variable on the dependent variable is nonlinear. For example, business psychologists expect a nonlinear relationship between amount of stress and productivity. As stress increases from very low levels, productivity at first increases. Beyond an optimal stress level, productivity actually declines as the excessive stress interferes with our mental capabilities.

## Estimating Regression Models

In this section, we have presented six regression models, Model 9.2–Model 9.7, but have not demonstrated how to estimate the population parameters, $\beta_0$, $\beta_1, \ldots \beta_k$. You first learned in Chapter 7 in the section, "Analyzing Quantitative Cross-Sectional Data" how to use the INTERCEPT and SLOPE function wizards to compute $b_0$ (which estimates $\beta_0$) and $b_1$ (which estimates $\beta_1$) to estimate the regression model, $E(y)=\beta_0+\beta_1 x_1$. The terms, $b_0$ and $b_1$, are sample regression coefficients and $\beta_0$ and $\beta_1$ are population parameters.

You should only use the INTERCEPT and SLOPE function wizards when there is only one predictor variable. But in Case II the analyst obtained data on two predictor variables, Sales and Type of Industry, and anticipated a Sales × Type of Industry interaction. The study therefore has three predictor variables. You should use Excel's regression data-analysis tool to obtain an *estimated* regression model that includes more than one predictor variable.

<hr>

[4] $E(y) = \beta_0 \cdot e^{\beta_1 \cdot x_1}$ is an example of a model that is nonlinear in the $\beta_1$ parameter.

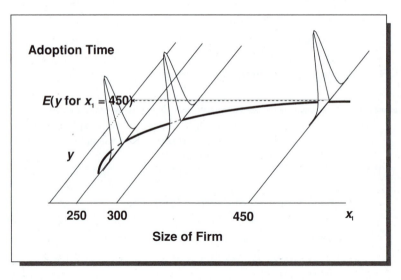

**Figure 9.4**
Curvilinear Regression Model

Table 9.2, which has been reproduced here, contains three changes. First, row and column headers from the Excel spreadsheet have been added. Second, Type of Industry has been coded as follows: $x_2 = 1$ if health care industry and 0 if electronics industry. Third, we added a Sales × Type of Industry data column to estimate the possible interaction.

| | A | B | C | D | E |
|---|---|---|---|---|---|
| 1 | Firm | Sales | Industry | Sales × Industry | Adoption Time |
| | | $x_1$ | $x_2$ | $x_1 x_2$ | $y$ |
| 2 | 1 | 200 | 0 | 0 | 8.16 |
| 3 | 2 | 150 | 0 | 0 | 5.44 |
| 4 | 3 | 250 | 0 | 0 | 10.62 |
| 5 | 4 | 300 | 0 | 0 | 13.43 |
| 6 | 5 | 340 | 0 | 0 | 14.65 |
| 7 | 6 | 250 | 0 | 0 | 12.07 |
| 8 | 7 | 175 | 0 | 0 | 5.89 |
| 9 | 8 | 405 | 0 | 0 | 11.10 |
| 10 | 9 | 235 | 1 | 235 | 9.75 |
| 11 | 10 | 325 | 1 | 325 | 6.50 |
| 12 | 11 | 205 | 1 | 205 | 10.05 |
| 13 | 12 | 395 | 1 | 395 | 4.55 |
| 14 | 13 | 155 | 1 | 155 | 12.35 |
| 15 | 14 | 175 | 1 | 175 | 14.55 |
| 16 | 15 | 305 | 1 | 305 | 7.00 |
| 17 | 16 | 400 | 1 | 400 | 2.50 |

**Table 9.4**
Adoption-Time Study Data (Recoded)

Below is the input screen for the regression data–analysis tool for the data in Table 9.4.

Excel's regression analysis tool provides the following *estimated* regression model for the data in Table 9.4.

$$\hat{y} = 2.205388 + 0.030781 \cdot x_1 + 17.27011 \cdot x_2 - 0.07112 \cdot x_1 x_2$$

**(9.8)**

where $\hat{y}$ represents the predicted adoption time in months

Model (9.8) is an estimate of the population regression model shown in Figure 9.3 based on one sample of 16 firms.

Rather than use the generic terms, $x_i$, for the predictor variables, good practice is to write the model using more meaningful terms. The result is

$$\hat{y} = 2.205388 + 0.030781 \cdot \text{SIZE} + 17.27011 \cdot \text{IND} - 0.07112 \cdot \text{SIZE} \times \text{IND}$$

You could use estimated Model (9.8) to predict adoption time *for the 16 firms* in the study based on the three predictor variables. But you may not be able to use it to predict adoption time *for all firms in the health care and electronics industries.* To draw conclusions about the population from which you selected the sample will require developing an estimated regression model (already done) *and* using a statistical inference procedure. The latter is our next topic.

# SCATTER DIAGRAMING AND THE ANALYSIS OF VARIANCE

An HR manager of a major accounting firm wants to know which variables affected the percent increase in salary for auditors last year, the dependent variable. He randomly selects 30 auditors and collects data on five predictor variables: gender, years of education, average performance rating for the past four quarters, stress level, and the previous year's goal-set level developed by each auditor. The HR manager wants to (1) determine which predictor variables are related to the percent increase in salary for *all* auditors and (2) predict percent increase in salaries based on one or more of the five predictor variables. By the end of this section, you should be able to

1. use the Chart Wizard function to construct *xy* scatter diagrams of each predictor variable versus the dependent variable;

2. use the *xy* scatter diagrams to suggest the inclusion of interaction terms and quadratic terms into the estimated regression model;

3. explain the role of the Analysis of Variance in determining if an estimated regression model is worth using at all;

4. explain how to use the coefficient of multiple determination to determine if you should add additional predictor variables to an estimated regression model; and

5. reduce the estimated standard error of the estimate by applying a screening procedure and explain why this procedure should be done when your goal is to use the estimated regression model for making predictions.

## Preliminary Analysis: Scatter Diagraming

Before computing estimated regression models draw scatter diagrams, one for each predictor variable against the dependent variable. First presented in Chapter 7, a scatter diagram is an *xy* plot of a predictor variable against a dependent variable. Scatter diagraming serves two purposes. First, it aids learning by providing a graphical representation of regression analysis. This is a "big plus" for visual learners. Second, scatter diagramming can suggest that you should add interaction terms or quadratic terms to the estimated regression model.

Figures 9.5–9.9 contain the five scatter diagrams of each predictor variable versus the dependent variable. See Table 9.3 for the data.

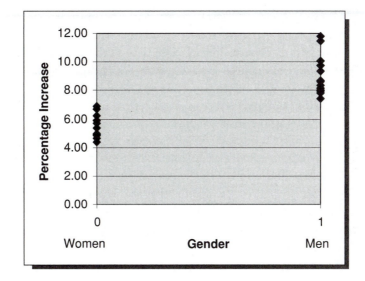

**Figure 9.5**
Gender versus Percent
Increase

Figure 9.5 indicates that for the specific sample of 30 auditors, women (coded as zero) received smaller percent increases than did their male counterparts. It does *not* mean that *in the population* of all auditors gender is related to percent increase. The HR manager cannot tell until he has completed the Analysis of Variance and screening procedure. However, Figure 9.5 does suggest that it was wise to include gender as a predictor variable.

Figure 9.6 indicates that for the specific sample of 30 auditors, years of education do not affect percent increase in salary. The sample data contains no systematic upward or downward pattern. Nor are any clusters evident. However, the HR manager should not discard this predictor variable until he has completed the Analysis of Variance and screening procedure.

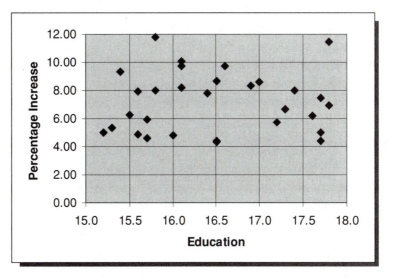

**Figure 9.6**
Years of Education versus
Percent Increase

Figure 9.7, rating versus percent increase, illustrates how a scatter diagram can suggest the inclusion of an additional predictor variable. Figure 9.7 has two distinct clusters. From Table 9.3, all the data points in the lower cluster refer to female auditors, and all the data points in the upper cluster refer to male auditors. Verify this before reading on. For example, a female auditor with a performance rating of 80 received a raise of slightly over 6%. A male with the same performance rating received almost a 10% raise. Similarly, two females who had performance ratings of 95 received between 6.5% and 7.0% raises. However, the male with the same performance rating received almost a 12% raise.

Most important, it appears that the slopes of the two clusters differ. That suggests that there may be an interaction between the gender and rating predictor variables. This means that for a particular performance rating, the percent raise an auditor received *depended* on his/her gender. The HR manager should include a gender x rating interaction term in the estimated regression model.

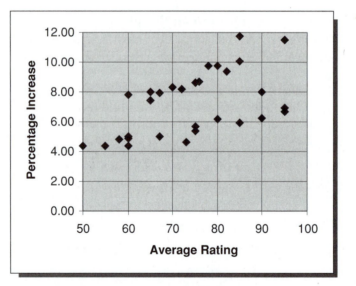

**Figure 9.7**
Average Performance
Rating versus Percent
Increase

It is not always apparent what causes clustering. In this case the two clusters were associated with gender. However, if gender had not explained the two clusters, the HR manager should consider other possible predictor variables.

Figure 9.8, stress level versus percent increase, again illustrates how a scatter diagram can suggest the inclusion of an additional term in the estimated regression model. For the specific sample of 30 auditors, there is a nonlinear, or quadratic, relationship between stress level and percent increase. As stress level increases, percent increase initially rises, then peaks, and finally turns downward. The curve's shape is near parabolic. Thus the HR manager should include a quadratic stress-level predictor variable term in the estimated regression model.

Figure 9.9 indicates that for the specific sample of 30 auditors, goal-set level is positively associated with the percent increase in salary. The swarm of data points is upward sloping to the right. It does not mean that in the population of all auditors, goal-set level is related to percent increase. The HR manager cannot tell until he has completed the Analysis of Variance and screening procedure. However, Figure 9.9 does suggest that the HR manager was correct in including goal-set level as a predictor variable.

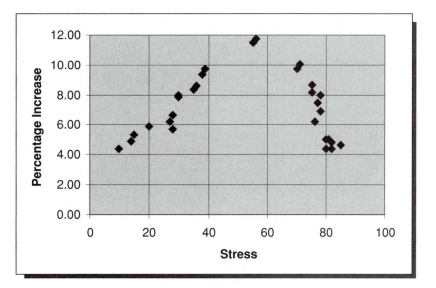

**Figure 9.8**
Stress Level versus
Percent Increase

Based on the scatter diagrams, the HR manager should add two terms to the estimated regression model: a Gender × Rating interaction term and a quadratic Stress Level term. Table 9.5 shows the inclusion of the two additional predictor variables.

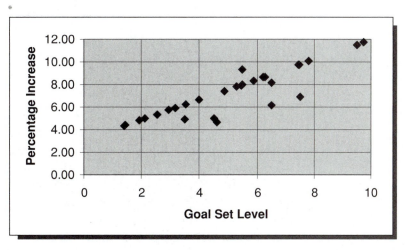

**Figure 9.9**
Goal-Set Level versus
Percent Increase

|   | A | B | C | D | E | F | G | H |
|---|---|---|---|---|---|---|---|---|
| 1 | Gender | Gen × Rat | Education | Avg. Rating | Stress | Stress$^2$ | Goal-Set | Percent |
| 2 | 0 | 0 | 17.7 | 55 | 10 | 100 | 1.5 | 4.40000 |
| 3 | 0 | 0 | 16.5 | 60 | 80 | 6400 | 1.5 | 4.40000 |
| 4 | 0 | 0 | 15.3 | 75 | 15 | 225 | 2.5 | 5.36667 |
| 5 | 0 | 0 | 15.7 | 85 | 20 | 400 | 3.2 | 5.91667 |
| 6 | 0 | 0 | 17.6 | 80 | 27 | 729 | 6.5 | 6.20000 |
| 7 | 0 | 0 | 15.6 | 60 | 14 | 196 | 3.5 | 4.88333 |
| 8 | 0 | 0 | 17.2 | 75 | 28 | 784 | 2.9 | 5.71667 |
| 9 | 0 | 0 | 15.7 | 73 | 85 | 7225 | 4.6 | 4.63333 |
| 10 | 0 | 0 | 17.7 | 67 | 81 | 6561 | 2.1 | 5.00000 |
| 11 | 0 | 0 | 15.5 | 90 | 76 | 5776 | 3.5 | 6.25000 |
| 12 | 0 | 0 | 15.2 | 60 | 80 | 6400 | 4.5 | 5.00000 |
| 13 | 0 | 0 | 16.5 | 50 | 82 | 6724 | 1.4 | 4.36667 |
| 14 | 0 | 0 | 16.0 | 58 | 82 | 6724 | 1.9 | 4.81667 |
| 15 | 0 | 0 | 17.3 | 95 | 28 | 784 | 4.0 | 6.66667 |
| 16 | 0 | 0 | 17.8 | 95 | 78 | 6084 | 7.5 | 6.91667 |
| 17 | 1 | 60 | 16.4 | 60 | 30 | 900 | 5.3 | 7.83000 |
| 18 | 1 | 75 | 17.0 | 75 | 36 | 1296 | 6.2 | 8.63000 |
| 19 | 1 | 67 | 15.6 | 67 | 78 | 6084 | 5.4 | 7.95000 |
| 20 | 1 | 76 | 16.5 | 76 | 75 | 5625 | 6.3 | 8.70000 |
| 21 | 1 | 65 | 17.7 | 65 | 77 | 5929 | 4.9 | 7.45000 |
| 22 | 1 | 72 | 16.1 | 72 | 75 | 5625 | 6.5 | 8.17000 |
| 23 | 1 | 70 | 16.9 | 70 | 35 | 1225 | 5.9 | 8.33000 |
| 24 | 1 | 65 | 17.4 | 65 | 30 | 900 | 5.5 | 8.00000 |
| 25 | 1 | 85 | 15.8 | 85 | 56 | 3136 | 9.7 | 11.77000 |
| 26 | 1 | 95 | 17.8 | 95 | 55 | 3025 | 9.5 | 11.50000 |
| 27 | 1 | 78 | 16.6 | 78 | 70 | 4900 | 7.4 | 9.73000 |
| 28 | 1 | 80 | 16.1 | 80 | 39 | 1521 | 7.5 | 9.75000 |
| 29 | 1 | 82 | 15.4 | 82 | 38 | 1444 | 5.5 | 9.35000 |
| 30 | 1 | 90 | 15.8 | 90 | 30 | 900 | 5.5 | 8.00000 |
| 31 | 1 | 85 | 16.1 | 85 | 71 | 5041 | 7.8 | 10.05000 |

$\overline{y} = 7.191\%$

**Table 9.5**
Final Database for Percent Raise Study

The Gen × Rat variable in column B is the product of the Gender and Rating variable values, column A times column D. The Stress$^2$ variable (column F) is the square of the Stress values in column E.

In summary, begin every regression analysis by plotting each predictor variable against the dependent variable. Although not a substitute for the Analysis of Variance, scatter diagramming does (1) confirm the inclusion of predictor variables in the estimated regression model and (2) suggest the inclusion of interaction terms or higher ordered terms.

## The ANalysis Of VAriance (ANOVA)

Begin by applying the regression data-analysis tool to the data in Table 9.5. The input screen is shown here. The values of the dependent variable are in column H, rows 1–31. The values of the predictor variables are in columns A–G, rows 1–31. The input data include the variables' labels and so we checked off the labels' box in the input screen.

Shown below in Table 9.6 is a portion of the output, the sample regression coefficients, based on the least squares equations.

|  | Coefficients |
|---|---|
| Intercept | 1.828351 |
| Gender | −0.76479 |
| Gen × Rat | 0.036868 |
| Education | −0.00606 |
| Avg. Quarterly Rating | 0.016553 |
| Stress Level | 0.092747 |
| Stress Squared | −0.00094 |
| Goal-Set Level | 0.31076 |

**Table 9.6**
Sample Regression
Coefficients

The estimated regression model is

$$\hat{y} = 1.828 - 0.7648\text{GENDER} + 0.0369\text{GEN} \times \text{RAT} - 0.0061\text{EDUC} + 0.0166\text{RAT} + 0.0927\text{STRESS} - 0.00094\text{STRESS}^2 + 0.3108\text{GOAL}$$

**(9.9)**

where $\hat{y}$ represents the predicted percent increase in salary

We cannot determine if the seven predictor variables are related to the dependent variable in the *population* by merely looking at the values of the sample regression coefficients. Even if the population regression coefficients, $\beta_i$, were equal to zero (no relationship), we would not expect the sample regression coefficients, $b_i$, to equal zero due to sampling variability. The Analysis of Variance is a formal statistical method of determining whether one or more predictor variables and the dependent variable are related *in the population*.

***Stating Hypotheses.*** We begin by stating the null and alternative hypotheses for the percent increase study. In regression analysis, the null is always the "no relationship" hypothesis.

| | Hypotheses | Action |
|---|---|---|
| $H_0$ | None of the predictor variables are statistically related to the dependent variable[5]<br><br>$\beta_1 = \beta_2 = \beta_3 \ldots = \beta_7 = 0$ | Seek other predictor variables. |
| $H_1$ | Not all $\beta_i$ equal zero | Use the estimated regression model to predict the dependent variable *if* the model's assumptions have not been violated *and* it provides precise-enough predictions. |

Based on the consequences of making a Type I error, the HR manager sets the significance level, $\alpha$, at 0.05.

***Decomposition of the Total Sum of Squares.*** The Analysis of Variance begins with a decomposition of the total sum of squares. Refer to the data in Table 9.5. Note that the dependent variable, percent increase, varies among the 30 auditors. How much variation is there about the mean percent increase of 7.191%? The variation is measured by the total sum of squares, SST. The general expression for SST for any dependent variable $y$ is

$$SST = \sum_i \left(y_i - \bar{y}\right)^2$$

(9.10)

---

[5]$\beta_1$ is the population regression coefficient that measures the impact of gender on percent increase holding all other predictor variables constant. $\beta_2$ to $\beta_7$ are similarly defined. Note that we not interested in $\beta_0$, the population intercept.

For the data in Table 9.5

$$\text{SST} = (4.40 - 7.191)^2 + (4.40 - 7.191)^2 + \ldots + (10.05 - 7.191)^2$$
$$= 134.334 \text{ units of variation}$$

What accounts for the 134.334 units of variation? There are two sources—the seven predictor variables in the estimated regression model or other variables not in the model. Sum of squares *regression* measures the variation in the dependent variable due to the seven predictor variables *plus* all other possible predictor variables not yet in the model. Sum of squares *residual* measures the variation in the dependent variable due *only* to all other possible predictor variables not yet in the model.

Table 9.7 is the Analysis of Variance output portion of the regression data-analysis tool for the data in Table 9.5. Of the 134.334 units of variation, the seven predictor variables account for 128.2813 units of variation. Only 6.0527 units of variation are due to predictor variables not yet in the model!

***Computing the F Ratio.*** After completing the decomposition in column 2, convert the sums of squares to *mean squares*, or variances (column 3). Remember the statistical method is called the analysis of *variance*. Divide the sum of squares by the degrees of freedom in column 1 to obtain the mean squares.

**Table 9.7**
Analysis of Variance
for Percent Increase
Study

| ANOVA | 1 | 2 | 3 | 4 | 5 |
|---|---|---|---|---|---|
| | *df* | *SS* | *MS* | *F* | *Significance F* |
| Regression | 7 | 128.2813 | 18.3259 | 66.6099072 | 2.E-13 |
| Residual | 22 | 6.0527 | **0.275123** | | |
| Total | 29 | 134.334 | | | |

1. The *total* degrees of freedom are $n - 1$, where $n$ equals the sample size. In the percent increase study, $30 - 1 = 29$.

2. The *regression* degrees of freedom equals the number of predictor variables, $k$. In the percent increase study, $k = 7$.

3. The *residual* degrees of freedom are the remainder, $n - k - 1$. In the percent increase study, $30 - 7 - 1 = 22$.

Next, the data-analysis tool computes the mean square regression and mean square residual. It divides each sum of squares term by its appropriate degrees of freedom. The mean square regression is 18.3259 and the mean square residual is 0.275123.

Finally, the package computes the *F ratio*. It is the mean square regression divided by the mean square residual.

$$F = \frac{\text{Mean Square(Regression)}}{\text{Mean Square(Residual)}}$$

**(9.11)**

Use the F ratio to test the null hypothesis that none of the predictor variables is related to the dependent variable.

The F ratio in Table 9.7 is 66.61. The mean square regression is 66.61 times as large as the mean square residual. Can we reject the null hypothesis at the $\alpha = 0.05$ level?

***Hypothesis Testing.*** Does an F ratio of 66.61 favor the null or alternative hypothesis? It will help if you understand what each mean square term measures. Mean square residual measures the impact on the dependent variable of all potential predictor variables other than the seven now in the estimated regression model. Mean square regression measures the impact of all potential predictor variables—those in the model (gender, gender × rating, rating, ... goal-set level) *plus* those not included.

If the null hypothesis is true and the seven predictor variables are not statistically related to the dependent variable, than except for sampling variability the numerator and denominator of the F ratio should be the same. If $H_0$ is true, the F ratio should be close to 1.0, but it is not! Mean square regression is over 66 times as large as mean square residual. Is this sufficiently large to reject the null hypothesis?

Column 5 in the Analysis of Variance table answers the question. If none of the seven predictor variables are related to the dependent variable, the probability of obtaining an F ratio of 66.61 or greater is 0.0000000000002.[6] Since this is smaller than the chosen significance level, $\alpha = 0.05$, the HR manager should reject the null hypothesis. The data have "*passed*" the Analysis of Variance. If the value in column 5 is larger than the chosen significance level of $\alpha = 0.05$, the HR manager should not reject the null hypothesis.

---

**Decision Rule**: If the significance F (*p*-value) is less than the chosen significance level, $\alpha$, reject the null hypothesis. Otherwise, do not reject the null hypothesis.

---

[6]Recall from Chapter 6, this is the study's **p-value**.

Having rejected the null hypothesis, the HR manager can now consider using the estimated regression model, Model (9.9), for making predictions on the percent increase in salary for all auditors provided the assumptions underlying the regression model are valid (see page 388). Even if the assumptions are valid, a regression model for making predictions is useful only if it generates precise-enough predictions.

Suppose the HR manager wants to predict next year's percent increase for an auditor who is a male (1), with a performance rating = 80, who has completed 18 years of schooling, whose stress level is 50, and whose goal set was rated as 8.0. The manager can use Model (9.9) to determine the *most likely* percent increase.

$$\hat{y} = 1.828 - 0.7648(1) + 0.0369(80) - 0.0061(18) + 0.0166(80) + 0.0927(50)$$
$$- 0.00094(50)^2 + 0.3108(8.0)$$
$$= 10.00\%$$

Consider the following two hypothetical intervals. Wouldn't you agree that an interval of 10% ± 0.05% would probably be precise enough for making meaningful predictions? However, an interval of 10% ± 9% would be much too wide.

***Standard Error of the Estimate.*** While the section, "Using the Estimated Regression Models for Making Predictions" beginning on page 395 will present a full discussion of making predictions, the width of prediction intervals depends, in large part, on an output from the ANOVA table. It is called the standard error of the estimate and is the square root of mean square residual term from the ANOVA table. From Table 9.7, the standard error of the estimate for the percent increase study is

$$\sqrt{0.275123} = 0.524521$$

What does the standard error of the estimate measure? It measures the impact on percent increase due to all variables excluded from the estimated model. If the database in Table 9.5 included every predictor variable that affected the dependent variable, the standard error of the estimate would equal zero. The larger the standard error of the estimate, the wider will be the prediction interval.

There are only two ways to reduce the standard error of the estimate.

1. Identify and add statistically significant predictor variables to the estimated regression model, Model (9.9).

2. Remove nonsignificant predictor variables from the estimated regression model (9.9) that has "passed" the ANOVA test. Recall that in rejecting

the null hypothesis, at least one of the predictor variables must be statistically significant. But all the predictor variables may not be significant!

The first strategy requires understanding the coefficient of multiple determination. The second strategy requires an understanding of the parameter estimate section of the Excel-generated output and a screening procedure.

## Coefficient of Multiple Determination

The coefficient of multiple determination[7] indicates how much of the dependent variable's total variation is accounted for by the seven predictor variables. It equals

$$\frac{\text{Sum of Squares(Regression)}}{\text{Sum of Squares(Total)}}$$

and is denoted as **R Square** in the Excel-generated output.

R Square measures the percentage of the variation in the dependent variable accounted for by the predictor variables in the estimated regression model. The range of possible values for R Square is 0 to 1.0 (or 0% to 100%).

R Square for the percent increase study is

$$\frac{128.2813}{134.334} = 0.954943$$

The seven predictor variables together account for 95.5% of the variation in the 30 auditors' percent salary increase data values. The remaining variation in the dependent variable, 5%, is due to all predictor variables other than the present seven and is still unaccounted for.

If the HR manager were to identify and add statistically significant predictor variables to the regression model, R Square would increase, the standard error of the estimate would decrease, and so would the width of the prediction interval.

Given that over 95% of the variation is already accounted for by the seven predictor variables, identifying additional predictor variables can be difficult. Therefore, let's consider removing nonsignificant predictor variables from Model 9.9.

---

[7] The Excel-generated output also provides for an adjusted R Square. This term factors in the number of predictor variables in the model. For the most part, the adjustment is minor and need not concern us.

When the coefficient of multiple determination is less than 50%–70%, consider brainstorming for additional predictor variables to include in the estimated regression model.

## Screening Procedure for Reducing the Standard Error

Use the screening procedure when the purpose of the regression analysis is to make predictions, and you desire the smallest width prediction intervals possible given your data. Shown here are the steps to the screening procedure applied to the percent increase study.

**1.** Take the absolute value of the t Stat values found in the parameter estimate section of the Excel-generated output. Ignore the intercept row of the table (see Table 9.8).

|  | *Coefficients* | *Standard Error* | *t Stat* |
|---|---|---|---|
| Gender | –0.76479 | 1.310221 | –0.58371 |
| Gen × Rat | 0.036868 | 0.017286 | 2.132758 |
| Education | –0.00606 | 0.118456 | **–0.05113** |
| Avg. Quarterly Rating | 0.016553 | 0.012545 | 1.319468 |
| Stress Level | 0.0920747 | 0.045304 | 2.047244 |
| Stress Squared | –0.00094 | 0.000448 | –2.107 |
| Goal-Set Level | 0.31076 | 0.083417 | 3.725377 |

**Table 9.8**
Parameter Estimate Section—All Seven Predictor Variables

**2.** Delete the predictor variable with the lowest absolute t Stat value provided it is less than 1.0.[8]

   The predictor variable with the lowest absolute t Stat value is Education, $|t \text{ Stat}| = 0.051$.

**3.** Use the regression data-analysis tool to reestimate the model with the remaining six predictor variables.[9] Repeat steps 2 and 3, one predictor variable at a time, until all the remaining predictor variables have $|t \text{ Stat}| \geq 1$.

---

[8]Deleting variables with t Stat values above 1.0 will actually widen the interval's width.

[9]Place the cursor in the Education column (column C). Click the Edit option on the menu bar and the Delete option on the pulldown menu. Then click the Entire Column Box and click OK. This will delete the Education column of data (column C).

The HR manager deleted the years of schooling variable and reran the regression data–analysis tool. Table 9.9 is the revised parameter estimate section.

|  | Coefficients | Standard Error | t Stat |
|---|---|---|---|
| Gender | –0.77278 | 1.272346 | **–0.60737** |
| Gen × Rat | 0.03702 | 0.016655 | 2.222707 |
| Avg. Quarterly Rating | 0.016581 | 0.012258 | 1.352624 |
| Stress Level | 0.09241 | 0.043839 | 2.107958 |
| Stress Squared | –0.00094 | 0.000433 | –2.17193 |
| Goal-Set Level | 0.310218 | 0.080926 | 3.833347 |

**Table 9.9**
Parameter Estimate Section with Education Deleted

Note that the absolute t Stat value for the gender variable is now less than 1, $|t\,Stat| = 0.607$. Eliminate the gender variable from the database, and rerun the regression. Table 9.10 is the revised parameter estimate section.

|  | Coefficients | Standard Error | t Stat |
|---|---|---|---|
| Gen × Rat | –0.027276 | 0.004419 | 6.17266 |
| Avg. Quarterly Rating | 0.020265 | 0.010511 | 1.928068 |
| Stress Level | 0.088808 | 0.042861 | 2.072004 |
| Stress Squared | –0.0009 | 0.000423 | –2.13518 |
| Goal-Set Level | 0.307797 | 0.079758 | 3.859136 |

**Table 9.10**
Parameter Estimate Section with Education and Gender Deleted

None of the predictor variables have absolute t Stat values below 1.0. The screening procedure is now complete.

The screening procedure produces the final estimated regression model, Model (9.12),

$$\hat{y} = 1.519 - 0.0273\text{GEN} \times \text{RAT} + 0.0203\text{RAT} + 0.0888\text{STRESS} - 0.0009\text{STRESS}^2 + 0.3078\text{GOAL}$$

(9.12)

where $\hat{y}$ represents the predicted percent increase in salary

The accompanying Excel output for Table 9.10 indicated that the standard error had dropped from $\sqrt{0.275123} = 0.524521$ (with seven predictor variables) to 0.50623 (with five predictor variables).

Why does this screening method work? First recall that the standard error of the estimate is

$$\sqrt{MSR(\text{esidual})} = \sqrt{\frac{SSR(\text{esidual})}{n-k-1}}$$

SSR(esidual) measures the impact of all potential predictor variables not yet in the model. As we delete a predictor variable from the model, SSR(esidual) must increase; the numerator of the standard error gets larger. However, each eliminated predictor variable also decreases $k$ and thereby increases the number of degrees of freedom by 1. Thus, the denominator of the standard error also gets larger.

If you eliminate a predictor variable with an absolute t Stat value of less than 1, the increase in SSR(esidual) is smaller than the relative increase in the degrees of freedom. As a consequence, the standard error will decrease. Table 9.11 illustrates this for the percent increase study.

**Table 9.11**
Impact on SSR(esidual) and Degrees of Freedom by Eliminating Predictor Variables with Absolute t Stat Values Less Than 1

| Predictor Variables | SSR(esidual) | $n - k - 1$ | MSR(esidual) | Standard Error |
|---|---|---|---|---|
| All Seven Variables | 6.0527 | 22 | 0.275123 | 0.524521 |
| Eliminate Education | 6.05342 | 23 | 0.263192 | 0.513023 |
| Eliminate Education and Gender | 6.150511 | 24 | 0.256271 | **0.506232** |

In summary, use the regression data-analysis tool to develop an ANOVA table. If you fail to reject the null, or no relationship, hypothesis, seek a new set of predictor variables that might impact the dependent variable. If you do reject the null and you want to minimize the width of your prediction intervals, use the absolute t Stat value screening procedure to obtain your final estimated model. Alternatively, include additional predictor variables if $R^2$ is relatively low; say, less than 50%–70%.

The HR manager should not yet use Model (9.12) for making predictions on the percent increase in salary. He should first evaluate the validity of the model's assumptions. And that is our next topic.

# EVALUATING THE REGRESSION MODEL ASSUMPTIONS: GRAPHICAL ANALYSIS OF RESIDUALS

This section presents how an examination of the prediction errors, or *residuals*, tests the assumptions underlying regression analysis. By the end of this section you should be able to

1. use the regression data-analysis tool to obtain residual plots;

2. identify residual plot patterns that suggest that the model's assumptions have been violated and take corrective action; and

3. use residual plots to identify omitted predictor variables from the estimated regression model.

Figure 9.10 illustrates that regression analysis assumes that the probability distributions of the dependent variable are (1) normal, (2) have equal variances, and (3) are statistically independent.

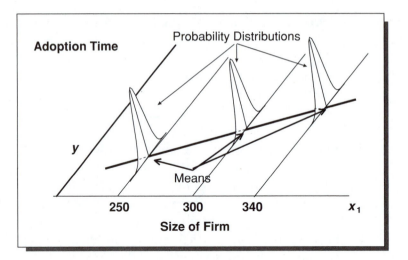

**Figure 9.10**
Pictorial Representation of the Simple Linear Regression Model

We use residual plots to determine whether an estimated regression model meets these three assumptions. A prediction error, or residual, is the difference between the actual value of $y$ and the value of $y$ predicted by the estimated regression model. There is one residual for each observation in the sample:

$$\text{Residual}_i = y_i - \hat{y}_i$$

Table 9.12 shows the residual output section for the Excel-generated analysis for Model (9.12).[10] Auditor 1's actual percent increase was 4.40%.

---

[10]We added column 2 showing the actual values of $y$ to aid understanding of the residuals.

Model (9.12) predicted she (GENder = 0) would obtain a 3.89% increase. The difference, or residual, is + 0.51, column 4. The standardized residuals in column 5 will be used to test the normality assumption and are discussed later.

$$\hat{y} = 1.519 + 0.0273\text{GEN} \times \text{RAT} + 0.0203\text{RAT} + 0.0888\text{STRESS}$$
$$- 0.0009\text{STRESS}^2 + 0.3078\text{GOAL}$$
$$= 1.519 + \left[0.0273 \cdot (0 \cdot 55)\right] + (0.0203 \cdot 55) + (0.0888 \cdot 10) - (0.0009 \cdot 100) + (0.3078 \cdot 1.5)$$
$$= 3.89\%$$

| Auditor | Actual Percent Increase | Predicted Percent Increase | Residuals | Standard Residuals |
|---|---|---|---|---|
| 1 | 4.40000 | 3.89343 | 0.50657 | 1.09998 |
| 2 | 4.40000 | 4.52311 | −0.12311 | −0.26733 |
| 3 | 5.36667 | 4.93771 | 0.42896 | 0.93145 |
| 4 | 5.91667 | 5.64185 | 0.27482 | 0.59674 |
| 5 | 6.20000 | 6.88086 | −0.68086 | −1.47844 |
| 6 | 4.88333 | 4.87890 | 0.00443 | 0.00961 |
| 7 | 5.71667 | 5.71061 | 0.00606 | 0.01315 |
| 8 | 4.63333 | 5.43989 | −0.80656 | −1.75138 |
| 9 | 5.00000 | 4.79309 | 0.20691 | 0.44929 |
| 10 | 6.25000 | 5.95483 | 0.29517 | 0.64093 |
| 11 | 5.00000 | 5.44650 | −0.44650 | −0.96955 |
| 12 | 4.36667 | 4.17476 | 0.19191 | 0.41672 |
| 13 | 4.81667 | 4.49078 | 0.32589 | 0.70764 |
| 14 | 6.66667 | 6.45450 | 0.21217 | 0.46072 |
| 15 | 6.91667 | 7.18688 | −0.27021 | −0.58673 |
| 16 | 7.83000 | 7.85481 | −0.02481 | −0.05388 |
| 17 | 8.63000 | 9.02026 | −0.39026 | −0.84741 |
| 18 | 7.95000 | 7.80059 | 0.14941 | 0.32443 |
| 19 | 8.70000 | 8.65349 | 0.04651 | 0.10100 |
| 20 | 7.45000 | 7.60275 | −0.15275 | −0.33168 |
| 21 | 8.17000 | 8.52488 | −0.35488 | −0.77059 |
| 22 | 8.33000 | 8.66551 | −0.33551 | −0.72853 |
| 23 | 8.00000 | 8.15408 | −0.15408 | −0.33457 |
| 24 | 11.77000 | 10.68781 | 1.08219 | 2.34989 |
| 25 | 11.50000 | 11.11308 | 0.38692 | 0.84017 |
| 26 | 9.73000 | 9.29770 | 0.43230 | 0.93870 |
| 27 | 9.75000 | 9.72138 | 0.02862 | 0.06215 |
| 28 | 9.35000 | 9.18158 | 0.16842 | 0.36571 |
| 29 | 8.00000 | 9.34262 | −1.34262 | −2.91539 |
| 30 | 10.05000 | 9.71511 | 0.33489 | 0.72718 |

**Table 9.12**
Residuals

Plot the residuals against the values of *each* predictor variable.[11] Figure 9.11 shows how each residual plot should look when the equal variance assumption is met. The residuals should vary within an equal–width horizontal band centered on zero and should display no systematic pattern of positive or negative residuals.

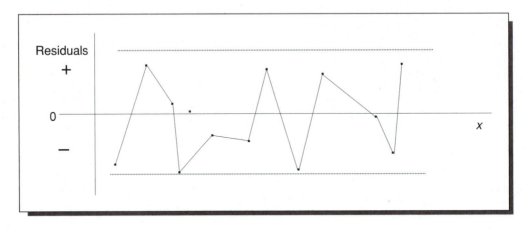

**Figure 9.11**
Residual Plot When Equal Variance and Normality Assumptions Met

If the probability distributions in Figure 9.10 are normally distributed, then the residuals should be centered about zero. Why? Because $\hat{y}$ is an estimate of the means of the probability distributions. For a normal distribution, 50% of the values lie above and 50% of the values lie below the mean. Thus, about half of the residuals should be positive and half should be negative.

***Equality of Variance?*** Figure 9.12 contains five residual plots, one for each predictor variable versus the residuals. With minor exceptions, each residual plot is a near-horizontal band centered about zero. The five plots were generated using Excel's regression data-analysis tool.

If any plot did violate the equal variance assumption, it would look trapezoidal as shown in Figure 9.13 (or a trapezoid that widens as $x$ increases).

---

[11] A residual plot against the predicted values of $y$, $\hat{y}$, is also effective.

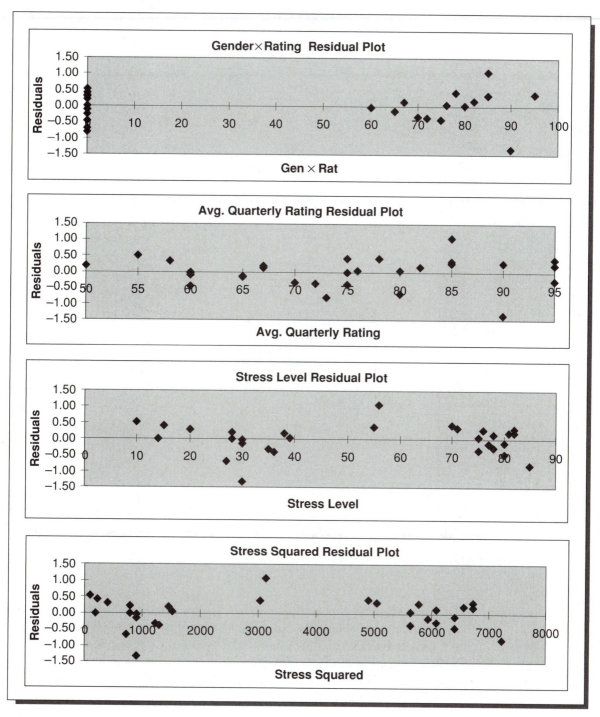

**Figure 9.12**
Five Residual Plots

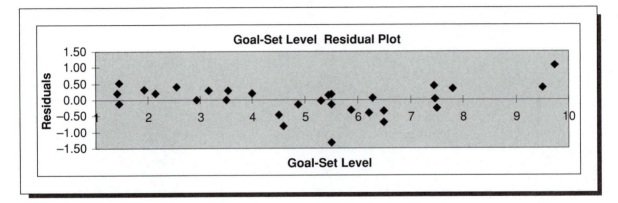

**Figure 9.12 (continued)**
Five Residual Plots

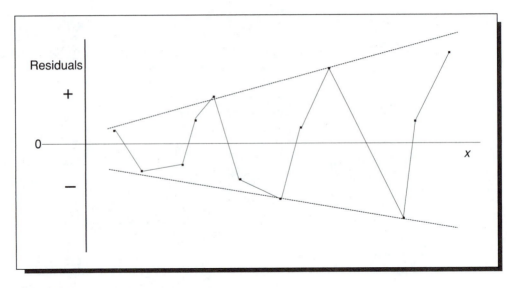

**Figure 9.13**
Residual Plot for Variance That Increases with $x$

When the residuals appear as in Figure 9.13, you might try transforming the dependent variable using either a square root or log base 10 transformation. That is, replace each $y$ value with its square root or log base 10 value. Then use the regression data-analysis tool to complete the analysis. If that does not provide residual plots that meet the equal variance assumption, seek help from a statistician.

***Normality?*** Use the standardized residuals from Table 9.12 to check for normality. A standardized residual is

Standardized Residual = Residual/Standard Error of the Estimate

Standardized Residual = 0.50657/0.506232 = 1.00067

If the probability distributions in Figure 9.10 are normal, about 68% of the standardized residuals should lie between −1 and +1. And about 95% should lie between −1.96 and +1.96. For the percent increase study

1.  Twenty-five of 30, or 83.3%, of the residuals lie between −1 and +1. Not close to 68%.

2.  Twenty-eight, or 93.3%, of the residuals lie between −1.96 and +1.96. Very close! The results are mixed.

If the data seriously violate the normality assumption (a judgment call), try transforming the dependent variable using the square root or log base 10 transformations. These transformations, that often equalize the variances, also tend to normalize the data.[12]

***Nonindependence.*** The salary increase study data are cross sectional, obtained at one point in time. However, when the data are time ordered (taken over time periods) it is good practice to plot the residuals versus time in addition to the residuals versus the predictor variables. When the residuals over time show a systematic pattern, the statistical independence assumption has been violated. If this occurs, obtain help from a statistician.

In addition to testing for the three assumptions, good practice requires two other assessments. We turn to these next.

***Outliers.*** Outliers are extreme values of the dependent variable that draw the estimated regression model away from the main body of data points. This, in turn, distorts the values of the sample regression coefficients, $b_i$, and produces poor estimates of the population regression coefficients, $\beta_i$.

One definition of an outlier is a standardized residual that is either less than −3.00 or greater than +3.00. If the data are normal, the probability of obtaining a standardized residual below −3.00 is only 0.00135 or above +3.00 is only .00135; to verify apply the NORMSDIST function wizard for a value of −3.00 or +3.00. So if you obtain a standardized residual either less than −3.00 or greater than +3.00, consider the standardized residual an outlier. Table 9.12 indicates that no outliers were present in the percent increase data.

---

[12] Excel provides a second "test" for normality, the normal probability plot. If the plot is linear, the data are normal. If the plot is nonlinear, especially the data points at the two ends of the line, the data are not normal.

How can we correct the problem of outliers if they occur? First, make sure that they are not the result of clerical errors. If so, delete the observations. If not, try using a log base 10 transformation on the dependent variable, develop a new estimated regression model, and check the standardized residuals again. If that does not work, seek expert statistical help.

**Omission of Important Predictor Variables.** Consider the plot of average quarterly ratings versus residuals reproduced as Figure 9.14. While the residuals indicate no violation of equal variance, why are some of the residuals positive and others negative? That is, what accounts for a positive residual for the employee whose quarterly rating is 55 (see circled residual)? What accounts for a negative residual for one of the employees whose rating is 90 (see circled residual)? Perhaps a predictor variable not yet in the model might explain all the positive and negative residuals.

Suppose you believe that the number of hours of internal training taken during the year might affect percent salary increase. Then next to each residual place the number of hours of training the auditor completed. (See the partially completed analysis in Figure 9.14.) Suppose all the positive residuals are associated with auditors who received extensive internal training during the year, and all the negative residuals are associated with auditors who received little or no training. That indicates that number of hours of training should be included in the estimated regression model. Add number of hours (HRS) to the present data base (Gen × Rat, Rating, Stress, Stress², and Goal-Set Level), and rerun the regression data-analysis tool. This should reduce MSR(esidual), and thereby reduce the width of prediction intervals.

Suppose there is no distinct residual pattern based on hours of training. Then it is not an important predictor variable and should not be added to the estimated regression model. In summary, looking for omitted predictor variables requires applying the above procedure to all residual plots.

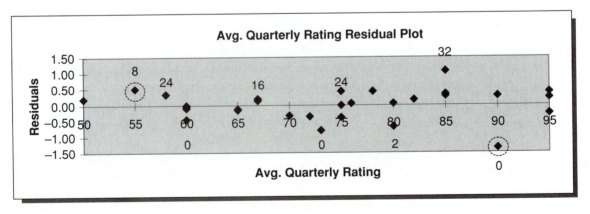

**Figure 9.14**
Using a Residual Plot to Identify Omitted Predictor Variables

# USING THE ESTIMATED REGRESSION MODELS FOR MAKING PREDICTIONS

Use an estimated regression model that is statistically significant (ANOVA) and that has met all the assumptions to make predictions about the dependent variable. By the end of this section you should be able to

1. distinguish between prediction and extrapolation;

2. explain the dangers of extrapolation;

3. explain when to construct a confidence interval or prediction interval;

4. interpret prediction and confidence intervals; and

5. explain how to reduce the width of prediction or confidence intervals.

## Prediction versus Extrapolation

Regression models help us estimate values of the dependent variable. There are two types of estimation. In the context of the auditor salary study, **prediction** means estimating the salary increase for values of the predictor variables *within* the range of the data. **Extrapolation** means estimating the salary increase for values of the predictor variables *outside* the range of the data. Extrapolation occurs if you use Model (9.12) to estimate the percent increase for an auditor with a performance rating of 100 or a goal-set level of 10. These two values are outside the range of data in the original study.

Extrapolation is risky because the estimated regression model may no longer provide valid predictions. For example, if you regressed advertising versus sales data, the resulting model would probably reveal a positive relationship between the two variables. Yet at some point, increasing advertising would not produce increasing sales. At some point all models cease to provide valid predictions.

When extrapolating, be prepared to explain why the estimated regression model still provides valid estimates outside the range of the original study. If you cannot make effective arguments, do not use the model for extrapolation.

An effective strategy is to select ranges of data for the predictor variables such that extrapolation will never be necessary. Unfortunately, this is not always possible.

## Differences between Prediction and Confidence Intervals

Which would be easier to do? Predict the mean class grade or predict a single student's score? Predicting the class mean is easier because it usually ranges between 75 and 85. A student's score could range anywhere from 0 to 100. Thus, estimation intervals for the mean should be narrower than for a single observation.

In regression analysis, we use *confidence intervals* to predict the mean values of the dependent variable. Graphically, we are estimating the means of the probability distributions in Figure 9.10. We use *prediction intervals* to predict a single value of *y*. Using the test grade example for insight, confidence intervals must be narrower than prediction intervals.

Suppose the HR manager wishes to develop a *prediction* interval on the percent increase for the following auditor:

| | |
|---|---|
| Gender | = Male = 1 |
| Rating | = 80 |
| Stress Level | = 50 |
| Goal-Set Level | = 9.5 |

Model (9.12), reproduced here, provides the *most likely* percent increase.

$$\hat{y} = 1.519 + 0.0273 \text{GEN} \times \text{RAT} + 0.0203 \text{RAT} + 0.0888 \text{STRESS} - 0.0009 \text{STRESS}^2 + 0.3078 \text{GOAL}$$
$$= 1.519 + \left[ 0.0273 \cdot (1 \cdot 80) \right] + (0.0203 \cdot 80) + (0.0888 \cdot 50) - (0.0009 \cdot 2500) + (0.3078 \cdot 9.5)$$
$$= 10.44\%$$

Unfortunately, Excel's regression data–analysis tool does not provide exact confidence or prediction intervals. You can use Expression (9.13) to construct approximate 95% intervals.[13] The approximate intervals underestimate the exact intervals' widths. The underestimation is greater for confidence intervals than for prediction intervals and becomes more severe as you include more predictor variables. Recall that the standard error in the expression is the square root of MSR(esidual) from the ANOVA table.

---

[13]Faculty can request a copy of a spreadsheet for generating exact intervals for distribution to their students.

$$\hat{y} \pm 2 \cdot \text{Standard Error} \cdot \sqrt{\frac{1}{n}}$$

**Confidence Interval**  $10.44 \pm \left( 2 \cdot 0.506232 \cdot \sqrt{\frac{1}{30}} \right)$

$$10.44 \pm 0.185$$

$$(10.26, 10.62)$$

$$\hat{y} \pm 2 \cdot \text{Standard Error} \cdot \sqrt{1 + \frac{1}{n}}$$

**Prediction Interval**  $10.44 \pm \left( 2 \cdot 0.506232 \cdot \sqrt{1 + \frac{1}{30}} \right)$

$$10.44 \pm 1.03$$

$$(9.41, 11.47)$$

**(9.13)**

The HR manager predicts that an individual male auditor whose performance rating is 80, whose stress level is 50, and whose goal-set level is 9.5 will receive a percent salary increase of between 9.41% and 11.47%.

The HR manager predicts that the mean percent increase of all male auditors whose performance ratings are 80, whose stress levels are 50, and whose goal-set levels are 9.5 will be between 10.26% and 10.62%.

Note that the prediction interval for percent increase of a single auditor is wider than the confidence interval for the mean increase for all auditors.

Prediction or confidence intervals—when does each make sense? That depends on your purpose. Is the goal to predict the performance of a single unit such as an auditor's percent increase or a single firm's adoption time? If so, construct prediction intervals. Or is the goal to predict the average performance of units such as the mean of all auditors' percent increases or the mean adoption time for all firms? If so, construct confidence intervals.

### Reducing the Width of Confidence or Prediction Intervals

One reason for building estimated regression models is to predict values of the dependent variable. Since a wide interval does not provide meaningful information, how do we reduce the width? Previously you learned two methods to reduce the standard error of the estimate: (1) add significant predictor variables to the estimated regression model or (2) remove nonsignificant predictor variables from the model. Expression (9.13) suggests an additional strategy. Increasing the sample size, $n$, will reduce the intervals' widths.

In summary, don't make predictions on the dependent variable until you have "passed" the Analysis of Variance test and verified the assumptions underlying regression analysis. While necessary, that is not sufficient. Your goal should be to obtain precise-enough intervals. This may require using the absolute t Stat value screening procedure, adding additional predictor variables, increasing the study's sample size, or using residual plots to identify omitted predictor variables. Remember, narrow intervals are more meaningful than wide intervals.

# MULTICOLLINEARITY

Business professionals use regression analysis to (1) make predictions on a dependent variable and (2) estimate the regression coefficients that measure the impact of the predictor variables on a dependent variable. Multicollinearity can pose serious problems for the latter. By the end of this section you should be able to

1. explain what multicollinearity is and why it is a problem;

2. detect multicollinearity; and

3. reduce the impact of multicollinearity.

### Multicollinearity and How to Detect It

Consider the following study to determine the impact of departmental square footage and number of full-time-equivalent sales associates on weekly sales, the dependent variable (see Table 9.13).

Before developing the estimated regression model, let's develop two scatter diagrams, one for each predictor variable against sales. Figure 9.15 indicates that for the specific sample, both square footage and the number of associates are *positively* related to sales. That is consistent with logic.

| Dept. | Footage | Associates | Weekly Sales |
|-------|---------|------------|--------------|
| 1 | 5500 | 5.50 | $ 51,500 |
| 2 | 6000 | 6.00 | $ 70,000 |
| 3 | 7500 | 7.50 | $ 87,500 |
| 4 | 8500 | 8.50 | $ 90,000 |
| 5 | 8000 | 8.00 | $105,000 |
| 6 | 6000 | 6.00 | $ 69,500 |
| 7 | 7500 | 7.50 | $ 86,500 |
| 8 | 7300 | 7.30 | $ 88,500 |
| 9 | 6700 | 6.70 | $ 81,000 |
| 10 | 9000 | 9.00 | $114,500 |
| 11 | 6000 | 5.50 | $ 75,000 |
| 12 | 5000 | 5.00 | $ 43,700 |
| 13 | 5800 | 6.50 | $ 69,500 |
| 14 | 9500 | 9.50 | $127,500 |
| 15 | 9500 | 9.90 | $122,500 |
| 16 | 6000 | 6.50 | $ 78,300 |
| 17 | 7500 | 7.50 | $ 86,300 |
| 18 | 6700 | 7.50 | $ 79,500 |
| 19 | 7600 | 7.60 | $ 87,000 |
| 20 | 6500 | 6.00 | $ 74,500 |
| 21 | 7200 | 7.20 | $ 81,700 |
| 22 | 7000 | 6.50 | $ 83,300 |
| 23 | 6500 | 6.50 | $ 80,000 |
| 24 | 8500 | 8.00 | $117,700 |
| 25 | 9500 | 9.50 | $115,000 |
| 26 | 7800 | 7.80 | $ 97,300 |
| 27 | 8000 | 9.00 | $ 97,500 |
| 28 | 8200 | 8.20 | $ 93,500 |
| 29 | 9000 | 9.50 | $ 80,000 |
| 30 | 8500 | 8.50 | $100,500 |

**Table 9.13**
Database to Illustrate
Multicollinearity

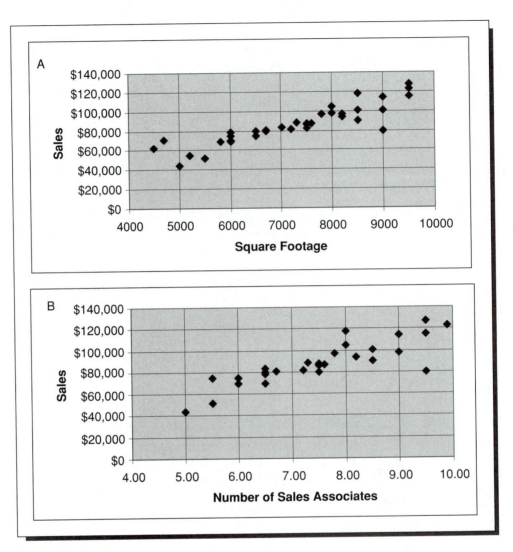

**Figure 9.15**
Two Scatter Diagrams

However, the highly significant estimated regression model (ANOVA not shown) shown below defies both logic and the two scatter diagrams.

$$\hat{y} = -143.38 + 17.3703 \cdot \text{FOOTAGE} - 3554.75 \cdot \text{ASSOCIATES}$$   **(9.14)**

where $\hat{y}$ is the predicted weekly sales.

Model (9.14) tells us that as the department size *increases* by 100 square feet, weekly sales increase by about $1737. That is consistent with diagram A in Figure 9.15. Model (9.14) also tells us that for each additional sales associate, weekly sales *decreases* by about $3555. That simply doesn't make any sense. The number of sales associates can't be negatively related to weekly sales! It defies scatter diagram B in Figure 9.15 and logic. What is happening?

Multicollinearity exists when pairs of predictor variables are highly correlated. When multicollinearity is present, one or more of the signs of the sample regression coefficients are often inconsistent with either their respective scatter diagrams or logic.

You can assess multicollinearity by computing a correlation matrix. Table 9.14 is the *correlation matrix* for the data in Table 9.13 and was produced by Excel's correlation data-analysis tool.

**Table 9.14**
Correlation Matrix for Data in Table 9.13

|              | *Footage* | *Associates* | *Weekly Sales* |
|--------------|-----------|--------------|----------------|
| Footage      | 1         |              |                |
| Associates   | 0.963514  | 1            |                |
| Weekly Sales | 0.900471  | 0.850087     | 1              |

From the section, "Correlation and Cross-Correlation" in Chapter 7, a correlation coefficient is a numerical measure of the strength of a *linear* relationship between two variables. Correlation coefficients can vary from −1 to + 1. Correlation coefficients near zero indicate that two variables are not linearly related. The correlation matrix provides the correlations among all pairs of variables in a study. The intersection of a row and column is the correlation coefficient for the two corresponding variables.

Let's analyze the correlation matrix in Table 9.14. The bottom row indicates the correlation of each predictor variable with the dependent variable. The two correlation coefficients indicate that for the specific sample, both predictor variables are strongly and positively related to weekly sales. That agrees with the two scatter diagrams in Figure 9.15. The correlation coefficient (shaded gray) measures the strength of the linear relationship between the *two predictor variables*. Note that its absolute value is greater than the absolute value of the other two correlation coefficients.

In plain English, the two predictor variables are more strongly related to each other than either predictor variable is to the dependent variable. When this occurs, multicollinearity is present. And often one or more of the signs of the sample regression coefficients are meaningless. While we can still make valid predictions on weekly sales, the model's face validity is compromised. That is, colleagues may question the negative regression coefficient in Model (9.14) and may not want to use it to make predictions.

**DEFINITION**

Severe multicollinearity occurs when two conditions are present.
Condition 1: When the *absolute value* of any correlation coefficient between a pair of predictor variables is higher than the *absolute values* of the correlations between predictor variables and the dependent variable.
Condition 2: One or more of the signs of the sample regression coefficients are the opposite of what logic would suggest.

How severe is the multicollinearity problem for the auditor's salary increase study? Table 9.15 provides the answer.

| | Gen × Rat | Avg. Rating | Stress Level | Stress Squared | Goal-Set Level | Percent Increase |
|---|---|---|---|---|---|---|
| Gen × Rat | 1 | | | | | |
| Avg. Rating | 0.27465 | 1 | | | | |
| Stress Level | 0.01034 | −0.10924 | 1 | | | |
| Stress Squared | −0.10311 | −0.18815 | 0.98854 | 1 | | |
| Goal-Set Level | 0.749001 | 0.585779 | 0.062798 | −0.05175 | 1 | |
| Percent Increase | 0.90395 | 0.54076 | −0.01738 | −0.14604 | 0.89692 | 1 |

**Table 9.15**
Correlation Matrix for Salary Increase Study

The bottom row indicates the correlation of each predictor variable with the dependent variable. The five correlation coefficients indicate that for the specific sample, three predictor variables are strongly and positively related to percent increase. It is not surprising that the two stress correlation coefficients are close to zero. Remember, correlation coefficients measure the strength of the *linear* relationship between two variables. But from Figure 9.8, it appears that stress is curvilinearly related to percent increase.

The values shaded in gray indicate the correlations among the five predictor variables. How strongly are the predictor variables related? Of the ten correlation coefficients, only three have higher absolute values than the correlations among the predictor and dependent variables. The very high correlation between the stress and stress–squared predictor variables is expected because the values of the latter predictor variable are the square of the former predictor variable values. Thus, only two predictor variables are strongly related. Since the estimated regression model reproduced below contains no sign reversals, we conclude that multicollinearity is not a serious problem.

$$\hat{y} = 1.519 + 0.0273\text{GEN} \times \text{RAT} + 0.0203\text{RAT} + 0.0888\text{STRESS}$$
$$- 0.00090\text{STRESS}^2 + 0.3078\text{GOAL}$$

Suppose the correlation matrix revealed severe multicollinearity. What can be done to reduce it? We turn to that topic next.

## Minimizing Multicollinearity

There are two commonly used strategies to minimize multicollinearity. One method is to discard highly correlated predictor variables. The t Stat screening procedure used to reduce the standard error of the estimate presented earlier can also be effective in reducing multicollinearity. Its effectiveness can be improved by adding one additional rule for removing predictor variables from an estimated regression model. To reduce multicollinearity, consider the following *enhanced* screening procedure:

**Recommendation** Remove predictor variables one at a time from the estimated regression model whose **absolute t Stat values** are less than one *or* whose **regression coefficient signs** are the opposites of your expectations.[14]

A more effective method requires obtaining additional data to "break the pattern." Let's return to the departmental sales study to illustrate this method. From Table 9.14, the correlation coefficient for square footage versus number of sales associates was $+0.963514$. Figure 9.16 displays the two predictor variables. There is a tight swarm of points upward sloping to the right; hence, the large positive correlation coefficient.

For the departmental sales study, seek additional observations (departments) that have (1) high square footage but few sales associates (cluster A) and (2) low square footage and many sales associates (cluster B). The additional observations break the linear pattern between square footage and number of sales associates. This will reduce the correlation coefficient, and thus the multicollinearity between the two predictor variables.

---

[14]It is possible that your expectations are incorrect.

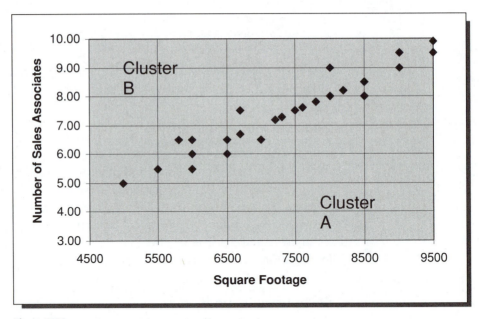

**Figure 9.16**
Square Footage versus Number of Sales Associates

Shown here are six additional observations to the data in Figure 9.16.

| Dept. | Footage | Number | Sales |
|-------|---------|--------|-----------|
| 31 | 9000 | 3.00 | $100,500 |
| 32 | 7500 | 4.50 | $82,000 |
| 33 | 8200 | 3.50 | $97,000 |
| 34 | 4500 | 8.00 | $62,000 |
| 35 | 5200 | 9.00 | $55,000 |
| 36 | 4700 | 7.50 | $70,550 |

Cluster A consists of departments 31–33 and cluster B consists of departments 34–36. If we add these six observations to Table 9.13 and recalculate the correlation matrix, the correlation between square footage and number of sales associates is reduced from 0.963514 to 0.366970. The estimated regression model will also no longer contain the negative sample regression coefficient for the number of sales associates predictor variable.

Breaking the pattern is not always possible. There may not be any departments that are in clusters A or B. Larger departments usually have more sales associates to service the customers. In general, breaking the pattern is difficult. And what is worse, multicollinearity can involve more than one pair of predictor variables.

# Chi-Square Test of Independence

Regression analysis and the chi-square test of independence are statistical tools for detecting relationships. Use the chi-square test when the predictor and dependent variables are both categorical. By the end of this section you should be able to

1. use the CHITEST function wizard to perform the test of independence; and

2. interpret the $p$-value output to determine if two categorical variables are statistically related in the population.

A product manager wants to know if a customer's race affects brand recognition for her product. Brand recognition is the dependent variable and race is the predictor variable. Both variables are categorical. She interviews 500 potential customers, asks them if they recognize the brand name, and displays the results in the 3 × 2 *contingency table* shown below. Is race related to brand recognition?

**Table 9.16**
Contingency Table:
**Actual** Frequency of
Race versus Brand
Recognition

|  | White | African American | Other | Total |
|---|---|---|---|---|
| Recognized | 100 | 50 | 5 | 155 d |
| Not Recognized | 100 | 150 | 95 | 345 e |
| Total | 200 a | 200 b | 100 c | 500 f |

The brand manager begins by stating the null and alternative hypotheses. As in regression analysis, the null is always the "no relationship" hypothesis. She also sets the significance level, $\alpha$, for the study. Based on the relative consequences of the Type I and II errors, she sets $\alpha = 0.025$.

Null hypothesis    Race and brand recognition are statistically independent (not related) *in the population.*

Alternative hypothesis    Race and brand recognition are statistically dependent (related) *in the population.*

Assuming the null is true, we can use the expressions shown below to determine the *expected* frequencies for the six cells shown in gray in Table 9.16.[15]

White and Recognized    $\left[\dfrac{a}{f}\right] \cdot \left[\dfrac{d}{f}\right] \cdot f = \dfrac{200}{500} \cdot \dfrac{155}{500} \cdot 500 = 62$

---

[15]Use these expressions to determine the expected frequencies in your spreadsheet. These are necessary inputs into the CHITEST function wizard. See the Appendix.

African American and
Recognized

$$\left[\frac{b}{f}\right] \cdot \left[\frac{d}{f}\right] \cdot f = \frac{200}{500} \cdot \frac{155}{500} \cdot 500 = 62$$

Other and Recognized

$$\left[\frac{c}{f}\right] \cdot \left[\frac{d}{f}\right] \cdot f = \frac{100}{500} \cdot \frac{155}{500} \cdot 500 = 31$$

White and Not Recognized

$$\left[\frac{a}{f}\right] \cdot \left[\frac{e}{f}\right] \cdot f = \frac{200}{500} \cdot \frac{345}{500} \cdot 500 = 138$$

African American and
Not Recognized

$$\left[\frac{b}{f}\right] \cdot \left[\frac{e}{f}\right] \cdot f = \frac{200}{500} \cdot \frac{345}{500} \cdot 500 = 138$$

Other and Not Recognized

$$\left[\frac{c}{f}\right] \cdot \left[\frac{e}{f}\right] \cdot f = \frac{100}{500} \cdot \frac{345}{500} \cdot 500 = 69$$

In general, to determine the expected frequency for any cell of a contingency table, compute the following expression:

$$\text{cell}_{ij} = \frac{\textbf{Total Row}_i \cdot \textbf{Total Column}_j}{\textbf{Total Sample Size}}$$

(9.15)

Table 9.17 shows the actual and expected frequencies for the brand recognition study. The actual frequencies are in the upper left corner of each cell; the expected frequencies are in the lower right corner. If the actual and expected frequencies are similar, then we cannot reject the null hypothesis. If the actual and expected frequencies are very different, then we will reject the null hypothesis and conclude that race and brand recognition are related in the population. But how different is "very different"?

**Table 9.17**
**Actual** and *Expected*
Frequencies for Brand
Recognition Study

|  | White | African American | Other | Total |
|---|---|---|---|---|
| Recognized | **100** | **50** | **5** | 155 |
|  | 62 | 62 | 31 |  |
| Not Recognized | **100** | **150** | **95** | 345 |
|  | 138 | 138 | 69 |  |
| Total | 200 | 200 | 100 | 500 |

Use the CHITEST function wizard to answer that question. The wizard screen is shown here.

CHITEST

| Actual_range | B1:D2 | = {100,50,5;100,150,' |
| Expected_range | B4:D5 | = {62,62,31;138,138,1 |

= 1.19354E-15

Returns the test for independence: the value from the chi-squared distribution for the statistic and the appropriate degrees of freedom.

**Expected_range** is the range of data that contains the ratio of the product of row totals and column totals to the grand total.

Formula result = 1.19354E-15

OK    Cancel

The study's $p$-value is shown as the Formula result. Since it is less than $\alpha = 0.025$, we reject the null hypothesis. If the null were true, the probability of obtaining the actual frequencies is 0.00000000000000119. Thus, we conclude that the different races exhibit different degrees of brand recognition *in the population*.

The CHITEST function wizard should *not* be used under the following conditions:

**1.** For a $2 \times 2$ contingency table when

    **a.** the sample size, f in Table 9.16, is less than 20.

    **b.** $20 < f < 40$ and any expected frequency is less than 5.

    **c.** $f > 40$ and any expected frequency is less than 1.

**2.** For larger than $2 \times 2$ contingency tables when

    **a.** more than 20% of the cells in the table have expected frequencies less than 5.

    **b.** any cell has an expected frequency less than 1.

In short, don't use the CHITEST wizard for a study with a small sample size.

# CHAPTER OVERVIEW

Both regression analysis and the chi-square test of independence are "relationship-detection" tools. Use the chi-square test of independence to determine if two categorical variables are related in the population. If the dependent variable is quantitative, then you use regression analysis. Regression analysis provides an estimated model to make predictions, whereas the chi-square test does not. In addition, regression analysis can handle one or more predictor variables, but the chi-square test handles only one predictor variable. In short, regression analysis is more powerful than the chi-square test of independence.

Figure 9.17 is a flowchart that describes the steps in a regression study.

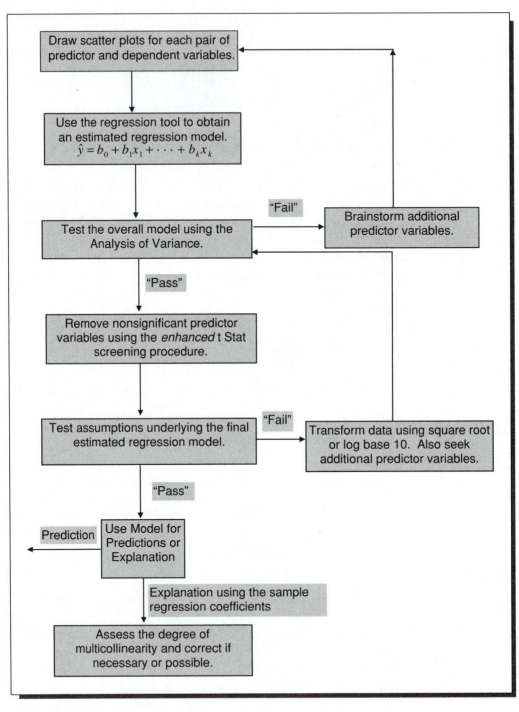

**Figure 9.17**
A Flowchart for Regression Analysis

# EXERCISES

**1.** Explain how $b_0$ and $b_1$ differ from $\beta_0$ and $\beta_1$. If we sampled the entire population, would $b_1$ equal $\beta_1$? Discuss.

**2.** Suppose the sample regression coefficients are not zero. Why can't we conclude that the predictor variables are statistically related to the dependent variable? Why must we do an ANOVA?

**3.** Explain the purpose of the t Stat screening procedure.

**4.** Explain what clusters are and why a simple correlation matrix may fail to detect them.

**5.** What must be true in order for the sum of squares residual, SSR(esidual), term to be zero?

**6.** You wish to determine if different market segments equally prefer two different types of advertising—informative or persuasive. Which relationship-detection tool should you use? Why?

**7.** When should a quadratic term be added to an estimated regression model?

**8.** When should an interaction term be added to an estimated regression model?

**9.** Explain the impact of severe multicollinearity on the sample regression coefficients.

**10.** Logically, why must prediction intervals be wider than confidence intervals?

**11.** We fit an estimated regression model and find a set of significant predictor variables. Even if the model meets the assumptions underlying regression analysis, does this guarantee that management will want to use the model for making predictions? Why?

**12.** If the original data are nonlinear and we fit a linear estimated regression model, what should the plot of the residuals versus the predictor variable look like?

*Problems 13–20 use the following data set.*

A staff manager runs a study to determine whether the size of the problem-solving group and the amount of group problem-solving training are related to performance on a group task, the dependent variable. He selects four groups of two, four, and six workers for a total of 12 groups. For each set of four groups, he provides two groups with four hours of training and two groups with no training. Shown are the data.

| GROUP | PERF | GROUPSIZE | TRAIN |
|-------|------|-----------|-------|
| 1 | 50 | 2 | 0 |
| 2 | 52 | 2 | 0 |
| 3 | 68 | 2 | 4 |
| 4 | 72 | 2 | 4 |
| 5 | 57 | 4 | 0 |
| 6 | 63 | 4 | 0 |
| 7 | 79 | 4 | 4 |
| 8 | 83 | 4 | 4 |
| 9 | 70 | 6 | 0 |
| 10 | 69 | 6 | 0 |
| 11 | 88 | 6 | 4 |
| 12 | 92 | 6 | 4 |

**13.** Draw a scatter diagram between performance and each predictor variable. Do the predictor variables appear to be related to performance?

**14.** Use the correlation data-analysis tool to generate the correlation matrix. Interpret the correlation coefficients of the dependent variable with each predictor variable.

**15.** Use the regression data-analysis tool to compute the estimated regression model with all predictor variables. Write the null and alternative hypotheses for testing the significance of the estimated regression model. Test the overall model using $\alpha = 0.05$.

**16.** Use the regression data-analysis tool and the t Stat screening procedure to produce a final estimated regression model that minimizes the standard error of the estimate. Explain the meaning of the standard error of the estimate in practical terms.

**17.** Interpret the meaning of the coefficient of multiple determination of the final model in the context of this problem.

**18.** Use the regression data-analysis tool to draw residual plots against each predictor variable in the final estimated model. Have the equal variance and normality assumptions been met? Are there any outliers? Discuss.

**19.** Develop an approximate 95% confidence interval on the mean task performance for a group of size three with two hours of training. Develop a prediction interval on the task performance for a single group of size three with two hours of training. Explain the difference between the two intervals in managerial terms.

**20.** Based on the correlation matrix for the final estimated regression model and the sample regression coefficients for that model, does multicollinearity appear to be a problem? Discuss.

*Problems 21–27 use the data in spreadsheet 921.xls.*

All publicly traded firms are required to have their financial statements audited by an independent CPA firm. When planning for the year's end, the comptroller is concerned about two things: the cost of the audit (in dollars) and the length of time the audit will take. The Board of Directors negotiates the audit contract. The comptroller, however, might be able to take steps to reduce audit time and therefore the disruption to normal activities.

An organization of 30 comptrollers has pooled data to measure the effects of three variables on the amount of time needed (Hours), the dependent variable, to complete an audit. The first variable is sales (in millions $)—the larger the company, the more time an audit is likely to require. The second is the number of hours spent on internal audit—a function carried out within the firm by the company's own employees. The feeling is that the more work done by the company's employees, the less time an outside auditor will need to spend. The third is the strength of internal controls—how tightly the accounting process is controlled on a day-to-day basis. For this study, the research team categorized controls as either strong (= 1) or weak (= 0).

**21.** Draw a scatter diagram between HOURS and each predictor variable. Do the predictor variables appear to be related to HOURS?

**22.** Use the correlation data-analysis tool to generate the correlation matrix. Interpret the correlation coefficients of the dependent variable with each predictor variable.

**23.** Use the regression data-analysis tool to compute the estimated regression model with all predictor variables. Write the null and alternative hypotheses for testing the significance of the estimated regression model. Test the model using $\alpha = 0.05$.

**24.** Use the regression data-analysis tool and the t Stat screening procedure to produce a final estimated regression model that minimizes the standard error of the estimate. Explain the meaning of the standard error of the estimate in practical terms.

**25.** Interpret the meaning of the coefficient of multiple determination of the final estimated model in the context of this problem.

**26.** Use the regression data-analysis tool to draw residual plots against each predictor variable in the final model. Have the equal variance and normality assumptions been met? Are there any outliers?

**27.** Based on the correlation matrix for the final estimated model and the sample regression coefficients for that model, does multi-collinearity appear to be a problem? Discuss.

**28.** Lenders who offer mortgages on single-family homes can usually get protection against borrower default by requiring mortgage guarantee insurance. One source of insurance is the Federal Housing Administration (FHA). The premium on such insurance becomes part of the purchaser's monthly payment.

In forecasting demand for loans, the FHA believes the number of loans (in thousands) insured (the dependent variable) varies directly with the loan-to-value ratio (the amount borrowed divided by the market value of the house), the length of the loan in years (TERM), and the interest rate of the loan. In addition, the FHA expects to insure fewer loans as the price of the insurance rises. The price of insurance is a fixed percentage of the loan.

The FHA collects data over a number of quarters and develops the following model to predict the number of mortgages that will require insurance.

| Variable | Coefficient | Standard Error | t Stat |
|---|---|---|---|
| INTERCEPT | −79.21 | 16.85 | −4.70 |
| LOAN-VALUE | 0.58 | .24 | 2.45 |
| TERM | 1.72 | .69 | 2.51 |
| INTEREST-RATE | 2.37 | .53 | 4.51 |
| INSURE-PRICE | −94.54 | 15.19 | −6.22 |
| Number of observations = 58 | | $R^2 = .82$ | |

**a.** If the purpose of the regression analysis was prediction, could the FHA reduce the standard error of the estimate by dropping any of the four predictor variables? Why?

**b.** Interpret each of the sample regression coefficients in terms a manager could understand.

**c.** Interpret the meaning of the coefficient of multiple determination in the context of this problem.

*Problems 29–36 use the following data.*

Shown below is a cross-sectional data set for 18 managers. It is a random sample of monthly salaries of managers at the same level within a major firm. The three predictor variables are months on the job, level of interpersonal communication skill along a 1 (poor) to 10 (good) scale, and the manager's gender. The firm wishes to predict monthly salary.

| | Monthly Salary | Months on the Job | Level of Communication Skill | Gender of Manager |
|---|---|---|---|---|
| 1 | 2000 | 14 | 3 | Female |
| 2 | 2100 | 14 | 2 | Female |
| 3 | 2150 | 12 | 3 | Female |
| 4 | 2200 | 25 | 4 | Female |
| 5 | 2300 | 27 | 6 | Female |
| 6 | 2200 | 30 | 5 | Female |
| 7 | 2400 | 32 | 7 | Female |
| 8 | 2300 | 36 | 8 | Female |
| 9 | 2500 | 40 | 9 | Female |
| 10 | 2700 | 15 | 1 | Male |
| 11 | 2800 | 16 | 3 | Male |
| 12 | 2900 | 22 | 4 | Male |
| 13 | 3200 | 27 | 5 | Male |
| 14 | 3200 | 26 | 5 | Male |
| 15 | 3100 | 30 | 6 | Male |
| 16 | 3400 | 34 | 8 | Male |
| 17 | 3600 | 32 | 7 | Male |
| 18 | 3900 | 38 | 9 | Male |

29. Plot monthly salary versus months on the job. Does there appear to be a linear relationship between the two variables?

30. Plot monthly salary versus level of communication skill. Does there appear to be a linear relationship between the two variables?

31. Label each of the data points in the two scatter diagrams in Problems 29 and 30 as male or female (the gender variable). Are there distinct clusters when we include the gender variable?

32. What can we conclude about the impact of gender on monthly salary?

33. Recode gender as follows: Female = 1 and Male = 0. Compute the correlation matrix for the four variables. Relate the correlation coefficients to the scatter diagrams in Problems 29 and 30.

34. Use the regression data-analysis tool to compute the estimated regression model with all predictor variables. Write the null and alternative hypotheses for testing the significance of the estimated regression model. Test the model using $\alpha = 0.05$.

35. Use the regression data-analysis tool and the t Stat screening procedure to produce a final estimated regression model that minimizes the standard error of the estimate. Explain the meaning of the standard error of the estimate in practical terms.

36 Develop an approximate 95% confidence interval on the mean monthly salary for all female managers who have been on the job for 20 months and whose communication skill level is 6.5. Also construct a 95% confidence interval on the mean monthly salary for all male managers who have been on the job for 20 months and whose communication skill level is 6.5. Does there appear to be gender discrimination?

37. Here are data on amount of stress and worker productivity.

| Stress Level | Worker Productivity |
|---|---|
| 10 | 15 pieces per hour |
| 20 | 22 |
| 30 | 27 |
| 40 | 32 |
| 50 | 32 |
| 60 | 28 |
| 70 | 24 |
| 80 | 17 |

a. Compute and interpret the correlation coefficient.

b. Plot a scatter diagram. Does there appear to be a linear relationship? Does there appear to be any relationship?

c. Reconcile your answers in parts (a) and (b).

d. Develop a second-order model, a polynomial of order 2. Test the estimated regression model at the $\alpha = 0.05$ level.

e. Develop an approximate 95% prediction interval for a worker whose stress level is 55. Interpret the interval.

*Problems 38–43 use the following data.*

Shown is a random sample of data on 12 physicians in the 45–50-year-old group. We have recorded their amount of life insurance, their annual income for the past year, and their marital status. We wish to predict amount of life insurance.

| Physician | Amount of Life Insurance (thousands of dollars) | Annual Income (thousands of dollars) | Marital Status |
|-----------|-------------------|------------------|----------------|
| 1 | 250 | 140 | Single |
| 2 | 350 | 155 | Single |
| 3 | 450 | 225 | Single |
| 4 | 500 | 190 | Single |
| 5 | 650 | 210 | Single |
| 6 | 800 | 240 | Single |
| 7 | 790 | 140 | Married |
| 8 | 950 | 160 | Married |
| 9 | 1200 | 170 | Married |
| 10 | 1300 | 200 | Married |
| 11 | 1400 | 220 | Married |
| 12 | 1350 | 230 | Married |

**38.** Plot a scatter diagram between amount of life insurance and annual income. Does there appear to be a linear relationship between the two variables?

**39.** Label each point in the scatter diagram with the marital status of the physician—single or married. Are there distinct clusters? What can we conclude about the impact of marital status on the amount of life insurance purchased?

**40.** Code Married as 1 and Single as 0. Use the regression data-analysis tool to compute the estimated regression model with all predictor variables. Write the null and alternative hypotheses for testing the significance of the estimated regression model. Test the model using $\alpha = 0.025$.

**41.** Interpret the meaning of the coefficient of multiple determination of the final model in the context of this problem.

**42.** Use the regression data-analysis tool and the t Stat screening procedure to produce a final estimated regression model that minimizes the standard error of the estimate. Explain the meaning of the standard error of the estimate in practical terms.

**43.** Use the regression data-analysis tool to draw residual plots against each predictor variable in the final estimated regression model. Have the equal variance and normality assumptions been met? Are there any outliers? Discuss.

**44.** Shown is a time-ordered data set on company sales (dependent variable) and disposable personal income.

| Quarter | Sales (millions of dollars) | Disposable Personal Income (billions of dollars) |
|---------|------------------|-------------------------------|
| 1 | 35.2 | 133.5 |
| 2 | 35.5 | 135.5 |
| 3 | 35.9 | 137.7 |
| 4 | 36.7 | 140.0 |
| 5 | 37.7 | 143.9 |
| 6 | 38.4 | 147.2 |
| 7 | 39.2 | 148.9 |
| 8 | 39.3 | 149.0 |
| 9 | 41.2 | 153.2 |
| 10 | 41.4 | 155.6 |
| 11 | 42.3 | 160.9 |
| 12 | 43.1 | 163.5 |

**a.** Use the regression data-analysis tool to develop an estimated first-order regression model.

**b.** Develop and interpret an ANOVA table. Test the significance of the estimated regression model at $\alpha = 0.10$.

**c.** Interpret the coefficient of multiple determination.

**d.** Interpret the standard error of the estimate.

**e.** Predict mean sales for a disposable personal income level of 150 billion dollars.

**f.** Draw a residual plot against time in quarters. Is the independence assumption reasonable? Discuss.

**45.** This exercise demonstrates how to use the regression data-analysis tool to develop an **autoregressive model with leading indicators** first presented in Chapter 7. Shown are 16 quarters of data. The dependent variable is sales and the predictor variable is housing starts (HS). We believe that housing starts is a two-quarter leading indicator. That is, housing starts in quarter $t$ affect sales in quarter $t + 2$. We also believe that sales in one quarter are affected by sales from the previous quarter.

| Time | Sales | Housing Starts |
|------|-------|----------------|
| 1    | 100   | 700            |
| 2    | 120   | 400            |
| 3    | 190   | 550            |
| 4    | 218   | 600            |
| 5    | 271   | 725            |
| 6    | 315   | 500            |
| 7    | 378   | 550            |
| 8    | 397   | 610            |
| 9    | 427   | 710            |
| 10   | 452   | 520            |
| 11   | 485   | 600            |
| 12   | 505   | 610            |
| 13   | 526   | 770            |
| 14   | 553   | 580            |
| 15   | 528   | 650            |
| 16   | 550   | 620            |

**a.** Since we believe that sales in one quarter affect sales in the next quarter, draw a scatter diagram of sales (quarters 1–15) versus sales (quarters 2–16). Do the two variables appear to be related?

**b.** Since we believe that housing starts is a two-quarter leading indicator, draw a scatter diagram of sales (quarters 3–16) versus housing starts (quarters 1–14). Do the two variables appear to be related?

**c.** Use the regression data-analysis tool to develop an estimated regression model of sales (quarters 3–16) versus sales

(quarters 2–15) and housing starts (quarters 1–14). At the $\alpha = 0.05$ level, does the overall estimated regression model "pass" the ANOVA test?

**d.** Use the t Stat screening procedure to reduce, if possible, the standard error of the estimate.

**e.** Develop the most likely sales forecast for quarter 17 using the final estimated regression model.

**46.** Consider the following estimated regression model.

$$\hat{y} = 60 - 2.5\text{STUDYHOURS} + 1.5\text{MATERDIFF}$$

where $\hat{y}$ is the predicted exam score and STUDYHOURS is the number of hours studied for the exam and MATERDIFF is an indicator variable: 1 if material is difficult, 0 otherwise

**a.** Would the above estimated regression model have high face validity?

**b.** What might cause the signs of the sample regression coefficients to be the reverse of logic?

**c.** Using logic alone, would you expect the two predictor variables to exhibit multicollinearity? Discuss.

**47.** Banks, like other firms, can follow a strategy of growth through acquisition. An important consideration in any acquisition is, of course, the price. The purchase price of an acquired bank can be above, equal to, or below the acquired bank's net asset value—the market value of the acquired bank's assets less the market value of its liabilities. If the purchase price is above the net asset value, then the acquired bank is selling at a premium. If the price is below net asset value, then the bank is selling at a discount.

Bankers believe that the growth rate of the bank to be acquired, as measured by the growth rate in deposits, has some influence on the purchase premium/discount. Another variable is profitability. In banking circles, one measure of profitability is the net interest spread (the difference between the rates paid depositors and the rates charged to borrowers). Finally, the tax status of the transaction (taxable = 0, nontaxable = 1) should also have some influence because shareholders of the acquired bank should demand a higher price to compensate for the additional taxes they will have to pay.

Data have been collected for a number of bank acquisitions and the following model developed to predict the dependent variable—premium or discount—measured in percent.

| Variable | Coefficient | Standard Error | t Stat |
|----------|-------------|----------------|--------|
| INTERCEPT | −42.95 | 20.26 | −2.12 |
| DEPOSIT GROWTH% | 4.03 | .85 | 4.72 |
| NET INTEREST SPREAD% | 11.21 | 3.96 | 2.83 |
| TAX STATUS | −16.37 | 7.78 | −2.10 |

$F = 12.57$    $R^2 = .53$
Number of observations = 64

**a.** If the purpose of the regression analysis was prediction, could we reduce the standard error of the estimate by dropping any of the three predictor variables? Why?

**b.** Interpret each of the sample regression coefficients in terms a manager would understand.

**c.** Does it appear that additional predictor variables should be added to the estimated regression model? Discuss.

*Problems 48–53 use the data in spreadsheet 948.xls.*

Data are collected for a random sample of 30 employees. Job satisfaction is the dependent variable. The predictor variables are (1) salary, measured in thousands of dollars; (2) years with the company; (3) age; (4) gender; (5) years of experience in a related field before joining the firm; and (6) management, an indicator variable that is equal to 1 if the employee has management responsibility and 0 if the employee has no management responsibility.

**48.** Plot a scatter diagram of job satisfaction and each of the six predictor variables listed above. Do the predictor variables appear to be related to job satisfaction?

**49.** Generate the correlation matrix. Interpret the simple correlation coefficients of the dependent variable with each predictor variable.

**50.** Use the regression data-analysis tool to compute the estimated regression model with all six predictor variables. Write the null and alternative hypotheses for testing the significance of the estimated regression model. Test the model using B = 0.01.

**51.** Use the regression data-analysis tool and the t Stat screening procedure to produce a final estimated regression model that minimizes the standard error of the estimate. Explain the meaning of the standard error of the estimate in practical terms.

**52.** Draw residual plots against each predictor variable in the final model. Have the equal variance and normality assumptions been met?

**53.** Based on the correlation matrix for the final estimated regression model and the sample regression coefficients for that model, does multicollinearity appear to be a problem? Discuss.

**54.** Suppose that a particular cancer is indicated by a test using a count of chromosome effects. There are two predictor variables: *cig* is the number of cigarettes an individual smokes each day; *alcoh* is the number of ounces of alcohol the individual drinks each day. The project manager has proposed the following estimated regression model:

$$\hat{y} = b_0 + b_1 \cdot CIG + b_2 \cdot ALCOH$$

where $\hat{y}$ is the predicted chromosome effects and $b_i$ will be obtained from the regression data–analysis tool

From previous studies, she knows that the combined effect of heavy smoking and drinking produces a higher count of chromosome effects than would be predicted by each predictor variable singly.

**a.** Is the above estimated regression model appropriate, given the known information?

**b.** Propose a more realistic estimated regression model that incorporates the idea that the combined effect of heavy smoking and drinking produces a higher count of chromosome effects than would be predicted by each predictor variable singly.

**55.** We wish to study whether female union members are earning the same salary as comparably situated male union members. Thus, we include a gender variable in the model. According to Title VII of the 1964 Civil Rights Act and empirical studies of lifetime earnings, the only economically and legally justifiable factor explaining earnings differential between the genders is seniority.

We use two measures of seniority: (1) years on job and (2) age in years. We propose the following estimated regression model:

$$\hat{y} = b_0 + b_1 \cdot AGE + b_2 \cdot YEARS + b_3 \cdot GENDER$$

where $\hat{y}$ is the predicted salary and $b_i$ will be obtained from the regression data-analysis tool.

**a.** If females are represented as GENDER = 0 and males as GENDER = 1, and if females receive significantly lower salaries than comparably situated males, should the sign of the sample regression coefficient, $b_3$, be positive or negative? Discuss.

**b.** If females are represented as GENDER = 0 and males as GENDER = 1, and if females receive the same salaries as comparably situated males, what will the population regression coefficient for the GENDER variable, $\beta_3$, equal? Discuss.

**c.** Given the three predictor variables, is multicollinearity likely to be a problem?

*Problems 56–60 use the data in spreadsheet 956.xls.*

A real estate appraiser collected the data in spreadsheet 956.xls for a random sample of 30 apartment units. He wants to use this information to predict rents. The appraiser believes that weekly rent is affected by the number of bedrooms, the size of the complex measured by the number of units, the age of the complex, whether all utilities are included (no = 0; yes = 1), and whether covered parking is provided (no = 0, yes = 1).

**56.** Draw a scatter diagram between weekly rent and each predictor variable. Do the predictor variables appear to be related to weekly rent?

**57.** Use the correlation data–analysis tool to generate the correlation matrix. Interpret the simple correlation coefficients of the dependent variable with each predictor variable.

**58.** Use the regression data-analysis tool to compute the estimated regression model with all predictor variables. Write the null and alternative hypotheses for testing the significance of the estimated regression model. Test the overall model using $\alpha = 0.05$.

**59.** Use the regression data-analysis tool and the t Stat screening procedure to produce a final estimated regression model that minimizes the standard error of the estimate. Explain the meaning of the standard error of the estimate in practical terms.

**60.** Based on the correlation matrix for the final estimated regression model and the sample regression coefficients for that model, does multicollinearity appear to be a problem? Discuss.

**61.** Best Dairy, Inc., knows that the Macho consumers have lower incomes than do the Status Seeker consumers. It wonders if Machos and Status Seekers also have different preferences for skim and whole milk. The marketing manager conducts a survey and asks the following question: "Do you prefer skim or whole milk?" He wants to verify that Best Dairy has meaningfully segmented its market. Best Dairy, Inc., interviews 200 customers and cross-classifies them by the following two categorical variables. Use the 0.05 significance level to determine whether the two categorical variables are related.

|       | Machos | Status Seekers | Total |
|-------|--------|----------------|-------|
| Skim  | 30     | 80             | 110   |
| Whole | 70     | 20             | 90    |
|       | 100    | 100            | 200   |

**62.** Zero coupon bonds (zeros) pay no annual interest but sell at a discount below par. This provides investors significant capital appreciation when the bond matures. Zeros are thought to be attractive because their yield is guaranteed even if interest rates drop. Thus, if investors believe interest rates will drop over the next five to ten years, they should be more interested in purchasing zeros. Is this true? A bond analyst selects 400 bond customers and cross-classifies them by their future interest rate prediction and type of bond preferred. The results are shown here. Use the 0.05 significance level to determine whether the two categorical variables are related.

|                              | Not a Zero Coupon Bond | Zero Coupon Bond |
|------------------------------|------------------------|------------------|
| Falling Interest             | 25                     | 75               |
| Steady or Increasing Interest | 200                    | 100              |

**63.** Is level of information systems technology related to bottom-line performance of firms? The American Computing Group (ACG) conducts a survey of 100 firms in the banking industry. Fifty banks are performing above the industry median; 50 are not. The ACG asks each firm to indicate the highest level of information systems technology it has achieved. Shown are the contingency table data. Use the 0.05 significance level to determine whether the two categorical variables are related.

| | Level of Information Technology | | |
|---|---|---|---|
| | Transaction Processing | Decision Support | Executive Support |
| Below median | 30 | 10 | 10 |
| Above median | 10 | 15 | 25 |

**64.** A human resource manager for a large firm wishes to know if the percentage of extroverts and introverts (as measured by the Myers–Briggs Type Indicator) varies by management level. She randomly selects 1000 managers, and cross-classifies them by level and Myers–Briggs type. Here are the data. Use an $\alpha = 0.05$ significance level to determine whether the two categorical variables are related.

|        | Extrovert | Introvert | Total |
|--------|-----------|-----------|-------|
| Upper  | 65        | 35        | 100   |
| Mid    | 250       | 150       | 400   |
| Lower  | 330       | 170       | 500   |
| Total  | 645       | 355       | 1000  |

**65.** Elizabeth Dole, former U.S. Secretary of Labor, referred to a "glass ceiling" that allegedly keeps women and minorities out of the top echelons of corporate management. The personnel manager of a large corporation wants to be sure that women and minorities are not discriminated against in promotion decisions in his corporation. He examines over 600 promotion decisions made over the past two years. The results are shown.

|              | White Males | Women and Minorities | Total |
|--------------|-------------|----------------------|-------|
| Promoted     | 220         | 60                   | 280   |
| Not promoted | 180         | 180                  | 360   |
| Total        | 400         | 240                  | 640   |

**a.** At a 5% significance level, does it appear that white males are favored in the promotion decision?

The personnel director reexamined the study data and divided the sample of 640 into those who had an MBA degree and those who did not. The sample results are shown.

| MBA Group | White Males | Women/Minorities |
|-----------|-------------|------------------|
| Promoted     | 120      | 40               |
| Not Promoted | 60       | 20               |

| No MBA Group | White Males | Women/Minorities |
|--------------|-------------|------------------|
| Promoted     | 100         | 20               |
| Not Promoted | 120         | 160              |

**b.** Having included the completion of the MBA degree as an intervening variable, is promotion now related to race/gender? Explain.

**66.** Is type of leadership related to level of worker job satisfaction? Shown are data for 500 workers.

|              | Autocratic Supervision | Participatory Supervision |
|--------------|------------------------|---------------------------|
| Satisfied    | 110                    | 260                       |
| Dissatisfied | 90                     | 40                        |

Perform the chi-square test of independence on the two categorical variables. Use a 0.05 significance level. What does the test tell you?

**67.** We study 1000 customers to determine whether level of product satisfaction is related to income level categories. Shown here are the data.

|              | Less than $30,000 | $30,000–$70,000 | More than $70,000 | Total |
|--------------|-------------------|-----------------|-------------------|-------|
| Satisfied    | 390               | 325             | 100               | 815   |
| Dissatisfied | 10                | 75              | 100               | 185   |
| Total        | 400               | 400             | 200               | 1000  |

Perform the chi-square test of independence on the two categorical variables. Use a 0.005 significance level. What does the test tell you?

**68.** This exercises demonstrates how to use the regression data-analysis tool to develop the **autoregressive model** first presented in Chapter 7. Shown are 20 quarters of data on ending inventory levels of cellular phones for a branch of a large electronics warehouse chain.

| Quarter | Inventory | Quarter | Inventory |
|---------|-----------|---------|-----------|
| 1 | 100 | 11 | 250 |
| 2 | 400 | 12 | 350 |
| 3 | 150 | 13 | 200 |
| 4 | 500 | 14 | 450 |
| 5 | 100 | 15 | 300 |
| 6 | 600 | 16 | 600 |
| 7 | 200 | 17 | 100 |
| 8 | 500 | 18 | 500 |
| 9 | 300 | 19 | 150 |
| 10 | 400 | 20 | 550 |

**a.** Draw a scatter diagram of inventory (quarters 1–19) versus inventory (quarters 2–20). Do the two variables appear to be related?

**b.** Use the regression data-analysis tool to develop an estimated regression model of inventory (quarters 2–20) versus inventory (quarters 1–19). At the $\alpha = 0.05$ level, does the overall estimated regression model "pass" the ANOVA test?

**c.** Develop the most likely inventory forecast for quarter 21.

**69.** Shown here is a small data set.

| Units Sold | Price | Advertising Level |
|------------|-------|-------------------|
| 8,000 | 10 | 20,000 |
| 10,000 | 20 | 40,000 |
| 14,000 | 30 | 40,000 |
| 13,000 | 40 | 60,000 |
| 17,000 | 50 | 80,000 |

**a.** Use the regression data-analysis tool to develop an estimated regression model for units sold. Test at the 0.10 significance level.

**b.** Do the sample regression coefficients make economic sense? Discuss.

**c.** Develop a scatter plot between the two predictor variables. What does it indicate?

**d.** Use the correlation matrix to verify that the predictor variables are highly related.

**e.** Add six data values to the original data set that should "break the pattern."

**f.** Rerun the regression data-analysis tool and the correlation data-analysis tool to verify that the additional data values did in fact reduce the degree of multicollinearity. Discuss.

**g.** Discuss the ease of obtaining data that would "break the pattern."

**h.** Would eliminating one of the predictor variables eliminate the unexpected signs of the sample regression coefficients? Rerun the regression data-analysis tool with only one predictor variable—price. Does the sign of the sample regression coefficient for the price predictor variable now make economic sense? Discuss.

**i.** Return to the original estimated regression model from part (a). Make a prediction on sales for PRICE = $32.50 and ADV = $42,500. Even though the model does not have high face validity, would the above prediction be valid? Discuss.

# CASE STUDY

Historically, Computer Technic's pay raises for AS/400 programmer/analysts consist of two components: (1) adjustment for the change in the consumer price index (CPI) and (2) adjustment for merit and performance. Each year an analyst predicts the following year's CPI. The CFO has also indicated that the merit percentage increase will vary next year between 0% and 8%.

The firm must estimate next year's change in the CPI. The economic forecaster obtains the consumer price index data for the most recent 28 years.

| Year | % Change in CPI | Year | % Change in CPI | Year | % Change in CPI | Year | % Change in CPI |
|------|------|------|------|------|------|------|------|
| t – 27 | 5.7 | t – 20 | 6.5 | t – 13 | 4.3 | t – 6 | 4.2 |
| t – 26 | 4.4 | t – 19 | 7.6 | t – 12 | 3.6 | t – 5 | 3.0 |
| t – 25 | 3.2 | t – 18 | 11.3 | t – 11 | 1.9 | t – 4 | 3.0 |
| t – 24 | 6.2 | t – 17 | 13.5 | t – 10 | 3.6 | t – 3 | 2.6 |
| t – 23 | 11.0 | t – 16 | 10.3 | t – 9 | 4.1 | t – 2 | 2.8 |
| t – 22 | 9.1 | t – 15 | 6.2 | t – 8 | 4.8 | t – 1 | 3.0 |
| t – 21 | 5.8 | t – 14 | 3.2 | t – 7 | 5.4 | t | 2.9 |

**Table 9.18**
CPI Data

The CFO must also develop a model or formula that generates the percentage increase for the merit portion of the raise. He will base it on the following data taken from last year in which the firm also gave a 0%–8% merit increase.

Predictor Variables:

Proportion of Improvement Projects Completed on Time and within Cost

Manager's Assessment of Quality of Work on 0 (well below standard) to 4 (well above standard) scale

Number of Hours of Continuing Education Taken during Year

Proportion of Programming Crises Handled within 24 Hours

Prepare a one-page report. The report should describe the expected percentage increase in the CPI for the upcoming year and describe the regression model to predict the merit percentage increase in salary for each AS/400 analyst. Use the data to support your position.

| Analyst | Percent Merit Increase | Proportion of Improvements | Work Quality | Hours of Education | Proportion Crises |
|---|---|---|---|---|---|
| 1 | 3.30 | 0.40 | 0 | 17 | 0.30 |
| 2 | 3.25 | 0.10 | 1 | 26 | 0.45 |
| 3 | 4.52 | 0.60 | 2 | 21 | 0.15 |
| 4 | 6.98 | 0.90 | 3 | 21 | 0.70 |
| 5 | 6.26 | 0.90 | 4 | 26 | 0.25 |
| 6 | 7.91 | 1.00 | 3 | 21 | 0.90 |
| 7 | 2.55 | 0.20 | 0 | 21 | 0.25 |
| 8 | 4.53 | 0.40 | 2 | 12 | 0.70 |
| 9 | 5.28 | 0.80 | 0 | 20 | 0.40 |
| 10 | 4.53 | 0.20 | 2 | 20 | 0.90 |
| 11 | 3.51 | 0.20 | 1 | 19 | 0.50 |
| 12 | 3.01 | 0.30 | 0 | 17 | 0.40 |
| 13 | 5.73 | 0.40 | 3 | 22 | 0.90 |
| 14 | 6.93 | 0.80 | 0 | 23 | 1.00 |
| 15 | 3.66 | 0.20 | 1 | 24 | 0.70 |
| 16 | 5.16 | 0.50 | 2 | 25 | 0.40 |
| 17 | 5.46 | 0.30 | 3 | 25 | 0.90 |
| 18 | 7.45 | 0.60 | 2 | 23 | 1.00 |
| 19 | 5.69 | 0.70 | 4 | 24 | 0.50 |
| 20 | 5.10 | 0.40 | 3 | 24 | 0.60 |
| 21 | 3.98 | 0.40 | 1 | 19 | 0.40 |
| 22 | 3.90 | 0.50 | 1 | 20 | 0.20 |
| 23 | 6.88 | 0.90 | 4 | 24 | 0.20 |
| 24 | 0.95 | 0.00 | 1 | 0 | 0.10 |
| 25 | 5.64 | 0.50 | 2 | 17 | 0.70 |

**Table 9.19**
Salary and Performance Data

# CHAPTER 9
# APPENDICES

## I. LISTING OF EXCEL TOOLS USED IN THIS CHAPTER

**1.** Regression data-analysis tool

**2.** Chart Wizard—XY Scatter Plot

**3.** Correlation data-analysis tool

**4.** CHITEST function wizard

## II. PERFORMING MULTIPLE REGRESSION ANALYSIS

| | A | B | C | D | E | F | G | H | I |
|---|---|---|---|---|---|---|---|---|---|
| **1** | Employee | Gender | Gen × Rat | Education | Rating | Stress | Stress$^2$ | Goal | Percent |
| **2** | 1 | 0 | 0 | 17.7 | 55 | 10 | 100 | 1.5 | 4.40 |
| **3** | 2 | 0 | 0 | 16.5 | 60 | 80 | 6400 | 1.5 | 4.40 |
| **4** | 3 | 0 | 0 | 15.3 | 75 | 15 | 225 | 2.5 | 5.37 |
| **5** | 4 | 0 | 0 | 15.7 | 85 | 20 | 400 | 3.2 | 5.92 |
| **6** | 5 | 0 | 0 | 17.6 | 80 | 27 | 729 | 6.5 | 6.20 |
| **7** | 6 | 0 | 0 | 15.6 | 60 | 14 | 196 | 3.5 | 4.88 |
| **8** | 7 | 0 | 0 | 17.2 | 75 | 28 | 784 | 2.9 | 5.72 |
| **9** | 8 | 0 | 0 | 15.7 | 73 | 85 | 7225 | 4.6 | 4.63 |
| **10** | 9 | 0 | 0 | 17.7 | 67 | 81 | 6561 | 2.1 | 5.00 |
| **11** | 10 | 0 | 0 | 15.5 | 90 | 76 | 5776 | 3.5 | 6.25 |
| **12** | 11 | 0 | 0 | 15.2 | 60 | 80 | 6400 | 4.5 | 5.00 |
| **13** | 12 | 0 | 0 | 16.5 | 50 | 82 | 6724 | 1.4 | 4.37 |

**1.** Arrange the data in columns with the seven predictor variables in the columns on the left (B through H) and the dependent variable in the column on the right (I). The seven predictor variables *must* be in adjacent columns. The spreadsheet only shows a portion of the data. See Table 9.5.

**2.** From the Tools menu, choose Data Analysis. In the Data-Analysis dialog box, scroll the list box, select Regression, and choose OK.

**3.** Input *y* range: Point to or enter the reference for the range containing values of the dependent variable (percent increase, I1:I31). Include the label above the data.

**4.** Input *x* range: Point to or enter the reference for the range containing values of the seven predictor variables (B1: H31). Include the labels above the data.

**5.** Other dialog box entries: Fill in the other check boxes and edit boxes as shown in the figure below. Then click OK.

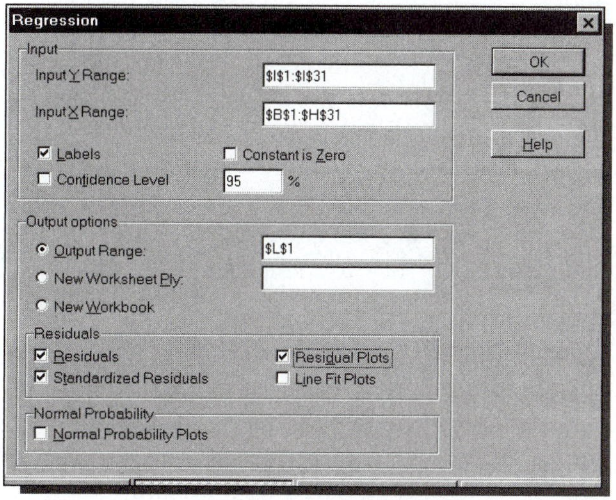

**6.** Optional: To change column widths so that all summary output labels are visible, select the cell containing the Adjusted R Square label and hold down the Control key while selecting cells containing the labels Coefficients, Standard Error, Significance F, and Upper 95%. From the Format menu, choose the Column command and select AutoFit Selection.

# III. Computing the Expected Frequencies for the CHITEST Function Wizard

The following steps describe how to construct the Actual Frequency and Expected Frequency tables. Excel's CHITEST wizard then computes the *p*-value for the study. Although the cell references shown are appropriate for a 3 × 3 contingency table, you can use this approach for any table.

The contingency table assesses if American, European, and Asian firms use the same financial strategies for meeting seasonal cash needs. The aggressive financial policy approach sells no marketable securities. The conservative approach meets all seasonal needs by the sale of marketable securities. The compromise plan sells some marketable securities to meet seasonal cash needs.

1. Enter all the labels shown in the figure below. Also insert the actual frequencies in the body of the contingency table (B3:E6).

2. Select the entire Actual Frequency table (B3:E6)—including title, labels, data, and marginal total—and click the Copy tool.

3. Select cell A8 and click the Paste tool.

4. Enter Expected Frequency in cell A8, replacing the original title.

5. Enter the formula using Expression (9.15) for the expected frequency for cell B10. Type the equal sign (=); then click on the Column total cell (B13) at the bottom of the table and press F4 twice to change the relative reference to a mixed reference (B$13, relative column reference and absolute row reference). Type the asterisk multiplication sign (*) and click on the Row Total cell (E10) and press F4 three times to change the relative reference to a mixed reference ($E10, absolute column reference and relative row reference). Type the division sign (/) and click on the Total Cell (E13) and press F4 once to change the relative reference to an absolute reference. Press Enter.

6. In the expected frequency table, copy the formula in cell B10 to the other eight cells in the *body of the contingency table*. Do *not* copy to the Column Total row or Row Total column.

7. To format, select all the numerical values in the body of the table and click the Decrease Decimal button repeatedly until you have the desired number of decimal places.

8. Enter the label, "*p*-value," into cell A15.

9. Select cell B15. Click the Function Wizard tool button. In step 1, select Statistical for the Function Category and select CHITEST as the Function Name. Click OK.

10. In step 2 of the function wizard, select the actual_range edit box and point to the appropriate cells on the worksheet (click B3 and drag to D5).

11. Select the expected_range edit box and point to the appropriate cells on the worksheet (click B10 and drag to D12). Click the OK button.

|    | A | B | C | D | E |
|----|---|---|---|---|---|
| 1 | **Actual Frequency** | | | | |
| 2 | | **US Firms** | **European Firms** | **Asian Firms** | **Row Total** |
| 3 | **Sell No Securities** | 100 | 125 | 10 | 235 |
| 4 | **Sell All Securities** | 100 | 125 | 70 | 295 |
| 5 | **Sell Some Securities** | 100 | 50 | 20 | 170 |
| 6 | **Column Total** | 300 | 300 | 100 | 700 |
| 7 | | | | | |
| 8 | **Expected Frequency** | | | | |
| 9 | | **US Firms** | **European Firms** | **Asian Firms** | **Row Total** |
| 10 | **Sell No Securities** | 100.71 | 100.71 | 33.57 | 235 |
| 11 | **Sell All Securities** | 126.43 | 126.43 | 42.14 | 295 |
| 12 | **Sell Some Securities** | 72.86 | 72.86 | 24.29 | 170 |
| 13 | **Column Total** | 300 | 300 | 100 | 700 |
| 14 | | | | | |
| 15 | **p-value** | 3.43E-13 | | | |

The $p$-value for the alternative financing policies versus American/Foreign firms study is 0.000000000000343. American versus European or Asian firms use different financing strategies.

# FORECASTING AND TIME SERIES ANALYSIS

## DATA PATTERNS AND FORECASTING

Managers develop quantitative forecasting models to predict the future. These models serve two purposes. First, they help set targets and goals for future performance. When actual future performance does not meet planned levels, managers must take corrective action. Second, they help develop production schedules and determine staff, raw material, and capital equipment needs. In summary, accurate forecasts are essential in establishing, achieving, and monitoring progress toward business goals. Developing accurate forecasts is the goal of this chapter.

We develop quantitative forecasts using *time-ordered* data. Time-ordered, or time series, data are data collected over time—data in chronological sequence. Forecasting begins by drawing a line graph of the historical data and examining the data pattern. Place time on the horizontal axis and the historical values of the variable to be forecasted on the vertical axis. A line graph can contain two distinctly different types of patterns—**meandering** or **seasonal.**

A **seasonal** pattern occurs when the data exhibit a repeating pattern on a regular basis. Although recurring patterns are often associated with the seasons (months or quarters) of the year, a seasonal pattern applies to any data that contains a repeating pattern.

Figure 10.1 is a line graph of 20 quarters of sales data. Note two observations. First, the data contain a trend. That is, the data exhibit a long-term increase (or decrease) over the 20 quarters. Second, there is a recurring pattern. The first and fourth quarters of each year are relatively weak sales periods and the second and third quarters are relatively strong sales periods. The pattern persists year after year. The *length* of the pattern is 1 year.

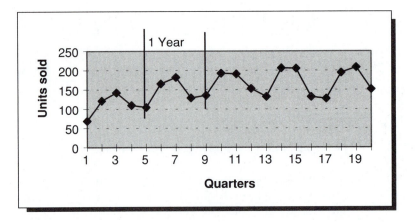

**Figure 10.1**
Data Containing a
Seasonal Pattern

Seasonal pattern lengths need not be one year. For example, a five-day seasonal pattern is common when analyzing daily percentage absenteeism data. Percentage absenteeism tends to be relatively high on Mondays and Fridays and relatively low on the other three days, week after week. Here the length of the seasonal pattern is five days. Remember, to qualify as a seasonal pattern, the pattern must repeat itself on a *regular* basis, not a yearly basis.

Figure 10.2 exhibits a meandering pattern. Note three observations. First, the data contain a trend. That is, the data exhibit a long-term increase (or decrease) over the 16 quarters. Second, there is a *no* recurring pattern. Finally, adjacent observations have values that are close to one another, but distant observations have very different values. In short, there is a meandering data pattern.

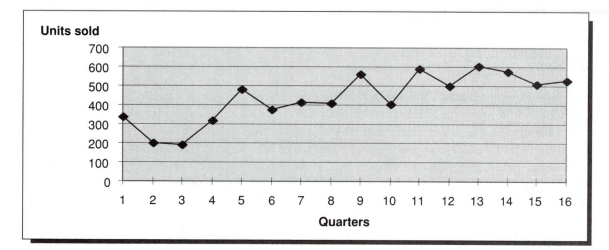

**Figure 10.2**
Data Containing a Meandering Pattern

**D E F I N I T I O N**  A meandering pattern occurs when adjacent observations have values that are usually close to one another but distant observations may have very different values. A meandering pattern does not contain any systematic or repeating pattern.

The appropriate quantitative forecasting method depends, in part, on the type of pattern—meandering or seasonal. It also depends on whether the forecaster wishes to use pattern-detection or relationship-detection tools.

***Relationship Detection.*** You are already familiar with relationship-detection tools. In Chapter 9 you used regression analysis to detect relationships between a dependent variable and a set of predictor variables. In this chapter you will develop forecasts by projecting these relationships into the future. For a valid forecast, the detected relationship based on historical data must continue into the future forecasting periods.

***Pattern Detection.*** Quantitative forecasting methods help identify patterns in the data—a trend and a seasonal pattern. You develop forecasts by projecting these patterns into the future forecasting periods. For a valid forecast, the detected patterns based upon historical data must continue into the future forecasting periods.

Which detection method in Table 10.1 should you use? Both pattern- and relationship-detection methods can produce accurate forecasts. If you wish only to make predictions, the forecast models based on pattern-detection methods are easier to build and maintain. If you also want to identify the predictor variables that affect the forecasted dependent variable, use regression analysis methods.

| Detection Method | Meandering Pattern | Seasonal Pattern |
|---|---|---|
| Relationship | Regression Analysis: <br> 1. Autoregressive Models: AR (1) or AR (2). | Regression Analysis: <br> 1. Autoregressive Models: AR (4) or AR (12). |
| | 2. Autoregressive Models That Include Coincident or Leading Predictor Variables | 2. Autoregressive Models That Include Coincident or Leading Predictor Variables |
| Pattern | 1. Linear or Nonlinear Trend Analysis | 1. Classical Time Series Decomposition Method |

**Table 10.1**
Relationship and Pattern Detection Tools

Although not presented here, there are qualitative forecasting methods as well. These include the Delphi method and the nominal group technique. In both methods, groups use intuition and judgment to arrive at a final forecast. The main difference is that in the Delphi method the group members are generally not aware of each other, and do not meet face to face. Both methods are especially useful in generating forecasts for distant events where there are little or no quantitative data and much uncertainty. For example, a qualitative forecasting method might be useful in predicting the year astronauts will land on Mars.

# MANAGEMENT SCENARIOS AND DATA SETS

Scenario I presents quarterly units sold and advertising expenditures data for four years. You want to make sales forecasts for the next four quarters. Table 10.2 contains the time-ordered data.

Figure 10.2 is a line graph of the 16 quarters of data. Note the meandering pattern. That is, adjacent observations have values that are close to one another, but distant observations have very different values. The meandering pattern does *not* contain any systematic or repeating pattern.

Scenario II presents 20 quarters of sales data (in dollars) and advertising data. Again you want to make sales forecasts for the next four quarters. Table 10.3 contains the time-ordered data.

| Quarter | Sales in 000s Units | Adv in $000s |
|---------|---------------------|--------------|
| 1 | 340 | 110 |
| 2 | 200 | 140 |
| 3 | 190 | 330 |
| 4 | 320 | 540 |
| 5 | 480 | 150 |
| 6 | 375 | 360 |
| 7 | 413 | 370 |
| 8 | 410 | 580 |
| 9 | 561 | 190 |
| 10 | 405 | 400 |
| 11 | 590 | 410 |
| 12 | 501 | 620 |
| 13 | 603 | 250 |
| 14 | 576 | 440 |
| 15 | 508 | 450 |
| 16 | 529 | 460 |

**Table 10.2**
Meandering Data for
Scenario I

| Sales in 000s | Adv |
|---------------|-----|
| 68.59 | $155,000 |
| 120.97 | 135,000 |
| 142.30 | 90,000 |
| 109.74 | 100,000 |
| 104.64 | 165,000 |
| 165.40 | 185,000 |
| 182.20 | 100,000 |
| 128.85 | 140,000 |
| 135.27 | 235,000 |
| 192.84 | 190,000 |
| 191.03 | 180,000 |
| 152.93 | 130,000 |
| 132.29 | 210,000 |
| 206.17 | 210,000 |
| 204.98 | 140,000 |
| 131.79 | 150,000 |
| 126.89 | 195,000 |
| 194.47 | 215,000 |
| 208.39 | 190,000 |
| 151.75 | 175,000 |

**Table 10.3**
Seasonal Data for
Scenario II

Figure 10.1 is a line graph of the 20 quarters of data. Note the seasonal pattern. That is, the data exhibit a repeating pattern on a regular basis. The length of the seasonal pattern is one year.

Determining visually whether a pattern is seasonal or meandering is some-times difficult. When in doubt, apply all the forecasting tools in Table 10.1 to the data to determine which forecasting method is most accurate.

# FORECASTING MEANDERING PATTERNS

In this section we examine how to use trend analysis and regression analysis to assess a meandering pattern and to make short-term forecasts. Use trend analysis when your only goal is to detect the underlying pattern in the data. Use regression analysis when your goal is to determine those predictor vari-ables that affect, or are related to, the dependent variable. Remember that both methods assume that the pattern or relationship found in the historical data will continue throughout the forecasting period. By the end of this unit you should be able to

1.  use Excel's Add Trendline tool to determine the best-fitting linear or nonlinear line to represent the meandering pattern; and

2.  compute and interpret the mean absolute percentage error (MAPE).

## TREND ANALYSIS

Begin a trend analysis by applying Excel's Trendline tool to the data.[1] The trendline tool generates the best-fitting linear line or best-fitting logarith-mic, polynomial, power, and exponential curves to the data. Recall from Chapter 9, the best-fitting linear line minimizes the sum of the squared deviations between the actual values of $y$ and the values of $y$ based on the linear equation, $\hat{y} = b_0 + b_1 \cdot x_1$. Similarly the Trendline tool obtains the sample regression coefficients for the other four classes, or types, of curves.

Figures 10.3–10.7 display the best-fitting lines for each of the five classes of curves. Included in each figure is the model's $R^2$ value, the coefficient of determination first learned in Chapter 9. Recall that it measures the amount of variation in the dependent variable (units sold) accounted for by the predictor variable (time).

---

[1] See Appendix II for instructions on how to use the Trendline tool.

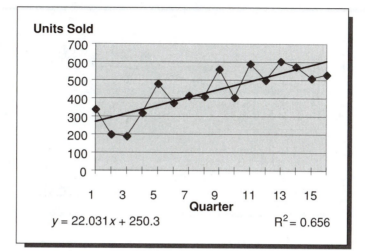

$y = 22.031x + 250.3$     $R^2 = 0.656$

**Figure 10.3**
Best-Fitting Linear Line
for 16 Quarters of
Sales Data

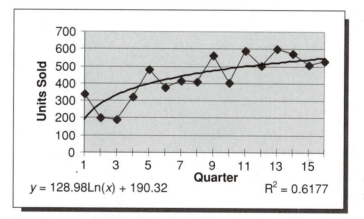

$y = 128.98\text{Ln}(x) + 190.32$     $R^2 = 0.6177$

**Figure 10.4**
Best-Fitting Logarithmic
Curve for 16 Quarters of
Sales Data

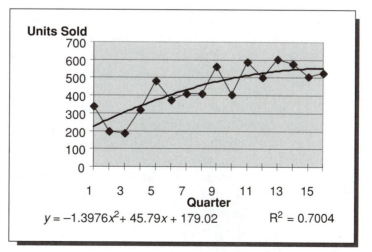

$y = -1.3976x^2 + 45.79x + 179.02$     $R^2 = 0.7004$

**Figure 10.5**
Best-Fitting Polynomial
of Order 2 Curve for 16
Quarters of Sales Data

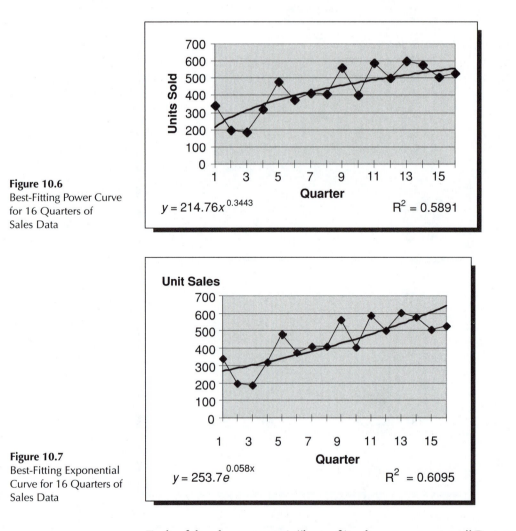

**Figure 10.6**
Best-Fitting Power Curve
for 16 Quarters of
Sales Data

$y = 214.76x^{0.3443}$    $R^2 = 0.5891$

**Figure 10.7**
Best-Fitting Exponential
Curve for 16 Quarters of
Sales Data

$y = 253.7e^{0.058x}$    $R^2 = 0.6095$

Each of the above curves is "best of its class, or curve, type." Best means that the model generated by the least squares equations has the highest possible $R^2$ value for its class.[2] For example, the linear model shown in Figure 10.3 is the best linear model in that any other linear model would have generated a lower $R^2$ value.

Which of the five models is "best of the best"? That is, which of the five curves should you use for making sales forecasts for the next four quarters? One criterion is to select the curve with the highest $R^2$.

Unfortunately, the $R^2$ values for all five curves are quite similar; they range from 59% to 70%. One or two curves do not emerge as the clear winners. Each curve type fits the historical data reasonably well (a perfect fit would have an $R^2$ of 1.00). However, Table 10.4 reveals that the five curves generate very different forecasts for quarters 17–20. Excel's Add Trendline tool generated the five equations in Table 10.4.

---

[2] Or the smallest standard error of the estimate for its curve type.

| Quarter | Log 190.32+128.98ln(X) | Polynomial 179.02+45.79X-1.3976X^2 | Linear 250.30+22.031X | Power 214.76X^.3443 | Exponential 253.7e^.058X |
|---------|------|------------|--------|-------|-------------|
| 17 | 555.75 | 553.54 | 624.83 | 569.64 | 680.04 |
| 18 | 563.12 | 550.42 | 646.86 | 580.96 | 720.65 |
| 19 | 570.09 | 544.50 | 668.89 | 591.87 | 763.68 |
| 20 | 576.71 | 535.78 | 690.92 | 602.42 | 809.29 |

**Table 10.4**
A Comparison of Forecasts for the Five "Best of the Best" Curves

Even when the first criterion suggests a single best curve, consider the following second criterion. Select that curve that has the smallest error over the most recent several quarters. The rationale is simple. Whatever curve has been most accurate in the *immediate* past will probably be most accurate into the near future. The second criterion calls for computing the **mean absolute percentage error (MAPE)**.

## Mean Absolute Percentage Error

The mean absolute percentage error is a commonly used measure of forecast accuracy. Here we use it to assess which of the five curves generated the most accurate "backcasts" for the most recent four quarters of data.[3]

Table 10.5 contains the data for calculating the MAPE for the linear model. Column 2 contains the actual units sold data for the last four quarters, quarters 13–16. Column 3 contains the predicted units sold based on the linear equation,

$$\hat{y}_{\text{LINEAR}} = 250.30 + 22.031\text{QUARTER}$$

Column 4 contains the residuals or deviations between the actual units sold and the predicted sales from the linear regression model. Column 5 contains the absolute percentage errors based on Expression (10.1). We computed the MAPE using Expression (10.2).

$$\text{APE}_i = \frac{|\text{Actual}_i - \text{Predicted}_i|}{\text{Actual}_i} \times 100$$

$$\text{APE}_i = \frac{|\text{Residual}_i|}{\text{Actual}_i} \times 100$$

**(10.1)**

where $\text{APE}_i$ is the absolute percentage error for time period $i$, $\text{Actual}_i$ is the actual value of the dependent variable for time period $i$, and $\text{Predicted}_i$ is

---

[3] We use the term "backcast" when referring to making forecasts for time periods that have already occurred. We can also compute the MAPE over all the time periods—16.

the predicted value of the dependent variable based on the model for time period $i$

$$MAPE = \frac{\sum_i APE_i}{n}$$

(10.2)

where $n$ is the number of time periods for which you have calculated the absolute percentage error

| Quarter (X) | Actual | Predicted from 250.30+22.031X | Residual | APE |
|---|---|---|---|---|
| 13 | 603 | 536.70 | 66.30 | 10.995 |
| 14 | 576 | 558.73 | 17.27 | 2.998 |
| 15 | 508 | 580.77 | -72.77 | 14.324 |
| 16 | 529 | 602.80 | -73.80 | 13.950 |
| | | | | |
| | | | | 10.567 |

**Table 10.5**
MAPE Calculation for the Linear Trend Line

Over the most recent four quarters, on average, the predicted units sold based on the linear model differed from the actual units sold by 10.57%.

Table 10.6 displays the MAPEs for the five "best of each class" curves.

**Table 10.6**
MAPE for "Best of Each Class" Type

| | Linear | Logarithmic | Polynomial | Power | Exponential |
|---|---|---|---|---|---|
| MAPE | 10.57% | 7.81% | 7.30% | 8.56% | 12.97% |

In conclusion, based on the second criterion—the minimum MAPE—either the logarithmic or polynomial model is the best of the best.

When the first two criteria do not yield a single "best of the best" model (as in this instance), use one of three approaches:

1. Select that model that is easiest to explain to others (the linear model if it is a contender).

2. Base your forecasts on the average of the two or more remaining models' forecasts.

3. Select the model for which you can provide the strongest support based on your knowledge and intuition.

The firm chose the logarithmic model for two reasons. First, its MAPE was the second smallest value for the five curves. Second, the firm rejected the polynomial model because it indicated that units sold had peaked and was heading down (see Table 10.4). That was inconsistent with the firm's intuition about the marketplace.

Before the firm uses the logarithmic model for forecasting, it should conduct a residual analysis to determine if the model satisfies the underlying assumptions.

In Chapter 9 you tested the model for normality, homogeneity of variance, and outliers. Whenever you have time-ordered data you must also plot the residual values against time.

Table 10.7 contains the 16 *residual values* for the logarithmic model. The residual plot for a model that satisfies the statistical independence assumption should be a horizontal band of residuals centered at zero that contain no pattern. Figure 10.8 suggests there is *no* pattern to the residuals over time. The firm can use the model for short-term forecasting. See column labeled "Log" in Table 10.4 for the forecast for the next four quarters.

**Table 10.7**
Residuals for Logarithmic Curve for 16 Quarters of Data

| Quarter | Actual | Predicted from Log Model | Residual |
|---|---|---|---|
| 1 | 340 | 190.32 | 149.68 |
| 2 | 200 | 279.72 | -79.72 |
| 3 | 190 | 332.02 | -142.02 |
| 4 | 320 | 369.12 | -49.12 |
| 5 | 480 | 397.91 | 82.09 |
| 6 | 375 | 421.42 | -46.42 |
| 7 | 413 | 441.30 | -28.30 |
| 8 | 410 | 458.53 | -48.53 |
| 9 | 561 | 473.72 | 87.28 |
| 10 | 405 | 487.31 | -82.31 |
| 11 | 590 | 499.60 | 90.40 |
| 12 | 501 | 510.82 | -9.82 |
| 13 | 603 | 521.15 | 81.85 |
| 14 | 576 | 530.71 | 45.29 |
| 15 | 508 | 539.60 | -31.60 |
| 16 | 529 | 547.93 | -18.93 |

Sometimes you will find one or more long strings of positive or negative residuals (five or more residuals) in the residual plot against time. When this occurs, the data are probably **autocorrelated.**

D E F I N I T I O N        Data are **autocorrelated** when a data value in one time period depends on the data values from one or more earlier time periods.

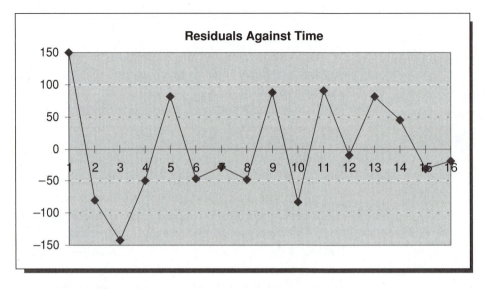

**Figure 10.8**
Plot of Residuals
against Quarters

This is a violation of the statistical independence assumption. When this violation occurs, we recommend shifting from the pattern-detection method of trend analysis to a relationship-detection tool called autoregressive modeling.

In summary, trend analysis requires determining the best-fitting linear line or best-fitting logarithmic, polynomial, power, and exponential curves. Use three criteria to determine which model to use for your short-term forecasts.

Criterion 1    Select the model(s) with the highest $R^2$ value.

Criterion 2    Select the model(s) with the lowest MAPE for the most recent time periods.

Criterion 3    Select the model that either is easiest to explain to others or use judgment or intuition. Alternatively, select the two or more most accurate models based on MAPE and develop a combination forecast.

Finally, before using any model for forecasting, compute the model's residuals and develop a residual plot against time. If the residual plot contains one or more long strings of positive or negative residuals, you should not use the trend analysis model for forecasting. Rather, consider developing an autoregressive model. That is our next topic.

## AUTOREGRESSIVE MODELING FOR MEANDERING PATTERNS

In Chapter 9 we used predictor variables to forecast the dependent variable for cross-sectional data. Recall that cross-sectional data are collected at one time period. This section extends regression analysis to time-ordered data.

By the end of this unit you should be able to

**1.** suggest when an autoregressive model, AR (1) or AR (2), should be considered;

**2.** generate, evaluate, and interpret an AR (1) or AR (2) model; and

**3.** include one or more coincident or lagging predictor variables into a forecasting model.

Regression analysis requires that you seek one or more predictor variables that explain the variation in units sold in Table 10.2. Because successive observations are close to one another, an obvious first choice for a predictor variable is units sold from the previous quarter. Should the forecast of units sold in one quarter be based, at least in part, on the units sold from one or more previous quarters? Is there a statistically significant relationship between units sold at time $t$, SALES $t$, and units sold at time $t - 1$, SALES $t - 1$ (or $t - 2$, $t - 3$)?

We answer this question by creating a new predictor variable, SALES $t - 1$ that is the value of units sold at time period $t - 1$. To determine whether there is a relationship between SALES $t$, and SALES $t - 1$, let's begin by drawing a scatter plot. Place SALES $t$, the dependent variable, on the vertical axis, and SALES $t - 1$, the predictor variable, on the horizontal axis.

Table 10.8 contains the data for the scatter plot. Note that the quarter $t = 2$ row contains SALES $t = 2$, which is 200, and SALES $2 - 1$, which is 340. The other 14 data values for the SALES $t - 1$ column are similarly obtained.

Figure 10.9 is the scatter plot of units sold for a period versus units sold for the previous period for quarters 2–16. The swarm of the 15 data points is upward sloping to the right. That suggests that SALES $t$ and SALES $t - 1$ are *positively* and *linearly* related. That is, if units sold in one quarter are low (high), units sold in the following quarter will also be low (high). While the correlation is positive, it is not, however, perfect. All the data values do not lie on a straight line. But the data are **positively autocorrelated** with a lag of one.

The term autocorrelation denotes a correlation between values of a variable and preceding values of the *same* variable. *Auto* means self or same.

---

**D E F I N I T I O N**    Autocorrelation of lag "$k$" denotes the correlation between values of a dependent variable at time period $t$ and values of the dependent variable at period $t - k$. The autocorrelation coefficient can vary from +1 to –1. If the data are either strongly positively or negatively autocorrelated, you should build an autoregressive model.

| Quarter | SALES t-1 | SALES t |
|---------|-----------|---------|
| 1 | NA | 340 |
| 2 | 340 | 200 |
| 3 | 200 | 190 |
| 4 | 190 | 320 |
| 5 | 320 | 480 |
| 6 | 480 | 375 |
| 7 | 375 | 413 |
| 8 | 413 | 410 |
| 9 | 410 | 561 |
| 10 | 561 | 405 |
| 11 | 405 | 590 |
| 12 | 590 | 501 |
| 13 | 501 | 603 |
| 14 | 603 | 576 |
| 15 | 576 | 508 |
| 16 | 508 | 529 |

**Table 10.8**
Table of Sales Data for Period $t$ versus Sales Data for Period $t-1$

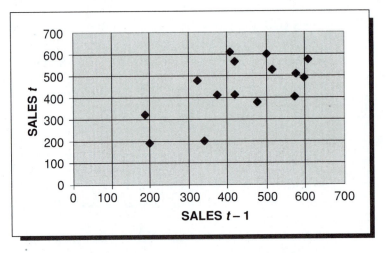

**Figure 10.9**
Scatter Plot of SALES $t-1$ versus SALES $t$

## Autoregressive Models, AR (1)

Can you use units sold in one quarter to forecast units sold in the next quarter? To find out, we use Excel's data–analysis regression tool to fit a linear regression model to the data in Table 10.8 for quarters 2–16. Expression (10.3) is an *autoregressive model with one-period lagged data, an AR (1) model.*

$$\hat{y}_t = 171.763 + 0.6311 \cdot \text{SALES } t - 1$$

(10.3)

where $\hat{y}_t$ is the predicted sales level for period $t$

From Expression (10.3), units sold in any quarter are equal to 171.763 plus 63.11% of the units sold the quarter before.

From the ANOVA table (not shown), the $p$-value for the model is 0.011. The residual plot against time does not exhibit any long strings of positive or negative residuals. Thus we can use Expression (10.3) to forecast units sold for the first quarter of the upcoming year, quarter 17. We use the actual units sold for quarter 16, 529.

$$\hat{y}_{17} = 171.763 + \left(0.6311 \cdot 529\right)$$
$$\hat{y}_{17} = 505.61$$

Compare this forecast of 505.61 to the logarithmic model's forecast from the trend analysis. From Table 10.4, the forecast for quarter 17 for the logarithmic model is 555.75.

You can use Expression (10.3) to forecast more than one quarter into the future. For example, to forecast quarter 18, you insert the *forecasted* SALES 18 − 1, or SALES 17, value into Expression (10.3).

$$\hat{y}_{18} = 171.763 + \left(0.6311 \cdot 505.61\right)$$
$$\hat{y}_{18} = 490.85$$

The greater the number of periods you forecast into the future with an autoregressive model, the greater is the likely forecast error. You based your forecast for quarter 18 on a *forecast* from quarter 17. This is risky.

If you believe that units sold in period $t$ also affect units sold two quarters later, you should develop an AR (2) model. This model would include a $t − 1$ and $t − 2$ term.

Could we develop a more accurate forecast by bringing an additional predictor variable such as amount of advertising into Expression (10.3)? From Excel's data-analysis regression tool, the simple coefficient of determination, $R^2$, is only 40% for the AR (1) model, Expression (10.3). Since that is relatively low, we should seek additional predictor variables.

## Leading and Coincident Predictor Variables

Let's try to improve the forecasting accuracy of Expression (10.3) by adding a new predictor variable—amount of advertising. We have also included one-period lagged values of advertising—ADV $t − 1$, in Table 10.9. Note that the database contains units sold and the three-predictor variables for quarters 2–16, not quarters 1–16. This is due to the inclusion of the SALES $t − 1$ and ADV $t − 1$ predictor variables.

ADV $t$ is a **coincident** predictor variable. We believe that advertising in time period $t$ affects units sold in the same time period. ADV $t-1$ is a **leading** (by one period) predictor variable. We believe that advertising in time period $t$ affects units sold one time period later.

Table 10.10 contains the output from Excel's data-analysis regression tool. The overall model with all three predictor variables has a $p$-value of 0.000156. Adding the ADV $t$ and ADV $t-1$ predictor variables increased the $R^2$ value, coefficient of multiple determination, from 40.4% to 82.9%.

However, recall from Chapter 9 that when your goal is prediction (as in forecasting) you should use the t Stat screening procedure to reduce the standard error of the estimate. To determine if you can reduce the standard error of the estimate, examine the t Stat values from the regression data-analysis tool.

$\longleftarrow$ Predictor Variables $\longrightarrow$

| Quarter | SALES t-1 | ADV t | ADV t-1 | SALES t |
|---|---|---|---|---|
| 2 | 340 | 140 | 110 | 200 |
| 3 | 200 | 330 | 140 | 190 |
| 4 | 190 | 540 | 330 | 320 |
| 5 | 320 | 150 | 540 | 480 |
| 6 | 480 | 360 | 150 | 375 |
| 7 | 375 | 370 | 360 | 413 |
| 8 | 413 | 580 | 370 | 410 |
| 9 | 410 | 190 | 580 | 561 |
| 10 | 561 | 400 | 190 | 405 |
| 11 | 405 | 410 | 400 | 590 |
| 12 | 590 | 620 | 410 | 501 |
| 13 | 501 | 250 | 620 | 603 |
| 14 | 603 | 440 | 250 | 576 |
| 15 | 576 | 450 | 440 | 508 |
| 16 | 508 | 460 | 450 | 529 |

**Table 10.9**
Quarterly Units Sold and Three Predictior Variables

| Regression Statistics | | | | | |
|---|---|---|---|---|---|
| Multiple R | 0.9106464 | | | | |
| R Square | 0.8292769 | | | | |
| Adjusted R Square | 0.7827161 | | | | |
| Standard Error | 61.209811 | | | | |
| Observations | 15 | | | | |
| | | | | | |
| ANOVA | | | | | |
| | df | SS | MS | F | Significance F |
| Regression | 3 | 2E+05 | 66730 | 17.81061 | 0.000156408 |
| Residual | 11 | 41213 | 3746.64 | | |
| Total | 14 | 2E+05 | | | |

**Table 10.10**
ANOVA and Accompanying Regression Statistics

Shown again are the steps to the t Stat screening procedure to reduce the standard error of the estimate.

**1.** Take the absolute value of the t Stat values found in the parameter estimate section of the Excel-generated output. Ignore the intercept row of the table.

|  | Coefficients | Standard Error | t Stat |
|---|---|---|---|
| ~~Intercept~~ | ~~19.5524646~~ | ~~70.15084042~~ | ~~0.279~~ |
| SALES t-1 | 0.51540686 | 0.132240663 | 3.897 |
| ADV t | 0.02303883 | 0.116635308 | 0.198 |
| ADV t-1 | 0.54324136 | 0.103884002 | 5.229 |

**2.** Delete the predictor variable with the lowest absolute t Stat value provided it is less than 1.0. The predictor variable with the lowest absolute t Stat value is ADV $t$, $|$ t Stat $| = 0.198$.

**3.** Delete the column containing the ADV $t$ variable. Use the regression data-analysis tool to reestimate the model with the remaining two predictor variables. Repeat steps 2 and 3, one predictor variable at a time, until all the remaining predictor variables have $|$ t Stat $| \geq 1$.

After deleting the ADV $t$ predictor variable and rerunning the data-analysis regression tool, the two remaining predictor variables both had absolute t Stat values greater than one. The $p$-value for the second model with the SALES $t - 1$ and ADV $t - 1$ predictor variables was 0.000025. Expression (10.4) is the estimated regression model.

$$\hat{y}_t = 25.8784 + 0.52337 \cdot \text{SALES } t - 1 + 0.54037 \cdot \text{ADV } t - 1$$

**(10.4)**

Expression (10.4) forecasts units sold for quarter 17 as follows:

$$\hat{y}_{17} = 25.8784 + 0.52337 \cdot \text{SALES } 17 - 1 + 0.54037 \cdot \text{ADV } 17 - 1$$

$$\hat{y}_{17} = 25.8784 + \left(0.52337 \cdot 529\right) + \left(0.54037 \cdot 460\right)$$

$$\hat{y}_{17} = 551.31$$

Before using Expression (10.4) we must examine the three residual plots (not shown here). The residual plot against SALES $t - 1$ and the residual plot against ADV $t - 1$ do not display long strings of either positive or negative residuals.

The residual analysis concludes with an examination of the normality assumption and looking for possible outliers. Table 10.11 displays the requirements to meet the normality assumption. It suggests that the model satisfied the normality assumption.

**Table 10.11**
Percentages of Standardized Residuals from Data-Analysis Tool

| Range of Standardized Residuals | Expected Percentage | Actual Percentage |
|---|---|---|
| –1 to +1 | 68% | 11/15 = 73% |
| –2 to +2 | 95% | 14/15 = 93% |
| –3 to +3 | 100% | 15/15 = 100% |

Finally, the standardized residuals reveal no outliers. In summary, the model satisfied all the assumptions underlying regression analysis. We can use Expression (10.4) for making one-quarter-ahead forecasts.

Since a major goal of using regression models for forecasting is to understand what predictor variables affect the dependent variable, you should assess multicollinearity. Table 10.12 displays the correlation matrix obtained from Excel's correlation data-analysis tool.

**Table 10.12**
Correlation Matrix for Model (10.4)

|  | SALES t-1 | ADV t-1 | SALES t |
|---|---|---|---|
| SALES t-1 | 1 |  |  |
| ADV t-1 | 0.16284 | 1 |  |
| SALES t | 0.632724 | 0.748768 | 1 |

Table 10.12 indicates that multicollinearity is not a problem because the correlation coefficient between the ADV $t - 1$ and SALES $t - 1$ predictor variables is only 0.16284. This is less than the correlations between the dependent variable, SALES $t$, and the two predictor variables.

The lack of multicollinearity is not a surprising finding. Note that the signs of the two sample regression coefficients in Model (10.4) were positive as theory and logic would suggest. That suggested that multicollinearity would not be a serious problem, and Table 10.12 corroborated that belief.

## SUMMARY

Table 10.13 contains the forecasts from three different models. Trend analysis generated one model, while regression analysis generated the other two models.

So which model should you use? It depends on whether your goal is only to forecast or to forecast *and* obtain insights into which predictor variables affect the dependent variable. Trend analysis can generate accurate forecasts; regression analysis can generate accurate forecasts and provide insights into "what affects what."

| Quarter | Log $190.32+128.98\ln(x)$ | AR(1) $171.763+.6311\text{SALES } t\text{-}1$ | AR(1) and Predictor Variable $25.87+.52\text{SALES } t\text{-}1 +.54\text{ADV } t\text{-}1$ |
|---|---|---|---|
| 17 | 555.75 | 505.62 | 554.31 |

**Table 10.13**
Forecasts for Quarter 17 from Three Different Models

Trend analysis and regression analysis use different approaches to determine the best model. In trend analysis, use the three criteria for selecting the best model. In regression analysis, use the ANOVA and the absolute t Stat screening procedure to determine the best model. Finally, for models with two or more predictor variables, assess the degree of muticollinearity. If severe, consult a professional statistician.

# FORECASTING SEASONAL PATTERNS

In this section we examine how to use (1) the classical decomposition method or (2) regression analysis to assess a seasonal and trend pattern and to make short-term forecasts. Use the decomposition method when your only goal is to detect the underlying patterns in the data. Use regression analysis when your goal is to determine those predictor variables that affect, or are related to, the dependent variable. Remember that both methods assume that the patterns or relationships found in the historical data will continue throughout the forecasting period. By the end of this unit you should be able to

1. compute and explain a centered moving average, raw seasonal indices, and typical seasonal indices;

2. explain the differences among a seasonal pattern, no detectable seasonal pattern, and no seasonal pattern;

3. derive and explain deseasonalized data;

4. decide which trend expression to use for forecasting; and

5. use the classical decomposition method to make short-term forecasts.

## THE CLASSICAL DECOMPOSITION METHOD

The classical decomposition method assumes that actual values of the dependent variable, $y$, are a multiplicative function of four components: (1) trend, (2) seasonal, (3) cycle, and (4) random fluctuation.

| |
|---|
| Actual data values = Trend $\times$ Seasonal $\times$ Cycle $\times$ Random fluctuation |

**(10.5)**

Expression (10.5) says that we multiply the values of the trend, seasonal, cyclical, and random fluctuation components to obtain the value of the forecasted variable, $Y$.

At most, forecasters can identify three of the four components in Expression (10.5).[4] Random fluctuation does not exhibit any systematic pattern and thus cannot be determined. Random fluctuation means that the data values are unpredictable.

We apply the classical decomposition method to the data in Table 10.3 that are displayed in Figure 10.1. The graph suggests a distinct upward trend and seasonal pattern with a one-year length. We begin by attempting to identify the **seasonal pattern.**

## The Seasonal Pattern

We use the **ratio to moving average** method to determine the seasonal component. Using the historical sales data, we compute a moving average that has the same length as the seasonal component in the data. For one-year seasonal patterns, the length of the moving average should be four quarters = one year (for quarterly data) or 12 months = one year (for monthly data).[5]

In Chapter 2 we first constructed moving averages. To compute a moving average of length four quarters (MA 4), take the first four values of the data set, add them, and compute the mean. The first moving average value is

$$\text{First moving average value} = \frac{68.59 + 120.97 + 142.30 + 109.74}{4} = 110.40$$

The firm sold 68.59 units as of the end of quarter 1, (the 90th day); 120.97 units as of the end of quarter 2 (the 180th day); 142.30 units as of the 270th day of the year; and 109.74 units as of the 360th day of the year. The mean of these four calendar dates is the 225th day of the year [(90 + 180 + 270 + 360)/4]. Thus, the moving average value of 110.40 units sold is the mean sales as of the 225th day of the year, August 15. See the first entry under MA 4 in Table 10.14.

To compute the second moving average value, delete the first data value from the MA 4 and add the fifth data value. Add the four terms and compute the mean.

$$\text{Second moving average value} = \frac{120.97 + 142.30 + 109.74 + 104.64}{4} = 119.41$$

The moving average value of 119.41 is the mean units sold as of the 315th day, November 15. This is the mean sales as of the 180th, 270th, 360th, and

---

[4]We will not attempt to identify the cyclical component, as it is difficult to forecast.

[5]The spreadsheet for calculating the ratio to moving average is in the chapter's appendix.

450th days. See the second entry in Table 10.14 in the MA 4 column. We computed the other 15 moving averages of length four in the same way; we deleted the first of the four values and added the next data value and then divided by four.

| Quarter | SALES $t$ | MA4 | Centered |
|---|---|---|---|
| 1 (90th day) | 68.59 | | Notice how original data and centered |
| 2 (180th day) | 120.97 | | moving average for quarter 3 "line up." |
| 225th | ← ————— | 110.40 | |
| 3 (270th day) | 142.30 | | 114.91 |
| 315th | ← ————— | 119.41 | |
| 4 (360th day) | 109.74 | | 124.97 |
| | | 130.52 | |
| 5 | 104.64 | | 135.51 |
| | | 140.50 | |
| 6 | 165.40 | | 142.89 |
| | | 145.28 | |
| 7 | 182.20 | | 149.11 |
| | | 152.94 | |
| 8 | 128.85 | | 156.37 |
| | | 159.80 | |
| 9 | 135.27 | | 160.90 |
| | | 162.01 | |
| 10 | 192.84 | | 165.01 |
| | | 168.02 | |
| 11 | 191.03 | | 167.65 |
| | | 167.27 | |
| 12 | 152.93 | | 168.94 |
| | | 170.61 | |
| 13 | 132.29 | | 172.35 |
| | | 174.09 | |
| 14 | 206.17 | | 171.45 |
| | | 168.81 | |
| 15 | 204.98 | | 168.13 |
| | | 167.46 | |
| 16 | 131.79 | | 166.00 |
| | | 164.53 | |
| 17 | 126.89 | | 164.96 |
| | | 165.39 | |
| 18 | 194.47 | | 167.88 |
| | | 170.38 | |
| 19 | 208.39 | | |
| 20 | 151.75 | | |

**Table 10.14**
Calculating an MA 4 and a Centered MA

Of the original four components in Expression (10.5), the moving average values in Column 3 of Table 10.14 contain only the T(rend) × C(ycle) components; we have eliminated the seasonal and random components.

Here's why. Figure 10.10 shows clearly that the MA 4 does not contain a seasonal component. The MA 4 also does not contain the random fluctuation component due to computing the means, or averaging.

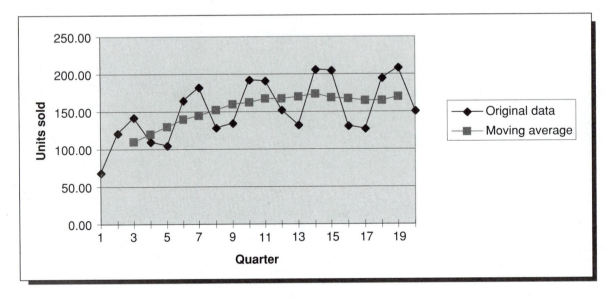

**Figure 10.10**
Original Units Sold and MA 4

Recall that our goal is to isolate (or identify) the seasonal component. Expression (10.6) indicates that we must divide the actual data (column 2) that contains all four components by the moving average that contains only the trend and cyclical components. The resulting values are the *raw seasonal indices* that contain only two components, seasonal and random fluctuation.

$$\text{Raw Seasonal Indices} = \frac{\textbf{Original Data}}{\textbf{Moving Average}} = \frac{T \times S \times C \times RF}{T \times C} = S \times RF \qquad \textbf{(10.6)}$$

where T represents Trend, S represents Seasonal, C represents Cycle, and RF represents Random Fluctuation

Expression (10.6) says to divide the original time series data values by the moving average values. Now a problem arises. The original data are quarterly units sold as of the 90th day, 180th day, 270th day, and 360th day of each year. But the moving average values are based on different calendar dates. For example, we cannot divide 142.30 (the 270th day) by 110.40 (the 225th day). However, by **centering** the moving average we can *line up* the moving average and original time series values. Only then is division meaningful.

Here is how to compute the **centered MA 4**. We compute the mean of the first two moving averages of Table 10.14. The first value of the centered moving average is (110.40 + 119.41)/2, or 114.90. We place this value halfway between the 225th day and the 315th day—that is, September 30th or the 270th day. Now the first value of the centered moving average *lines up* with the September 30th calendar date of the original time series. See Table 10.14. The second value of the centered moving average is (119.41 + 130.52)/2, or 124.97. After centering the moving average, notice how all the values of the centered moving average line up with the data in the original data set, SALES *t*. Now we can divide the two time series as per Expression (10.6).

***Raw Seasonal Indices.*** Raw seasonal indices measure the level of activity of a specific period (day, quarter, or month) compared to the average activity for that year. From Expression (10.6), the raw seasonal indices include the seasonal component and the random fluctuation component—S × RF. For the data in Table 10.15, the raw seasonal index for quarter 3 of year 1 is the actual time series data for quarter 3 (column 2) divided by the centered moving average for quarter 3 (column 4):

$$\text{Raw seasonal index for year 1 quarter 3} = \frac{142.30}{114.91} = 1.2384$$

How do we interpret the raw seasonal index for year 1, quarter 3? The actual units sold was 23.8% higher than the centered moving average for the same quarter. In other words, the seasonal and random fluctuation components account for a 23.8% increase in sales. *If* the random fluctuation component is small (and we determine this next), the seasonal pattern explains most of the 23.8% increase. Simply put, units sold was strong in the third quarter of year 1—about 23.8% above the centered moving average.

The raw seasonal index for quarter 4 of year 1 is 0.8782. Actual units sold were only 87.8% of the centered moving average. In short, quarter 4 was a weak sales period—below-average sales.

Table 10.15 contains the 16 raw seasonal index calculations. Note that the raw seasonal indices for the four quarters over the five years are as follows:

First quarter     quarters 5, 9, 13, 17     (cannot compute for quarter 1)

Second quarter    quarters 6, 10, 14, 18    (cannot compute for quarter 2)

Third quarter     quarters 3, 7, 11, 15     (cannot compute for quarter 19)

Fourth quarter    quarters 4, 8, 12, 16     (cannot compute for quarter 20)

From Table 10.15, you can see that it is not possible to compute raw seasonal indices for the first two quarters of year 1 and the last two quarters of year 5. When determining raw seasonal indices using the ratio to the moving average method, you always lose the ability to compute either four quarters or 12 months of raw seasonal indices.

| Quarter | SALES *t* | MA4 | Centered | Raw Seasonal | |
|---------|-----------|------|----------|--------------|---|
| 1 | 68.59 | | | | |
| 2 | 120.97 | | | | |
| | | 110.40 | | | Raw seasonal index |
| 3 | 142.30 | | 114.91 | 1.2384 | for quarter 3 of year |
| | | 119.41 | | | 1 = 142.30/114.90 |
| 4 | 109.74 | | 124.97 | 0.8782 | |
| | | 130.52 | | | Raw seasonal index |
| 5 | 104.64 | | 135.51 | 0.7722 | for quarter 1 of year |
| | | 140.49 | | | 2 = 104.64/135.51 |
| 6 | 165.40 | | 142.89 | 1.1576 | |
| | | 145.27 | | | |
| 7 | 182.20 | | 149.11 | 1.2219 | |
| | | 152.93 | | | |
| 8 | 128.85 | | 156.37 | 0.8242 | |
| | | 159.79 | | | |
| 9 | 135.27 | | 160.90 | 0.8407 | |
| | | 162.00 | | | |
| 10 | 192.84 | | 165.01 | 1.1686 | |
| | | 168.02 | | | |
| 11 | 191.03 | | 167.65 | 1.1395 | |
| | | 167.27 | | | |
| 12 | 152.93 | | 168.94 | 0.9052 | |
| | | 170.61 | | | |
| 13 | 132.29 | | 172.35 | 0.7676 | |
| | | 174.09 | | | |
| 14 | 206.17 | | 171.45 | 1.2025 | |
| | | 168.81 | | | |
| 15 | 204.98 | | 168.13 | 1.2192 | |
| | | 167.46 | | | |
| 16 | 131.79 | | 166.00 | 0.7939 | |
| | | 164.54 | | | |
| 17 | 126.89 | | 164.96 | 0.7692 | |
| | | 165.39 | | | |
| 18 | 194.47 | | 167.88 | 1.1584 | |
| | | 170.38 | | | |
| 19 | 208.39 | | | | |
| 20 | 151.75 | | | | |

**Table 10.15**
Calculating the Raw Seasonal Indices—S and RF Components

The format of Table 10.15 makes it difficult to see if there is a seasonal pattern. We transferred the raw seasonal indices of Table 10.15 into Table 10.16—a *year-by-quarter* table. Note that the first entry in Table 10.16 is for quarter 3 of year 1.

**Table 10.16**
Year-by-Quarter Table of Raw Seasonal Indices

| Year | Quarter 1 | Quarter 2 | Quarter 3 | Quarter 4 |
|------|-----------|-----------|-----------|-----------|
| 1 | Cannot determine | | 1.2384 | 0.8782 |
| 2 | 0.7722 | 1.1576 | 1.2220 | 0.8241 |
| 3 | 0.8407 | 1.1687 | 1.1395 | 0.9052 |
| 4 | 0.7676 | 1.2025 | 1.2192 | 0.7939 |
| 5 | 0.7692 | 1.1584 | Cannot determine | |

Before completing the seasonal pattern analysis, compare the two sets of raw seasonal indices in Table 10.17 with the actual indices in Table 10.16. Which set exhibits a seasonal pattern, which set exhibits wide variation from quarter to quarter but no seasonal pattern, and which set exhibits no seasonal pattern at all? Please think about it before continuing.

Set A

| Year | Quarter 1 | Quarter 2 | Quarter 3 | Quarter 4 |
|------|-----------|-----------|-----------|-----------|
| 1 | Cannot determine | | 1.410 | 0.410 |
| 2 | 1.150 | 0.869 | 0.977 | 0.309 |
| 3 | 1.357 | 0.790 | 0.831 | 1.210 |
| 4 | 0.105 | 1.502 | 1.511 | 1.345 |
| 5 | 0.453 | 1.679 | Cannot determine | |

Set B

| Year | Quarter 1 | Quarter 2 | Quarter 3 | Quarter 4 |
|------|-----------|-----------|-----------|-----------|
| 1 | Cannot determine | | 1.000 | 0.999 |
| 2 | 1.007 | 0.990 | 1.001 | 1.002 |
| 3 | 0.999 | 1.002 | 0.999 | 0.999 |
| 4 | 1.000 | 0.999 | 1.000 | 1.000 |
| 5 | 0.999 | 1.003 | Cannot determine | |

**Table 10.17**
Two Additional Year-by-Quarter Tables of Raw Seasonal Indices

The raw seasonal indices in Table 10.16 exhibit a seasonal pattern. In each year, units sold are relatively low in the first and fourth quarters and relatively high in the second and third quarters. The pattern is stable and repeatable over the five years of data.

In contrast, Set A in Table 10.17 has much variability but no repeatable pattern—no detectable seasonal pattern. There is much variation within each quarter between years. But there is no stable pattern from year to year.

Set B suggests no seasonal pattern at all! All indices are close to 1.0 in each quarter. Set B is typical of staples such as bread sales. Unlike ice cream or jewelry sales, bread sales are not seasonal. Lack of variation within and between quarters over the five years indicates *no seasonal pattern*.

Let's return to Table 10.16 and quantify the seasonal pattern. From Expression (10.6), each number in Table 10.16 consists of two components—seasonal and random fluctuation. Now we must isolate the seasonal component by computing *typical seasonal indices*.

***Typical Seasonal Indices.*** Raw seasonal indices measure the level of activity of a *specific period* compared to the mean activity for that year. We speak of the raw seasonal index for the third quarter of year 1 or year 4. Typical seasonal indices measure the level of activity of a *typical period* compared to the mean activity for a typical year. We speak of a typical seasonal index for the third quarter or the first quarter. The raw seasonal indices contain the seasonal and random fluctuation components whereas the typical seasonal indices contain only the seasonal component.

To obtain the typical seasonal indices, we must eliminate random fluctuation from the raw seasonal indices. One way to do this is by computing *trimmed means*. Referring to Table 10.16, we eliminate the high and low raw seasonal indices for a quarter and then compute the mean of the remaining values. For example, to compute the trimmed mean for quarter 1, we eliminate the year 3 (the highest) and the year 4 (the lowest) first quarter raw seasonal indices. The trimmed mean is the mean of the remaining two indices, $(0.7722 + 0.7692)/2 = 0.7707$.[6] See Table 10.18 for the calculations for the typical seasonal indices for each quarter.

Here is the logic behind using the trimmed means. The differences among the raw seasonal indices for a given quarter over the five years are due to random fluctuation. By computing the trimmed means, we eliminate random fluctuation.

| Year | Quarter 1 | Quarter 2 | Quarter 3 | Quarter 4 | |
|---|---|---|---|---|---|
| 1 | Cannot determine | | 1.2384 | 0.8782 | |
| 2 | 0.7722 | 1.1576 | 1.2219 | 0.8242 | |
| 3 | 0.8407 | 1.1686 | 1.1395 | 0.9052 | |
| 4 | 0.7676 | 1.2025 | 1.2192 | 0.7939 | |
| 5 | 0.7692 | 1.1584 | Cannot determine | | |
| Trimmed means | 0.7707 | 1.1635 | 1.2206 | 0.8512 | 4.006 |
| Typical seasonal indices | **0.7695** | **1.1618** | **1.2187** | **0.8499** | **4.0000** |

**Table 10.18**
Typical Seasonal Indices Calculations

---

[6] We would compute trimmed means in the same way for monthly data.

We must adjust the trimmed means to obtain the typical seasonal indices. The sum of the four trimmed means in Table 10.18 should be 4.00 for the following reason. Units sold will be relatively strong in some quarters and the trimmed means will greater than 1. Units sold will be relatively weak in other quarters and the trimmed means will be less than 1. Strong quarters cancel out weak quarters and the mean of the four typical seasonal indices must be 1, or the sum must be 4.00. From Table 10.18, the sum of the four trimmed means is 4.006. The reason the sum is not 4 (or 12 for monthly data) is that we eliminated the lowest and highest raw seasonal indices within each quarter before computing the trimmed means. To make the adjustment, multiply each trimmed mean by 0.9985 (i.e., 4.000/4.006) to obtain the four typical seasonal indices.

▶ **WARNING**  *Do not* compute typical seasonal indices unless you have five or more years of quarterly or monthly data. First, in computing the typical seasonal indices you cannot determine the raw seasonal indices of the first two quarters of year 1 and the last two quarters of year 5 (see Table 10.18). Second, you discard two years of raw seasonal indices in computing the trimmed means. That leaves only two raw seasonal indices for each quarter (or month), which is barely enough to compute a meaningful typical seasonal index.

In summary, by using the ratio to moving average method we have identified the following seasonal component:

**1.** Typical Seasonal Index for Quarter 1  0.7695

**2.** Typical Seasonal Index for Quarter 2  1.1618

**3.** Typical Seasonal Index for Quarter 3  1.2187

**4.** Typical Seasonal Index for Quarter 4  0.8499

Having identified the seasonal component, let's turn our attention to identifying the trend (T) component.

### Deseasonalized Data

Before determining the trend pattern we *deseasonalize* the data by removing the seasonal pattern from the original time series values. Deseasonalized data are also known as seasonally adjusted data.

$$\text{Deseasonalized Data} = \frac{\textbf{Original Data}}{\textbf{Typical Seasonal Indices}} = \frac{T \times S \times C \times RF}{S} = \textbf{T} \times \textbf{C} \times \textbf{RF}$$

(10.7)

Expression (10.7) says to divide the original data values by the typical seasonal indices to obtain the deseasonalized data. From Table 10.19, the deseasonalized data value for quarter 1 is $68.59/0.7695 = 89.14$.

| Quarter | SALES $t$ | Typical Seasonal | Deseasonalized |
|---------|-----------|------------------|----------------|
| 1 | 68.59 | 0.7695 | 89.14 |
| 2 | 120.97 | 1.1618 | 104.12 |
| 3 | 142.30 | 1.2187 | 116.76 |
| 4 | 109.74 | 0.8499 | 129.12 |
| 5 | 104.64 | 0.7695 | 135.98 |
| 6 | 165.40 | 1.1618 | 142.37 |
| 7 | 182.20 | 1.2187 | 149.50 |
| 8 | 128.85 | 0.8499 | 151.64 |
| 9 | 135.27 | 0.7695 | 175.79 |
| 10 | 192.84 | 1.1618 | 165.98 |
| 11 | 191.03 | 1.2187 | 156.75 |
| 12 | 152.93 | 0.8499 | 179.94 |
| 13 | 132.29 | 0.7695 | 171.92 |
| 14 | 206.17 | 1.1618 | 177.46 |
| 15 | 204.98 | 1.2187 | 168.20 |
| 16 | 131.79 | 0.8499 | 155.07 |
| 17 | 126.89 | 0.7695 | 164.90 |
| 18 | 194.47 | 1.1618 | 167.39 |
| 19 | 208.39 | 1.2187 | 170.99 |
| 20 | 151.75 | 0.8499 | 178.55 |

**Table 10.19**
Deseasonalized, or
Seasonally Adjusted, Data

In Figure 10.11, the graph of the deseasonalized data is *smoother* than that of the original data because the deseasonalized data do not contain the seasonal pattern. In fact, the trend pattern literally jumps out at us from the deseasonalized data.[7] We will do the trend analysis next and quantify the observed trend pattern.

▶ **WARNING**   *Do not* deseasonalize the data if there is no stable seasonal pattern (see Table 10.17, Set A) or if there is no seasonal pattern at all (see Table 10.17, Set B). Deseasonalizing does not make sense when there is no seasonal pattern. Instead of using deseasonalized data for the trend analysis, you would use the *original* data, SALES *t*.

---

[7] We could also apply the trend analysis to the MA (4) data. Remember that it only contains a trend and cyclical component—see Expression (10.6).

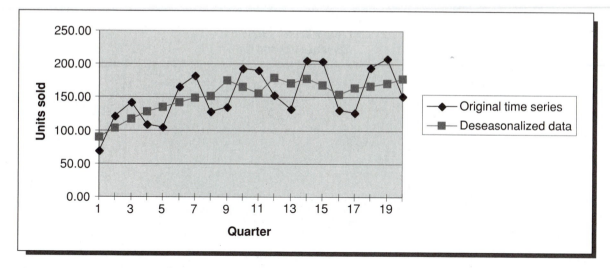

**Figure 10.11**
Original Data and Deseasonalized Data

## THE TREND PATTERN

Table 10.19, column 4, contains the data for determining the best-fitting trend line. Again use Excel's Add Trendline option to determine the best of five different types of models—linear, logarithmic, polynomial of order 2, power, and exponential. Figure 10.12 displays the five best curves together with their regression equations.

Recall that you use three criteria to determine the "best of the best" curve.

Criterion 1    Select the model(s) with the highest $R^2$ value.

Criterion 2    Select the model(s) with the lowest MAPE for the most recent time periods.

Criterion 3    Select the model that either is easiest to explain to others or use your judgment and intuition. Alternatively, you can choose the two or more most accurate models and develop a combination forecast.

Based upon the three criteria, the firm selected the log trend model to represent the trend component.

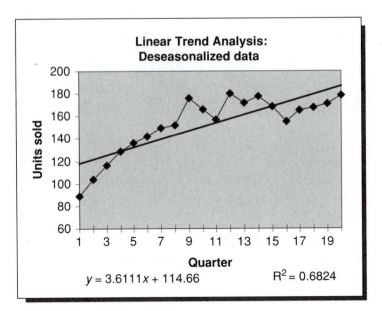

**Figure 10.12a**
Best of the Linear Trend
Curve Class

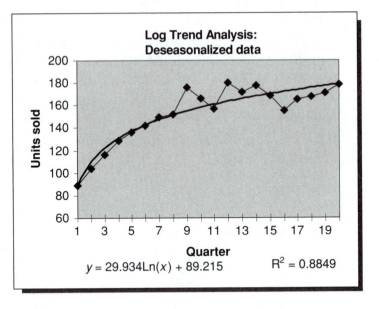

**Figure 10.12b**
Best of the Logarithmic
Curve Class

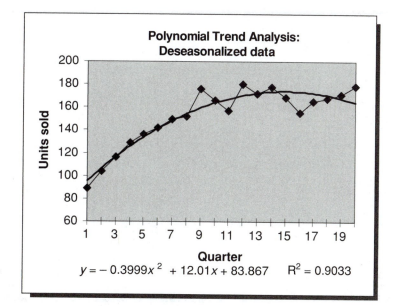

**Figure 10.12c**
Best of the Polynomial of
Order 2 Curve Class

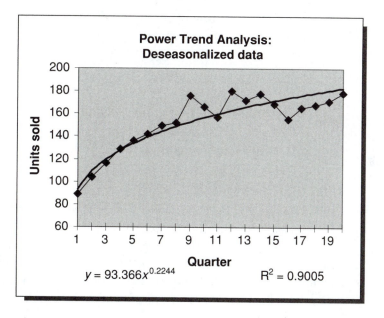

**Figure 10.12d**
Best of the Power Curve
Class

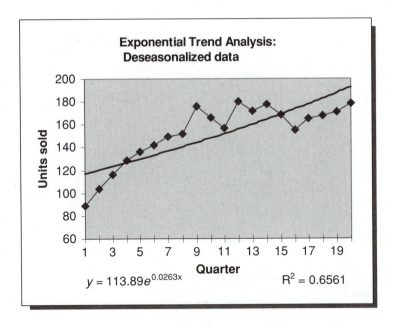

**Figure 10.12e**
Best of the Exponential
Curve Class

In summary, we have now identified the two major components of the original time series data—the seasonal (S) and trend (T) components:

**Seasonal Component**

| | |
|---|---|
| Typical Seasonal Index for Quarter 1 | 0.7695 |
| Typical Seasonal Index for Quarter 2 | 1.1618 |
| Typical Seasonal Index for Quarter 3 | 1.2187 |
| Typical Seasonal Index for Quarter 4 | 0.8499 |

**Trend Component**   $\hat{y}_t = 89.215 + [29.934 \cdot \text{Ln(QUARTER)}]$

### Short-Term Forecasting

We have isolated a logarithmic trend pattern and the typical seasonal indices. Let's prepare a forecast for the next four quarters, 21–24.

Table 10.20 shows how to prepare the forecast. Column 2 contains the four typical seasonal indices obtained by the ratio to moving average method. Column 3 contains the trend values for quarters 21–24 based on the logarithmic model, $89.215 + [29.934 \cdot \text{Ln(QUARTER)}]$. Column 4 is the product of columns 2 and 3.

**Table 10.20**
Forecast Using Log Trend
Model and Typical
Seasonal Indices

| Quarter | Typical Seasonal | Log Trend 89.215+[29.934LN(QUARTER)] | Forecast |
|---|---|---|---|
| 21 | 0.7695 | 180.35 | 138.78 |
| 22 | 1.1618 | 181.74 | 211.15 |
| 23 | 1.2187 | 183.07 | 223.11 |
| 24 | 0.8499 | 184.35 | 156.68 |

Table 10.20 provides a four-quarter forecast based on the trend and seasonal patterns. We could forecast additional quarters into the future, but that is risky. The classical decomposition method provides reasonably accurate forecasts for four to six quarters into the future. Beyond that, the assumption that the historical patterns will continue into the future is questionable.

Update the forecast every quarter or two. That is, add the latest data values to the original time series, and then recalculate the typical seasonal indices and the best trend pattern. You can then forecast four to six quarters into the future using the newly quantified seasonal and trend patterns.

### Summary of the Decomposition Method

Figure 10.13 summarizes the major steps of the decomposition method. After isolating and quantifying the seasonal and trend components, you can multiply the typical seasonal indices by the trend values from the best trend model to make forecasts for four to six quarters into the future.

Use the decomposition method when your goal is to detect the underlying pattern in the data to make short-term forecasts. You identify and quantify the seasonal and trend components. We ignored the cyclical component because it is not as well behaved as the seasonal component. While the length of the seasonal component is one year, the lengths of cycles are often unpredictable and thus unsuitable for forecasting.

You can then use the quantified trend and seasonal patterns to make forecasts up to six quarters into the future.

If your twin goals are forecasting and determining those predictor variables that affect the dependent variable, use regression analysis, not the classical decomposition method.

## AUTOREGRESSIVE MODELING FOR SEASONAL PATTERNS

Earlier in the chapter you used AR (1) or AR (2) autoregressive models to forecast meandering patterns. In addition to forecasting, regression-based models provide insight into those predictor variables that affect the forecasted variable. You can also use autoregressive models to forecast seasonal patterns. However, since the length of the seasonal pattern is one year, use **autoregressive models with four-period lagged data, AR (4) models** when you have quarterly data.[8] To improve the accuracy of an AR (4) model consider including coincident or leading predictor variables. By the end of this unit you should be able to

**1.** generate, evaluate, and interpret an AR (4) model; and

**2.** use the t Stat screening procedure to eliminate one or more coincident or leading predictor variables from an autoregressive model.

---

[8] Or AR (12) models for monthly data.

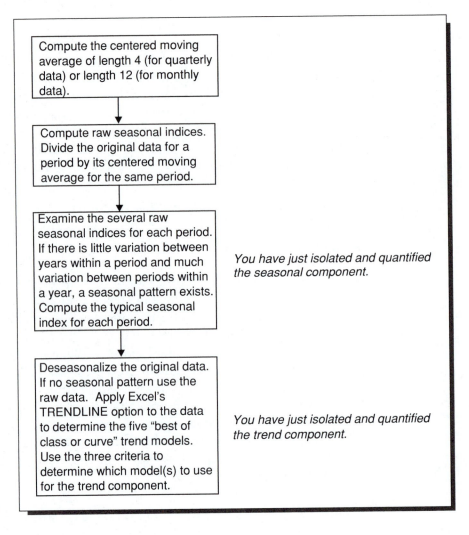

**Figure 10.13**
Flowchart for the
Decomposition Method

Because the data in Figure 10.1 contain a seasonal pattern of length one year, the units sold data in period $t$ will be related to the units sold data from four periods earlier, $t - 4$. To verify this, we developed the scatter plot in Figure 10.14. The data for the scatter plot are SALES $t - 4$ (predictor variable) and SALES $t$ (dependent variable) for quarters $t = 5$–20.

Figure 10.14 clearly shows the positive relationship between SALES $t$ versus SALES $t - 4$. That is, if units sold was relatively low (high) in one period, it was also relatively low (high) four periods earlier.

When the data contain a seasonal pattern of length one year you should construct an AR (4) model (see Table 10.21). First, this will allow you to determine if the forecasted variable, SALES $t$, is related to SALES $t - 4$. Second, you can also determine if SALES $t$ is related to SALES $t - 1$, SALES $t - 2$, and SALES $t - 3$.

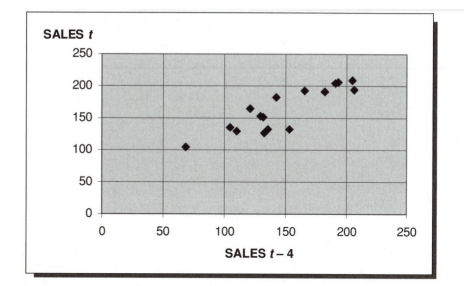

**Figure 10.14**
Scatter Plot of SALES
$t-4$ vs. SALES $t$

| | | | Predictor Variables | | |
|---|---|---|---|---|---|
| Quarter | SALES $t$ | SALES $t-1$ | SALES $t-2$ | SALES $t-3$ | SALES $t-4$ |
| 5 | 104.64 | 109.74 | 142.30 | 120.97 | 68.59 |
| 6 | 165.40 | 104.64 | 109.74 | 142.30 | 120.97 |
| 7 | 182.20 | 165.40 | 104.64 | 109.74 | 142.30 |
| 8 | 128.85 | 182.20 | 165.40 | 104.64 | 109.74 |
| 9 | 135.27 | 128.85 | 182.20 | 165.40 | 104.64 |
| 10 | 192.84 | 135.27 | 128.85 | 182.20 | 165.40 |
| 11 | 191.03 | 192.84 | 135.27 | 128.85 | 182.20 |
| 12 | 152.93 | 191.03 | 192.84 | 135.27 | 128.85 |
| 13 | 132.29 | 152.93 | 191.03 | 192.84 | 135.27 |
| 14 | 206.17 | 132.29 | 152.93 | 191.03 | 192.84 |
| 15 | 204.98 | 206.17 | 132.29 | 152.93 | 191.03 |
| 16 | 131.79 | 204.98 | 206.17 | 132.29 | 152.93 |
| 17 | 126.89 | 131.79 | 204.98 | 206.17 | 132.29 |
| 18 | 194.47 | 126.89 | 131.79 | 204.98 | 206.17 |
| 19 | 208.39 | 194.47 | 126.89 | 131.79 | 204.98 |
| 20 | 151.75 | 208.39 | 194.47 | 126.89 | 131.79 |

**Table 10.21**
Data for Developing
an AR (4) Model for
Seasonal Pattern Data
from Table 10.3

Although the overall regression model has a $p$-value of 0.00001, we can reduce the standard error of the estimate by applying the following t Stat screening procedure.

**1.** Take the absolute value of the t Stat values found in the parameter estimate section of the Excel-generated output. Ignore the intercept row of the table.

|  | Coefficients | Standard Error | t Stat |
|---|---|---|---|
| ~~Intercept~~ | ~~115.4357842~~ | ~~29.04223285~~ | ~~3.974755827~~ |
| Sales t − 1 | 0.165655218 | 0.236402524 | 0.700733711 |
| Sales t − 2 | −0.495992715 | 0.199790732 | −2.482561182 |
| Sales t − 3 | 0.129313256 | 0.251170665 | 0.514842194 |
| Sales t − 4 | 0.533501938 | 0.206085859 | 2.588736276 |

**2.** Delete the predictor variable with the lowest absolute t Stat value provided it is less than 1.0.

The predictor variable with the lowest absolute t Stat value is SALES $t − 3$, with $|t \text{ Stat}| = 0.515$.

**3.** Delete the column containing the SALES $t − 3$ data. Use the regression data-analysis tool to reestimate the model with the remaining three predictor variables. Repeat steps 2 and 3, one predictor variable at a time, until all the remaining predictor variables have $|t \text{ Stat}| \geq 1$.

Upon completing the t Stat screening procedure, only two predictor variables remained in the autoregressive model. Table 10.22 displays the regression statistics and parameter estimate sections for the final model.

| Regression Statistics | |
|---|---|
| Multiple R | 0.951906871 |
| R Square | 0.906126691 |
| Adjusted R Square | 0.891684644 |
| Standard Error | 11.24680668 |
| Observations | 16 |

**Table 10.22**
Parameter Estimate Section of Excel-Generated Output

|  | Coefficients | Standard Error | t Stat |
|---|---|---|---|
| Intercept | 126.8979631 | 20.85364525 | 6.085169358 |
| Sales t − 2 | −0.38493793 | 0.08877596 | −4.336060439 |
| Sales t − 4 | 0.650870449 | 0.077557444 | 8.39210803 |

From Table 10.22, do not remove either predictor variable, SALES $t − 2$ and SALES $t − 4$, from the model. Thus, Expression (10.8), given below, minimizes the standard error of the estimate. The coefficient of multiple determination, $R^2$, is 90.6%. That is, the two predictor variables, SALES $t − 2$ and SALES $t − 4$, account for 90.6% of the variation in units sold in period $t$.

$$\hat{y}_t = 126.898 − 0.3849 \cdot \text{SALES } t − 2 + 0.6509 \cdot \text{SALES } t − 4$$

**(10.8)**

Table 10.23 displays the forecast for quarters 21–22 using Expression (10.8). To forecast quarter 23 you must use the *forecasted* units sold for quarter 21 and the known past value of units sold for quarter 19. As mentioned earlier, it is not good practice to use forecasted values to make forecasts.

| Quarter | SALES $t$ | Forecast |
|---------|-----------|----------|
| 17 | 126.89 | |
| 18 | 194.47 | |
| 19 | 208.39 | |
| 20 | 151.75 | |
| 21 | | $129.28 = 126.898 - 0.3849(208.39) + 0.6509(126.89)$ |
| 22 | | $195.07 = 126.898 - 0.3849(151.75) + 0.6509(194.47)$ |

**Table 10.23**
Forecast for
Quarters 21–22
using AR (4) Model

### Leading and Coincident Predictor Variables

Let's try to reduce the standard error of Expression (10.8) by adding a new predictor variable—amount of advertising—see Table 10.24. We have also included one-period lagged values of advertising—ADV $t - 1$. Note that the database contains units sold and the four predictor variables for quarters 5–20. This is due to the inclusion of the SALES $t - 4$ predictor variable.

The t Stat screening method suggested removing the ADV $t$ predictor variable from the model. The inclusion of the ADV $t - 1$ predictor variable reduced the standard error from 11.245 to only 6.91. The $R^2$ increased from 90.6% to 96.7%. Expression (10.9) is the forecasting model.

$$\hat{y}_t = 93.241 - 0.30528 \cdot \text{SALES } t - 2 + 0.38332 \cdot \text{SALES } t - 4 + 0.000356 \cdot \text{ADV } t - 1$$

**(10.9)**

Here is the forecast for quarter 21.

$$\hat{y}_{21} = 93.241 - 0.30528 \cdot \text{SALES } 21 - 2 + 0.38332 \cdot \text{SALES } 21 - 4 + 0.000356 \cdot \text{ADV } 21 - 1$$
$$\hat{y}_{21} = 93.241 - 0.30528 \cdot \text{SALES } 19 + 0.38332 \cdot \text{SALES } 17 + 0.000356 \cdot \text{ADV } 20$$
$$\hat{y}_{21} = 140.54$$

| Quarter | SALES t | SALES t-2 | SALES t-4 | ADV t-1 | ADV t |
|---------|---------|-----------|-----------|---------|-------|
| 5 | 104.64 | 142.30 | 68.59 | 100000 | 165000 |
| 6 | 165.40 | 109.74 | 120.97 | 165000 | 185000 |
| 7 | 182.20 | 104.64 | 142.30 | 185000 | 100000 |
| 8 | 128.85 | 165.40 | 109.74 | 100000 | 140000 |
| 9 | 135.27 | 182.20 | 104.64 | 140000 | 235000 |
| 10 | 192.84 | 128.85 | 165.40 | 235000 | 190000 |
| 11 | 191.03 | 135.27 | 182.20 | 190000 | 180000 |
| 12 | 152.93 | 192.84 | 128.85 | 180000 | 130000 |
| 13 | 132.29 | 191.03 | 135.27 | 130000 | 210000 |
| 14 | 206.17 | 152.93 | 192.84 | 210000 | 210000 |
| 15 | 204.98 | 132.29 | 191.03 | 210000 | 140000 |
| 16 | 131.79 | 206.17 | 152.93 | 140000 | 150000 |
| 17 | 126.89 | 204.98 | 132.29 | 150000 | 195000 |
| 18 | 194.47 | 131.79 | 206.17 | 195000 | 215000 |
| 19 | 208.39 | 126.89 | 204.98 | 215000 | 190000 |
| 20 | 151.75 | 194.47 | 131.79 | 190000 | 175000 |

The top of the table has a spanning header over SALES t-2, SALES t-4, and ADV t-1: ← Predictor Variables →

**Table 10.24**
Quarterly Units Sold and
Four Predictor Variables

To forecast quarter 22 you must use the *known values* of units sold for quarters 18 and 20 and the *anticipated* level of advertising for quarter 21. Using the anticipated level of advertising presents no problems because management controls this variable. Do not confuse using the **anticipated** level with using the **forecasted** level of a variable. The former is okay, but the latter is not!

$$\hat{y}_{22} = 93.241 - 0.30528 \cdot \text{SALES } 22 - 2 + 0.38332 \cdot \text{SALES } 22 - 4 + 0.000356 \cdot \text{ADV } 22 - 1$$
$$\hat{y}_{22} = 93.241 - 0.30528 \cdot \text{SALES } 20 + 0.38332 \cdot \text{SALES } 18 + 0.000356 \cdot \text{ADV } 21$$

# SUMMARY

This chapter has presented how to forecast meandering patterns and seasonal patterns. Both patterns are similar in that they often contain a trend component—either upward or downward sloping to the right. Both patterns are different in that the seasonal pattern contains a seasonal component— often of length one year.

The appropriate forecasting model depends on the pattern type. To detect meandering patterns, you can use trend analysis or autoregressive models, typically AR (1) or AR (2), with or without coincident or leading predictor variables. To detect seasonal patterns you can use the classical decomposition method or autoregressive models, typically AR (4) or AR (12), with or without coincident or leading predictor variables.

While there are sophisticated statistical methods to determine if patterns are seasonal or meandering, a simple approach is to generate a line graph of the time-ordered data. Based on your line graph make a judgment call as to the type of pattern, and then use the appropriate methods to quantify it. Remember, for valid forecasts you must assume that the detected historical pattern or relationship will continue on into the near future.

# EXERCISES

1. Distinguish between a regression model and an autoregressive model.

2. Why must we center the moving average?

3. Distinguish between a meandering pattern and a seasonal pattern.

4. Why can't we compute a centered moving average for the first two and last two data points for quarterly data?

5. Why can't all the typical seasonal indices be greater than 1?

6. What are seasonally adjusted data?

7. What is one advantage of a regression-based forecasting model over a trend analysis–based forecasting model?

8. If you have daily closing prices for 30-year bonds and suspect that bond prices have a 15-day seasonal pattern, what type of autoregressive model, AR $(n)$, should you construct? Why?

9. What problems will you have if you use the decomposition method on a data set that contains only three years of quarterly data?

10. Explain why a trend model with the highest $R^2$ might not have the lowest MAPE over the most recent several quarters.

11. Shown here are units sold for the last 20 quarters.

| Year/Quarter | 1 | 2 | 3 | 4 |
|---|---|---|---|---|
| 1 | 8500 | 13,300 | 13,600 | 9400 |
| 2 | 10,400 | 15,400 | 16,600 | 11,500 |
| 3 | 11,200 | 18,400 | 17,500 | 14,000 |
| 4 | 13,600 | 20,500 | 21,000 | 14,400 |
| 5 | 14,800 | 22,900 | 23,700 | 17,000 |

a. Develop a line graph of the 20 quarters of data. Do the data contain a seasonal pattern or a meandering pattern?

b. Construct a centered moving average of length four. Plot the centered moving average on the line graph containing the original data. Characterize the "smoothness" of the centered moving average in comparison to the original data.

c. Compute the typical seasonal indices for the four quarters. Do the data contain a stable seasonal pattern? Explain what the typical seasonal indices mean.

d. Deseasonalize the data. Explain in nontechnical language the term "deseasonalized data."

e. Using the $R^2$ criterion, determine the best-fitting line for the deseasonalized data.

f. Develop a four-quarter forecast using the model with the highest $R^2$ and the typical seasonal indices.

**12.** Consider the data in Exercise 11. Develop an AR (4) model for the data and use the t Stat screening method to minimize the standard error of the estimate. Develop a forecast for the next four quarters.

**13.** Shown here are quarterly data on the discount rate charged by the Federal Reserve Bank of New York from 1980 to 1985. The discount rate is the interest rate that the Fed charges its commercial bank customers to borrow money and is one of several tools it uses to manage the overall economy.

| Year/Quarter | 1 | 2 | 3 | 4 |
|---|---|---|---|---|
| 1 | 13.00% | 11.00% | 11.00% | 13.00% |
| 2 | 13.75 | 14.00 | 13.00 | 12.00 |
| 3 | 12.00 | 11.50 | 10.00 | 9.00 |
| 4 | 8.50 | 8.50 | 8.75 | 8.75 |
| 5 | 9.00 | 9.00 | 8.50 | 8.00 |
| 6 | 7.75 | 7.50 | 7.50 | 7.00 |

**a.** Develop a line graph of the 24 quarters of data. Do the data contain a seasonal pattern or a meandering pattern?

**b.** Develop an AR (1) model. Is the model significant at the 95% level of confidence?

**c.** Compute the MAPE over the 24 quarters of data.

**d.** Prepare a forecast for the first quarter of year 7 (1986).

**14.** Shown here are 60 months of hypothetical data on the number of users for one Internet service provider.

**a.** Develop a line graph of the 60 months of data. Do the data contain a seasonal pattern or a meandering pattern?

**b.** Construct a centered moving average. Plot the centered moving average on the line graph containing the original data. Characterize the "smoothness" of the centered moving average in comparison to the original data.

**c.** Compute the typical seasonal indices. Do the data contain a stable seasonal pattern? Explain what the typical seasonal indices mean.

**d.** Deseasonalize the data. Explain in nontechnical language the term "deseasonalized data."

**e.** Using the $R^2$ criterion, determine the best-fitting line for the deseasonalized data.

**f.** Develop a 12-month forecast using the model with the highest $R^2$ and the typical seasonal indices.

| Month/Year | 1 | 2 | 3 | 4 | 5 |
|---|---|---|---|---|---|
| Jan | 900 | 1700 | 3100 | 5700 | 10,400 |
| Feb | 1100 | 1900 | 3700 | 6100 | 11,400 |
| March | 1100 | 2000 | 3700 | 6700 | 12,000 |
| April | 1200 | 2200 | 3900 | 7000 | 15,800 |
| May | 1300 | 2100 | 3800 | 7000 | 12,700 |
| June | 1300 | 2300 | 4100 | 7800 | 14,700 |
| July | 1400 | 2600 | 4700 | 8600 | 15,600 |
| Aug | 1600 | 2900 | 5200 | 9800 | 17,300 |
| Sept | 1800 | 3400 | 6000 | 10,900 | 19,900 |
| Oct | 1800 | 3200 | 5700 | 10,500 | 19,100 |
| Nov | 1900 | 3500 | 6500 | 11,500 | 19,000 |
| Dec | 1900 | 3500 | 6400 | 11,600 | 21,000 |

**15.** Consider the data in Exercise 14. Develop an AR (12) model for the data and use the t Stat screening method to minimize the standard error of the estimate. Develop a forecast for as many months as your final model will allow.

**16.** We have fitted the following AR (1) model to the monthly closing Dow-Jones Industrial Index for the years 1976 to 1981. The market peaked in December 1976 at about 980 and bottomed out two years later at about 800. By March 1981 the market again had climbed into the 960 range.

$$\hat{y}_t = 101 + 0.886 \cdot \text{DJI} - 1$$

The analysis of variance indicated that the model was significant. Explain in nontechnical language the meaning of the positive sample slope for the AR (1) model.

17. Obtain the monthly closing data for the Dow-Jones Industrial Index for the years 1992–1997. Develop an AR (1) model. Conduct an analysis of variance on the model. Compare the sample intercept and slope of your model with the model in Exercise 16. What do the two sample intercepts and sample slopes reveal about the stock market from 1976 to 1981 versus 1992 to 1997?

18. Shown here are the daily closing prices of the Kaufman Fund, a highly successful aggressive growth mutual fund, over a 30 day period—mid-July to mid-August 1997. (Read across).

| | | | | | | |
|---|---|---|---|---|---|---|
| $6.16 | 6.15 | 6.15 | 6.20 | 6.20 | 6.22 | 6.23 |
| 6.25 | 6.30 | 6.33 | 6.35 | 6.40 | 6.37 | 6.35 |
| 6.34 | 6.33 | 6.37 | 6.39 | 6.40 | 6.40 | 6.39 |
| 6.41 | 6.43 | 6.45 | 6.49 | 6.50 | 6.78 | 6.49 |
| 6.50 | 6.53 | | | | | |

a. Plot the time series.

b. Develop an AR (1) model. Is the model significant at the 95% confidence level?

c. Prepare a forecast for the day 31 closing price.

19. Shown here are the average miles per gallon of cars from 1976 to 1990. (*Source: Federal Highway Administration*—Department of Transportation)

| | | | | |
|---|---|---|---|---|
| 1976 | 13.5 | | 1983 | 17.1 |
| 1977 | 13.8 | | 1984 | 18.3 |
| 1978 | 14.0 | | 1985 | 19.2 |
| 1979 | 14.4 | | 1986 | 20.3 |
| 1980 | 15.5 | | 1987 | 21.7 |
| 1981 | 15.9 | | 1989 | 21.7 |
| 1982 | 16.7 | | 1990 | 21.6 |

a. Plot the time series.

b. Using the TRENDLINE option, determine the best-fitting model for the data. Select the model with the highest $R^2$ and develop a forecast for 1991.

20. Shown here are quarterly sales data in 1000s of units.

| | Quarter 1 | Quarter 2 | Quarter 3 | Quarter 4 |
|---|---|---|---|---|
| Year 1 | 2215 | 3035 | 3589 | 2885 |
| Year 2 | 2215 | 3254 | 3980 | 3263 |
| Year 3 | 2574 | 3585 | 4212 | 3646 |
| Year 4 | 2750 | 3805 | 4645 | 4212 |
| Year 5 | 3188 | 4390 | 4747 | 3552 |

a. Plot the time series.

b. Develop an appropriate forecasting model.

c. Prepare a forecast for the upcoming four quarters.

21. Suppose the typical seasonal indices are as shown:

| | | | |
|---|---|---|---|
| TSI 1 = 1.25 | TSI 2 = 1.00 | TSI 3 = .90 | TSI 4 = .85 |

Based on 30 quarters of data, the trend pattern is $\hat{y}_t = 894.11 + (8.85 \cdot \text{QUARTER})$ Prepare a forecast for the upcoming four quarters.

22. Shown here are quarterly sales data.

| Quarter | Sales $t$ | Quarter | Sales $t$ |
|---|---|---|---|
| 1 | 686 | 11 | 1910 |
| 2 | 1210 | 12 | 1530 |
| 3 | 1423 | 13 | 1330 |
| 4 | 1095 | 14 | 2060 |
| 5 | 1045 | 15 | 2050 |
| 6 | 1650 | 16 | 1320 |
| 7 | 1820 | 17 | 1270 |
| 8 | 1290 | 18 | 1950 |
| 9 | 1350 | 19 | 2080 |
| 10 | 1930 | 20 | 1520 |

**a.** Plot the time series.

**b.** Develop an appropriate forecasting model.

**c.** Prepare a forecast for the upcoming four quarters.

**23.** Shown here are 20 quarters of sales data.

| Quarter | Sales $t$ | Quarter | Sales $t$ |
|---------|-----------|---------|-----------|
| 1 | 470 | 11 | 575 |
| 2 | 650 | 12 | 815 |
| 3 | 450 | 13 | 685 |
| 4 | 640 | 14 | 935 |
| 5 | 540 | 15 | 640 |
| 6 | 745 | 16 | 900 |
| 7 | 510 | 17 | 755 |
| 8 | 725 | 18 | 1030 |
| 9 | 610 | 19 | 705 |
| 10 | 840 | 20 | 990 |

**a.** Develop a line graph of the 20 quarters of data. Do the data contain a seasonal pattern or a meandering pattern?

**b.** Construct a centered moving average of length four. Plot the centered moving average on the line graph containing the original data. Characterize the "smoothness" of the centered moving average in comparison to the original data.

**c.** Compute the typical seasonal indices for the four quarters. Do the data contain a stable seasonal pattern? Explain what the typical seasonal indices mean.

**d.** Deseasonalize the data. Explain in nontechnical language the term "deseasonalized data."

**e.** Using the lowest MAPE for the most recent four-quarters criterion, determine the best-fitting linear line for the deseasonalized data.

**f.** Develop a four-quarter forecast using the model with the lowest MAPE and the typical seasonal indices.

**24.** Shown here are quarterly sales data for the past five years.

| | Quarter 1 | Quarter 2 | Quarter 3 | Quarter 4 |
|---|-----------|-----------|-----------|-----------|
| Year 1 | 254.0 | 292.4 | 297.8 | 330.5 |
| Year 2 | 291.6 | 327.8 | 321.5 | 354.6 |
| Year 3 | 304.8 | 348.9 | 350.6 | 374.9 |
| Year 4 | 319.8 | 361.5 | 369.4 | 395.1 |
| Year 5 | 332.0 | 383.8 | 384.6 | 407.7 |

**a.** Plot the time series.

**b.** Develop an appropriate forecasting model.

**c.** Prepare a forecast for the upcoming four quarters.

**25.** We believe that the number of people below the poverty level and the number of prisoners executed impact the dependent variable—the number of violent crimes (murder, rape, aggravated assault, and battery) each year. Our data include 1979–1988. *Sources: Crime in the United States*, U.S. Federal Bureau of Investigations; *Correctional Projections in the United States*, U.S. Bureau of Justice Statistics.

| Year | VIOLENT (in millions) | POVERTY (in millions) | EXECUTE |
|------|-----------------------|-----------------------|---------|
| 1979 | 1.208 | 26.1 | 1 |
| 1980 | 1.345 | 29.3 | 1 |
| 1981 | 1.362 | 31.8 | 1 |
| 1982 | 1.322 | 34.4 | 2 |
| 1983 | 1.258 | 35.3 | 5 |
| 1984 | 1.273 | 33.7 | 21 |
| 1985 | 1.329 | 33.1 | 18 |
| 1986 | 1.489 | 32.4 | 18 |
| 1987 | 1.484 | 32.3 | 25 |
| 1988 | 1.566 | 31.9 | 11 |

Consider the following three predictor variables, VIOLENT $t - 1$, POVERTY, and EXECUTE. Use the t Stat screening method to determine if all the predictor variables are significantly related to the dependent variable—VIOLENT $t$.

**26.** Below are quarterly data on sales over five years.

| Year/Quarter | 1 | 2 | 3 | 4 |
|---|---|---|---|---|
| 1 | 2540 | 2924 | 2978 | 3303 |
| 2 | 2911 | 3276 | 3213 | 3545 |
| 3 | 3040 | 3485 | 3510 | 3745 |
| 4 | 3190 | 3615 | 3695 | 3955 |
| 5 | 3325 | 3835 | 3835 | 4075 |

**a.** Develop a line graph of the 20 quarters of data. Do the data contain a seasonal pattern or a meandering pattern?

**b.** Construct a centered moving average of length four. Plot the centered moving average on the line graph containing the original data. Characterize the "smoothness" of the centered moving average in comparison to the original data.

**c.** Compute the typical seasonal indices for the four quarters. Do the data contain a stable seasonal pattern? Explain what the typical seasonal indices mean.

**d.** Deseasonalize the data. Explain in nontechnical language the term "deseasonalized data."

**e.** Using the lowest MAPE for the most recent four quarters criterion, determine the best-fitting line for the deseasonalized data.

**f.** Develop a four-quarter forecast using the model with the lowest MAPE and the typical seasonal indices.

**27.** Refer to Exercise 26. Construct an AR (4) model and use the t Stat screening procedure to reduce the standard error of the estimate. Develop a four-quarter forecast.

**28.** Below are monthly data on average hourly wages for workers in the electronics industry. (Read across.)

| | | | |
|---|---|---|---|
| $15.71 | $15.63 | $15.66 | $15.69 |
| $15.61 | $15.63 | $15.63 | $15.74 |
| $15.96 | $15.85 | $16.07 | $16.09 |
| $16.04 | $16.15 | $16.20 | $16.15 |

Using the Add TRENDLINE option, determine the best-fitting model for the data. Select the model with the highest $R^2$ and develop a one-month forecast. What is a problem in developing a three-month forecast?

**29.** Refer to Exercise 28. Select the model with the lowest MAPE over the past four months and develop a forecast for next three months.

**30.** Refer to Exercise 19. Using the Add TRENDLINE option determine the best-fitting model for the data. Select the model with the lowest MAPE over the past four years and develop a forecast for 1991.

# CASE STUDY

Computers Unlimited, Inc., sells computer equipment to many small- to medium-sized firms in the Chicago area. A decision science intern recently developed an AR (12) monthly sales forecasting model. The firm has been using it for several months and it has generated rather poor forecasts. The owner, Pam Vexler, calls a meeting of her staff to discuss the problem.

| | |
|---|---|
| Vexler | We are here to discuss why our new model is generating such poor forecasts. I have asked our intern to make a presentation. |
| Intern | Thank you. After you gave me the assignment I first line-graphed the eight years of monthly sales data. It seemed to me that there was a seasonal pattern rather than a meandering pattern. |
| Jones | What do you mean by a seasonal pattern? |
| Intern | The data contained a repetitive, or recurring, pattern. So that suggested that I construct an AR (12) model because I had monthly data and the definition of a seasonal pattern is one whose length is one year. |
| Vexler | What exactly does an AR (12) mean? |
| Intern | It means that sales in any month, say $t$, is related to sales in $t + 12$ months later. In any case I developed an AR (12) model. |
| Jones | Did you do any evaluation of your model? |
| Intern | I wanted to but I ran out of time. I was planning to do some "backcasting." That's where you use the model to predict sales for periods that have already occurred. I would have used the mean absolute percentage error criterion to evaluate the model. Anyway, the sales manager suggested that we simply use the model for several months and see what happens. Well, now we know. For some reason my forecasts are inaccurate. |
| Vexler | Can we see your original line graph? |
| Intern | Sure. Here it is. |

After studying the line graph for a while, Vexler says, "I think I know what the problem is."

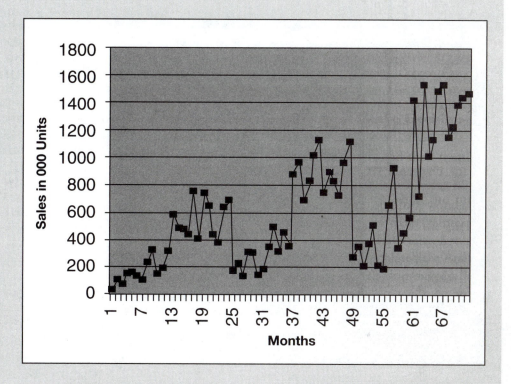

Assignment:

Prepare a one-page report on why the model generated such poor forecasts. What type of autoregressive model, AR (k), would you recommend?

# CHAPTER 10
# APPENDICES

## I. LISTING OF EXCEL TOOLS USED IN CHAPTER

**1.** Add TRENDLINE option

**2.** Chart Wizard—Line Graph

**3.** Chart Wizard—XY Scatter Plot

**4.** Regression data-analysis tool

**5.** Correlation data-analysis tool

## II. ADD TRENDLINE

**1.** Click at one of the corners of the line chart to activate it for editing. Eight small black squares appear in the chart.

**2.** From the Chart menu, choose the Add Trendline option.

**3.** On the Trendline Type tab, click on the desired icon (linear, logarithmic, etc.).

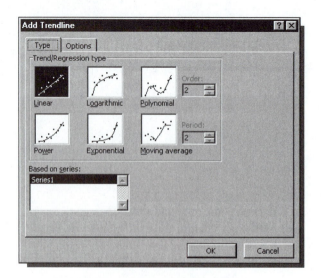

**4.** Click the Options tab of the Trendline dialog box shown here. Click to put checks in the Display Equation on Chart and Display R-squared Value on Chart. Then click OK.

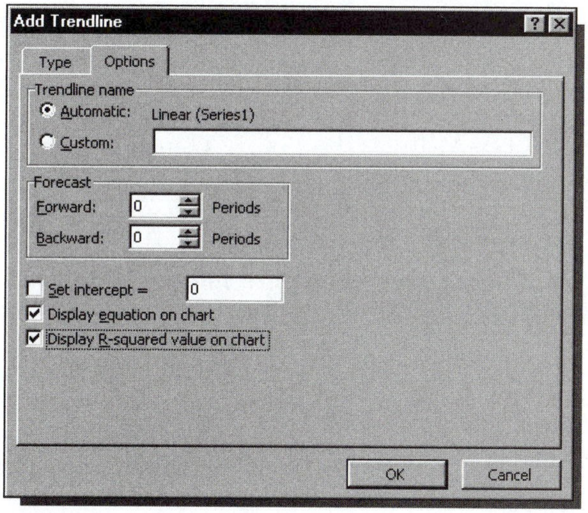

# III. GENERATE RAW SEASONAL INDICES

Below are the steps to develop a moving average of length four, a centered moving average, and the typical seasonal indices for quarterly data.

**1.** Enter the data shown in columns A and B as shown below.

**2.** Enter the labels shown in columns C, D, and E.

|    | A       | B       | C      | D      | E     |
|----|---------|---------|--------|--------|-------|
| 1  | Quarter | SALES t | MA(4)  | CMA    | RSI   |
| 2  | 1       | 68.59   |        |        |       |
| 3  |         |         |        |        |       |
| 4  | 2       | 120.97  |        |        |       |
| 5  |         |         | 110.40 |        |       |
| 6  | 3       | 142.30  |        | 114.90 | 1.238 |
| 7  |         |         | 119.41 |        |       |
| 8  | 4       | 109.74  |        | 124.96 | 0.878 |
| 9  |         |         | 130.52 |        |       |
| 10 | 5       | 104.64  |        | 135.51 | 0.772 |
| 11 |         |         | 140.49 |        |       |
| 12 | 6       | 165.40  |        | 142.88 | 1.158 |
| 13 |         |         | 145.27 |        |       |
| 14 | 7       | 182.20  |        |        |       |
| 15 |         |         |        |        |       |
| 16 | 8       | 128.85  |        |        |       |

**3.** Select cell C5 and enter the formula = AVERAGE(B2:B8). This is the average of the first four quarters of data and is the average sales associated with a point in time between quarter 2 and quarter 3.

**4.** Copy cell C5 and paste into C7, then C9, then C11, and then C13. Cell C13 is the last cell for which you have four quarters of data for computing the average.

**5.** To compute the centered moving average, select cell D6 and enter the formula =AVERAGE(C5:C7). This is the centered moving average for the third quarter of year 1.

**6.** Copy cell D6 and paste into D8, D10, and D12.

**7.** To compute the raw seasonal indices, select cell E6 and enter the formula =B6/D6. This is the raw seasonal index for quarter 3 of year 1.

**8.** Copy cell E6 and paste into E8, E10, and E12.

# Chapter 11

---

# QUALITY IMPROVEMENT AND STATISTICAL PROCESS CONTROL

## QUALITY IMPROVEMENT, PRODUCTIVITY, AND BUSINESS SUCCESS

An effective quality improvement program can increase productivity and reduce cost. Consider this scenario. A firm manufactures 1000 components per day. The first-pass yield is 75%. That is, 75% of the process output meets the design requirements and 25% does not. Of the 25% unacceptable components, the firm can rework 60% and they scrap the rest. The direct manufacturing cost for the component is $25 and the cost of reworking a component is $5. The present manufactured cost per good part is

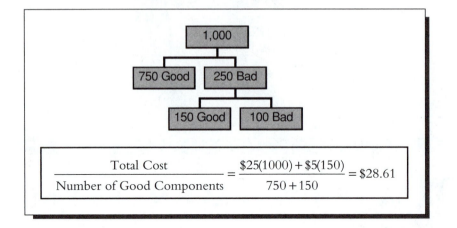

After the firm installs a statistical control procedure the first-pass yield increases from 75% to 95%. Of the 5% unacceptable components, the firm can still rework 60%. The revised manufactured cost per good part is

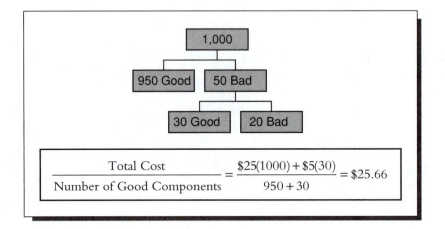

The quality effort reduced manufactured cost by over 10% and increased productivity by almost 9%. And all it took was installing an inexpensive statistical control procedure.

That is not all. The quality of a firm's products or services is important to its strategic success. Research by the Strategic Planning Institute (SPI) of Cambridge, Massachusetts, shows that firms that stress product quality have higher returns on investment.[1] SPI asked 2700 businesses to identify key

---

[1]Brandley, Gale, *Quality as a Strategic Weapon*. Cambridge: The Strategic Planning Institute, 1985.

product and service attributes (except price) and weight them in terms of customer importance. Relative quality was the only variable that was correlated with return on investment (ROI). Firms with the poorest relative quality product scores had a mean return on investment of about 12%. Firms with the highest relative quality product scores had a mean return on investment above 30%. Superior quality is a key to business success. As SPI noted, "Quality comes close to being a panacea (for business success)."

# TYPES OF QUALITY

What is quality? Are there different types of quality? Who defines quality? Whose responsibility is it to monitor quality? By the end of this section you should be able to

**1.** distinguish among the three views of quality;

**2.** explain the nominal value and the lower and upper specification limits; and

**3.** explain the quality function deployment method.

Every product or service possesses a number of potential quality characteristics. There are two major categories of quality characteristics:

**Variables**   A quality characteristic that you **measure** on a continuous scale is a variable. Examples include length of time before component failure, component weight, degree of service satisfaction, job completion time, etc.

**Attributes**   A quality characteristic that you judge by assessing whether a product or service possesses certain desirable characteristics is an attribute. Examples include the absences of (1) errors in invoice forms, (2) scratches on eyeglasses, (3) failed soldering connections in printed circuit boards, etc. You **count** attributes.

Managers use three definitions that focus on either the *quality of conformance* or the *quality of design*.

***Quality of Conformance.***   The traditional definition of quality is conformance to specifications (specs). If a Mercedes–Benz conforms to its design specifications, it is a quality car. If a Hyundai conforms to its design specifications, it too is a quality car.

Conformance to specs is called *manufactured quality*. Assume that a customer will accept a one-foot ruler that is $12 \pm .01$ inches for a cost of $0.39. Manufactured quality is the ability to produce rulers to that design specification. Improving quality of conformance often reduces cost.

Several definitions are essential when discussing the quality of conformance.

**D E F I N I T I O N**    The **nominal**, or **target, value** is the most desired level of a product characteristic.

The nominal value for a one-foot ruler is 12 inches. Here the firm bases the nominal value on the definition of one foot.

Having established a target value, firms should have some flexibility in achieving it. They do this by setting **specification limits**. The limits indicate the range of measurements of the product or service that the customer will find acceptable. This leads to two other important definitions.

**D E F I N I T I O N**    The **upper specification limit (USL)** is the largest allowable value that a quality characteristic can have and still be acceptable to the consumer.

**D E F I N I T I O N**    The **lower specification limit (LSL)** is the smallest allowable value that a quality characteristic can have and still be acceptable to the consumer.

Returning to the 12-inch ruler illustration, the LSL would be $12.00 - 0.01 = 11.99$ inches, and the USL would be $12.00 + 0.01 = 12.01$. Any ruler between 11.99 and 12.01 inches would be a *conforming* product. Any ruler outside of specs would be a *nonconforming* product. Two-sided specs indicate that a quality characteristic should be *between* two specific values.

Some products or services have only a single specification limit. For example, the breaking strength of the plastic housing for a desk phone would only have a lower specification limit. After all, customers will not complain if the firm increases the breaking strength (unless they raise the price too). Alternatively, accounts receivable processing time would only have an upper specification limit (perhaps 30 days to take advantage of the discounts). One-sided specs indicate that a quality characteristic should be *at least* (LSL) or *at most* (USL) some specific value.

Who decides what a product or service's nominal value will be? Traditionally, in manufacturing, engineering departments set the nominal value. Today, manufacturing firms are asking their customers. In the service sector, it would be hard *not* to involve the customer in setting the target value or specification limits. Recently firms have begun to use *quality function deployment* (QFD) in setting specifications.

Telrad Telecommunications and Electronic Industries Ltd. used QFD to reexamine its design specifications.[2] It identified seven engineering objectives. See the columns in Figure 11.1. Telrad then designed a questionnaire to assess these engineering objectives. See the rows of Figure 11.1 (only two questions shown). Note that each question relates to one or more engineering objectives. The three symbols indicate the degree of relationship between a question and an engineering objective.

Telrad then asked a random sample of 150 customers to use a 1 (worst) to 5 (best) point scale to answer each question. Figure 11.1 displays the distribution of the 150 responses (the numbers in the five right-most columns) for questions 1 and 4. The mean score for question 1 is

$$\frac{\left(1\cdot 1\right)+\left(7\cdot 2\right)+\left(34\cdot 3\right)+\left(67\cdot 4\right)+\left(41\cdot 5\right)}{1+7+34+67+41}=3.9$$

The overall quality score for the handset transmission objective is the product of the mean scores for questions 1 and 4 multiplied by their respective weights.[3]

$$(9 \cdot 3.9) + (3 \cdot 4.2) = 47.7$$

After computing the six other quality scores, Telrad engineers could then decide what design changes, if any, they should make.

### *Quality of Design.*

**Quality of Design.** Dr. J. M. Juran, a pioneer in the field, defines quality as "fitness for use."[4] Fitness for use is the design quality definition. Producing one-foot rulers with a LSL = 10 inches and a USL = 14 inches is unacceptable because customers would not purchase such rulers at any price.

Design quality often means higher initial costs. However, such costs are actually *prevention costs* and do prevent quality problems at later stages of the product's life cycle. In sum, design quality makes the product or service right the first time.

---

[2]Glushkovsky, E., Florescu, R., Hershkovits, A., and Sipper, D., "Avoid a Flop: Use QFD with Questionnaires," *Quality Progress*, June 1995, Vol. 28(6), pp. 57–64.

[3]Glushkovsky et al., incorrectly used weighted averages such as
$$\left[9\cdot (3.9) + 3\cdot (4.2)\right]\big/9 + 3 = 4.0$$ to determine the importance of the seven engineering objectives.

[4]Juran, J. M., ed., *Quality Control Handbook*. 3rd edition. New York: McGraw-Hill, 1974.

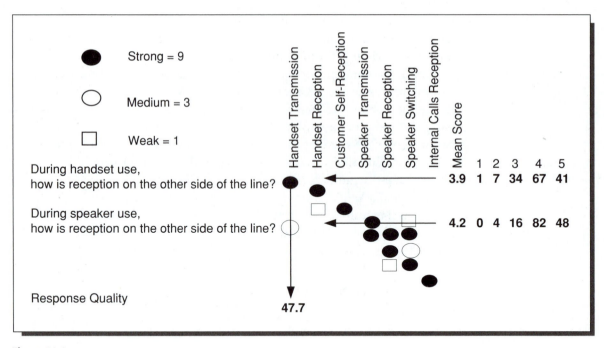

**Figure 11.1**
QFD Questionnaire and Response Calculation

***Taguchi's Loss Function.*** Japanese engineer Dr. Genichi Taguchi defines quality as the loss imparted to society when a product or service quality characteristic varies from its nominal value. Costs include the energy and time to fix the problem, the payment for replacement parts or services, or the loss of goodwill or market share.

In the conformance to specification view of quality, any product with a quality characteristic within specs is conforming. Suppose that the LSL for a one-foot ruler is 11.99 inches and the USL is 12.01 inches. Ruler lengths close to the nominal value of 12.00 inches are no better than ones near, but not outside, one of the specification limits.

Taguchi disagrees. A ruler that is within specs, say 11.995 inches, still produces a loss for society because it is not 12 inches, its nominal or target value. Taguchi quantifies the loss by using a quadratic function.[5]

---

[5]See Farnum, N., *Modern Statistical Quality Control and Improvement.* Belmont, CA: Duxbury Press, 1994.

# THE "BIG 8" QUALITY IMPROVEMENT TOOLS

Monitoring and improving quality is a full-time job. Fortunately, management and hourly employees have eight tools available for this. Most are very simple to use. However, two tools, control charting and design of experiment, will require additional explanation.

## PROCESS DIAGRAMS

How can you improve a process if you don't know where the bottlenecks or critical steps are? A process diagram identifies the process flow, potential bottlenecks, critical steps, and potential control points. Begin by simply listing all the steps in a process. Then draw a process flowchart and ask,

1. What is the purpose of each step?

2. Could any steps be combined or eliminated?

3. Could any steps be done simultaneously?

4. Which steps have the greatest number of mistakes?

Through such questions, you can "streamline" the process or eliminate or redesign those steps that have the greatest number of mistakes.

Figure 11.2 displays the process of opening a checking account. Included are several measures of the process quality.

## CHECK SHEET

How many errors have occurred in each process step? A check sheet spots potential problem areas by frequency, type, or cause. List the type of errors and then record the number of each type.

Table 11.1 records the monthly number of errors made by bank personnel in opening checking accounts.

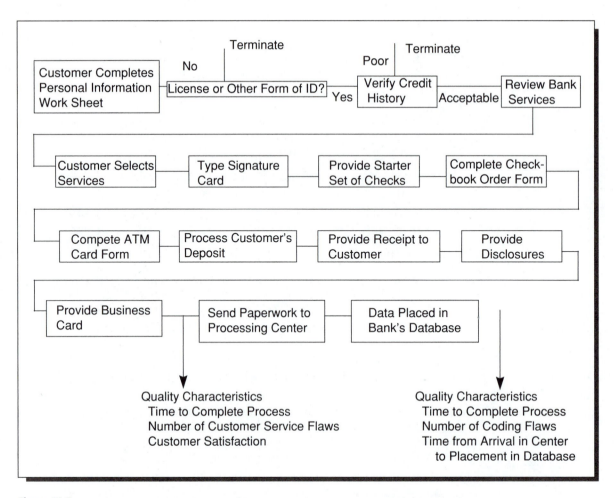

**Figure 11.2**
Process Flow Diagram for Opening a Checking Account

**Table 11.1**
Check Sheet for Errors (or Flaws) for First Six Months

| Error Category | J | F | M | A | My | J | Total |
|---|---|---|---|---|---|---|---|
| Improper Credit Check | 2 | | 1 | | 1 | | 4 |
| Unsigned Signature Card | 4 | 3 | 2 | 3 | 4 | 2 | 18 |
| Starter Checks Not Provided | 4 | | 1 | | 1 | | 6 |
| Disclosures Not Provided | | 1 | 1 | | | 1 | 3 |
| Checks Not Ordered | 2 | | 4 | 3 | 2 | 5 | 16 |
| Paperwork Lost at DP Center | 1 | | 1 | | | | 2 |
| Incorrect Data Entry at DP | 2 | | 2 | | | | 4 |

# PARETO CHART

What process steps exhibit the most frequent or most costly errors? A Pareto chart will tell us. A Pareto chart is simply a graph of the check sheet data. Begin by rank ordering the frequency of error data in the total column of Table 11.1. The most frequent error or service flaw is unsigned signature cards, followed by unordered checks. The least frequent error is lost paperwork at the data processing center. Then, use Excel's chart wizard (column chart) to display the data. Figure 11.3 shows that unsigned signature cards and unordered checks account for about 64% of the errors.

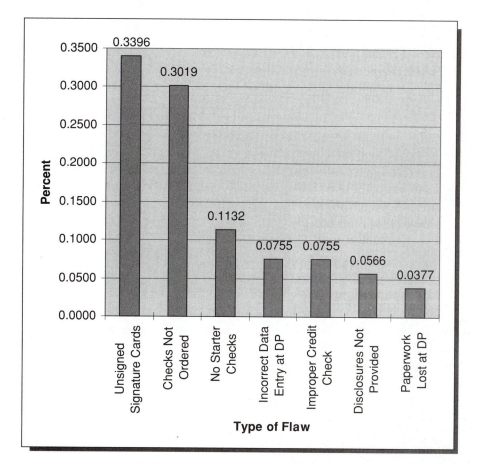

**Figure 11.3**
Pareto Chart for Errors in Opening Checking Accounts

Although the Pareto chart resembles the relative frequency histogram from Chapter 2, there is one major difference. In a relative frequency histogram, the horizontal axis displays values of a quantitative variable such as income level, claims processed, or days to complete a project. The horizontal axis for a Pareto chart displays type of error, a qualitative variable. The vertical axis for both graphical tools is the percentage occurrence.

Given Figure 11.3, should the bank focus its process redesign efforts to eliminate the two most frequently occurring problems? The answer is yes, but it might also want to focus on the *most costly* process flaws.

Consider developing a *cost-based* Pareto chart that highlights the most costly errors. Simply multiply the total number of each type of flaw in Table 11.1 by its associated cost. Then, rank order the cost data and use Excel's chart wizard (column chart) to construct a Pareto chart based on the total costs associated with each type of error.

## CAUSE-AND-EFFECT DIAGRAMS

Now that you have identified the most frequent or most costly error, how do you solve it? A fishbone, or Ishikawa, diagram is a visual and creative problem-solving tool. Let's use a fishbone diagram to solve the unordered check problem.

Place into the goal box of Figure 11.4 the desired goal(s)—ensuring that checks are ordered. Next, generate three or four potential *major* causes. You can use either logic or creative methods to generate the potential major causes. These are the "large bones" in Figure 11.4. Good sources for major causes for manufacturing processes are the four M's: methods, manpower, materials, and machines. For service processes, generate your own list. Starting with each major bone, brainstorm two to six possible specific causes, or "small bones." Then rank the specific causes and evaluate the most promising ones. Possible solutions from Figure 11.4 include the following:

1. Provide additional training for personal bankers.

2. Provide incentives for customers to place their own orders.

3. Place enlarged facsimile of a check in a large framed picture where personal bankers can see it when they are opening accounts.

4. Program a "software warning pop-up" to remind personal banker to place order for permanent checks.

5. Checks are automatically ordered when first starter check clears.

6. Checks are automatically ordered when customer data are entered into the bank's database.

7. Have branch manager spot-audit the process.

8. Post a check sheet to provide personal bankers with feedback on how well they are doing.

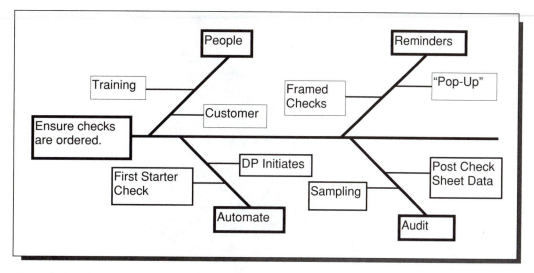

**Figure 11.4**
Fishbone Diagram for Solving the Unordered Checks Problem

## HISTOGRAM

Consider drawing a histogram for a quantitative quality characteristic. Place the classes or bins for the quantitative variable on the horizontal axis and the frequency of occurrence on the vertical axis. You can then compare the distribution of actual performances against the target value and the specification limits.

Figure 11.5 is a frequency histogram of paperwork completion time (a quantitative quality characteristic) for the last 98 accounts. Figure 11.5 contains the target value of 15 minutes and the upper specification limit of 25 minutes. There is only an upper specification limit as customers will not complain if the bank completes the paperwork very quickly.

The process needs improvement. More than 5% of the accounts (5/98) took longer than the maximum acceptable time. Over 50% of the transactions took longer than the 15-minute target value. The bank should develop a fishbone diagram or plot scatter diagrams to seek ways to reduce paperwork completion time.

## SCATTER DIAGRAM

What variables affect paperwork completion time? If the variables are quantitative, consider drawing a scatter diagram. Scatter diagrams show possible associations between two quantitative variables.

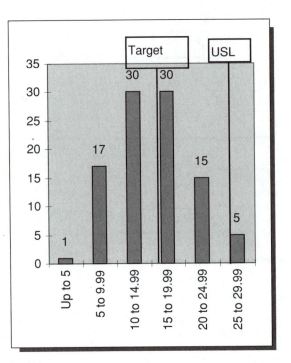

**Figure 11.5**
Frequency Histogram for
Time to Complete
Paperwork

Suppose the bank manager believes that the number of interruptions increases paperwork completion time. He generates Figure 11.6 that displays the number of interruptions $(x_i)$ and paperwork completion time $(y_i)$ for the last 18 customers. For each customer, he records the number of interruptions experienced and the total time to complete the paperwork. He constructs Figure 11.6 using Excel's chart wizard $xy$ scatter plot.

Note that the swarm of data points slopes upward to the right. The greater the number of interruptions, the longer it generally takes to complete the paperwork. Eliminating interruptions should reduce paperwork completion time and make it possible to bring the process within specs (no data values above the USL in Figure 11.5).

## DESIGN OF EXPERIMENT

Another major process improvement tool is the *planned change study*. Managers first identify one or more factors that they believe will improve the product or process. They then run a small-scale study, and if the planned changes are an improvement, they implement them permanently.

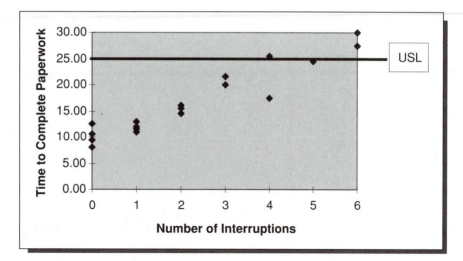

**Figure 11.6**
Scatter Diagram on Number of Interruptions and Completion Time

Here we describe how design of experiment reduced the soldering time for printed circuit boards. Before the study soldering time for the 800 connections on a circuit board was 160 milliseconds. The engineering staff believed that they could reduce it without increasing the proportion of improperly soldered connections. Reducing soldering time would significantly improve productivity.

Members of the team ran a planned change study. First, they identified three factors that they thought significantly affected soldering time. These were

**1.** conveyor speed that transports boards to the wave soldering machine (the current speed was 6.0 feet per minute);

**2.** preheat chamber temperature where the boards are heated prior to soldering the 800 connections (the current temperature was 140°); and

**3.** incline angle as the boards entered the soldering machine (the current incline angle was 6°).

The team then determined the variations (or factor levels) of each factor it wanted to test. These were

|  | **Factor** | **Variations** |
|---|---|---|
| 1. | Conveyor Speed | 5 feet per minute and 7 feet per minute |
| 2. | Chamber Temperature | 120° and 160° |
| 3. | Incline Angle | 5° and 7° |

The study required running eight different factor level combinations, shown as cells 1–8 in Table 11.2. The team ran five circuit boards under each of the eight combinations for a total sample size of 40. The dependent variable was soldering speed.

**Table 11.2**
Experimental Layout for
Three-Factor Study

|  | 5 feet per minute | | 7 feet per minute | |
|---|---|---|---|---|
|  | 5° | 7° | 5° | 7° |
| 120° | 1 | 2 | 3 | 4 |
| 160° | 5 | 6 | 7 | 8 |

After completing the study, the team analyzed the results. The fastest wave soldering occurred at factor level combination 6: a five-feet-per-minute conveyor speed, a 160° preheat chamber temperature, and a 7° incline angle. On average, this combination reduced soldering time from 160 to 104 milliseconds without increasing the proportion of the 800 connections that had failed solders. The team then ran a larger scale confirmatory, or validation, study before implementing the study's findings on the production floor.

In summary, one small-scale study reduced wave soldering time by 35%. Such is the power of design of experiment (see Chapter 12).

## CONTROL CHARTS

This section introduces the basics of control charting and shows how to use a control chart as an "early warning system" to detect changes in process quality. In the section, "Control Charts for Variables: $\bar{x}$ and Standard Deviation" later in this chapter, we present how to construct control charts.

Figure 11.7 is a control chart. The horizontal axis measures time or the subgroup number. The vertical axis measures an important quality characteristic that you wish to improve or control, such as

**1.** the *mean* time to open a checking account or

**2.** the *standard deviation* in the soldering times for printed circuit boards.

At appropriate intervals (every hour, every half-day, or every day) you select a subgroup of size $n$, record the quality characteristic, and compute sample statistics such as the mean and standard deviation. You then plot each sample statistic in a separate control chart.

The control chart contains three important lines. The **center line (CL)** represents the mean of the recorded data. The **lower control limit (LCL)** and the **upper control limit (UCL)** are usually three standard deviations above and below the center line.

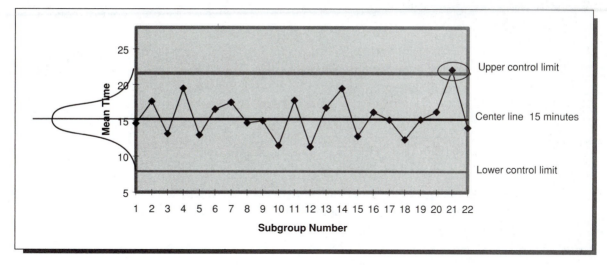

**Figure 11.7**
Control Chart on the Sample Mean Time to Open an Account

***In-Control Process.*** A process is under statistical control when the plotted values fall between the lower and upper control limits and there is no systematic pattern to the plotted values. From Figure 11.7, time to open an account was in control for the first 20 days. When a process is in control, workers or management need not take any corrective action, for the process is "not broken." From Chapter 1, only *common-cause* variation is present.

***Out-of-Control Process.*** When a plotted value falls either above the upper control limit or below the lower control limit the process is no longer in control.[6] *Assignable-cause* variation is present, the process is broken, and workers or management must fix it.

From Figure 11.7, the process went out of control on day 21. The personal banker must have determined the assignable cause(s) because the process was again in control on day 22. Had he not corrected the process, the plotted data value for day 22 would have also fallen outside the control limits.

Do not confuse the target value and specification limits with the center line and the control limits. Based on customers' wants and needs, *management and customers* determine the target value and specification limits. As you will see in the section, "Control Charts for Variables," the *process* itself determines the center line and control limits.

---

[6] A process is also out of control if there are strings of eight or more values all above or all below the center line even when all the values are between the lower and upper control limits. We discussed this idea in Chapter 1.

Since most processes do not operate in a state of statistical control, control charts are necessary and serve three purposes.

1. Control charts provide an early warning system that a process that was in control has just gone out of control. It warns us that the process warrants attention.

2. Charts detect the presence of assignable-cause variation. If you can eliminate these sources of variation, you can reduce the overall process variation. Low variation means greater uniformity, less rework, and improved productivity.

3. Control charts help assess **process capability** which is the ability of a process to deliver conforming goods and services to the customer.

This chapter presents one pair of commonly used control charts for variables and two commonly used control charts for attributes.

In summary, you have now learned the "Big 8" quality improvement tools. Use

| | |
|---|---|
| **Process Diagram** | to identify potential bottlenecks and critical steps to streamline a process. |
| **Check Sheet** | to record the number of different types of errors or service flaws. |
| **Pareto Chart** | to identify the most frequent or most costly type of errors. |
| **Cause-and-Effect Diagram** | to generate potential solutions to the most frequent or costly errors. |
| **Histogram** | to display the distribution of an important quality characteristic to find areas in need of improvement. |
| **Scatter Diagram** | to assess potential causes for an identified problem. |
| **Design of Experiment** | to improve product quality or service by running planned change studies. |
| **Process Charting** | to warn when a process goes out of control and must be fixed. |

# MANAGEMENT SCENARIOS AND DATA SETS

Table 11.3 presents three cases that illustrate how managers use time-ordered data to construct and maintain control charts for variables and attributes.

| Process | Quality Characteristic | Type | Control Charts |
|---|---|---|---|
| Completing Rental Car Paperwork | Time | Variable | Mean and Standard Deviation |
| Writing Sales Invoices | Absence of Errors | Attribute | Fraction Nonconforming |
| Filling Orders | Absence of Different Types and Seriousness of Errors | Attribute | Demerit |

**Table 11.3**
Scenarios and Data Sets

The Los Angeles Airport (LAX) agency manager for Quality Car Rental monitors how long it takes its reservation clerks to complete the rental car paperwork. She has set an *upper specification limit of 14 minutes* and a *target value of 10 minutes.* Customers who wait longer than 14 minutes may become disgruntled (even 10 minutes seems like a lifetime when waiting in line). The quality measure is the number of minutes to complete the rental car paperwork from the time the customer enters the queue to the time he or she leaves the counter.

Each day, each clerk completes 35–45 forms. Table 11.4 contains the number of minutes it took one specific clerk to process five successive customers at randomly chosen times each day over a 30-day period. The quality characteristic is a variable in that we measure time on a continuous scale. We will use this data to construct a mean chart and a standard deviation chart.

Table 11.5 contains the fraction of sales invoices that have one or more errors. The error could be an incorrect address, order quantity, or part number. Each day employees at Rent-2-Own Furniture process about 300 sales invoices. They record the number of invoices with one or more errors. Their goal is to reduce the proportion of invoices with one or more errors to under 0.005. From Table 11.5, they have a long way to go.

The quality characteristic is an attribute. A conforming sales invoice is one with no errors and a nonconforming invoice is one with one or more errors. We will use this data to construct a fraction nonconforming chart.

| Subgroup | Observations | | | | |
|---|---|---|---|---|---|
| 1 | 11.6 | 9.3 | 9.8 | 9.2 | 10.5 |
| 2 | 11.3 | 12.5 | 9.4 | 11.8 | 13.6 |
| 3 | 10.4 | 9.4 | 8.2 | 11.5 | 9.6 |
| 4 | 12.1 | 9.7 | 10.0 | 9.0 | 10.0 |
| 5 | 12.6 | 10.8 | 12.8 | 12.0 | 11.1 |
| 6 | 11.8 | 9.2 | 9.0 | 9.6 | 9.8 |
| 7 | 9.8 | 11.6 | 9.2 | 10.3 | 9.0 |
| 8 | 11.9 | 7.7 | 11.4 | 8.4 | 8.3 |
| 9 | 9.7 | 9.9 | 9.4 | 9.9 | 9.5 |
| 10 | 10.4 | 12.4 | 12.0 | 12.4 | 12.1 |
| 11 | 8.5 | 7.9 | 10.0 | 10.1 | 11.5 |
| 12 | 11.8 | 9.1 | 8.0 | 8.8 | 9.1 |
| 13 | 9.5 | 11.6 | 8.3 | 10.8 | 10.4 |
| 14 | 9.5 | 10.0 | 10.0 | 10.0 | 7.2 |
| 15 | 10.1 | 10.5 | 9.8 | 9.7 | 10.8 |
| 16 | 11.2 | 10.0 | 9.6 | 8.5 | 8.7 |
| 17 | 8.6 | 10.3 | 9.2 | 11.7 | 8.2 |
| 18 | 10.4 | 9.0 | 8.2 | 8.6 | 10.4 |
| 19 | 11.0 | 11.0 | 8.4 | 7.2 | 10.7 |
| 20 | 10.8 | 9.4 | 9.4 | 10.6 | 11.2 |
| 21 | 10.2 | 9.7 | 8.3 | 12.2 | 7.6 |
| 22 | 8.7 | 10.7 | 11.0 | 10.7 | 8.9 |
| 23 | 10.7 | 9.7 | 8.1 | 9.8 | 9.1 |
| 24 | 9.1 | 9.9 | 9.7 | 9.5 | 10.2 |
| 25 | 10.9 | 10.6 | 9.0 | 10.8 | 9.0 |
| 26 | 10.2 | 11.6 | 10.3 | 10.0 | 8.3 |
| 27 | 11.3 | 9.0 | 9.9 | 7.8 | 10.7 |
| 28 | 9.1 | 7.2 | 11.6 | 6.4 | 9.2 |
| 29 | 8.9 | 10.4 | 10.8 | 8.6 | 9.7 |
| 30 | 9.5 | 9.0 | 10.1 | 12.1 | 10.8 |

**Table 11.4**
Customer Processing
Time in Minutes

The quality characteristic is an attribute because we cannot measure it on a continuous scale. Rather, we determine the quality characteristic by *counting* the number of invoices with one or more errors.

| Day | Examined | Nonconforming | Proportion |
|-----|----------|---------------|------------|
| 1 | 286 | 10 | 0.035 ◀——— 10/286 |
| 2 | 281 | 9 | 0.032 |
| 3 | 310 | 8 | 0.026 |
| 4 | 313 | 11 | 0.035 |
| 5 | 305 | 14 | 0.046 |
| 6 | 307 | 13 | 0.042 |
| 7 | 295 | 15 | 0.051 |
| 8 | 311 | 10 | 0.032 |
| 9 | 294 | 9 | 0.031 |
| 10 | 300 | 10 | 0.033 |
| 11 | 305 | 17 | 0.056 |
| 12 | 295 | 8 | 0.027 |
| 13 | 290 | 12 | 0.041 |
| 14 | 302 | 8 | 0.026 |
| 15 | 296 | 10 | 0.034 |
| 16 | 306 | 12 | 0.039 |
| 17 | 305 | 12 | 0.039 |
| 18 | 300 | 7 | 0.023 |
| 19 | 305 | 5 | 0.016 |
| 20 | 298 | 13 | 0.044 |

**Table 11.5**
Fraction of
Nonconforming
Purchase Orders over
20 Days

A newly inaugurated shopping channel processes about 5000 orders per day. It selects a sample of 1000 order forms each day and does a complete audit to determine if the item(s) purchased have the correct item number, quantity purchased, and unit price. Table 11.6 contains the number of three different types of errors found in 20 successive subgroups of 1000 order forms. The three types of errors, wrong part number, incorrect quantity, and wrong price, do not have the same degree of severity (see bold-faced numbers in Table 11.6). For each subgroup of 1000 forms the firm computes a demerit score that reflects the numbers of each type of error weighted by its degree of severity. The firm's goal is to reduce the overall demerit score for the ordering process.

The quality characteristic is an attribute because we do not measure it on a continuous scale. Rather, we determine the demerit score by *counting* the number of different types of errors in each sample of 1000 forms and then weighting them by their degrees of severity.

| Day | Part No. | Quantity | Price | Demerit |
|-----|----------|----------|-------|---------|
|     | 5.00     | 1.00     | 3.00  |         |
| 1   | 8        | 5        | 1     | 48 ◄——— $(8 \cdot 5) + (5 \cdot 1) + (1 \cdot 3) = 48$ |
| 2   | 3        | 6        | 1     | 24      |
| 3   | 2        | 8        | 8     | 42      |
| 4   | 5        | 6        | 4     | 43      |
| 5   | 6        | 3        | 5     | 48      |
| 6   | 2        | 4        | 7     | 35      |
| 7   | 4        | 5        | 8     | 49      |
| 8   | 6        | 5        | 3     | 44      |
| 9   | 4        | 7        | 5     | 42      |
| 10  | 2        | 4        | 3     | 23      |
| 11  | 2        | 9        | 5     | 34      |
| 12  | 2        | 6        | 11    | 49      |
| 13  | 4        | 5        | 3     | 34      |
| 14  | 6        | 8        | 6     | 56      |
| 15  | 3        | 10       | 4     | 37      |
| 16  | 2        | 3        | 5     | 28      |
| 17  | 3        | 1        | 3     | 25      |
| 18  | 5        | 5        | 7     | 51      |
| 19  | 3        | 7        | 5     | 37      |
| 20  | 7        | 5        | 3     | 49      |

**Table 11.6**
Demerit Chart Data for
20 Successive Days

# CONTROL CHARTS FOR VARIABLES: $\bar{x}$ AND STANDARD DEVIATION

Two common control charts for variables are the mean and standard deviation charts. Develop two separate charts when charting variables. One monitors the process variation (an $s$ chart) and the other monitors the process mean (an $\bar{x}$ chart). There are four steps to constructing control charts for variables:

1. Select an important quality characteristic;

2. Obtain a **rational subgroup** and determine the sample size per subgroup;

3. Select 15–30 subgroups to establish the **initial** control limits; and

4. Look for assignable-cause variation and revise the control limits if you find causes.

Once constructed, use the control charts to monitor the process on an on-going basis. By the end of this section you should be able to

1. determine which quality characteristics to control chart;

2. select a rational subgroup and appropriate sample size;

3. construct mean and standard deviation control charts;

4. use these charts to monitor a process;

5. compute the nonconformance rate;

6. compute and interpret the $C_{pk}$ process capability index;

7. explain the logic of the 3-Sigma rule;

8. explain when an out-of-control signal indicates an opportunity, not a problem; and

9. determine when to discontinue control charting a process.

## SELECTING THE QUALITY CHARACTERISTIC TO CHART

Any process contains many possible quality measures. However, use control charts to track only the most important ones. Management can determine the important measures by asking its customers. Firms use surveys or the quality function deployment method to assess what is a quality service or product. Alternatively, a firm could use a check sheet and Pareto chart to determine the most frequent or most costly problem areas and use control charts to reduce these problems.

## SELECTING RATIONAL SUBGROUPS AND DETERMINING SAMPLE SIZE

**Rational subgroups** are samples from a process that are as homogeneous as possible on the quality characteristic being measured. Homogeneous means that the firm produces the services or products under essentially the same conditions.

Use the **instant-time** method to select a rational subgroup. At a randomly determined time, select $n$ successive products or services and measure the quality characteristic. This method minimizes the chance of assignable-cause variation being present within the subgroup data values. This approach provides a process "snapshot" at each point in time when you collect data.

Quality Car Rental's LAX station manager selected a rational subgroup of size five. At a randomly determined time of day she monitored five consecutive customers from a single clerk and recorded paperwork completion times. The only variation in the five data values should be common-cause variation. The manager has minimized the possibility of clerk-to-clerk and time-within-day sources of assignable-cause variation.

A subgroup consisting of five customer completion times each processed by a different clerk at different times of the day would not be a rational subgroup. The five data values would exhibit both common-cause and systematic clerk-to-clerk and time-within-day assignable-cause variation. If the manager wishes to monitor all five clerks, she must construct a control chart for each clerk.

The subgroup sample size depends on how much process variation there is and the sampling cost. Suppose the time to process customers exhibits very little variability; say, $10.0 \pm 0.5$ minutes. How large a sample is needed from such a process to accurately predict the next result? Clearly, the answer is a very small sample, perhaps $n = 1$. Alternatively, suppose the process exhibits much variability; say, $10 \pm 10$ minutes. Here you will need a larger sample size.

Cost plays a role in determining the sample size per subgroup. When sampling is costly, consider small sample sizes of four or less. For sample mean and standard deviation charts, firms frequently use sample sizes of 3 to 10.

In summary, rational subgroups increase the chances that only common-cause variation is present within a subgroup. This makes it easier to detect assignable-cause variation; it sticks out like a "mountain among the hills."

## ESTABLISHING INITIAL CONTROL LIMITS FOR THE $\bar{x}$ AND $s$ CHARTS

Unlike specification limits that customers set, the process itself determines the values for a control chart's three critical lines (LCL, CL, and UCL).

To establish control charts for customer completion time, begin by obtaining between 15–30 subgroups of five data values each (see Table 11.4). First, construct a standard deviation chart to monitor process variation. Table 11.4 reproduced below contains the sample means and standard deviations for the $k = 30$ subgroups of size five. Also shown are the overall mean, $\bar{\bar{x}}$, of the 30 sample means and the mean standard deviation, $\bar{s}$, of the 30 sample standard deviations. We have not included the data values for subgroup 3–subgroup 28 to reduce the table's "clutter."

Expression (11.1) provides the center line for a standard deviation chart. The variable $s_i$ represents the sample standard deviations for each of the $k = 30$ subgroups of five data values. Again, $\bar{s}$ is simply the mean of the $k = 30$ sample standard deviations, $s_i$.

Use Expressions (11.2) and (11.3) to compute the upper and lower control limits for the s chart. Appendix II contains the control chart constants, $B_3$ and $B_4$. For subgroups of size five, $B_3$ and $B_4$ are zero and 2.089, respectively.

| Subgroup | Observations | | | | | Mean | Std. Dev. |
|---|---|---|---|---|---|---|---|
| 1 | 11.6 | 9.3 | 9.8 | 9.2 | 10.5 | 10.08 | 0.993 |
| 2 | 11.3 | 12.5 | 9.4 | 11.8 | 13.6 | 11.72 | 1.558 |
| 3 | | | | | | 9.82 | 1.226 |
| 4 | | | | | | 10.16 | 1.159 |
| 5 | | | | | | 11.86 | 0.888 |
| 6 | | | | | | 9.88 | 1.119 |
| 7 | | | | | | 9.98 | 1.040 |
| 8 | | | | | | 9.54 | 1.953 |
| 9 | | | | | | 9.68 | 0.228 |
| 10 | | | | | | 11.86 | 0.835 |
| 11 | | | | | | 9.60 | 1.425 |
| 12 | | | | | | 9.36 | 1.436 |
| 13 | | | | | | 10.12 | 1.268 |
| 14 | | | | | | 9.34 | 1.216 |
| 15 | | | | | | 10.18 | 0.466 |
| 16 | | | | | | 9.60 | 1.089 |
| 17 | | | | | | 9.60 | 1.416 |
| 18 | | | | | | 9.32 | 1.026 |
| 19 | | | | | | 9.66 | 1.754 |
| 20 | | | | | | 10.28 | 0.832 |
| 21 | | | | | | 9.60 | 1.790 |
| 22 | | | | | | 10.00 | 1.105 |
| 23 | | | | | | 9.48 | 0.960 |
| 24 | | | | | | 9.68 | 0.415 |
| 25 | | | | | | 10.06 | 0.974 |
| 26 | | | | | | 10.08 | 1.178 |
| 27 | | | | | | 9.74 | 1.387 |
| 28 | | | | | | 8.70 | 2.022 |
| 29 | 8.9 | 10.4 | 10.8 | 8.6 | 9.7 | 9.68 | 0.942 |
| 30 | 9.5 | 9.0 | 10.1 | 12.1 | 10.8 | 10.30 | 1.210 |
| | | | | | | **9.97 min** | **1.16 min** |

**Table 11.7**
Customer Processing
Time for 30 Subgroups
of Size Five

Center line
$$\bar{s} = \sum_i \frac{s_i}{k} = \sum_i \frac{s_i}{30} = 1.16\,\text{min}$$
    **(11.1)**

Upper Control Limit
$$B_4\bar{s} = (2.089)(1.16) = 2.42\,\text{min}$$
    **(11.2)**

Lower Control Limit
$$B_3\bar{s} = (0)(1.16) = 0\,\text{min}$$
    **(11.3)**

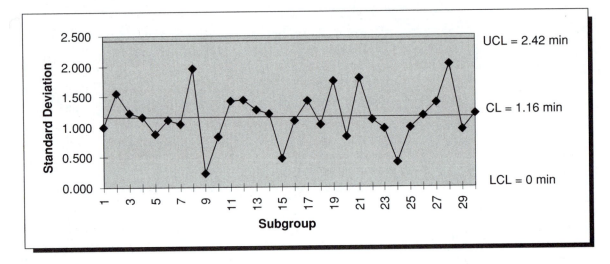

**Figure 11.8**
Initial Control Chart for Standard Deviation of Processing Times

Even though neither of the control chart constants, $B_3$ and $B_4$ equal three, the upper and lower control limits are three standard deviations from the center line. It can be shown that

$$\bar{s} + 3\hat{\sigma}_s = B_4 \cdot \bar{s}$$

$$\bar{s} - 3\hat{\sigma}_s = B_3 \cdot \bar{s}$$

However, that is beyond the scope of this book.[7] Years ago, statisticians developed the $B_3$ and $B_4$ factors so practitioners would not have to compute $\hat{\sigma}_s$ directly. This has really simplified constructing control charts.

***Examining the Preliminary* s *Chart.*** Are any plotted values outside the control limits? If so, assignable cause is present. If the branch manager or

---

[7]$\hat{\sigma}_s$ is simply the standard deviation for the $k = 30$ standard deviations in Table 11.7.

clerk can determine the reasons for the assignable cause, he or she should eliminate the subgroups from Table 11.7 and recompute the initial control limits. From Figure 11.8, the process variation was never out of control for the 30 subgroups so the clerk does not have to revise the control limits.

Once the process variability is under control, construct a control chart for the sample mean. Expression (11.4) provides the center line for the $\bar{x}$ chart where $\bar{x}_i$ represents the sample means for each of the $k = 30$ subgroups of five data values. Again, $\bar{\bar{x}}$ is simply the mean of the $k = 30$ sample means. Then

$$\text{Center line} \quad \boxed{\bar{\bar{x}} = \sum_i \frac{\bar{x}_i}{k} = \sum_i \frac{\bar{x}_i}{30} = 9.97 \text{ min}}$$

**(11.4)**

Use Expressions (11.5) and (11.6) to compute the upper and lower control limits for the $\bar{x}$ chart. Appendix II provides the $A_3$ value. For a subgroup of size five, $A_3 = 1.427$.

$$\text{Upper Control Limit} \quad \boxed{\bar{\bar{x}} + A_3 \cdot \bar{s} = 9.97 + \left(1.427 \cdot 1.16\right) = 11.62 \text{ min}}$$

**(11.5)**

$$\text{Lower Control Limit} \quad \boxed{\bar{\bar{x}} - A_3 \cdot \bar{s} = 9.97 - \left(1.427 \cdot 1.16\right) = 8.31 \text{ min}}$$

**(11.6)**

Even though $A_3$ does not equal three, the upper and lower control limits are three standard deviations from the center line. It can be shown that

$$\bar{\bar{x}} + 3\hat{\sigma}_{\bar{x}} = \bar{\bar{x}} + \left(A_3 \cdot \bar{s}\right)$$

$$\bar{\bar{x}} - 3\hat{\sigma}_{\bar{x}} = \bar{\bar{x}} - \left(A_3 \cdot \bar{s}\right)$$

However, that too is beyond this book's scope.[8]

### *Examining the Preliminary $\bar{x}$ Chart.*

After constructing a preliminary $\bar{x}$ control chart, check for *two* conditions. First, is the center line close to the target value? If not, the branch manager and clerk must do intensive problem solving to bring the center line close to the target value. Figure 11.9 shows that the center line of 9.97 minutes is very close to the target value of 10 minutes (mentioned in the earlier section, "Management Scenarios and Data Sets").

---

[8] $\hat{\sigma}_{\bar{x}}$ is simply the standard deviation for the $k = 30$ means in Table 11.7.

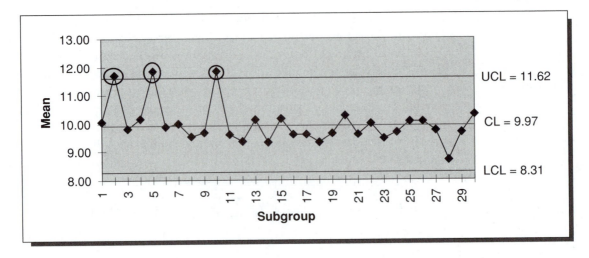

**Figure 11.9**
Initial Control Chart for Sample Mean Processing Times

Second, the manager must determine if any sample means are outside the control limits. If so, the manager and clerk must determine the assignable causes. If they determine the causes, the manager can then revise the control limits for the $\bar{x}$ chart.

***Revising Initial Control Limits.*** Figure 11.9 shows that sample means for subgroups 2, 5, and 10 are above the upper control limit. The process is not yet under statistical control in the mean.

The branch manager investigated. She found that for day 2 the clerk had not used the standard procedures for completing the paperwork. On day 5 the clerk had made many data-entry errors due to working a double shift. On day 10 the clerk's computer terminal was experiencing intermittent problems throughout the day.

The branch manager then eliminated subgroups 2, 5, and 10 from Table 11.7, and recomputed a new center line and control limits for the $\bar{x}$ control chart. Eliminating the three subgroups changed $\bar{\bar{x}}$ from 9.97 to 9.76 minutes—see new center line in Figure 11.10. Eliminating these subgroups caused $\bar{s}$ to change from 1.16 minutes to 1.17 minutes.

| Revised Upper Control Limit | 11.43 min = 9.76 + (1.427 · 1.17) |
|---|---|
| Revised Center Line | 9.76 min |
| Revised Lower Control Limit | 8.09 min = 9.76 − (1.427 · 1.17) |

If the manager had not determined the causes, she would not have discarded the subgroups and revised the limits.

Figure 11.10 is the revised control chart for the sample mean. The branch manager will now use it with a *revised s* chart to monitor the paperwork completion time at the LAX branch.

The manager must eliminate subgroups 2, 5, and 10 and recompute $\bar{s}$, the center line, and the lower and upper control limits. The revised limits for the *s* chart are

Revised Upper Control Limit          2.44 minutes

Revised Center Line          1.17 minutes

Revised Lower Control Limit          0 minutes

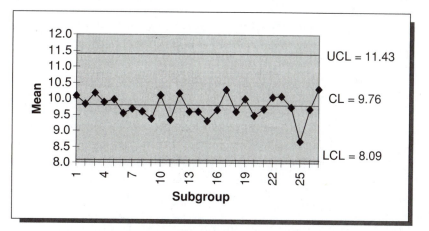

**Figure 11.10**
Revised Control Chart for Sample Mean Processing Times

The preliminary phase has ended, and now the manager will use the two revised charts as early warning systems to notify her when either the mean or standard deviation in customer completion times go out of control. At some point, they probably will.

***Using Control Charts to Monitor a Process.*** Every day at a randomly determined time the branch manager will record how long it took the clerk to service five successive customers. She will then compute the sample mean and sample standard deviation and plot these two data values on their respective control charts. The manager will investigate the process when either of the following occurs.

**1.** one sample mean falls outside its control limits[9]

The process mean has shifted either upwards or downwards from the target value. Investigate why!

_____

[9] There are additional rules to detect an out-of-control process. For example, eight successive points above (or below) the center line or any nonrandom pattern signals the presence of assignable-cause variation.

If the sample mean falls above the upper control limit, management must take action to return the process mean to the target value. It does not want to increase the customer processing time.

If the sample mean falls below the lower control limit, management should determine the assignable causes. If successful, it could permanently reduce the mean time from its present 9.76 minutes. Customers who are quickly serviced are happy customers!

An important point: An out-of-control signal can indicate an emerging opportunity as well as an emerging problem.

2. one sample standard deviation falls above the upper control limit

   This indicates the process variation has increased. Management must take action to reduce the process variation. Customers want consistent service times.

   Given that the chart's lower control limit is zero, the manager can never obtain a signal that could help her permanently reduce process variation.

   There are two solutions for a LCL of zero for a standard deviation chart. From Appendix II if the manager increases the subgroup size to six or more, the lower limit for the standard deviation chart will not equal zero. Second, she could construct a standard deviation chart with probability limits, but that is beyond the scope of this book.

In summary, an out-of-control signal can suggest an emerging opportunity or an emerging problem. In any case, management and service providers must investigate to determine the assignable causes.

## ESTIMATING PROCESS CAPABILITY

Process control and process capability are different ideas. Process control determines whether there is only common-cause variation present in a process. That is, is the process under statistical control? Process capability determines whether an in-control process can produce a sufficiently large number of parts or services within design specification limits.

***Estimating Nonconformance Rates.*** Here you determine the proportion of quality measurements that fall above the upper **specification** (not control) limit or below the lower **specification** limit; that is, nonconforming products or services.

Proportion above USL $\boxed{P(x > \text{USL})}$

**(11.7)**

$$\text{Proportion below LSL} \quad \boxed{P(x < \text{LSL})}$$

**(11.8)**

If the proportion from the two expressions above is acceptably low, the process is capable of meeting customer wants and needs. Do not assess process capability until a process is under statistical control.

Let's compute the proportion of customers who will have to wait more than the upper specification limit of 14 minutes to complete the rental car paperwork. From Expression (11.7),

$$P(x > 14 \text{ min})$$

This is the only calculation needed since there is no lower specification limit for the car rental paperwork process.

Use Excel's NORMDIST function wizard first discussed in Chapter 4 to compute the above probability. Shown below are the NORMDIST wizard inputs.

1. $x = 14$ minutes, which is the upper specification limit.

2. The mean is 9.76 minutes, $\bar{\bar{x}}$, which is the center line of the mean chart.

3. The estimated process standard deviation that we do not yet know.

4. The cumulative input is always shown as TRUE.

What does the estimated process standard deviation actually measure and what is its value? The estimated process standard deviation, $\hat{\sigma}$, is the "natural" variation of the process. There is variation in all processes. For example, is your travel time to a mall precisely the same every trip? Of course not! It will depend on weather conditions, traffic conditions, etc. Similarly, a business process has a natural variation. Here's how to estimate it.

The revised mean of the standard deviation control chart, $\bar{s} = 1.17$ minutes, does *not* equal the estimated process standard deviation, $\hat{\sigma}$, but it is close.

The estimated process standard deviation, $\hat{\sigma}$, measures differences among products (or services) *within* a subgroup and *between* subgroups. But you compute $\bar{s}$ by taking the mean of the $k = 30$ standard deviations within each subgroup (see Table 11.7). Therefore, $\bar{s}$ does not measure possible variation between subgroups; it only measures the variation within each subgroup. Thus, $\bar{s}$ *underestimates* the estimated process standard deviation, $\hat{\sigma}$.

Use Expression (11.9) to estimate the process standard deviation.

$$\hat{\sigma} = \frac{\bar{s}}{c_4}$$

(**11.9**)

The $c_4$ factor depends on the sample size per subgroup and is given in Appendix II. Since the $c_4$ values are less than one, the estimated process standard deviation, $\hat{\sigma}$, will always be larger than the mean standard deviation, $\bar{s}$.

For the car rental process the estimated process standard deviation is:

$$\hat{\sigma} = \frac{1.17}{0.9400} = 1.24 \text{ minutes}$$

Now insert 1.24 into the NORMDIST function wizard for the standard deviation.

NORMDIST provides the *cumulative* probability, $P(x \leq 14 \text{ minutes})$. Thus, the desired probability is $1 - 0.999686 = 0.000314$. That is, for every 10,000 customers about 3.1 $(0.000314 \cdot 10,000)$ will have to wait in line more than 14 minutes. That level of nonconformance is very good (but not outstanding) in today's highly competitive environment.[10]

---

[10]Motorola, a winner of the Malcolm Baldrige National Quality Award, has achieved a nonconformance rate in some of its manufacturing processes of under one part per *million*.

If the nonconformance rate had been too high, Quality Car Rental would have two choices. First, it could seek ways to reduce the overall mean time from the present 9.76 minutes. A process flowchart would be critical. Alternatively, it could reduce the estimated process standard deviation below its present 1.24 minutes. Both options would have required either redesigning the process or intensive capital investment in personnel or technology.

**Computing the $C_{pk}$ Index.** The $C_{pk}$ index is a commonly used measure of process capability.

$$C_{pk} = \text{minimum}\left[\frac{\text{USL} - \bar{\bar{x}}}{3\hat{\sigma}}, \frac{\bar{\bar{x}} - \text{LSL}}{3\hat{\sigma}}\right]$$

**(11.10)**

The numerator measures the *allowable* spread from the center line to each specification limit. The denominator measures the *actual* spread within which half of 99.73% of the process data will lie assuming normally distributed data. Recall that 99.73% of the data will lie within $\pm$ 3 standard deviations of the mean.

For processes with two-sided specifications, the $C_{pk}$ index is the smaller of the two computed terms in Expression (11.10). For processes with a one-sided specification, compute the appropriate term in Expression (11.10).

For the car rental paperwork process, the $C_{pk}$ index is

$$C_{pk} = \frac{14 - 9.76}{3 \cdot 1.24} = 1.14$$

A $C_{pk}$ index of 1.00 or higher is acceptable. However, a common goal in many companies is to achieve a $C_{pk}$ greater than 1.33. Companies that strive for world-class quality often design processes with $C_{pk}$ values above 2.00.

## UNDERSTANDING THE 3-SIGMA RULE

According to Walter Shewhart, a pioneer in the quality assurance field, a process is out of control when a subgroup mean or standard deviation falls outside the 3-sigma limits. Here's the logic of his 3-Sigma rule. From Chapters 2 and 4, if the plotted value ($\bar{x}$ or $s$) is normally distributed, 99.73% of the data values should fall within $\pm$ 3 standard deviations of the mean. The area between the lower and upper control limits should equal 0.9973. Thus the area outside of the control limits is

$$1.00 - 0.9973 = 0.0027$$

So if a plotted data value falls outside the control limits, the chance that it is due to common-cause variation is only 0.0027. The probability that it is due to an assignable cause is 0.9973 (see Figure 11.11).

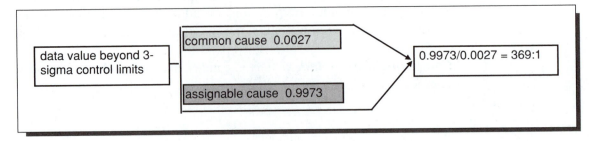

**Figure 11.11**
Implications for One Data Value beyond the 3-Sigma Limits

The odds that one data value outside the 3-sigma limits signifies assignable-cause variation versus common-cause variation are 0.9973/0.0027, or 369 to 1 odds. In short, the odds are 369:1 that the process is broken and must be fixed![11]

## DISCONTINUING A CONTROL CHART

Periodically revise the control chart limits. Select a particular time period (a week, month, quarter, etc.) and use the most recent data to revise the center line and control limits for the mean and standard deviation charts. As you obtain out-of-control signals and "fix the process," the process mean or variation can change over time. The revision frequency depends on the process stability. For processes that frequently go out of control, the revision cycle should be short.

When you have used a chart for a long time two things can happen. First, the presence of assignable-cause variation remains a problem. Continue to chart but frequently revise the limits. Second, the process never goes out of control. At that point, consider eliminating the chart and focusing on other quality characteristics of the process or other critical processes.

This section concludes with an important flow diagram that addresses two key ideas (see Figure 11.12):

**1.** Is the process under statistical control?

**2.** Is the process capable?

---

[11]The probability of obtaining eight data points in a row above (or below) the center line is approximately 0.0027.

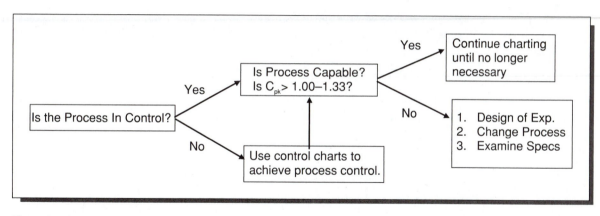

**Figure 11.12**
Flowchart for Statistical Process Control (SPC)

Do not assess process capability until you have achieved statistical process control. Use control charts to identify and correct assignable-cause variation. Look for plotted values outside the control limits or any nonrandom pattern in the data.

Once the process is under statistical control, then assess the process capability using either the nonconformance rate or the $C_{pk}$ index. If the process is capable, use control charts to monitor the process to warn against the occurrence of any new assignable causes that could degrade process performance.

If the process is not yet capable, consider three strategies.

**1.** Design studies either to change the process mean in the desired direction or reduce process variation.

**2.** If that doesn't work, reexamine the specification limits. Perhaps the firm set them tighter than the customers demanded. But don't change them without consulting your customers.

**3.** As a last resort, consider redesigning the process.

# CONTROL CHARTS FOR PROPORTION NONCONFORMING

In the previous section you learned to construct and use control charts on variables (data that you *measure*). You cannot always determine product or service quality by measuring quality characteristics. In control charts on attributes, you use count, or yes or no, data to assess process quality. Here are a few examples of business processes and their attribute quality indicators.

| Process | Quality Characteristic (Count, or Yes/No, Data) |
|---------|--------------------------------------------------|
| 1. Mold handset | Phone handsets without blemishes |
| 2. Do surgery | Postsurgical complications each week |
| 3. Travel on airline | Flights that arrive on time |
| 4. Fill purchase order | Orders without errors |
| 5. Design software | Number of errors in 1000 lines of computer code (KLOC) |

By the end of this section you should be able to

1. construct and interpret a proportion nonconforming, $p$, chart;

2. explain how to deal with variable subgroup sizes; and

3. determine the subgroup size such that the lower control limit will be greater than zero.

Each day, Rent-2-Own Furniture processes about 300 purchase orders. Management audits every purchase order to check for errors. Table 11.5 (reproduced here) contains the number of purchase orders examined each day and the proportion, $\hat{p}_i$, of nonconforming orders (containing one or more *errors* or *nonconformities*). You plot the $\hat{p}_i$ values in a proportion non-conforming control chart.

***Constructing a Control Chart.*** To establish a control chart, select between 15–30 subgroups of size $n$ (see Table 11.5a). Use Expression (11.11) to compute the center line for the chart.

$$\text{Center line} \quad \boxed{\bar{p} = \frac{x_1 + x_2 + x_3 + \cdots + x_k}{n_1 + n_2 + n_3 + \cdots + n_k} = \frac{213}{6004} = 0.0355}$$

(11.11)

$x_1, x_2, x_3, \ldots, x_k$ are the number of nonconforming items in subgroups $n_1$, $n_2$, $n_3, \ldots, n_k$.

Use Expressions (11.12) and (11.13) to compute the upper and lower control limits for the proportion nonconforming chart. The two expressions show that the control limits are indeed three standard deviations from the center line.[12]

---

[12]In Chapters 4 and 5 you learned the expression for the standard error of the proportion, $\sqrt{\dfrac{p \cdot (1 - p)}{n}}$.

| Day | Examined | Nonconforming | Proportion |
|-----|----------|---------------|------------|
| 1 | 286 | 10 | 0.035 |
| 2 | 281 | 9 | 0.032 |
| 3 | 310 | 8 | 0.026 |
| 4 | 313 | 11 | 0.035 |
| 5 | 305 | 14 | 0.046 |
| 6 | 307 | 13 | 0.042 |
| 7 | 295 | 15 | 0.051 |
| 8 | 311 | 10 | 0.032 |
| 9 | 294 | 9 | 0.031 |
| 10 | 300 | 10 | 0.033 |
| 11 | 305 | 17 | 0.056 |
| 12 | 295 | 8 | 0.027 |
| 13 | 290 | 12 | 0.041 |
| 14 | 302 | 8 | 0.026 |
| 15 | 296 | 10 | 0.034 |
| 16 | 306 | 12 | 0.039 |
| 17 | 305 | 12 | 0.039 |
| 18 | 300 | 7 | 0.023 |
| 19 | 305 | 5 | 0.016 |
| 20 | 298 | 13 | 0.044 |
| | 6004 | 213 | 0.0355 |

$\hat{p}_1 = 10/286 = 0.035$

**Table 11.5a**
Daily Records of
Number and Proportion
of Nonconforming
Orders

$$\text{Upper control limit} \quad \boxed{\bar{p} + 3\sqrt{\frac{\bar{p} \cdot (1 - \bar{p})}{n}}} \tag{11.12}$$

$$\text{Lower control limit}^{13} \quad \boxed{\bar{p} - 3\sqrt{\frac{\bar{p} \cdot (1 - \bar{p})}{n}}} \tag{11.13}$$

Given that the sample size varies over the 20 subgroups, what sample size
"$n$" should you use for the two expressions? There are two choices.

**1.** You can use the actual sample size per subgroup. Because it varies, the
upper and lower control limit lines will vary. These disjointed lines are
distracting, so consider a second option.

---

[13]Note that if the computed LCL from Expression 11.13 is less than zero, set the LCL
to zero.

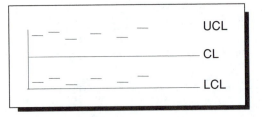

2.  When the range of sample sizes is less than 15%, use the mean sample size over the $k$ subgroups. This ensures that the upper and lower control limits will be straight lines or constant. That is the approach Rent-2-Own followed because the range of sample sizes ($313 - 281 = 32$) was less than 15% ($32/281$). The mean sample size is $\dfrac{6004}{20} = 300.2$, or simply $n = 300$.

The upper and lower control limits for the proportion nonconforming chart are

$$\text{Upper control limit}\quad 0.0355 + 3\sqrt{\frac{0.0355 \cdot \left(0.9645\right)}{300}} = 0.0675$$

$$\text{Lower control limit}\quad 0.0355 - 3\sqrt{\frac{0.0355 \cdot \left(0.9645\right)}{300}} = 0.0034$$

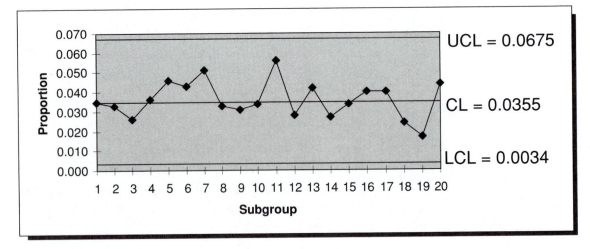

**Figure 11.13**
Initial Control Chart for Proportion of Nonconforming Items

***Examining the Preliminary p Chart.*** Are any plotted values outside the control limits? Are there any nonrandom patterns in the 20 data points? If so, assignable cause is present. If the manager or clerk can determine the reasons for the assignable cause, they should eliminate the subgroups from Table 11.5a and recompute the initial control limits. From Figure 11.13, the process was never out of control for the 20 subgroups, so the manager does not have to revise the control limits.

***An Important Note.*** Even though the process is in control, the mean proportion of nonconforming purchase orders per day, 0.0355, is too high. On average, 300·(0.0355) = 10.65 orders will have one or more errors. Management must reduce $\bar{p}$ from its present level of 0.0355. This will require redesigning the purchase order forms or improvements in training and technology.

***Monitoring the Process.*** While Rent-2-Own management seeks ways to improve the process, it should use the control chart in Figure 11.13 to monitor the process.

Why should management be interested if the subgroup proportion, $\hat{p}$, falls below the lower control limit? After all, isn't that good? Why must it determine why the proportion nonconforming has dropped so low? Think about it before continuing!

A plotted subgroup proportion falling below the lower control limit means there is an assignable cause for the very low proportion of nonconforming purchase orders. If the firm could determine the causes, it could permanently reduce the proportion nonconforming. Now unless the manager had sought an assignable cause, he would have lost an opportunity to make a permanent process improvement.

It is important to detect a plotted value, $\hat{p}_i$, below the lower control limit. However, often the lower control limit for a $p$ chart is zero. To keep from obtaining an LCL of zero, select a sample size, $n$, such that:

$$\bar{p} - 3\sqrt{\frac{\bar{p}(1 - \bar{p})}{n}} > 0$$

$$\bar{p} > 3\sqrt{\frac{\bar{p}(1 - \bar{p})}{n}}$$

$$n > \frac{9(1 - \bar{p})}{\bar{p}}$$

(11.14)

So before conducting a process control study, estimate the mean proportion, $\bar{p}$, for a process. Then use Expression (11.14) to determine the minimum sample size.

Rent-2-Own wanted to know if a sample of 300 orders each day would be sufficient to ensure that the lower control limit would be greater than zero. It anticipated that the mean proportion of nonconforming purchase orders would be no lower than 0.03. Substituting $\bar{p} = 0.03$ into Expression (11.14), the minimum sample size should be 291. Management selected an average sample size of 300.

In summary, a product or service that has one or more defects or *non-conformities* is a nonconforming item. Construct a proportion nonconforming chart and investigate if $\hat{p}_i$ is above the UCL or below the LCL. If you obtain a $\hat{p}_i$ below the LCL, seek to determine the assignable causes to permanently lower the proportion of nonconforming products or services. In short, process control charts not only control processes, but can sometimes lead to process improvements.

# CONTROL CHARTS FOR THE NUMBER OF NONCONFORMITIES: THE DEMERIT CHART

In the previous section a purchase order was nonconforming whether it had only one defect or five defects. Sometimes you are interested in monitoring *the number of nonconformities, or errors,* not whether the product or service is *conforming.* Furthermore, not all defects are equally serious. For example, in manufacturing a car a failed transmission is a much more serious defect than a cracked windshield. And both of these defects are more serious than a squeaky door.

This section presents the demerit control chart. It is a commonly used attribute chart where the system can produce many different nonconformities with different severity levels. By the end of this section you should be able to construct and interpret a demerit control chart.

The Shop-Ease Channel processes about 5000 orders per day. The firm selects a subgroup sample of 1000 order forms (KOF) each day and does an audit to determine if the item(s) purchased have the correct item number, quantity purchased, and total price. Table 11.6 reproduced here contains the numbers of the three different types of errors found in 20 successive subgroups of 1000 order forms each. The firm used Expression (11.15) to compute the demerit score for each subgroup, $D_i$. You will plot these values in the demerit control chart.

$$D_i = \sum_i w_i c_i = w_1 c_1 + w_2 c_2 + w_3 c_3$$

**(11.15)**

where $c_i$ is the number of different types of nonconformities and $w_i$ is the severity of each type of nonconformity

Table 11.6a also provides the mean number of different types of errors or nonconformities per KOE.

| | |
|---|---|
| Mean Number of Incorrect Part Numbers | $\bar{c}_1 = 3.95$ |
| Mean Number of Incorrect Order Quantities | $\bar{c}_2 = 5.60$ |
| Mean Number of Incorrect Unit Prices | $\bar{c}_3 = 4.85$ |

| Subgroup | Incorrect Part No. | Incorrect Quantity | Incorrect Price | Demerits | |
|---|---|---|---|---|---|
| | [5] | [1] | [3] | | |
| 1 | 8 | 5 | 1 | 48 | $(8 \cdot 5) + (5 \cdot 1) + (1 \cdot 3) = 48$ |
| 2 | 3 | 6 | 1 | 24 | |
| 3 | 2 | 8 | 8 | 42 | |
| 4 | 5 | 6 | 4 | 43 | |
| 5 | 6 | 3 | 5 | 48 | |
| 6 | 2 | 4 | 7 | 35 | |
| 7 | 4 | 5 | 8 | 49 | |
| 8 | 6 | 5 | 3 | 44 | |
| 9 | 4 | 7 | 5 | 42 | |
| 10 | 2 | 4 | 3 | 23 | |
| 11 | 2 | 9 | 5 | 34 | |
| 12 | 2 | 6 | 11 | 49 | |
| 13 | 4 | 5 | 3 | 34 | |
| 14 | 6 | 8 | 6 | 56 | |
| 15 | 3 | 10 | 4 | 37 | |
| 16 | 2 | 3 | 5 | 28 | |
| 17 | 3 | 1 | 3 | 25 | |
| 18 | 5 | 5 | 7 | 51 | |
| 19 | 3 | 7 | 5 | 37 | |
| 20 | 7 | 5 | 3 | 49 | |
| Mean Number of Defects | 3.95 | 5.60 | 4.85 | 39.90 | |

**Table 11.6a**
Demerit Chart Data for 20 Successive Days of Subgroups of 1000 Orders Each

**Constructing a Preliminary Control Chart.** To establish a control chart, select between 15–30 subgroups of size $n$ (see Table 11.6a). Use Expression (11.16) to compute the center line for the chart.

$$\bar{D} = \frac{\sum_i D_i}{k} = \frac{\sum_i D_i}{20} = 39.90$$

(11.16)

Use Expressions (11.17) and (11.18) to compute the upper and lower control limits for the demerit chart. The two expressions show that the control limits are indeed three standard deviations from the center line.

$$\text{Upper control limit} \quad \boxed{\overline{D} + 3\sqrt{\sum_i w_i^2 \cdot \overline{c}_i}}$$

(11.17)

$$\text{Lower control limit} \quad \boxed{\overline{D} - 3\sqrt{\sum_i w_i^2 \cdot \overline{c}_i}}$$

(11.18)

The upper and lower limits for the data in Table 11.6a are

$$39.90 + 3\sqrt{\left(5^2 \cdot 3.95\right) + \left(1^2 \cdot 5.60\right) + \left(3^2 \cdot 4.85\right)} = 76.40$$

$$39.90 - 3\sqrt{\left(5^2 \cdot 3.95\right) + \left(1^2 \cdot 5.60\right) + \left(3^2 \cdot 4.85\right)} = 3.40$$

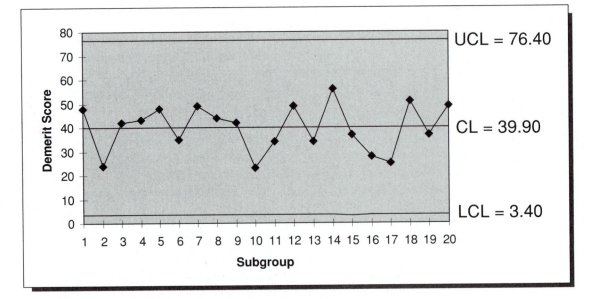

**Figure 11.14**
Initial Control Chart for Demerit Scores

***Examining the Preliminary Demerit Chart.*** Are any plotted values outside the control limits? Is there a nonrandom data pattern? If so, assignable cause is present. If management can determine the reasons for the assignable cause, it should eliminate the subgroups from Table 11.6a and recompute the initial control limits. From Figure 11.14 the process was never out of control for the 20 subgroups, so management need not revise the control limits.

**An Important Note.** Even though the process is in control, the mean number of demerits is too high. Management must reduce $\bar{D}$ from its present level of 39.90. This will take redesigning the purchase order forms or improvements in training and technology.

**Monitoring the Process.** While the ShopEase Channel management seeks ways to improve the process, it should use the control chart in Figure 11.14 to monitor the process.

There are many variations of the basic demerit chart. For example, in complex products such as cars, computers, or major appliances you can use the following demerit scheme:

| | |
|---|---|
| **Class A Defects** | This denotes a very serious problem. The unit is unfit for service or could cause personal injury or property damage. $w_1 = 100$ |
| **Class B Defects** | This denotes a serious problem. The unit may suffer a Class A operating failure. It most certainly will have a reduced life or increased maintenance cost. $w_2 = 50$ |
| **Class C Defects** | This denotes a moderately serious problem. The unit may have increased maintenance costs or major defects in the finish or appearance. $w_3 = 10$ |
| **Class D Defects** | This unit has only minor defects in the finish or appearance. $w_4 = 1$ |

In summary, consider demerit charts when you wish to monitor or improve a process in which different errors with different severity levels can occur. While it is good practice to augment the demerit chart with individual $c$ charts (one for each type of defect), we will not present $c$ charts here.

# IDEAS AND OVERVIEW

This chapter concludes with Table 11.8, which compares and contrasts the four control charts. Three bases for comparison establish important similarities and three bases establish important differences.

| Bases for Comparison | Mean | Standard Deviation | Proportion Nonconforming | Demerit |
|---|---|---|---|---|
| What Is Measured? | Variable (Measure) | Variable (Measure) | Attribute (Count) | Attribute (Count) |
| What Is Monitored? | Process Center | Process Variation | Proportion of Nonconforming Products or Services | Weighted Score of Type of Defect and Its Severity |
| Typical Subgroup Size | 3–10 | 3–10 | $n > 200$ | $n > 200$ |
| Rational Subgroup | Yes | Yes | Yes | Yes |
| Use 3-Sigma Limits or Other Rules? | Yes | Yes | Yes | Yes |
| Reasons for Charting | Monitor or Improve Process | Monitor or Improve Process | Monitor or Improve Process | Monitor or Improve Process |

**Table 11.8**
Compare and Contrast Table for Four Control Charts

The customer has the right to a high-quality product or service. For this to be more than a slogan, firms must adopt the philosophy that quality is more than just $\bar{x}$, $s$, $p$, or demerit charts. It is also more than techniques such as Pareto charts, fishbone diagrams, and the like. Rather, it is an attitude. Quality occurs when hourly employees and management commit themselves to controlling and improving quality in the long run.

# E X E R C I S E S

1. Distinguish between design and manufactured quality.

2. If a process is under statistical control, doesn't that ensure that the process is also capable of producing products or services with very low nonconformance rates?

3. What are two effective remedies for a process with a $C_{pk}$ of 0.5? The process has a two-sided specification.

4. If a plotted value ($\bar{x}$, $s$, $\hat{p}$, or $D$) falls above or below the 3-sigma limit, is it possible that there is no assignable cause? How often will this happen?

5. What problem might you have if you use a fishbone diagram without first clearly defining the problem?

6. How do basic Pareto charts differ from relative frequency histograms?

7. Should (or can) ensuring manufactured quality be the responsibility only of a quality control department?

8 When should you use a proportion nonconforming chart versus using a demerit chart?

9. When should you use mean and standard deviation charts versus using a proportion nonconforming chart?

**10.** Distinguish (how similar and how different) between the standard deviation per subgroup, the mean standard deviation for "*k*" subgroups, and the estimated process standard deviation.

**11.** Below are two figures. Which figure reflects Juran's view of manufactured quality and which figure reflects Taguchi's view? The loss associated with a product being within or outside of specifications is shown as the bold-faced lines. Discuss.

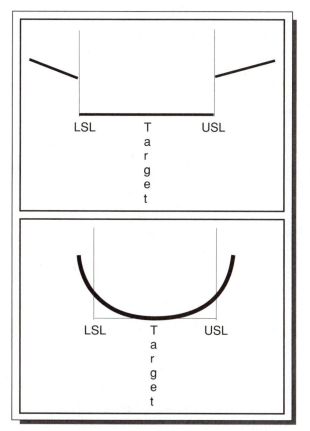

**12.** Given that a process only contains common-cause variation, comment on the appropriateness of the following action. Management places signs in the work area that say, "Quality is job 1—Hunker down and improve quality." According to Deming and most other quality experts this would be stupid and ineffective. Discuss.

**13.** Suggest a process (service or manufacturing) where the project manager would establish (1) an LSL only, (2) a USL only, and (3) both an LSL and USL. Defend your answers.

**14.** Journal adjustments are made at the monthly closing only when there have been incorrect entries posted in the journal accounts. Shown is the number of adjusting entries made for the first ten monthly closings for four major accounts. Each account has over 20,000 postings each month.

| | Accounts | | | |
|---|---|---|---|---|
| **Month** | **1** | **2** | **3** | **4** |
| January | 100 | 98 | 102 | 94 |
| February | 96 | 95 | 104 | 100 |
| March | 102 | 104 | 103 | 98 |
| April | 90 | 100 | 100 | 98 |
| May | 103 | 100 | 100 | 93 |
| June | 100 | 95 | 100 | 101 |
| July | 104 | 103 | 100 | 97 |
| August | 101 | 99 | 104 | 102 |
| September | 104 | 100 | 103 | 99 |
| October | 93 | 97 | 103 | 102 |

**a.** Set up control limits for the mean and standard deviation.

**b.** Given is the number of adjusting entries for the four journal accounts for the next ten months.

| **Month** | **1** | **2** | **3** | **4** |
|---|---|---|---|---|
| November | 96 | 95 | 103 | 96 |
| December | 100 | 96 | 105 | 99 |
| January | 102 | 101 | 100 | 105 |
| February | 101 | 95 | 102 | 104 |
| March | 110 | 85 | 103 | 91 |
| April | 104 | 97 | 101 | 102 |
| May | 99 | 99 | 99 | 99 |
| June | 102 | 104 | 102 | 99 |
| July | 95 | 102 | 96 | 104 |
| August | 98 | 96 | 98 | 96 |

According to the $\bar{x}$ or $s$ charts, was the process ever out of control?

c. Even if the process is under control, should management be satisfied with the current process? Discuss.

15. A firm produces wooden handles for umbrellas. The standard reads: The handles shall be free of blemishes or rough spots. Each shift, the inspector selects $n = 500$ handles and inspects them for blemishes and rough spots. Shown are the data for the first ten shifts.

| Subgroup | Sample Size | Number of Nonconforming Handles |
|---|---|---|
| 1 | 500 | 3 |
| 2 | 500 | 4 |
| 3 | 500 | 2 |
| 4 | 500 | 5 |
| 5 | 500 | 3 |
| 6 | 500 | 4 |
| 7 | 500 | 2 |
| 8 | 500 | 5 |
| 9 | 500 | 3 |
| 10 | 500 | 5 |

a. Determine the sample proportion nonconforming for the first ten subgroups.

b. Compute $\bar{p}$ for the first ten shifts. Determine the LCL and UCL. Construct a control chart for the proportion nonconforming.

c. Shown are the numbers of nonconforming umbrella handles for the next 15 shifts.

| Subgroup | Sample Size | Number of Nonconforming Handles |
|---|---|---|
| 11 | 500 | 3 |
| 12 | 500 | 4 |
| 13 | 500 | 3 |
| 14 | 500 | 2 |
| 15 | 500 | 3 |
| 16 | 500 | 4 |
| 17 | 500 | 10 |
| 18 | 500 | 11 |
| 19 | 500 | 10 |
| 20 | 500 | 4 |
| 21 | 500 | 3 |
| 22 | 500 | 5 |
| 23 | 500 | 2 |
| 24 | 500 | 3 |
| 25 | 500 | 2 |

Was the process ever out of control for the next 15 subgroups?

d. If it was, was the firm able to correct the problem? Explain.

16. In a statistics class a key measure of success is the attentiveness or alertness of the students. Suppose you take one sample of size five from the student body of two classes (two students from a 1:15–3:30 PM class and three students from a 7:55–10:05 PM class) each class day throughout the term. You measure student alertness on a 100 point scale from dazed or catatonic (0) to highly alert (100). You then compute the mean and standard deviation in alertness scores for the 20 class periods of sample size five and use the data to construct $\bar{x}$ and $s$ control charts. Why would the above sampling procedure for subgroups of size five violate the principal of rational subgrouping?

17. Below are two Pareto charts that capture the types of errors in typed documents in a major law firm. The Before column reflects the breakdown of errors before the firm began a major quality improvement effort. The After column reflects the breakdown of errors after the initial effort.

|  | Before | After |
| --- | --- | --- |
| spelling errors | 50% | |
| missing words | 35 | |
| improper punctuation | 10 | 70% |
| improper formatting | 3 | 20 |
| additional words | 1 | 5 |
| incorrect case | 1 | 5 |

a. Was the initial quality effort successful?

b. Has there been in drop in the overall number of typing errors?

c. Now what action should the firm take to improve the typing process?

18. Compare and contrast the standard deviation and mean charts. That is, complete the following table. Two bases must show how the mean and standard deviation charts are *similar*, and two bases must establish how the mean and standard deviation charts are *different*. Use bases different from those in Table 11.8.

| Bases | Mean Chart | s Chart |
| --- | --- | --- |
| 1. | | |
| 2. | | |
| 3. | | |
| 4. | | |

19. Given the following subgroups of size four, compute the five subgroup means and standard deviations and then determine the LCLs, CLs, and UCLs for the mean and standard deviation charts.

| Subgroup | Observations Taken during Subgroup | | | |
| --- | --- | --- | --- | --- |
| 1 | 40 | 35 | 41 | 40 |
| 2 | 42 | 39 | 40 | 38 |
| 3 | 40 | 36 | 42 | 41 |
| 4 | 35 | 41 | 42 | 40 |
| 5 | 38 | 42 | 44 | 41 |

20. Shown are data on the amount of time (in minutes) needed for a pill to enter into the bloodstream. Each half-hour, an inspector selects four successive pills and runs diffusion tests.

| | Observation | | | |
| --- | --- | --- | --- | --- |
| Subgroup | 1 | 2 | 3 | 4 |
| 1 | 2.00 | 1.98 | 2.02 | 1.98 |
| 2 | 2.02 | 1.98 | 2.02 | 2.00 |
| 3 | 2.00 | 1.97 | 2.02 | 1.97 |
| 4 | 2.00 | 1.98 | 2.03 | 2.00 |
| 5 | 2.00 | 1.98 | 2.02 | 1.96 |
| 6 | 2.00 | 1.98 | 2.02 | 2.00 |
| 7 | 2.03 | 1.98 | 2.02 | 2.00 |
| 8 | 2.00 | 1.98 | 2.02 | 2.00 |
| 9 | 2.35 | 2.33 | 2.35 | 2.31 |
| 10 | 2.37 | 2.33 | 2.36 | 2.33 |
| 11 | 2.33 | 2.30 | 2.34 | 2.33 |
| 12 | 2.35 | 2.30 | 2.35 | 2.31 |
| 13 | 2.32 | 2.32 | 2.35 | 2.31 |
| 14 | 2.38 | 2.34 | 2.33 | 2.35 |
| 15 | 2.33 | 2.30 | 2.35 | 2.31 |

Construct control charts for the mean and standard deviation. Are the mean and standard deviation of the process under statistical control? Explain.

21. The traffic at a major shopping mall dropped about 20% between March of one year and March of the following year. Use a fishbone diagram and your general business knowledge to generate possible root causes. Identify four major bones and several subbones.

**22.** Use Excel's data-analysis tool (random number generator) to develop a spreadsheet of 20 subgroups of size five based on a uniform distribution with a range of values between 75 and 125.

    **a.** Determine the LCLs, CLs, and UCLs for the $\bar{x}$ and $s$ charts.

    **b.** Draw the two control charts and identify any out-of-control data points.

    **c.** Estimate the process standard deviation, $\hat{\sigma}$.

**23.** Construct the control limits for the following demerit data. Given the Shewhart 3-Sigma rule, was the process ever out of control?

| Subgroup | | Class A<br>w = 100 | Class B<br>w = 50 | Class C<br>w = 10 | Class D<br>w = 10 |
|---|---|---|---|---|---|
| 1 | | 0 | 6 | 2 | 5 |
| 2 | | 0 | 4 | 3 | 5 |
| 3 | | 1 | 3 | 3 | 5 |
| 4 | | 4 | 3 | 4 | 6 |
| 5 | | 3 | 4 | 2 | 6 |
| 6 | | 0 | 2 | 4 | 7 |
| 7 | | 1 | 4 | 6 | 7 |
| 8 | | 2 | 5 | 6 | 4 |
| 9 | | 2 | 2 | 5 | 7 |
| 10 | | 3 | 3 | 5 | 7 |

**24.** Compare and contrast control limits and specification limits. Develop one *important* basis that establishes a similarity and one *important* basis that establishes a difference. Describe the similarity and difference.

| Bases of<br>Comparison | Control<br>Limits | Specification<br>Limits |
|---|---|---|
| 1. | | |
| 2. | | |

**25.** An overnight parcel delivery service wishes to develop a control chart for the proportion of overnight parcels that are not delivered within the specified time limit. Shown are data for a small shipping center.

| Subgroup | Number of<br>Overnight<br>Parcels | Number Not<br>Delivered on Time<br>(Nonconforming) |
|---|---|---|
| 1 | 10,000 | 10 |
| 2 | 9000 | 7 |
| 3 | 9000 | 10 |
| 4 | 11,000 | 10 |
| 5 | 13,000 | 12 |
| 6 | 12,000 | 14 |
| 7 | 9000 | 9 |
| 8 | 10,000 | 8 |
| 9 | 15,000 | 16 |
| 10 | 12,000 | 9 |

    **a.** In terms of late deliveries, the firm has set a desired target value proportion of 0.002 or less. Has it met its target over the past ten days?

    **b.** Set up an LCL and UCL for the proportion of overnight parcels that fail to arrive within the specified time. Use 10,000 for the normal or typical sample size. Was the process ever out of control?

    **c.** Suppose the firm wants to reduce late deliveries. What quality improvement tool(s) should it use? Discuss what analysis the firm should carry out.

**26.** Below are the daily records of the numbers of tested and rejected circuit boards. A circuit board is defined as nonconforming (rejected) if it has one or more nonconformities.

| Subgroup | Rejected | Tested |
|----------|----------|--------|
| 1 | 14 | 301 |
| 2 | 22 | 296 |
| 3 | 16 | 290 |
| 4 | 9 | 305 |
| 5 | 16 | 310 |
| 6 | 14 | 290 |
| 7 | 18 | 298 |
| 8 | 8 | 301 |
| 9 | 22 | 311 |
| 10 | 17 | 315 |
| 11 | 16 | 305 |
| 12 | 21 | 296 |
| 13 | 9 | 289 |
| 14 | 11 | 299 |
| 15 | 18 | 312 |
| 16 | 13 | 305 |
| 17 | 19 | 295 |
| 18 | 23 | 315 |
| 19 | 7 | 320 |
| 20 | 16 | 305 |
| 21 | 19 | 297 |
| 22 | 13 | 297 |
| 23 | 16 | 290 |
| 24 | 8 | 316 |
| 25 | 21 | 308 |
| 26 | 23 | 305 |
| 27 | 17 | 299 |
| 28 | 12 | 309 |
| 29 | 14 | 306 |
| 30 | 18 | 294 |

**a.** Construct a proportion nonconforming chart and graph the plotted values. Use the mean sample size to determine the control limits.

**b.** Was the process ever out of control?

**27.** A software firm records the number of errors (nonconformities) per 1000 lines of code (KLOC) for a very large program. It classifies each error into one of two categories: (1) major coding problem or (2) minor coding problem. Below are data for the past 20 working days. Develop and plot the control chart for the following data. Was the process ever out of control?

| Subgroup | Major Problem ($w_1 = 10$) | Minor Problem ($w_2 = 2.5$) |
|----------|----------------------------|------------------------------|
| 1 | 2 | 4 |
| 2 | 2 | 5 |
| 3 | 2 | 5 |
| 4 | 1 | 5 |
| 5 | 3 | 5 |
| 6 | 2 | 4 |
| 7 | 1 | 4 |
| 8 | 3 | 5 |
| 9 | 0 | 8 |
| 10 | 2 | 0 |
| 11 | 2 | 3 |
| 12 | 1 | 4 |
| 13 | 1 | 3 |
| 14 | 1 | 2 |
| 15 | 1 | 2 |
| 16 | 2 | 2 |
| 17 | 3 | 1 |
| 18 | 2 | 4 |
| 19 | 3 | 4 |
| 20 | 1 | 5 |

**28.** A firm produces car batteries. Each shift, an inspector selects five consecutive five batteries. She determines how long an engine will crank (in seconds) at 30 degrees before needing to be recharged. The firm has set a lower specification limit of 85 seconds and an upper specification limit of 115 seconds. The center line for the $s$ chart is 1.98 seconds. The center line for the mean chart is 89.89 seconds.

**a.** Compute the $C_{pk}$ index.

**b.** Compute the nonconformance rate in parts per million.

**c.** Suggest two ways to increase the process capability index.

**29.** A sample of $n = 4$ items was selected each hour over a five-hour period and the lengths were measured. The mean of the five sample standard deviations was 0.10 cm. The mean of the five sample means was 17.5 cm.

   **a.** What would be the proportion of defective items produced by the process if you began production? The lower and upper specification limits are 15.0 and 20.0 cm. respectively. Assume the process data are normally distributed.

   **b.** Compute the $C_{pk}$ index.

**30.** Spreadsheet 1130.xls contains 20 rational subgroups of four observations each.

   **a.** Construct a mean chart and a standard deviation chart.

   **b.** Compute the estimated process standard deviation.

   **c.** Was the process ever out of control within the first 20 subgroups?

**31.** You use a standard deviation chart to monitor process variation. For the last 19 subgroups the $s$ chart is as below.

   Does the chart indicate that the process is under statistical control? That is, if the 19 standard deviation values are normally distributed within the control limits, would you expect all 19 values to be very close to the center line if only common-cause variation were present? Discuss.

**32.** Spreadsheet 1132.xls contains 20 subgroups of $n = 300$ each. Shown also are the number of items with one or more nonconformities.

   **a.** Construct a preliminary proportion non-conforming chart.

   **b.** Was the process ever out of control? If so, delete these subgroups and recompute the control limits for the chart.

**33.** Suppose a drive-in fast-food restaurant has a five-minute burger preparation time (from time of order to time of pickup). Suppose that a completion time of $y = 3$ minutes would produce a loss of $0.02 and a completion time of $y = 7$ minutes would produce a loss of $0.08 based on loss of future business. The Taguchi loss function is as follows:

$$L = k_1(y - 5)^2 \text{ if } Y \le 5 \text{ minutes}$$
$$L = k_2(y - 5)^2 \text{ if } Y \ge 5 \text{ minutes}$$

where $L$ is the loss

   **a.** Determine the values for $k_1$ and $k_2$.

   **b.** Plot the loss function.

   **c.** Explain in nontechnical language what information the loss function provides.

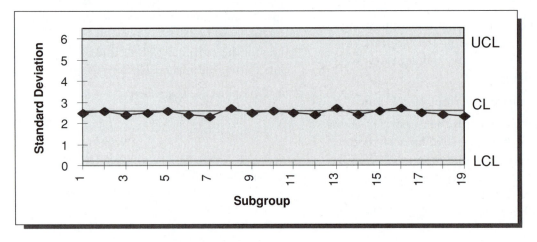

**d.** The above loss function is nonsymmetrical because completion times below the target value produce only lukewarm food whereas as completion times above the target value produce impatient customers. Provide an example from the manufacturing sector where you might expect a nonsymmetrical loss function.

**34.** A sample of ten items was selected each hour over an eight-hour period. Inspectors measured the shatter strength. The mean of the eight standard deviations was 100 ppsi. The mean of the eight sample means was 2800 ppsi. The LSL and USL are 2400 ppsi and 3200 ppsi respectively. The target value is 2800 ppsi.

**a.** Compute the $C_{pk}$ index.

**b.** Compute the proportion of nonconforming parts (in parts per million) for the above process.

**35.** The process of making ignition keys for automobiles consists of trimming and pressing raw key blanks, cutting grooves, cutting notches, and plating. An important quality measurement is the groove dimension in inches. Every 20 minutes, the operator selects five consecutive keys and measures the groove dimension. Spreadsheet 1135.xls contains the data.

**a.** The target value is 0.0080 inches. Does the center line for the mean chart indicate that the process is centered? That is, is the overall mean very close to the target value?

**b.** The LSL is 0.0010 and the USL is 0.0150. Compute the $C_{pk}$ index.

**c.** Construct a sample mean chart and a sample standard deviation chart.

**d.** Was the process ever out of control in the mean or the standard deviation?

**36.** You are preparing to construct a proportion nonconforming chart. You want to ensure that the lower control limit is above zero. You anticipate that the mean proportion of nonconforming items will be about 0.02. What size sample per subgroup must you have to ensure that the lower control limit is above zero?

**37.** Consider a control chart where the specification limits are inside the control limits. What does this tell us about the nonconformance rate (or rejects in parts per million)?

**38.** The following $\bar{x}$ and $s$ charts are based on a subgroup sample size of four. The mean and standard deviation are under statistical control.

| $\bar{x}$ chart | $s$ Chart |
|---|---|
| UCL = 508.20 | UCL = 3.420 |
| CL = 506.00 | CL = 1.738 |
| LCL = 503.80 | LCL = 0.052 |

**a.** Estimate the process standard deviation.

**b.** If the specification limits are 505 ± 15 and the process output is normally distributed, what will be the nonconformance rate in parts per million?

**39.** Construct a flowchart for purchasing a car. Use the steps shown below.

Read Brochures
Decide Down Payment
Buy Car
Visit Dealer
Brag to Others
Discuss Deal
Study Monthly Payments
Wait for New Car Prep
Check *Consumer Reports*
Check on Loan Rates
Inspect Cars on Lot
Drive It Home
Choose Car to Test

Check on Used Car Price for Present Auto
Test-Drive Car
Inspect before Driving Home
Narrow Choices and Price Range

**40.** Frozen orange juice concentrate is packed in 6-oz cardboard cans. When filled, either the can will leak (nonconforming) or will not leak (conforming). You wish to construct a control chart to reduce the proportion of nonconforming cans. Every four hours you select 100 cans and test them for leakage. Spreadsheet 1140.xls contains the data.

**a.** Construct a control chart for the proportion of nonconforming cans.

**b.** Was the process ever out of control? If so, delete the subgroup(s) and recompute the control chart center line and control limits.

**c.** After recomputing the limits, was the process now in control?

**d.** Even if the process is under statistical control, should the firm be satisfied with the overall proportion of nonconforming cans? Discuss.

**41.** You work in customer service for MCI. Describe the steps in constructing a "reason for switching to AT&T Long Distance Service" Pareto chart.

**42.** You use histograms to display the individual measurements. From this you can see the proportion of products or services that are outside of specifications (see Figure 11.5). You use control charts to chart the sample statistics you wish to improve or control; for example, the process mean or standard deviation. This exercise helps you discover the connection between these two graphs.

You track the amount of time it takes for a help desk person to respond to a customer call. Given here are the data.

Target = 300 seconds
USL   = 360 seconds
LCL   = 270 seconds
UCL   = 330 seconds

Draw a frequency histogram and a control chart that illustrates the following conditions (use the above specification limit and control limits to draw your histogram and control chart):

**a.** A centered process that will produce very few nonconforming services and the process is under statistical control.

**b.** A centered process that will produce very few nonconforming services but the process is not yet under statistical control.

**43.** Use Excel's XY scatter plot Chart Wizard to determine if increasing the hours of training in creative methods increases the number of solutions developed when using the fishbone diagram. Below are the data.

| Hours of Training | Number of Solutions |
|---|---|
| 0 | 10 |
| 7 | 30 |
| 14 | 50 |
| 0 | 15 |
| 3.5 | 15 |
| 7 | 25 |
| 14 | 45 |
| 7 | 35 |
| 10.5 | 40 |

**44.** Consider the data with the severity weights shown below. Construct a demerit chart and determine the center line and control limits. Was the process ever out of control? Discuss.

| Subgroup | Type I (10) | Type II (5) | Type III (3) |
|----------|-------------|-------------|--------------|
| 1 | 1 | 2 | 0 |
| 2 | 1 | 0 | 0 |
| 3 | 1 | 1 | 0 |
| 4 | 0 | 1 | 4 |
| 5 | 2 | 1 | 0 |
| 6 | 0 | 2 | 0 |
| 7 | 2 | 0 | 1 |
| 8 | 2 | 0 | 1 |
| 9 | 1 | 0 | 1 |
| 10 | 1 | 1 | 0 |

**45.** A proportion nonconforming chart presently has a center line of 0.01, UCL = 0.0399, LCL = 0, and $n = 100$. If 3-sigma limits are used, find the smallest sample size that would produce a positive lower control limit value.

**46.** A proportion nonconforming chart indicates that the current process proportion is 0.03. The sample size is 200 per subgroup. Determine the 3-sigma limits for this chart.

**47.** Under what conditions, if any, can the actual lower control limit for a demerit chart be less than zero? Discuss.

**48.** You have learned four control charts in this chapter—mean, standard deviation, proportion, and demerit charts. Develop a flowchart that a manager could use to help him or her determine when to use each control chart.

**49.** What does the $\bar{x}$ chart provide that the standard deviation chart does not? What does the standard deviation chart provide that the $\bar{x}$ chart does not?

**50.** For subgroup sizes less than $n = 6$, the LCL for the standard deviation chart will be zero. Thus it is not possible for a standard deviation of a subgroup to be below the LCL. Why is this a serious weakness of the standard deviation chart? Discuss.

## CASE STUDY

Nikcoat, Inc., is a small firm that specializes in nickel-coating steel. The nickel plate is deposited by electrolysis in a nickel solution. The nickel plate minimizes corrosion and also adds a decorative finish. Two common problems are depositing a (1) too light or (2) too heavy nickel plate.

Several months ago the engineering department set a new specification to minimize both problems. The specification reads as follows: "The nickel concentration in the electrolysis bath shall be $4.6 \pm 1$ ounce per gallon at the beginning of the shift."

About one month ago Nikcoat started using a control chart to monitor the nickel-coating process. At the beginning of each of the two daily shifts the technician takes one sample of nickel solution, determines its concentration, and then plots the data value on a control chart. Recently the purchasing manager has complained that Nikcoat is using more nickel concentration than it should given its production volume.

Herman Santana, Nikcoat's CEO, calls a meeting in his office to discuss the problem.

| Herman | I've called you here at Dick's request to discuss the increased cost for the nickel-plating operation. Dick tells me that we are using more nickel than we should given our production volume. |
|---|---|
| Dick | Yes, that is true. I thought we were control charting the nickel concentration level so that this would not happen. Joe—what does the control chart reveal? |
| Joe | As you know, the chart has three critical lines. We set the center line at 4.60, which is our target value. The lower control limit is 4.3 ounces per gallon and the upper control limit is 4.90 ounces per gallon. The control limits are 3-sigma on either side of the center line. |
| Herman | That's interesting, but does the control chart reveal any out-of-control signals over the past 30 days or 60 subgroups? |
| Joe | That's the odd thing. My chart does not indicate any data points outside the 3-sigma limits. So the process is under statistical control. It seems to me that if we are using more nickel, we should have had one or more data points above the upper control limit of 4.90. Yet all the data points lie within the control limits. I am stumped. Maybe these types of charts aren't too useful? |
| Herman | Let's not badmouth the chart just yet. Could I please see the chart? |

Several minutes elapse.

| Herman | I think I see what the problem is. The process is really out of control. And that explains the increased usage of nickel recently. |
| Joe | I disagree. None of the 60 data points are outside the limits. |

Assignment:

1. Is the process out of control? Who is right—Herman or Joe?

2. What changes, if any, should Nikcoat make in how it detects the presence of assignable-cause variation using the control chart?

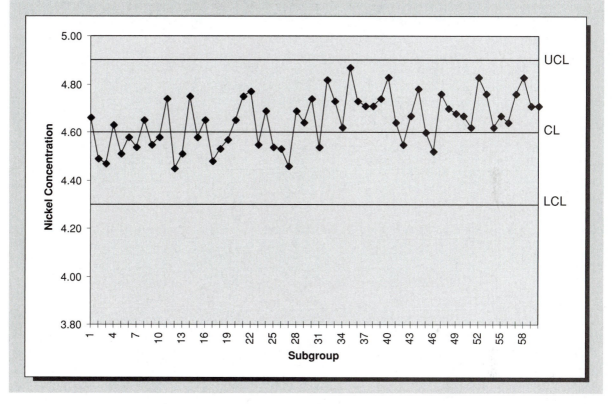

# CHAPTER 11
# APPENDICES

## I. LISTING OF EXCEL TOOLS USED IN CHAPTER

1. Chart Wizard—Column Chart
2. Histogram data-analysis tool
3. Chart Wizard—XY Scatter Plot
4. NORMDIST function wizard

## II. CONTROL CHART FACTORS

| Subgroup Size | $B_3$ | $B_4$ | $A_3$ | $c_4$ |
|---|---|---|---|---|
| 3 | 0 | 2.568 | 1.954 | 0.8862 |
| 4 | 0 | 2.266 | 1.628 | 0.9213 |
| 5 | 0 | 2.089 | 1.427 | 0.9400 |
| 6 | 0.030 | 1.970 | 1.287 | 0.9515 |
| 7 | 0.118 | 1.882 | 1.182 | 0.9594 |
| 8 | 0.185 | 1.815 | 1.099 | 0.9650 |
| 9 | 0.239 | 1.761 | 1.032 | 0.9693 |
| 10 | 0.284 | 1.716 | 0.975 | 0.9727 |

## III. USING EXCEL TO CONSTRUCT CONTROL CHARTS

Below are the steps to construct an $\bar{x}$ control chart.

1. Enter the labels in row I as shown in the table below. Enter the label Observations in cell B1 and then center by selecting B1:Fl and clicking the Center Across Columns button.

Input Data for a Control Chart on the Mean

| | A | B | C | D | E | F | G | H | I | J | K |
|---|---|---|---|---|---|---|---|---|---|---|---|
| **1** | Subgroup | | Observations | | | | Mean | CL | SD | UCL | LCL |
| **2** | 1 | 10.07 | 9.89 | 10.01 | 9.61 | 11.85 | 10.29 | 9.89 | 0.89 | 11.08 | 8.70 |
| **3** | 2 | 8.30 | 9.28 | 8.99 | 9.75 | 9.81 | 9.23 | 9.89 | 0.62 | 11.08 | 8.70 |
| **4** | 3 | 9.58 | 10.84 | 9.63 | 8.66 | 7.34 | 9.21 | 9.89 | 1.30 | 11.08 | 8.70 |
| **5** | 4 | 9.67 | 9.22 | 9.34 | 9.06 | 9.40 | 9.34 | 9.89 | 0.22 | 11.08 | 8.70 |
| **6** | 5 | 9.93 | 11.11 | 9.89 | 9.15 | 10.72 | 10.16 | 9.89 | 0.77 | 11.08 | 8.70 |
| **7** | 6 | 10.95 | 10.95 | 10.14 | 9.16 | 10.58 | 10.35 | 9.89 | 0.75 | 11.08 | 8.70 |
| **8** | 7 | 10.02 | 9.66 | 10.26 | 10.19 | 10.01 | 10.03 | 9.89 | 0.23 | 11.08 | 8.70 |
| **9** | 8 | 11.19 | 11.32 | 9.29 | 10.78 | 8.47 | 9.21 | 9.89 | 1.26 | 11.08 | 8.70 |
| **10** | 9 | 12.00 | 9.11 | 8.45 | 9.25 | 10.85 | 9.93 | 9.89 | 1.46 | 11.08 | 8.70 |
| **11** | 10 | 9.66 | 11.43 | 9.39 | 9.97 | 10.62 | 10.21 | 9.89 | 0.82 | 11.08 | 8.70 |
| **12** | | | | | | | | | | | |
| **13** | | | | | | CL | 9.89 | | 0.83 | | |

2. Arrange your data as shown in cells B2:F11.

3. In cell G2 compute the mean of the subgroup by using the formula, =AVERAGE(B2:F2). Select cell G2, click the fill handle in the lower right corner, and drag down to cell G11.

4. To prepare a control chart, select the sample means (G2:G11), click the Chart Wizard button, and select Line chart type and click Next. In step 2 click on Next.

5. In step 3 type in labels for the category X and Y axes. Click on Legend tab and click on Show legend box. Click on Finish.

6. Activate the chart by clicking on one of the corners of the embedded chart. Double click on the vertical axis. In the Format Axis dialog box, click the Scale tab. Clear the Auto check box for Minimum and type 8.5 and then clear the Auto check box for Maximum and type 11.5. Then click OK.

7. To compute the overall mean for the $k = 10$ subgroups, select cell G13 and enter the formula, =AVERAGE(G2:G11).

8. To add the center line (CL), select cell H2, and enter the formula, =G$13. To copy this value to the other cells, select Cell H2. Click the fill handle in the lower right corner, and drag down to cell H11. Format for two decimal places.

Control Chart

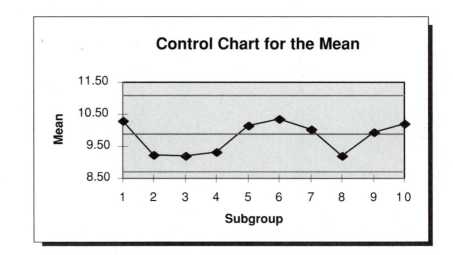

**9.** To add the center line to the control chart, select the CL values (H2:H11). Move the pointer near the edge of the selected range until the pointer becomes an arrow. Then click, drag the CL values to the chart, and release the mouse button. The center line appears in the chart.

**10.** The control limits for the $\bar{x}$ chart depend on the mean standard deviation observed in the subgroups. To determine the standard deviations, select cell I2, and enter the formula, =STDEV(B2:F2). Select cell I2, click the fill handle in the lower right corner, and drag down to cell I11.

**11.** To compute the mean standard deviation, select cell I13 and enter the formula, =AVERAGE(I2:I11).

**12.** To determine the upper control limit (UCL), use Expression (11.5). Select cell J2, and enter the formula, =G$13+1.427*I$13. To copy the formula to the other cells, select cell J2, click the fill handle in the lower right corner, and drag down to cell J11. Format the number of decimal places to 2.

**13.** To determine the lower control limit (LCL), use Expressions (11.5). Select cell K2, and enter the formula, =G$13−1.427*I$13. To copy the formula to the other cells, select cell K2, click the fill handle in the lower right corner, and drag down to cell K11. Format the number of decimal places to 2.

**14.** To add the lower and upper control limits to the control chart, select the LCL and UCL values (J2:K11). Move the pointer near the edge of the selected range until the pointer becomes an arrow. Then click, drag the values to the chart, and release the mouse button. The lower and upper control limits appear on the chart.

# DESIGN OF EXPERIMENT

## THE ROLE OF EXPERIMENTATION IN PROCESS AND PRODUCT IMPROVEMENT

Experimentation is essential to determining the root causes of disturbance, or crisis, problems. A disturbance problem is a sudden and significant deviation from historical or planned performance levels, such as a sudden increase in rework or a major drop in service levels. Faced with a disturbance problem, a manager must be able to

1. separate the symptoms from the facts—*problem definition*;

2. identify potential root causes—*problem diagnosis*; and

3. determine which are the true root causes—*problem solving*.

Experimentation is effective in diagnosing and solving problems.

Solving disturbance problems does not necessarily lead to improved performance. For example, putting out a fire in a hotel is critical, but it doesn't lead to better service or performance. Managers must also continually seek ways to improve product, service, or quality.

In short, experimentation fixes today's crisis problems and improves tomorrow's product, performance, or service.

# MANAGEMENT SCENARIOS AND DATA SETS

The two scenarios illustrate the one-factor and two-factor designs, respectively. The first scenario demonstrates how experimentation can improve or promote a product, service, or process. The second case shows how experimentation can help solve a disturbance problem.

In Scenario I, a product manager evaluates the effectiveness of three advertising strategies for a digital broadcast satellite (DBS) service. The manager identifies 75 potential customers, all of whom have expressed interest in purchasing a satellite system. She conducts a one-factor three-level completely random study (see the section, "Designing Experiments" later in this chapter). She randomly assigns 25 potential customers to one of three different advertisements. Each participant views one of three 60-second advertisements once a day, at 8:00 PM, for seven days during the test week. Afterward, each person indicates his or her intent to buy the firm's DBS service on a scale from 0 (definitely will not buy) to 100 (definitely will buy).

Pioneer product advertising (variation one) creates awareness of the DBS service. It promotes the advantages of the firm's DBS service versus local cable systems. Retentive product advertising (variation two) summarizes the major benefits of the system, helps customers evaluate their purchase decisions, and reduces postpurchase doubt. Comparative product advertising (variation three) persuades customers that the firm's DBS service has features that outstrip its competitors such as USSB, DirecTV, or Primestar Partners.

Table 12.1 displays the results of the advertising study. The mean intent to purchase scores for the three types of advertising are 77.4 (pioneer), 61.2 (retentive), and 80 (comparative). In the section, "One-Factor Completely Random Design" the product manager will analyze the data using the analysis of variance and select one or more types of advertisements to launch the firm's DBS service.

| **Experimental Factor:** | **Treatments:** |
|---|---|
| **Type of Advertising** | **Pioneer, Retentive, and Comparative** |

Scenario II illustrates the role of experimentation in determining root causes. Apex produces three sizes of drawers or compartments for computer tables sold by Contemporary Office Furniture. Model A has a 4-inch-deep drawer, model B has a 7-inch-deep drawer, and model C has a 10-inch-deep drawer.

There are three steps in manufacturing drawers. At blanking, workers cut the raw material to the approximate drawer size. Next, workers use stamping presses that bend the blanked metal to form the drawer. Stamping press 3 makes the 4-inch drawer, presses 1 and 4 make the 7-inch drawer, and press 2 makes the 10-inch drawer. Finally, workers inspect for cracks and other damage. Apex then ships defect-free drawers to Contemporary Office Furniture.

| Pioneer | Retentive | Comparative | |
|---------|-----------|-------------|---|
| 75 | 90 | 80 | |
| 80 | 65 | 60 | |
| 75 | 30 | 75 | |
| 75 | 65 | 70 | |
| 60 | 40 | 85 | |
| 95 | 90 | 55 | |
| 75 | 30 | 80 | |
| 90 | 70 | 85 | |
| 75 | 65 | 90 | |
| 95 | 80 | 75 | |
| 55 | 55 | 85 | |
| 90 | 90 | 100 | |
| 50 | 70 | 70 | |
| 80 | 60 | 95 | |
| 85 | 65 | 75 | |
| 55 | 60 | 60 | |
| 75 | 45 | 100 | |
| 70 | 75 | 60 | |
| 70 | 65 | 95 | |
| 100 | 60 | 75 | |
| 60 | 55 | 85 | |
| 75 | 65 | 95 | |
| 95 | 20 | 85 | |
| 95 | 70 | 75 | |
| 85 | 50 | 90 | |
| **77.4** | **61.2** | **80** | **72.867 Sample means** |

**Table 12.1**
Impact of Advertising on Intent to Purchase Digital Broadcast Satellite Service

Cracking sometimes happens during stamping. It occurs at the lower corners of the drawer where the metal undergoes the maximum deformation and therefore stress. Over the past several months, 1% of the drawers had cracks.

At 8:00 AM on Tuesday, stamping press 2 started producing about 6% cracks. The line supervisor had engineering check the press, but found no problems. After the morning break (10:00 AM), stamping press 1 started producing about 4% cracks. Finally at 11:00 AM, stamping press 4 started producing about 4% cracks. At noon, only stamping press 3 was still producing 1% cracks.

Apex has a severe disturbance problem. Why has there been a fourfold and sixfold increase in cracking rates on three of the four stamping presses? What is going on?

Before Apex can take corrective action it must understand the disturbance problem. The operations manager should use an effective problem diagnostic tool that complements intuition and experience.

The Kepner-Tregoe method is an effective problem definition and diagnostic tool.[1] It transforms ambiguous symptoms, facts, and assumptions into a clear problem statement. To define the problem, start by asking and answering the following questions:

What is the deviation (versus what isn't it)?

When is the deviation (versus when isn't it)?

Where did the deviation occur (versus where didn't it occur)?

How much, how many, and to what extent did the deviation occur (versus to what extent didn't it occur)?

Reject vague phrases. "Something is wrong" is an unacceptable answer to a "what is" question. Also avoid useless adjectives such as "We have *a lot of* cracks." Be specific. Be precise. If the information is vague or imprecise, do more detective work before entering the data into a Kepner-Tregoe worksheet (see Table 12.2).

**Table 12.2**
Kepner-Tregoe Worksheet for the Cracked Drawer Problem

|  | The Deviation Is | The Deviation Is Not |
|---|---|---|
| WHAT | 4%, 6% cracks on 7" and 10" drawers | Excessive scratches<br>Bent drawers<br>4%, 6% for 4" drawers |
| WHEN | 8:00 AM on press 2<br>10:00 AM on press 1<br>11:00 AM on press 4 | On press 2 before 8:00 AM<br>On press 1 before 10:00 AM<br>On press 4 before 11:00 AM |
| WHERE | Presses 1, 2, 4<br>Lower four corners of drawers | Press 3<br>Cracks randomly distributed<br>At blanking operation |
| EXTENT | Press 2: 6%<br>Presses 1, 4: 4%<br>Instantaneous jump | Press 3: normal 1%<br>Gradual rise in defect rate |

Based on the Kepner-Tregoe analysis, the operations manager believed that there were two root causes of excessive cracked drawers: (1) the new material and (2) the drawer depth. The plant had started using material from a new vendor as the material from the old vendor was depleted. The drawer depth could also be a cause since the excessive cracking did not occur on the 4-inch-deep drawers, but did occur on the deeper 7-inch and 10-inch drawers.

---

[1]Kepner, B. and Tregoe, C., *The New Rational Manager*. Princeton, New Jersey. Princeton Research Press, 1988.

The manager conducted a two-factor completely random study (see the section, "Two-Factor Completely Random Design" later in this chapter). The factors are material supplier and drawer depth. The raw material factor has *two* levels, or variations: old and new material supplier. The drawer depth factor has *three* levels: 4-inch, 7-inch, and 10-inch drawer depth. This is a 2 × 3 factorial, or multifactor, study.

| **Experimental Factor:** **Material** | **Treatments:** **Old and New Material** |
|---|---|
| **Experimental Factor:** **Stamping Depth** | **Treatments:** **4 inch, 7 inch, and 10 inch** |

The manager tested all six (2 × 3 = 6) combinations of material and stamping depths. He ran each combination five times for one hour each. He randomly selected enough old raw material to make 15 one-hour runs and randomly assigned the old material to the three stamping depths. Next, the manager randomly selected enough new raw material to make 15 one-hour runs and randomly assigned the new material to the three stamping depths. He randomly determined the sequence of the six runs or combinations and recorded the percentage of cracked drawers for each one-hour run.

Table 12.3 displays the results of the 2 × 3 factorial study. We have also included the sample mean percent cracked drawers for the six combinations.

| Combination | Percent Cracked |
|---|---|
| old material and 4-inch drawer | 1.010% |
| old material and 7-inch drawer | 0.970% |
| old material and 10-inch drawer | 1.036% |
| new material and 4-inch drawer | 1.086% |
| new material and 7-inch drawer | 4.096% |
| new material and 10-inch drawer | 6.262% |

| | | 4 inch | 7 inch | 10 inch |
|---|---|---|---|---|
| | | 1.00 | 0.20 | 0.20 |
| | | 0.43 | 1.90 | 1.82 |
| **Old** | | 1.96 | 0.70 | 1.25 |
| **Material** | | 0.01 | 1.40 | 0.35 |
| | | 1.65 | 0.65 | 1.56 |
| | | 0.30 | 4.51 | 7.50 |
| | | 1.96 | 2.21 | 3.56 |
| **New** | | 0.15 | 4.65 | 6.85 |
| **Material** | | 2.13 | 2.57 | 5.90 |
| | | 0.89 | 6.54 | 7.50 |

**Table 12.3**
Results of 2 × 3
Factorial Study for
the Cracked Drawer
Problem

**Overall mean = 2.410**

In the section, "Two-Factor Completely Random Design," the operations manager will analyze the $2 \times 3$ factorial study using the analysis of variance to verify the root causes and take corrective action.

# DESIGNING EXPERIMENTS

Running a study requires more than merely analyzing data that you have already collected. It requires planning and involves *gathering* data. By the end of this section you should be able to

**1.** define experimental design terms;

**2.** distinguish between an experiment and a nonexperiment; and

**3.** explain how randomization helps rule out alternative explanations and why it is important.

## Basic Terminology

What is an experiment? The "scientist image" represents experimentation in chemistry, physics, or psychology. However, managers also must run experiments to determine if planned changes do improve performance, service, or quality. So, what is an experiment? It's simply a *controlled study* in which a manager varies one or more factors and then measures the effects on the dependent variable.

*Experimental Factor.* In business, factors, or treatments, are the planned changes that managers believe will improve performance, service, or quality or solve a disturbance problem. Factors could include types of advertising, brands of computers, types of rewards systems, stamping depths, types of leadership, types of soldering fluxes, and so forth.

*Level.* Each variation of a planned change factor is a factor, or treatment, level. A marketing manager may try three different advertising approaches—three treatment levels. A plant manager may try two different soldering fluxes—two treatment levels. An IT manager may evaluate five brands of computers—five treatment levels.

*Experimental Unit.* The entities that experience the planned change are the experimental units. They can be people, groups of people, or items on a production line. When the units are people, we call them subjects.

*Dependent Variable.* Dependent variables are quantities that the manager measures to determine if the planned change has had the desired impact. We will limit our discussion to experiments that have only one dependent variable. Examples of possible dependent variables include intent to purchase scores, percentage of cracked drawers, soldering times, job productivity, and so forth.

**Extraneous Factor.** These are factors that the manager is not interested in or cannot control. However, extraneous factors can affect the dependent variable. In a study of types of advertising (experimental factor) on intent to purchase (dependent variable), three extraneous factors are (1) customers' income levels, (2) customers' ages, and (3) the programs that carry the advertisements.

## Experiments versus Nonexperiments

To run a valid experiment, the manager must

1. assign experimental units to different factor levels, introduce a planned change, and measure the impact;

2. control for extraneous factors; and

3. use randomization within the study.

The first scenario meets none of the three requirements.

**Scenario 1.** The manager of information technology wants to determine which of the firm's desktop computers is least expensive to maintain—IBM, COMPAQ, Dell, or Gateway. He plans to drop the brand(s) that has the highest maintenance cost. The manager collects the maintenance records for the past year and then computes the total cost for each brand. Since the firm owns an equal number of each brand and type (Pentium and so forth), the manager compares the costs directly. Here are the results.

| IBM | COMPAQ | Dell | Gateway |
|---|---|---|---|
| $39,500 | $51,000 | $53,000 | $45,000 |

The IT manager has not conducted an experiment. First, there is no experimental factor since the manager did not vary anything. Second, all he did was examine historical records. This is an *observational study* in which the manager collects data on an event that has already happened.

Observational studies are not experiments and are difficult to interpret. The observational study suggests that IBM computers have the lowest maintenance cost. If the manager were naive, he would purchase only IBM computers to reduce his maintenance costs. However, that may be an incorrect strategy! The low maintenance cost may be due to extraneous factors,

factors beyond the computer itself. Generate a list of possible extraneous factors. Please don't look ahead.

1. Hours of usage differences for each brand

2. End-user differences ("pounders," "tinkers")

3. Application differences

4. Operating environment differences (dust, etc.)

5. Regular maintenance differences (dust covers, disk optimization, etc.)

Simply stated, the manager cannot determine why IBM computers had the lowest maintenance cost. It may be that IBM is indeed the least expensive computer to maintain. Alternatively, its low cost may be due to at least five other reasonable alternative explanations.

Choose experiments over observational studies whenever possible as observational studies cannot control for extraneous factors. However, simply introducing a planned change and measuring its effects does not control for extraneous factors either.

*Scenario 2.* A university professor compares two teaching methods (the experimental factor), lecture versus case, for an advanced business law course. Since he now teaches two sections, he uses the lecture method in the first section and the case method in the second section. After six weeks, he gives a different version of a chapter test to each section. The mean score in the lecture class is 83, as compared with a mean of 65 for the case method. *Question:* Has the professor run an experiment? Think about it before continuing!

The professor has introduced a planned change and measured the effects. He has taught sections using the case and lecture methods. He has measured the impact of different teaching methods by an examination. Therefore, he has met the first requirement of an experiment. However, his study is still not a valid experiment.

A valid experiment ensures that the measured effects result from the planned change, or experimental factors, and not extraneous factors, factors outside the control or interest of the professor. The professor has not controlled for *any* potential extraneous factors. For example,

1. The professor may be a better lecturer than case teacher.

2. Students in the lecture class were smarter, more alert, or more motivated than students in the case method class.

3. The final exam in the lecture class was easier.

4. The lecture class met in the late morning and the case class met in the late evening. Students cannot think as clearly in the late evening.

Therefore, he has not conducted a valid experiment. Now compare this study with Scenario 3.

***Scenario 3.*** Using *simple random sampling,* the professor selects two sections of business law from the five sections being taught at 10:00 AM. The sections are scheduled in different buildings on campus. Students cannot register for an individual class, merely the 10:00 AM class time. The professor selects a colleague who, like himself, is equally effective in both teaching approaches. The professor determines *randomly* which section his colleague will teach and which section he will teach. The professor then *randomly* assigns students to the two sections. During the first class, the instructors give students in both sections the same pretest on business law fundamentals to determine entry-level knowledge. After six weeks, the instructors give the same posttest to both sections. Here are the results.

|  | Section 1: Case Method | | | Section 2: Lecture Method | | |
|  | Pretest | Posttest | Difference | Pretest | Posttest | Difference |
| --- | --- | --- | --- | --- | --- | --- |
| Mean | 48 | 76 | +28 | 45 | 95 | +50 |

This is a valid experiment. The instructor has controlled for the four previously mentioned extraneous factors. He used two different approaches: (1) eliminating potential extraneous factors and (2) randomization. Examples of the former approach are his use of the same pretest and posttest and selecting sections taught at the same time of day. The professor used randomization when he selected two 10:00 AM sections, subdivided the students into two groups, assigned them to the two sections, and assigned the two instructors.

## The Importance of Randomization

Randomization is essential to running a valid study. Randomization minimized the chances that two groups of students will systematically differ due to extraneous factors. In other words, randomization tends to equalize the groups on most potential extraneous factors. For example, randomization minimizes the chances that most of the better prepared, highly motivated, or smarter students are in the lecture method course. Thus, if we find a difference in the groups' performances, it must be due to the planned change, not extraneous factors.

Randomize to the fullest extent possible in a study. Use randomization to (1) select experimental units, (2) subdivide them into groups, (3) assign the groups to the factor levels or treatment combinations, and (4) determine the sequence of experimental runs.

This section concludes with several basic experimental design principles:

PRINCIPLE 1:   Choose experiments over observational studies whenever possible. Observational studies collect past data and do not generate new data. They are after-the-fact studies and are not experiments.

PRINCIPLE 2:   Conduct a valid experiment by *randomly* assigning experimental units to different treatment levels, introducing a planned change, and measuring the impact.

PRINCIPLE 3:   Control extraneous factors by using randomization and eliminating possible extraneous factors from the experiment. Both approaches ensure that the experimental factors caused the improvement in the product or service, and not extraneous factors. This is the RO principle of Ruling Out extraneous factors.

# THE ONE-FACTOR COMPLETELY RANDOM DESIGN

The one-factor $k$-level study is the simplest experimental design. We vary one factor or treatment and determine the impact on the dependent variable. To determine if performance has improved, we conduct an analysis of variance (ANOVA).[2] By the end of this section you should be able to

**1.** develop null and alternative hypotheses;

**2.** assess the assumptions underlying the ANOVA using Excel's SKEW, KURT, and VAR function wizards;

**3.** explain why there are only two sources of variation that account for the total sum of squares in a one-factor $k$-level completely random study;

**4.** interpret the ANOVA output from the Excel ANOVA: Single Factor data-analysis tool; and

**5.** explain the need for, construct, and interpret Tukey confidence intervals.

The advertising study is a one-factor three-level experiment. The factor is type of advertising and the levels are the three types of ads, pioneer ($A_1$), retentive ($A_2$), and comparative ($A_3$).

## Null and Alternative Hypotheses

Recall from Chapter 6 that a statistical hypothesis is a testable claim or statement about one or more population parameters. The null hypothesis is

---

[2]We first presented the ANOVA in Chapter 9 on regression analysis.

always the claim of "no difference," "no change," or "no improvement." We also define a second hypothesis—alternative hypothesis—that we hope or suspect is true. Shown below are the null and alternative hypotheses for the advertising study.

| Hypotheses | Managerial Actions |
|---|---|
| $H_0$  In the *population*, the mean intent to purchase is the same for the three types of advertisements. *(no difference)*<br><br>$\mu_{PIONEER} = \mu_{COMPARATIVE} = \mu_{RETENTIVE}$ | Failure to reject the null hypothesis means that no one advertisement is more effective than the others. Select one type of ad on another criteria (cost, etc.). |
| $H_1$  In the *population*, the mean intent to purchase is not the same for the three types of advertisements. *(a difference)*<br>Not all $\mu$ the same | Determine which type of ad is most effective and implement it. |

**Table 12.4**
Null and Alternative Hypotheses for Type of Advertising Study

The null and alternative hypotheses focus on the mean intent to purchase the digital broadcast satellite service for *all* potential customers, not merely the 75 who participated in the study. The product manager is not interested in the specific sample of 75 participants.

Based on the cost of making the Type I error and the most likely Type II error, the product manager sets the significance level, $\alpha$, at 0.05.

Before doing the analysis of variance you should assess its underlying assumptions.

## Assessing Assumptions Underlying the Analysis of Variance

There are three assumptions underlying the analysis of variance.

Assumption 1:   The observations within each of the three treatment levels are independent random samples.

Assumption 2:   The observations within each of the three treatment levels are near-normally distributed.

Assumption 3:   The variances within each of the three treatment levels are the same or nearly so.

The first assumption is true because the product manager used randomization in the study. She randomly divided the 75 participants into three groups of 25 members each. She randomly assigned each group of 25 to a different type of advertisement. Randomization ensures that the first assumption is met.

Is the second assumption reasonable? First, compute the 25 residuals for each of the three treatment levels. A residual is simply the difference between an actual data value and its column mean. See Table 12.5, which is based on Table 12.1.

| Pioneer | Retentive | Comparative |
|---|---|---|
| $75 - 77.4 = -2.4$ | $90 - 61.2 = 22.8$ | $80 - 80 = 0$ |
| 2.6 | 3.8 | −20 |
| −2.4 | −31.2 | −5 |
| −2.4 | 3.8 | −10 |
| −17.4 | −21.2 | 5 |
| 17.6 | 28.8 | −25 |
| −2.4 | −31.2 | 0 |
| 12.6 | 8.8 | 5 |
| −2.4 | 3.8 | 10 |
| 17.6 | 18.8 | −5 |
| −22.4 | −6.2 | 5 |
| 12.6 | 28.8 | 20 |
| −27.4 | 8.8 | −10 |
| 2.6 | −1.2 | 15 |
| 7.6 | 3.8 | −5 |
| −22.4 | −1.2 | −20 |
| −2.4 | −16.2 | 20 |
| −7.4 | 13.8 | −20 |
| −7.4 | 3.8 | 15 |
| 22.6 | −1.2 | −5 |
| −17.4 | −6.2 | 5 |
| −2.4 | 3.8 | 15 |
| 17.6 | −41.2 | 5 |
| 17.6 | 8.8 | −5 |
| 7.6 | −11.2 | 10 |
| −0.28617706 | −0.543555531 | −0.284505459 |
| −0.777566537 | 0.330816083 | −0.776379285 |

**Table 12.5**
Residuals for Type of Advertising Study

Second, apply Excel's KURT and SKEW function wizards to the 25 residuals within each treatment level in Table 12.5. If the SKEW and KURT values are between −1 and +1 for each treatment level, the normality assumption is reasonable. Table 12.5 displays the skewness and kurtosis values (bottom two rows) for the three treatment levels. The data are approximately normally distributed.

Is the third assumption reasonable? First, apply Excel's VAR function wizard to the three columns of data. The three *sample* variances are 196.08, 329.75, and 164.58, respectively. Given that the largest sample variance is two times greater than the smallest sample variance, is the homogeneity of variance assumption reasonable?

The Hartley ratio is a very simple test for the equality of variances when the sample sizes per treatment level are equal. Compute the following ratio:

$$H_{max} = \frac{s^2_{largest}}{s^2_{smallest}} = \frac{329.75}{164.58} = 2.003$$

Second, compare the $H_{max}$ value to $H_{critical}$ (number of treatment levels, degrees of freedom for each level) found in Table 12.6.

---

**Decision Rule:** At the 95% confidence level, the variances are homogeneous if $H_{max}$ is less than $H_{critical}$.

---

Interpolating Table 12.6, $H_{critical}$ (3 levels, 24 df) is 2.73. Since $H_{max}$ of 2.003 is less than 2.73, the manager is at least 95% confident that the homogeneity of variance assumption is true.[3]

$H_{critical}$(3 levels, 20 df) = 2.95

$$H_{critical}\left(3, 24\right) = 2.95 - \frac{24 - 20}{30 - 20} \cdot \left(2.95 - 2.40\right) = 2.73$$

$H_{critical}$(3 levels, 30 df) = 2.40

| DF at Each Level | Three Levels | Four Levels | Five Levels | Six Levels |
|---|---|---|---|---|
| 4 | 15.50 | 20.60 | 25.20 | 29.50 |
| 5 | 10.80 | 13.70 | 16.30 | 18.70 |
| 6 | 8.38 | 10.40 | 12.10 | 13.70 |
| 7 | 6.94 | 8.44 | 9.70 | 10.80 |
| 8 | 6.00 | 7.18 | 8.12 | 9.03 |
| 9 | 5.34 | 6.31 | 7.11 | 7.80 |
| 10 | 4.85 | 5.67 | 6.34 | 6.92 |
| 12 | 4.16 | 4.79 | 5.30 | 5.72 |
| 15 | 3.54 | 4.01 | 4.37 | 4.68 |
| 20 | 2.95 | 3.29 | 3.54 | 3.76 |
| 30 | 2.40 | 2.61 | 2.78 | 2.91 |
| 60 | 1.85 | 1.96 | 2.04 | 2.11 |

**Table 12.6**
Hartley $H_{critical}$ Values: 95% Confidence Level

Given that the data have met the three assumptions underlying the analysis of variance, we may continue the formal statistical analysis. If the data

---

[3]Moderate departures from the homogeneity of variance assumption are not serious and should be ignored. The analysis of variance is a *robust* test.

violate either of the last two assumptions, consult a professional statistician for alternative analyses.

## The Analysis of Variance

As in Chapter 9, the analysis of variance begins with a decomposition of the total sum of squares. Refer to Table 12.1. Note that the dependent variable, intent to purchase scores, varies among the 75 participants. How much variation is there about the overall mean score of 72.867? The total sum of squares, SST, measures this variation. The general expression for SST for any dependent variable $y$ is:

$$\text{SST} = \sum_{i \text{ levels}}^{k} \sum_{j \text{ obs}}^{n} \left(y_{ij} - \overline{\overline{y}}\right)^2$$

**(12.1)**

For the data in Table 12.1, there are $k = 3$ treatment levels and $n = 25$ observations per level. The SST for the data in Table 12.1 requires 75 squared calculations and equals

$$\text{SST} = (75 - 72.867)^2 + (80 - 72.867)^2 + \cdots + (75 - 72.867)^2 + (90 - 72.867)^2$$
$$= 21{,}758.67 \text{ units of variation}$$

What accounts for the 21,758.67 units of variation? There are two sources. The total variation is either due to the three levels of the experimental factor (sum of squares between groups) or it is not (sum of squares within groups).

---

**D E F I N I T I O N**    **Sum of squares between groups** measures the variation in the dependent variable due to the "$k$" levels of the experimental factor.

---

**D E F I N I T I O N**    **Sum of squares within groups**[4] measures the variation in the dependent variable *only* due to all extraneous factors.

---

Although you will use Excel's data-analysis tool to compute the sums of squares between and within, it is informative to understand how we compute each. First, consider the sum of squares within groups. Why don't the 25 values for the pioneer advertising equal the mean of 77.4? After all, all 25 subjects received the same type of advertising. Any variation within each

---

[4]In regression analysis these were the sum of squares regression and sum of squares residual, respectively.

treatment level must be due to extraneous factors. Thus, we compute the sum of squares within groups as follows.

| SS Within—Pioneer | SS Within—Retentive | SS Within—Comparative |
|---|---|---|
| $(75 - 77.4)^2$ | $(90 - 61.2)^2$ | $(80 - 80)^2$ |
| $(80 - 77.4)^2$ | $(65 - 61.2)^2$ | $(60 - 80)^2$ |
| $\vdots$ | $\vdots$ | $\vdots$ |
| $(95 - 77.4)^2$ | $(70 - 61.2)^2$ | $(75 - 80)^2$ |
| $(85 - 77.4)^2$ | $(50 - 61.2)^2$ | $(90 - 80)^2$ |
| 4706 | 7914 | 3950 |

SS within groups = 4706 + 7914 + 3950 = 16,570 units of variation

The greater the spread of data values within each treatment level, the greater is the impact of extraneous factors on the dependent variable and the greater is the SS within groups.

The sum of squares between groups measures the impact of the "$k$" treatment levels on the dependent variable. What numbers best represent the impact of the different treatment levels? The three sample means! The sum of squares between measures how different the three sample means are from the overall mean of 72.867, weighted by the sample size per treatment level, 25.

$$25\left[\left(77.4 - 72.867\right)^2 + \left(61.2 - 72.867\right)^2 + \left(80 - 72.867\right)^2\right]$$

SS between groups = 5,188.67 units of variation

The greater the spread in the sample means and the greater the sample size per treatment level, the greater is the sum of squares between groups.

In summary, of the 21,758.67 units of variation, the three levels of the experimental factor account for 5,188.67 units of variation. The remaining 16,570 units of variation are due to all extraneous factors.

Below is the input screen for the ANOVA: Single Factor data-analysis tool.

Table 12.7 is the ANOVA: Single Factor data-analysis tool output for the data in Table 12.1.

***Computing the F Ratio.*** After completing the decomposition in column 1, the data-analysis tool converts the sums of squares to *mean squares*, or variances (column 3). It divides the sums of squares by their respective degrees of freedom in column 2.

**Table 12.7**
ANOVA for the Type of Advertisement Study

| *Source of Variation* | **1** SS | **2** df | **3** MS | **4** F | **5** P-value | **6** F crit |
|---|---|---|---|---|---|---|
| Between Groups | 5188.67 | 2 | **2594.333** | **11.2729** | **5.51E-05** | 3.123901 |
| Within Groups | 16,570 | 72 | **230.1389** | | | |
| Total | 21,758.67 | 74 | | | | |

The breakdown of degrees of freedom is as follows.

1. The *total* degrees of freedom is $N - 1$, where $N$ equals the total sample size. In the type of advertising study, $75 - 1 = 74$.

2. The *between groups* degrees of freedom equals $k - 1$, where $k$ is the number of levels of the experimental factor. In the type of advertising study, $k - 1 = 2$.

3. The *within groups* degrees of freedom is the remainder, $k(n - 1)$ where $n$ is the sample size per treatment level. There are $25 - 1$ or 24 degrees of freedom for each treatment level. As there are three treatment levels, there are $3(24) = 72$ degrees of freedom.

Next, the data-analysis tool computes the mean squares between and within groups. It divides each sum of squares term by its appropriate degrees of freedom. The mean square between groups is 2594.333 and the mean square within groups is 230.1389.

Finally, the tool computes the *F ratio*. It is the mean square between divided by the mean square within.

$$F = \frac{\text{Mean Square (Between Groups)}}{\text{Mean Square (Within Groups)}}$$

(12.2)

The F, or variance, ratio measures the size of the mean square between groups to the mean square within groups. We use the F ratio to test the null hypothesis that

$$\mu_{\text{PIONEER}} = \mu_{\text{RETENTIVE}} = \mu_{\text{COMPARATIVE}}$$

The F ratio in Table 12.7 is $\dfrac{2594.33}{230.1389} = 11.2729$. The mean square between groups is 11.27 times as large as the mean square within groups. Can we reject the null hypothesis at the $\alpha = 0.05$ level?

***Hypothesis Testing.*** Does an F ratio of 11.27 favor the null or alternative hypothesis? Mean square within groups measures the impact of all potential factors other than the three types of advertisements on the purchase scores. Mean square between groups measures the impact of all factors—the experimental factor *plus* all extraneous factors not included in the study.

If the null hypothesis is true, then except for sampling variability the numerator and denominator of the F ratio should be the same. In short, if $H_0$ is true, the F ratio should be close to 1.0. But it is not! Mean square between groups is over 11 times as large as mean square within groups. Is this sufficiently large to reject the null hypothesis?

Column 5 in Table 12.7 answers the question. If the experimental factor did not affect the dependent variable, the probability of obtaining an F ratio of 11.27 or greater would be only 0.000055 or 55 in one million. Since this is smaller than the chosen significance level, $\alpha = 0.05$, the product manager should reject the null hypothesis. If the *p*-value in column 5 is larger than the chosen significance level, $\alpha = 0.05$, the product manager should not reject the null hypothesis.[5]

**Decision Rule:** If the *p*-value is less than the significance level set by the manager, reject the null hypothesis. Otherwise do not reject the null hypothesis.

In summary, the analysis of variance indicates that not all types of advertisements are equally effective in persuading the *population* of potential customers to purchase the firm's DBS service.

Which type (or types) of advertisement is (are) most effective in the *population*? The analysis of variance really doesn't answer that question. After rejecting the null hypothesis, you must do additional statistical analyses.

## Tukey Honestly Significance Difference (HSD) Confidence Intervals

The analysis of variance (ANOVA) does not always provide the answers that managers need. Remember, the alternative hypothesis says that *not* all $k$ population means are the same. However, the analysis of variance does not rank order the treatment levels; it does not tell us which treatment level is best.

---

[5]The Excel tool also provides F-critical (column 6). The F value (column 4) must be larger than F-critical to reject the null hypothesis at the stated significance level, $\alpha$.

But managers must know which treatment level is best, which is second best, and so forth. Use Tukey intervals to rank order the treatment levels.

Use Expression (12.3) to construct Tukey HSD confidence intervals:

$$\bar{x}_i - \bar{x}_j \pm \text{Margin of Error}$$

$$\bar{x}_i - \bar{x}_j \pm q\left(df_{within}, \text{number of levels}\right) \cdot \sqrt{\frac{\text{MS Within}}{n}}$$

(12.3)

where $\bar{x}_i$ is the sample mean for treatment level $i$

The ANOVA table provides MS Within (230.1389) and the degrees of freedom within (72).

$n$ is the sample size for each treatment level, 25.

The number of levels is 3.

The term q(72 df, 3) is the value of the Studentized range distribution from Table 12.8.

The interpolated Studentized range statistic value for q(72, 3) equals:

$$3.40 - \frac{72-60}{120-60} \cdot \left(3.40 - 3.36\right) = 3.392$$

| df$_{within}$ | Number of Levels | | | | |
| | 2 | 3 | 4 | 5 | 6 |
|---|---|---|---|---|---|
| 10 | 3.15 | 3.88 | 4.33 | 4.65 | 4.91 |
| 11 | 3.11 | 3.82 | 4.26 | 4.57 | 4.82 |
| 12 | 3.08 | 3.77 | 4.20 | 4.51 | 4.75 |
| 13 | 3.06 | 3.73 | 4.15 | 4.45 | 4.69 |
| 14 | 3.03 | 3.70 | 4.11 | 4.41 | 4.64 |
| 16 | 3.00 | 3.65 | 4.05 | 4.33 | 4.56 |
| 18 | 2.97 | 3.61 | 4.00 | 4.28 | 4.49 |
| 20 | 2.95 | 3.58 | 3.96 | 4.23 | 4.45 |
| 24 | 2.92 | 3.53 | 3.90 | 4.17 | 4.37 |
| 30 | 2.89 | 3.49 | 3.84 | 4.10 | 4.30 |
| 40 | 2.86 | 3.44 | 3.79 | 4.04 | 4.23 |
| 60 | 2.83 | 3.40 | 3.74 | 3.98 | 4.16 |
| 120 | 2.80 | 3.36 | 3.69 | 3.92 | 4.10 |

**Table 12.8**
Table of Studentized Range Statistic Values for 95% Intervals

Following are confidence intervals on intent to purchase scores for all pairs of treatment levels.

1. Pioneer advertising (77.4) versus retentive advertising (61.2)

2. Comparative advertising (80) versus pioneer advertising (77.4)

3. Comparative advertising (80) versus retentive advertising (61.2)

| Interval | Construction of Interval | Interpretation |
|---|---|---|
| Pioneer vs. vs. Retentive[6] | $77.4 - 61.2 \pm$ Margin of Error <br><br> $77.4 - 61.2 \pm q\sqrt{\dfrac{230.1389}{25}}$ <br> $16.2 \pm q(72,3) \cdot 3.034$ <br><br> $16.2 \pm 3.392 \cdot 3.034$ <br> $16.2 \pm 10.29$ <br> lower limit $= +\ 5.91$ <br> upper limit $= +26.49$ | Interval does not include zero. *In the population* pioneer advertising produces higher intent to purchase scores than retentive advertising by between 5.91 and 26.49.[7] |
| Comparative vs. Pioneer | $80 - 77.4 \pm 10.29$ <br> lower limit $= -\ 7.69$ <br> upper limit $= +12.89$ | Interval does include zero. There is no difference in the two population mean intent to purchase scores at the 95% level of confidence. |
| Comparative vs. Retentive | $80 - 61.2 \pm 10.29$ <br> lower limit $= +\ \ 8.51$ <br> upper limit $= +\ 29.09$ | Interval does not include zero. *In the population* comparative advertising produces higher intent to purchase scores than retentive advertising by between 8.51 and 29.09. |

Here is how to interpret a Tukey confidence interval. First, determine if the confidence interval contains the value of zero. A value of zero within the confidence interval indicates *no, or zero difference* in the two *population* column means. If the interval does not contain zero, then one population mean is different from the other. Second, from the lower and upper limits of the

---

[6] For ease of interpretation, place the larger sample mean first in Expression (12.3).

[7] See Appendix for a spreadsheet that computes the margin of error in Expression (12.3) directly.

confidence interval you can determine how different the two population means are (and which treatment level is better from a managerial viewpoint).

Here is another way to view the confidence interval. The interval, $16.2 \pm 10.29$, consists of two parts. The value of 16.2 tells us that pioneer advertising resulted in a higher mean intent to purchase score than retentive advertising *in the sample.* Is this difference statistically significant? Compare it to the margin of error. The margin of error of 10.29 represents the impact of all extraneous factors on the intent to purchase scores. Figure 12.1 indicates that pioneer advertising's superior performance over retentive advertising outweighs the impact of all extraneous factors. Thus, pioneer advertising is more effective than retentive advertising *in the population.*

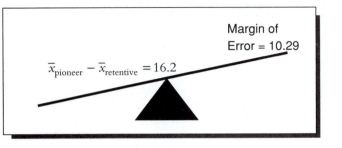

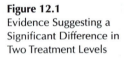
**Figure 12.1**
Evidence Suggesting a Significant Difference in Two Treatment Levels

Figure 12.2 illustrates a situation wherein you cannot tell if one type of advertising is better than another type *in the population.* That's because the difference in sample means is less than the impact due to extraneous factors.

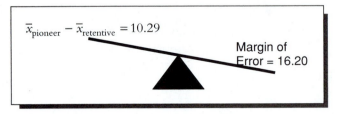

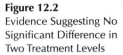
**Figure 12.2**
Evidence Suggesting No Significant Difference in Two Treatment Levels

While the *sample* data suggest that pioneer advertising is better than retentive advertising, its impact on intent to purchase scores is less than the impact of all extraneous factors. Thus, you cannot be 95% confident that pioneer advertising is more effective than retentive advertising *in the population.*

Based on the three Tukey confidence intervals, the marketing manager is 95% confident that

**1.** Pioneer and comparative advertising are both the most effective forms of advertising as measured by intent to purchase scores.

**2.** Retentive advertising is less effective than either of the other two advertising methods.

The marketing manager should now choose between pioneer or comparative advertising (or use both) to launch the digital broadcast satellite service.

# THE TWO-FACTOR COMPLETELY RANDOM DESIGN

The two-factor study is the simplest form of the factorial, or multifactor, experimental design. We vary two factors or treatments and determine the impact on the dependent variable.

**DEFINITION**

**Factorial experiments** permit a manager to evaluate the combined effect of two or more experimental factors when used simultaneously. You evaluate every level of one factor at all levels of all other factors.

To determine if performance has *significantly* improved, we conduct an analysis of variance (ANOVA). By the end of this section you should be able to

**1.** develop sets of null and alternative hypotheses;

**2.** Use Excel to draw profile graphs and determine if you are *likely* to reject (or fail to reject) the null hypothesis of no interaction effect;

**3.** interpret and explain the ANOVA output from the Excel ANOVA: Two-Factor with Replication data-analysis tool;

**4.** explain what a statistically significant interaction is and what are its decision-making implications; and

**5.** construct and interpret Tukey confidence intervals.

Return to the case of the cracked table drawers discussed earlier. Apex's plant manager suspected that the combination of new material and deep stamping depth had caused excessive cracking. So he ran a two-factor study. Factor A, material, has two treatment levels, or variations, and factor B, stamping depth, has three levels.

| | |
|---|---|
| Factor A | $A_1$ Old Material |
| | $A_2$ New Material |
| Factor B | $B_1$ 4-inch drawer depth |
| | $B_2$ 7-inch drawer depth |
| | $B_3$ 10-inch drawer depth |

This is a 2 (levels of Factor A) × 3 (levels of Factor B) factorial study. The manager will run the six treatment combinations of material and stamping depths, or cells. The dependent variable is the percentage of cracked drawers.

## The Interaction Effect

The factorial study introduces a new concept—the interaction effect. Table 12.9 illustrates an interaction effect. Table 12.9 displays a hypothetical and incomplete data set for a 2 × 3 factorial study to reduce cracking. The tabled values are the means for five of the six treatment combinations.

**Table 12.9**
Data Set to Illustrate the Absence or Presence of an Interaction Effect

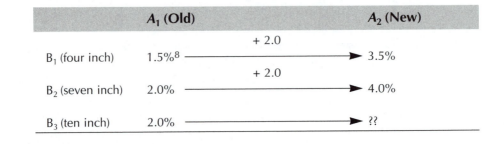

| | $A_1$ (Old) | $A_2$ (New) |
|---|---|---|
| $B_1$ (four inch) | 1.5%[8] $\xrightarrow{+2.0}$ | 3.5% |
| $B_2$ (seven inch) | 2.0% $\xrightarrow{+2.0}$ | 4.0% |
| $B_3$ (ten inch) | 2.0% $\longrightarrow$ | ?? |

If the two experimental factors (material and drawer depth) do not statistically interact, you can predict the mean for the $AB_{23}$ treatment combination (the cell labeled ??) simply based on the other five values in Table 12.9. The cell mean should be about 4.0%. Why? Because at the 4-inch depth ($B_1$ level), going from old material ($A_1$) to $A_2$ increased the mean value of the dependent variable by 2.0. At the $B_2$ level, going from $A_1$ to $A_2$ increased the mean value of the dependent variable also by 2.0. If there is no interaction you should expect the same increase at the 10-inch depth ($B_3$) level as well. Thus 2.0 + 2.0 = 4.0.

**D E F I N I T I O N**    Lack of a **statistical interaction** occurs when the impact of one factor on the dependent variable does not depend on the level of another factor. The impact of the two factors on the dependent variable is *additive*.

*Subject to statistical verification* by the analysis of variance, there is no interaction between the two experimental factors.

Suppose the mean of the $AB_{23}$ treatment combination were 10%. You could not have predicted this from the other five entries in Table 12.9. The

---

[8]The manager used the old material ($A_1$) in combination with the 4-inch-deep drawers ($B_1$). The percentage of drawers that cracked was 1.5%.

impact of the two factors on the dependent variable is not additive. Nonadditive means

1.  At the $B_1$ level, the mean value of the dependent variable increases by 2.0 going from the $A_1$ to $A_2$ level.

2.  At the $B_2$ level, the mean value of the dependent variable also increases by 2.0 going from the $A_1$ to $A_2$ level.

3.  However, at the $B_3$ level, the mean value of the dependent variable increases by 8.0.

The important point is that the impact of Factor A on the dependent variable depends on the level of Factor B. It is different at the $B_3$ level versus the $B_1$ or $B_2$ levels.

**D E F I N I T I O N**     A **statistical interaction** occurs when the impact of one factor on the dependent variable *does depend* on the level of another factor.

*Subject to statistical verification* by the analysis of variance, there is an interaction between the two experimental factors.

Interactions are common in industry and education studies. Often the best advertising strategy *depends* on the market segment. There may be no one best marketing strategy for all consumers. Often the best teaching method *depends* on the students' learning styles or aptitudes. Often the best leadership style *depends* on the workers' demographics or preferences. Interactions are prevalent in industry, and you can run factorial experiments to detect them.

Let's return now to the $2 \times 3$ cracked drawer study and begin the statistical analysis of the data in Table 12.3.

## NULL AND ALTERNATIVE HYPOTHESES

In all factorial studies there are two sets of null and alternative hypotheses. The first null hypothesis states there is no statistically significant interaction. You test for the presence of a statistically significant interaction first. If one is found, do not test for the impact of Factors A and B on the dependent variable for there is no one best level of Factor A or Factor B. The best level of Factor A (or B) depends on the level of Factor B (or A); that is what an interaction means.

However, if you fail to reject the no interaction hypothesis, then test for the impact of each experimental factor individually on the dependent variable—the main effects. Use the second set of null and alternative hypotheses to test for the two main effects—Factor A and Factor B (see Table 12.10).

| Hypotheses | Managerial Actions |
|---|---|
| *Set I: The Interaction Effect*<br>$H_0$ In the *population* there is *no* interaction effect. | Failure to reject the null hypothesis requires testing the two main effects: material and stamping depth. |
| $H_1$ In the *population* there is an interaction effect. | Determine if the interaction is consistent with the problem diagnosis that the combination of the new material and deep stamping depths caused the increased cracking percentage. |
| *Set II: The Main Effects*<br>$H_0$ In the *population* the mean percentage of cracked drawers is the same for both materials and for all three stamping depths. | Failure to reject the null hypothesis means that neither stamping depth or material individually affect the percentage of cracked drawers.<br><br>Brainstorm additional factors that could affect the percentage of cracked drawers. |
| Factor A<br>$\mu_{\text{OLD MATERIAL}} = \mu_{\text{NEW MATERIAL}}$ | |
| Factor B<br>$\mu_{\text{4-INCH}} = \mu_{\text{7-INCH}} = \mu_{\text{10-INCH}}$ | |
| $H_1$ In the *population* the mean percentage of cracked drawers is not the same for all materials or for all stamping depths. | Determine which material or stamping depth produces the lowest percentage of cracked drawers. |
| Factor A<br>$\mu_{\text{OLD MATERIAL}} \neq \mu_{\text{NEW MATERIAL}}$ | |
| Factor B<br>Not all $\mu_{\text{DEPTHS}}$ are the same. | |
| The manager sets the significance level, $\alpha$, at 0.05. | |

**Table 12.10**
Sets of Null and Alternative Hypotheses for the Cracked Drawer Study

The five bold-faced values in Table 12.11 are the row means for the two materials and the column means for the three stamping depths. The overall mean is 2.410. The six cell means and variances are shown in Table 12.12.

| | $B_1$ 4-inch | $B_2$ 7-inch | $B_3$ 10-inch | |
|---|---|---|---|---|
| **$A_1$ Old Material** | 1.00<br>0.43<br>1.96<br>0.01<br>1.65 | 0.20<br>1.90<br>0.70<br>1.40<br>0.65 | 0.20<br>1.82<br>1.25<br>0.35<br>1.56 | **1.005** |
| **$A_2$ New Material** | 0.30<br>1.96<br>0.15<br>2.13<br>0.89 | 4.51<br>2.21<br>4.65<br>2.57<br>6.54 | 7.50<br>3.56<br>6.85<br>5.90<br>7.50 | **3.815** |
| | **1.048** | **2.533** | **3.649** | 2.410 |

**Table 12.11**
Data for 2 × 3 Study to Determine Causes of the Cracked Drawer Problem

| Cell | Treatment Combination | Mean | Variance |
|---|---|---|---|
| $AB_{11}$ | old material  and   4-inch drawer | 1.010% | 0.662 |
| $AB_{12}$ | old material  and   7-inch drawer | 0.970% | 0.455 |
| $AB_{13}$ | old material  and 10-inch drawer | 1.036% | 0.526 |
| $AB_{21}$ | new material and   4-inch drawer | 1.086% | 0.847 |
| $AB_{22}$ | new material and   7-inch drawer | 4.096% | 3.084 |
| $AB_{23}$ | new material and 10-inch drawer | 6.262% | 2.711 |

**Table 12.12**
Cell Means and Variances for 2 × 3 Factorial Study

## EXPLORING DATA THROUGH PROFILE GRAPHS

Begin an exploration of Table 12.11 by constructing a material (or stamping depth) profile graph. Profile graphs effectively display and explore (but do not test for) an interaction effect.

To construct a material profile graph, place the levels of the other experimental factor—drawer depth—on the horizontal axis. Figure 12.3 displays the 4-inch, 7-inch, and 10-inch depths. The vertical axis represents the dependent variable, the percentage of cracked drawers.

Draw two lines, an old material profile and a new material profile. The old material line displays the cell means for the old material at the 4-inch-, 7-inch-, and 10-inch-deep drawers. The new material line displays the cell means for the new material at the 4-inch-, 7-inch-, and 10-inch-deep drawers. Use Excel's Chart Wizard Line Graph to plot the three cell mean values for each profile.[9]

Figure 12.3 is a material profile graph. It displays the impact of the two materials on the percentage of cracked drawers at the three stamping depths.

---

[9]See the chapter's Appendix IV for instructions on how to construct a profile graph.

The profiles are clearly nonparallel. Nonparallel profiles indicate the possibility of an interaction. A significant interaction would not necessarily support the diagnosis that the new material–deeper stamping depths caused the excessive cracked drawer problem. But the *shape* of the profiles does! The profile shape is consistent with the problem diagnosis. From Figure 12.3, note:

1. For the old material, the percentage of cracked drawers does not increase with increasing drawer depth; it remains about 1%.

2. For the new material, the percentage of cracked drawers does increase with increasing drawer depth, but is 1% at the 4-inch depth.

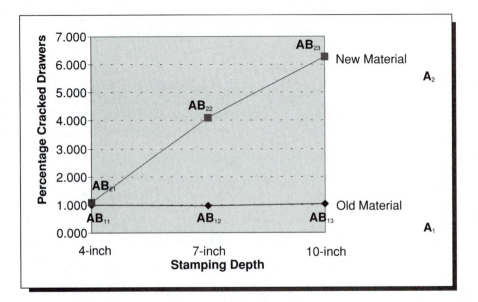

**Figure 12.3**
Material Profile (New and Old Material) Graph for Cracked Drawer Data

In summary, when a profile graph displays nonparallel profiles, it indicates, *subject to verification by the analysis of variance*, a statistical interaction between the two experimental factors. However, you must conduct the analysis of variance to draw a conclusion about the population. After all, you are not interested in the specific sample selected for the study, but all desk drawers in the population!

Before conducting the analysis of variance it is good practice to test its three underlying assumptions presented in the previous section. To test for normality, compute the five residual values for each of the six treatment combinations. A residual is a cell data value minus its *cell* sample mean. Then apply Excel's KURT and SKEW function wizards to the six sets of five residuals to assess normality. If the six SKEW and KURT values are all between −1 and +1, the data are normal. As we presented this earlier in the chapter, we will not present it again here.

Also, assess the homogeneity of variance assumption. First, compute the ratio of the largest treatment combination, or cell, variance to the smallest treatment combination variance, and apply the Hartley test. From Table 12.12

$$H_{max} = \frac{s^2_{largest}}{s^2_{smallest}} = \frac{3.084}{0.455} = 6.78$$

Second, compare $H_{max}$ against the $H_{critical}$ (number of **treatment combinations**, degrees of freedom for each cell) value from Table 12.6. $H_{critical}$ (6 combinations, 4df per cell) is 29.50. Since $H_{max} = 6.78$ is less than 29.50, the manager is at least 95% confident that the homogeneity of variance assumption is true.

## The Analysis of Variance

As in the one-factor study, the analysis of variance begins with a decomposition of the total sum of squares. Refer to the data in Table 12.11. Note that the dependent variable, percentage of cracked drawers, varies among the 30 data values. How much variation is there about the overall mean of 2.410? The total sum of squares, SST, measures the total variation.

The SST for the data in Table 12.11 requires 30 squared calculations and equals

$$SST = (1.00 - 2.410)^2 + (0.43 - 2.410)^2 + \ldots + (5.90 - 2.410)^2 + (7.50 - 2.410)^2$$
$$= 159.912 \text{ units of variation}$$

What accounts for the 159.912 units of variation? There are two sources. The first source reflects the experimental factors and consists of three components: (1) Factor A (material), (2) Factor B (stamping depth), and (3) the AB interaction. The second source is due to all extraneous factors that could affect the cracked drawer percentages. Sum of squares *sample, columns,* and *interaction* measure the variation in the dependent variable due to the two experimental factors and their interaction. Sum of squares *within* measures the variation in the dependent variable due to all extraneous factors such as worker differences, age of machinery, temperature or humidity, and so forth.

Below is the input screen for the ANOVA: Two-Factor with Replication data-analysis tool. There are five observations for each treatment combination, or cell.

Table 12.13 is the ANOVA: Two-Factor with Replication data-analysis tool output for the data in Table 12.11. Of the 159.912 units of variation, the three stamping depths (columns) account for 34.05294 units of variation, the two materials (sample) account for 59.19265, and the AB interaction accounts for 33.52917. The remaining 33.13724 units of variation are due to all extraneous factors.

***Computing the F Ratio.*** After completing the decomposition in column 1, the data–analysis tool converts the sums of squares to *mean squares*, or variances (column 3).

**Table 12.13**
ANOVA for 2 × 3 Factorial Study on Cracked Drawers

| ANOVA | 1 | | 2 | 3 | 4 | 5 | 6 |
|---|---|---|---|---|---|---|---|
| *Source of Variation* | *SS* | | *df* | *MS* | *F* | *P-value* | *F crit* |
| Sample | 59.19265 | | 1 | 59.19265 | 42.87091 | 9.01E-07 | 4.259675 |
| Columns | 34.05294 | | 2 | 17.02647 | 12.3316 | 0.000207 | 3.402832 |
| Interaction | 33.52917 | | 2 | 16.76458 | 12.14193 | 0.000227 | 3.402832 |
| Within | 33.13724 | | 24 | 1.380718 | | | |
| Total | 159.912 | | 29 | | | | |

Divide the sums of squares by their degrees of freedom in column 2 to obtain the mean squares.

The breakdown of degrees of freedom is as follows.

1. The *total* degrees of freedom is $N - 1$, where $N$ equals the total sample size. In the cracked drawer study, $30 - 1 = 29$.

2. The *sample (material)* degrees of freedom equals the number of levels of the material experimental factor minus one, $2 - 1 = 1$.

3. The *columns (stamping depth)* degrees of freedom equal the number of levels of the drawer depth experimental factor minus one, $3 - 1 = 2$.

4. The *interaction* degrees of freedom equals the degrees of freedom for material *times* the degrees of freedom for depth, $2 \cdot 1 = 2$.

**5.** The *within* degrees of freedom is the remainder, $29 - [1 + 2 + 2] = 24$. Alternatively, there are five observations per cell. Thus there are four degrees of freedom per cell. There are six cells, so there are $4 \cdot 6 = 24$ degrees of freedom.

Next, the data-analysis tool computes the mean squares. It divides each sum of squares term by its appropriate degrees of freedom. Finally, the tool computes the three *F ratios*.

Begin by first testing for a significant interaction effect. The appropriate F ratio is $MS_{INTERACTION}/MS_{WITHIN}$:

$$F = \frac{16.76458}{1.380718} = 12.14193$$

Can we reject the "no interaction" null hypothesis at the $\alpha = 0.05$ level?

***Hypothesis Testing.*** Does an F ratio of 12.14 favor the first null hypothesis—that there is no interaction effect? Column 5 in Table 12.13 answers the question. If there was no interaction effect, the probability of obtaining an F ratio of 12.14 or greater is only 0.000227, or 227 in one million. Since this is smaller than the chosen significance level, $\alpha = 0.05$, the manager should reject the "no interaction" null hypothesis.

As there is a statistically significant interaction, do not test for the significance of the two main effects. If the *p*-value in column 5 is larger than the chosen significance level, $\alpha = 0.05$, the manager would fail to reject the "no interaction" null hypothesis. He should then assess the two F ratios

| Material | $MS_{MATERIAL}/MS_{WITHIN}$ |
| Stamping Depth | $MS_{DEPTH}/MS_{WITHIN}$ |

by interpreting their two associated *p*-values.

## Applying Tukey Confidence Intervals

As in the previous section, we use Tukey confidence intervals to conduct a post–ANOVA analysis when you reject either the "no interaction" or "no main effects" null hypotheses.

Here we examine how to construct and interpret Tukey intervals following the rejection of the "no interaction" null hypothesis. You can construct Tukey confidence intervals between all possible pairs of means within a *logical grouping*.

| | |
|---|---|
| For a significant interaction | A logical grouping includes all pairs of cell means within a single row ($A_1$ or $A_2$) or single column ($B_1$, $B_2$, $B_3$) of a factorial study. |
| For a significant main effect | A logical grouping includes all pairs of row or column means. |

The manager wanted to determine if, *for the new material*, the percentage of cracked drawers increased for increasing stamping depths: 4-inch to 7-inch to 10-inch. Thus he chose as his logical grouping, the single row, $A_2$, the new material, to construct Tukey intervals. He used Expression (12.4) to construct three Tukey confidence intervals.

$$\bar{x}_{AB_{2i}} - \bar{x}_{AB_{2j}} \pm q\left(df_{within}, \text{number of levels}\right) \cdot \sqrt{\frac{MS_{within}}{n_{cell}}}$$

(12.4)

where

$\bar{x}_{AB_{2i}}$ are the cell means at the $A_2$ level to be compared: 1.086, 4.096, and 6.262

$n$ is the sample size per treatment combination or cell: $n$ equals 5
$df_{within}$ is from the ANOVA table and equals 24.

number of levels to be compared is three: $AB_{21}$, $AB_{22}$, and $AB_{23}$.

$MS_{within}$ is from the ANOVA table and equals 1.380718
$q(24,3) = 3.53$ from Table 12.8

| Interval | Construction of Interval | Interpretation |
|---|---|---|
| 7-inch vs. 4-inch[10] | $4.096 - 1.086 \pm 3.53 \cdot \sqrt{\dfrac{1.380718}{5}}$ <br><br> $3.01 \pm 1.85$ <br> lower limit: 1.16 <br> upper limit: 4.86 | The interval does not include zero. Or the difference of 3.01 is greater than the margin of error. The percentage of cracked drawers is greater at the 7-inch depth than at the 4-inch depth (by between 1.16% and 4.86%). |

---

[10]For ease of interpretation, place the larger sample mean first in Expression (12.4).

| 10-inch vs. 4-inch | $6.262 - 1.086 \pm 1.85$<br>$5.176 \pm 1.85$ | The interval does not include zero. Or the difference of 5.176 is greater than the margin of error.<br>The percentage of cracked drawers is greater at the 10-inch depth than at the 4-inch depth (by between 3.33% and 7.03%). |
| --- | --- | --- |
| 10-inch vs. 7-inch | $6.262 - 4.096 \pm 1.85$<br>$2.166 \pm 1.85$ | The interval does not include zero. Or, the difference of 2.166 is greater than the margin of error.<br>The percentage of cracked drawers is greater at the 10-inch depth than at the 7-inch depth (by between .32% and 4.02%). |

The operations manager is 95% confident that, for the new material, the highest percentage of cracking occurs at the 10-inch depth, the second highest percentage at the 7-inch depth, and the lowest percentage at the 4-inch depth. This is consistent with the problem diagnosis that for the new material the percentage of cracked drawers increases with increasing drawer depth.

Even without constructing Tukey intervals, clearly there is no difference in the percentage of cracked drawers at the three stamping depths for the old material. However, let's construct the intervals to illustrate two important ideas. From Table 12.11 and Expression (12.4) the three intervals are

$$1.010 - 0.970 \pm 1.85 \qquad 1.036 - 1.010 \pm 1.85 \qquad 1.036 - 0.970 \pm 1.85$$

Point 1    All three confidence intervals include the values of zero. At the 95% confidence level, there is no difference in the percentage of cracked drawers in the population at the three stamping depths.

Point 2    The confidence level for the three intervals for the new material and old material are *each* $100 - 5 = 95\%$. The *overall* confidence level for the *family* of six intervals, three for the old material and three for the new material, is $100 - 2 \cdot 5 = 90\%$.

If the confidence level for intervals for one single row (or column) is $100 - 5 = 95\%$, the overall confidence level for all intervals for "$k$" rows (or columns) is $100 - 5 \cdot k$.

The manager took immediate corrective action by switching back to the firm's old material vendor. The percentage of cracked drawers immediately returned to about 1.00% at all stamping depths.

You can construct Tukey intervals if either one or both of the main effects are significant. Use Expression (12.5).

$$\bar{x}_i - \bar{x}_j \pm q\left(df_{within}, \text{number of levels}\right) \cdot \sqrt{\frac{MS_{within}}{n_{R/C}}}$$

(12.5)

where

$\bar{x}_i$ is the row (or column) sample mean

$n_{R/C}$ is the sample size per row (or column)

number of levels is number of rows or columns

For example, let's *pretend* that the interaction had not been significant, but the main effect due to stamping depth had been significant. You could use Expression (12.5) to construct three Tukey confidence intervals to compare the percentage of cracked drawers at the

**1.** 4-inch versus 7-inch stamping depths,

**2.** 4-inch versus 10-inch stamping depths, and

**3.** 7-inch versus 10-inch stamping depths.

Shown below are the calculations. Remember to use (1) the column sample means, not the cell sample means, and (2) the sample size per column [10], not the sample size per treatment combination [5].

$$\text{7-inch vs. 4-inch} \quad 2.533 - 1.048 \pm q(24,3) \cdot \sqrt{\frac{1.380718}{10}}$$

$$\text{10-inch vs. 4-inch} \quad 3.649 - 1.048 \pm q(24,3) \cdot \sqrt{\frac{1.380718}{10}}$$

$$\text{10-inch vs. 7-inch} \quad 3.649 - 2.533 \pm q(24,3) \cdot \sqrt{\frac{1.380718}{10}}$$

However, you should not construct these three intervals because the interaction in the cracked drawer study was significant at the $\alpha = 0.05$ level.

## Flowchart for Conducting Analysis of Variance and Constructing Tukey Intervals

Figure 12.4 is a flowchart that illustrates how to analyze sequentially a two-factor study. First, test for the significance of the AB interaction effect. If significant, use Expression (12.4) to construct Tukey intervals on all pairs of cell sample means within one or more rows or columns. Constructing these intervals will help you understand the meaning of the interaction and help you explain it to others. *Caution:* Constructing Tukey intervals within multiple row or columns will reduce the overall confidence level of the family of intervals; the overall confidence level for the family of intervals is (100 − 5·number of rows or columns)%.

If the AB interaction is not significant, then test for the significance of both main effects, Factor A and Factor B. If one or both main effects are significant, then use Expression (12.5) to construct Tukey intervals on either the column or row sample means or both. If no interaction or main effects are significant, the study has been a failure. Brainstorm additional experimental factors and rerun the study.

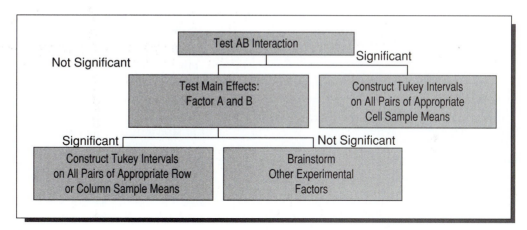

**Figure 12.4**
Analysis Flowchart for Two-Factor Study

# EXERCISES

**1.** Explain why as the F ratio increases, the chances of rejecting the null hypothesis increases.

**2.** If the lines in a profile graph are nonparallel, why is it necessary to conduct the analysis of variance to determine if there is a statistical interaction?

**3.** If you were only interested in drawing conclusions about the specific sample, would you need to do the analysis of variance?

**4.** Distinguish between an experimental factor, its levels, and an extraneous factor.

**5.** If we reject the null hypothesis in a one-factor analysis of variance, why is it necessary to compute Tukey confidence intervals? That is, what information do the intervals provide that the analysis of variance does not?

**6.** What does the expression, "there is no one best way," mean in a statistical sense?

**7.** Provide a business example where you would suspect an interaction between two experimental factors.

**8.** Correct if necessary: If a Tukey confidence interval contains the value of zero, conclude at the 95% confidence level that the two sample means do differ.

**9.** If you fail to reject the no interaction null hypothesis, why must you then test for the significance of the Factor A and Factor B main effects?

**10.** If you reject the no interaction null hypothesis, why shouldn't you then test for the significance of the main effects: Factor A and Factor B?

**11.** An electronics store selects 15 customers who recently purchased a compact disk player. They ask the customers to rate the sound quality of three brands of speakers (one customer to a brand of speakers) on a scale from 0 (poor) to 100 (outstanding). Below are the sample results.

| Polk | Fisher | Pioneer |
|------|--------|---------|
| 95 | 95 | 90 |
| 55 | 95 | 50 |
| 75 | 85 | 85 |
| 60 | 70 | 95 |
| 90 | 75 | 85 |

**a.** Compute the sample means and sample variances for the three levels of the experimental factor.

**b.** Based on the three *sample* means, does it appear that there is a difference in the three *population* mean sound qualities? How did you arrive at your conclusion?

**c.** Conduct an analysis of variance for the sound quality study. Use an $\alpha$ level of 0.05. Does the analysis of variance support your conclusion from part (b)? If not, why did you draw the incorrect conclusion in part (b)?

**12.** An HR manager wishes to determine which of three creativity methods is best. Best is defined as the method that maximizes the quantity of different solutions for a given problem. She randomly selects 21 employees within the same department. Each member receives training in one of the three methods. The employees then work on a common problem. Below are the number of different solutions generated for the common problem.

| Brainstorming | Analogy | Manipulative Verbs |
|---------------|---------|--------------------|
| 15 | 34 | 10 |
| 21 | 38 | 15 |
| 25 | 41 | 12 |
| 22 | 38 | 16 |
| 26 | 35 | 17 |
| 25 | 40 | 12 |
| 27 | 44 | 18 |

**a.** Compute the sample means and sample variances for the three levels of the experimental factor.

**b.** Based on the three *sample* means, does it appear that there is a difference in the three *population* mean number of alternatives generated? How did you arrive at your conclusion?

**c.** Conduct an analysis of variance for the creativity study. Use an $\alpha$ level of 0.05. Does the analysis of variance support your conclusion from part (b)? If not, why did you draw the incorrect conclusion in part (b)?

**d.** Based on 95% Tukey confidence intervals, which creativity method(s) is best? Discuss.

**13.** During the product development cycle, Mr. Koffee, Inc., often asks potential customers to rate product features at various costs. It can then include product features that consumers want at a price they are willing to pay. An important feature of coffee makers is the brew capacity. Mr. Koffee selects 30 potential consumers. Ten customers each are given one of the three prototype coffee makers described below. They rate their intent to purchase the coffee maker along a scale ranging from 0 (absolutely certain not to buy) to 100 (absolutely certain to buy).

| Prototype | Brew Capacity | Cost |
|---|---|---|
| 1 | 4-cup capacity | $19.99 |
| 2 | 6-cup capacity | $25.99 |
| 3 | 8-cup capacity | $34.99 |

| 4-cup | 6-cup | 8-cup |
|---|---|---|
| 50 | 70 | 35 |
| 45 | 75 | 30 |
| 50 | 80 | 40 |
| 40 | 85 | 40 |
| 55 | 90 | 35 |
| 40 | 80 | 35 |
| 45 | 75 | 30 |
| 45 | 80 | 35 |
| 50 | 80 | 35 |
| 45 | 75 | 35 |

**a.** State the null and alternative hypotheses.

**b.** Compute the 30 residuals and assess the normality assumption underlying the analysis of variance.

**c.** Use the Hartley test to assess the homogeneity of variance assumption underlying the analysis of variance.

**d.** Conduct an analysis of variance. Use an $\alpha$ level of 0.05.

**e.** Use the Tukey interval procedure to make all pairwise comparisons on the three population mean intent to purchase scores. At the 95% confidence level which coffee maker(s) is most preferred? Discuss.

**14.** Do all states have the same population mean cost per day for a hospital stay? A public policy watchdog group chooses three states—Alaska, South Dakota, and Georgia. It randomly selects six very similar community hospitals and determines their mean cost per day. Below are the sample data.

| Alaska | South Dakota | Georgia |
|---|---|---|
| 892 | 318 | 456 |
| 808 | 350 | 500 |
| 910 | 370 | 425 |
| 880 | 280 | 450 |
| 901 | 325 | 460 |
| 870 | 300 | 470 |

**a.** Compute the sample means and sample variances for the three levels of the experimental factor.

**b.** Based on the three *sample* means, does it appear that there is a difference in the three *population* mean costs per day? How did you arrive at your conclusion?

**c.** Conduct an analysis of variance for the hospital study. Use an $\alpha$ level of 0.05. Does the analysis of variance support your conclusion from part (b)? If not, why did you draw the incorrect conclusion in part (b)?

**d.** Based on 95% Tukey confidence intervals, which state has the least expensive hospital costs? Discuss.

**15.** During the product development cycle, Mr. Koffee, Inc., often asks potential customers to rate product features at various costs. It can then include product features that consumers want at a price they are willing to pay. Two important features of coffee makers are (1) brew capacity and (2) brew time. Mr. Koffee selects 18 potential consumers. Two customers are each given one of the nine prototype coffee makers described below. They must rate their intent to purchase the coffee maker along a scale ranging from 0 (absolutely certain not to buy) to 100 (absolutely certain to buy).

| Prototype | Brew Capacity (cups) | Brew Time (minutes) | Cost |
|---|---|---|---|
| 1 | 4 | 3 | $24.99 |
| 2 | 4 | 5 | 27.99 |
| 3 | 4 | 7 | 33.99 |
| 4 | 6 | 3 | 26.99 |
| 5 | 6 | 5 | 29.99 |
| 6 | 6 | 7 | 35.99 |
| 7 | 8 | 3 | 29.99 |
| 8 | 8 | 5 | 32.99 |
| 9 | 8 | 7 | 38.99 |

Below are the data on the $3 \times 3$ factorial study.

| | $A_1$ 4-cup | $A_2$ 6-cup | $A_3$ 8-cup |
|---|---|---|---|
| $B_1$ 3 minutes | 55 | 40 | 50 |
| | 65 | 50 | 45 |
| $B_2$ 5 minutes | 50 | 80 | 30 |
| | 70 | 90 | 40 |
| $B_3$ 7 minutes | 55 | 10 | 50 |
| | 65 | 30 | 70 |

**a.** Conduct an analysis of variance. Use a significance level of 0.05.

**b.** Explore the significant brew capacity–brew time interaction by drawing brew time profiles. What do the profiles suggest?

**16.** Consider the $3 \times 3$ experiment in Exercise 15. Develop one data set—two observations per cell for a total of 18 observations—for a study that will produce

**1.** A nonsignificant AB interaction at the 0.05 level.

**a.** Compute the nine cell means for your data.

**b.** Before conducting the analysis of variance, draw a brew time profile graph and ensure that the three brew time lines are reasonably parallel. Recall that parallel profiles *suggest* no interaction.

**c.** Verify your profile graph by conducting an analysis of variance. The ANOVA table should indicate a nonsignificant AB interaction.

**2.** A significant AB interaction at the 0.05 level. Do parts (a)–(c) again.

**17.** A manager investigates the impact of quality circles and top management support on the number of defects per 100 cars in three plants that produce the Ford Taurus. Below are the weekly number of defects per 100 cars for 21 work groups six months after the start of the study. All 21 teams were randomly selected and have the same years of work experience and demographics.

| No Quality Circle | QC— No Top Support | QC— Top Support |
|---|---|---|
| 80 | 79 | 56 |
| 85 | 85 | 61 |
| 85 | 82 | 64 |
| 89 | 88 | 58 |
| 82 | 84 | 64 |
| 78 | 85 | 61 |
| 75 | 76 | 60 |

**a.** State the null and alternative hypotheses.

**b.** Compute the seven residuals per treatment level and assess the normality assumption underlying the analysis of variance.

**c.** Use the Hartley test to assess the homogeneity of variance assumption underlying the analysis of variance.

**d.** Conduct an analysis of variance. Use an $\alpha$ level of 0.05.

**e.** Use the Tukey interval procedure to make all pairwise comparisons on the three population mean number of defects per 100 car data. At the 95% confidence level, which type of quality circle has the lowest number of defects per 100 cars? Discuss.

**18.** A firm seeks to increase the tensile strength of its plastic housing for cellular phones by varying injection molding temperature and pressure. Shown are the results of a $2 \times 2$ factorial study with three observations per cell. Present operating conditions are 1200 degrees and 500 kilograms (kg).

|  | $A_1$ 1200 degrees | $A_2$ 1250 degrees |
|---|---|---|
| $B_1$ 500 kg | 4750 | 4725 |
|  | 4775 | 4750 |
|  | 4800 | 4800 |
|  | 4775 | 4760 |
| $B_2$ 600 kg | 4525 | 4925 |
|  | 4500 | 4950 |
|  | 4550 | 4950 |
|  | 4510 | 4940 |

**a.** Compute the cell means and plot pressure profiles.

**b.** Conduct an analysis of variance. Use a significance level of 0.05.

**c.** Explain the significant interaction in terms that an operations manager could

understand. What now would be the best manufacturing conditions?

**19.** Below is a one-factor five-level study on the impact of different bearing brands on the vibration (in microns) of electric motors. The larger the number, the greater is the vibration and the worse the bearing.

| Brand 1 | Brand 2 | Brand 3 | Brand 4 | Brand 5 |
|---|---|---|---|---|
| 13.1 | 16.3 | 13.7 | 15.7 | 13.5 |
| 15.0 | 15.7 | 13.9 | 13.7 | 13.4 |
| 14.0 | 17.2 | 12.4 | 14.4 | 13.2 |
| 14.4 | 14.9 | 13.8 | 16.0 | 12.7 |
| 14.0 | 14.4 | 14.9 | 13.9 | 13.4 |
| 11.6 | 17.2 | 13.3 | 14.7 | 12.3 |

**a.** State the null and alternative hypotheses.

**b.** Compute the six residuals per treatment level and assess the normality assumption underlying the analysis of variance.

**c.** Use the Hartley test to assess the homogeneity of variance assumption underlying the analysis of variance.

**d.** Conduct an analysis of variance. Use an $\alpha$ level of 0.05.

**e.** Use the Tukey interval procedure to make all pairwise comparisons on the five population mean vibration values. At the 95% confidence level, which bearing brand(s) provide(s) the least vibration? Discuss.

**20.** Below is a partially completed analysis of variance table for a $5 \times 5$ factorial study with three observations per cell.

| Source | SS | df | MS | F |
|---|---|---|---|---|
| Factor A | 20 | — | — | — |
| Factor B | — | — | — | — |
| AB | — | — | — | 8.1 |
| Within | — | — | 2 | |
| Total | 500 | 74 | | |

**a.** After completing the table, use Excel's FDIST function wizard to determine the p-value for the AB interaction. In FDIST, degrees of freedom 1 refer to the degrees of freedom in the numerator of the F ratio.

**b.** Given the p-value for the interaction, should you test for the main effects, Factor A and Factor B? Discuss.

**21.** In the following study a researcher seeks to reduce cholesterol level (mg/dL). She randomly selects 24 patients with cholesterol levels between 300 and 320. She randomly assigns the patients to one of three treatment levels. After six months, she determines each patient's drop in cholesterol level.

| Diet/Exercise | Exercise | Diet |
|---|---|---|
| 45 | 10 | 15 |
| 50 | 15 | 15 |
| 55 | 12 | 20 |
| 60 | 10 | 10 |
| 55 | 15 | 15 |
| 65 | 20 | 20 |
| 60 | 15 | 10 |
| 55 | 18 | 19 |

**a.** Compute the sample means and sample variances for the three levels of the experimental factor.

**b.** Based on the three *sample* means, does it appear that there is a difference in the three *population* mean reductions in cholesterol levels? How did you arrive at your conclusion?

**c.** Conduct an analysis of variance for the cholesterol study. Use an $\alpha$ level of 0.05. Does the analysis of variance support your conclusion from part (b)? If not, why did you draw the incorrect conclusion in part (b)?

**d.** Based on 95% Tukey confidence intervals, which method produces the greatest drop in cholesterol levels? Discuss.

**22.** Based on the results of the study in Exercise 18, the firm sought to further increase the tensile strength of the housing for its cellular phones. Shown are the results of a second $2 \times 2$ factorial study with four observations per cell.

| | $A_1$ 1250 degrees | $A_2$ 1300 degrees |
|---|---|---|
| $B_1$ 600 kg | 4930 | 4825 |
| | 4930 | 4810 |
| | 4940 | 4815 |
| | 4930 | 4815 |
| $B_2$ 650 kg | 4815 | 4790 |
| | 4800 | 4795 |
| | 4790 | 4810 |
| | 4800 | 4800 |

**a.** Compute the cell means and plot pressure profiles.

**b.** Conduct an analysis of variance. Use a significance level of 0.05.

**c.** What combination of injection temperature and pressure produces the highest tensile strengths? Discuss.

**23.** We run a study to determine which type of clothes dryer, gas or electric, dries clothes fastest. The effectiveness of each dryer was measured by the percentage of moisture that remained in the test clothing after 35 minutes. The data for a $3 \times 2$ factorial study with five observations per cell follow on page 569.

**a.** Plot a type of dryer, gas versus electric, profile graph. Does it appear that there is an interaction between dryer brand and type? Explain what an interaction would mean in practical terms.

|          | $A_1$<br>Brand A        | $A_2$<br>Brand B     | $A_3$<br>Brand C        |
|----------|-------------------------|----------------------|-------------------------|
| $B_1$<br>Gas Dryer | 17, 13, 21,<br>19, 15 | 7, 10, 6,<br>5, 7 | 12, 9, 13,<br>11, 15 |
| $B_2$<br>Electric  | 15, 11, 18,<br>12, 19 | 8, 12, 5,<br>8, 7 | 11, 8, 15,<br>10, 11 |

**b.** Perform an analysis of variance. Use a 0.05 significance level.

**c.** Which brand of dryer is fastest? Defend.

**24.** Consider the following data from a $2 \times 2$ factorial study. The dependent variable is the number of lost bags per 10,000 passengers over five successive weeks. Present practice at Air Georgia is that counter personnel receive 20 hours of check-in training and manually tag baggage. The airline's goal is zero lost bags per 10,000 passengers.

| Factor A | $A_1$ Manual Tag | $A_2$ Computer Tag |
|----------|------------------|--------------------|
| $B_1$<br>20 hours | 10, 8, 9, 9, 9 | 8, 6, 7, 6, 8 |

| Factor B | | |
|----------|-----------------|----------------|
| $B_2$<br>40 hours | 9, 9, 9, 8, 10 | 0, 2, 1, 1, 1 |

**a.** Compute the cell means and plot hours of training profiles.

**b.** Conduct an analysis of variance. Use a significance level of 0.05.

**c.** What combination of training hours and tag system produces the fewest lost bags per 10,000 passengers? Discuss.

**25.** A manager investigates the impact of job switching (job rotation) on the amount of rework (%) at a plant. Below are the weekly data for 27 randomly selected work groups one month after the start of the study.

**a.** State the null and alternative hypotheses.

**b.** Compute the nine residuals per treatment level and assess the normality assumption underlying the analysis of variance.

**c.** Use the Hartley test to assess the homogeneity of variance assumption underlying the analysis of variance.

| Job Switch<br>Daily | Job Switch<br>Weekly | No Job<br>Switch |
|---------------------|----------------------|------------------|
| 1.83 | 2.06 | 4.10 |
| 1.64 | 1.67 | 4.42 |
| 1.54 | 1.56 | 4.15 |
| 1.75 | 1.86 | 3.55 |
| 1.85 | 1.96 | 3.75 |
| 1.75 | 1.92 | 4.02 |
| 1.90 | 1.80 | 3.96 |
| 1.75 | 1.92 | 3.91 |
| 1.80 | 1.90 | 3.75 |

**d.** Conduct an analysis of variance. Use an $\alpha$ level of 0.05.

**e.** Use the Tukey interval procedure to make all pairwise comparisons on the three population mean percent of rework values. At the 95% confidence level which type of job switching generates the least amount of rework? Discuss.

**26.** We have conducted a $3 \times 2$ factorial study with nine observations per cell to improve test score grades. The two factors are

Factor A, Type of Teaching
  $A_1$ Lecture          $A_2$ Case
  $A_3$ Cooperative Groups

Factor B, Students' SAT Scores
  $B_1$ Less than 950     $B_2$ More than 1150

Here are the test score data.

|  | $A_1$ | $A_2$ | $A_3$ |
|---|---|---|---|
| $B_1$ less than 950 | 85, 84, 81<br>81, 84, 78<br>78, 81, 77 | 70, 65, 75<br>73, 75, 68<br>68, 72, 74 | 75, 76, 70<br>75, 72, 73<br>74, 72, 70 |
| $B_2$ more than 1150 | 80, 81, 79,<br>83, 82, 78<br>80, 85, 84 | 88, 90, 91<br>91, 88, 92<br>90, 88, 85 | 95, 96, 90<br>95, 98, 99<br>90, 95, 99 |

**a.** Compute the cell means and plot teaching method profiles.

**b.** Conduct an analysis of variance. Use a significance level of 0.05.

**c.** Can we say that there is one best teaching method? Discuss.

**27.** Firms use the Watson-Glaser Critical Thinking Appraisal to measure problem-solving ability. Firms also use the Myers-Briggs Type Indicator to determine an employee's problem-solving style. The HR manager suspects there may be an interaction between problem-solving type and level of critical thinking on problem-solving time. He runs a $2 \times 3$ factorial study with five observations per cell. The dependent variable is time in minutes to solve a complex problem.

Factor A, Problem-Solving Style
   $A_1$ Sensing-Judger    $A_2$ Intuitive-Perceptor

Factor B, Problem-Solving Ability
   $B_1$ Low        $B_2$ Medium        $B_3$ High

**a.** Compute the cell means and levels of critical thinking profiles.

**b.** Conduct an analysis of variance. Use a significance level of 0.05.

**c.** Describe in plain English the relationship between problem-solving style and critical thinking ability on time to solve a complex problem. Discuss.

|  | $A_1$ Sensing-Judger | $A_2$ Intuitive-Perceptor |
|---|---|---|
| $B_1$ Low Scores | 25 min.<br>28 min.<br>30 min.<br>25 min.<br>27 min. | 35 min.<br>30 min.<br>33 min.<br>32 min.<br>34 min. |
| $B_2$ Medium Scores | 22 min.<br>23 min.<br>20 min.<br>21 min.<br>22 min. | 22 min.<br>19 min.<br>18 min.<br>20 min.<br>21 min. |
| $B_3$ High Scores | 18 min.<br>17 min.<br>16 min.<br>17 min.<br>18 min. | 8 min.<br>7 min.<br>10 min.<br>11 min.<br>9 min. |

**28.** Which of three types of sales displays generates the largest revenue? Shown are the data from a one-factor three-level study conducted at three similar stores over five consecutive days.

| Display A | Display B | Display C |
|---|---|---|
| $1350 | $1050 | $1295 |
| 1250 | 1005 | 1200 |
| 1175 | 980 | 1350 |
| 1060 | 1475 | 990 |
| 975 | 1350 | 1050 |

**a.** State the null and alternative hypotheses.

**b.** Compute the five residuals per treatment level and assess the normality assumption underlying the analysis of variance.

**c.** Use the Hartley test to assess the homogeneity of variance assumption underlying the analysis of variance.

**d.** Conduct an analysis of variance. Use an $\alpha$ level of 0.05. What can you conclude from the study?

**29.** A manager runs a one-factor three-level study on the impact of blade coatings on the number of smooth shaves before the blade must be discarded. Here are the data. The sample size per treatment level is ten observations.

| Plastic | Lubricant | Standard |
|---------|-----------|----------|
| 15 | 15 | 7 |
| 17 | 14 | 9 |
| 15 | 17 | 11 |
| 14 | 15 | 10 |
| 18 | 16 | 9 |
| 17 | 17 | 8 |
| 17 | 14 | 9 |
| 17 | 16 | 10 |
| 18 | 19 | 11 |
| 17 | 14 | 8 |

**a.** State the null and alternative hypotheses.

**b.** Compute the ten residuals per treatment level and assess the normality assumption underlying the analysis of variance.

**c.** Use the Hartley test to assess the homogeneity of variance assumption underlying the analysis of variance.

**d.** Conduct an analysis of variance. Use an $\alpha$ level of 0.05.

**e.** Use the Tukey interval procedure to make all pairwise comparisons on the three population mean number of smooth shaves. At the 95% confidence level which type of blade lasts the longest? Discuss.

**30.** Groupthink is the tendency of groups to reach a too-quick consensus and generate poor decisions. Groupthink happens to groups under severe stress that have poor leadership. Shown is a 2 × 2 factorial study that tests for the necessity of both conditions: severe stress and poor leadership. The dependent variable is the number of symptoms of groupthink that each group exhibits as it solves a complex business case.

| | $A_1$ Poor Leadership | $A_2$ Good Leadership |
|---|---|---|
| $B_1$ Low Stress | 2 | 1 |
| | 1 | 0 |
| | 1 | 2 |
| | 0 | 1 |
| $B_2$ Severe Stress | 7 | 0 |
| | 6 | 1 |
| | 7 | 1 |
| | 6 | 0 |

**a.** Compute the cell means and plot the level of stress profiles.

**b.** Conduct an analysis of variance. Use a significance level of 0.05.

**c.** Does the shape of the significant interaction support the researcher's belief that both negative factors must be present for groupthink to occur? Discuss.

**31.** An IT manager wishes to evaluate the impact of a computerized support system for improving creativity. She believes that the impact of the computerized brainstorming creativity support depends on a person's level of computer literacy. For computer literate personnel, the creativity support system will be very effective at increasing the number of problem definitions to a complex problem. This is not so for computer illiterate personnel. Their lack of familiarity with computers will cause then to lose out on the potential benefits of the creativity support system.

Factor A, Level of Computer Literacy
  $A_1$ Low          $A_2$ High

Factor B, Type of Creativity Support
  $B_1$ No Creativity     $B_2$ Creativity Support

There are five subjects per cell for the 2 × 2 or $2^2$ factorial study. The dependent variable is the number of different problem definitions generated during the study. Below are the data for a $2^2$ factorial study.

**a.** Compute the cell means and plot the level of computer literacy profiles.

**b.** Conduct an analysis of variance. Use a significance level of 0.05.

**c.** Does the shape of the significant interaction support the researcher's belief that the impact of creativity support depends on a person's level of computer literacy? Discuss.

|       | $A_1$ | $A_2$ |
|-------|-------|-------|
|       | 1     | 1     |
|       | 2     | 2     |
| $B_1$ | 1     | 2     |
|       | 2     | 1     |
|       | 1     | 1     |
| $B_2$ | 2     | 7     |
|       | 1     | 8     |
|       | 2     | 8     |
|       | 1     | 9     |
|       | 2     | 8     |

**32.** An HR manager wishes to evaluate four different benefits packages. He randomly selects 40 people from the plant and randomly subdivides the 40 people into four groups of ten people each. Each group reviews an HR benefits package with different elements, and rates the desirability of the package on a scale from 0 (unacceptable) to 100 (outstanding). Below are the data.

**a.** State the null and alternative hypotheses.

**b.** Compute the sample means and variances for the four levels.

**c.** Does it appear that the manager will be able to reject the "no difference in the population desirability of the four HR packages" null hypothesis?

**d.** Conduct an analysis of variance. Use an $\alpha$ level of 0.05.

| $A_1$ Package 1 | $A_2$ Package 2 | $A_3$ Package 3 | $A_4$ Package 4 |
|-----------------|-----------------|-----------------|-----------------|
| 65 | 70 | 70 | 70 |
| 70 | 70 | 80 | 80 |
| 70 | 80 | 80 | 60 |
| 70 | 70 | 70 | 60 |
| 70 | 70 | 70 | 65 |
| 75 | 70 | 80 | 75 |
| 60 | 65 | 85 | 70 |
| 70 | 75 | 80 | 70 |
| 75 | 70 | 65 | 70 |
| 70 | 65 | 85 | 65 |

**33.** Refer to Exercise 29. Develop a set of data (30 data values) that will fail to reject the null hypothesis. Determine the sample means for the three treatment levels. Why do you believe that your data set will not cause rejection of the null hypothesis? Explain in terms of variance between versus variance within. Now use Excel's ANOVA single factor tool to verify that your data set does indeed fail to reject the null hypothesis. Let $\alpha$ 0.05.

**34.** Refer to Exercise 29. Develop a set of data (30 data values) that will fail to meet the assumption of normality for each treatment level. The data set should also fail to meet the assumption of homogeneity of variance. Use Excel's SKEW and KURT function wizards to verify the lack of normality. Apply the Hartley test to verify the variances are not homogeneous.

**35.** A firm evaluates the effectiveness of brand labels, grade labels, and informative labels on a consumer product. Chiquita stickers on bananas are an example of a brand label. A grade label identifies the product quality by a letter, number, or a word such as "prime." An informative label provides written information about the product's ingredients, use, care, or life expectancy.

Which type of labeling do consumers prefer? The dependent variable is the interest level in the product on a scale from 0 (very disinterested) to 100 (very interested). Nine randomly selected potential customers for a product are shown a product with one type of labeling. They then rank product desirability on the 0–100 scale. As there are three types of labels, the study requires 27 subjects.

| Brand Label $A_1$ | Grade Label $A_2$ | Informative Label $A_3$ |
|---|---|---|
| 50 | 60 | 40 |
| 60 | 50 | 60 |
| 70 | 60 | 50 |
| 50 | 70 | 70 |
| 60 | 40 | 40 |
| 40 | 80 | 80 |
| 60 | 60 | 50 |
| 80 | 80 | 70 |
| 40 | 40 | 40 |

At $\alpha = 0.05$ what can you conclude? Discuss.

36. Below are data sets from two studies. In one data set you will reject the no difference in treatment levels null hypothesis, and in one study you will fail to reject the null hypothesis. *Without doing the analysis of variance,* determine the data set for which you will reject the null hypothesis and explain why. *Hint:* Recall what the sum of squares within groups and between groups measure.

| $A_1$ | $A_2$ | $A_3$ | $A_1$ | $A_2$ | $A_3$ |
|---|---|---|---|---|---|
| 1 | 3 | 5 | 0 | 1 | 5 |
| 1 | 3 | 5 | 2 | 5 | 9 |
| 1 | 3 | 6 | 0 | 1 | 1 |
| 1 | 3 | 4 | 2 | 5 | 5 |

Now verify using Excel's ANOVA: Single Factor data-analysis tool. Set $\alpha = 0.05$.

37. *From the profile graph,* does there appear to be a significant interaction or significant Factor A or Factor B main effects? Explain.

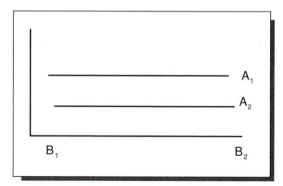

38. *From the profile graph,* does there appear to be a significant interaction or significant Factor A or Factor B main effects? Explain.

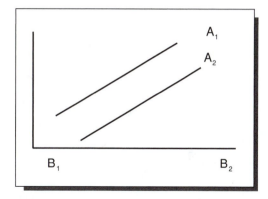

39. *From the profile graph,* does there appear to be a significant interaction or significant Factor A or Factor B main effects? Explain.

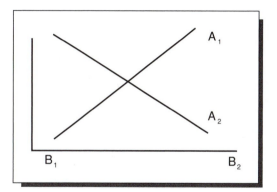

**40.** The diagram at right illustrates the results of a Tukey HSD confidence interval. Can you conclude that the population mean for treatment level $A_1$ is significantly greater than the population mean for treatment level $A_2$? Explain in nontechnical terms a manager could understand.

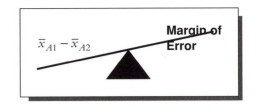

## CASE STUDY

Worldwide Optical Company is a major producer of ophthalmic lenses. It has 20 plants worldwide and its headquarters are located in Danbury, Connecticut. It is the quality leader in the field. Worldwide has been trying to improve the surface finish of its Prestige series. Worldwide defines surface finish as the number of *microscopic* scratches per square inch that can be seen using a 10× magnifying lens. While the Prestige series has the fewest scratches in the industry, Worldwide believes that it can further reduce the number from its present average of 1.6 scratches per square inch. The quality control manager calls a meeting to discuss the improvement project.

| | |
|---|---|
| Manager | I've called this meeting to explore how to reduce the number of scratches on our Prestige lenses. The R&D people tell me that we should be able to reduce the number to less than 1 per square inch. I've asked the production manager of the Prestige series to give a briefing. |
| Production | Last week we had a meeting of Engineering, R&D, my staff, and the operating personnel. We brainstormed several factors that could affect the number of scratches. The group decided two factors are critical: (1) the polishing compound for the final polishing operation and (2) the micron size of the diamonds used to rough cut the lenses. So we asked Engineering to run some preliminary studies. Let me turn the discussion over to Engineering. |
| Engineering | We decided to run a series of sequential studies. In our first study we held all factors constant except the polishing compound. In a controlled study we used both the present ferrous oxide compound and a new synthetic compound from the same vendor. Let me show you the results. |

| Ferrous Oxide | Synthetic Compound |
|---------------|--------------------|
| 1.69 | 1.93 |
| 1.95 | 1.93 |
| 1.81 | 1.49 |
| 1.26 | 1.19 |
| 1.94 | 1.30 |
| 1.41 | 1.48 |
| 1.14 | 1.02 |
| 1.78 | 1.03 |
| 1.16 | 1.56 |
| 1.57 | 1.97 |
| 1.80 | 1.76 |
| 1.47 | 1.14 |
| 1.56 | 1.81 |
| 1.41 | 1.43 |
| 1.46 | 2.64 |
| 1.47 | 1.81 |
| 1.47 | 1.49 |
| 0.92 | 1.71 |
| 1.23 | 1.05 |
| 1.83 | 1.76 |
|  |  |
| 1.52 | 1.58 |

We ran an analysis of variance and concluded that both polishing compounds produced the same number of scratches per square inch. By the way, the average number for both compounds was the same as we had been getting all along, about 1.6. That indicates that nothing happened during the experiment that could "foul up" the results.

Manager         So what did you do next?

Engineering     Well, the synthetic compound was a bit more costly than our present ferrous oxide. We decided not to switch over to the synthetic compound.

Manager         That makes sense. Did you run a study on the size of the diamonds used to cut the lenses?

Engineering    I was just getting to that. We then ran a second study in which we compared the present 120 micron tools against a finer cut 80 micron tool. Of course, we kept all other factors constant and used the ferrous oxide polishing compound for the final polishing operation. Let me show you the results of the second study.

| 120 Micron | 80 Micron |
|---|---|
| 1.12 | 1.28 |
| 1.76 | 1.75 |
| 1.20 | 1.72 |
| 1.45 | 2.28 |
| 1.76 | 1.60 |
| 1.52 | 1.55 |
| 1.28 | 1.43 |
| 1.70 | 1.66 |
| 1.30 | 1.96 |
| 1.85 | 1.31 |
| 1.52 | 1.02 |
| 1.69 | 1.74 |
| 1.36 | 1.70 |
| 1.51 | 1.77 |
| 1.90 | 1.02 |
| 1.58 | 1.46 |
| 1.72 | 1.55 |
| 1.54 | 1.87 |
| 1.58 | 1.64 |
| 1.61 | 1.50 |
|  |  |
| 1.55 | 1.59 |

We ran an analysis of variance and concluded that both micron sizes produced the same number of scratches per square inch. Again, the average number for both micron sizes was the same as we had been getting all along. That indicates that nothing happened during the experiment that could "foul up" the results.

Production     The results don't make any sense! R&D assures us that these two factors are the critical ones. And yet we ran two valid studies and neither factor significantly reduced the number of scratches. Could R&D be wrong?

Manager        I don't think so. Perhaps there is a major flaw in our strategy for running the studies. Let's think about it and reconvene in an hour.

Write a one-page memo that addresses the following issues.

1. What flaws, if any, do you see in Worldwide Optical's study strategy?

2. How would you have conducted the study if you had been given the assignment?

# CHAPTER 12
# APPENDICES

## I. LISTING OF EXCEL TOOLS USED IN CHAPTER

1. SKEW function wizard

2. KURT function wizard

3. VAR function wizard

4. ANOVA: Single Factor data-analysis tool

5. ANOVA: Two-Factor with Replication data-analysis tool

6. Chart Wizard—Line Chart

## II. ANOVA: SINGLE FACTOR

1. Enter the labels and data shown below into a sheet of a workbook.

|    | A | B | C |
|----|---------|-----------|-------------|
| 1  | Pioneer | Retentive | Competitive |
| 2  | 75 | 90 | 80 |
| 3  | 80 | 65 | 80 |
| 4  | 75 | 30 | 75 |
| 5  | 75 | 65 | 70 |
| 6  | 60 | 40 | 85 |
| 7  | 95 | 90 | 55 |
| 8  | 75 | 30 | 80 |
| 9  | 90 | 70 | 85 |
| 10 | 75 | 65 | 90 |
| 11 | 95 | 80 | 75 |

**2.** From the Tools menu, choose Data Analysis. In the Data–Analysis dialog box, double click Anova: Single Factor. Fill in the entries in the dialog box as shown below and click OK.

**Anova: Single Factor**

Input

Input Range: $A$1:$C$11

Grouped By:
- ⦿ Columns
- ○ Rows

☑ Labels in First Row

Alpha: 0.05

Output options
- ⦿ Output Range: $E$1
- ○ New Worksheet Ply:
- ○ New Workbook

OK  Cancel  Help

The output appears as shown below.

|    | E | F | G | H | I | J |
|----|---|---|---|---|---|---|
| 1 | Anova: Single Factor | | | | | |
| 2 | | | | | | |
| 3 | SUMMARY | | | | | |
| 4 | *Groups* | *Count* | *Sum* | *Average* | *Variance* | |
| 5 | Pioneer | 10 | 795 | 79.5 | 119.1667 | |
| 6 | Retentive | 10 | 625 | 62.5 | 501.3889 | |
| 7 | Competitive | 10 | 775 | 77.5 | 95.83333 | |
| 8 | | | | | | |
| 9 | | | | | | |
| 10 | ANOVA | | | | | |
| 11 | *Source of Variation* | *SS* | *df* | *MS* | *F* | *P-value* |
| 12 | Between Groups | 1726.667 | 2 | 863.3333 | 3.615355 | 0.040625 |
| 13 | Within Groups | 6447.5 | 27 | 238.7963 | | |
| 14 | | | | | | |
| 15 | Total | 8174.167 | 29 | | | |

# III. ANOVA: TWO-FACTOR WITH REPLICATION

**1.** Enter the labels and data shown below into a sheet of a workbook.

|    | A | B | C | D |
|----|---|------|------|-------|
| **1** |  | **4 inch** | **7 inch** | **10 inch** |
| **2** |  | 1.00 | 0.20 | 0.20 |
| **3** |  | 0.43 | 1.90 | 1.82 |
| **4** | **Old** | 1.96 | 0.70 | 1.25 |
| **5** | **Vendor** | 0.01 | 1.40 | 0.35 |
| **6** |  | 1.65 | 0.65 | 1.56 |
| **7** |  | 0.30 | 4.51 | 7.50 |
| **8** |  | 1.96 | 2.21 | 3.56 |
| **9** | **New** | 0.15 | 4.65 | 6.85 |
| **10** | **Vendor** | 2.13 | 2.57 | 5.90 |
| **11** |  | 0.89 | 6.54 | 7.50 |
| **12** |  |  |  |  |

**2.** From the Tools menu, choose Data Analysis. In the Data–Analysis dialog box, double click Anova: Two-Factor with Replication. Fill in the entries in the dialog box as shown below and click OK.

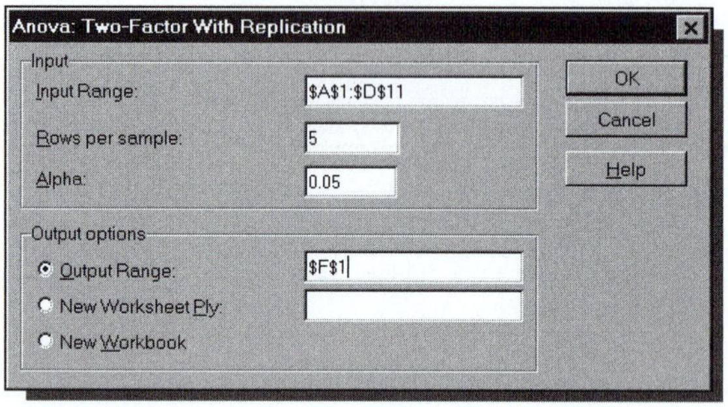

**Anova: Two-Factor With Replication**

Input
Input Range: $A$1:$D$11
Rows per sample: 5
Alpha: 0.05

Output options
⦿ Output Range: $F$1
○ New Worksheet Ply:
○ New Workbook

OK
Cancel
Help

**3.** The output appears as shown below.

| | F | G | H | I | J | K | L |
|---|---|---|---|---|---|---|---|
| 1 | Anova: Two-Factor With Replication | | | | | | |
| 2 | | | | | | | |
| 3 | SUMMARY | 4 inch | 7 inch | 10inch | Total | | |
| 4 | | | | | | | |
| 5 | Count | 5 | 5 | 5 | 15 | | |
| 6 | Sum | 5.05 | 4.85 | 5.18 | 15.08 | | |
| 7 | Average | 1.01 | 0.97 | 1.036 | 1.005333 | | |
| 8 | Variance | 0.66215 | 0.4545 | 0.52613 | 0.470155 | | |
| 9 | | | | | | | |
| 10 | | | | | | | |
| 11 | Count | 5 | 5 | 5 | 15 | | |
| 12 | Sum | 5.43 | 20.48 | 31.31 | 57.22 | | |
| 13 | Average | 1.086 | 4.096 | 6.262 | 3.814667 | | |
| 14 | Variance | 0.84653 | 3.08428 | 2.71072 | 6.724084 | | |
| 15 | | | | | | | |
| 16 | Total | | | | | | |
| 17 | Count | 10 | 10 | 10 | | | |
| 18 | Sum | 10.48 | 25.33 | 36.49 | | | |
| 19 | Average | 1.048 | 2.533 | 3.649 | | | |
| 20 | Variance | 0.672129 | 4.287201 | 9.02501 | | | |
| 21 | | | | | | | |
| 22 | | | | | | | |
| 23 | ANOVA | | | | | | |
| 24 | Source of Variation | SS | df | MS | F | P-value | F crit |
| 25 | Sample | 59.19265 | 1 | 59.19265 | 42.87091 | 9.01E-07 | 4.259675 |
| 26 | Columns | 34.05294 | 2 | 17.02647 | 12.3316 | 0.000207 | 3.402832 |
| 27 | Interaction | 33.52917 | 2 | 16.76458 | 12.14193 | 0.000227 | 3.402832 |
| 28 | Within | 33.13724 | 24 | 1.380718 | | | |
| 29 | | | | | | | |
| 30 | Total | 159.912 | 29 | | | | |

Remember, in the Sources of Variation column, Sample refers to the experimental factor in the rows of the study. Column refers to the experimental factor in the columns of the study.

# IV. PROFILE GRAPH

The following steps describe how to construct a profile graph for the significant AB interaction.

|    | A | B | C | D | E | F | G | H |
|----|---|---|---|---|---|---|---|---|
| 1  |   | 4-INCH | 7-INCH | 10-INCH | Old | 1.01 | 0.97 | 1.04 |
| 2  |   | 1.00 | 0.20 | 0.20 | New | 1.09 | 4.10 | 6.2E |
| 3  |   | 0.43 | 1.90 | 1.82 |   |   |   |   |
| 4  | Old Mat | 1.96 | 0.70 | 1.25 |   |   |   |   |
| 5  |   | 0.01 | 1.40 | 0.35 |   |   |   |   |
| 6  |   | 1.65 | 0.65 | 1.56 |   |   |   |   |
| 7  |   | 0.30 | 4.51 | 7.50 |   |   |   |   |
| 8  |   | 1.96 | 2.21 | 3.56 |   |   |   |   |
| 9  | New Mat | 0.15 | 4.65 | 6.85 |   |   |   |   |
| 10 |   | 2.13 | 2.57 | 5.90 |   |   |   |   |
| 11 |   | 0.89 | 6.54 | 7.50 |   |   |   |   |
| 12 |   |   |   |   |   |   |   |   |
| 13 |   |   |   |   |   |   |   |   |
| 14 |   |   |   |   |   |   |   |   |
| 15 |   |   |   |   |   |   |   |   |
| 16 |   |   |   |   |   |   |   |   |
| 17 |   |   |   |   |   |   |   |   |
| 18 |   |   |   |   |   |   |   |   |
| 19 |   |   |   |   |   |   |   |   |
| 20 |   |   |   |   |   |   |   |   |
| 21 |   |   |   |   |   |   |   |   |
| 22 |   |   |   |   |   |   |   |   |
| 23 |   |   |   |   |   |   |   |   |
| 24 |   |   |   |   |   |   |   |   |

1. Enter the labels (bold-faced) for the 2 × 3 factorial study as shown above.

2. Enter the data for the study into cells B2 to D11.

3. Compute the six cell means. Place the cursor in cell F1. Click the Function Wizard tool. Click the statistical function category. Click the Average function name. Click OK. Select the data (cells B2:B6). Click OK. Point to the fill handle in the lower right-hand corner of the cell. The pointer changes to a cross. Click and drag the fill handle to cell H1. Release the mouse. Place the cursor in cell F2. Click the Function Wizard tool. Click the statistical function category. Click the Average function name. Click OK. Select the data (cells B7:B11). Click OK. Drag to fill the range to cell H2.

4. Select the cell mean data including the labels (cells E1:H2). Click the ChartWizard button and select the Line Chart. Click the Next button.

**5.** In step 2, click on Next. In step 3, type in Stamping Depth for Category X axis and Percentage Cracking for Category Y axis. Click on Finish.

# V. TUKEY INTERVALS FOR ONE-FACTOR ANOVA

**1.** Type Table 12.8 into spreadsheet cells J3:O15 (not shown). Include the DF column but you can exclude the bold-faced "Number of Levels."

**2.** Highlight cells J3:O15. Then click the Name box at the left end of the formula bar. Type in the name for the cells—qstat.

**3.** Type in all labels in column A as shown in the figure below.

|    | A | B | C | D | E | F | G |
|----|---|---|---|---|---|---|---|
| 1 | Number of | 5 | Maximum of 6 | | | | |
| 2 | Treatments | | | | | | |
| 3 | | | | | | | |
| 4 | Sample Size | 9 | | | | | |
| 5 | per Treatment | | | | | | |
| 6 | | | | | | | |
| 7 | Within DF | 40 | Minimum of 10 | | | | |
| 8 | | | | | | | |
| 9 | MSWithin Groups | 245.1944 | From ANOVA Table | | | | |
| 10 | | | | | | | |
| 11 | q-stat | 4.04 | Does not interpolate q-Stat Table | | | | |
| 12 | | | | | | | |
| 13 | Approximate MOE | 21.08703 | Difference in Two Sample Means ± MOE | | | | |

**4.** Type in cell B7 the following expression: $= (B4 - 1) \cdot B1$.

**5.** Type in cell B11 the following expression: =VLOOKUP(B7,qstat, B1). This function will do the look up in the qstat table that you named in step 2.

**6.** Type in cell B13 the following expression: =B11·SQRT(B9/B4).

You must insert the number of treatment levels in cell B1 and the sample size per treatment level in cell B4. You must also insert the $MS_{within}$ from the ANOVA table in cell B9. The spreadsheet will then determine the degrees of freedom, the qstat statistic from Table 12.8, and the margin of error.

*Note:* VLOOKUP does not interpolate the Studentized range table. That is why cell B13 is labeled Approximate Margin of Error. The margin of error is exact for the degrees of freedom shown in Table 12.8.

The spreadsheet provides margins of error for up to six treatment levels. The degrees of freedom for within must be 10 or larger.

# INDEX

## NUMBERS